Kodak Cameras

THE FIRST HUNDRED YEARS

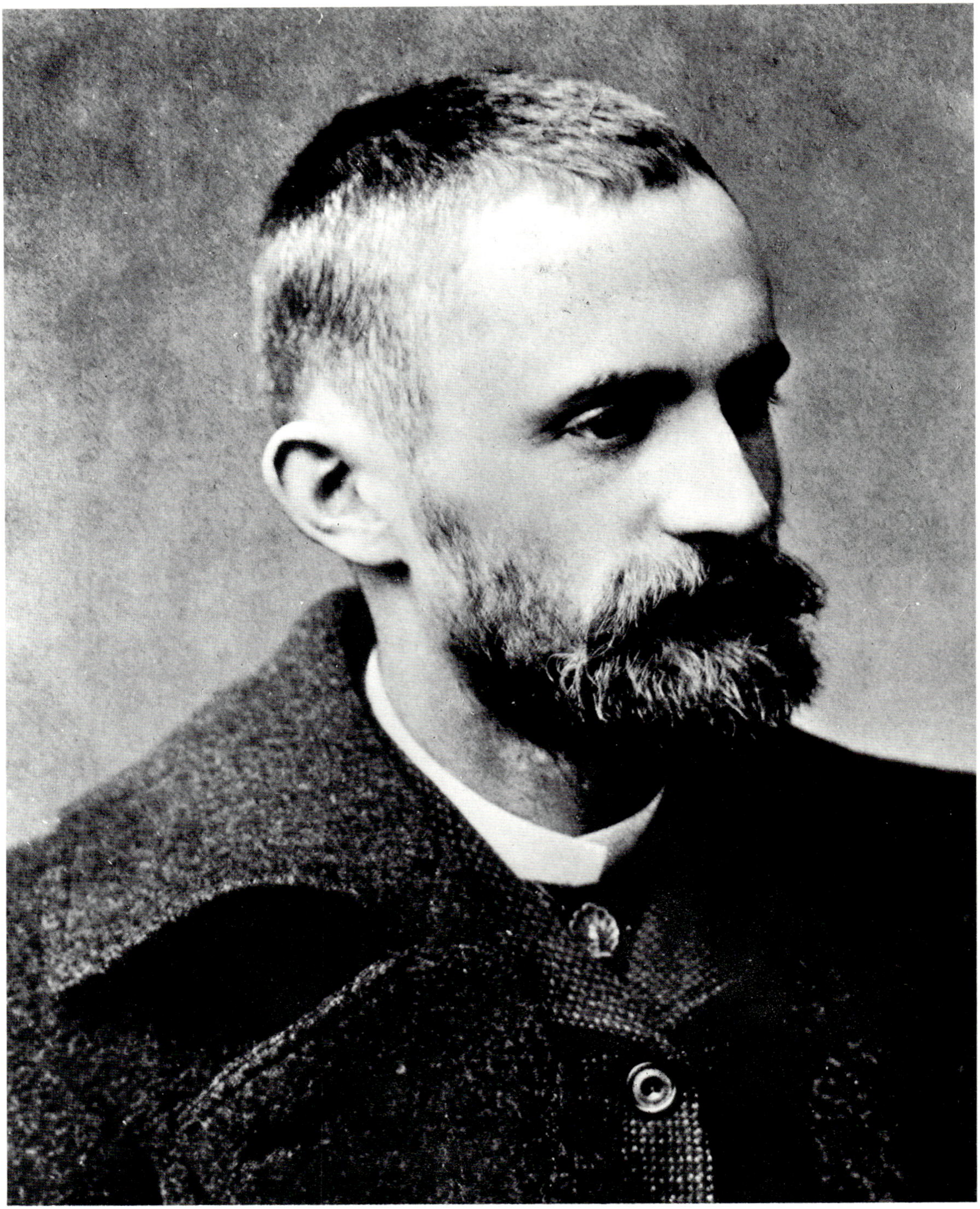

George Eastman. KP

Kodak Cameras

THE FIRST HUNDRED YEARS

BRIAN COE

HOVE
FOTO
BOOKS

Kodak Cameras – The First Hundred Years
Brian Coe
ISBN 0–906447–44–5
First published in Great Britain 1988
Hove Foto Books
34 Church Road,
Hove, East Sussex
BN3 2GJ

U.S.A. Distribution:
Seven Hills Books
49 Central Avenue, Suite 300,
Cincinnati, Ohio 45202, U.S.A.

Typesetting by Alphabet Workshop, Eastbourne.
Printed in Great Britain by Purnell Book Production Ltd.

British Library Cataloguing in Publication Data

Coe, Brian, *1930-*
Kodak cameras : the first 100 years.
1. Kodak cameras, to 1987
I. Title
771.3'1
ISBN 0-906447-44-5

Contents

Preface

A hundred years of camera production by the world's largest photographic organisation amounts to a lot of cameras! Not only have there been many hundreds of basic models, but many of them existed in a very wide range of variations. To attempt to list them all is no easy task. Paradoxically, more information has survived about the production of the earliest models than is available for many of the later productions. Catalogues, Sales Plans, Trade Circulars and advertisements all yield information. The chronological lists of Kodak cameras, started by Vic Moyes of the Kodak Patent Department Museum in Rochester and continued and expanded by the late Don Ryon and his successor David Gibson have provided the basis of several publications dealing with Kodak cameras. As a result these have tended to concentrate only on those cameras made or sold in the United States. There are very many, often quite different, Kodak cameras which have been manufactured in England, Germany and France.

From 1969 to 1985 the author was Curator of the Kodak Museum, which was then at the Kodak factory in Harrow, England. Much of the research upon which this book is based was carried out there, using material held in the Museum and, particularly, in the Kodak Research Laboratory Library. The before-mentioned chronology of Kodak cameras inevitably provided the framework on which information from other sources could be assembled. While every attempt has been made to include all Kodak cameras and their variations, it is inevitable that some will have been missed. None the less, the listings in this book are the most comprehensive yet to be published. To keep the project to a manageable size, the listings concentrate on the 'mainstream' Kodak and Brownie cameras. Those cameras made under trade names acquired when Eastman bought other companies – Premo, Hawk-Eye, Folmer & Schwing, etc. – are listed briefly in Appendix 1. Only those cameras made for the amateur or mass markets are covered; professional studio, field, scientific or technical cameras are not included.

In compiling the information on which this book is based, over a period of almost twenty years, many people have helped in many ways. The late Don Ryon, curator of the Kodak Patent Department Museum in Rochester, provided me with much information, and provided me with access to the extensive files during visits to the United States. His successor, David Gibson, has been especially helpful, particularly his significant extension and improvement of the chronological listing of Kodak cameras. His many kindnesses are much appreciated, particularly his provision of many illustrations for this book at a time when he was under considerable pressure from more important work. I know that many American collectors share with me a high regard for what he has done for Kodak camera history. My former colleague, Christine Lucas, Assistant Curator at the Kodak Museum in the 1970s, did a valuable job in creating a chronological listing of cameras made by Kodak Limited, a task which involved many hours of painstaking research though catalogues, Sales Plans and Trade Circulars. Her work saved me a great deal of time which would have had to be spent covering the same ground.

Since I left the Kodak Museum, on its transfer in 1985 to the National Museum of Photography, Film and Television at Bradford under the curatorship of Roger Taylor, I have had cause to be grateful to former colleagues. Peter Sutherst, of Kodak Customer Relations, as always, has been helpful in providing information about recent Kodak cameras, and in supplying illustrations. Chris Roberts, of the Information Group of the Kodak Research Laboratory, was good enough to give me access to the Kodak Archive, which had been separated from the Kodak Museum on its move to Bradford, enabling me to check information on camera production in England. Joe Pokorny, of Kodak AG in Germany, helped in providing illustrations, and arranged for the provision of information concerning some Kodak AG cameras by Karl Otto Kemmler, to whom I am especially grateful.

Thurman (Jack) Naylor of Boston, whose remarkable personal photo-history collection is of international museum standard, has helped in many ways over the years, not least in providing illustrations of many Kodak cameras. I value Jack's friendship and respect his considerable knowledge in this field. John Ward, a valued colleague at the Science Museum in London, helped greatly by giving access to some of the Kodak cameras held there.

The photographs which illustrate this book have been collected over a period of almost twenty years. Most were photographed by, or for, me from the originals held in various collections. They are attributed as follows:

KM – The Kodak Museum, which has the largest collection of Kodak cameras outside America, and is now housed at the National Museum of Photography, Film and Television in Bradford, England.

KP – Kodak press and publicity photographs.

KAG – Kodak AG, Stuttgart, West Germany.

PDM – The Kodak Patent Department Museum, Rochester, New York, USA.

RPS – The Royal Photographic Society, Bath, England.

SM – The Science Museum, London, England.

TN – The Thurman Naylor Collection, Boston, Massachusetts, USA.

I have tried to make this book as comprehensive an account as possible of the Kodak cameras produced in this first century, but it is inevitable that examples of models or variations not listed will come to light.

Acknowledgement – The Kodak Museum

The story of popular photography is closely linked to the long history of camera manufacture by the Eastman Kodak Company.

The Kodak Museum at the National Museum of Photography, Film and Television, Bradford, England, will trace the story of popular photography in its extensive new galleries and displays. These open to the public in April 1989 as a contribution to the 150th Anniversary of photography's first public announcement.

Many of the cameras illustrated in this book will be on display.

Publisher's Notes

1. The contents of this work have not been reviewed by Eastman Kodak Company or its subsidiaries, which as a consequence can accept no responsibility for the accuracy thereof.
2. Many of the illustrations in this book have been provided by Eastman Kodak Company and its subsidiaries. We acknowledge with gratitude their help in this respect.

Introduction George Eastman and the Kodak Company

The Kodak organisation was founded by a young American, George Eastman, who worked as a bookkeeper in the Rochester Savings Bank in New York State. He became interested in photography in 1877, taking lessons from a local Rochester photographer, George Monroe, using the wet plate process which had been in general use for the previous 26 years. He was soon dissatisfied with the need to carry around, as he put it, "a pack-horse load" of equipment required to coat and process plates on the spot. In 1878 he read in the *British Journal of Photography* of Charles Bennett's improvements on the gelatine dry-plate process, first suggested by Dr Richard Leach Maddox in 1871. He began to experiment with the coating of gelatine dry-plates, and by the end of the year he had been sufficiently successful as to consider the manufacture of plates for sale. By June 1879 he had invented a machine for coating plates, which he patented first in England, in July 1879, and subsequently in America and elsewhere. Some income from the sale of licences to use his invention enabled him to prepare for manufacture of his own brand of plate, and he rented the third floor of a building in Rochester for this purpose. He got financial backing from a buggy-whip manufacturer, Colonel Henry A. Strong, who invested $1000 in the new project, and on 1st January 1881 the Eastman Dry Plate Company was formed. E. & H.T. Anthony, the leading photographic supply house, became agents for Eastman's plates, and after surviving some early setbacks, the business prospered.

The new dry plates simplified the business of photography, doing away with much of the paraphernalia of the earlier process, but still heavy and fragile glass plates were needed. Eastman turned to the idea of using paper as a base for the negative, reviving a principle from the earliest days of photography. Eastman Negative Paper was launched in 1884; special adapters enabled the sheets of sensitive paper to be used in the conventional plate holder. In that year, the business was turned into a corporation, The Eastman Dry Plate and Film Company, working from a four-storey building in State Street, Rochester. In 1885, Eastman launched a new product which he had developed with William H. Walker, a camera maker who had joined the company the previous year. The new device was a rollholder which attached to the ordinary plate camera, enabling it to take a roll of negative paper, sufficient for 24 exposures. Its weight and size was very much less than the equivalent number of glass plates in their holders. Although there had been earlier rollholders, none had been very successful, mainly because of unsatisfactory sensitive materials. The combination of precision manufacture of the rollholder and the good quality of the negative paper made Eastman's product popular with photographers. Later in 1885 he was able to market a new product, American Film, a paper base coated with a layer of soluble gelatine, then a layer of collodion and finally a gelatine emulsion. The exposed and developed negative image could be separated from the paper base during processing and laid down on glass or thick gelatine sheets. The product combined the light weight and flexibility of paper with the transparency glass for printing.

To sell the new products in Europe, Eastman sent Walker over to London in 1885 to manage a wholesale business, and advertised widely in photographic journals. The rollholder was well received, being favourably reviewed and awarded medals and prizes. Eastman had designed a continuous coating machine to make the new American film, and this greatly reduced production costs. In the belief that many more people would take up photography if it could be simplified, Eastman decided to combine the rollholder with a small hand-held camera.

His first, but not successful, design was the Eastman Detective Camera (see Chapter 9). His second attempt got things right. The Kodak camera, marketed in 1888, combined the simplicity of a point-and-shoot rollfilm box camera with a developing and printing service which did away with the need for the camera user to have a darkroom. Although by today's standards it was a primitive (and expensive) device, it was the beginning of popular photography. New, larger models followed the following year, when Eastman was also able to introduce the first commercial celluloid rollfilm, flexible, tough and transparent, without the disadvantages of paper. In 1889 the Company's name was changed to The Eastman Company, and changed again, finally, in 1892 to the Eastman Kodak Company.

Eastman's first attempt to produce a daylight loading camera (all the early models had to be loaded in the dark) was not very successful; the Daylight Kodak cameras of 1891 (see Chapter 1) did not sell in significant numbers. The answer to this problem was found by Samuel N. Turner in 1892. He invented a rollfilm in which the sensitive material was attached to a longer length of black paper and wound on a spool. The backing paper was printed with white exposure numbers which could be read through a red window in the back of the camera. The idea was first incorporated in the Boston Camera Manufacturing Company's "Bull's-Eye" camera of 1892; it had only modest success. Eastman saw the potential of the idea, and arranged a licence from Turner to use it, launching the Bullet and Pocket Kodak cameras (see Chapter 1) in 1895. In that year he bought the rights to the patent from Turner, and acquired the Boston Camera Manufacturing Company in August, thus adding the "Bull's-Eye" trademark to that of "Kodak".

A key figure in the development of the early Kodak cameras was Frank Brownell. He had begun his career as a cabinet maker, turning to the manufacture of cameras in the early 1880s. His stand cameras were of sound design and quality construction, and impressed Eastman, who commissioned Brownell to manufacture the wooden parts of the rollholder in 1885. He subsequently designed most of the early Kodak cameras and his company manufactured all of them until 1902. In 1915 Eastman said of Brownell "He is the greatest camera designer that ever lived. Practically all the hand cameras are made after his designs today, throughout the world." The simplest, yet most influential, design that Brownell created for Eastman was the Brownie camera (see Chapter 2). The low cost of the Brownie camera, made possible by mass production techniques and simple yet effective design, brought snapshot photography within the reach of the masses for the first time.

Eastman's organisation never looked back from this point, continuing to develop innovatory cameras based on the philosophy of the first Kodak camera sales slogan: "You Press the Button,

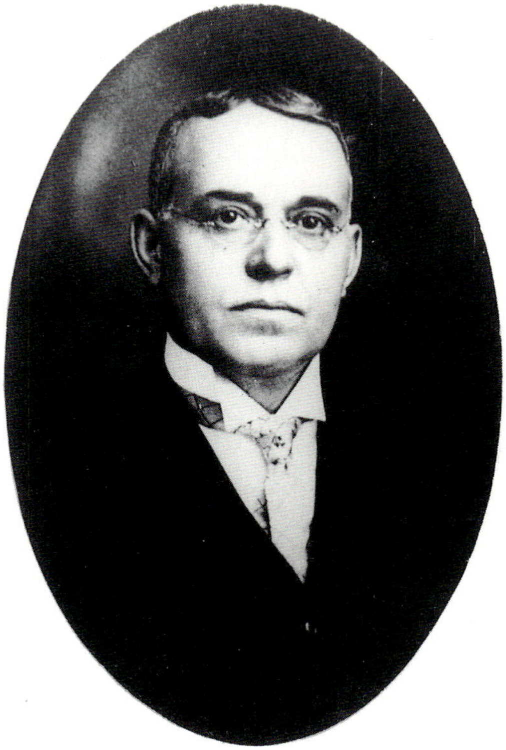

Frank Brownell

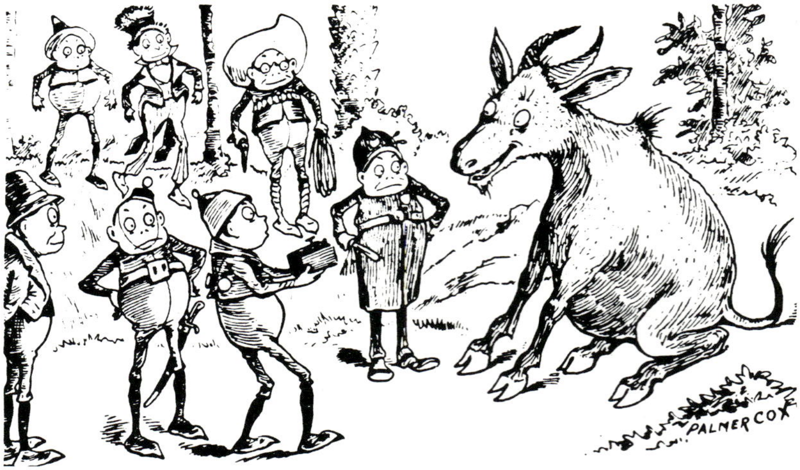

The 'Brownies'

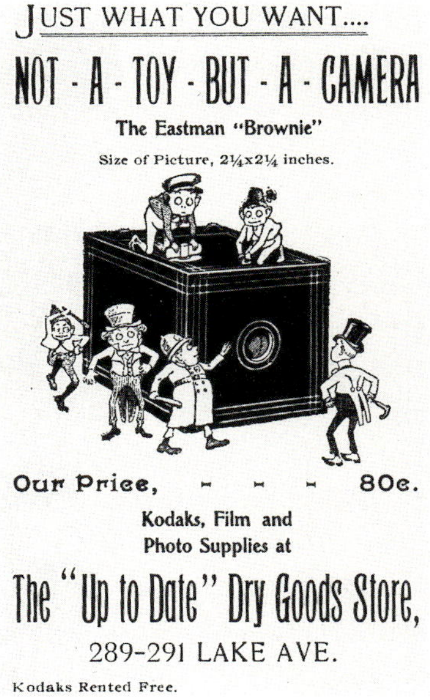

Early Brownie advertisement

We do the Rest". In the 1920s Eastman progressively relinquished control of the Company, while still taking an active interest. In 1932, suffering from terminal cancer, and having settled all his affairs and having over the years disposed of his considerable fortune in various charitable ways, he shot himself through the heart, leaving a note: "To my friends: My work is done. Why wait? G.E.". The organisation he left behind survived the shock, and to the present day continues to develop cameras for the mass market.

From the early years of the century, the manufacture of Kodak cameras was carried out in Rochester at the Kodak plant, although items like lenses and shutters were often bought in, usually from Bausch & Lomb, another Rochester company. A manufacturing facility was also set up in Toronto, Canada, just over the border from Rochester. The Canadian Kodak Company's products were normally identical to those made in the United States, but being "Empire Made" were not subject to heavy import tariffs when shipped to the United Kingdom.

The Kodak presence in Britain had developed from the wholesale importing agency set up in 1885, with the formation of the Eastman Photographic Materials Company in 1889, set up to manufacture and market Eastman's products, taking over the business and markets of the Company outside north and south America. At the factory at Harrow, (then) outside London, photographic film and paper was manufactured, and the developing and printing of customer's films was carried out. At first, no cameras were manufactured in Britain, all those sold being imported from Rochester or, later, Canada. However, as can be seen in the camera listings in later chapters, a very large number of local variations of lens and shutter combinations were offered in many models of folding camera. This reflects the influence that the advanced amateur users had in the British and Continental markets; they wanted something more elaborate than the models which satisfied the general public in America. It is likely that these lens and shutter changes were carried out in the camera repair department at the Head Office; factory organisation charts of the time show no separate section with this function. Another indication of the importance of the London operation is seen the the manufacture at Rochester of several camera models sold exclusively in Europe. Models such as the Flat Folding Kodak camera and the Flush-Back Kodak camera (see Chapter 3) had no American counterpart, like the quarter-plate versions of the Kodet cameras (see Chapter 8).

The English company had become Kodak Limited in 1898; for a short time the new Company had a controlling interest in the whole organisation, owning 98% of the business, until during the Boer War the English tax authorities tried to tax the Company on its world-wide, rather than its local, earnings. Control returned swiftly to Rochester after that! Kodak Limited handled the marketing of Kodak products throughout Europe (including Russia), Africa and India.

In 1915, during World War One, the McKenna Duty imposed considerable restrictions on the import of luxury goods into Britain, and the effect of this was felt well into the 1920s, when there was no longer the same advantage to be had in importing goods from Canada. The decision was made to begin camera manufacture in England. In 1927 Kodak Limited acquired the New Zealand Pavilion which had been erected for the British Empire Exhibition in 1926 at Wembley, and moved it, in sections, to the Harrow factory. Manufacture began with the assembly of Cartridge Hawkeye and Brownie box cameras from imported parts, but from 1929 Harrow-designed models were produced, starting with the No 2 Portrait Brownie camera (see Chapter 2). From now on, until the discontinuation of manufacture in the United Kingdom in 1982, Kodak Limited manufactured cameras which were entirely original, or which differed significantly from their American counterparts.

The third major camera manufacturing facility in the Kodak organisation was created in December 1931 with the acquisition by Kodak AG in Germany of the Dr Nagel-Werke in Stuttgart. Kodak's German presence had begun in 1896 simply as a distribution agency for the products of the American and English factories, initially controlled from London. In 1927 Kodak acquired Glanzfilm AG in Koepenick, Berlin, and was able to begin the production of photographic materials, with the formation of Kodak Aktiengesellschaft. Dr August Nagel was a talented camera designer whose first company was Drexler & Nagel, formed in 1908. This became the famous Contessa Kamera-werke in 1909, and with the acquisition of the Nettel

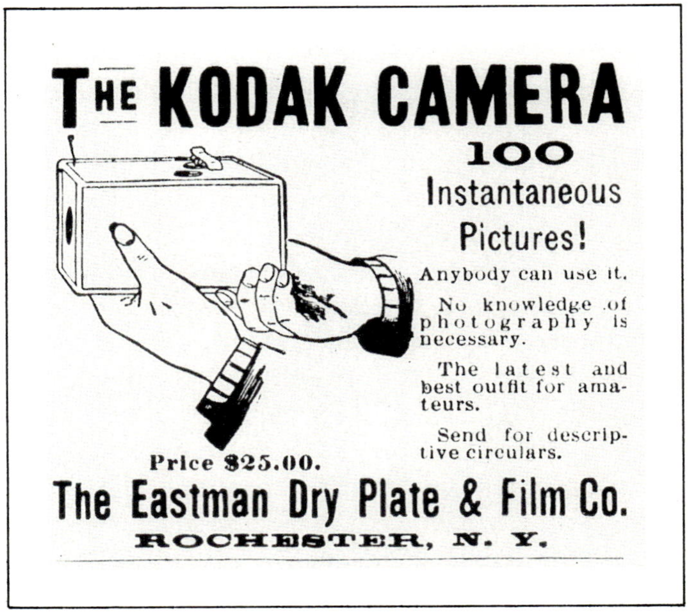

1888 Kodak advertisement

Kamera-werke in 1919 Contessa-Nettel AG was formed. The hard times in the 1920s, after the ravages of World War One, saw the disappearance or merger of many companies, and Contessa-Nettel, Ernemann, Goerz and Ica combined with Zeiss to form Zeiss Ikon AG in 1926. Within two years, Nagel was itching to be independent again, and he resigned to form his own company, Dr. August Nagel-Werke, in Stuttgart in 1928. He manufactured high precision folding plate and rollfilm cameras, and when Kodak AG was looking for a company with experience of precision camera making and a high reputation, Nagel's company was a natural choice. Nagel sacrificed his independence once again in return for the financial resources and distribution network of a world-wide organisation, at a time of economic depression when many German companies were going to the wall. The first new major product designed by Nagel for Kodak was the Retina camera (see Chapter 5). By producing a quality 35mm camera at a price far less than the Leica or Contax cameras he put miniature camera photography into the hands of the man in the street. "Die Kodak Volks-kamera" – The People's Camera– it was called. Kodak AG in Stuttgart continued to manufacture cameras until almost the present day. Dr Nagel's brother Hugo joined Kodak Limited in 1932 and set up a camera design team at Harrow. He was responsible for many of the 1930s models, and in 1939 had completed the design of a new all-metal range of Six-20 Brownie box cameras which eventually appeared after World War Two was over.

The American/Canadian, English and German factories between them produced the vast majority of Kodak cameras. Small numbers of cameras were produced in France by Kodak-Pathé in the post-World War Two years, to overcome import restrictions; more recently, cartridge loading cameras have been made or assembled in other countries, notably Brazil, Spain and Australia. Apart from the country of origin and local language inscriptions, these cameras have been virtually identical to American-made models. Since 1986 a range of 35mm compact cameras (see Chapter 5) has been produced for Kodak by companies in Hong Kong and Japan – the first time since the beginning of the century that all camera production has not been carried out within the Kodak organisation.

Using the Listings

The entries in the listings are divided into chapters by camera type – Kodak folding cameras, Brownie box cameras, Kodak 35mm cameras and so on. It is easy to place almost all Kodak cameras into one of these categories. Within each chapter the cameras are listed alphabetically. Virtually all Kodak cameras have the model name on them somewhere. It may be on the lens panel or baseboard of a folding camera, or on or inside the camera back, or in the film spool compartment, or stamped on the carrying handle. There are very few exceptions to this rule. The first is the first Kodak camera. This is not likely to be mistaken for anything else, if you are lucky enough to come across one. The next generation of 'string-set' Kodak box cameras had the model name on a paper strip glued in the bottom of the lens compartment, behind the removable front panel. Sometimes, this paper strip has become detached or defaced, but these early cameras are very distinctive, and the particular model can be deduced from the picture size and other clues. The Kodet plate or rollfilm cameras have no model identification on them – in a way, this is how they may be identified! Following the introduction of the daylight loading cartridge cameras in 1895, all Kodak cameras have model identification, except the very rare limited production Cone cameras, and some examples of the Vest Pocket Kodak camera, whose 'lazy-tongs' cross strut construction is sufficiently distinctive not to be confused with anything else.

Within the listings, each named model – eg Folding Pocket Kodak camera – is listed in model number order. The model numbers do not relate to order of introduction, as is sometimes believed, but to picture size. These numbers are used consistently for roll film cameras from 1895 on, but there are anomalies between the Kodak and the Brownie ranges. Here are the most common model numbers, with picture sizes in inches:

Kodak cameras	*Brownie cameras*	*Picture size*
0	0	1⅝ × 2½
1	2	2¼ × 3¼
1A	2A	2½ × 4¼
2C	2C	2⅞ × 4⅞
3	3	3¼ × 4¼
3A	3A	3¼ × 5½
4	–	4 × 5
4A	–	4¼ × 6½
5	–	7 × 5

Within each numbered model, any structural variations are listed, generally in chronological order, and where lens and shutter options were available, these are given with their dates of availability. These are separated into American and UK groups – the latter often being of considerable size.

So: determine camera type and select the chapter; find the camera name and model number; select the entry.

The dates of introduction and discontinuation will be found, and the lens/shutter combination, or design variation, may in some cases enable a closer date to be determined.

Many of the earlier Kodak cameras carry patent numbers and dates. These are only of use in giving an earliest production date for a particular example, since clearly a camera with a 1915 patent date cannot have been made before that year (but may well have been made long after it). They frequently refer to patents issued many years before, sometimes for features which are not present on the particular camera. A few Kodak cameras, mostly box cameras made between 1895 and 1900, are identified as "Model of '98", for example.

For cameras made before 1920, the serial number may be useful in closer dating, since production information about design changes related to serial numbers has survived, and is given where known. Not all Kodak cameras had serial numbers; most Brownie cameras did not. On folding cameras, the serial number is often to be found on the folding support foot on the baseboard. Early cameras may have the number stamped into the leather covering, or into the wood of the case, or inside the camera back, or elswhere. In most cases, the serial numbers were straightforward, although the starting number varied from model to model – it could be 1, or 501, or 1001 or whatever. A few cameras have a more complicated system, notably the No 3 Folding Pocket Kodak camera, which had several serial number ranges, some running simultaneously, and the result of this can be great confusion.

The production numbers of Kodak cameras are mostly not known, or available, for cameras made after 1920. Figures for earlier models are given where they are known. However, it is safe to assume that with very few exceptions, Kodak cameras were made in large numbers. Production runs of several million were not unknown, and runs of tens or hundreds of thousands were commonplace.

The materials from which Kodak cameras have been made are many and varied. Only the earliest models, before 1900, have any unplated brass metal parts. Nickel or chromium plating was the standard finish. Camera bodies were covered with real or imitation leather until the introduction of self-coloured plastic moulded cameras. Only one, the Ordinary Kodak camera of 1891 (see Chapter 1) was made in uncovered wood. Many early cameras had bodies of wood, or card in the case of the cheap Brownie cameras. During the early years of the century aluminium progressively replaced wood in the construction of most Kodak cameras, and by the mid 1920s all Kodak cameras were fabricated from metal, with the exception of low-cost Hawkeye cameras made for premium sales, which continued to be made from wood and strawboard into the late 1930s. Eastman had used aluminium from early days, soon after new methods of production had made it an economic material. The first Pocket Kodak cameras of 1895 had aluminium film carriers, and the Folding Pocket Kodak camera of 1897 had an aluminium back. The development of Bakelite urea-formaldehyde plastic, which made moulding of camera parts possible, was first used by Kodak in the manufacture of side plates for some of the Autographic Kodak Special cameras in 1915. The first complete Kodak camera to be made from moulded Bakelite was the No 2 Hawkette camera of 1930, made by Kodak Limited. The Baby Brownie camera of 1934 was the first moulded plastic camera to be made by Eastman Kodak in America. From this time on, an increasing number of Kodak cameras employed this method of contruction which became almost universally used after the development of new plastics and precision injection moulding techniques in the 1950s. The bellows of folding cameras were made of leather or light-tight fabric, depending on the cost. Up to 1911, most of the Kodak and Brownie folding cameras had red leather bellows; these were phased out from 1911, starting with batches exported to London, and from 1912 all cameras were supplied with black bellows (except, of course, for the cameras in fashion colours, in the late 1920s). However, it should be noted that early models may have had their red bellows replaced with black during servicing.

Finally, a word about roll film sizes. Before 1913, Kodak roll films were identified by the name of the camera which they fitted – No 2 Bull's-Eye, No 1 Folding Pocket Kodak, and so on. As the number of models proliferated, many of them using the same size film, this method became unwieldy. Eastman Kodak decided to rationalize the situation by giving a number to each film size. Starting with 101, films were numbered in the order in which they had been introduced, starting with the Pocket Kodak camera in 1895. The number sequence reached 127, for the recently introduced Vest Pocket Kodak camera. Numbers 128 and 129 were allocated to films made to fit the popular Ensignette cameras made in England by Houghton. The next film size to be introduced was 130, for the No 2C Autographic Kodak camera in 1916; after this the logical numbering system was dropped. The next new films, 620 and 616, in 1931 were identical to 120 and 116 sizes, but on a slimmer metal spool. 135 was given to the 35mm disposable film cassette in 1934, and 828 to the new Bantam 35mm wide rollfilm launched in 1935 (8 exposures 28mm high). No new film sizes were introduced until 1963, with the launch of the Instamatic cameras. The "Kodapak" cartridge was numbered 126, producing occasional problems when customers, who had asked for a 126 film, complained that it did not fit the No 4A Folding Kodak camera they had inherited! The pocket Instamatic cameras which followed in 1972 used a cartridge numbered 110. The Kodak Instant cameras introduced in 1976 used PR10 film packs, later changed to PR144 and HS144. The Kodak disc cameras used HR and VR disc films. A full listing of all Kodak roll film numbers and their dates of introduction is given in Appendix 2. The Autographic Kodak cameras made between 1914 and 1932 could take a special rollfilm which enabled data to be 'written' on the film in the camera; these films were identical in size to the standard type, but with an "A" prefix. After 1913, the roll film size is given on the majority of Kodak cameras – "Use 120 film" etc.

CHAPTER 1 *Kodak Box and Solid Body Cameras*

Most of the early Kodak cameras in the late 1880s and 1890s were box cameras of fairly basic construction. After the introduction of the Brownie camera in 1900, this simple construction passed to the new name,and most plain Kodak cameras were folding models. In the 1930s, a new breed of non-folding cameras began to appear, with eyelevel direct vision finders and fixed lens panels, or with lenses on telescoping tubes or helical screw mounts. After World War Two the development of precision plastic moulding techniques accelerated this trend.

This section deals with the Kodak cameras of this type; the Brownie cameras are dealt with in the next chapter.

No 2 Bullet Kodak

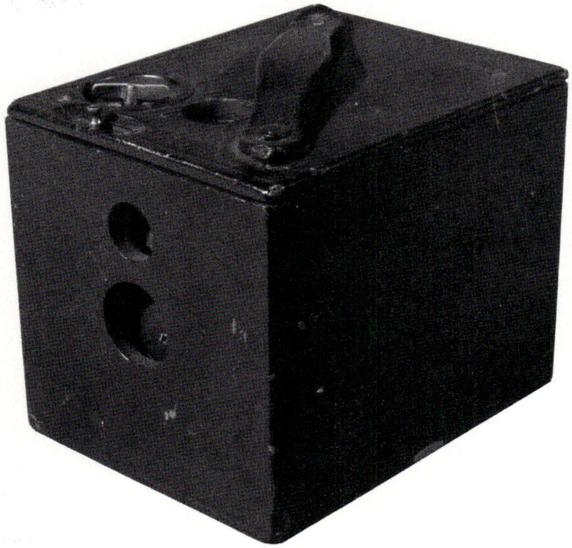

1895 Model. KM

Type Box rollfilm
Introduced March 1895
Discontinued 1902
Film size 101
Picture size 3½ × 3½in.

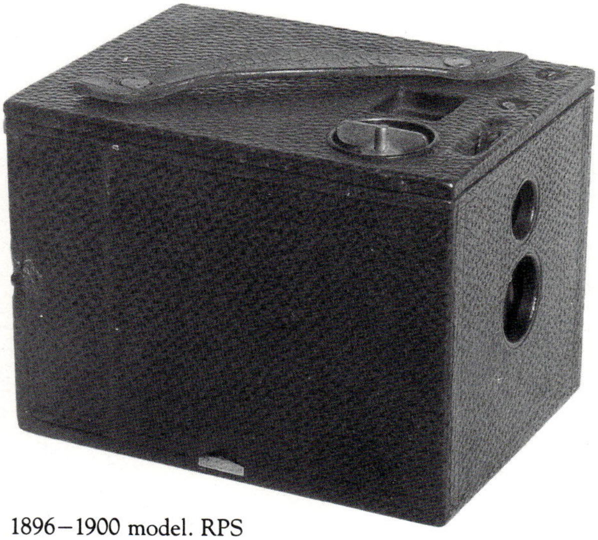

1896–1900 model. RPS

Manufactured US
Lens Achromatic
Shutters 1895–1896: Tisdell
1896–1902: Rotary
Numbers made 30,000 approximately

Description/Remarks

The No 2 Bullet was 'aimed' at the Boston Camera Company's Bull's-Eye camera, which was marketed from 1892, incorporating S.N. Turner's invention of the numbered paper-backed rollfilm. It was the first Kodak camera to use the 'cartridge' rollfilm.

Leather covered wooden casing; the early Tisdell shutter had a single button for setting time and instantaneous exposures and for taking, while the later rotary shutter had a separate pull-up control to set for time exposures.

Variations

1895–May 1896: Round finder; Tisdell shutter, fixed aperture; from serial number 351.

May 1896–Aug. 1900: Improved model; rotary shutter, 3 apertures on pull-up strip, square finder; provision for single plateholder through door in side. *Sept. 1897:* Fittings changed from brass to nickel, from serial number 17,941. *Apr. 1898:* Case changed from spruce to cherry wood, from serial number 19,111. *May 1899:* Noiseless winding key fitted, from serial number 25,120. *Aug. 1900:* Brilliant finder; provision for double plateholder, from serial number 27,501.

No 2 Bullet Special Kodak

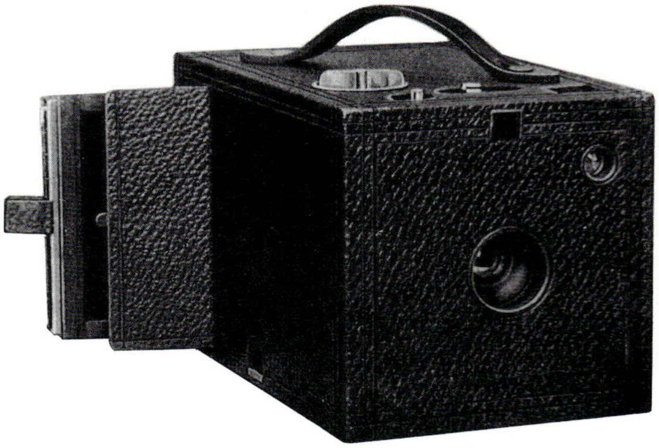

Type Box rollfilm
Introduced May 1898
Discontinued April 1904
Film size 101
Picture size 3½ × 3½in.
Manufactured US
Lens Rapid Rectilinear – but see below
Shutter Eastman Triple Action
Numbers made 4,000+

Description/Remarks

Similar in appearance to No 2 Bullet camera, but with opening front to give access for shutter setting, and finder on right (seen from front) instead of centre. Provision for use of double plate holder, through side door; from serial number 1.

Variations

Aug. 1899: Noiseless winding key fitted, from serial number 2,998. *June 1900:* Brilliant finder fitted.

UK VARIATIONS
1901–1907: Goerz Doppel Anastigmat lens. *1901:* Beck-Steinheil Orthostigmat lens.

No 4 Bullet Kodak

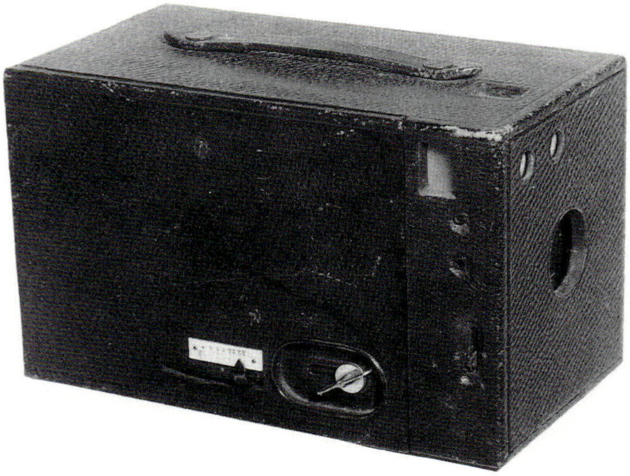

RPS

Type Box rollfilm
Introduced 1896
Discontinued 1900
Film size 103
Picture size 4 × 5in.
Manufactured US
Lens Achromatic
Shutter Rotary
Numbers made 10,000 approximately

Description/Remarks

Leather covered wooden box; two reflecting finders;

pull-out sliding controls for aperture and shutter setting; provision for use of single plate holder; lever focusing; from serial number 1.

Variations

Sept. 1896: guide rollers for film fitted from serial number 219. *May 1898:* Wood of box changed from spruce to cherry and fittings from brass to nickel, from serial number 5,422. *July 1899:* Noiseless winding key fitted, from serial number 8,930.

No 4 Bullet Special Kodak

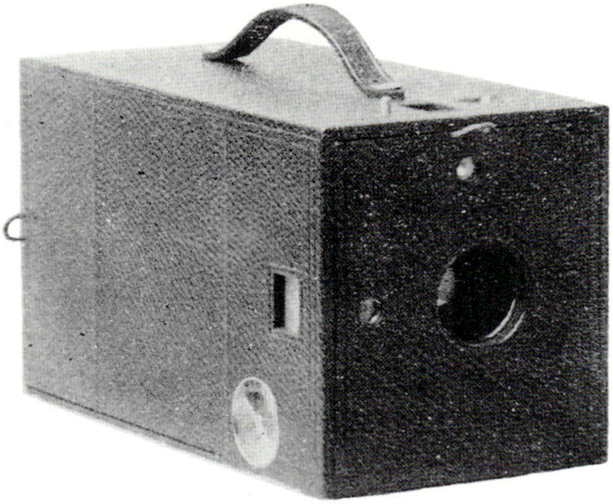

First model, 1898–1900

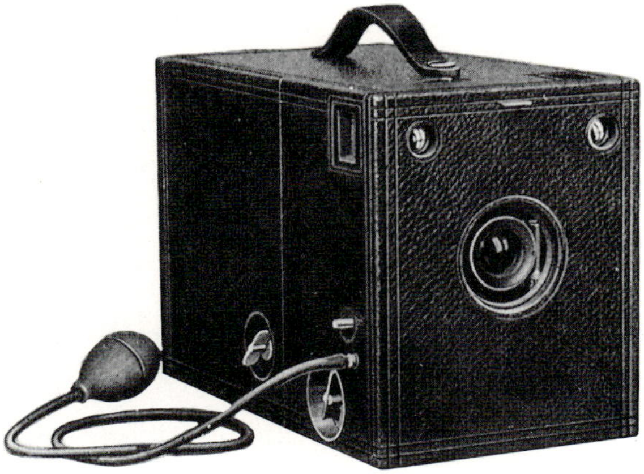

Model C, 1901–1904

Type Box rollfilm
Introduced May 1898
Discontinued April 1904
Film size No 4 Cartridge Roll Holder or 103
Picture size 4 × 5in.
Manufactured US
Lens Rapid Rectilinear
Shutter Eastman Triple Action
Numbers made 6,000+

Description/Remarks

Leather covered wooden box; provision for using double plate holder; front opening for shutter setting; two reflecting finders; rack and pinion focusing; from serial number 2.

Variations

1898–1900: Detachable No 4 horizontal Cartridge Roll Holder fitted; the camera could be supplied for plate use without roll holder; shutter release on top; reflecting finders on centre top and centre side.

Apr. 1901–Apr. 1904: Model C; redesigned, with integral roll holder using 103 rollfilm; brilliant finders on top left and right; pneumatic shutter release and finger release on side; from serial number 5,001.

UK VARIATIONS
1901: Beck-Steinheil Orthostigmat lens. *1901–1904:* Goerz Doppel Anastigmat lens.

No 2 Bulls-Eye Kodak

Type Box rollfilm
Introduced August 1895
Discontinued 1913
Film size 101
Picture size 3½ × 3½in.
Manufactured US
Lens Achromatic
Shutter Rotary
Numbers made 257,000

Description/Remarks

This camera was first manufactured by the Boston Camera Mfg. Company in 1892, the first to use S.N.

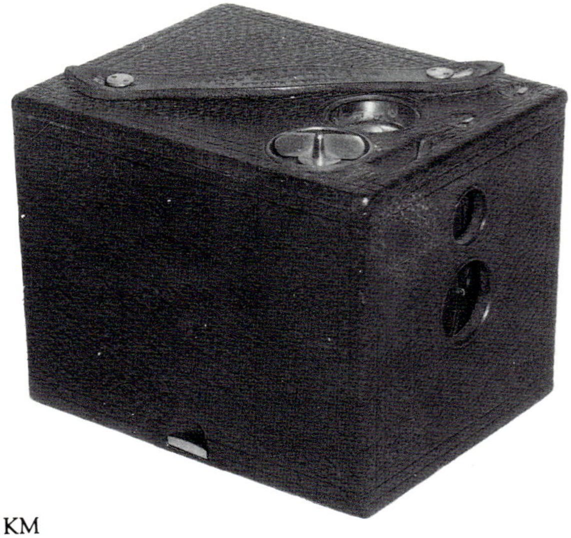

KM

Turner's invention of the numbered paper-backed rollfilm. The company was bought by Eastman in August 1895, and the cameras continued under the Kodak name, but somewhat changed in design, although a few of the first to carry the Kodak name had the D-shaped red window and detachable back and hinged sides of the earlier version.

Variations

Model designations 1896, 1897, 1898, C and D. Leather covered wooden box with lift-out film carrier; circular reflecting finder; fixed focus; from serial number 800.

Aug. 1897: fittings changed from brass to nickel, from serial number 60,025. *Apr. 1898:* wood changed from spruce to cherry; conical light guard fitted; from serial number 83,030. *Mar. 1899:*Noiseless winding key fitted, from serial number 119,900. *Sept. 1900:* Brilliant finder fitted, from serial number 145,311. *Oct.1903:* Film guide rollers blackened.

No 2 Bulls-Eye Special Kodak

Type Box rollfim
Introduced 1898
Discontinued April 1904
Film size 101
Picture size 3½ × 3½in.
Manufactured US
Lens Rapid Rectilinear
Shutter Eastman Triple Action
Numbers made 17,000+

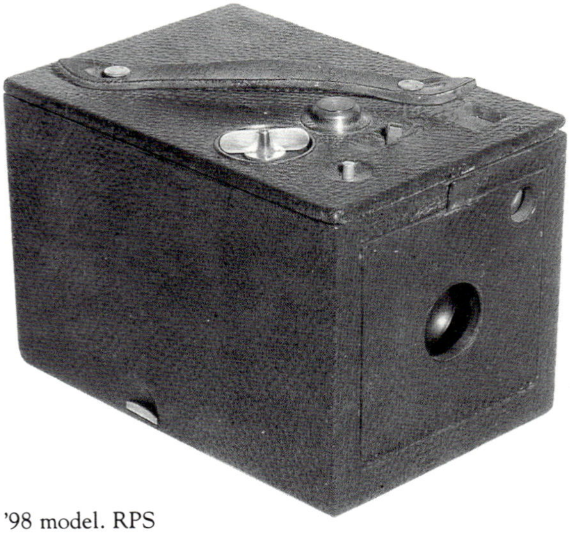

'98 model. RPS

Description/Remarks

Leather covered wooden box; square reflecting finder; fixed focus; front hinged for access to shutter and aperture scales; from serial number 1.

Variations

Model designations 1898, 1899 and C.
June 1898: Conical light guard fitted; from serial number 3,764. *Feb. 1901:* Brilliant finders fitted. *July 1901:* Noiseless winding key fitted, from serial number 16,109.

UK VARIATIONS
1901: Beck-Steinheil Orthostigmat lens. *1901–1904:* Goerz Doppel Anastigmat lens.

No 3 Bulls-Eye Kodak, Model A

Type Box rollfilm
Introduced March 1908
Discontinued 1913
Film size 124
Picture size 3¼ × 4¼in.

Manufactured US
Lens Achromatic
Shutter Rotary
Numbers made 23,000

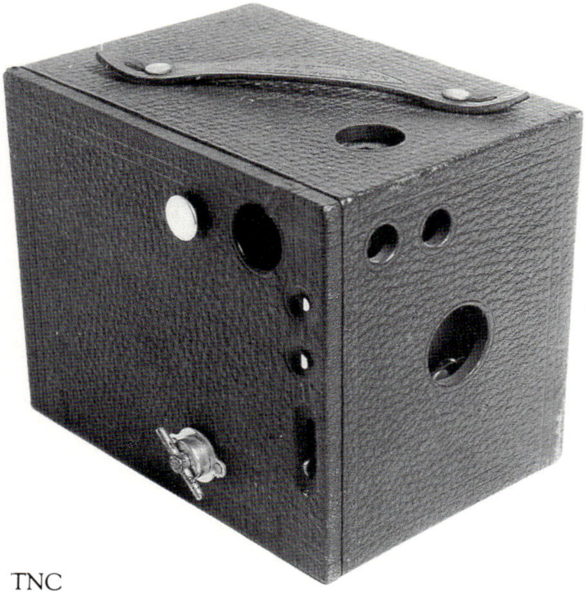

TNC

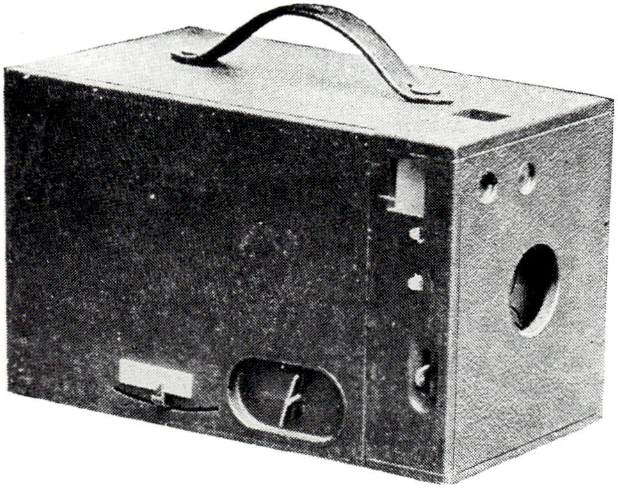

Variations

Model designations 1896, 1897, 1898, C and D.
Sept. 1899: Noiseless winding key fitted; improved case lock; from serial number 22,399. *July 1900:* Brilliant finders fitted; from serial number 25,409. *Dec. 1903:* Lens mount fastened so that it can be removed from the back: from serial number 36,506.

Description/Remarks

Seal-grain leather covered wooden box; brilliant finders; pull-out aperture and shutter setting strips; from serial number 1.

No 4 Bulls-Eye Kodak

Type Box rollfilm
Introduced 1898
Discontinued 1904
Film size 103
Picture size 4 × 5in.
Manufactured US
Lens Achromatic
Shutter Rotary
Numbers made 37,000

Description/Remarks

Leather covered wooden box; two reflecting finders; lever focusing; pull-out aperture and shutter setting strips; from serial number 251.

No 4 Bulls-Eye Special Kodak

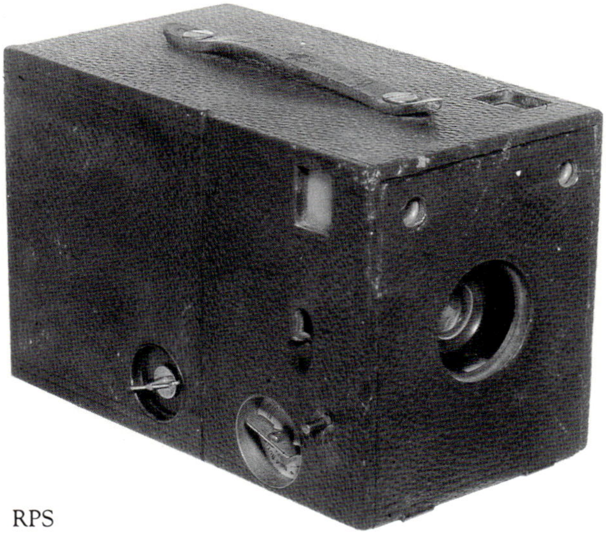

RPS

Type Box rollfilm
Introduced 1898
Discontinued April 1904
Film size 103
Picture size 4 × 5in.
Manufactured US
Lens Rapid Rectilinear
Shutter Eastman Triple Action
Numbers made 10,000

Description/Remarks

Leather covered wooden box; recessed key operated focusing; hinged front for access to shutter and aperture scales; two reflecting finders; from serial number 1.

Variations

Model designations 1898 and C.

Feb. 1901: Brilliant finders fitted; from serial number 7,007.

UK VARIATIONS
1901: Beck-Steinheil Orthostigmat lens. *1901–1904:* Goerz Doppel Anastigmat lens.

Century of Progress World's Fair Souvenir

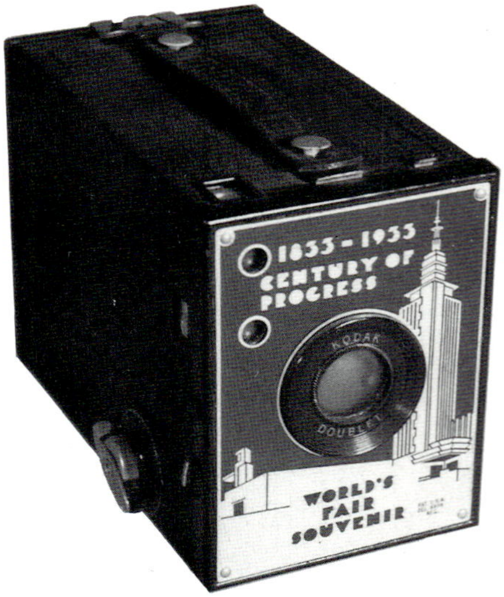

PDM

Type Box rollfilm
Introduced 1933
Discontinued 1933
Film size 120
Picture size 2¼ × 3¼in.
Manufactured US
Lens Doublet
Shutter Rotary
Numbers made 2,000 approximately

Description/Remarks

Special version of Brownie Special No 2 camera with decorative front panel.

No 1 Cone (or Cone Pocket Kodak)

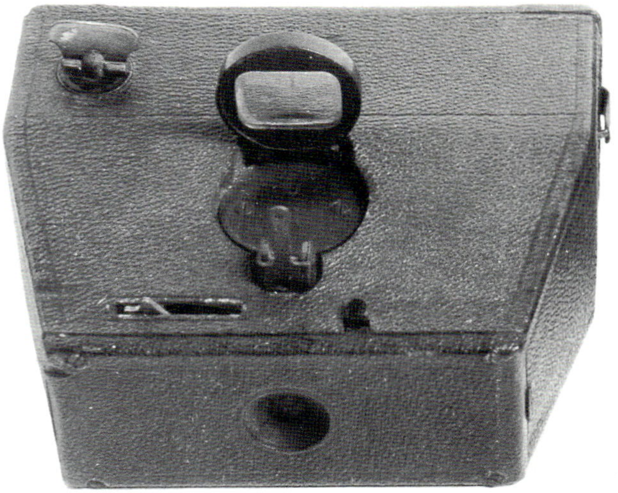

TNC

Type Box rollfilm
Introduced Shipped January 1898
Discontinued –
Film size 102
Picture size 1 × 1½in.
Manufactured US, for UK market only
Lens Meniscus
Shutter Rotary
Numbers made 1,000

Description/Remarks

Tapered box body, red leather covering; folding optical finder; 3 apertures on pull-up strip. No Kodak identification, marked "Made in USA"; not included in any catalogue. The cameras may have been produced as a token batch to establish a presence for a new design in the European market; a London manager's notebook recorded in 1898 "Cone Pockets sent to Paris, Feb., to stop competition". Several have survived, and the cameras were clearly sold somewhere.

No 2 Cone

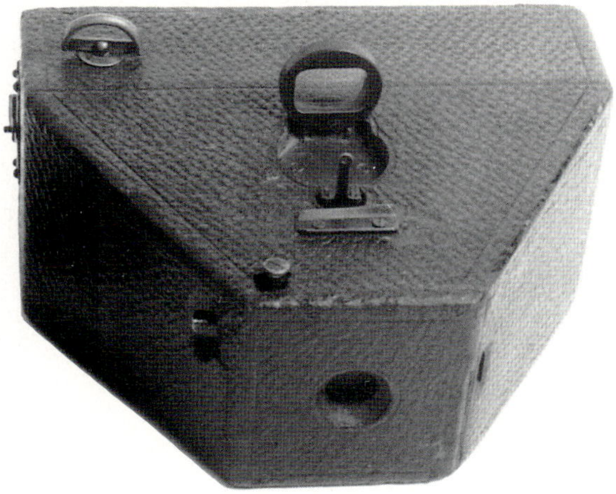

TNC

Type Box rollfilm
Introduced Shipped November 1898
Discontinued –
Film size 105
Picture size $2\frac{1}{4} \times 3\frac{1}{4}$in.
Manufactured US, for UK market only
Lens Meniscus
Shutter Eastman Automatic
Numbers made 500

Description/Remarks

Black leather covered tapered wooden box; folding optical finder; 3 apertures on pull-out strip. No Kodak identification; marked "Made in USA". Presumably produced for the same purpose as the No 1 Cone (q.v.).

'A' Daylight Kodak

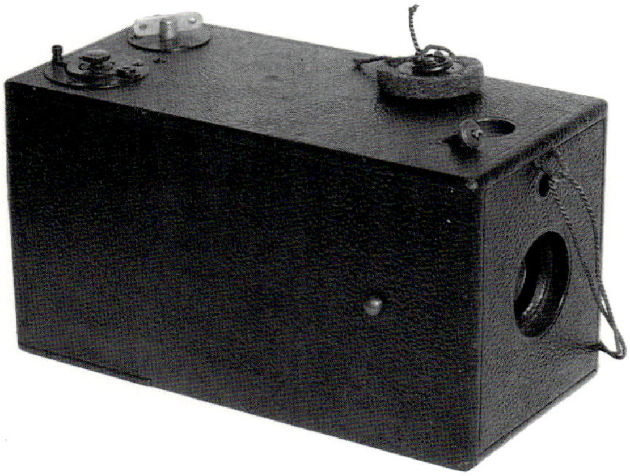

Type Box rollfilm
Introduced December 1891
Discontinued 1895
Film size 24 exposure special daylight loading
Picture size $2\frac{3}{4} \times 3\frac{1}{4}$in.
Manufactured US
Lens Single, fixed aperture and focus
Shutter Special Sector Type
Numbers made 2,350

Description/Remarks

Leather covered wooden box; single reflecting finder; string-set shutter; film in card cartons, with black cloth leader, permitting loading in subdued light; automatic lock on film wind; exposure counter.

'B' Daylight Kodak

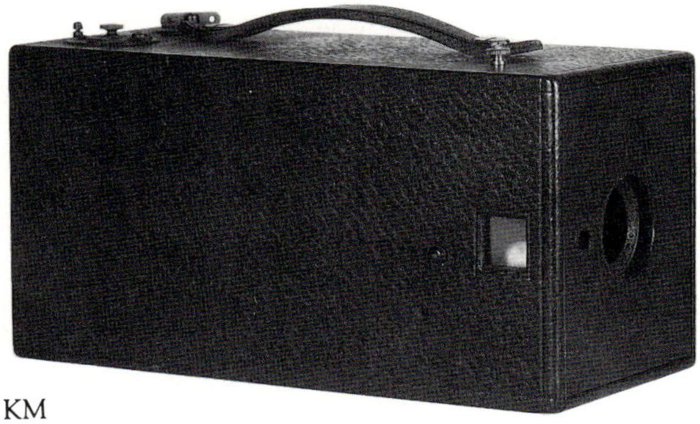

KM

Type Box rollfilm
Introduced Dec. 1891
Discontinued 1895
Film size 24 exposure special daylight loading
Picture size 3½ × 4in.
Manufactured US
Lens Double lens, fixed focus, wheel stops
Shutter Special Sector Type
Numbers made 3,100

Description/Remarks

Leather covered wood box; single reflecting finder; string-set shutter; film in card cartons, with black cloth leader, permitting loading in subdued light; automatic lock on film wind; exposure counter.

'C' Daylight Kodak

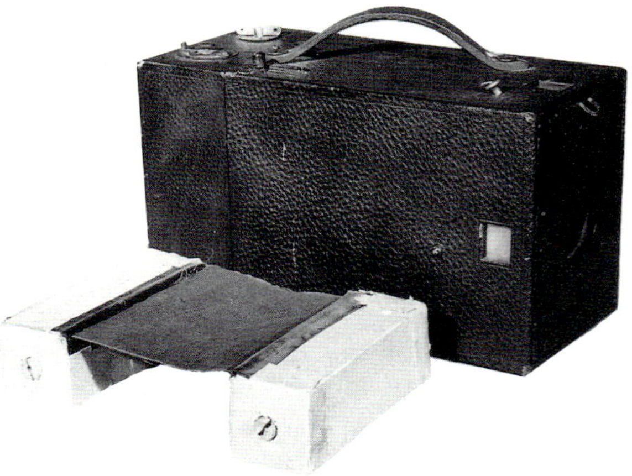

KM

Type Box rollfilm
Introduced December 1891
Discontinued 1895
Film size 24 exposure special daylight loading
Picture size 4 × 5in.
Manufactured US
Lens Double lens, wheel stops
Shutter Special Sector Type
Numbers made 2,475

Description/Remarks

Leather covered wood box; two reflecting finders; string-set shutter; film in card carton, with black cloth leader, permitting loading in subdued light; automatic lock on film wind; exposure counter; glass plate attachment available, interchangeable with detachable film holder.

The Eastman Anniversary

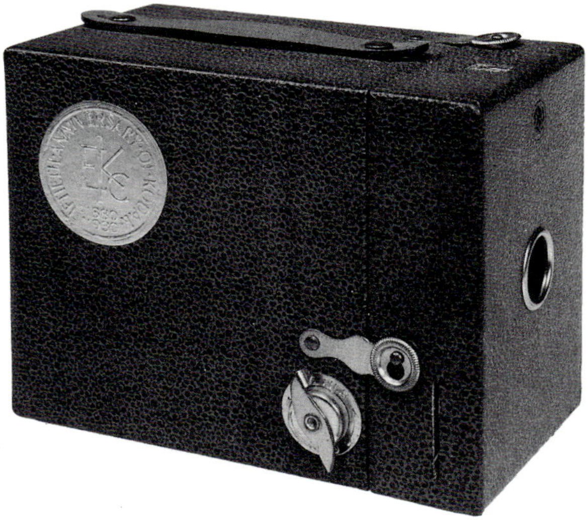

KM

Type Box rollfilm
Introduced May 1930
Discontinued –
Film size 120
Picture size 2¼ × 3¼in.
Manufactured US
Lens Meniscus
Shutter Rotary
Numbers made 557,000

Description/Remarks

A special model created to celebrate the 50th anniversary of Eastman's company. It was based on the No.2 Hawk-Eye premium camera. Tan leatherette covering, with gilt fittings and gold foil anniversary badge. The cameras were distributed free through Kodak dealers in America and Canada to children who were twelve years old in 1930. All went in two or three days.

Eastman Bullet

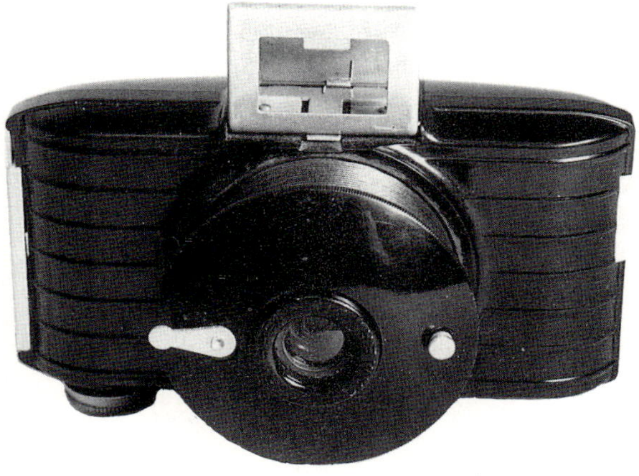

KM

Type Solid body rollfilm
Introduced October 1936
Discontinued October 1942
Film size 127
Picture size 1⅝ × 2½in.
Manufactured US
Lens Meniscus
Shutter Rotary
Numbers made ?

Description/Remarks

Moulded Bakelite plastic body, lens on helical thread extending tube; folding frame finder.

No 2 Eureka

Type Box rollfilm
Introduced June 1897
Discontinued 1899
Film size 106 Cartridge Roll Holder
Picture size 3½ × 3½in.
Manufactured US
Lens Achromatic
Shutter Rotary
Numbers made 14,000

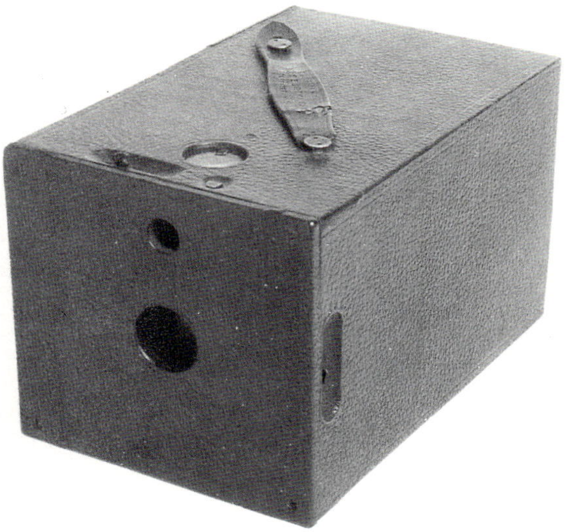

TNC

Description/Remarks

Plate camera, adapted for film with Cartridge Roll Holder; fine grain leather-covered wood box; reflecting finder; pull-up strips for aperture and shutter setting; space in back for three double plate holders or rollholder; from serial number 1.

Variations

Mar. 1898: fitted with improved Bulls-Eye rotary shutter, from serial number 6,000.

No 4 Eureka

Type Box rollfilm
Introduced 1899
Discontinued 1899
Film size 109 Cartridge Roll Holder
Picture size 4 × 5in.
Manufactured US
Lens Achromatic
Shutter Rotary
Numbers made 4,500

Description/Remarks

Plate camera adapted for rollfilm with Cartridge Roll Holder. Fine grain leather covered wood box; two reflecting finders; rack and pinion focusing by recessed

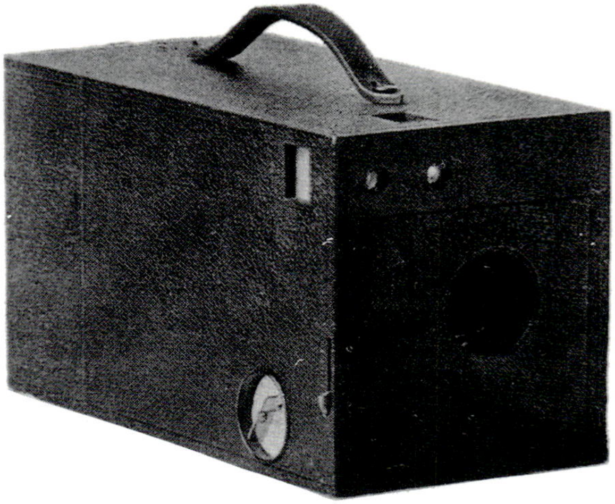

key; space in back for roll holder or three double plateholders; from serial number 200.

Variations

Owing to the existing use of the name Eureka by another manufacturer, W.W. Rouch & Co., this camera was sold on the UK market as the No 4 Zenith camera from October 1899 to 1900.

Falcon Kodak

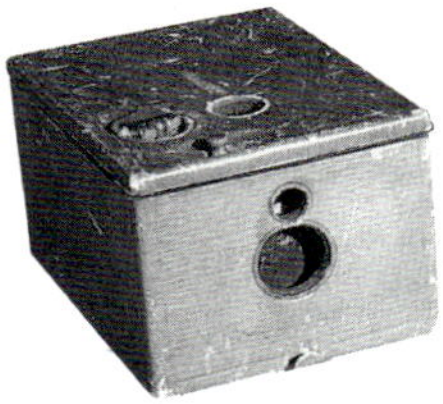

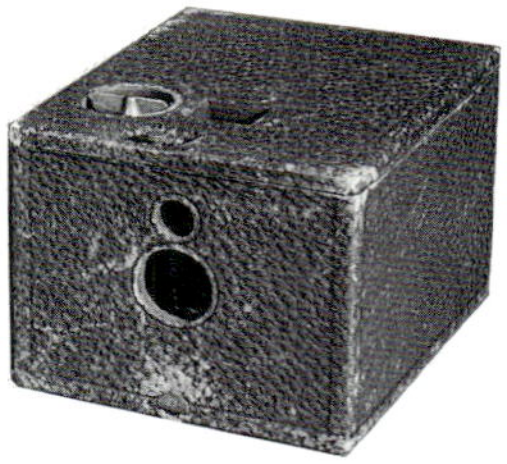

Left: Pocket Kodak camera. Right: Falcon Kodak camera. KM

Type Box rollfilm
Introduced 1897
Discontinued 1898
Film size Special Falcon
Picture size 2 × 2½in.
Manufactured US
Lens Achromatic
Shutter Rotary
Numbers made 2,500

Description/Remarks

Very similar construction to the Pocket Kodak camera, but larger; top lifts out with film carrier and Tisdell shutter; single finder.

No 2 Falcon Kodak

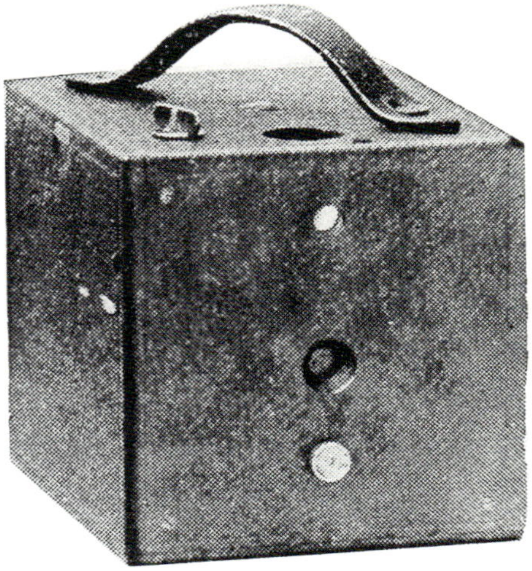

Type Box rollfilm
Introduced September 1897
Discontinued December 1899
Film size 101
Picture size 3½ × 3½in.
Manufactured US
Lens Achromatic
Shutter Rotary
Numbers made 35,000

Description/Remarks

Leather covered wood box; circular reflecting finder; top and sides lift off film carrier; separate shutter; pull-up strip for aperture setting.

This camera was redesigned and renamed No 2 Flexo in April 1899.

Variations

June 1898: conical light guard fitted.

Early 1899: a small number of redesigned cameras,

with removable sides, back released by a catch in the finder lens opening and integral shutter, were redesignated "Improved No 2 Falcon Kodak"; soon afterwards the name was changed to No 2 Flexo Kodak.

No 2 Flexo Kodak

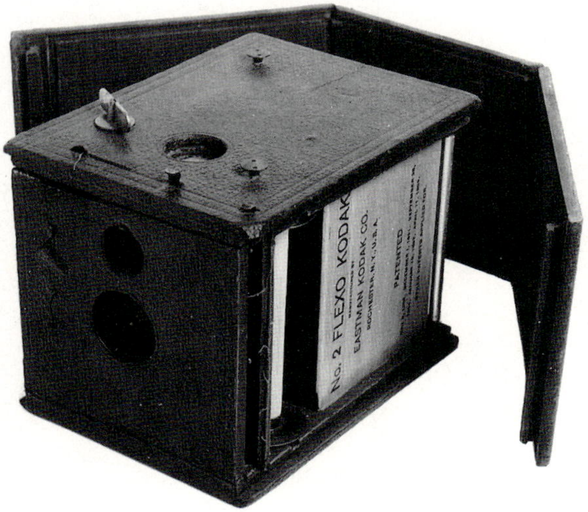

TNC

Type Box rollfilm
Introduced December 1899
Discontinued April 1913
Film size 101
Picture size 3½ × 3½in.
Manufactured US
Lens Achromatic
Shutter Rotary
Numbers made 118,800

Description/Remarks

New version of the No 2 Falcon Kodak camera. Grained leather covered wood box; back and sides released by catch in large finder window; circular reflecting finder; pull-up strips for aperture and shutter setting; from serial number 35,000. The camera was named No 2 Plico Kodak for the UK market.

The Kodak

Type Box darkroom loaded rollfilm
Introduced June 1888
Discontinued 1889
Film size 100 exposure darkroom loaded
Picture size 2½in. diameter circular
Manufactured US
Lens Periscopic
Shutter Cylindrical barrel
Numbers made 5,200+

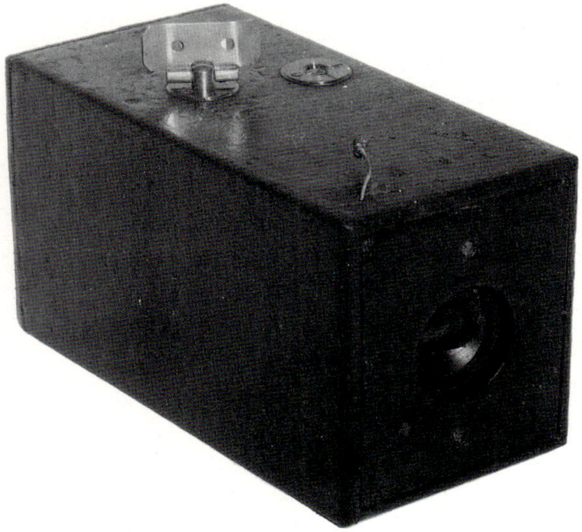
RPS

Description/Remarks

The first Kodak camera; smooth black morocco leather covered wooden box; roll holder removed by unscrewing winding key; revolving exposure indicator in peep-hole in top; no exposure counter; string-set shutter; no finder,but V sighting lines on camera top; release button above centre on right (seen from front); felt lens plug for time exposures; two screws fix front panel; initially took darkroom loaded paper negative stripping film until the introduction of celluloid rollfilm in late 1889.

No 1 Kodak

Type Box darkroom loaded rollfilm
Introduced 1889
Discontinued 1895
Film size 100 exposure darkroom loaded

Picture size 2½in. diameter circular
Manufactured US
Lens Periscopic
Shutter Sector type
Numbers made 10,000+

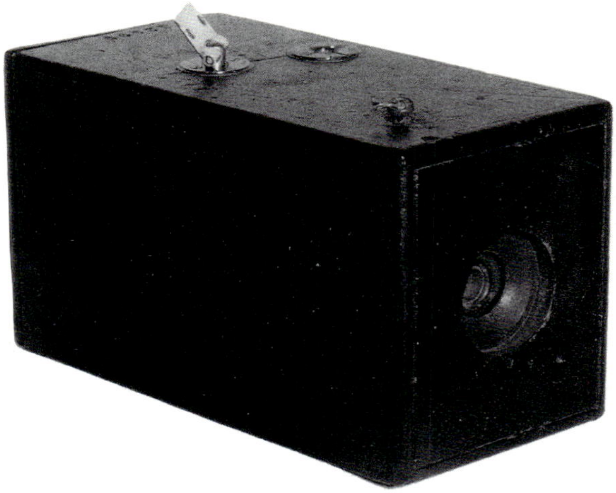

RPS

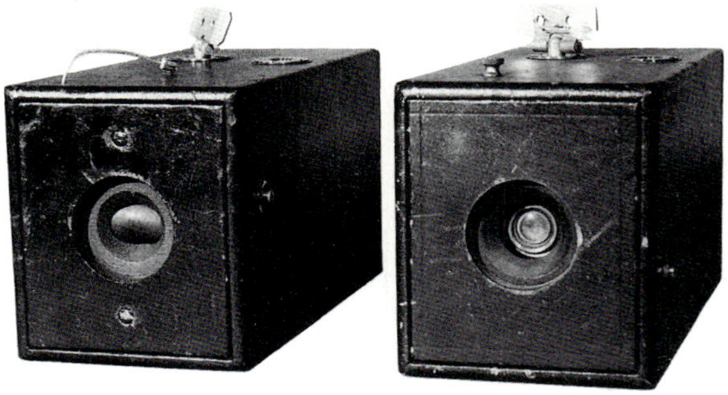

Left: The Kodak camera. Right: No 1 Kodak camera. KM

Description/Remarks

During 1889 the cylindrical shutter on the Kodak camera, which was expensive to manufacture, was replaced by a simpler sector shutter. Appearance differs from original model in having no screws on front panel, lens always visible, shutter release below centre on right (seen from front), cocking string further back and to the right. After October 1889 and the introduction of the No 2 Kodak camera, this model was known as the No 1 Kodak camera. Serial numbers in sequence from original model.

No 2 Kodak

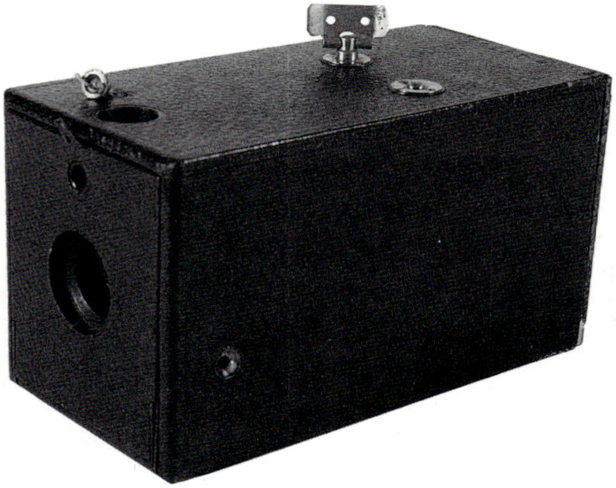

KM

Type Box darkroom loaded rollfilm
Introduced October 1889
Discontinued 1897
Film size 60 or 100 exposure darkroom loaded
Picture size 3½in. diameter circular
Manufactured US
Lens Periscopic
Shutter Sector type
Numbers made 19,000+

Description/Remarks

Leather covered wood box; circular reflecting finder; fixed focus lens; aperture adjusted by removing front panel; string-set shutter; rotating exposure indicator, no counter until 1892; integral rollholder.

No 3 Kodak

Type Box darkroom loaded rollfilm
Introduced December 1889
Discontinued 1897
Film size 60 or 100 exposure darkroom loaded
Picture size 4¼ × 3¼in.
Manufactured US
Lens Bausch & Lomb Universal
Shutter Sector type
Numbers made 4,050

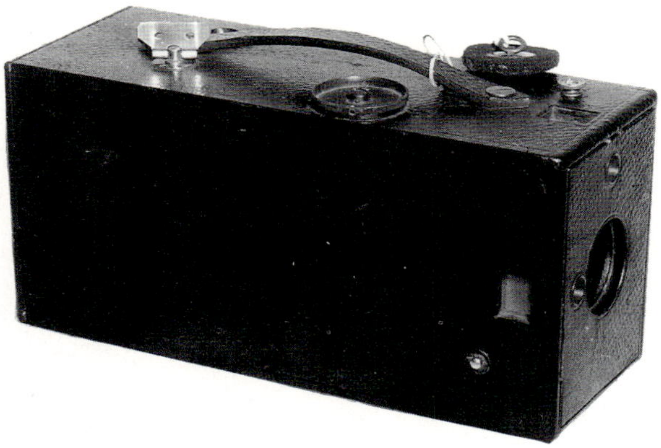

RPS

Description/Remarks

Leather covered wooden box; two reflecting finders; front panel removes to adjust aperture and shutter speed; string-set shutter; rack and pinion focusing, control on camera top; rotating exposure indicator, no counter until 1892; tripod sockets; integral roll holder.

No 4 Kodak

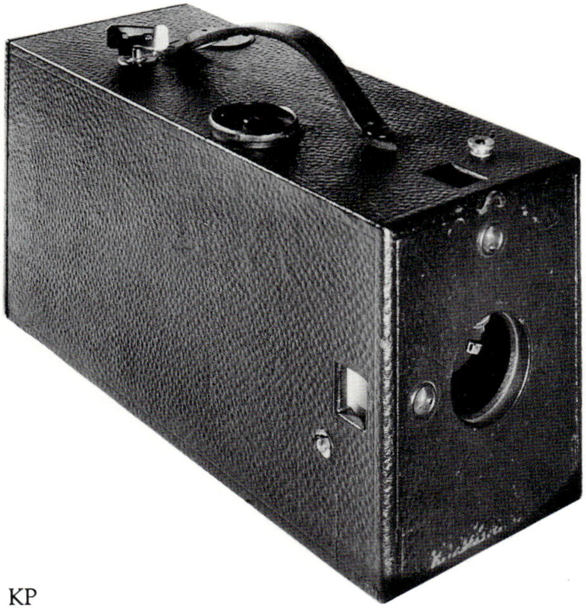

KP

Type Box darkroom loaded rollfilm
Introduced November 1889
Discontinued 1897
Film size 48 or 100 exposure darkroom loaded
Picture size 5 × 4in.
Manufactured US
Lens Bausch & Lomb Universal
Shutter Sector type
Numbers made 4,850

Description/Remarks

Leather covered wood box; two reflecting finders; front panel removes to adjust aperture and shutter; string-set shutter; rack and pinion focusing, control on camera top; tripod sockets; rotating exposure indicator, no counter until 1892; integral rollholder.

Kodak Autosnap

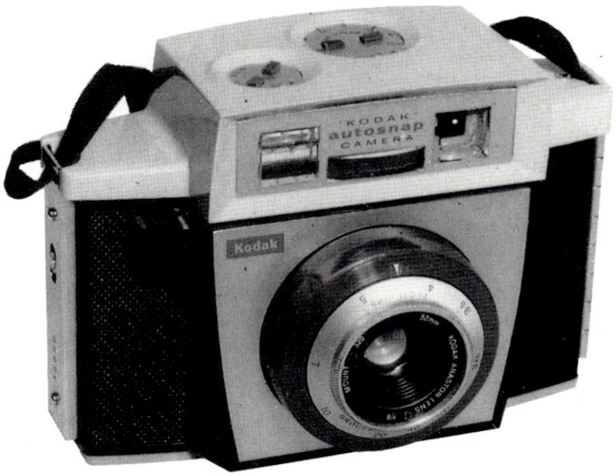

RPS

Type Automatic solid body eyelevel rollfilm
Introduced May 1962
Discontinued 1964
Film size 127
Picture size 1⅝ × 1⅝in.
Manufactured UK
Lens Anaston f/8, 50mm
Shutter Single speed (1/40) sec.
Numbers made ?

Description/Remarks

Moulded plastic body; automatic exposure setting by photocell, manual setting for flash; low light warning in direct vision optical finder; pin and screw flash sockets; front cell focusing; lever film wind.

Kodak Bantam f/8

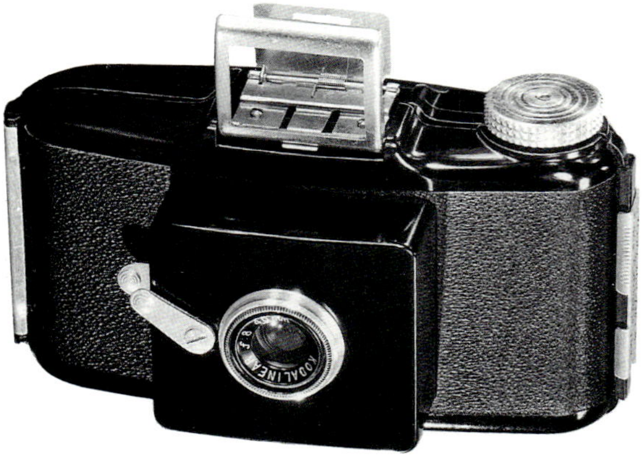

KP

Type Solid body eyelevel rollfilm
Introduced July 1938
Discontinued October 1942
Film size 828
Picture size 28 × 40mm
Manufactured US
Lens Kodalinear f/8
Shutter Built-in
Numbers made ?

Description/Remarks

Moulded Bakelite plastic body; lens on square section telescoping tube; folding frame finder.

Kodak Bantam Colorsnap

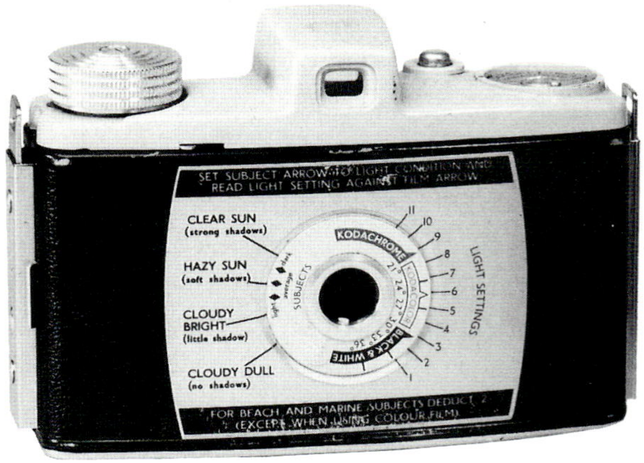

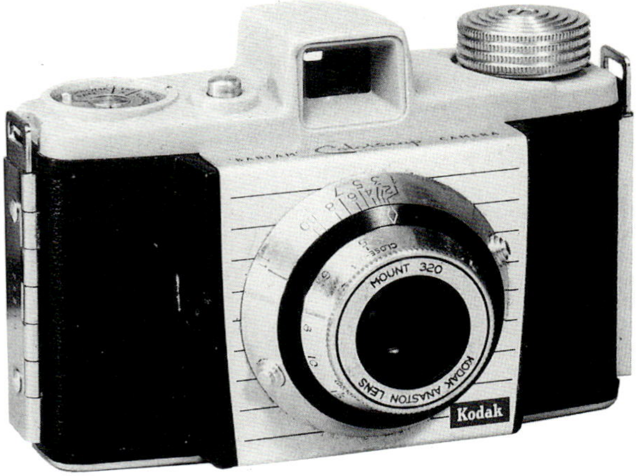

KM

Type Solid body eyelevel rollfilm
Introduced May 1955
Discontinued September 1959
Film size 828
Picture size 28 × 40mm
Manufactured UK
Lens Kodak Anaston f/4.5
Shutter Dakon self-setting
Numbers made ?

Description/Remarks

Designed to make colour photography with Kodachrome film simple for the non-expert; dial-the-weather exposure calculator on back; EV scale; direct vision optical finder; double exposure prevention, with over-ride control on models from 1958; alloy body with plastic top; front cell focusing.

Kodak Bantam Colorsnap II

Type Solid body eyelevel rollfilm
Introduced September 1959
Discontinued July 1961
Film size 828
Picture size 28 × 40mm
Manufactured UK
Lens Kodak Anaston f/4.5, 51mm
Shutter Dakon self-setting
Numbers made ?

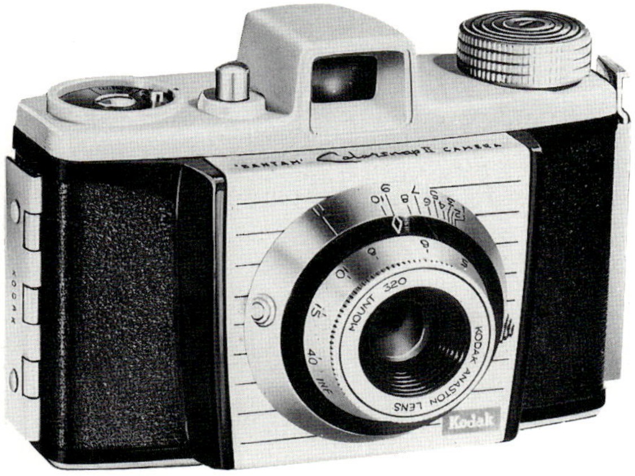

KP

Description/Remarks

Similar to original Colorsnap camera but with moulded plastic body; Kodacolor film included on exposure guide.

Kodak Bantam Colorsnap 3

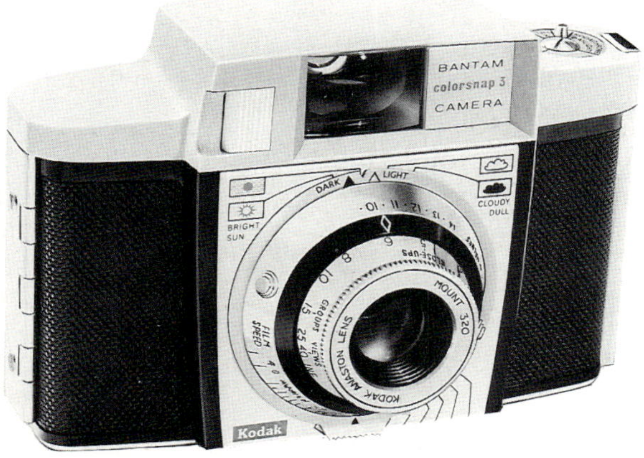

KM

Type Solid body eyelevel rollfilm
Introduced October 1961
Discontinued 1963
Film size 828
Picture size 28 × 40 mm
Manufactured UK
Lens Kodak Anaston f/3.9, 43.9mm
Shutter Single speed (1/40) sec.
Numbers made ?

Description/Remarks

Restyled, with more angular moulded plastic body; exposure guide on camera front; direct vision optical finder; press-in shutter release; double exposure prevention with over-ride; lever film wind; pin and screw flash contacts; front-cell focusing.

Kodak Bantam RF

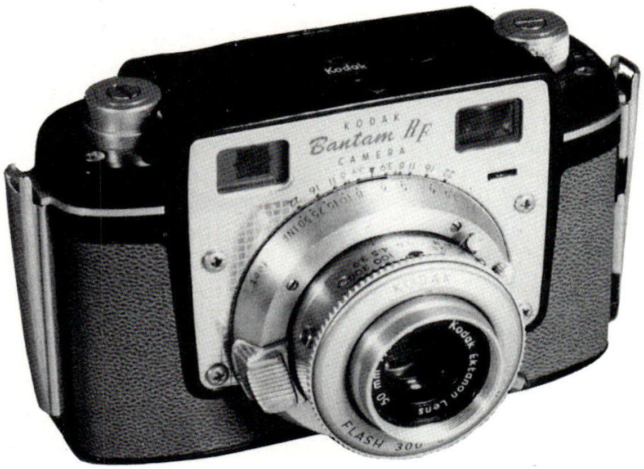

PDM

Type Solid body eyelevel rollfilm
Introduced October 1953
Discontinued January 1957
Film size 828
Picture size 28 × 40mm
Manufactured US
Lens Kodak Ektanon f/3.9
Shutter Kodak Flash 300
Numbers made ?

Description/Remarks

Sold with case and flash holder as the Kodak Town and Country Outfit. The camera was sold alone from April 1954. Coupled rangefinder combined with direct vision optical finder; flash synchronised.

Kodak Box 620

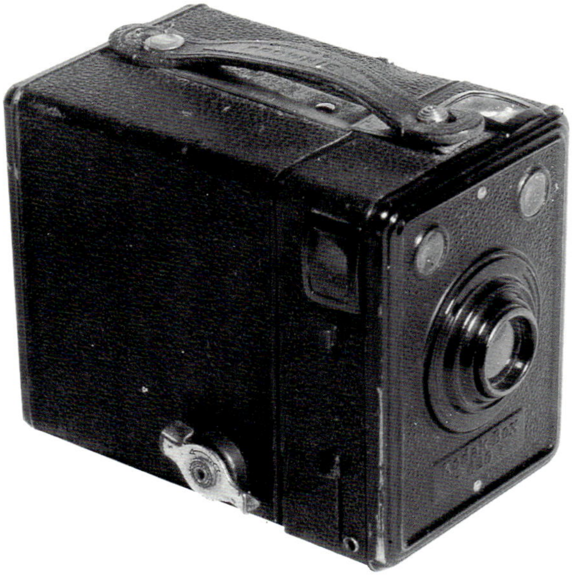

RPS

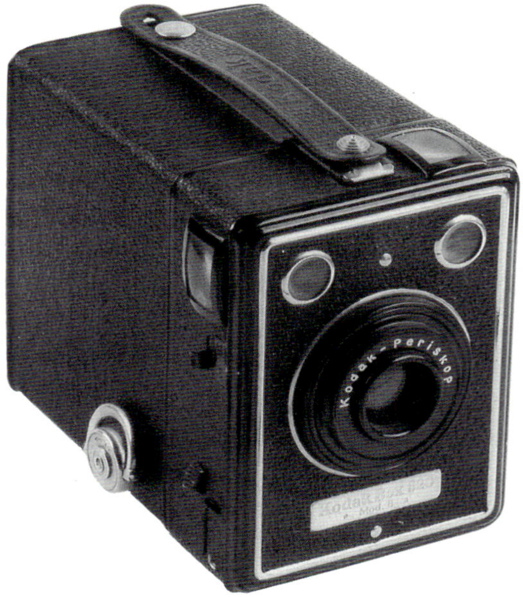

Model B, 1937–1939. KAG

Type Box rollfilm
Introduced 1936
Discontinued 1939
Film size 620
Picture size 6 × 9cm
Manufactured Germany
Lenses 1936–1939: Meniscus
1937–1939: Periskop (Model B)
Shutter Single speed
Numbers made 425,000

Description/Remarks

Metal body; two brilliant finders; two tripod sockets. Model B (1937–1939) had nickel plated trim and accidental exposure prevention.

Kodak Chevron

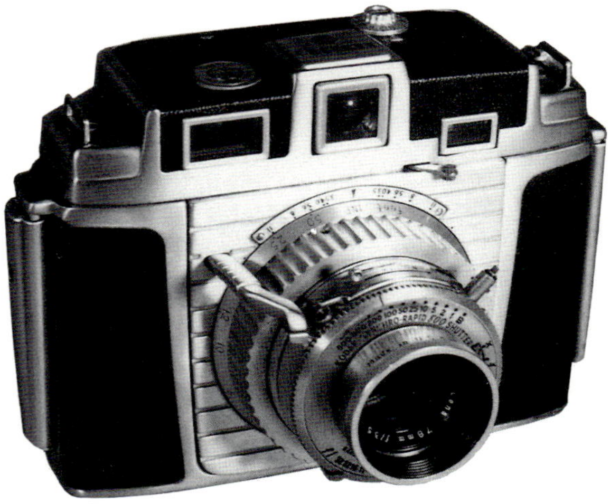

PDM

Type Solid body eyelevel rollfilm
Introduced October 1953
Discontinued December 1956
Film size 620
Picture size 2¼ × 2¼in.
Manufactured US
Lens Kodak Ektar f/3.5
Shutter Synchro-Rapid 800
Numbers made ?

Description/Remarks

Advanced specification with between-lens shutter

with a maximum speed of 1/800 sec. Coupled rangefinder; separate direct vision optical finder; bayonet flash contacts.

Kodak Duaflex

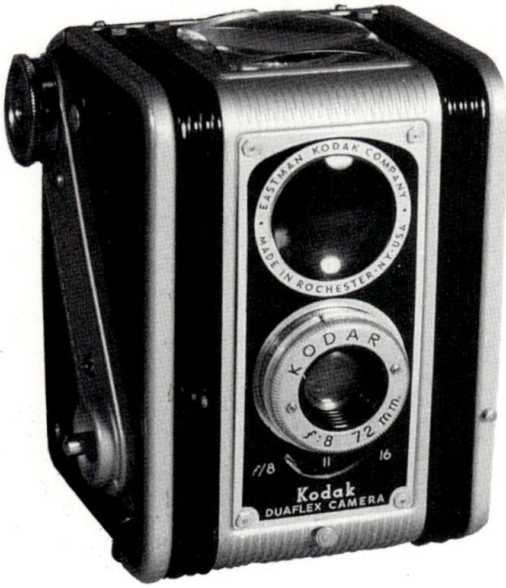

US model. PDM

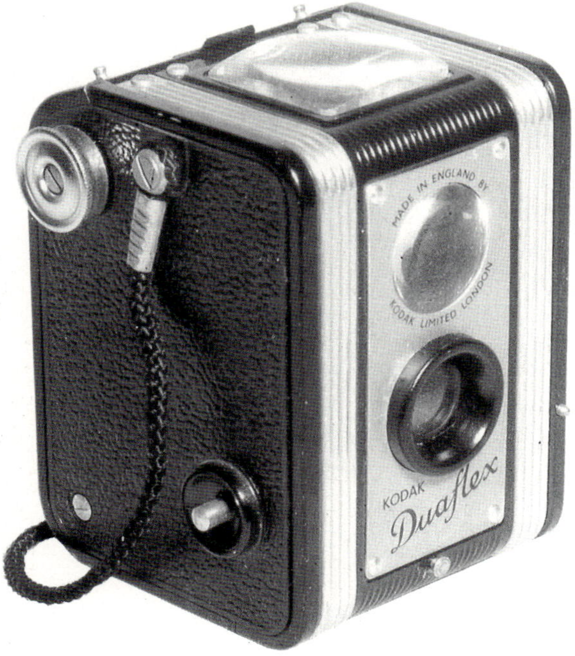

UK model. RPS

Type Box rollfilm
Introduced December 1947 (1949 in UK)
Discontinued September 1950 (1955 in UK)
Film size 620
Picture size 2¼ x x2¼in.
Manufactured US, UK
Lenses Kodet meniscus f/15 fixed focus
March 1949–1950: Kodar f/8 focusing (US only)
Shutter Built-in, flash synchronised
Numbers made ?

Description/Remarks

'Twin-lens reflex' style box camera with large reflecting finder; 2-pin flash contacts; f/8 lens model with double exposure prevention feature.

Kodak Duaflex II

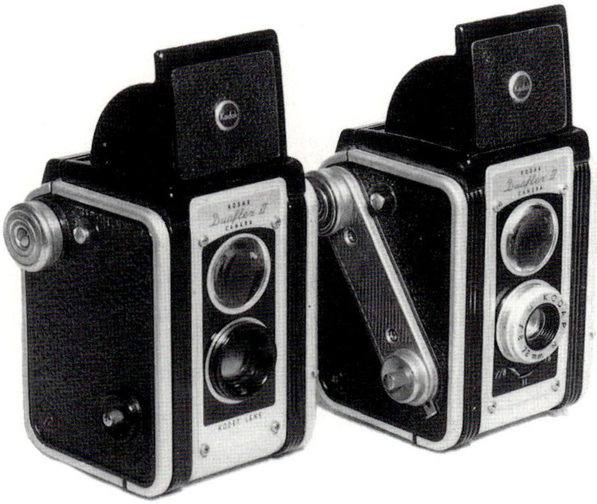

US models. RPS

Type Box rollfilm
Introduced June 1950 (July 1955 in UK)
Discontinued May 1954 (1960 in UK)
Film size 620
Picture size 2¼ x 2¼in.
Manufactured US, UK
Lenses Kodet meniscus f/15 fixed focus
Kodar f/8 focusing (US only)
Shutter Built-in, flash synchronised
Numbers made ?

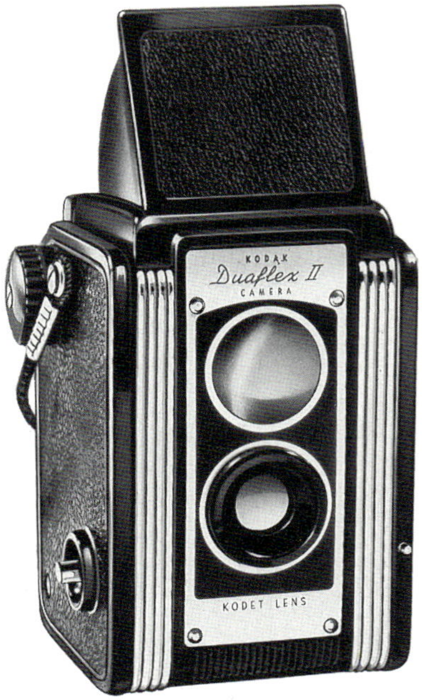

UK model. KP

Description/Remarks

Improved model; large reflecting finder with folding hood; 2-pin flash contacts; f/8 model has double exposure prevention feature.

Variations

Jan. 1953: "B" altered to "L" on time exposure setting (US model).

Kodak Duaflex III

Type Box rollfilm
Introduced March 1954
Discontinued January 1957
Film size 620
Picture size 2¼ × 2¼in.
Manufactured US
Lenses Kodet meniscus f/15 fixed focus
  Kodar f/8 focusing
Shutter Built-in flash synchronised
Numbers made ?

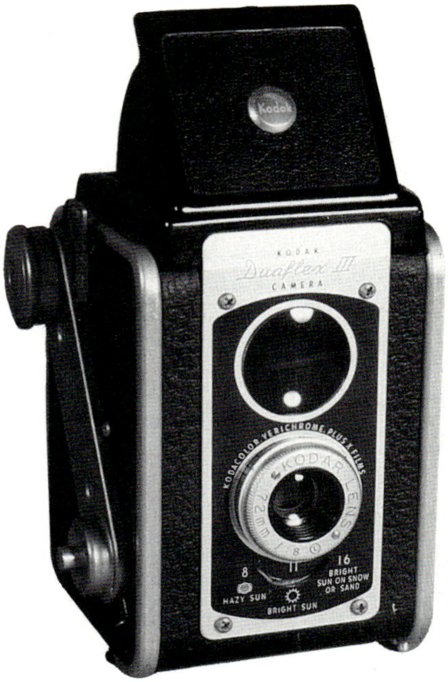

PDM

Description/Remarks

Similar to Duaflex II camera, but screw and pin flash contacts. Both models with double exposure prevention.

Kodak Duaflex IV

Type Box rollfilm
Introduced September 1955
Discontinued March 1960
Film size 620
Picture size 2¼ × 2¼in.
Manufactured US
Lenses Kodet meniscus f/15 fixed focus
  Kodar f/8 focusing (to January 1957)
Shutter Built-in flash synchronised
Numbers made ?

Description/Remarks

Restyled front plate with zone focusing scale on f/8 model; brown and tan finish; double exposure prevention; pin and screw flash contacts.

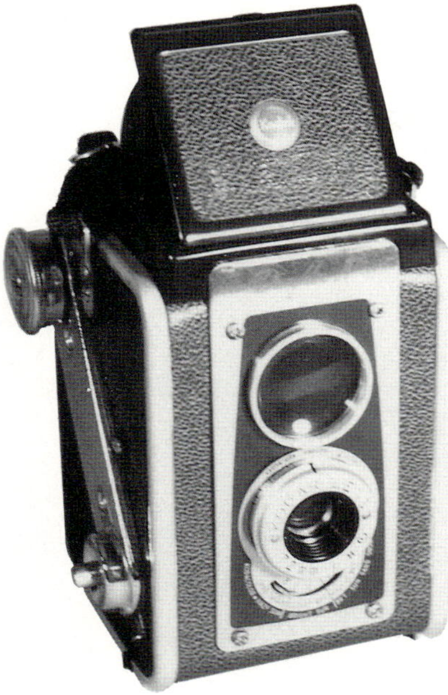

PDM

Kodak Duex

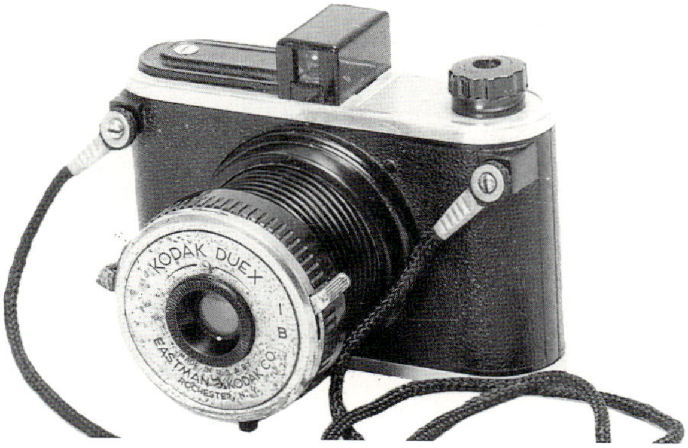

KM

Type Solid body eyelevel rollfilm
Introduced June 1940
Discontinued November 1942
Film size 620
Picture size 1⅝ × 2½in.
Manufactured US
Lens Periscopic Doublet
Shutter Built-in
Numbers made ?

Description/Remarks

Moulded plastic body, metal top and bottom plates; lens on helical screw extending tube; direct vision optical finder; 16 exposures on 620 film.

No 3 Kodak Junior

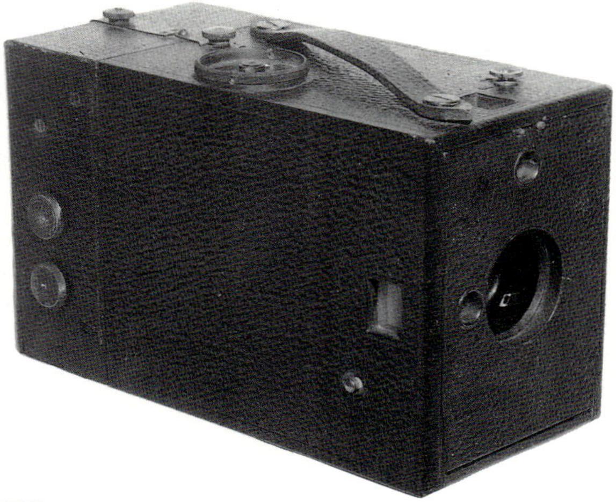

RPS

Type Box darkroom loaded rollfilm
Introduced December 1889
Discontinued 1897
Film size 60-exposure darkroom loaded
Picture size 3¼ × 4¼in.
Manufactured US
Lens Bausch & Lomb Universal
Shutter Sector type
Numbers made 4,100

Description/Remarks

Leather covered wood box; detachable rollholder; two reflecting finders; string-set shutter; rack and pinion focusing, control on top; front opens to set shutter and aperture; rotating exposure indicator.

Variations

1892: exposure counter added (earlier models could be converted), and glass plate attachment available. The camera could be bought without rollholder as the Junior Glass Plate Kodak camera from 1892.

No 4 Kodak Junior

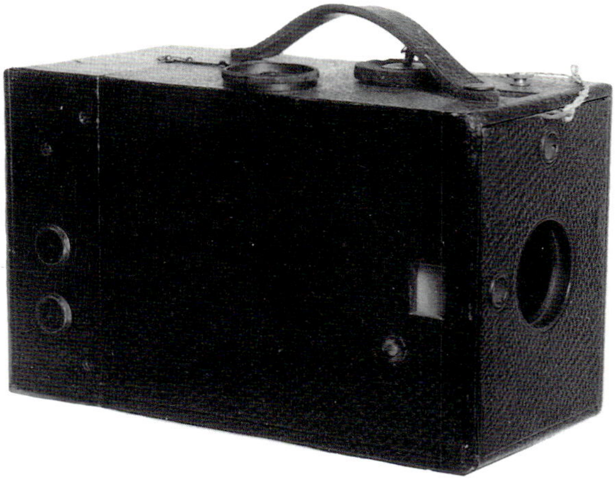

SM

Type Box darkroom loading rollfillm
Introduced December 1889
Discontinued 1897
Film size 48 exposure darkroom loading
Picture size 4 × 5in.
Manufactured US
Lens Bausch & Lomb Universal
Shutter Sector type
Numbers made 4,200

Description/Remarks

Leather covered wood box; detachable rollholder; rotating exposure indicator; front opens for setting aperture and shutter; rack and pinion focusing, control on camera top; stringset shutter.

Variations

1892: Exposure counter fitted (older models could be converted); plate attachment available. The camera was sold without the rollholder, for plates only, as the Junior Glass Plate Kodak camera.

Kodak Medalist

Type Solid body eyelevel rollfilm
Introduced July 1941
Discontinued June 1948
Film size 620
Picture size 2¼ × 3¼in.
Manufactured US
Lens Kodak Ektar f/3.5
Shutter Supermatic
Numbers made ?

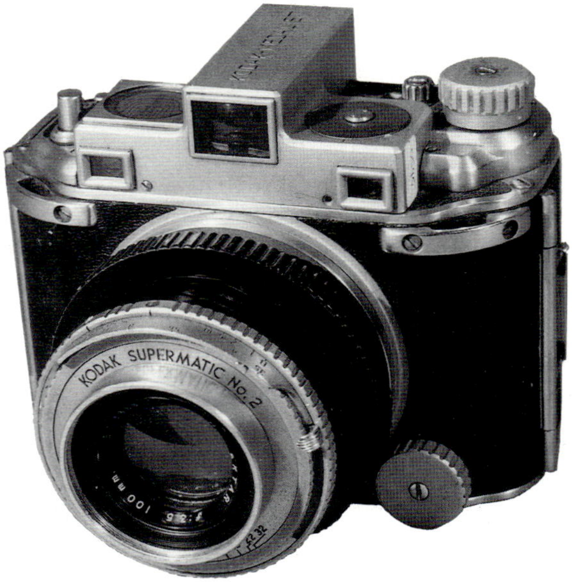

KM

Description/Remarks

Advanced specification; coupled long-base rangefinder; direct vision optical finder with automatic parallax correction; lens extension on double helical tube, with fine focus wheel; accessory back for plates or cut film.

Variations

Lens tube anodised black during World War Two.

Kodak Medalist II

Type Solid body eyelevel rollfilm
Introduced March 1946
Discontinued April 1953
Film size 620
Picture size 2¼ × 3¼in.
Manufactured US
Lens Kodak Ektar f/3.5

Shutter Flash Supermatic
Numbers made ?

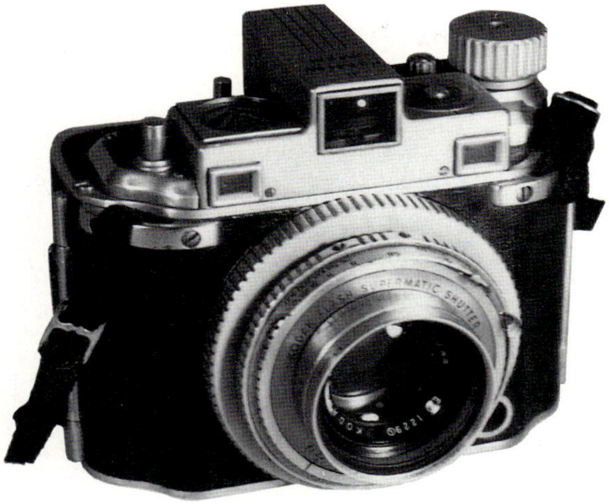

PDM

Description/Remarks

Similar to Medalist I camera, but with flash synchronisation socket replacing fine focus wheel.

Kodak Pony 828

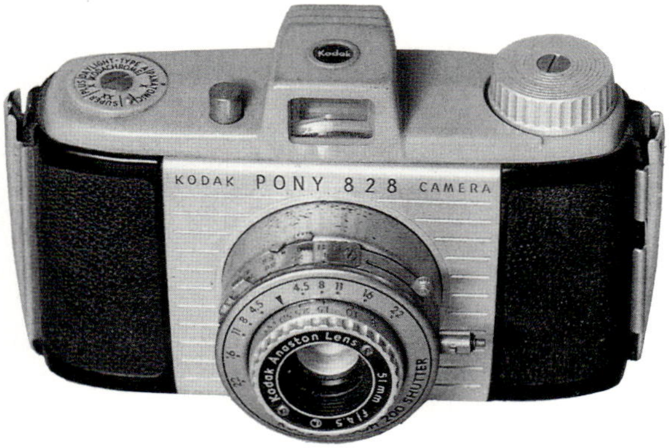

KM

Type Solid body eyelevel rollfilm
Introduced November 1949
Discontinued October 1959
Film size 828
Picture size 28 × 40mm
Manufactured US
Lens Kodak Anaston f/4.5
Shutter Kodak Flash 200
Numbers made ?

Description/Remarks

Moulded plastic body; direct vision optical finder; lens on pull-out tube; flash contacts.

Kodak Pupille

Type Solid body eyelevel rollfilm
Introduced 1931
Discontinued 1935
Film size 127
Picture size 3 × 4cm
Manufactured Germany
Lens Schneider Xenar f/3.5, 5cm – but see below
Shutter Compur
Numbers made 5,000 approximately, (991 from 1933)

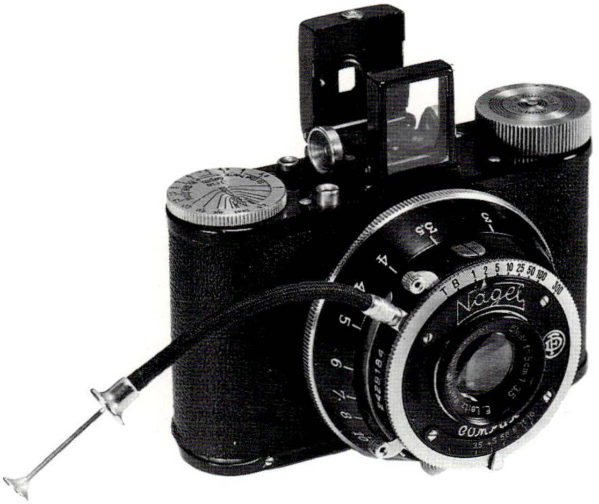

Leitz Elmar lens model. KP

Description/Remarks

First manufactured by Nagel-Werke, then by Kodak AG from 1932. Lens on helical focusing tube, focusing to

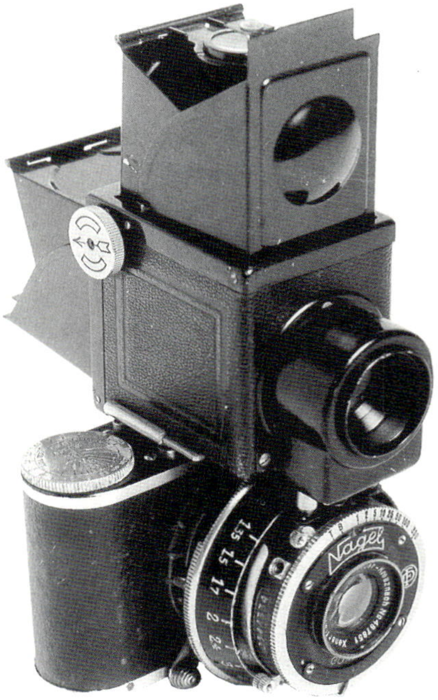

Fitted with Nagel mirror reflex focusing device. TNC

around 13 inches; folding optical frame finder; depth of field scale. Sold by R.F. Hunter in UK in early 1930s under the name Rolloroy.

Variations

1931–1935: Schneider Xenon f/2.0, 4.5cm; Schneider Xenar f/2.9,5cm; Leitz Elmar f/3.5, 5cm.
1932–1935: Zeiss Tessar f/3.5, 5cm; Zeiss Tessar f/2.8, 5cm.

Kodak Ranca No 46 and 46/I

Type Solid body eyelevel rollfilm
Introduced 1930
Discontinued 1934
Film size 127
Picture size 3 × 4cm
Manufactured Germany
Lens Nagel Anastigmat f/4.5, 5cm
Shutters Nagel (model 46)
Ibsor or Pronto (model 46/I)
Numbers made 2,200 approximately

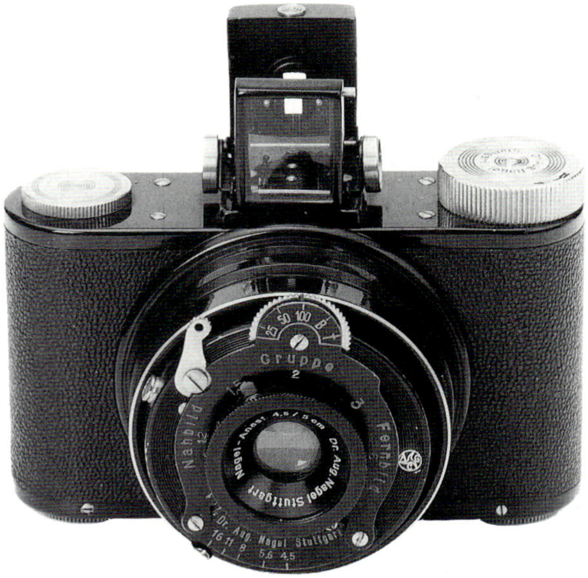

Model 46/1. KAG

Description/Remarks

Inexpensive version of Pupille camera; model 46/I had the same helical focusing lens mount and folding optical frame finder; model 46 had front-cell focusing and folding frame finder. Made before Kodak AG acquired Nagel-Werke, but sold under the Kodak name from 1932 to 1934.

Kodak Reflex

Type Twin-lens reflex rollfilm
Introduced April 1946
Discontinued January 1949
Film size 620
Picture size 2¼ × 2¼in.
Manufactured US
Lens Kodak Anastigmat f/3.5
Shutter Flash Kodamatic
Numbers made ?

Description/Remarks

True twin-lens reflex camera with gear-coupled viewing and taking lenses; hooded reflex screen. Click stops added to aperture setting from June 1948.

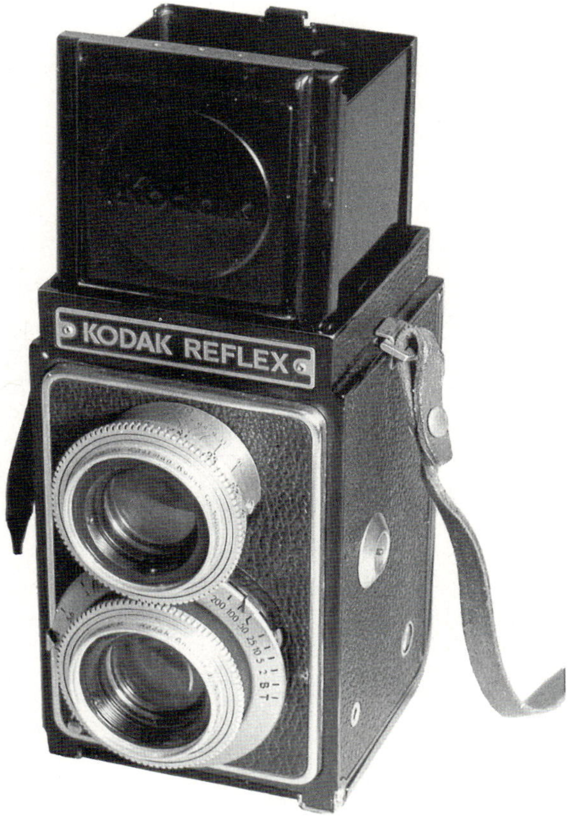

KM

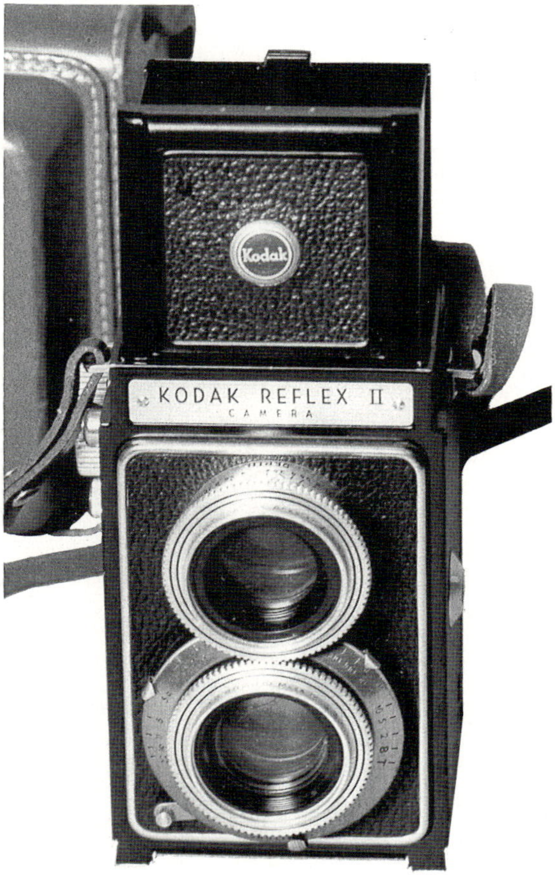

KM

Kodak Reflex II

Type Twin-lens reflex rollfilm
Introduced December 1948
Discontinued September 1949
Film size 620
Picture size 2¼ × 2¼in.
Manufactured US
Lens Kodak Anastar f/3.5
Shutter Flash Kodamatic
Numbers made ?

Description/Remarks

Similar to Kodak Reflex camera but restyled; Ektalite field lens in finder from September 1949.

Kodak Startech

Type Solid body eyelevel rollfilm

Special version of Brownie Starflash camera (q.v.)

Kodak World's Fair Flash

Type Solid body eyelevel rollfilm
Introduced March 1964
Discontinued January 1966
Film size 127
Picture size 1⅝ × 1⅝in.
Manufactured US
Lens Meniscus achromat f/13.5, 50mm
Shutter Single speed, flash synchronised
Numbers made ?

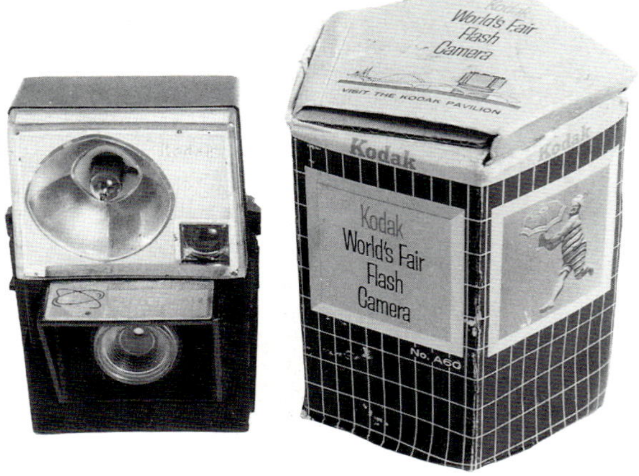

TNC

Description/Remarks

Moulded plastic body; direct vision optical finder; lens shade with 'atom' motif; built-in flash gun for AG1 bulbs. Sold at New York World's Fair 1964-1965.

Kodet cameras

See Chapter 8

New York World's Fair Bullet

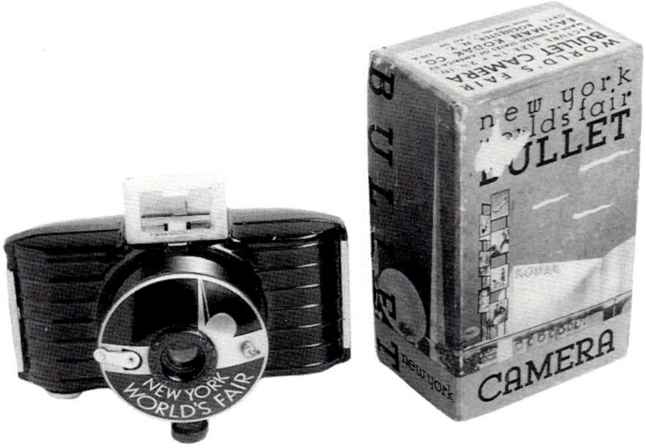

TNC

Type Solid body eyelevel rollfilm
Introduced April 1939
Discontinued October 1940
Film size 127
Picture size 1⅝ × 2½in.
Manufactured US
Lens Meniscus
Shutter Rotary
Numbers made ?

Description/Remarks

Moulded plastic body, lens on helical thread lens tube; folding frame finder. Identical to Eastman Bullet camera, but with "New York World's Fair" on lens plate.

'A' Ordinary Kodak

Type Box darkroom loaded rollfilm
Introduced 1891
Discontinued 1895
Film size 24 exposure darkroom loaded
Picture size 2¾ × 3¼in.
Manufactured US
Lens Single
Shutter Special sector type
Numbers made 2,050

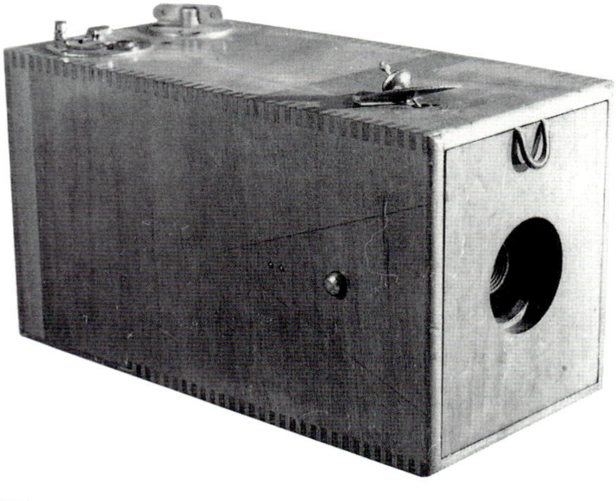

KM

Description/Remarks

Polished natural wood box; fixed focus; no finder, but

V sighting lines on top; string-set shutter; exposure counter and automatic lock.

Lens Single, with wheel stops
Shutter Special sector type
Numbers made 2,025

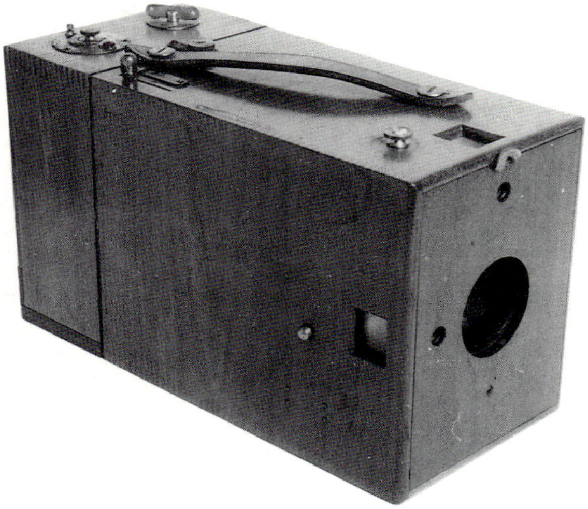

TNC

Description/Remarks

Polished natural wood box; reflecting finder; front removes for aperture and shutter setting; lever focusing; string-set shutter; exposure counter and automatic lock; detachable rollholder, glass plate attachment available – camera sold without rollholder as 'C' Ordinary Glass Plate Kodak camera.

'B' Ordinary Kodak

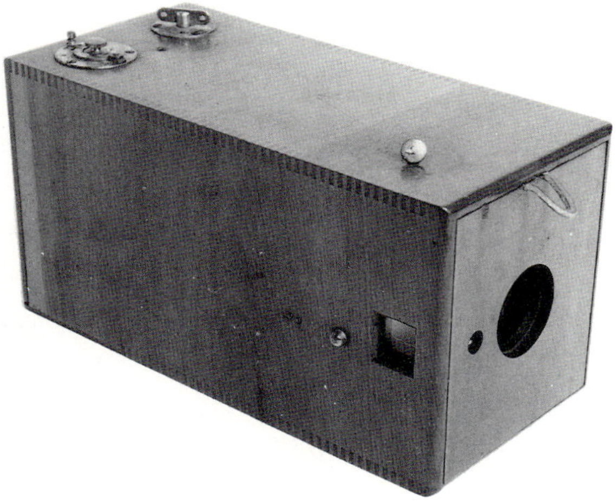

TNC

Type Box darkroom loaded rollfilm
Introduced 1891
Discontinued 1895
Film size 24 exposure darkroom loaded
Picture size 3½ × 4in.
Manufactured US
Lens Single, with wheel stops
Shutter Special sector type
Numbers made 1,900

Description/Remarks

Polished natural wood box; reflecting finder; front panel removes for aperture setting; exposure counter and automatic lock; string-set shutter; fixed focus.

'C' Ordinary Kodak

Type Box darkroom loaded rollfilm
Introduced 1891
Discontinued 1895
Film size 24 exposure darkroom loaded
Picture size 4x5in.
Manufactured US

No 1 Panoram Kodak

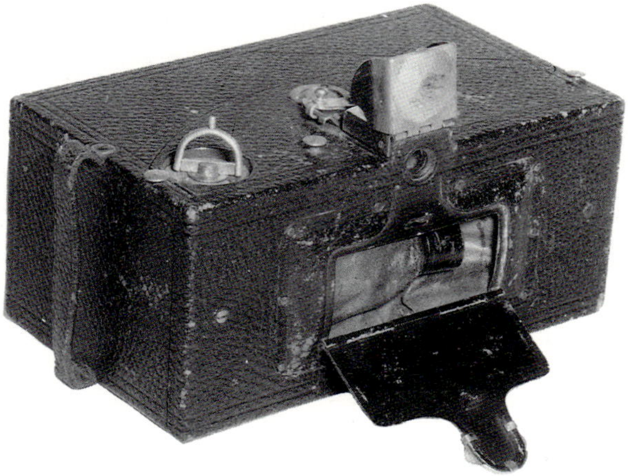

First model, 1900–1901. RPS

Type Box rollfilm
Introduced April 1900
Discontinued May 1926
Film size 105
Picture size 2¼ × 7in.
Manufactured US
Lenses 1900–1901: Rapid Rectilinear
1901–1925: Meniscus – but see below
Shutter Swinging lens tube with focal plane slot
Numbers made ? but over 22,000

Description/Remarks

Leather covered box; swivelling lens records 112 degree panoramic view; brilliant finder and V sighting lines; from serial number 101.

Variations

June 1901: Model B; metal rim on back of rollholder; undressed kid bellows; from serial number 11,183.

1903: Model C; tripod socket and level for vertical use added; from serial number 15,532. *1905–1907:* Diaphragm stops supplied for lens.

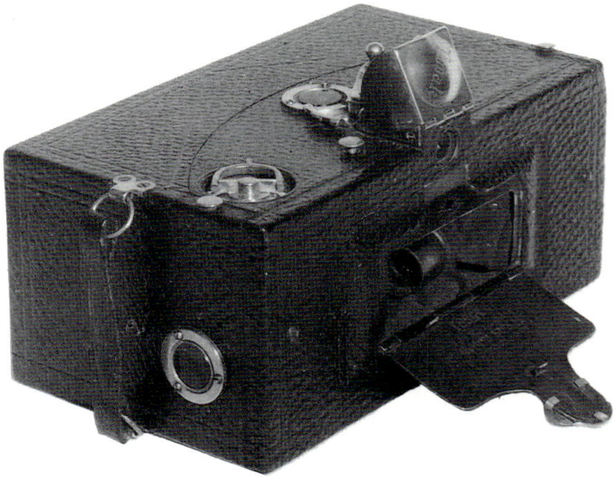

Model C. RPS

Apr. 1905: version with oil-retarded shutter with variable speeds (1/50) – 1 sec., with iris diaphragm.

Aug. 1907: Model D; removable rigid back replaced by side and end opening for film loading; levels omitted; from serial number 16,360.*Nov. 1917:* Levels refitted; new shutter speed governor; from serial number 20,501.

UK VARIATIONS
1906: Goerz Anastigmat. *1910:* Cooke Series II f/4.5; Beck Series II f/5.8; Goerz Dagor f/6.8. *1912–1915:* Zeiss Tessar IIbf/8.4. *1916–1925:* Ross Homocentric Series IV f/6.8.

No 3A Panoram Kodak

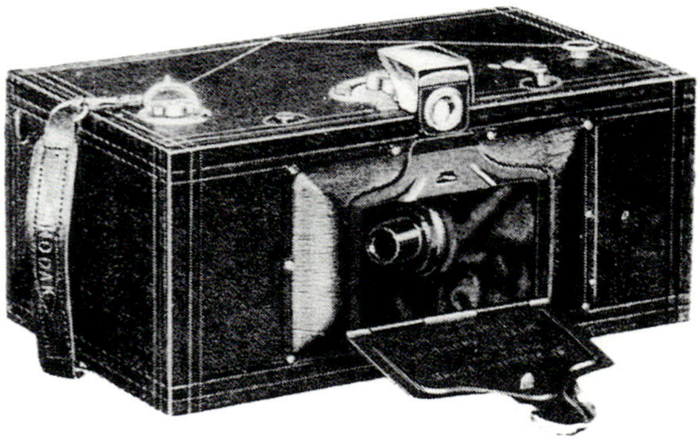

Type Box rollfilm
Introduced May 1926
Discontinued 1928
Film size 122
Picture size 3¼ × 10⅜in.
Manufactured US
Lens Meniscus f/12.8, 133mm
Shutter Swinging lens with focal plane slot, (1/10) and (1/50) sec.
Numbers made ?

Description/Remarks

Panoramic camera with swinging lens covering 120 degree angle of view. Leather covered wood box; brilliant finder with mirror for eyelevel use inhood; V sighting lines; T-shaped spirit level.

UK VARIATIONS
1927–1930: Ross Homocentric f/6.3, 133mm; Zeiss Tessar f/6.8,130mm.

No 4 Panoram Kodak

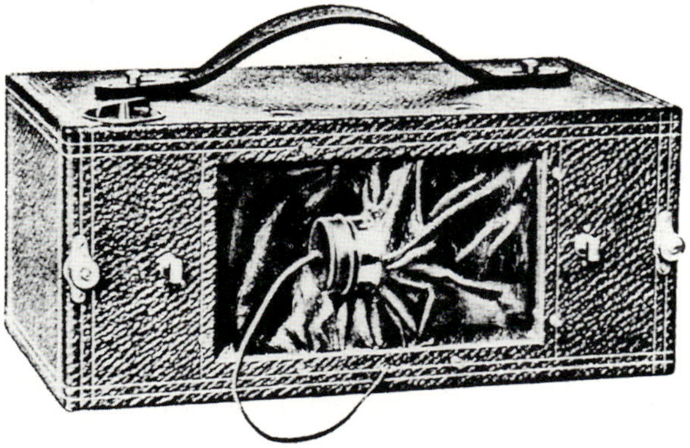

First model, 1899–1900.

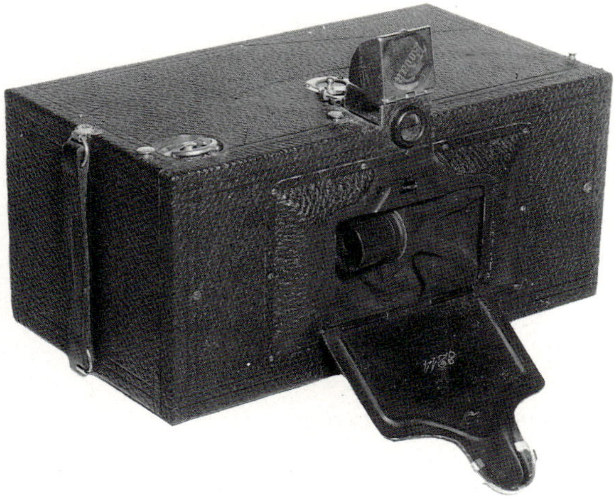

Model B, 1900–1904. RPS

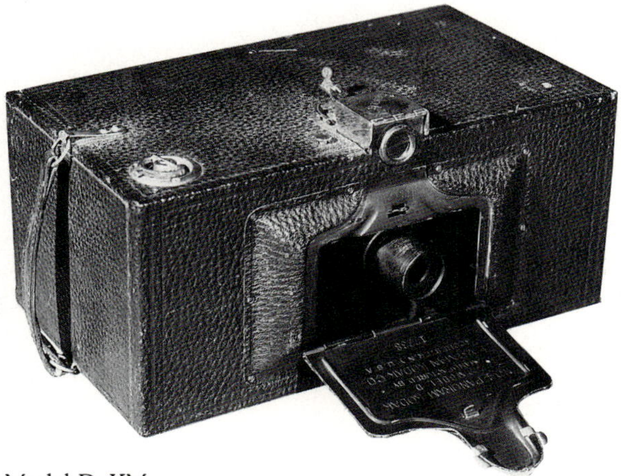

Model D. KM

Type Box rollfilm
Introduced 1899
Discontinued June 1924
Film size 103
Picture size 3½ × 12in.
Manufactured US
Lenses 1899–1902: Rapid Rectilinear f/10, 5 inch
1902–1924: Meniscus
Shutter Swinging lens with focal plane slot
Numbers made ? but well over 18,000

Description/Remarks

Swinging lens panoramic camera taking 142 degree field of view; leather covered wood box; brilliant finder (from 1900), with V sighting lines; two traversing speeds (from 1900); from serial number 101.

Variations

1899–Nov. 1900: No lens cover or finder; single traversing speed; loaded by unscrewing front.

Nov. 1900: Model B; hinged lens cover, brilliant finder; two traversing speeds; loaded by removing back; from serial number 2,001.

Mar. 1901: Metal rim on back of rollholder; from serial number3,009. *July 1901:* Undressed kid bellows fitted; from serial number 4,515.

Apr. 1904: Model C: level and tripod socket for vertical pictures;from serial number 9,700.

Apr. 1905: Version with oil-retarded shutter with variable speeds (1/50) – 1 sec.; iris diaphragm.

May 1907: Model D; ends and sides open for loading film; levels omitted; from serial number 11,702. *Oct. 1917:* Levels refitted; from serial number 16,511.

UK VARIATIONS
1906: Goerz Anastigmat. *1910:* Ross Homocentric f/6.8. *1916–1924:* Ross Homocentric Series IV f/6.8.*1912–1915:* Zeiss Tessar Series IIb f/8.4.

No 2 Plico Kodak

Type Box rollfilm
Introduced March 1901
Discontinued 1913
Film size 101
Picture size 3½ × 3½in.

Manufactured US, for UK market only
Lens Achromatic
Shutter Rotary
Numbers made 20,100

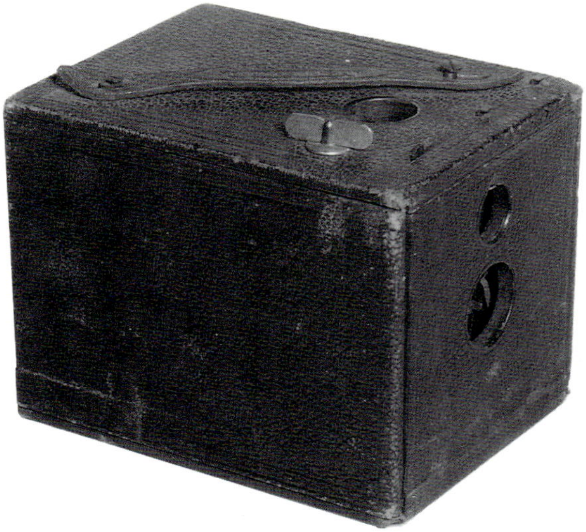

RPS

Description/Remarks

UK market version of No 2 Flexo camera. Grained leather covered wood box; back and sides released by catch in large finder window; circular reflecting finder; pull-up strips for aperture and shutter setting; from serial number 1,001.

Pocket Bulls-Eye

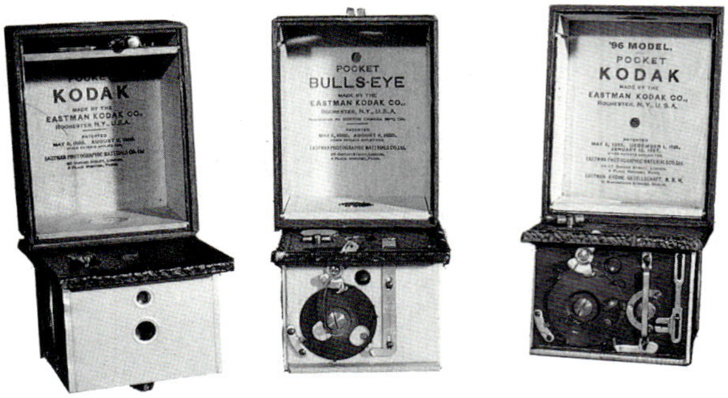

Centre, compared with 1895 (left) and 1896 (right) models of the Pocket Kodak camera. KM

Type Box rollfilm
Introduced ? 1896
Discontinued
Film size 102
Picture size 1½ × 2in.
Manufactured US
Lens Meniscus
Shutter Rotary – Bulls-Eye type
Numbers made ?

Description/Remarks

Black leather covered wood box; single circular finder; shutter fixed to wooden film carrier, like the 1896 rotary shutter version of the Pocket Kodak camera, but with no aperture adjustment. No record exists of any sale of this model; an example in the Kodak Museum collection in England may be a prototype only, although it has all the signs of a production model.

Pocket Kodak

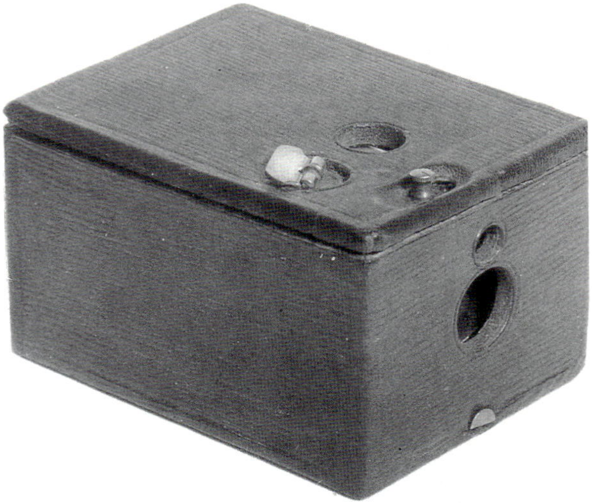

First model, 1895. RPS

Type Box rollfilm
Introduced July 1895
Discontinued 1900
Film size 102
Picture size 1½ × 2in.
Manufactured US

Lens Meniscus
Shutters 1895–June 1896: Tisdell
June 1896–1900: Rotary
Numbers made 147,000

Description/Remarks

Small leather covered wood box; reflecting finder; provision for taking single plate. Enormously successful camera – 100,000 sold in first year, an extraordinarily large number for that time.

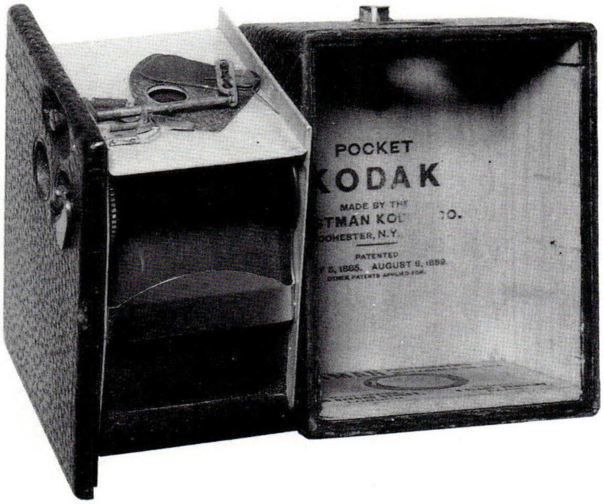

1895, first version. RPS

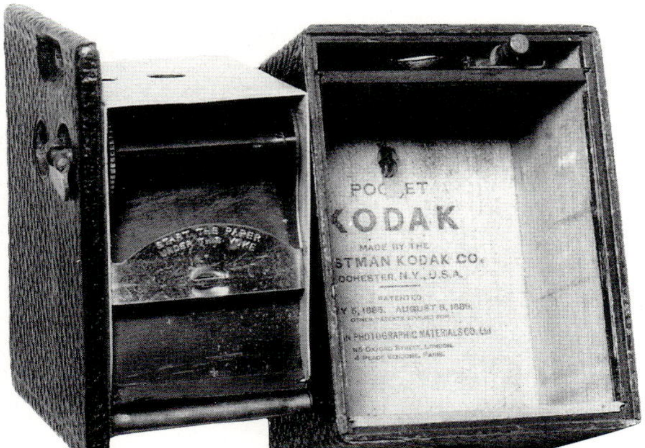

1895, third version. RPS

Variations

Model designations: '96, '97, '98, 99, and D

July 1895–June 1896: Round reflecting finder; fine grained red or coarse grained black leather; aluminium film carrier; Tisdell sector shutter with single lever for cocking and firing shutter.

Four changes during first year: **1st model:** Felt film guides, plain metal flaps on spool compartments, shutter first attached to film carrier, then separate. **2nd model:** Felt guides, printing on flaps.**3rd model:** Roller film guides, printed or plain flaps. **4th model:** Roller guides, shutter attached to film carrier.

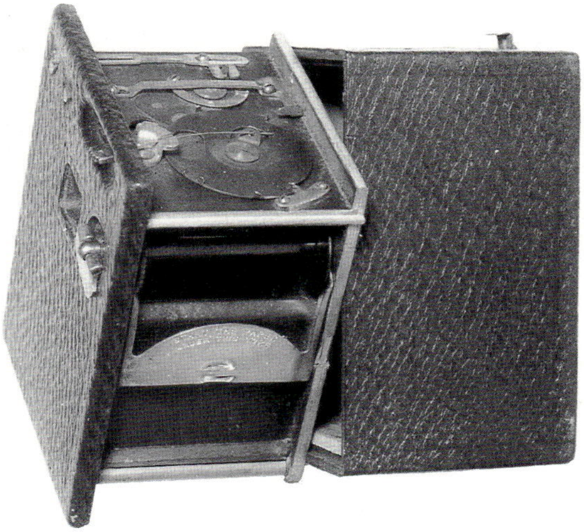

1895, fourth version. RPS

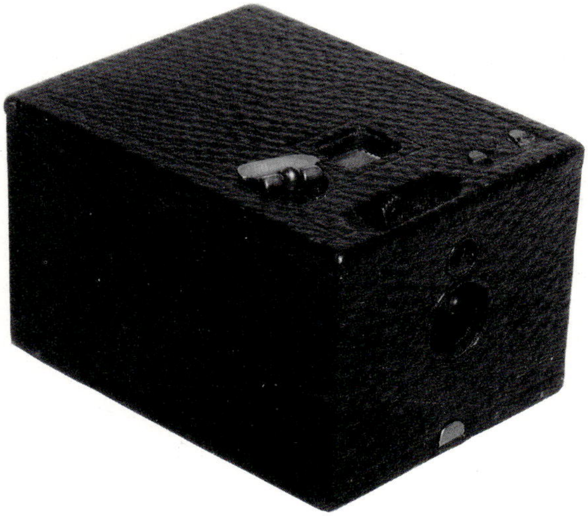

1896 model. RPS

June 1896: Rectangular finder; wooden film carrier; coarse grained black leather; attached rotary shutter with pull-up strips for aperture and shutter setting. *June 1898:* internal light guard fitted.

3B Quick Focus Kodak

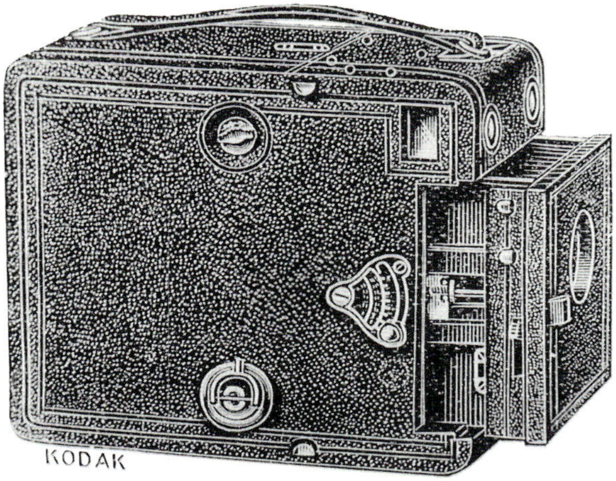

Model A.

Type Box rollfilm
Introduced July 1905
Discontinued April 1911
Film size 125
Picture size 3¼ × 5¼in.
Manufactured US
Lens Meniscus achromat
Shutter Eastman rotary
Numbers made 9,000+

Description/Remarks

Leather covered wooden box; sprung lens panel extends automatically to pre-set focusing distance by pressing a button; two brilliant finders; from serial number 101-K.

Variations

July 1905: Model A; quadrant-shaped focus scale; short front handle catch.

June 1906: Model B; metal bearing for extending lens panel; longer handle catch; from serial number 3,075-K.

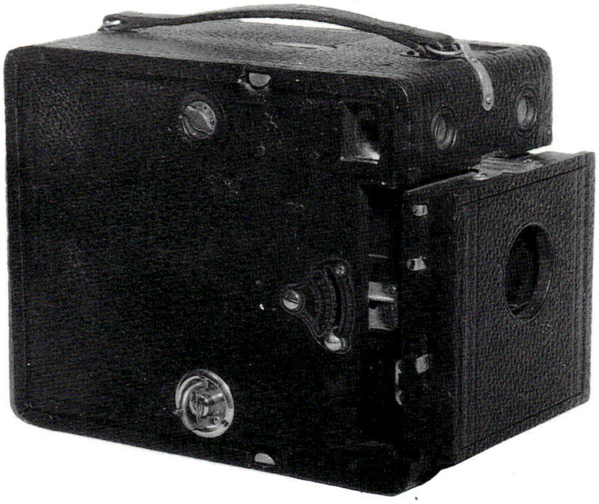

Model B. RPS

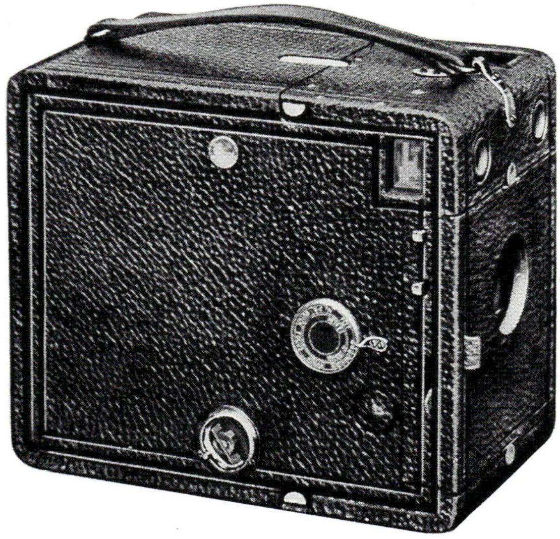

Model C.

Nov. 1906: Model C; circular focus dial; new spool centre pins, disc rather than key shape; from serial number 5,100-K.

No 2 Stereo Kodak

Type Stereoscopic box rollfilm
Introduced October 1901
Discontinued 1905 (1908 in UK)

Film size 101
Picture size Two $3\frac{1}{2} \times 3\frac{1}{2}$in.
Manufactured US
Lens Two Rapid Rectilinear
Shutter Special version of Eastman Automatic
Numbers made 2,500+

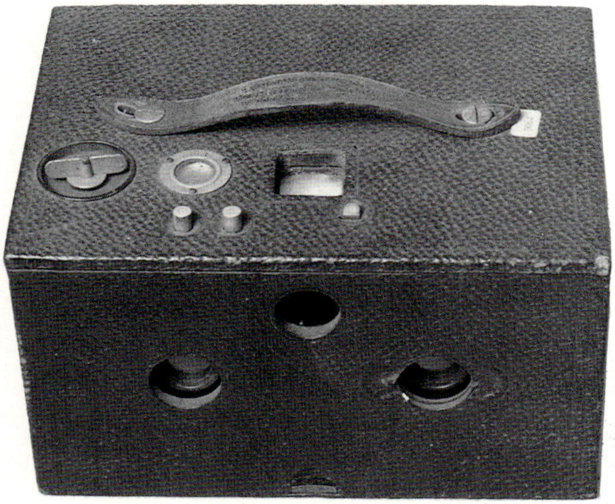

KM

Description/Remarks

Seal grain leather covered wooden box; brilliant finder; single exposures possible by closing blind on right lens (seen from front); separate time and instantaneous exposure buttons; spirit level; from serial number 101.

No 3 Zenith

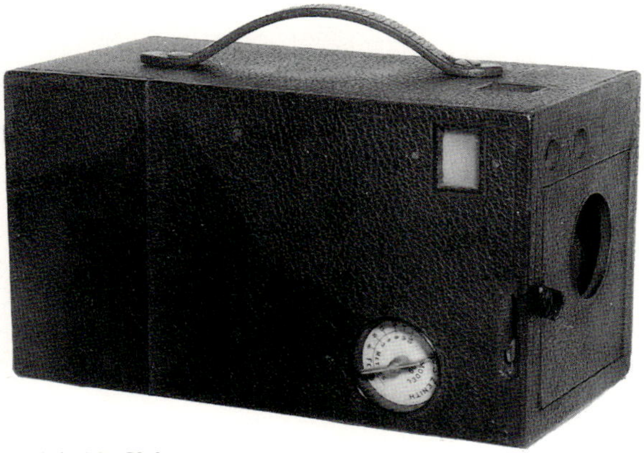

Model '99. SM

Type Box rollfilm
Introduced March 1899
Discontinued 1900
Film size Cartridge roll holder
Picture size
Manufactured US, for UK market only
Lens Achromatic
Shutter Rotary
Numbers made 2,000

Description/Remarks

A quarter-plate version of the Eureka camera made for the UK market only, where the Eureka name was already in use by W. W. Rouch & Co. Plate camera adapted for rollfilm with Cartridge Roll Holder; reflecting finders; from serial number 200.

A version for 9×12cm pictures was produced for the Continental market – 1,000 were shipped in 1899.

No 4 Zenith

Type Box rollfilm
Introduced October 1899
Discontinued 1900
Film size 109 Cartridge Roll Holder
Picture size
Manufactured US, for UK market only
Lens Achromatic
Shutter Rotary
Numbers made 1,000

Description/Remarks

A version of the No 4 Eureka camera produced for the UK market, where the name was already in use by W. W. Rouch & Co. Plate camera adapted for rollfilm with Cartridge Roll Holder. Leather covered wood box; 2 reflecting finders; rack and pinion focusing by recessed key; space in back for 3 double plateholders or rollholder; from serial number 701.

CHAPTER 2 *Brownie Box Cameras*

In 1898 Eastman asked his camera designer and manufacturer, Frank Brownell, to design the least expensive camera possible, consistent with its being effective and reliable. Eastman saw that if the cost could be reduced, more people, and in particular children, might take up photography. Brownell came up with the Brownie camera, launched in 1900. It was named after the little characters created by the Canadian author and illustrator Palmer Cox. His doggerel verse and entertaining drawings had been highly popular with children throughout the 1890s, and by adopting the name, and using the characters in advertising, Eastman, shrewd as always, gained a major marketing advantage. That in itself would not have ensured the long-term success of the cameras, if they had not also been of good value and reliable. For the next 80 years the name Brownie was synonymous with popular photography. Several generations of famous photographers acknowledged that their interest began through first using a Brownie box camera. From the first cardboard and wood model in 1900, to the last, a compact moulded plastic cartridge loading pocket camera made by Kodak Limited in 1980, almost 100 cameras bore the famous name.

Baby Brownie

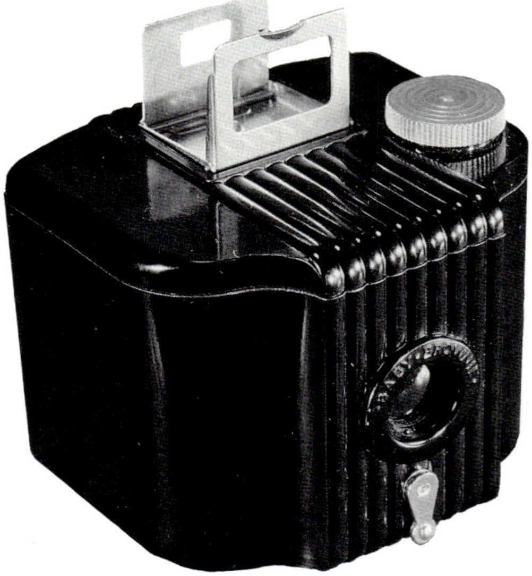

KP

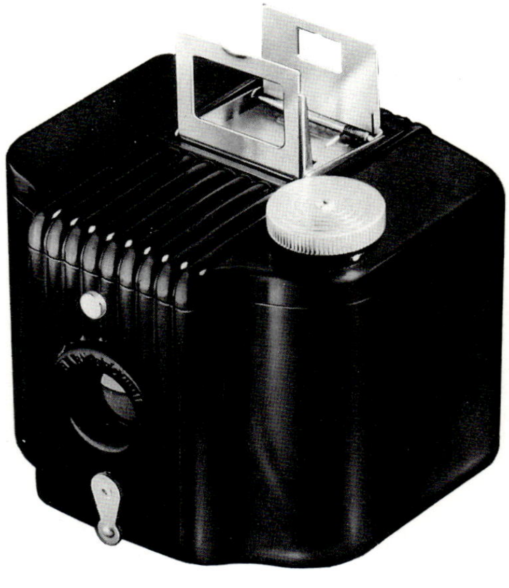

Export model. KP

Type Solid body eyelevel rollfilm
Introduced July 1934 (1948 in UK)
Discontinued 1941 (1952 in UK)
Film size 127
Picture size 1⅝ × 2½in.
Manufactured US and UK
Lens Meniscus lens
Shutter Rotary shutter
Numbers made ?

Description/Remarks

Moulded plastic body, styled by Walter Dorwin Teague; folding frame finder; export models from 1936 to 1939 had a button for brief time exposures.

Kodak Limited manufactured the camera for export only after World War Two; the brief time button was added from 1951.

Baby Brownie Special

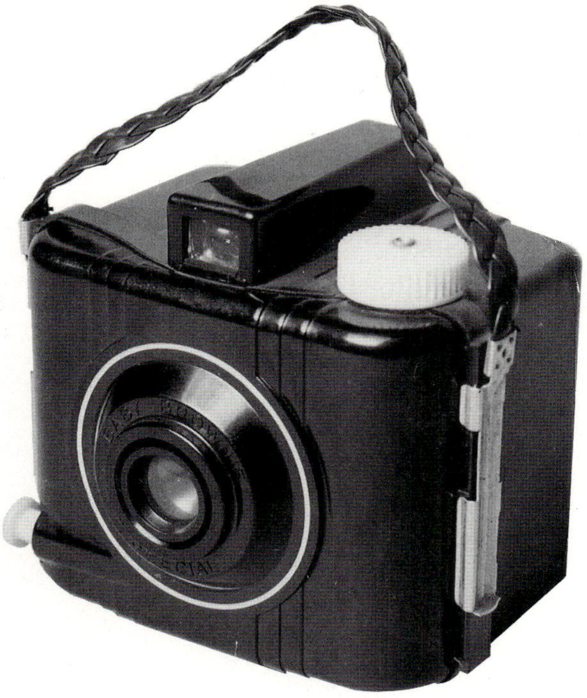

KM

Type Solid body eyelevel rollfilm
Introduced September 1939
Discontinued 1954
Film size 127
Picture size 1⅝ × 2½in.
Manufactured US
Lens Meniscus
Shutter Rotary
Numbers made ?

Description/Remarks

Moulded plastic box with direct vision optical finder; braided strap. Export models in 1939 had button for brief time exposures.

No 2 Beau Brownie

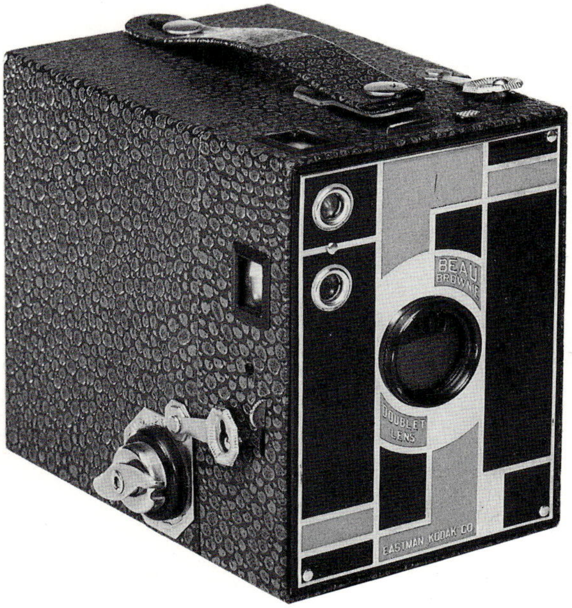

KM

Type Box rollfilm
Introduced October 1930
Discontinued 1933
Film size 120
Picture size 2¼ × 3¼in.
Manufactured US
Lens Doublet
Shutter Rotary
Numbers made ?

Description/Remarks

Metal body, styled by Walter Dorwin Teague with two-tone enamelled geometric Art Deco design front panel, in five colours – black, blue, rose, green and tan, with matching leatherette covering (green and rose models sold only in 1930 and 1931, and were not available in UK, although a maroon version was available). The doublet lens allowed a shorter body than with the usual Brownie boxes.

No 2A Beau Brownie

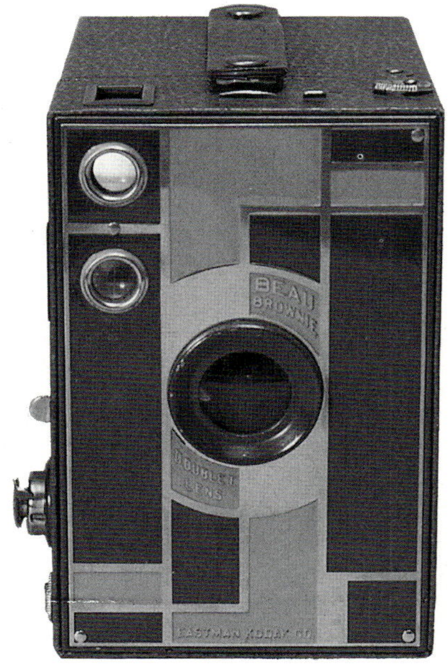

KM

Type Box rollfilm
Introduced October 1930
Discontinued 1933
Film size 116
Picture size 2½ × 4¼in.
Manufactured US
Lens Doublet
Shutter Rotary
Numbers made ?

Description/Remarks

Metal body box styled by Walter Dorwin Teague with two-tone enamelled geometric Art Deco design front panel in five colours – black, tan, rose, green, blue – with matching leatherette covering. Green and rose models sold only in 1930 and 1931. The doublet lens allowed a shorter body than with usual Brownie boxes.

Boy Scout Brownie

Type Box rollfilm
Introduced October 1932
Discontinued 1932
Film size 120
Picture size 2¼ × 3¼in.
Manufactured US
Lens Meniscus
Shutter Rotary
Numbers made ?

Description/Remarks

Front panel with geometric pattern and American Boy Scout emblem.

The Brownie

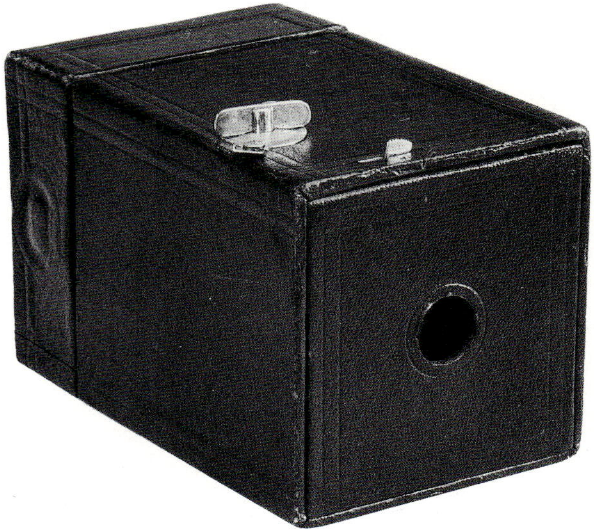

First model with box-lid back. KM

Type Box rollfilm
Introduced February 1900
Discontinued October 1901
Film size 117
Picture size 2¼ × 2¼in.
Manufactured US
Lens Meniscus
Shutter Rotary
Numbers made 245,000 approximately

Description/Remarks

Card box with wood film carrier; no finder, but V sighting lines on top (a clip-on accessory reflecting finder was available from July 1900); detachable film winding key. This camera introduced the 2¼in. square format.

Variations

The first batch of about 15,000 had push-on box-lid backs which proved unreliable. Most of this first batch was sent to Kodak Limited, and examples are therefore more common in Europe.

Mar. 1900: Bottom-hinged back with sliding latch on top.

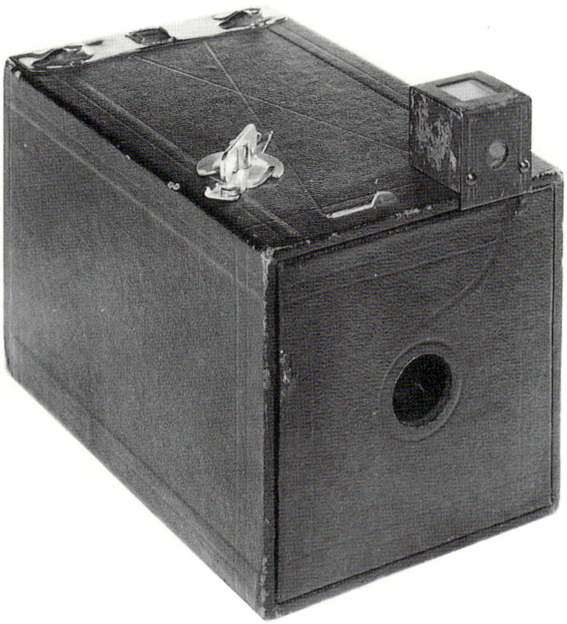

Improved model with latch back. KP

No 0 Brownie

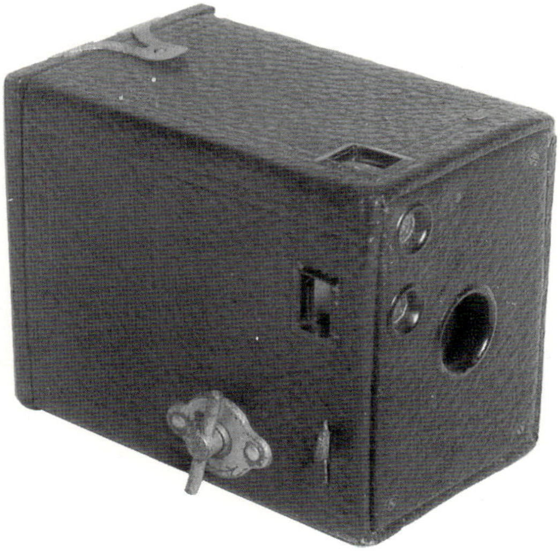

RPS

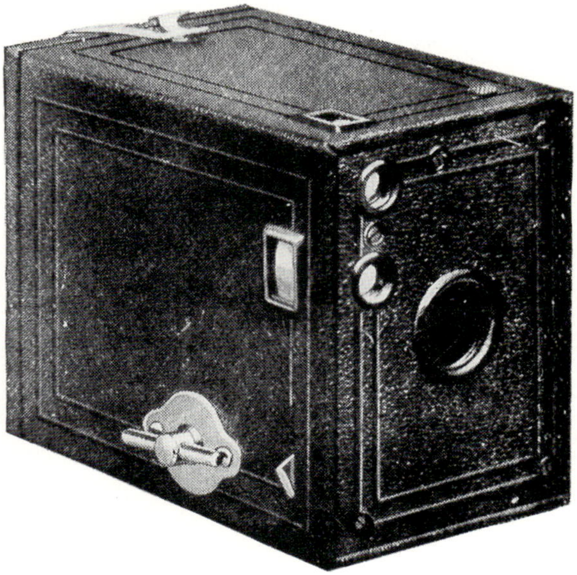

Late model, from c.1928.

Type Box rollfilm
Introduced May 1914
Discontinued April 1935
Film size 127
Picture size 1⅝ × 2½in.
Manufactured US, assembled in UK 1929-1930

Lens Meniscus
Shutter Rotary
Numbers made ?

Description/Remarks

Card and wood construction; two reflecting finders; hinged back with triangular catch.

Variations

July 1917: Film tension springs bearing on ends rather than centre of spool; direction arrows added to winding key plate. *c.1928:* Double crossed line embossed decoration replaced by double rectangles.

No 1 Brownie

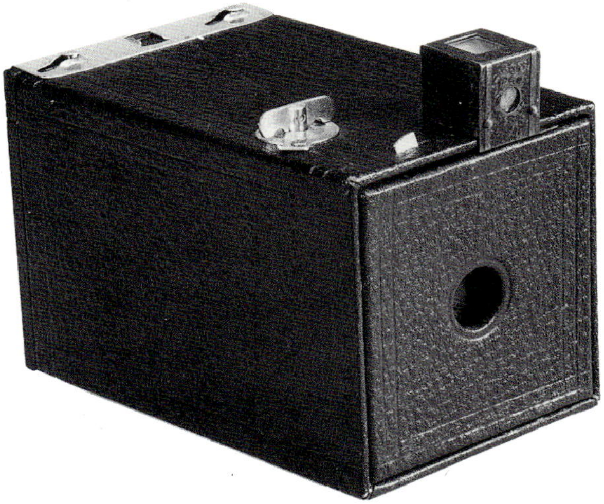

1904–1916 model with grained covering. KM

Type Box rollfilm
Introduced October 1901
Discontinued 1916
Film size 117
Picture size 2¼ × 2¼in.
Manufactured US
Lens Meniscus
Shutter Rotary
Numbers made 522,000 approximately

Description/Remarks

Identical to the Brownie camera, but renamed with the introduction of the No 2 Brownie camera.

Variations

April 1904: smooth leathercloth covering changed for more grained version.

No 2 Brownie

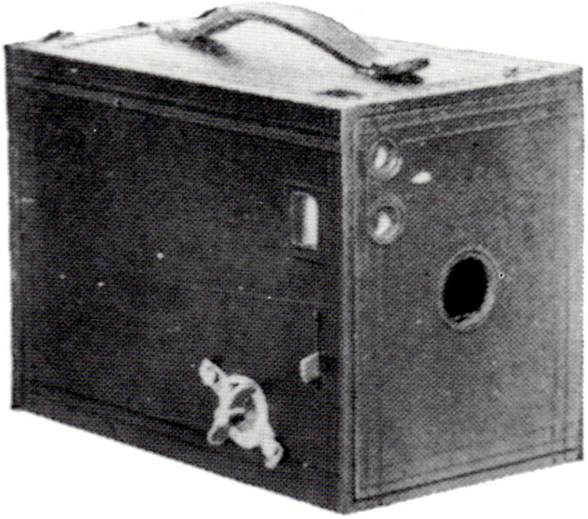

First model, 1901–1902.

Type Box rollfilm
Introduced October 1901
Discontinued 1933
Film size 120
Picture size 2¼ × 3¼in.
Manufactured US, UK from 1928-1935
Lens Meniscus
Shutter Rotary
Numbers made Several million
(over 2,500,000 before 1921)

Description/Remarks

Leatherette covered card or, from 1924, metal box; two reflecting finders.

Variations

1901–early 1902: detachable winding keys similar to Brownie camera. *Early 1902:* fixed, pull-out winding key.

Feb. 1904: Model B; fine grain leatherette covering replaced by coarser grain; metal eyelets fitted to lens and finder windows.

Apr. 1907: Model C; spool centres fitted.

Dec. 1914: Model D; during the run of this model the sliding latch for hinged back was replaced by a spring catch; mask in back omitted.*June 1917:* Film tension springs bearing on spool ends instead of centre. *Dec. 1917:* metal name plate on back.

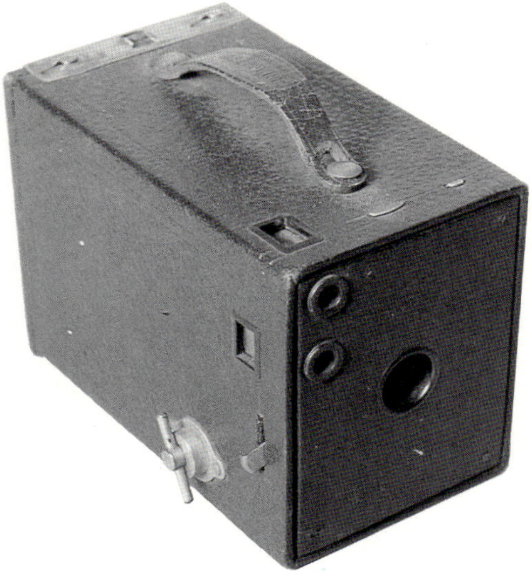

Model B. KM

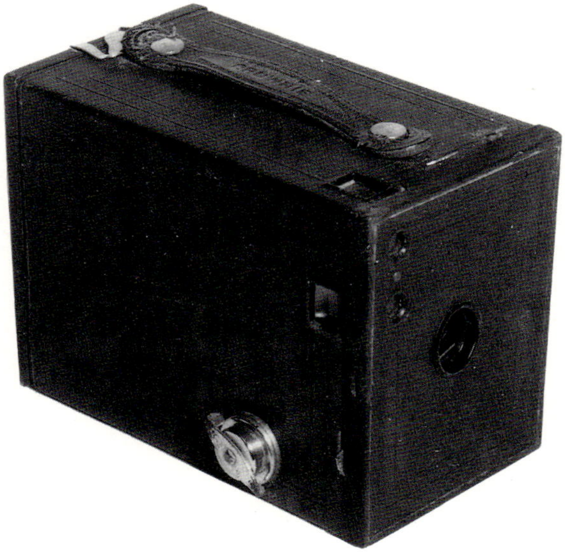

Model F – US version. RPS

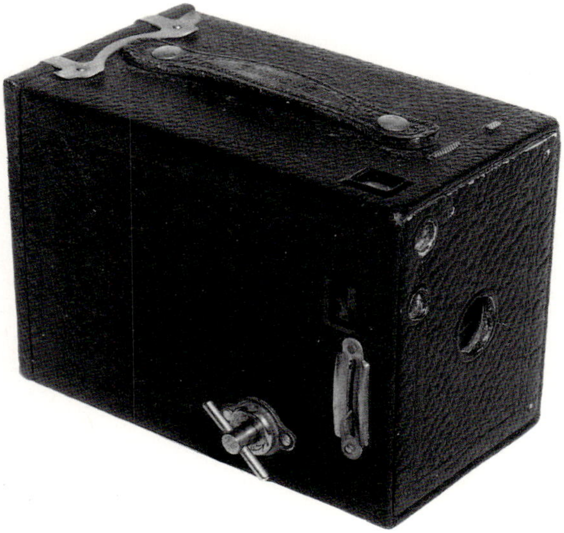

Model E, 1919. RPS

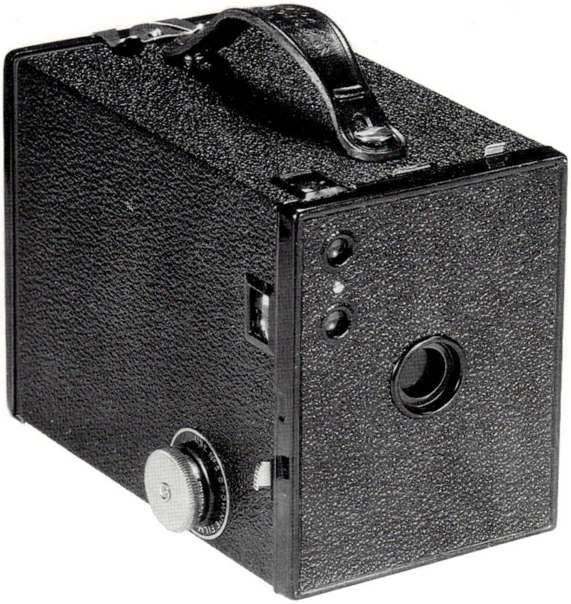

Model F – UK version, 1931. KM

Mar. 1919: Model E; metal film carrier instead of wood, card outer casing. *Mar. 1920:* Trigger guard fitted.

Feb. 1924: Model F; aluminium case replaced card; tripod sockets added; no trigger guard; finer grained leatherette covering.

Apr. 1929–1933: US models in five colour finishes – Red, grey, green, blue, brown – as well as black. *1929–1933:* UK models in six colour finishes – red, brown, claret, green, blue, grey as well as black.

From 1931: knob replaced winding key; 1931 models had double rectangular line decoration of earlier models; thereafter plain finish.

1934–1935: UK models in two colour finishes – grey or black. Silver model produced for Silver Jubilee of King George V in 1935. *Nov. 1930:* UK model in special Modernist finish, black with slight relief, wax-like feel; made only in limited numbers for the Christmas season. (See No.2 Portrait Brownie Camera)

No 2A Brownie

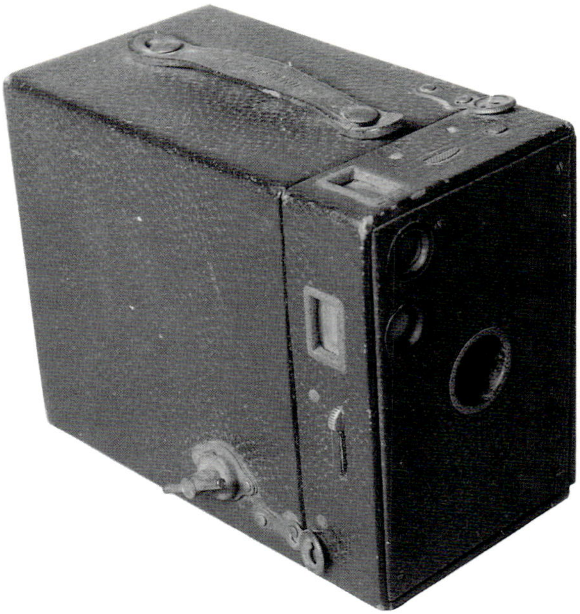

Model B, 1917–1920. KM

Type Box rollfilm
Introduced April 1907
Discontinued 1933
Film size 116
Picture size 2½ × 4¼in.
Manufactured US, UK from 1930-1936
Lens Meniscus
Shutter Rotary
Numbers made Several millions
(over 2,100,000 before 1921)

Description/Remarks

Leatherette covered card or, after 1924, metal box; metal film carrier; two reflecting finders. Case removed for loading by releasing two pivoted catches and pulling out winding key.

Variations

Aug. 1909: Eyelets fitted to lens and finder windows.

Oct. 1911: Model B; internal changes to lens board etc.*June 1917:* Film tension springs bearing on spool ends rather than centre. *Oct. 1917:* improved case latches with rounded ends with milled edges. *Jan. 1918:* Metal nameplate on back. *Mar.1920:* trigger guard fitted.

Apr. 1924: Model C; aluminium body; tripod sockets; hinged back with spring catch; finer grain leatherette covering.

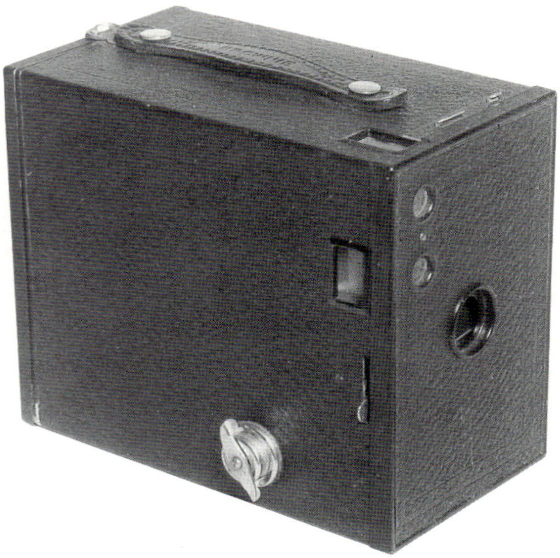

Model C, 1924 on. RPS

Apr. 1929–1933: US models available in five colours – red, grey, green, brown or blue – as well as black. *1930–1936:* UK models available in four colours – brown, blue, claret and green – as well as black. Black was discontinued in 1935, and blue in 1936. From 1932 winding key replaced by knob.

No 2C Brownie

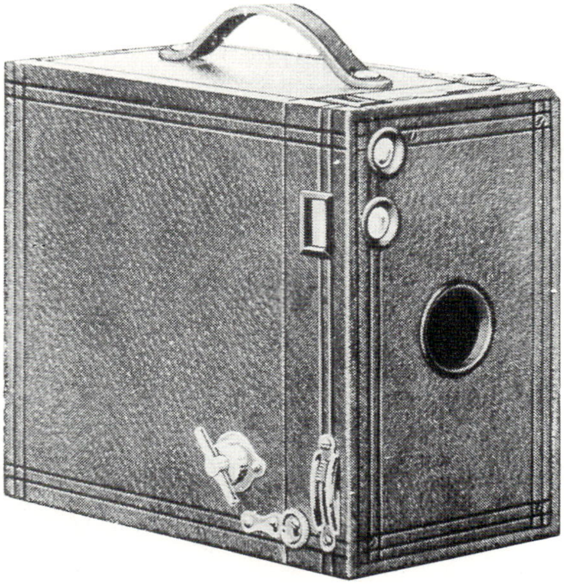

Type Box rollfilm
Introduced July 1917
Discontinued 1934
Film size 130
Picture size 2⅞ × 4⅞in.
Manufactured US
Lens Meniscus achromat
Shutter Rotary
Numbers made ? but probably over half million

Description/Remarks

Leatherette covered card case; metal film carrier; case removed for loading by releasing two pivoted catches and pulling out winding key; two reflecting finders; tripod sockets; trigger guard.

No 3 Brownie

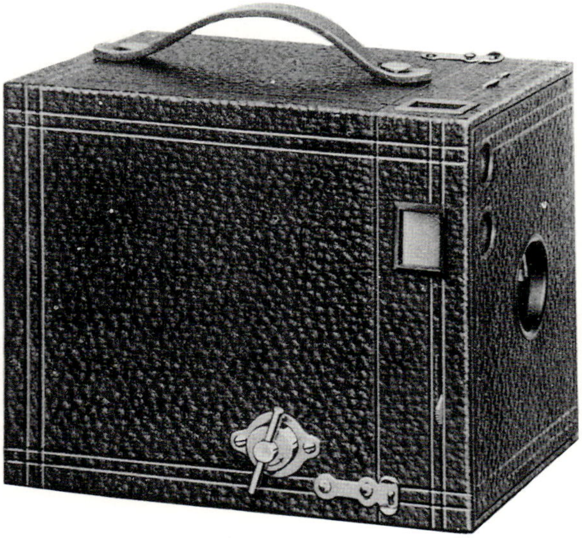

First model, 1908–1911.

Type Box rollfilm
Introduced November 1908
Discontinued 1934
Film size 124
Picture size 3¼ × 4¼in.
Manufactured US
Lens Meniscus achromatic
Shutter Rotary
Numbers made Probably over 1,000,000 (470,000 before 1921)

Description/Remarks

Leatherette covered card case; metal film carrier; two reflecting finders; case removed for loading by releasing pivoted catches and pulling out winding key.

Variations

Aug. 1911: Model B; internal changes to lens board etc. *Aug. 1917:* Film tension springs bearing on spool ends rather than centre. *Oct. 1917:* New case latches with rounded, milled ends. *1920:* Trigger guard fitted. *1926:* Coarse grained leatherette changed for fine grain.

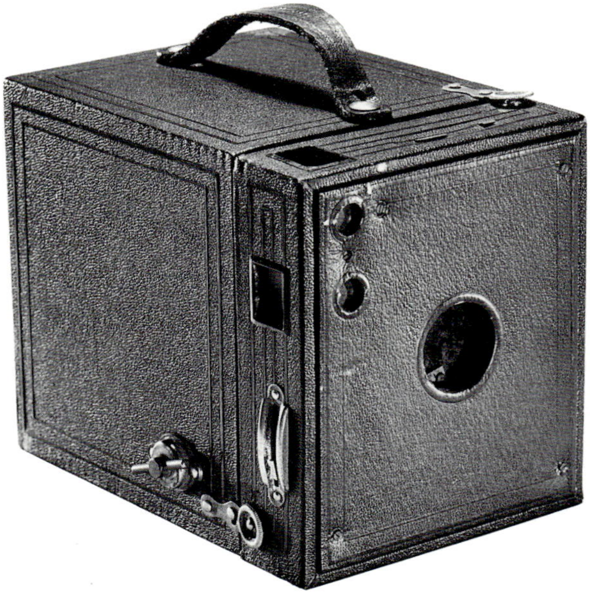

1926 model. KM

Brownie Auto 27

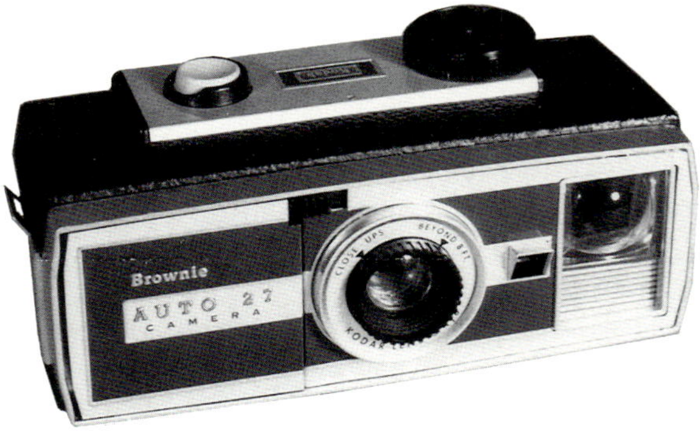

PDM

Type Solid body eyelevel rollfilm
Introduced August 1963
Discontinued June 1965
Film size 127
Picture size $1\frac{5}{8} \times 1\frac{5}{8}$in.
Manufactured US
Lens Kodar f/8
Shutter Two-speed
Numbers made ?

Description/Remarks

Optical direct vision finder; automatic exposure control; concealed built-in flash gun for AG1 bulbs.

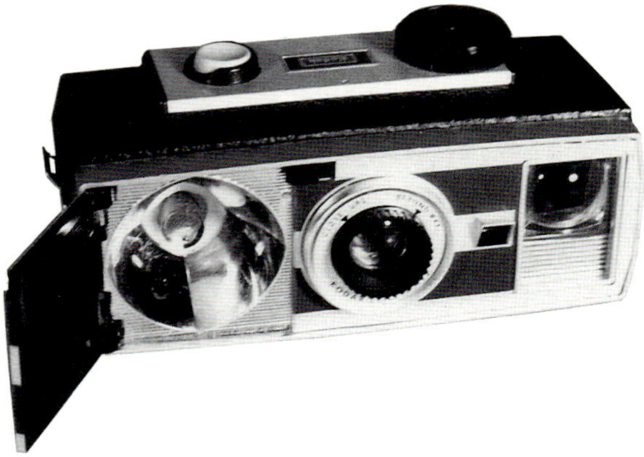

With flash cover open. PDM

Brownie Bullet

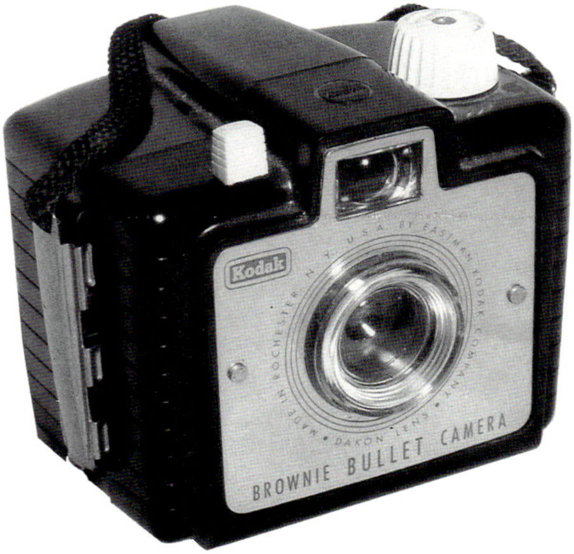

RPS

Type Solid body eyelevel rollfilm
Introduced September 1957
Discontinued 1964

Film size 127
Picture size 1⅝ × 2½in.
Manufactured US, Brazil
Lens Dakon
Shutter Rotary
Numbers made ?

Description/Remarks

Premium version of Brownie Holiday camera; moulded black plastic body with white controls and faceplate. Also known as Camara Brownie Chiquita.

Brownie Bullet II

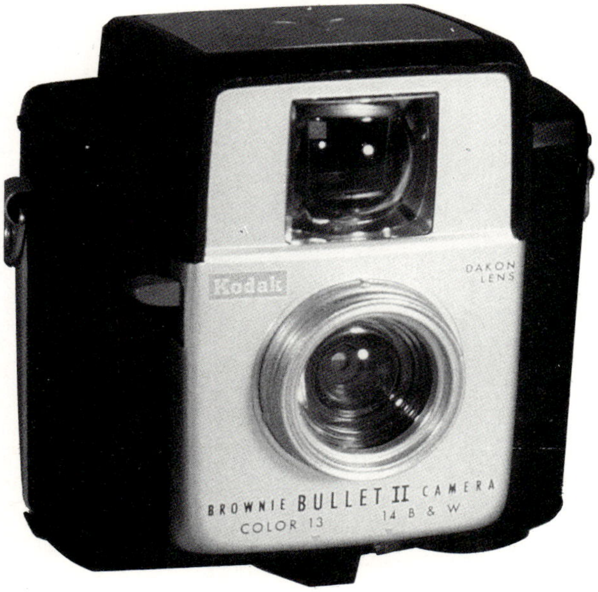

PDM

Type Solid body eyelevel rollfilm
Introduced August 1961
Discontinued November 1968
Film size 127
Picture size 1⅝ × 1⅝in.
Manufactured US
Lens Dakon
Shutter Rotary
Numbers made ?

Description/Remarks

Continuation of Brownie Starlet camera, but without flash contacts.

Brownie Bulls-Eye

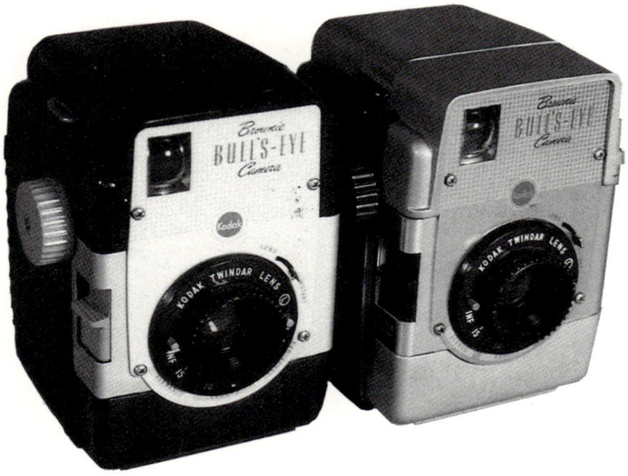

Left: 1954–1958 model. Right: 1957–1960 model. PDM

Type Solid body eyelevel rollfilm
Introduced August 1954
Discontinued October 1960
Film size 620
Picture size 2¼ × 3¼in.
Manufactured US
Lens Twindar
Shutter Rotary
Numbers made ?

Description/Remarks

Moulded plastic; optical direct vision finder; pin and screw flash contacts.

Variations

1954–Aug. 1958: Black and silver-grey model. *Sept. 1957–Oct. 1960:* Gold enamelled with brass colour front plate.

Brownie Cresta

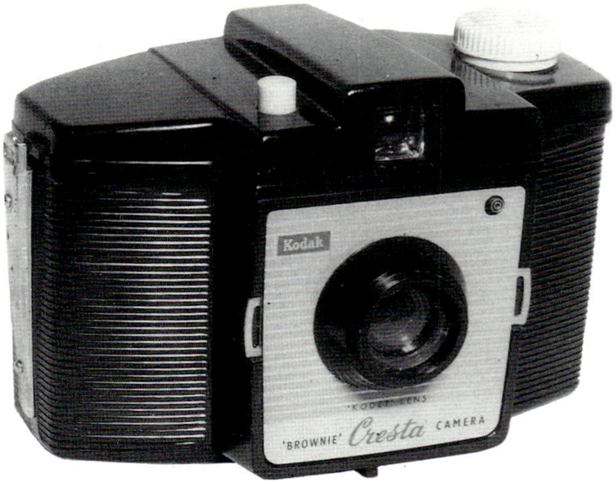

RPS

Type Solid body eyelevel rollfilm
Introduced 1955 (export only 1955)
Discontinued 1958
Film size 120
Picture size 2¼ × 2¼in.
Manufactured UK
Lens Kodet f/14 fixed focus, with close-up lens
Shutter Single speed (1/40) sec.
Numbers made ?

Description/Remarks

Black moulded plastic body with horizontal ribbing; optical direct vision finder; coaxial flash socket; yellow cloud filter.

Brownie Cresta II

Type Solid body eyelevel rollfilm
Introduced March 1956 (export only until July 1958)
Discontinued 1959
Film size 120
Picture size 2¼ × 2¼in.
Manufactured UK
Lens Kodet f/11, with close-up lens
Shutter Single speed (1/40) sec.
Numbers made ?

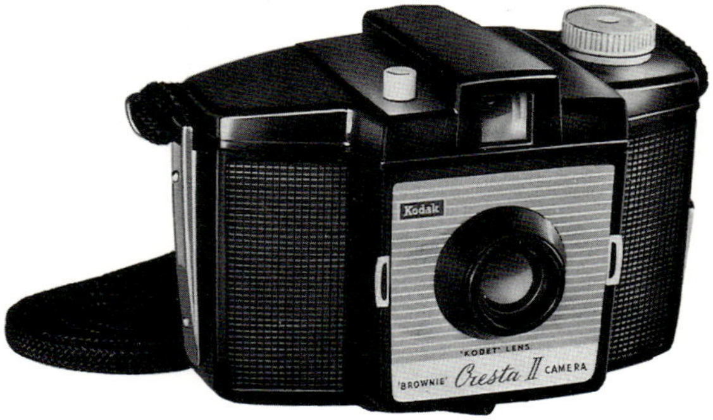

KP

Description/Remarks

Black moulded plastic body with crossed ribbing; screw and pin flash contacts; otherwise similar to first model.

Brownie Cresta 3

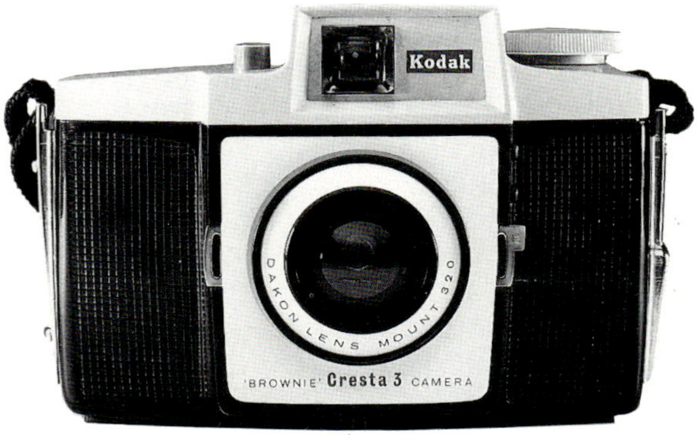

KP

Type Solid body eyelevel rollfilm
Introduced 1960
Discontinued 1965
Film size 120
Picture size 2¼ × 2¼in.
Manufactured UK
Lens Dakon f/11, with close-up lens
Shutter Single speed (1/40) sec.
Numbers made ?

Description/Remarks

Redesigned Brownie Cresta II, with more angular style moulded black plastic body with grey top and plain lens panel; optical direct vision finder with bright line corner marks for Superslide format; pin and screw flash contacts; two apertures.

Brownie Fiesta

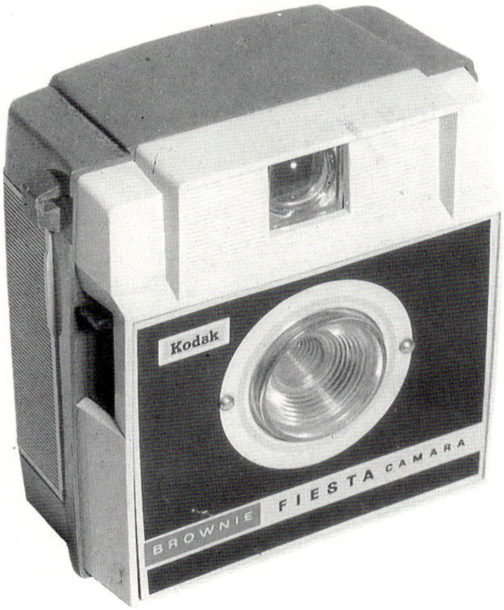

Spanish version. RPS

Type Solid body eyelevel rollfilm
Introduced March 1962
Discontinued March 1970
Film size 127
Picture size $1\frac{5}{8} \times 1\frac{5}{8}$in.
Manufactured US, Spain
Lens Meniscus f/11
Shutter Built-in
Numbers made ?

Description/Remarks

Moulded plastic body with clear plastic front over lens plate; optical direct vision finder.

Variations

1962–Oct. 1965: Two-tone grey and silver. *May 1965–June1966:* Two-tone dark and light blue.

Mar. 1966–Mar. 1970: Model R4; grey front, silver lens plate; flashcube socket.

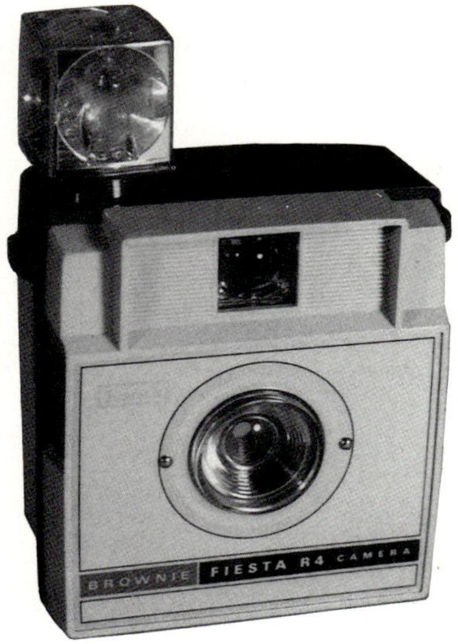

Model R4. PDM

Brownie Flash B

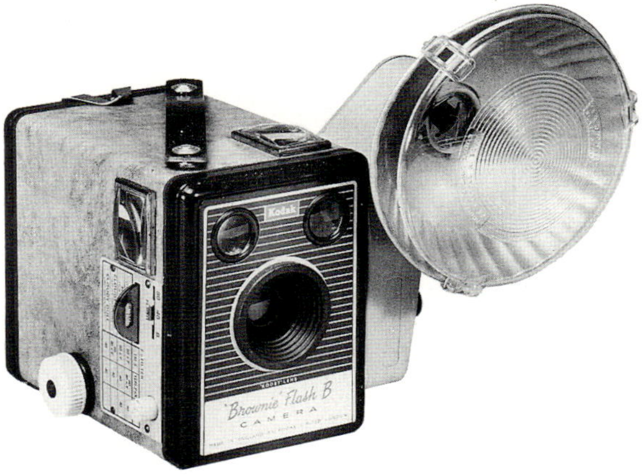

KM

Type Box rollfilm
Introduced May 1958

Discontinued 1960
Film size 620
Picture size 2¼ × 3¼in.
Manufactured UK
Lens Meniscus f/11, with close-up lens
Shutter Two-speed (1/40) and (1/80) sec.
Numbers made

Description/Remarks

Light brown leatherette covering and horizontally striped front panel; two brilliant finders; pin and screw flash contacts; cloud filter; exposure guide.

Brownie Flash II

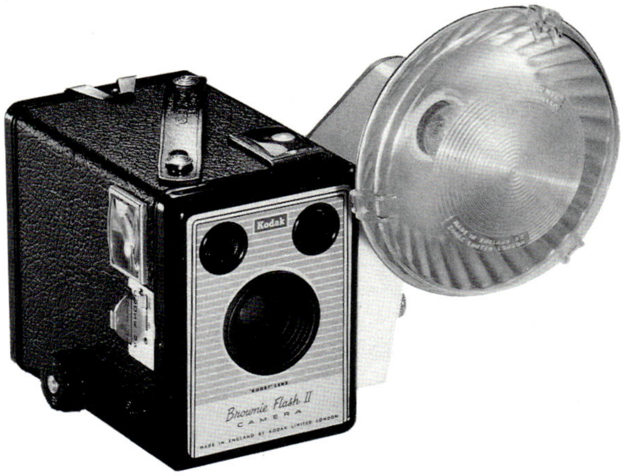

KP

Type Box rollfilm
Introduced July 1957
Discontinued 1960
Film size 620
Picture size 2¼ × 3¼in. rollfilm
Manufactured UK
Lens Kodet f/14, with close-up lens
Shutter Single blade
Numbers made

Description/Remarks

Imitation leather covered metal box, with horizontally striped front panel; two brilliant finders; pin and screw flash contacts.

Brownie Flash III

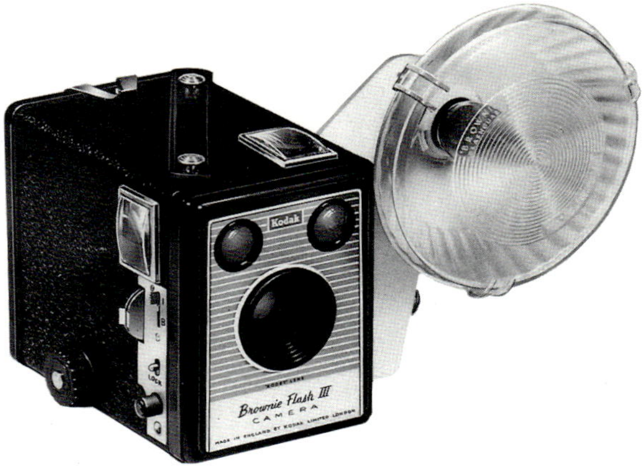

KP

Type Box rollfilm
Introduced May 1957
Discontinued 1960
Film size 620
Picture size 2¼ × 3¼in.
Manufactured UK
Lens Kodet f/14, with close-up lens
Shutter Single blade
Numbers made ?

Description/Remarks

Black imitation leather covering on metal box; two brilliant finders; yellow cloud filter; shutter lock; tripod socket; cable release socket.

Brownie Flash IV

Type Box rollfilm
Introduced September 1957
Discontinued 1959
Film size 620
Picture size 2¼ × 3¼in.
Manufactured UK
Lens Kodet f/14, with close-up lens

Shutter Single blade shutter
Numbers made ?

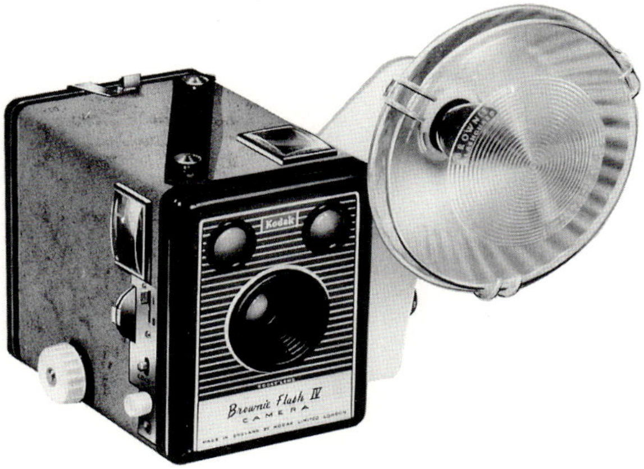

KP

Description/Remarks

De luxe version of Brownie Flash III camera, with light brown leatherette covering and gilt metalwork; otherwise similar.

Brownie Flash Six-20

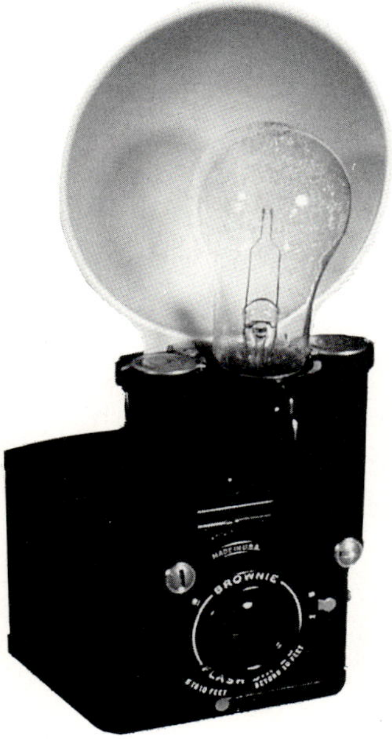

PDM

Type Solid body eyelevel rollfilm
Introduced July 1946
Discontinued January 1955
Film size 620
Picture size 2¼ × 3¼in.
Manufactured US
Lens Meniscus
Shutter Rotary
Numbers made ?

Description/Remarks

Metal box body; optical direct vision finder; accepts cumbersome flashgun. Renamed from Six-20 Flash Brownie camera.

Brownie Flash 20

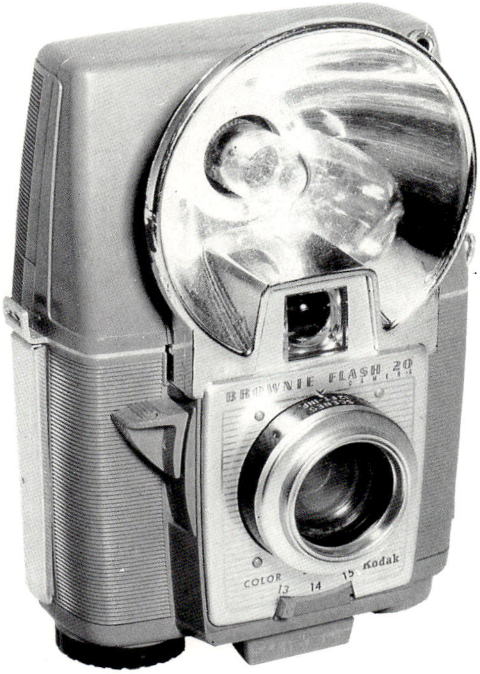

RPS

Type Solid body eyelevel rollfilm
Introduced April 1959
Discontinued October 1962
Film size 620
Picture size 2¼ × 2¼in.

Manufactured US, assembled in UK 1960–1961
Lens Meniscus, f/11, 3 apertures
Shutter Single speed
Numbers made ?

Description/Remarks

Moulded blue plastic body; direct vision optical finder; built-in capacitor flash gun for capless bulbs.

Brownie Flashmite 20

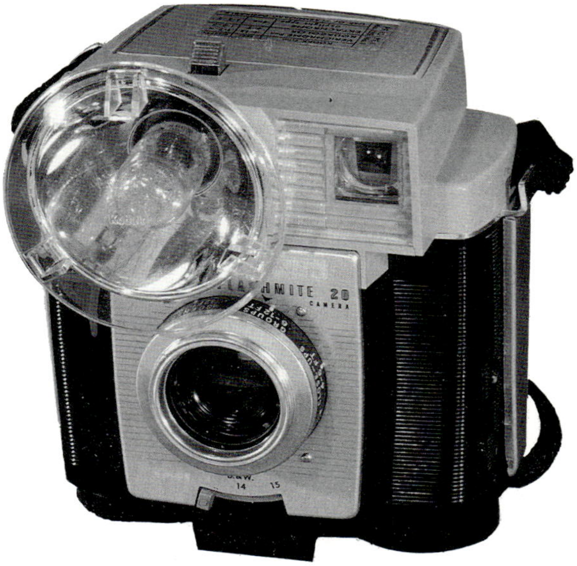

KP

Type Solid body eyelevel rollfilm
Introduced April 1960
Discontinued June 1965
Film size 620
Picture size 2¼ × 2¼in.
Manufactured US, assembled in UK May 1961–1964
Lens Meniscus f/11
Shutter Single speed
Numbers made ?

Description/Remarks

Moulded plastic body; optical direct vision finder; built-in flash gun for AG1 bulbs.

Brownie 44A

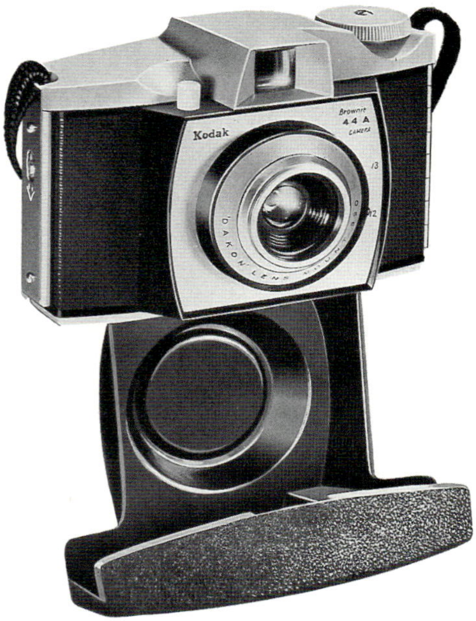

KP

Type Solid body eyelevel rolllfilm
Introduced September 1959
Discontinued 1965
Film size 127
Picture size 1⅝ × 1⅝in.
Manufactured UK
Lens Dakon, EV12 or EV13 (+ EV14 from 1964)
Shutter Single speed (1/40) sec.
Numbers made ?

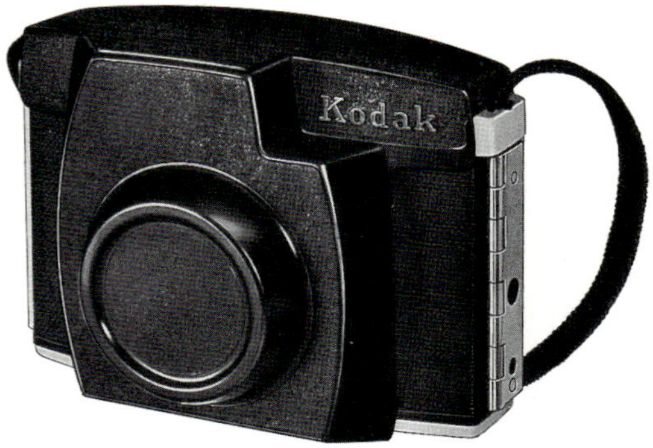

Description/Remarks

Designed by Kenneth Grange, with black moulded plastic body, grey 'sculptured' top and fabric covered aluminium back, integral flexible plastic ever-ready cover; optical direct vision finder; pin and screw flash contacts.

Brownie 44B

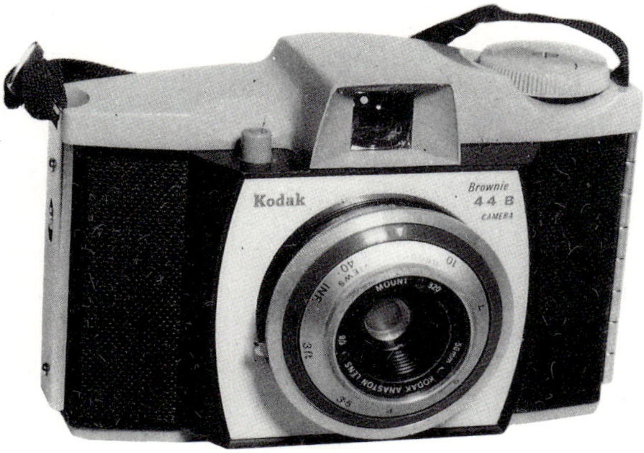

RPS

Type Solid body eyelevel rollfilm
Introduced May 1961
Discontinued September 1963
Film size 127
Picture size 1⅝ × 1⅝in.
Manufactured UK
Lens Anaston f/8, three apertures, focusing
Shutter Two speed, (1/30) and (1/60) sec.
Numbers made ?

Description/Remarks

Similar styling to Brownie 44A camera, but without integral ever-ready cover; optical direct vision finder; double exposure prevention; pin and screw flash contacts.

Brownie Hawkeye

Type Box rollfilm
Introduced May 1949
Discontinued July 1961
Film size 620
Picture size 2¼ × 2¼in.
Manufactured US, France (Flash model)
Lens Meniscus
Shutter Rotary
Numbers made ?

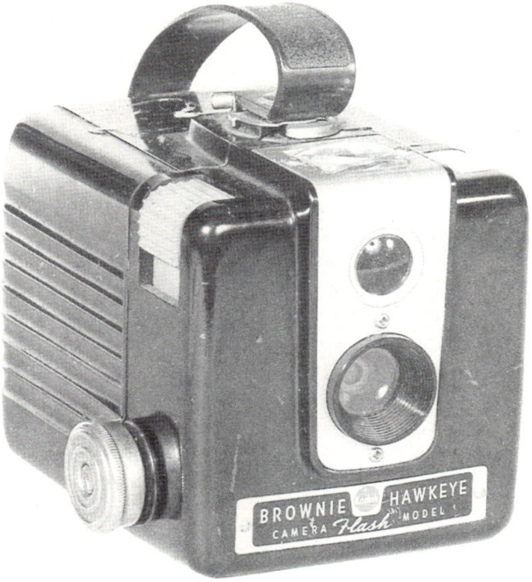

Flash model. KM

Description/Remarks

Moulded plastic body; brilliant finder; *May 1949–Nov. 1951:* non-synchronised model. *Sept. 1950–July 1961:* Flash Model; also manufactured in France as Brownie Flash camera.

Brownie Holiday

Type Solid body eyelevel rollfilm
Introduced October 1953
Discontinued April 1962
Film size 127
Picture size 1⅝ × 2½in.
Manufactured US
Lenses 1953–1955: Kodet
1955–1962: Dakon plastic
Shutter Rotary
Numbers made ?

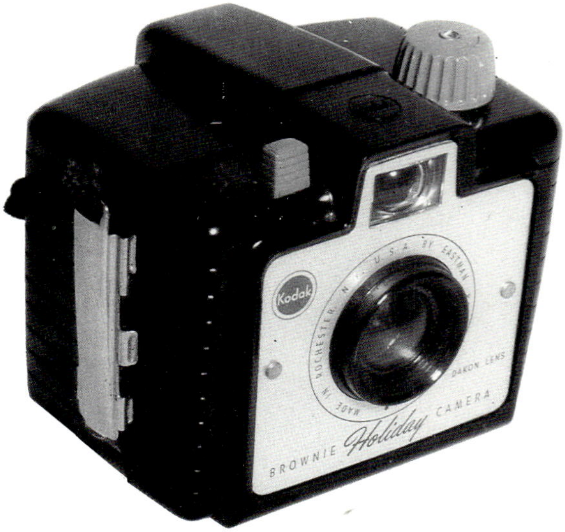

1953–1957. RPS

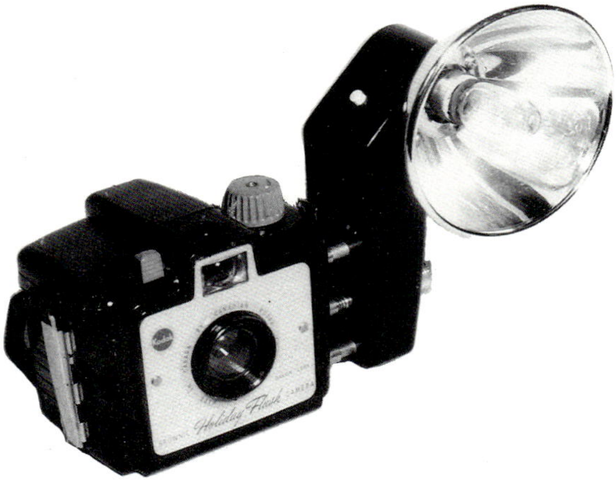

Flash model, 1954–1962. RPS

Description/Remarks

Moulded brown and tan plastic body; optical direct vision finder. *1953–Sept. 1957:* Non-synchronised model. *Oct. 1954–Apr.1962:* Flash model.

No 2 Brownie Junior

Type Box rollfilm
Introduced January 1930
Discontinued January 1933
Film size 120
Picture size 2¼ × 3¼in.
Manufactured UK
Lens Meniscus
Shutter Eastman Rotary
Numbers made ?

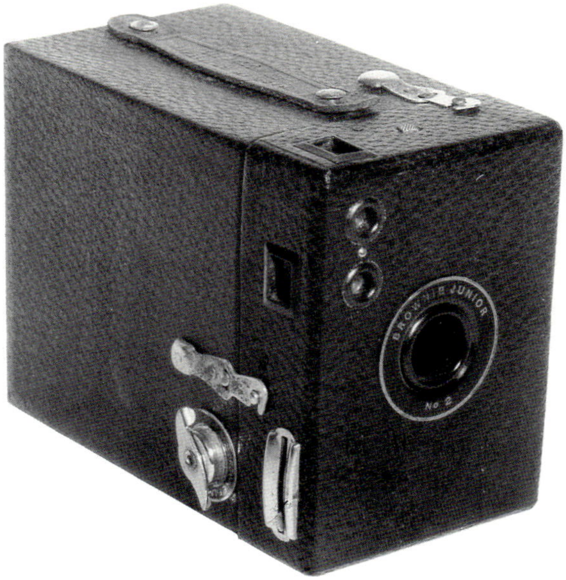

RPS

Description/Remarks

Leatherette covered card box; 2 reflecting finders; trigger guard; 2 pivoted side catches. *1930:* "No 2 Brownie Junior" on top of lens surround. *1931–1932:* "Brownie Junior" above, "No 2" below on lens surround.

Brownie Junior 620

Type Box rollfilm
Introduced 1934
Discontinued 1936
Film size 620
Picture size 6 × 9cm
Manufactured Germany
Lens Meniscus, three apertures
Shutter Box-shutter
Numbers made 90,500

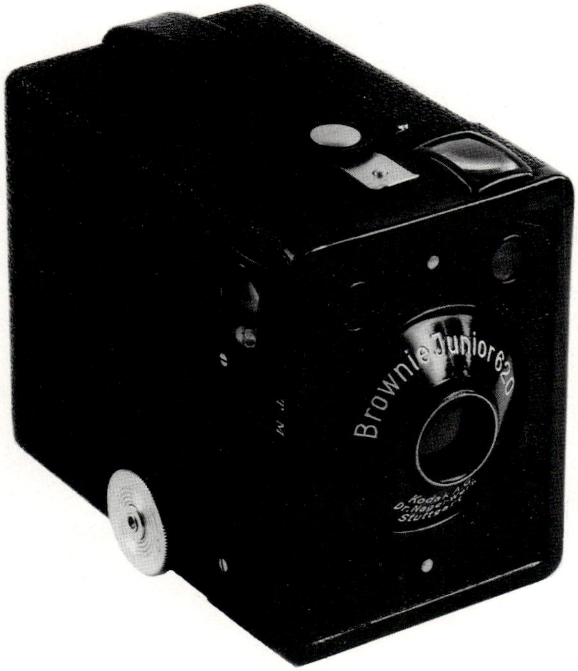

KAG

Type Box rollfilm
Introduced May 1957
Discontinued 1959
Film size 620
Picture size 2¼ × 3¼in.
Manufactured UK
Lens Kodet f/14 fixed focus
Shutter Rotary
Numbers made ?

Description/Remarks

Morocco grained imitation covering on metal body; horizontally striped front panel; two brilliant finders.

Description/Remarks

Black leatherette covered metal box; large conical lens mount; two brilliant finders.

Brownie Model I

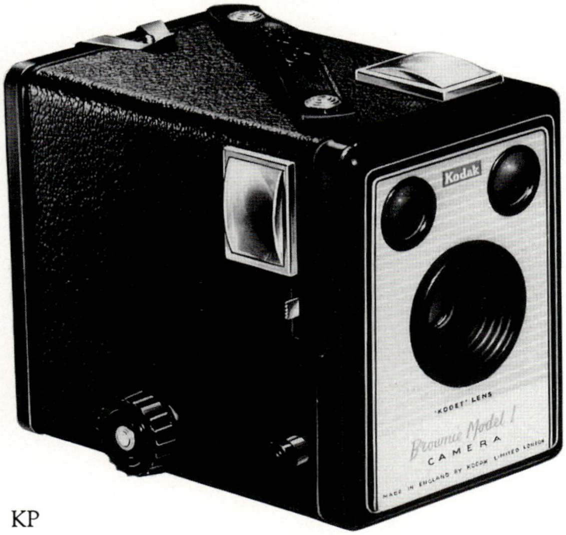

KP

Brownie 127

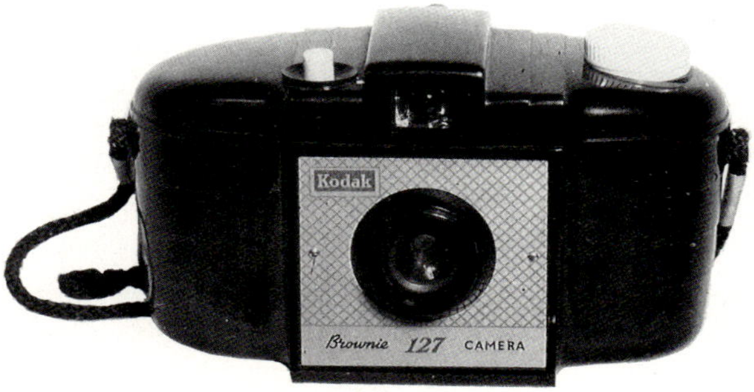

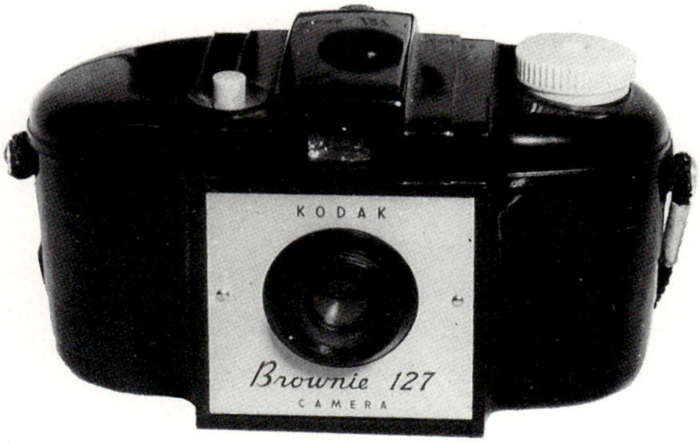

Below: 1952–1955. Above: 1956–1959.

Type Solid body eyelevel rollfilm
Introduced 1952
Discontinued 1959
Film size 127
Picture size 1⅝ × 2½in.
Manufactured UK

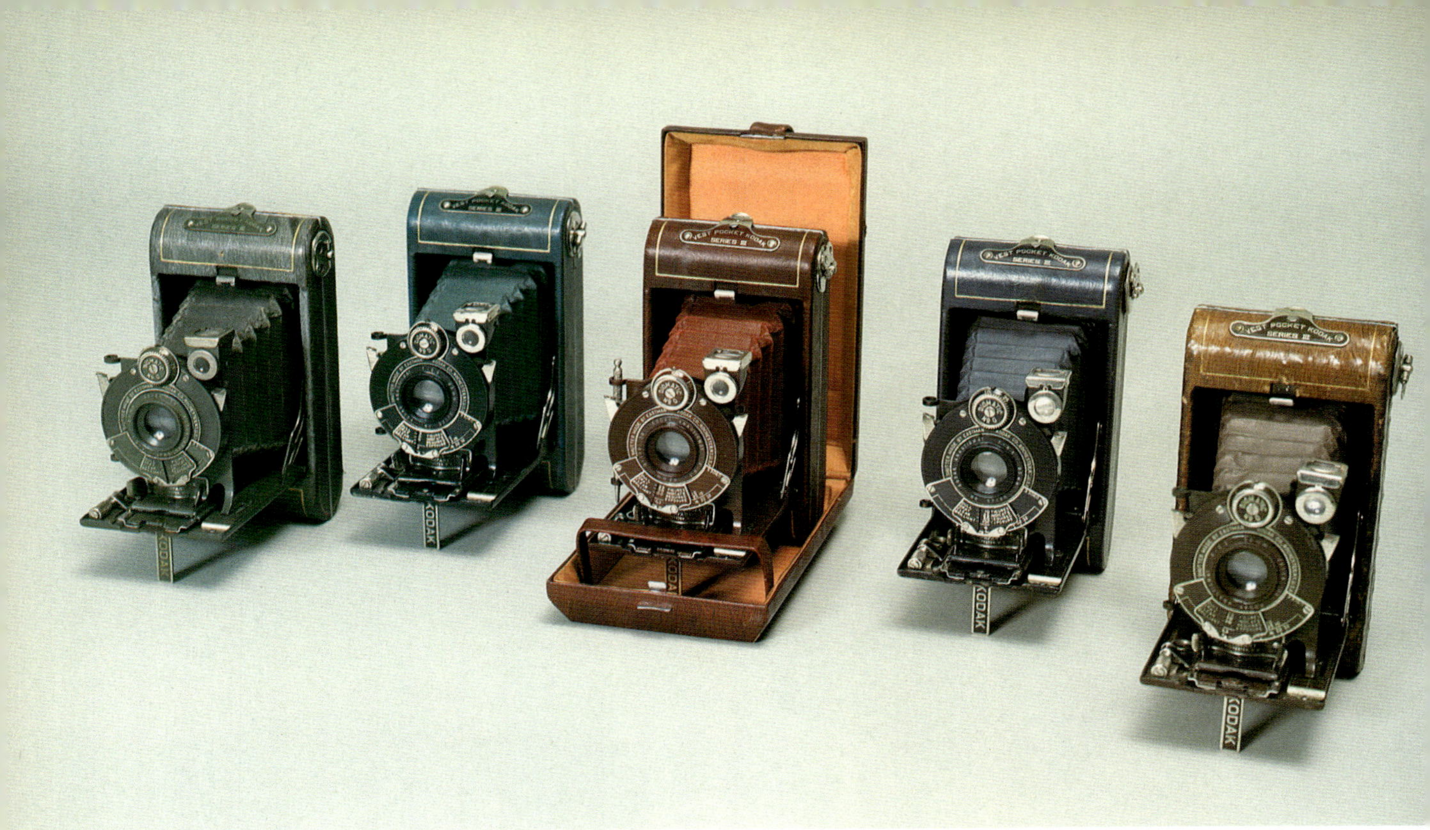

Above: The Vanity Kodak cameras in five colours (see page 167). KM   Below: No.1 Cone camera (see page 6). TNC

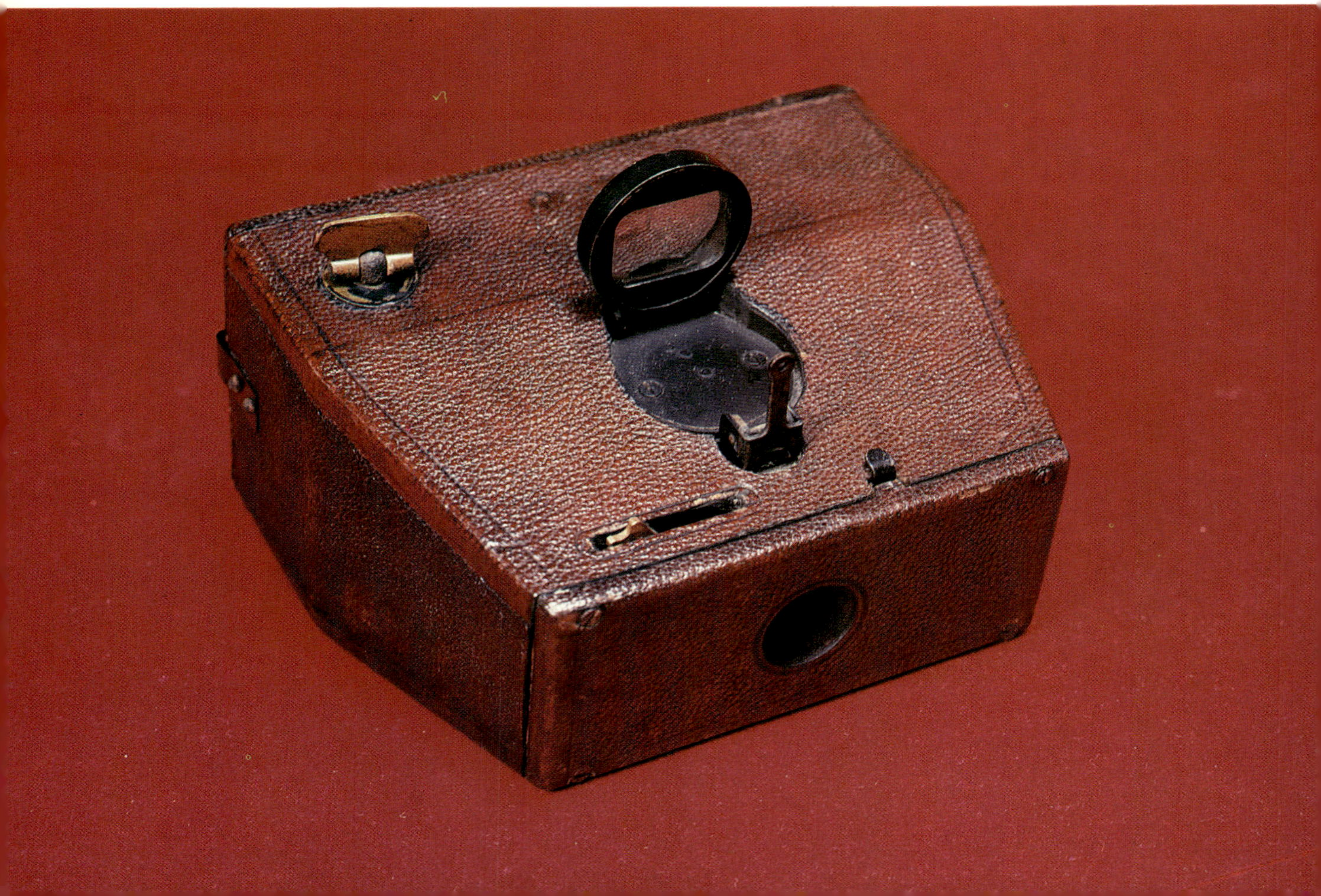

Lens   Meniscus f/14, 65mm
Shutter   Single speed 1/50 sec.
Numbers made   Several million
(1,000,000 made by August 1954)

Description/Remarks

Moulded smooth plastic body with broad horizontal steps; optical direct vision finder. Between May 1953 and September 1954 263,000 of these cameras were exported to America.

Variations

1952–1955: Plain lens face plate. *1956–1959:* Cross-hatched lens face plate.

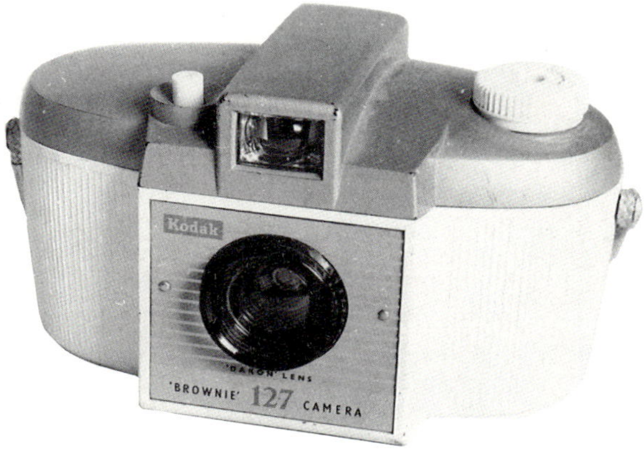

'Albino' version, c.1959. RPS

Variations

c1959: An 'albino' version with white body and grey top was produced for field testing; about 5,000 were sold in the Channel Islands. No more were made, as the grooved white body rapidly became dirty-looking.

Brownie 127, second model

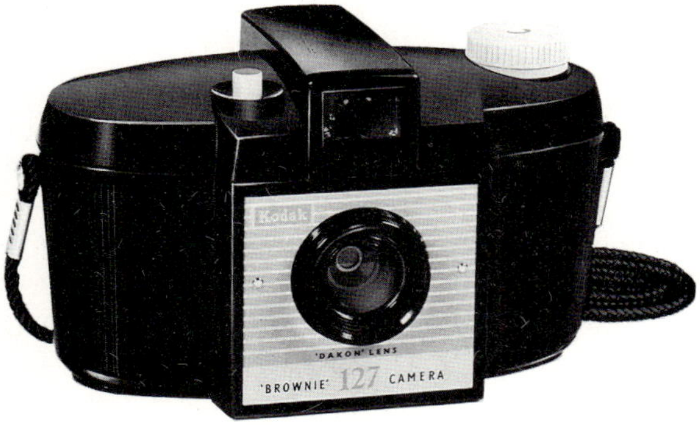

1959–1963 model. KP

Type   Solid body eyelevel rollfilm
Introduced   April 1959
Discontinued   1963
Film size   127
Picture size $1\frac{5}{8} \times 2\frac{1}{2}$in.
Manufactured   UK
Lens   Dakon f/11 plastic
Shutter   Rotary single speed
Numbers made   Probably several million

Description/Remarks

Moulded plastic body with vertical ribbing, smooth top. Optical direct vision finder; horizontally striped lens faceplate.

Brownie 127, third model

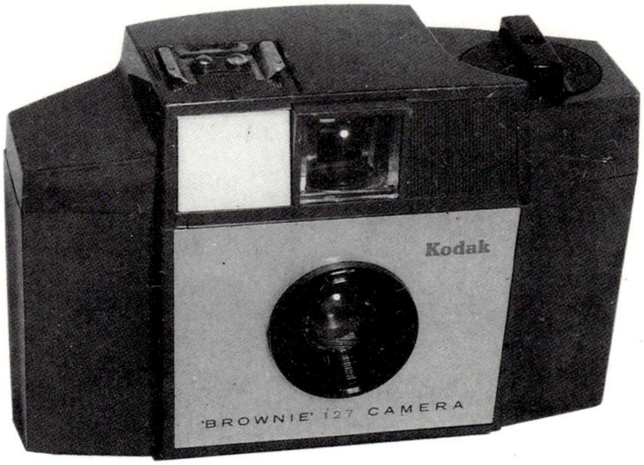

RPS

Type   Solid body eyelevel
Introduced   November 1965
Discontinued   November 1967

Film size 127
Picture size 1⅝ × 1⅝in.
Manufactured UK
Lens Plastic f/14, 50.6mm
Shutter Single speed (1/40) sec.
Numbers made Probably 1,000,000+

Description/Remarks

Completely restyled, with more angular plastic moulded body; optical direct vision finder with film wind-on reminder; hot shoe for Instamatic flasholder; double exposure prevention.

Brownie Reflex

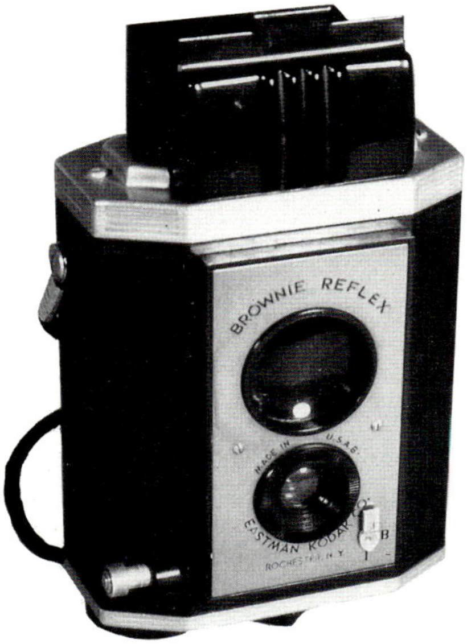

US model. PDM

Type Box rollfilm
Introduced May 1940 (1946 in UK)
Discontinued May 1952 (May 1960 in UK)
Film size 127
Picture size 1⅝ × 1⅝in.
Manufactured US and UK
Lens Meniscus
Shutter Rotary
Numbers made ?

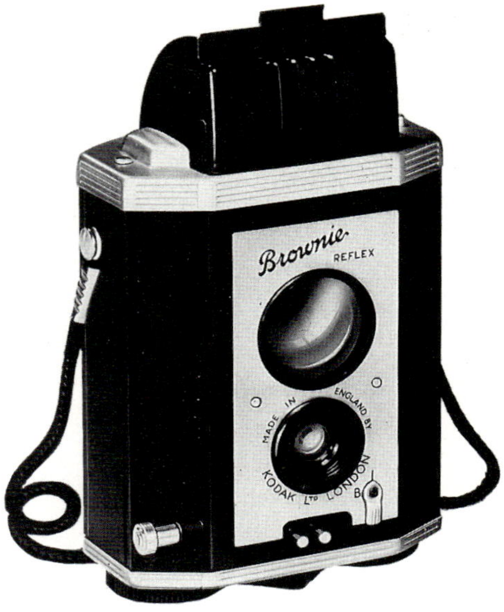

UK model. KP

Description/Remarks

'Twin-lens reflex' pattern; large brilliant finder with folding hood. *1940–Aug. 1941:* non-synchronised model. *Sept.1941–May 1952:* Synchro Model; with 2-pin flash contacts. Made in UK 1946–1960.

Brownie Reflex 20

Type Box rollfilm
Introduced April 1959
Discontinued January 1966
Film size 620
Picture size 2¼ × 2¼in.
Manufactured US, assembled in UK 1960–1965
Lens Meniscus f/11
Shutter Single speed (1/40) sec.
Numbers made ?

Description/Remarks

Moulded plastic body; 'twin-lens reflex' pattern with large brilliant finder with hood; pin and screw flash contacts.

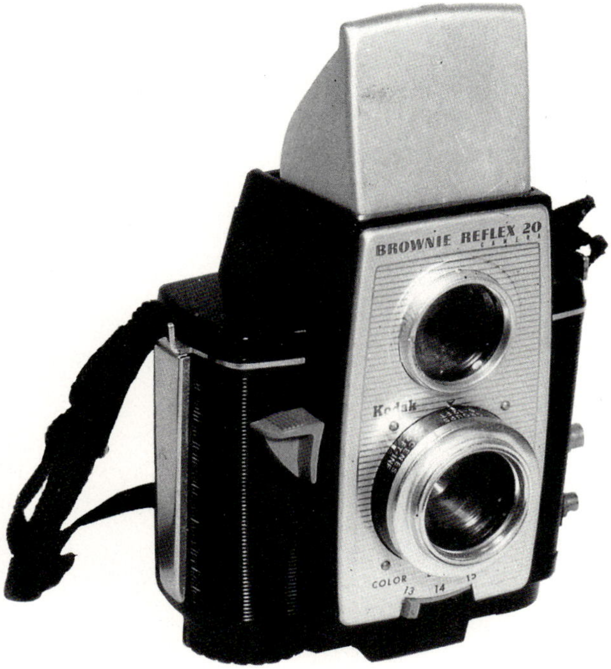

Type Box rollfilm
Introduced 1933
Discontinued 1936
Film size 620
Picture size 6 × 9cm
Manufactured Germany
Lenses 1933: Doublet f/8
1934–1936: f/11
With two close-up lenses
Shutter Box-shutter
Numbers made 27,000

Description/Remarks

Black leatherette covered metal box, with geometric design in black enamel and nickel-chrome on front; two brilliant finders; shutter release lock.

RPS

Brownie 620

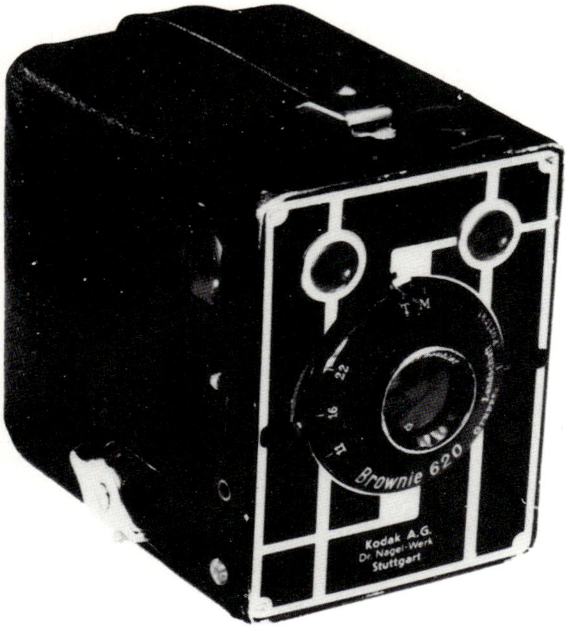

Brownie Special No 2

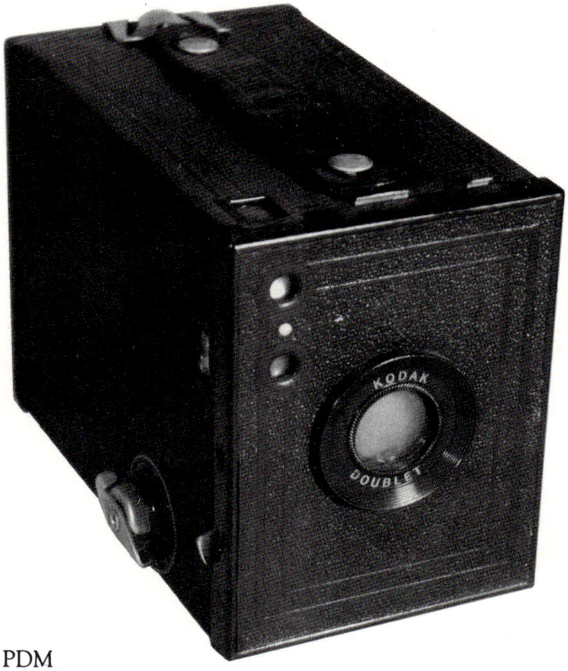

PDM

Type Box rollfilm
Introduced November 1933
Discontinued February 1934
Film size 120
Picture size 2¼ × 3¼in.

Manufactured US
Lens Doublet
Shutter Rotary
Numbers made ?

Description/Remarks

Two reflecting finders

Brownie Starflash

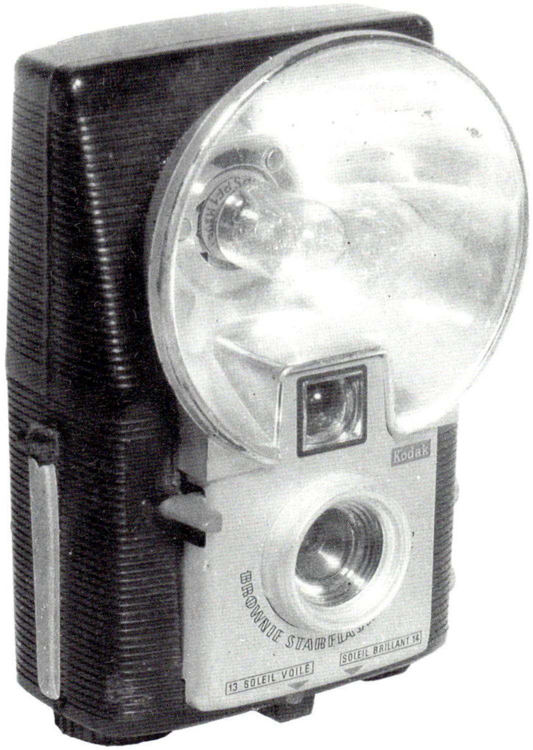

French model. RPS

Type Solid body eyelevel rollfilm
Introduced March 1957
Discontinued June 1965
Film size 127
Picture size 1⅝ × 1⅝in.
Manufactured US, France
Lens Dakon
Shutter Rotary
Numbers made ?

Description/Remarks

Moulded plastic body; optical direct vision finder; built-in flash gun for capless bulbs.

Mar. 1957–June 1965: black model. *Mar. 1958–Oct. 1960:* red model. *Mar. 1958–Aug. 1962:* white model. *Mar. 1958–Feb. 1962:* blue model. *Oct. 1959–Dec. 1961:* with Coca-Cola motif.

The French version was in white, black, grey or blue colours.

Variations

This camera was supplied in an outfit for close-up photography as the Kodak Startech camera.

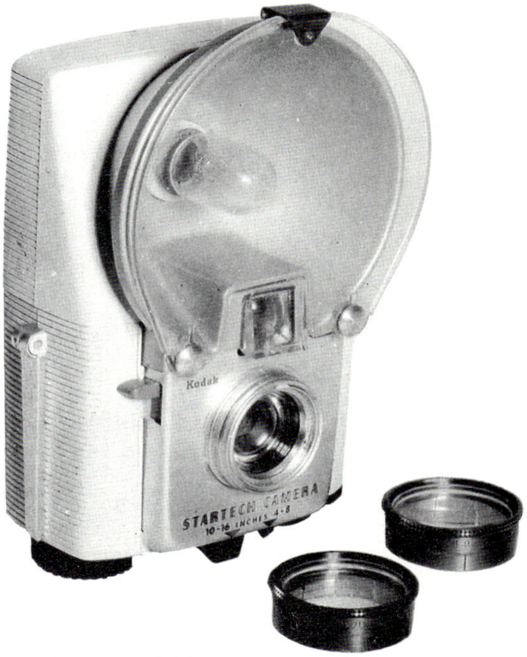

Kodak Startech version. RPS

Brownie Starflex

Type Box rollfilm
Introduced March 1957
Discontinued September 1964
Film size 127
Picture size 1⅝ × 1⅝in.
Manufactured US

Lens Dakon
Shutter Rotary
Numbers made ?

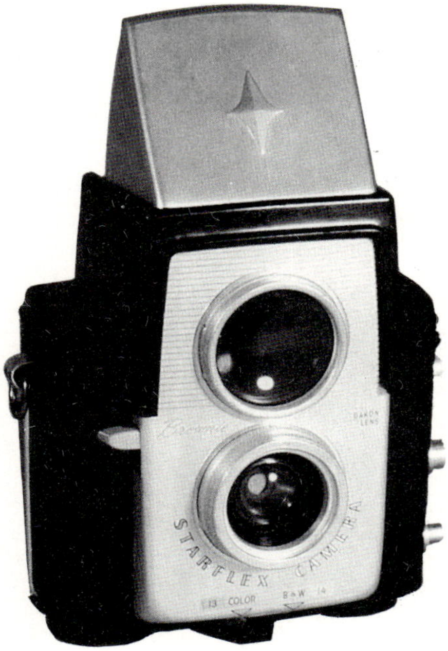

PDM

Description/Remarks

Moulded plastic body; 'twin-lens reflex' pattern with large brilliant finder with hood; screw and pin flash contacts.

Brownie Starlet

Type Solid body eyelevel rollfilm
Introduced May 1956
Discontinued August 1956
Film size 127
Picture size 1⅝ × 2½in.
Manufactured UK, for export to US
Lens Meniscus
Shutter Rotary
Numbers made ?

Description/Remarks

Version of the UK Brownie 127 camera (first model) for the US market.

Brownie Starlet, US model

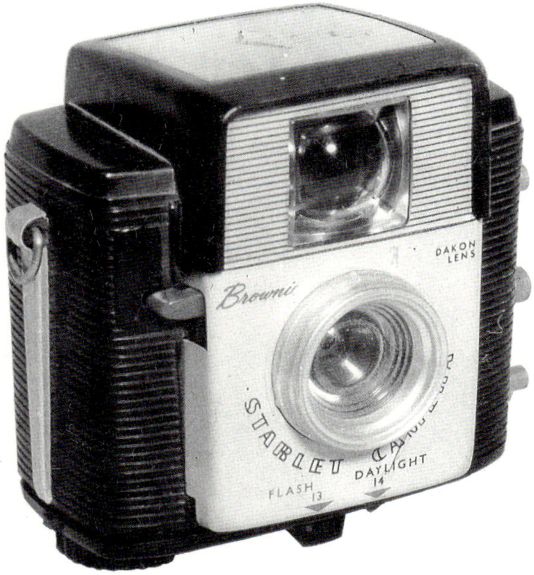

US model. RPS

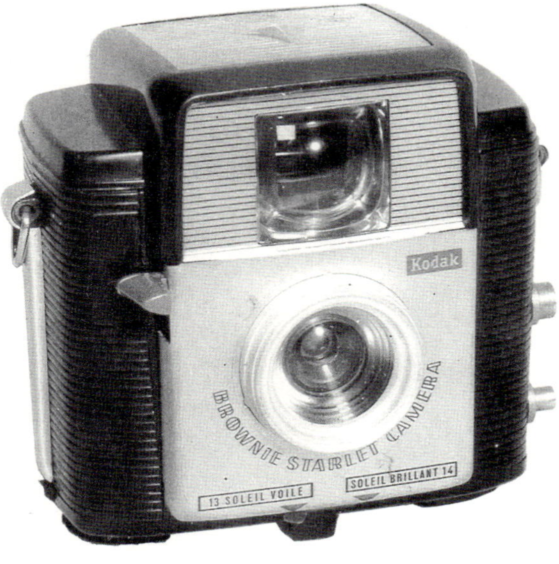

French model. RPS

Type Solid body eyelevel rollfilm
Introduced July 1957
Discontinued June 1962
Film size 127
Picture size 1⅝ × 1⅝in.

Manufactured US, France
Lens Dakon
Shutter Rotary
Numbers made ?

Description/Remarks

Moulded plastic body; optical direct vision finder; screw and pin flash contacts. This model continued as the Brownie Bullet II camera from 1961.

Brownie Starluxe II

Type Solid body eyelevel rollfilm

French version of Brownie Starmite II camera (q.v.).

Brownie Starmatic

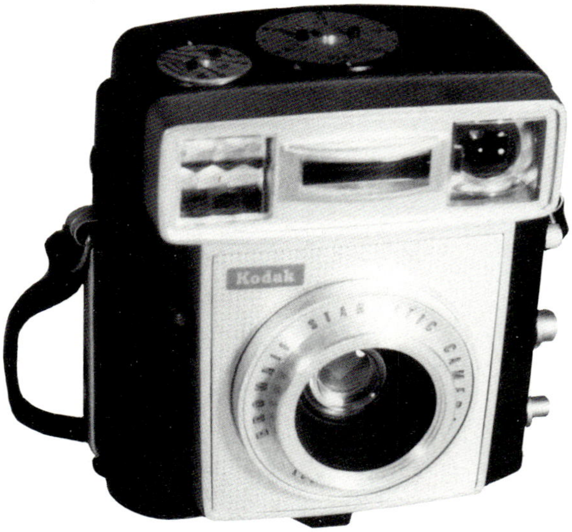

PDM

Type Automatic solid body eyelevel rollfilm
Introduced April 1959
Discontinued August 1963
Film size 127
Picture size 1⅝ × 1⅝in.
Manufactured US
Lens Kodar f/8
Shutter Rotary
Numbers made ?

Description/Remarks

Moulded plastic body; optical direct vision finder; automatic exposure setting by photocell; pin and screw flash contacts.

From Aug. 1961–Aug. 1963: Starmatic II, with two-tone grey body, 2-speed shutter.

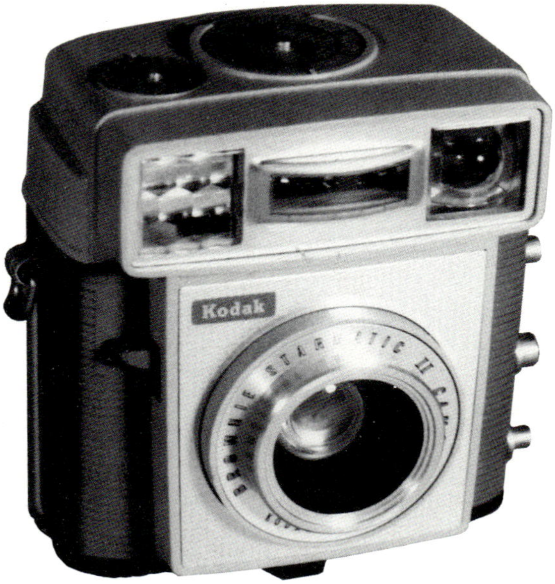

PDM

Brownie Starmeter

Type Solid body eyelevel rollfilm
Introduced April 1960
Discontinued November 1965
Film size 127
Picture size 1⅝ × 1⅝in.
Manufactured US
Lens Kodar f/8
Shutter Rotary
Numbers made ?

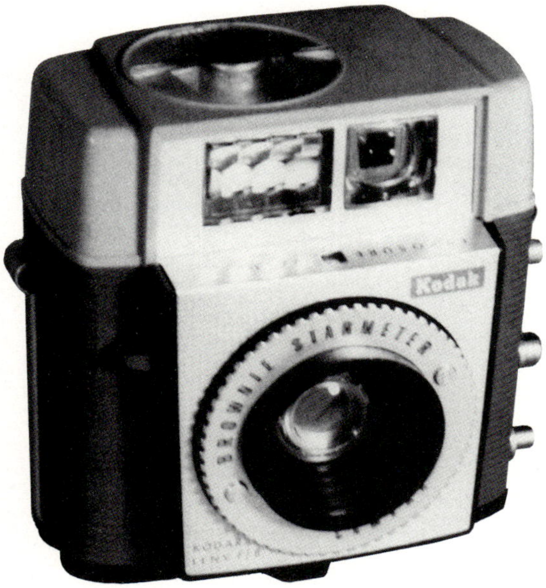

PDM

Description/Remarks

Moulded plastic body; optical direct vision finder; built-in meter; pin and screw flash contacts.

Brownie Starmite

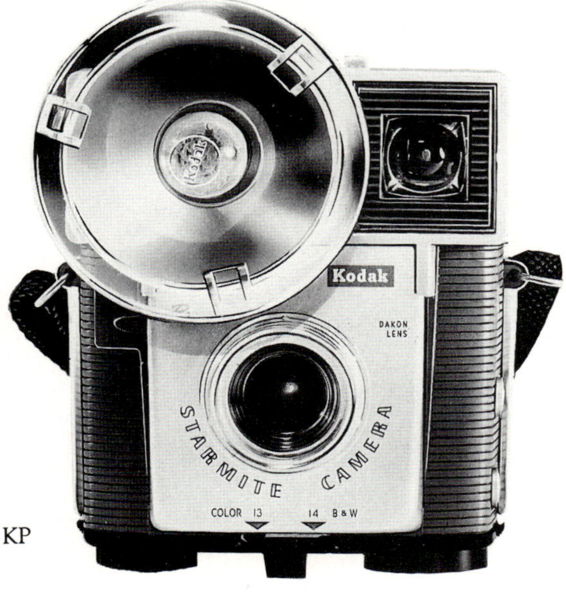

KP

Type Solid body eyelevel rollfilm
Introduced April 1960
Discontinued June 1963
Film size 127
Picture size 1⅝ × 1⅝in.
Manufactured US, assembled in UK May 1961-1965
Lens Fixed focus f/11
Shutter Rotary
Numbers made ?

Description/Remarks

Moulded plastic body; optical direct vision finder; built-in flash gun for capless bulbs

Brownie Starmite II

Type Solid body eyelevel rollfilm
Introduced November 1962
Discontinued August 1967
Film size 127
Picture size 1⅝ × 1⅝in.
Manufactured US, France
Lens Fixed focus f/11
Shutter Rotary
Numbers made ?

Description/Remarks

Moulded plastic body; optical direct vision finder; built-in flash gun with rectangular reflector for AG1 bulbs.

A version was assembled in France under the name Brownie Starluxe II camera.

Brownie Super 27

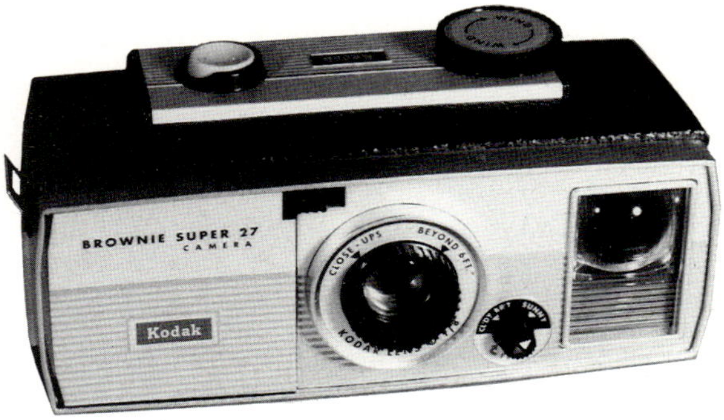

PDM

Type Solid body eyelevel rollfilm
Introduced August 1961
Discontinued June 1965
Film size 127
Picture size 1⅝ × 1⅝in.
Manufactured US
Lens Kodar f/8
Shutter Two-speed
Numbers made ?

Description/Remarks

Moulded plastic body; optical direct vision finder; concealed flash gun for AG1 bulbs.

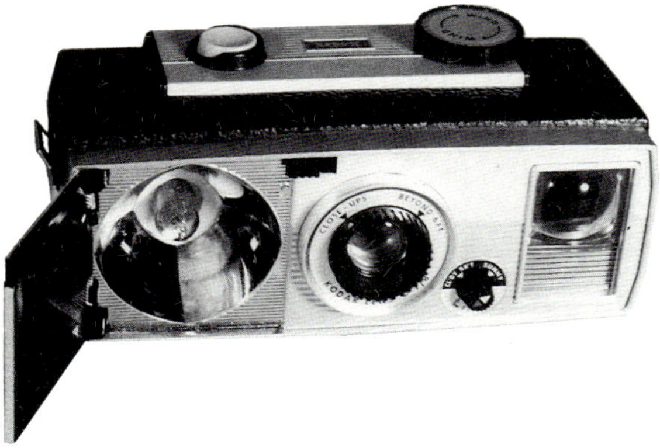

With flash cover open. PDM

Brownie Target Six-16

Type Box rollfilm
Introduced July 1946
Discontinued November 1951
Film size 616
Picture size 2½ x4¼in.
Manufactured US
Lens Meniscus
Shutter Rotary
Numbers made ?

Description/Remarks

Metal body box; 2 brilliant finders; vertical line design on front panel. Developed from Target Brownie Six-16 camera.

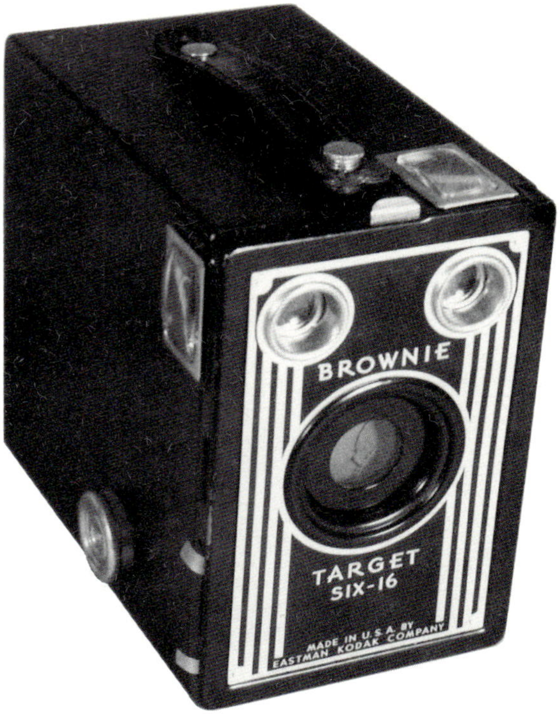

PDM

Brownie Target Six-20

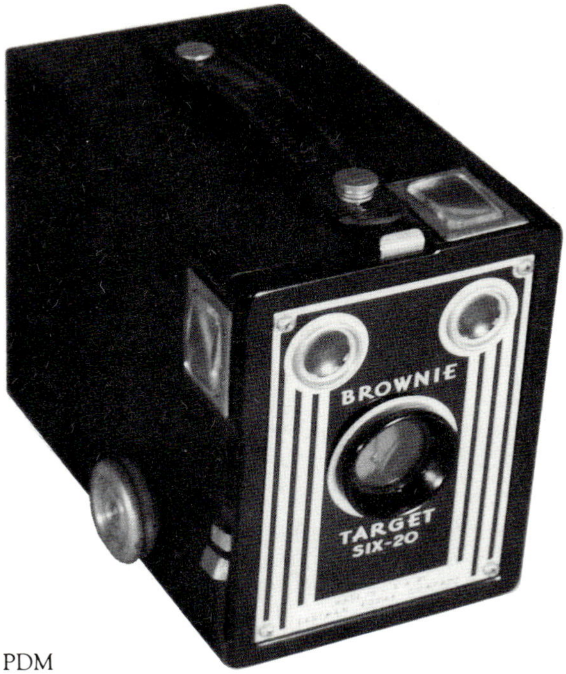

PDM

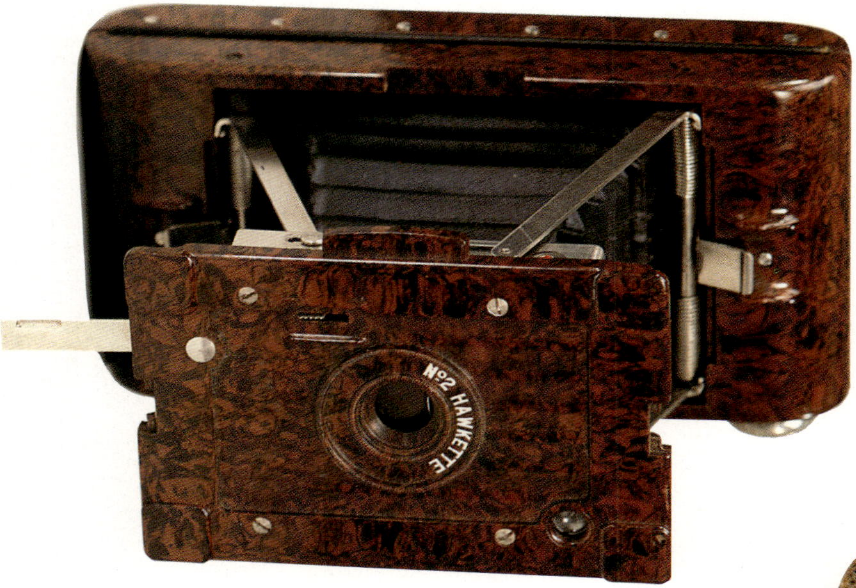

No.2 Hawkette camera (see page 115). KM

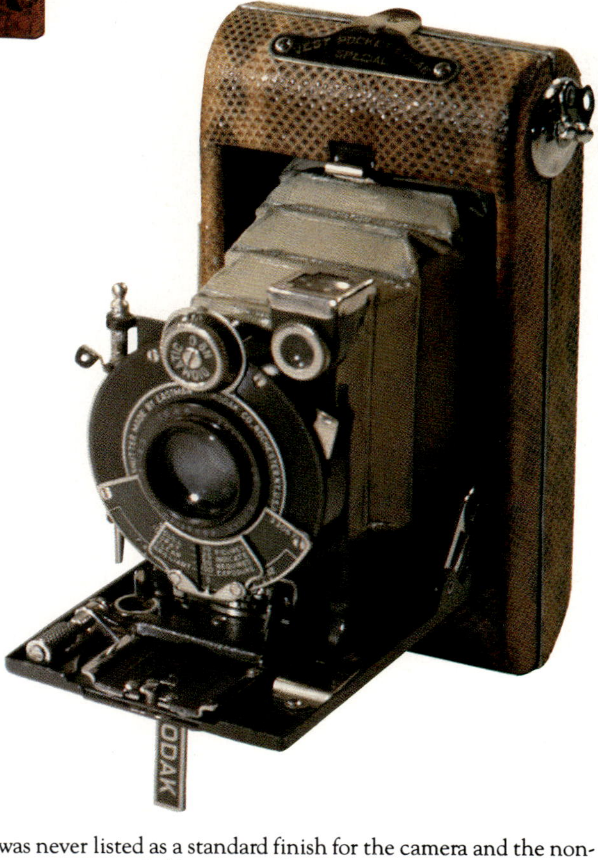

Vest Pocket Kodak Special camera in lizard-skin covering. This was never listed as a standard finish for the camera and the non-Kodak appearance of the rivets attaching the nameplate indicate it was probably a one-off modification carried out in an independent workshop (see also page 292 for another example of an independent modification). Private collection.

Type Box rollfilm
Introduced July 1946
Discontinued May 1952
Film size 620
Picture size 2¼ × 3¼in.
Manufactured US
Lens Meniscus
Shutter Rotary
Numbers made ?

Description/Remarks

Metal box; two brilliant finders; vertical line design on front panel. Developed from Target Brownie Six-20 camera.

Brownie Twin 20

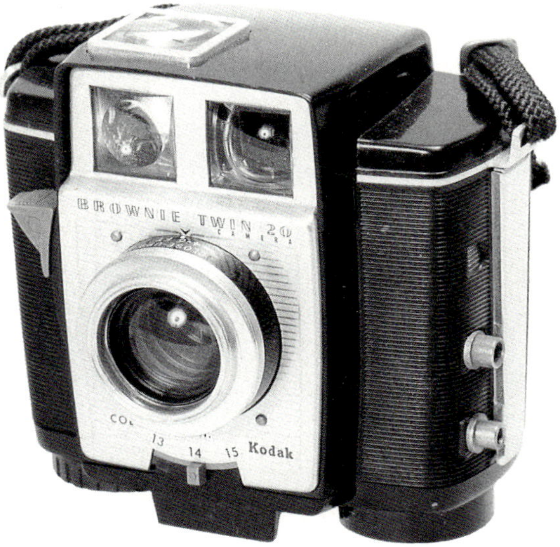

KM

Type Solid body eyelevel rollfilm
Introduced April 1959
Discontinued September 1964
Film size 620
Picture size 2¼ × 2¼in.
Manufactured US, assembled in UK February 1960–1964
Lens Meniscus f/11
Shutter Rotary
Numbers made ?

Description/Remarks

Moulded plastic body; optical direct vision and brilliant finders; screw and pin flash contacts.

Brownie Vecta

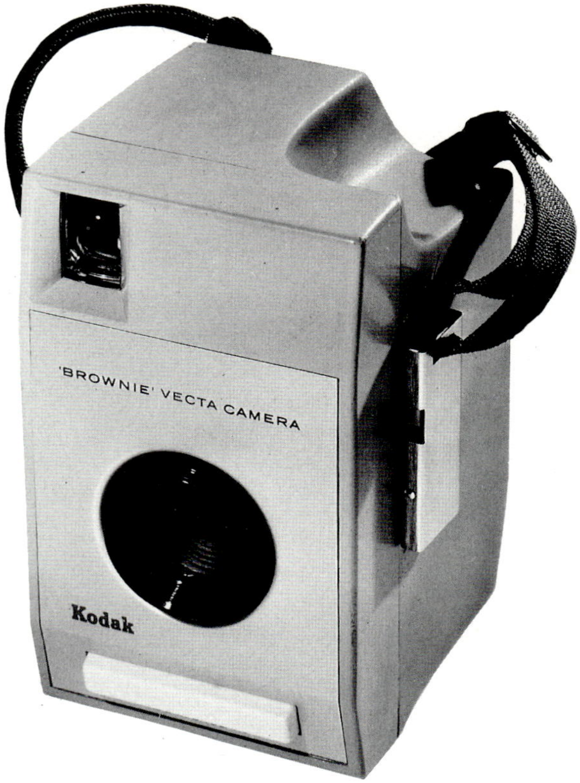

KP

Type Solid body eyelevel rollfilm
Introduced September 1963
Discontinued 1966
Film size 127
Picture size 1⅝ × 2½in.
Manufactured UK
Lens Plastic f/14
Shutter Single speed
Numbers made ?

Description/Remarks

Designed by Kenneth Grange, moulded grey plastic upright box with 'sculptured' finger recesses to minimise camera shake; optical direct vision finder; bar shutter release.

New York World's Fair Baby Brownie

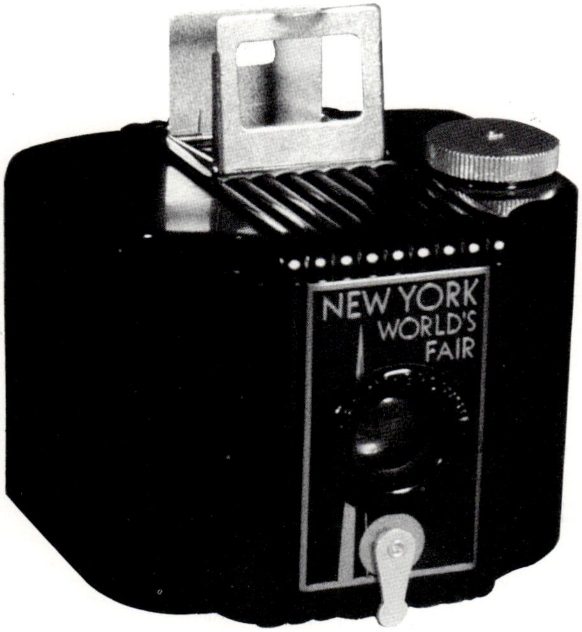

PDM

Type Solid body eyelevel rollfilm
Introduced April 1939
Discontinued 1940
Film size 127
Picture size 1⅝ × 2½in.
Manufactured US
Lens Meniscus
Shutter Rotary
Numbers made ?

Description/Remarks

Moulded plastic body; identical to Baby Brownie except for special lens plate. Available only at the World's Fair.

No 2 Portrait Brownie

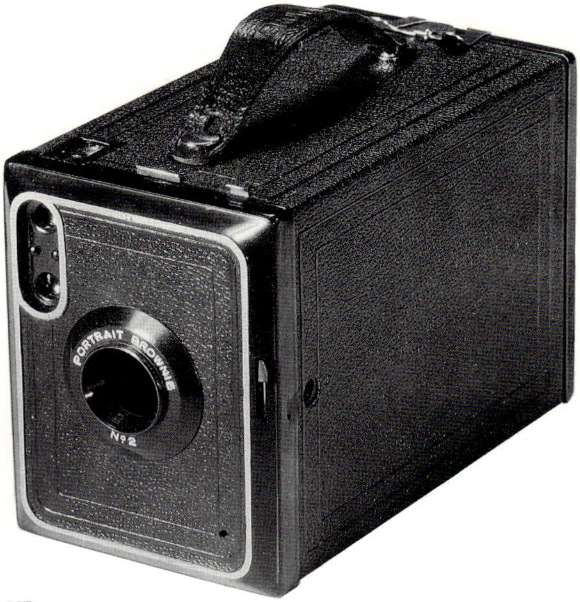

KP

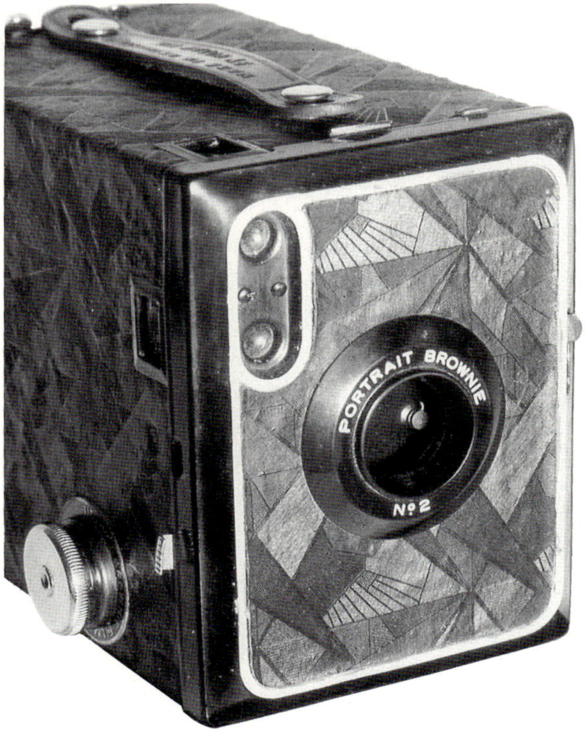

Modernist finish, 1930. RPS

Type Box rollfilm
Introduced February 1929
Discontinued 1935
Film size 120
Picture size 2¼ × 3¼in.
Manufactured UK
Lens Meniscus, with portrait lens
Shutter Eastman Rotary
Numbers made ?

Description/Remarks

First design from the new Kodak camera factory at Harrow. Metal body with angled edges to front panel with bright line border and edge to finder window. Two brilliant finders.

Made in range of coloured finishes: *1929–1935:* Grey, claret, brown, red. *1929–1934:* Green. *1929–1933:* Blue, black.

Nov. 1930: Black Modernist covering, slight relief, wax-like feel – special line for Christmas sale, limited numbers only.

Popular Brownie

See Six-20 Popular Brownie

Six-16 Brownie

Type Box rollfilm
Introduced March 1933
Discontinued April 1941
Film size 616
Picture size 2½ × 4¼in.
Manufactured US
Lens Diway lens, with close-up lens
Shutter Rotary
Numbers made ?

Description/Remarks

Leatherette covered metal box, front panel with geometric Art Deco design; two brilliant finders.

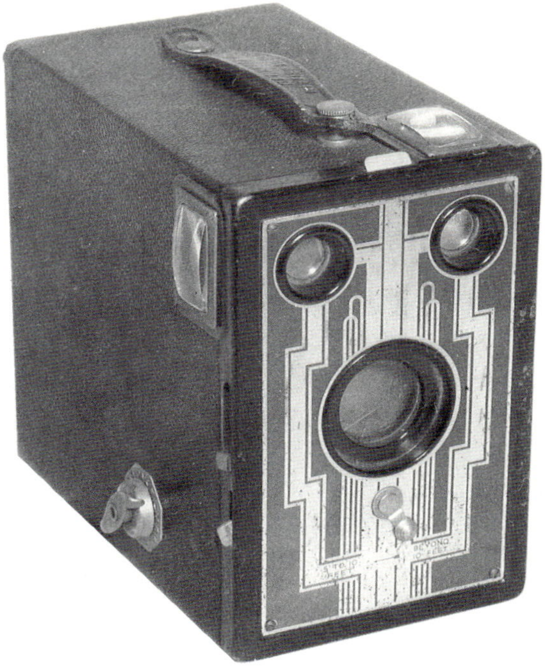

RPS

Six-16 Brownie Junior

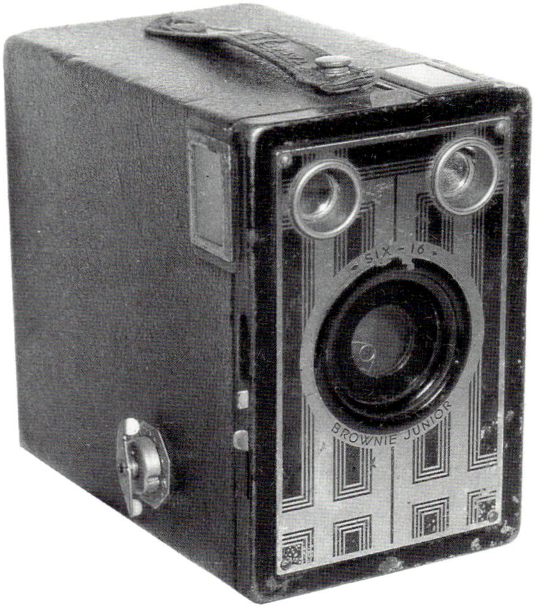

RPS

Type Box rollfilm
Introduced February 1934
Discontinued October 1942

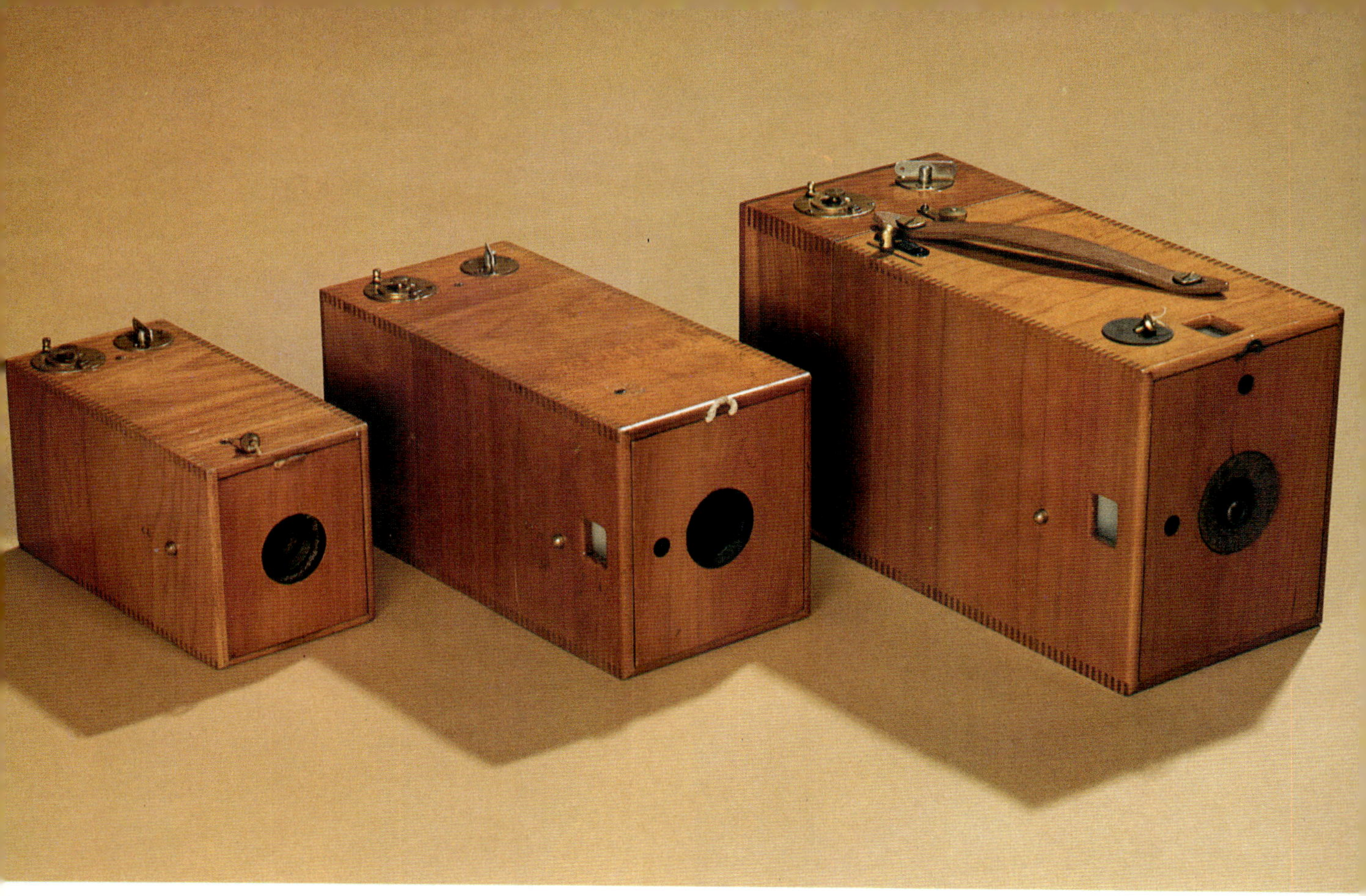

Above: The A, B, and C Ordinary Kodak cameras (see pages 24/25). PDM. Below: 2 and 2A Beau Brownie cameras (see page 33). KM

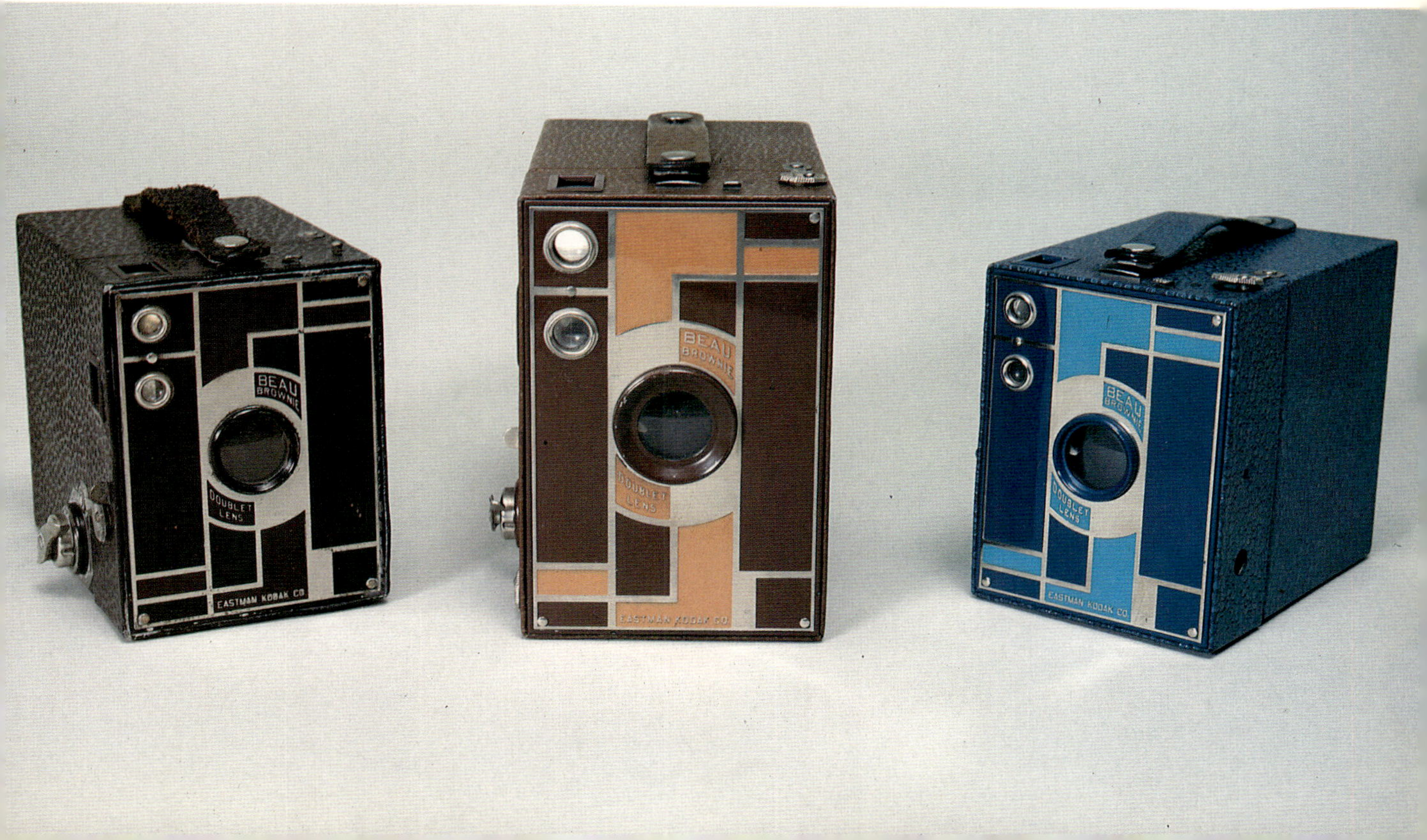

Film size 616
Picture size 2½ × 4¼in.
Manufactured US
Lens Meniscus
Shutter Rotary
Numbers made ?

Description/Remarks

Leatherette covered metal box, front panel black with embossed design or gilt with geometric Art Deco pattern; two reflecting finders.

Six-16 Brownie Special

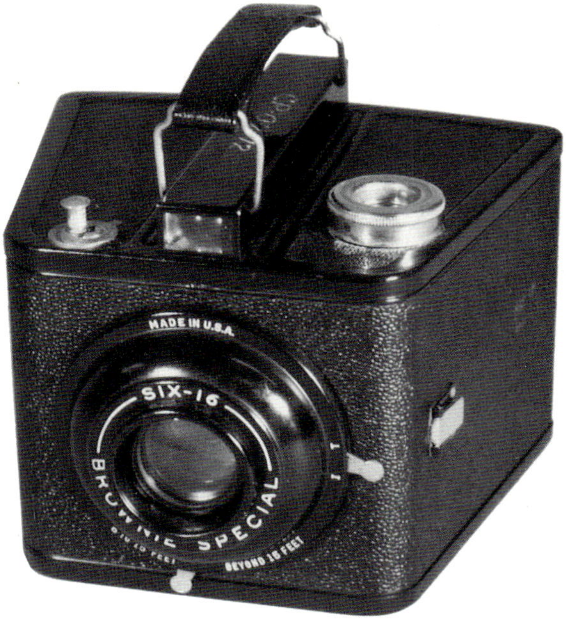

PDM

Type Solid body eyelevel
Introduced September 1938
Discontinued July 1942
Film size 616
Picture size 2½ × 4¼in.
Manufactured US
Lens Meniscus
Shutter Rotary
Numbers made ?

Description/Remarks

Moulded plastic body; optical direct vision finder.

Six-20 Boy Scout Brownie

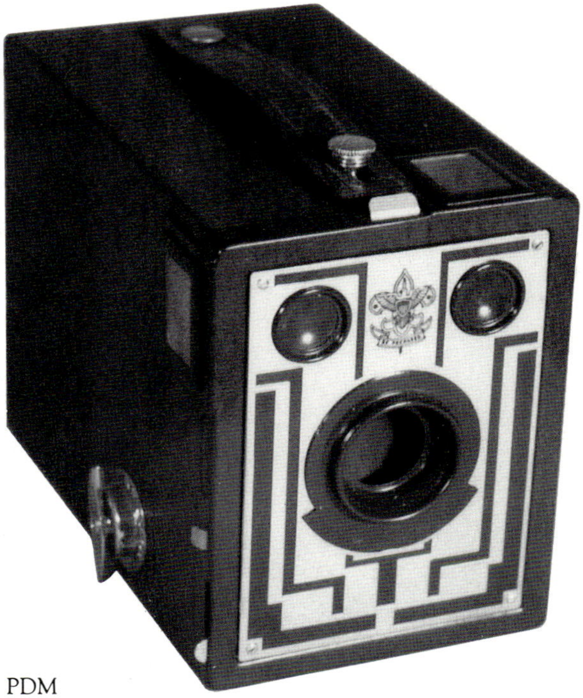

PDM

Type Box rollfilm
Introduced January 1933
Discontinued 1934
Film size 620
Picture size 2¼ × 3¼in.
Manufactured US
Lens Meniscus
Shutter Rotary
Numbers made ?

Description/Remarks

Metal body with front panel with geometric design and American Boy Scout emblem.

Six-20 Brownie (US model)

Type Box rollfilm

Introduced March 1933
Discontinued April 1941
Film size 620
Picture size 2¼ × 3¼in.
Manufactured US
Lens Diway, with close-up lens
Shutter Rotary
Numbers made ?

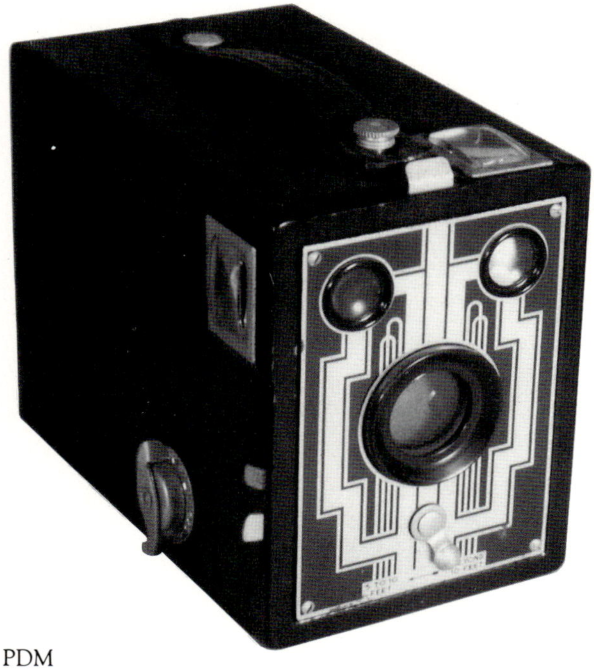

PDM

Description/Remarks

Leatherette covered metal body with front panel with geometric Art Deco design; two brilliant finders.

Six-20 Brownie (UK model)

Type Box rollfilm
Introduced New Year 1934
Discontinued 1941
Film size 620
Picture size 2¼ × 3¼in.
Manufactured UK
Lens Doublet f/11, focusing
Shutter Single speed shutter
Numbers made ?

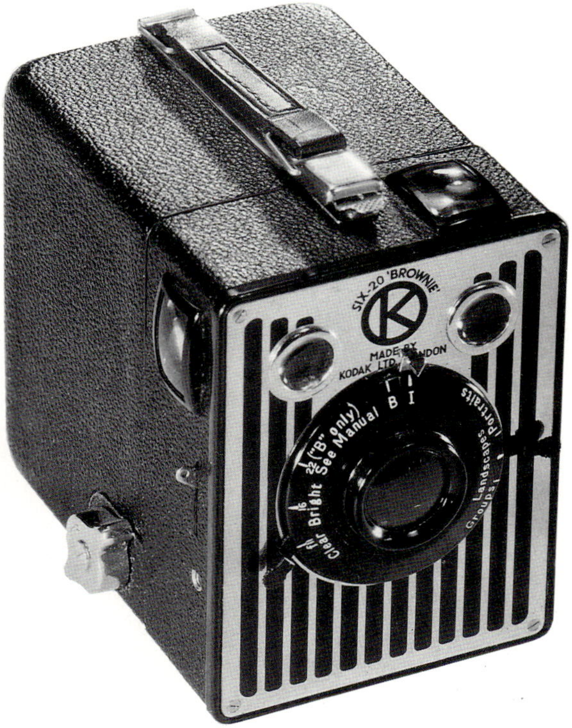

UK model, 1934–1937. KP

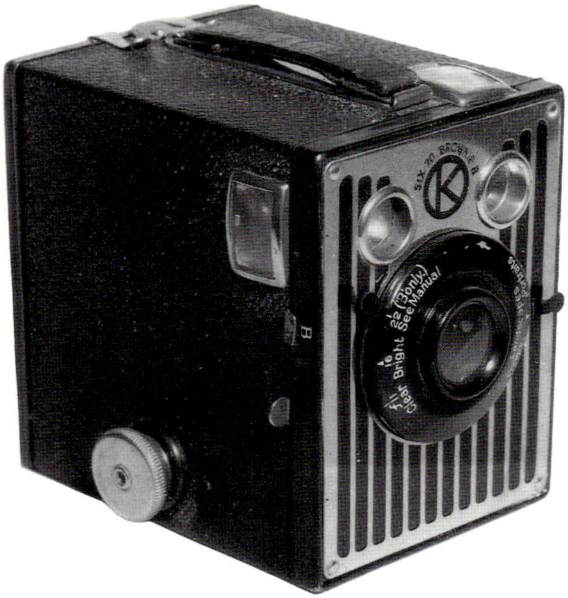

Model B, 1937–1941. RPS

Description/Remarks

Metal body, front panel with 'Kodak Girl' vertical stripe pattern in black enamel and bright stainless metal; two brilliant finders. *1934–1937:* camera opens in two halves, linked by hinged arms,for loading.

1937–1941: Model B; redesigned, more angular case, with same front panel design; fitted with older pattern hinged back with springcatch.

Six-20 Brownie model C

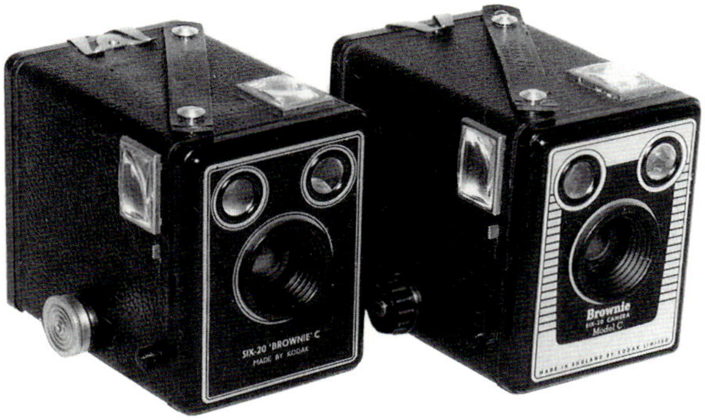

Left: 1946–1953. Right: 1953–1957. RPS

Type Box rollfilm
Introduced 1946
Discontinued 1957
Film size 620
Picture size 2¼ × 3¼in.
Manufactured UK
Lens Meniscus f/11, 100mm
Shutter Single blade
Numbers made ?

Description/Remarks

Morocco-grained imitation leather covered metal body; two brilliant finders.

1946–1953: plain matt enamel front; metal wind knob and release button. *1953–1957:* horizontally striped front; plastic wind knob and release button; triangular spring back catch.

Six-20 Brownie model D

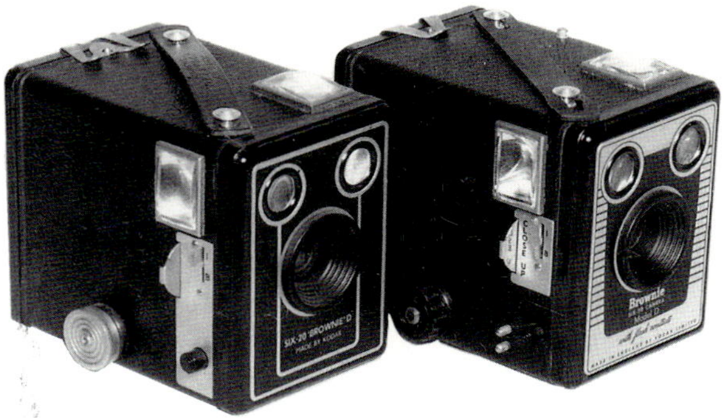

Left: 1946–1953. Right: 1953–1957. RPS

Type Box rollfilm
Introduced 1946
Discontinued 1957
Film size 620
Picture size 2¼ × 3¼in.
Manufactured UK
Lens Meniscus f/11, 100mm, with portrait lens
Shutter Single blade
Numbers made ?

Description/Remarks

Pearl-grained imitation leather; two brilliant finders; hinged back with spring catch.

1946–1953: plain matt enamel front; metal windknob and release button. *1953–1957:* horizontally striped front; plastic wind knob and release button; 2-pin flash contacts; triangular spring back catch.

Six-20 Brownie model E

Type Box rollfilm
Introduced 1947
Discontinued 1957
Film size 620
Picture size 2¼ × 3¼in.
Manufactured UK
Lens Meniscus f/11, 100mm, with portrait lens
Shutter Single blade
Numbers made ?

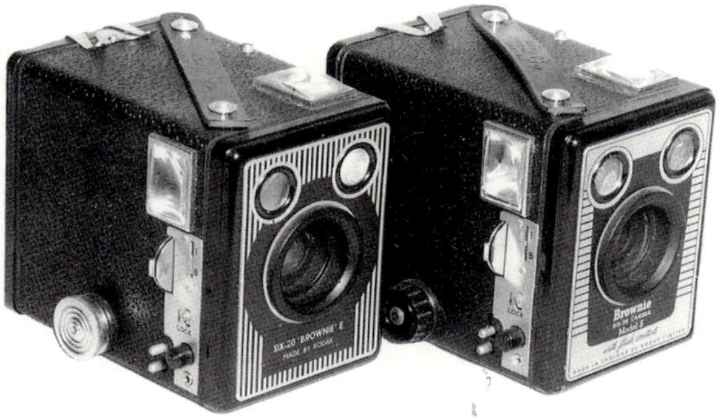

Left: 1947–1953. Right: 1953–1957. RPS

Description/Remarks

Imitation-pigskin covered metal body; two brilliant finders; yellow filter; 2-pin flash contacts; shutter safety catch; tripod sockets; cable release socket.

1947–1953: vertically striped front, metal wind knob and release button. *1953–1957:* horizontally striped front, plastic wind knob and release button, triangular spring back catch.

Six-20 Brownie model F

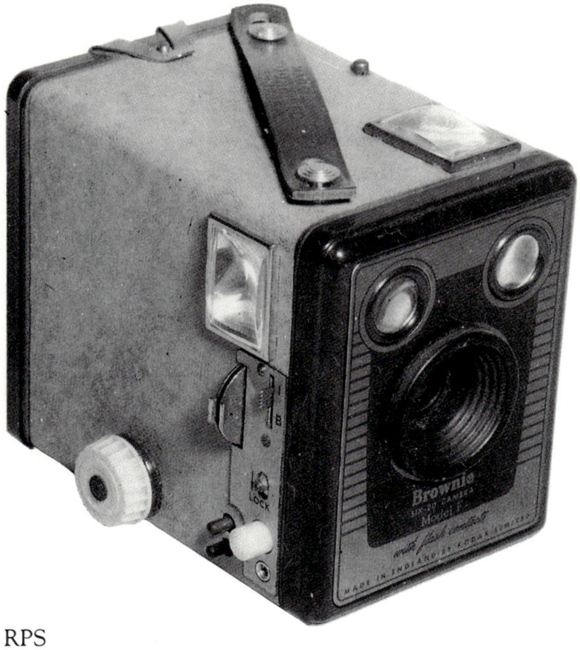

RPS

Type Box rollfilm
Introduced 1955
Discontinued 1957
Film size 620
Picture size 2¼ × 3¼in.
Manufactured UK
Lens Meniscus f/11, with portrait lens
Shutter Everset single speed
Numbers made ?

Description/Remarks

De Luxe version of Six-20 model E camera, with light brown leather cloth covering and gilt metalwork.

Six-20 Brownie Junior (US model)

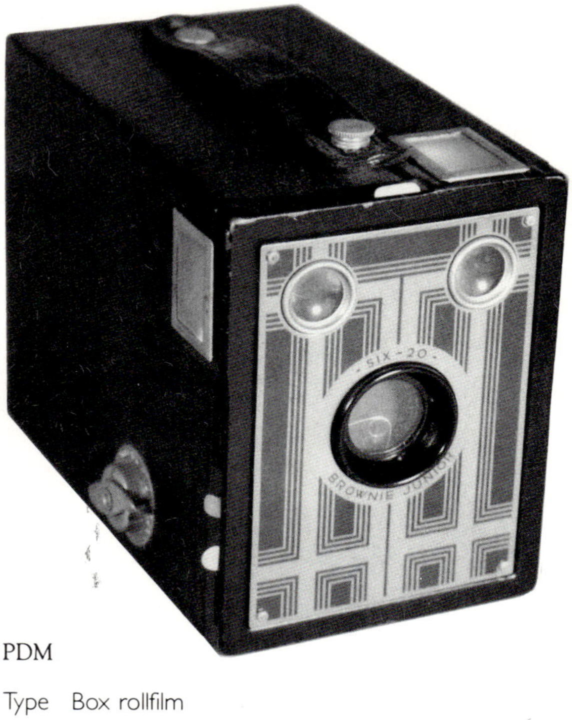

PDM

Type Box rollfilm
Introduced February 1934
Discontinued October 1942
Film size 620
Picture size 2¼ × 3¼in.
Manufactured US

Lens Meniscus
Shutter Rotary
Numbers made ?

Description/Remarks

Leatherette covered metal body with geometric Art Deco design on front panel; two reflecting finders.

Six-20 Brownie Junior (UK Model)

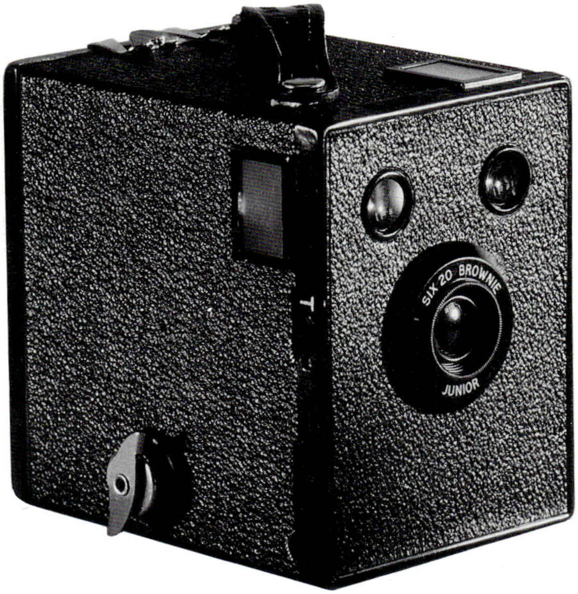

KP

Type Box rollfilm
Introduced New Year 1934
Discontinued 1938
Film size 620
Picture size 2¼ × 3¼in.
Manufactured UK
Lens Meniscus f/11
Shutter Single speed
Numbers made ?

Description/Remarks

Metal body; 2 reflecting finders; hinged back with spring catch.

Six-20 Brownie Junior (portrait model)

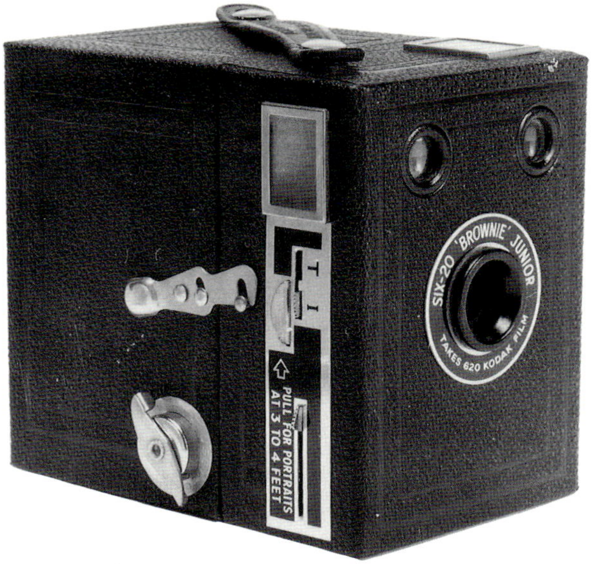

KP

Type Box rollfilm
Introduced 1939
Discontinued 1943
Film size 620
Picture size 2¼ × 3¼in.
Manufactured UK
Lens Meniscus, portrait lens on pull-out slide
Shutter Simple single speed
Numbers made ?

Description/Remarks

Grained leatherette card body; two reflecting finders; detachable body with long side catches.

Six-20 Brownie Junior Super Model

Type Box rollfilm
Introduced January 1935
Discontinued 1940
Film size 620
Picture size 2¼ × 3¼in.

Manufactured UK
Lens Meniscus
Shutter Eastman Rotary
Numbers made ?

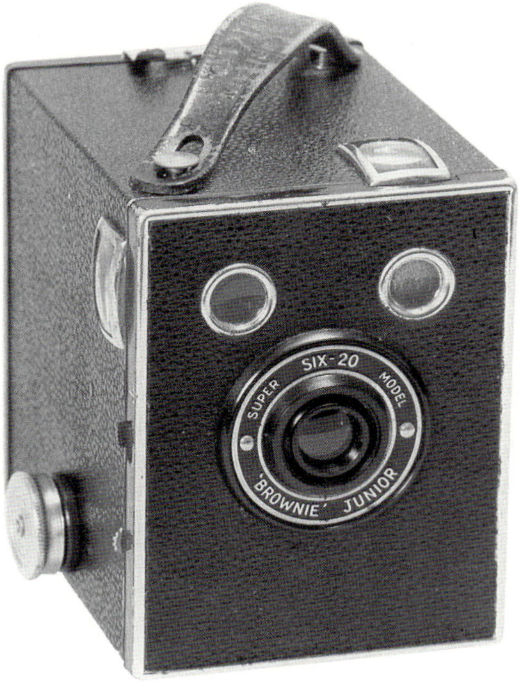

KP

Description/Remarks

Pearl-grained leatherette covered metal body; two brilliant finders; winding knob; hinged back with spring catch, removable roll holder.

Six-20 Brownie Minor

Type Box rollfilm
Introduced 1935
Discontinued 1935
Film size 620
Picture size 2¼ × 3¼in.
Manufactured UK
Lens Meniscus lens
Shutter Simple shutter
Numbers made ?

Description/Remarks

Made for premium sales only. Card box; two reflecting finders.

Six-20 Brownie Senior

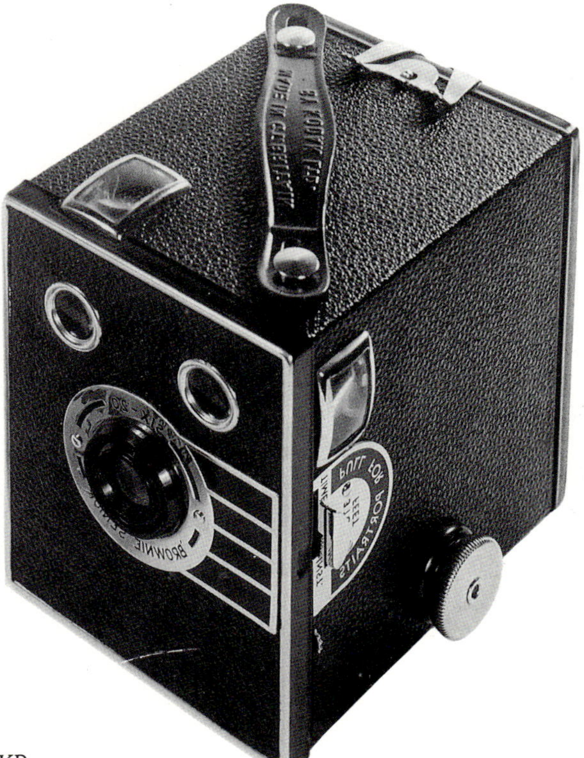

KP

Type Box rollfilm
Introduced June 1939
Discontinued 1940
Film size 620
Picture size 2¼ × 3¼in.
Manufactured UK
Lens Meniscus, with portrait lens
Shutter Eastman Rotary
Numbers made ?

Description/Remarks

Metal body; two brilliant finders; portrait lens. Very similar to Six-20 Portrait Brownie camera.

Six-20 Brownie Special

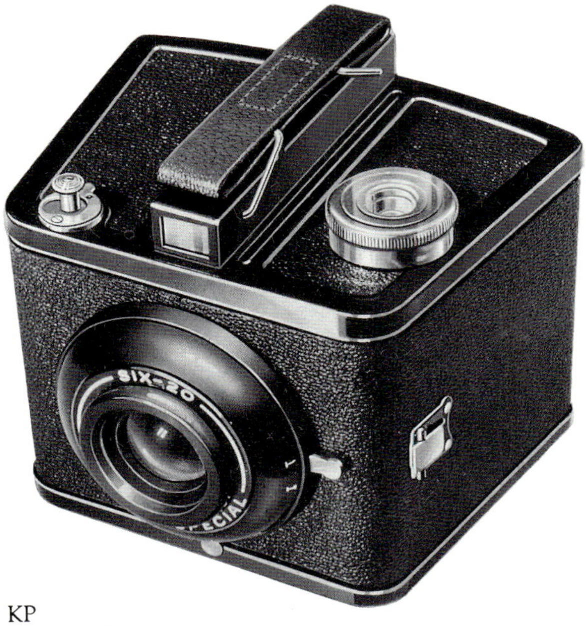

KP

Type Solid body eyelevel rollfilm
Introduced September 1938
Discontinued October 1942
Film size 620
Picture size 2¼ × 3¼in.
Manufactured US
Lens Meniscus
Shutter Rotary
Numbers made ?

Description/Remarks

Metal body; optical direct vision finder.

Six-20 Bulls-Eye Brownie

Type Solid body eyelevel rollfilm
Introduced July 1938
Discontinued 1941
Film size 620
Picture size 2¼ × 3¼in.
Manufactured US
Lens Meniscus
Shutter Single action
Numbers made ?

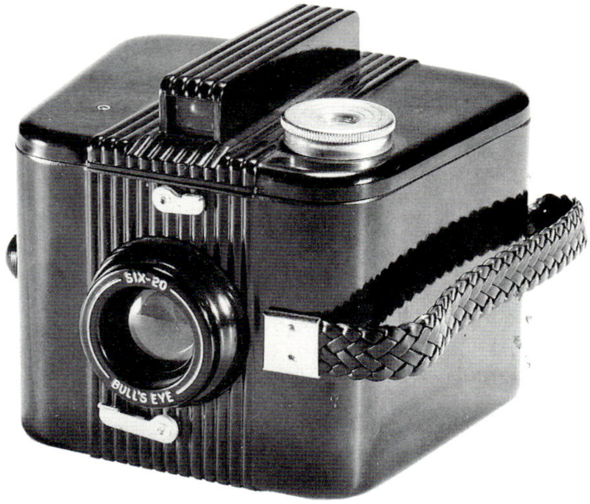

KP

Description/Remarks

Moulded plastic body; optical direct vision finder; braided strap.

Six-20 Flash Brownie

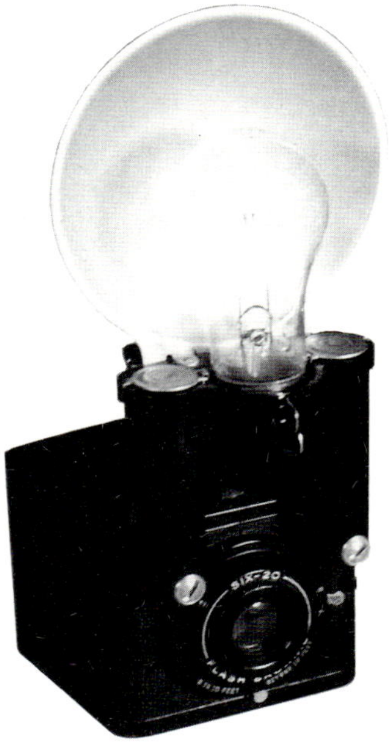

PDM

Type Solid body eyelevel rollfilm
Introduced December 1940
Discontinued 1946

Film size 620
Picture size 2¼ × 3¼in.
Manufactured US
Lens Meniscus
Shutter Rotary
Numbers made ?

Description/Remarks

Metal body; optical direct vision finder; flash synchronised, taking cumbersome flash gun.

Six-20 Popular Brownie

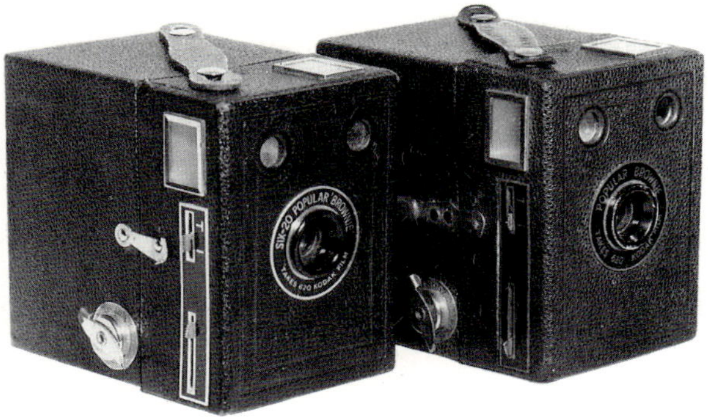

Right: 1937–1938 model. Left: 1939–1943 model. RPS

Type Box rollfilm
Introduced January 1937
Discontinued 1943
Film size 620
Picture size 2¼×3¼in.
Manufactured UK
Lens Meniscus
Shutter Simple
Numbers made ?

Description/Remarks

Grained leatherette covered card body; two reflecting finders.

1937–1938: "Popular Brownie", long side catches. *1939–1943:* "Six-20 Popular Brownie", short side catches, double rectangles embossed on front.

Six-20 Portrait Brownie

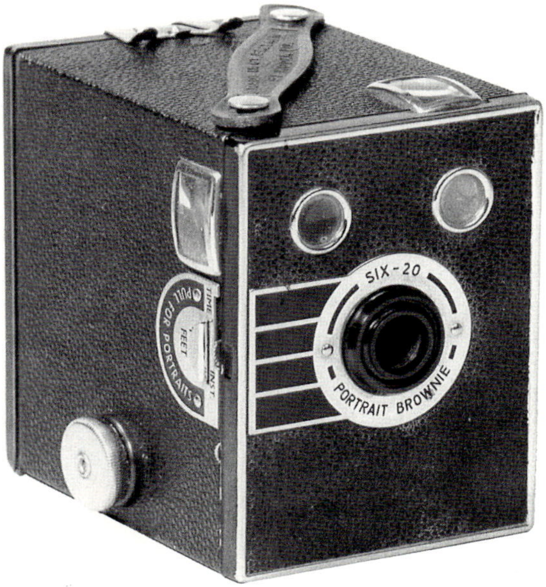

KP

Type Box rollfilm
Introduced February 1936
Discontinued 1940
Film size 620
Picture size 2¼ × 3¼in.
Manufactured UK
Lens Meniscus, with portrait lens on pull-out slide.
Shutter Eastman Rotary
Numbers made ?

Description/Remarks

Leatherette covered metal body, with nickel plated trim, band of horizontal lines on left of camera front; two brilliant finders; winding knob.

Target Brownie Six-16

Type Box rollfilm
Introduced April 1941
Discontinued 1946
Film size 616
Picture size 2½ × 4¼in.
Manufactured US

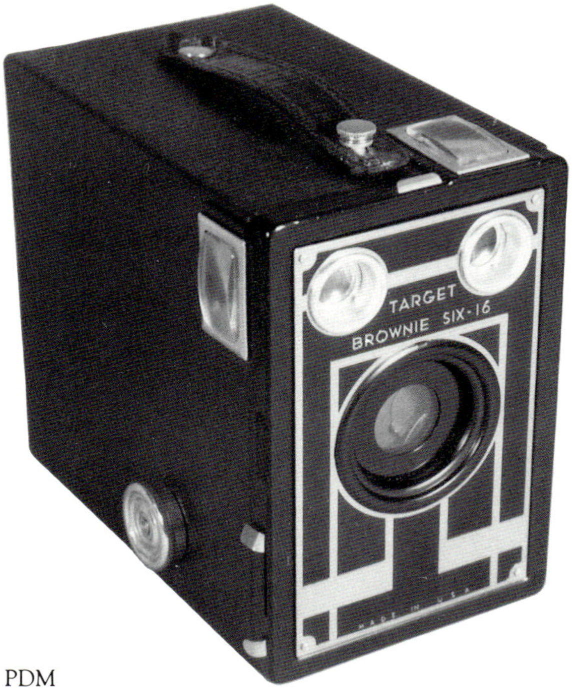

PDM

Lens Meniscus
Shutter Rotary
Numbers made ?

Description/Remarks

Leatherette covered box with geometric design on front panel; two brilliant finders.
Became Brownie Target Six-16 from 1946.

Target Brownie Six-20

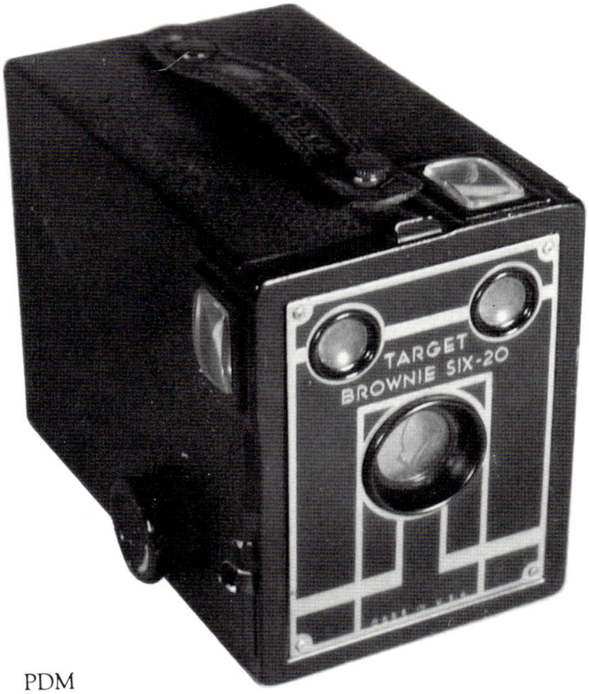

PDM

Type Box rollfilm
Introduced April 1941
Discontinued 1946
Film size 620
Picture size 2¼ × 3¼in.
Manufactured US
Lens Meniscus
Shutter Rotary
Numbers made ?

Description/Remarks

Metal body with geometric design on front panel.
Became Brownie Target Six-20 camera in 1946.

CHAPTER 3 *Kodak Folding Rollfilm Cameras*

The first Kodak folding rollfilm models, the Folding Kodak cameras, were introduced 1n 1890. The last was the Kodak 66 camera, made by Kodak Limited and discontinued in 1960. In that 70 year period almost 200 basic models were introduced, many of them in a wide range of variations.

Under this heading this listing covers two types of construction. One is the straight folding camera, with a hinged baseboard which pulls down to provide a bed along which the lens panel can be drawn into the operating position. Some of these are self-erecting, the lens panel moving into position automatically as the baseboard is lowered. The other type has been designated 'collapsing', in which no baseboard is fitted, and the lens panel is pulled straight out and held in position by side struts. All the cameras covered in this chapter have bellows; cameras in which the lens is on a telescoping tube will be found in Chapter 1. Folding Brownie cameras are in Chapter 4.

A group of cameras sold between 1914 and 1932 incorporated the Autographic feature. This idea was patented by Henry J. Gaisman in 1913 and 1914, and it permitted the photographer to 'write' information on the film at the time of exposure. Gaisman proposed that the rollfilm should carry a tissue, rather like typewriting carbon paper, between the backing paper and the film. Pressure on the backing paper with a metal stylus would make the tissue transparent at that point, and light filtering through the backing paper would expose the sensitive film, giving a record which would appear when the film was developed. Eastman saw the potential of this invention, and bought the rights from Gaisman for $300,000, a considerable sum at the time. The first Autographic Kodak cameras were based on the popular Folding Pocket Kodak camera series. Access to the film backing paper was provided through a hinged flap on the camera back. The first form of Autographic feature had the flap held closed by a sliding latch, which also held the metal stylus in a recess in the flap. This design was soon changed for an improved version with the flap held by a sprung hinge, with the stylus held in loops on the flap edge. In some later models, the stylus was held in loops on the side of the lens panel.

Autographic replacement backs were supplied for a number of earlier Folding Pocket Kodak cameras, including the No 4 and 4A sizes which were not made in special Autographic models. There may be some confusion caused by this. Generally, those cameras made as Autographic models will have the Autographic name on the camera body as well as on the back. Cameras made around the time of the introduction of this feature may carry both names, however. The serial numbers may help in determining whether a particular camera was made as or converted to an Autographic model.

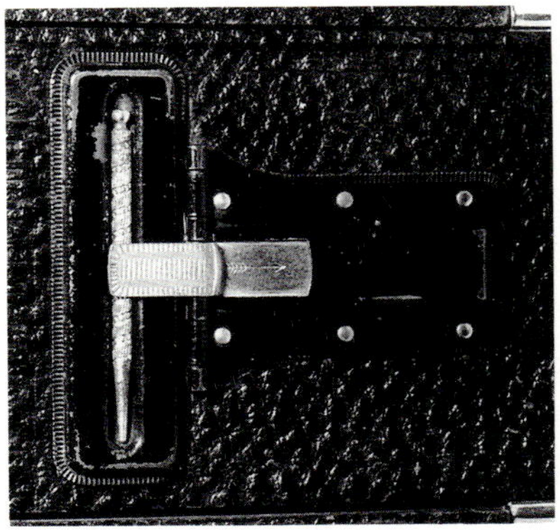

Autographic feature.
First type, 1914–1916. RPS

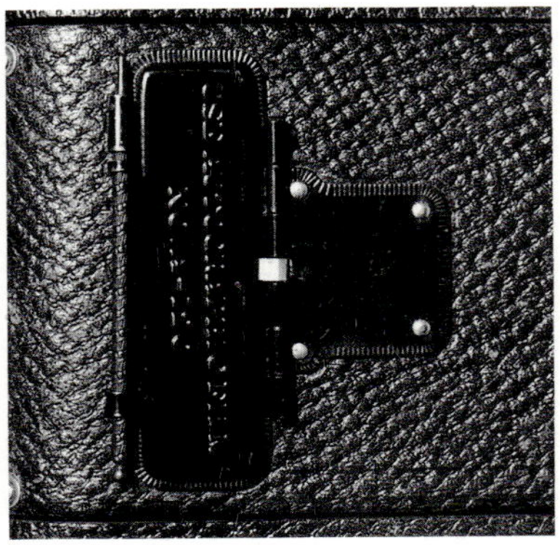

Second type, from 1916. RPS

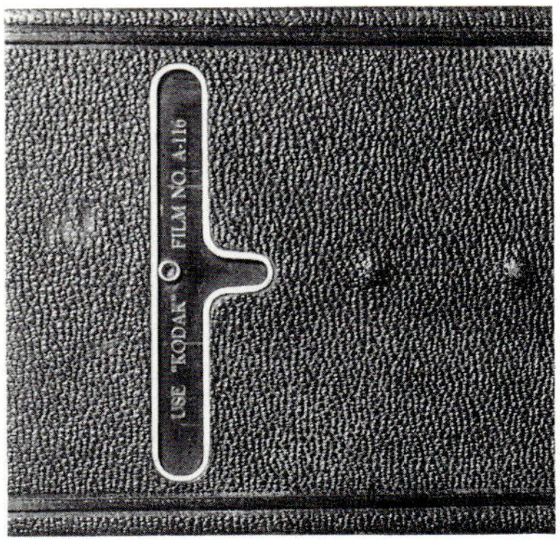

Third type, 1920s. RPS

No 1 Autographic Kodak Junior

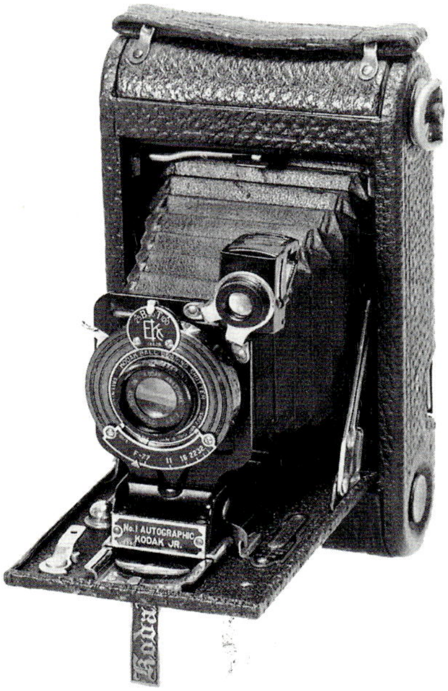

1916–1919 model. KM

Type Folding rollfilm
Introduced December 1914
Discontinued January 1927
Film size A120
Picture size 2¼ × 3¼in.

Manufactured US
Lenses December 1914–1927: Achromatic, fixed focus
April 1916–1927: focusing model – but see below
Shutters 1914–1924: Kodak Ball Bearing
1925–1927: Kodex – but see below
Numbers made Well over 800,000

Description/Remarks

Autographic version of No 1 Kodak Junior camera; first

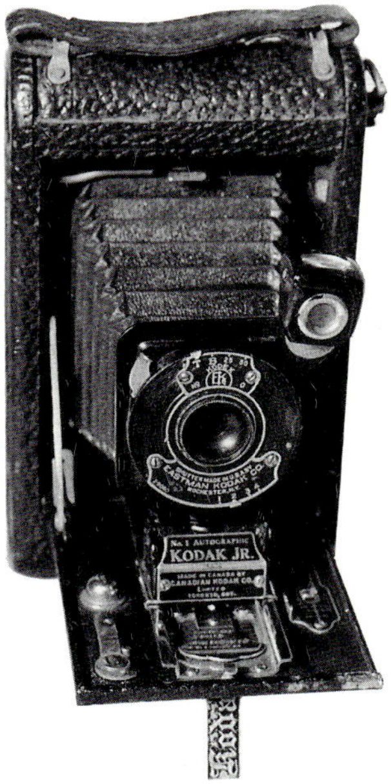

Late model, from 1920. KM

serial number 33,901. More basic specification than the standard Autographic models. J-shaped back with side catches below centre line.

Variations

Mar. 1916: New Autographic attachment, from serial number 94,701. *Aug. 1919:* New grooved base release button replaced concealed button, from serial number 295,101. *1920:* Collapsible finder replaced by enclosed version.

Rapid Rectilinear: *Dec. 1914–1924:* Ball Bearing shutter; *1925:*Kodex shutter.

Kodak Anastigmat f/7.7: *Apr. 1915–1924:* Ball Bearing shutter; Sept. 1924–1926 Diomatic shutter.

Kodar f/7.9: *May 1925–1926:* Kodex shutter.

UK VARIATIONS

Zeiss Tessar f/6.3: *1926–1927:* Compur shutter.

Anastigmat, f/6.3: *1926–1927:* Kodex shutter.

No 1 Autographic Kodak Special model A

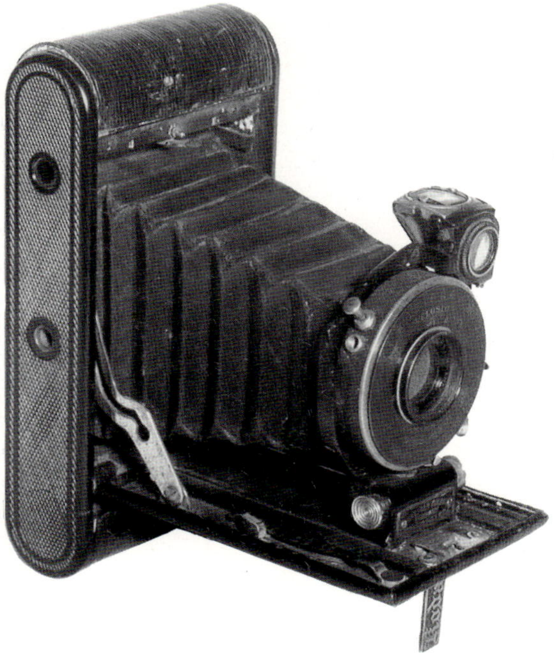

RPS

Type Folding rollfilm
Introduced April 1915
Discontinued 1920
Film size A120
Picture size 2¼ × 3¼in.
Manufactured US
Lenses Bausch & Lomb Zeiss Tessar f/6.3 or f/4.5 – but see below
Shutter Optimo
Numbers made 18,000 approximately

Description/Remarks

Lever focusing; side panels of moulded bakelite; covered with long grain calf leather. No rising front. Collapsible finder with revolving mask. Back opens in a sliding motion from the centre.

Variations

Early examples do not have "Model A" designation. *After May 1916:* the name "Zeiss" omitted from the Tessar lenses, to minimise the German connection during the War.

Apr. 1915–1916: Cooke Kodak Anastigmat f/6.3.
Apr. 1915–1916: Zeiss Kodak Anastigmat f/6.3.
July 1915–July 1916: Bausch & Lomb Anastigmat
Apr. 1916–1920: Bausch & Lomb Kodak Anastigmat f/6.3.
Dec. 1915–1920: Kodak Anastigmat f/6.3.
July 1916–1920: Bausch & Lomb Anastigmat Special f/6.3.

UK VARIATIONS

In Velosto shutter:
Nov. 1915–1923: Bausch & Lomb Anastigmat f/6.3.
1916–1923: Ross Homocentric f/6.3, Cooke Series III f/6.5.
1921–1923 Cooke Aviar f/4.5, Ross Xpres f/4.5.
Feb. 1917: Lacour-Berthiot Olor Anastigmat f/5.7.
From 1921: the first five lenses were also supplied in Compur shutter.

No 1 Autographic Kodak Special Model B

Type Folding rollfilm

Introduced April 1921
Discontinued April 1926
Film size A120
Picture size 2¼ × 3¼in.
Manufactured US
Lens Kodak Anastigmat f/6.3 – but see below
Shutters Kodamatic or, before May 1922, Ilex shutter – but see below
Numbers made ?

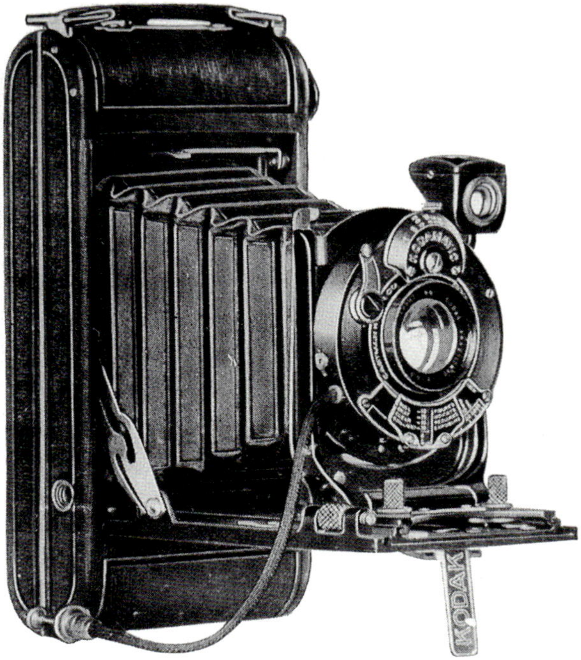

Description/Remarks

Redesigned back, overlapping sides. Lever operated rising front; rack and pinion focusing, 1921, then screw focusing, from May 1922. Autographic back countersunk. Covered in seal leather. Enclosed reversible finder.

Variations

Bausch & Lomb Tessar f/6.3: *Apr. 1921–1924:* Kodamaticshutter. *1921:* Ilex shutter.
Bausch & Lomb Tessar f/4.5: *Apr. 1921–Apr. 1926:* Kodamatic shutter. *1921:* Ilex shutter.
Bausch & Lomb Kodak Anastigmat f/6.3: *Apr. 1921–1924:* Kodamatic shutter. *1921:* Ilex shutter.

UK VARIATIONS
In Kodamatic or, *from 1925*, Compur shutter:
1925–1926: Zeiss Tessar f/6.3, f/4.9, f/4.5.
1924–1926: Ross Homocentric f/6.3.
1924–1926: Ross Xpres f/4.5.
1924–1926: Cooke Aviar f/4.8.
1924–1925: Cooke Aviar f/6.3.
1924–1925: Cooke Series III f/6.5.

No 1A Autographic Kodak

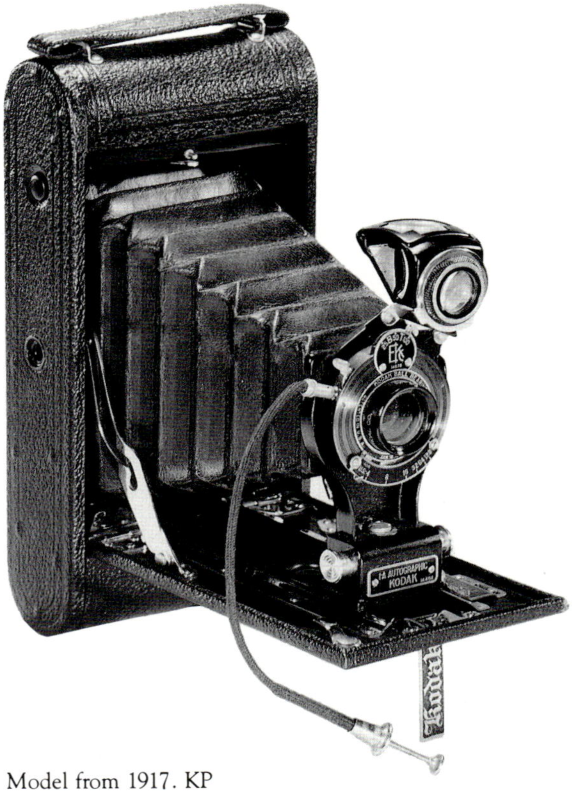

Model from 1917. KP

Type Folding rollfilm
Introduced September 1914
Discontinued July 1924
Film size A116
Picture size 2¼ × 4¼in.
Manufactured US
Lens Rapid Rectilinear – but see below
Shutters Kodak Ball Bearing or 1914–1916 Kodak Automatic – but see below
Numbers made More than 80,000

Description/Remarks

Essentially the same as the 1A Folding Pocket Kodak camera, R.R. type, but with Autographic back. First serial number 79,808.

Variations

Oct. 1916: fitted with new Autographic attachment, from serial number 100,801. *Apr. 1917:* Redesigned, new back, without side cutouts, no hood on larger finder, lens panel rounded, without 'ears'. First serial number 140,001. *After Dec. 1917:* "1917 Model" omitted from nameplate.

Cooke Kodak Anastigmat f/6.3: *1914:* Compound shutter.
Kodak Anastigmat f/8: *Nov. 1914–Apr. 1915:* Ball Bearing shutter.
Kodak Anastigmat f/7.7: *Apr. 1915–July 1924:* Ball Bearing shutter.

UK VARIATION
TTH-Kodak Anastigmat f/6.8: *1916–1917:* Kodak Automatic shutter.

No 1A Autographic Kodak Junior

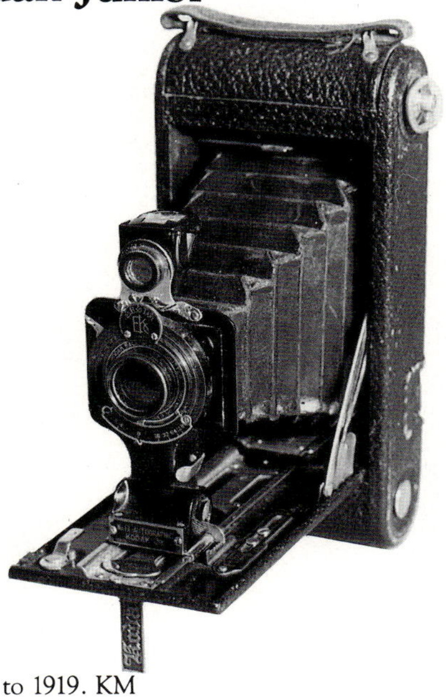

Model to 1919. KM

Type Folding rollfilm
Introduced December 1914
Discontinued January 1927
Film size A116
Picture size 2½ × 4¼in.
Manufactured US
Lenses 1914–1924: Achromatic, fixed focus; 1916–1927: focusing – but see below
Shutters 1914–1924: Kodak Ball Bearing
January 1925–January 1927: Kodex – but see below
Numbers made At least 780,000

Description/Remarks

Autographic version of No 1A Kodak Junior camera, from serial number 49101. More basic specification than the No 1A Autographic Kodak; no rising front. J-shaped back with catches below centre line.

Variations

Mar. 1916: New Autographic attachment, from serial number 94,701. *Aug. 1919:* New grooved base release button replaced concealed button, from serial number 403,001. *1920:* Collapsible finder replaced by enclosed version.

Kodak Anastigmat f/7.7: *Apr. 1915–Jan. 1925:* Ball Bearing shutter (*after Dec. 1916:* lettering on front of lens mount rather than around, from serial number 200,301). *1923–Jan. 1925:* Ilex shutter. *1924:* multiple speed shutter. *Jan. 1925–Feb.1927:* Diomatic shutter.
Rapid Rectilinear: *Dec. 1914–May 1925:* Ball Bearing shutter. *1925:* Kodex shutter.
Kodar f/7.9: *May 1925–Dec. 1926:* Kodex shutter.

UK VARIATIONS
Zeiss Tessar f/6.3: *1926:* Compur shutter.
Anastigmat f/6.3: *1926–1927:* Kodex shutter.

No 1A Autographic Kodak Special

Type Folding rollfilm
Introduced September 1914
Discontinued 1916
Film size A116

Picture size 2¼ × 2½in.
Manufactured US
Lens Bausch & Lomb Zeiss Tessar f/6.3 – but see below
Shutters Compound, to 1915, then Compur, 1916
Numbers made 2,500 approximately

Description/Remarks

Autographic version of No 1A Kodak Special camera. First serial number 2686. Rising front; reversible finder with level; rack and pinion focusing.

Variations

May 1916: fitted with new Autographic attachment.

In Bausch & Lomb Compound shutter:
1914–1915: Zeiss Kodak Anastigmat f/6.3, Cooke Series IIIa f/6.5, Cooke Kodak Anastigmat f/6.3.
In Bausch & Lomb Compur shutter:
1916: Bausch & Lomb Kodak Anastigmat f/6.3, Kodak Anastigmat f/6.3, Cooke Kodak Anastigmat f/6.3

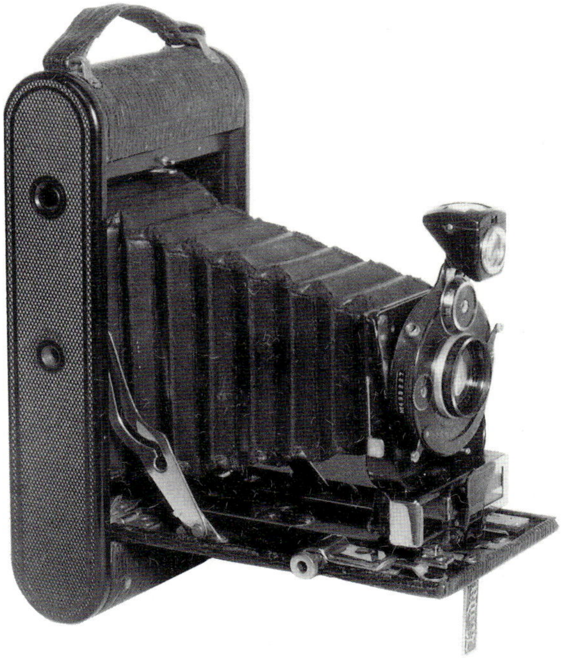

1917 model. SM

UK VARIATIONS
Zeiss Tessar f/6.3: *1915:* Compound or Koilos shutter.
Cooke Anastigmat Series III f/6.5: *1915–1916:* Velosto or Kodak Automatic shutter.
Ross Homocentric f/6.3: *1915–1916:* Velosto or Kodak Automatic shutter.
Kodak Anastigmat f/6.3: *1917:* Velosto shutter; Lacour-Berthiot Olor Anastigmat f/5.7, Velosto shutter.

No 1A Autographic Kodak Special + rangefinder

Type Folding rollfilm
Introduced April 1917
Discontinued April 1926
Film size 116
Picture size 2½ × 4¼in.
Manufactured US
Lens Kodak Anastigmat f/6.3 – but see below
Shutter Optimo – but see below
Numbers made ?

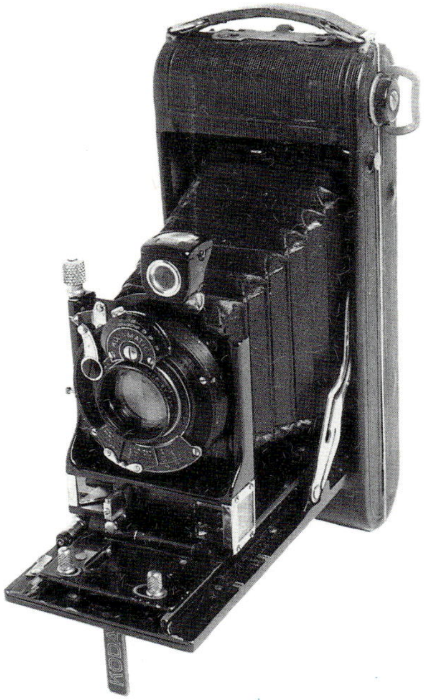

Model B. TNC

Description/Remarks

Coupled rangefinder version of 1A Autographic Kodak Special camera. Bakelite side panels; lever rising front; finder to one side; rack and pinion focusing; long-grained calf covering. *From Aug. 1923:* model B had an overlapping back; screw rising front; central finder; screw focusing; seal leather covering.

Variations

Kodak Anastigmat f/6.3, 5in: *Apr. 1921–Apr. 1926:*Kodamatic shutter. *Apr. 1921–Aug. 1923:* Ilex shutter.
Bausch & Lomb Kodak Anastigmat f/6.3: *Apr. 1917–1923:* Optimo shutter. *Apr. 1921–1923:* Kodamatic or Ilex shutter.
Bausch & Lomb Tessar f/6.3: *Apr. 1917–1923:* Optimo, Kodamatic or Ilex shutter.

UK VARIATIONS
Kodak Anastigmat f/6.3, 5in: *1921:* Velosto shutter. *1921–1926:* Compur shutter.
Ross Homocentric f/6.3: *1921:* Velosto shutter. *1921–1926:* Compur shutter. *1926 (model B):* Kodamatic shutter.
Cooke Aviar f/6.3: *1924–1926:* Compur shutter. *1926 (model B):* Kodamatic shutter.
Zeiss Tessar f/6.3: *1925–1926:* Compur shutter. *1926 (model B):* Kodamatic shutter.
Bausch & Lomb Kodak Anastigmat f/6.3: *1924:* Compur shutter.

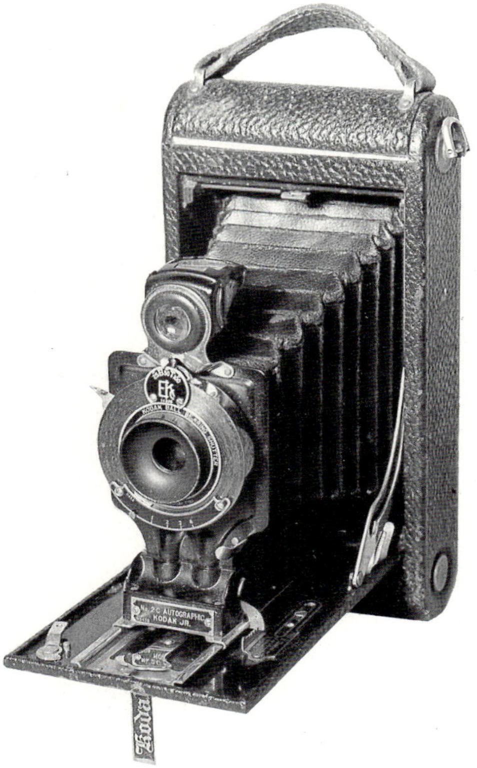

Model from 1916 to 1919. KM

No 2C Autographic Kodak Junior

Type Folding rollfilm
Introduced June 1916
Discontinued January 1927
Film size A130
Picture size 2⅞ × 4⅞in.
Manufactured US
Lenses Achromatic or (until August 1925) Rapid Rectilinear – but see below
Shutters 1916–1924: Kodak Ball Bearing 1925–1927: Kodex – but see below.
Numbers made At least 200,000

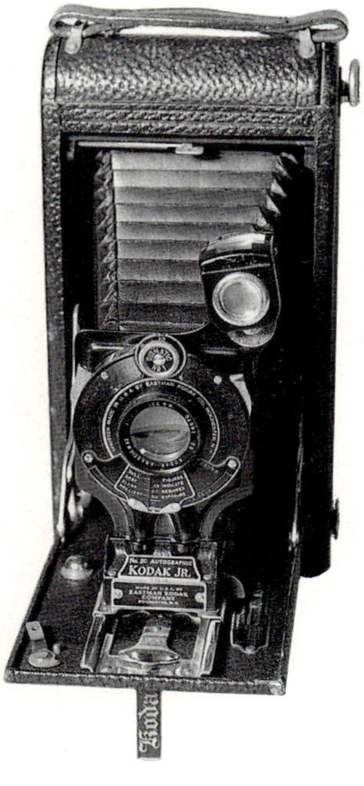

Model from 1920. KM

Description/Remarks

J-shaped back with catches below centre line. Simple specification; no rising front. Automatically locking focusing scale. Serial numbers start from 951.

Variations

1920: Collapsible finder replaced by enclosed version and moved from centre to right of lens panel; new name plate with sloping sides.

Kodak Anastigmat f/7.7: *June 1916–Jan. 1925:* Ball Bearing shutter. *May 1922–1923:* Ilex Universal shutter. *1924:* multiple speed shutter. *Jan. 1925–1926:* Diomatic shutter.
Kodar f/7.9:*May 1925–Feb. 1927:* Kodex shutter.

UK VARIATION
Zeiss Tessar f/6.3:*1926:* Compur shutter.

No 2C Autographic Kodak Special

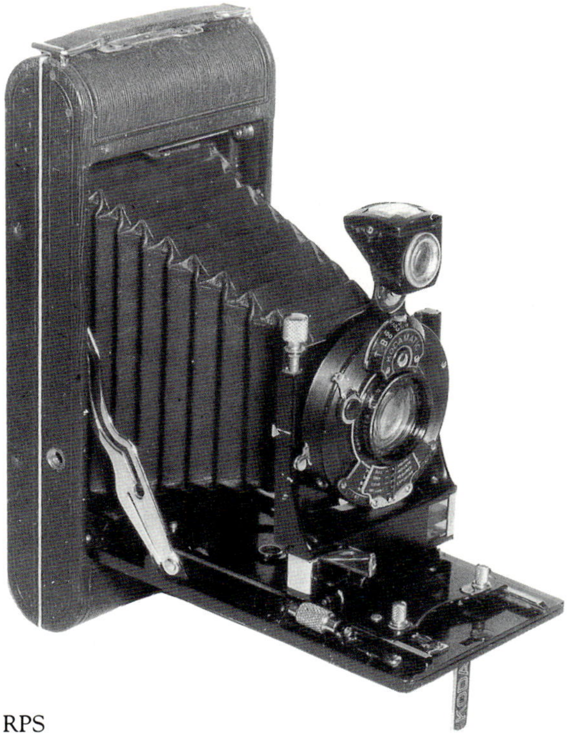

RPS

Type Folding rollfilm
Introduced 1923
Discontinued 1928 (1932 in UK)
Film size A130
Picture size 2⅞ × 4⅞in.
Manufactured US
Lens Kodak Anastigmat f/6.3 – but see below
Shutter Kodamatic – but see below
Numbers made ?

Description/Remarks

Coupled rangefinder; back with recessed Autographic feature; screw rising front and focusing; seal leather covering.

UK VARIATIONS
Kodak Anastigmat f/6.3: *1923–1932:* Compur shutter.
Cooke Aviar f/6.3, 6in: *1924:* Kodamatic shutter. *1925–1931:* Compur shutter.
Ross Homocentric f/6.3, 6in: *1924:* Kodamatic shutter. *1925–1931:* Compur shutter.
Zeiss Tessar f/6.3, 15cm: *1925–1931:* Compur shutter.
Zeiss Tessar f/4.9, 15cm: *1925–1928:* Compur shutter.

In 1930 and 1931 catalogues the camera was called No 2C Pocket Kodak Special, but reverted to original name in 1932, after which it was discontinued.

No 3 Autographic Kodak

Type Folding rollfilm
Introduced 1914
Discontinued 1925
Film size A118
Picture size 3¼ × 4¼in.
Manufactured US
Lens Rapid Rectilinear
Shutter Kodak Ball Bearing
Numbers made Well over 100,000

Description/Remarks

Autographic version of No 3 Folding Pocket Kodak camera models G and H; serial numbers from 120,939.

Note: many No 3 Folding Pocket Kodak cameras were converted by fitting accessory Autographic backs.

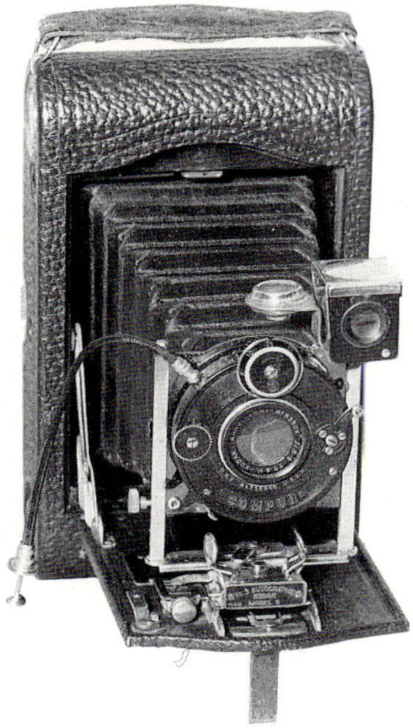

Model G. KM

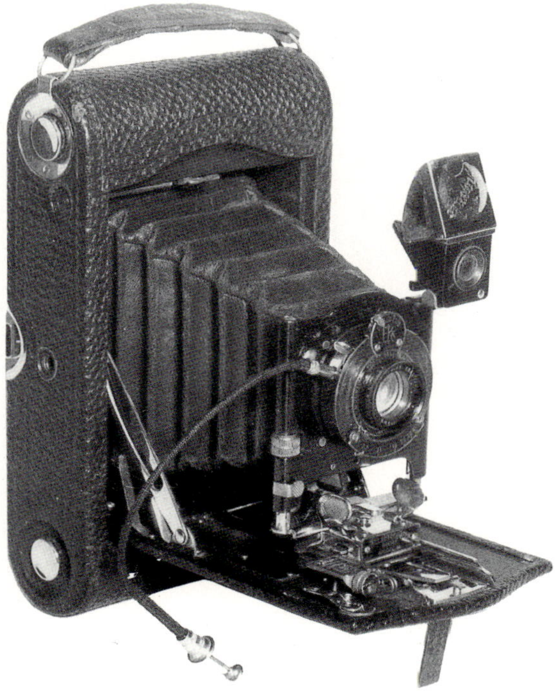

Model H. RPS

Variations

From May 1916: fitted with new Autographic attachment, serial number 124,101.

Cooke Kodak Anastigmat f/6.3:*1914:* Compound shutter.
Rapid Rectilinear:*Sept. 1914–Nov. 1917:* Kodak Automatic shutter.
Kodak Anastigmat f/8:*Nov. 1914–Apr. 1915:* Ball Bearing shutter.
Kodak Anastigmat f/7.7:*Apr. 1915–May 1925:* Ball Bearing shutter. *May 1925–Apr. 1926:* Diomatic shutter.
Kodar f/7.9:*May 1925–Apr. 1926:* Kodex shutter.

UK VARIATIONS
TTH-Kodak Anastigmat f/6.8, 5in.: *1914–1917:* Kodak Automatic shutter. *1918–1924:* Kodak Ball Bearing shutter. *1925* Compur shutter.
Kodak Anastigmat f/6.3, 5in.: *1924–1925:* Kodamatic or Compur shutter.
Cooke Anastigmat f/6.5, 5in.: *1924–1925:* Kodamatic or Compur shutter.
Ross Homocentric f/6.3, 5in.: *1924–1925:* Kodamatic (1924) or Compur shutter.
Zeiss Tessar f/6.3: *1925:* Compur shutter.
Cooke Aviar f/6.3: *1925:* Compur shutter.

No 3 Autographic Kodak Special

Type Folding rollfilm
Introduced September 1914
Discontinued January 1926
Film size A118
Picture size 3¼ × 4¼in.
Manufactured US
Lens Zeiss Kodak Tessar f/6.3 (renamed after April 1916 Bausch & Lomb Kodak Anastigmat) – but see below
Shutters 1914–1915: Bausch & Lomb Compound
1916: Bausch & Lomb Compur April 1917–1924: Optimo
April 1921–January 1926: Kodamatic
April 1921–1924: Ilex – but see below
Numbers made ?

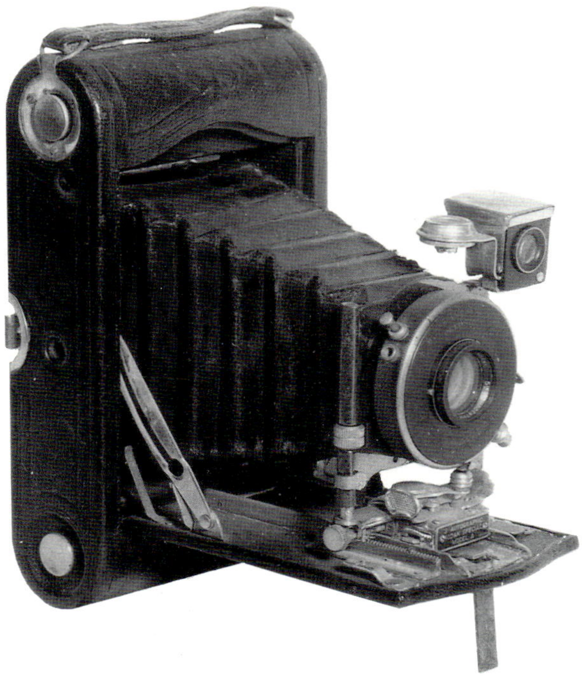

SM

Description/Remarks

Autographic version of No 3 Special Kodak camera, from serial number 4,949. Persian morocco covering; reversible reflecting finder with level; new style Autographic attachment from serial 6,601.

Variations

Cooke Series IIIa f/6.5: *Sept. 1914–1915:* Bausch & Lomb Compound shutter.
Cooke Kodak Anastigmat f/6.3: *1915:* Bausch & Lomb Compound shutter. *1916:* Bausch & Lomb Compur shutter.
Kodak Anastigmat f/6.3: *1916:* Bausch & Lomb Compur shutter. *Apr. 1917–1924:* Optimo shutter. *Apr. 1921–Apr.1925:* Kodamatic shutter. *Apr. 1921 – 1924:* Ilex shutter.
Bausch & Lomb Tessar f/6.3: *Apr. 1921–Apr. 1925:* Optimo or Kodamatic shutter. *Apr. 1921–1924:* Ilex shutter.

UK VARIATIONS
Cooke Series IIIa f/6.5: *1915:* Compound or Koilos shutter. *1916–1921:* Velosto shutter. *1916–1917:* Kodak Automatic shutter. *1921–1924:* Compur shutter.
Zeiss Tessar f/6.3: *1915:* Compound or Koilos shutter.
Zeiss Tessar f/4.9: *1925:* Compur shutter.
Ross Homocentric f/6.3: *1916–1921:* Velosto shutter. *1921–1925:* Compur shutter. *1917:* Kodak Automatic shutter.
Ross Xpres f/4.5: *1924:* Compur shutter. *1925:* Kodamatic shutter.
Cooke Aviar f/6.3: *1924–1925:* Compur shutter.
Cooke Aviar f/4.5: *1925:* Compur shutter.
Kodak Anastigmat f/6.3: *1917–1921:* Velosto shutter. *1921–1925:* Compur shutter.
Lacour-Berthiot Olor f/5.7: *1917:* Velosto shutter.
Bausch & Lomb Kodak Anastigmat f/6.3: *1921:* Velosto shutter. *1921 – 1924:* Compur shutter.

No 3A Autographic Kodak

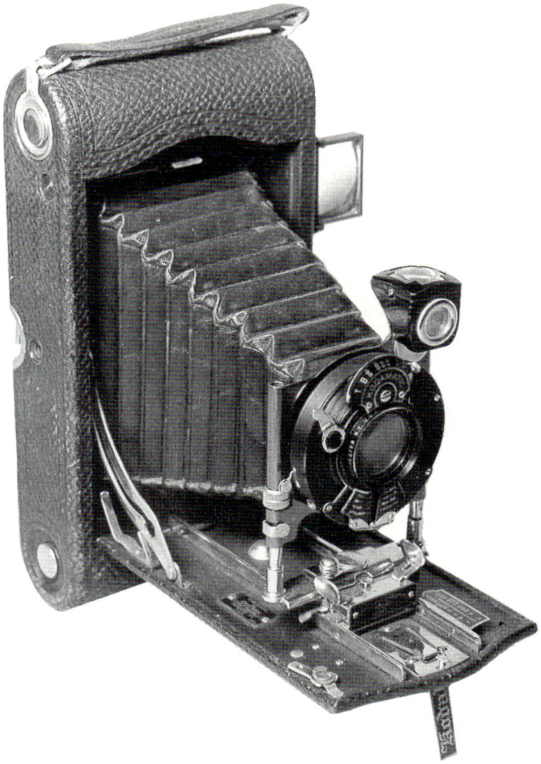

KM

Type Folding rollfilm
Introduced July 1914
Discontinued 1934
Film size A122

Picture size 3¼ × 5½in.
Manufactured US
Lens 1914–1924 Rapid Rectilinear – but see below
Shutters 1914–1924 Kodak Ball Bearing
1914–November 1917 Kodak Automatic – but see below
Numbers made Well over 300,000

Description/Remarks

Autographic version of No 3A Folding Pocket Kodak camera. Rising front; preset stop for sliding focusing. Serial numbers from 368,668.

Variations

Straight edge to baseboard front until 1920, curved thereafter. Hood to reflecting finder until 1921. *Mar. 1916:* new Autographic attachment, from serial number 426,7011.

Cooke Kodak Anastigmat f/6.3: *July 1914–1914:* Compound shutter.
Kodak Anastigmat f/7.7: *Apr. 1915–Dec. 1924:* Ball Bearing shutter; *Apr. 1915–Nov. 1917:* Kodak Automatic shutter; *May 1922–Dec. 1924:* Ilex Universal shutter; *1924:* multiple speed shutter; *Dec. 1924–May 1926:* Diomatic shutter.
Rapid Rectilinear: *1925:* Kodex shutter.
Kodar f/7.9 *May 1925–Nov. 1933:* Kodex shutter.
Kodak Anastigmat f/6.3: *May 1926–1931:* Ilex Universal shutter.
Kodak Anastigmat f/6.3: *1932–1934:* multiple speed shutter.

UK VARIATIONS
TTH-Kodak Anastigmat f/6.8: *1917–1920:* Kodak Automatic shutter; *1921–1926:* Kodak Ball Bearing shutter; *1924–1926:* Kodamatic shutter; *1924–1928:* Compur shutter.
Cooke Anastigmat f/6.5: *1924:* Kodamatic or Compur shutter.
Cooke Aviar f/6.3: *1926* Kodamatic shutter. *1926–1930:* Compur shutter.
Zeiss Tessar f/6.3: *1926* Kodamatic shutter. *1926–1933:* Compur shutter.
Ross Homocentric f/6.3: *1926* Kodamatic shutter. *1926–1933:* Compur shutter.
Kodak Anastigmat f/6.3: *1924–1933:* Compur shutter.

No 3A Autographic Kodak Junior

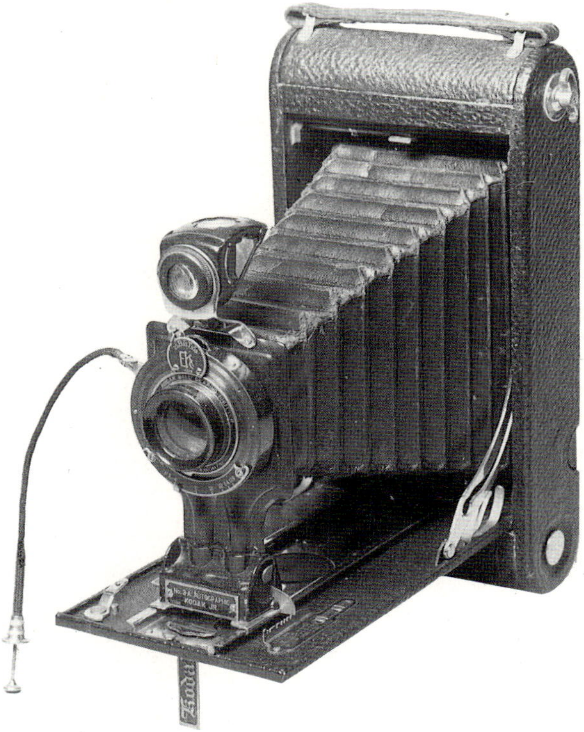

KM

Type Folding rollfilm
Introduced April 1918
Discontinued February 1927
Film size A122
Picture size 3¼ × 5½in.
Manufactured US
Lenses Achromatic or, until 1925, Rapid Rectilinear – but see below.
Shutters 1918–1924: Kodak Ball Bearing
January 1925–December 1926: Kodex – but see below
Numbers made ?

Description/Remarks

J-shaped back with side catches below centre line. Focusing lock. Serial numbers from 1001. Collapsible finder centred above lens.

Variations

Kodak Anastigmat f/7.7: *Apr. 1918–Jan. 1925:* Ball Bearing shutter. *May 1922–Jan. 1925:* Ilex Universal shutter.*1924:* multiple speed shutter. *Jan. 1925–Feb. 1927:* Diomatic shutter.
Kodar f/7.9 *May 1925–Feb. 1927:* Kodex shutter.

UK VARIATION
Zeiss Tessar f/6.3: *1926:* Compur shutter.

No 3A Autographic Kodak Special

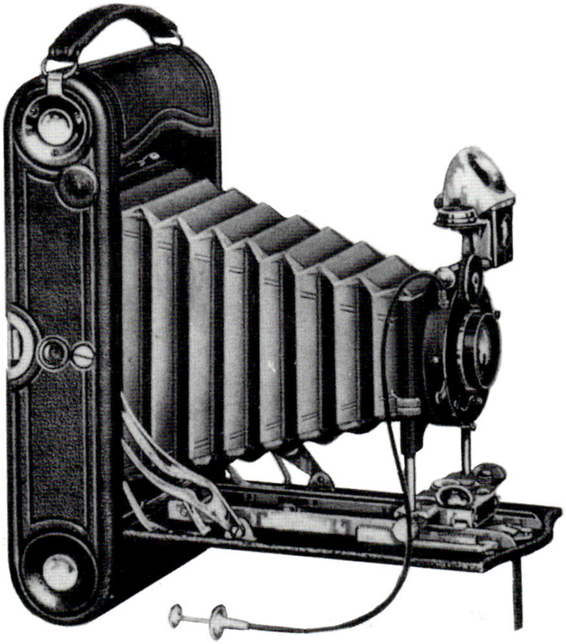

Type Folding rollfilm
Introduced July 1914
Discontinued February 1916
Film size A122
Picture size 3¼ × 5½in.
Manufactured US
Lens Zeiss Kodak Anastigmat f/6.3 – but see below
Shutter Bausch & Lomb Compound
Numbers made 4,000+

Description/Remarks

Autographic version of No 3A Special Kodak camera, from serial number 18,246. Reversible finder with level, Persian morocco leather covering.

Variations

July 1914–1915: Cooke series IIIa f/6.5, Bausch & Lomb Zeiss Tessar f/6.3. *1915:* Cooke Kodak Anastigmat f/6.3. All in Bausch & Lomb Compound shutters.

UK VARIATIONS
Cooke series III f/6.5: *1915:* Koilos or Compound shutter. *1916–1917:* Velosto or Kodak Automatic shutter.
Zeiss Tessar f/6.3: *1915:* Koilos or Compound shutter.
Ross Homocentric f/6.3: *1916–1917:* Velosto or Kodak Automatic shutter.
Kodak Anastigmat f/6.3: *1917:* Velosto shutter.
Bausch & Lomb Kodak Anastigmat f/6.3: *1917:* Velosto or Compur shutter.
Lacour-Berthiot Olor f/5.7: *1917:* Velosto shutter.

No 3A Autographic Kodak Special + rangefinder

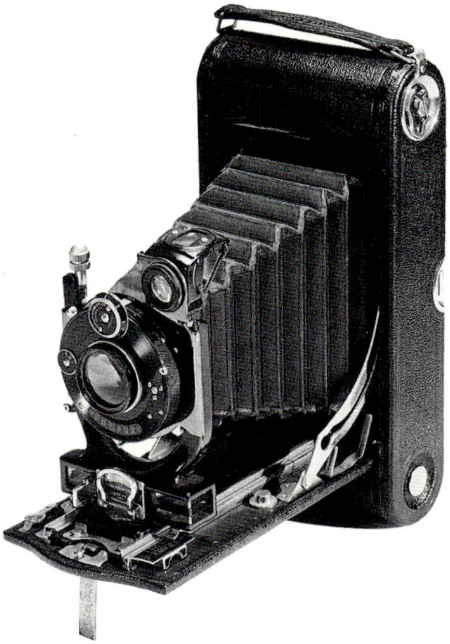

KP

Type Folding rollfilm
Introduced February 1916
Discontinued 1937
Film size A122
Picture size 3¼ × 5½in.
Manufactured US
Lens Zeiss Kodak Anastigmat f/6.3 (renamed Bausch & Lomb Kodak Anastigmat f/6.3, April 1916), February 1916–December 1925 – but see below
Shutter Optimo (1916–1924) or Kodamatic (1921–1925) – but see below
Numbers made ?

Description/Remarks

As No 3A Autographic Kodak Special, with added coupled rangefinder – the first camera to have this feature. *From Oct. 1919:* baseboard release button grooved, replacing the earlier concealed button. *From 1921:* folding reflecting finder replaced by a rigid enclosed version.

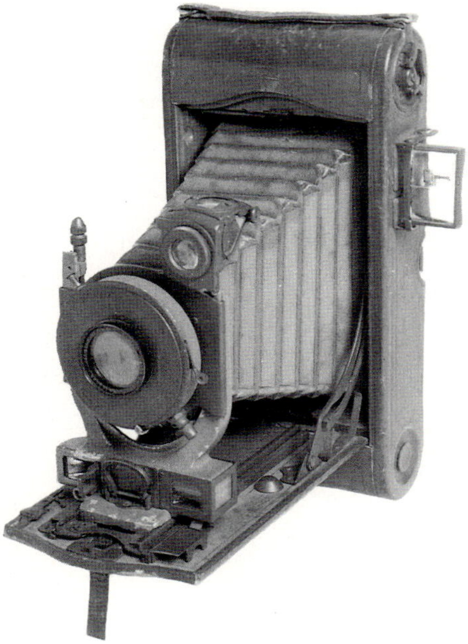

US Army Signal Corps model. TNC

Variations

During the First World War military versions were supplied with brown leather and brass or anodised fittings instead of nickel plating.

Bausch & Lomb Zeiss Tessar f/6.3: *Feb. 1916–Apr. 1916:* Optimo shutter.
Bausch & Lomb Tessar Anastigmat f/6.3: *Apr. 1916–1924:* Optimo shutter. *1921–1925:* Kodamatic shutter. *1921–1924:* Ilex shutter.
Kodak Anastigmat f/6.3: *Apr. 1916–1924:* Optimo shutter. *1921–1934:* Kodamatic shutter. *1921–1924:* Ilex shutter.

UK VARIATIONS
Zeiss Tessar f/6.3: *1925–1931, 1935:* Compur shutter. *1926:* Kodamatic shutter.
Zeiss Tessar f/5.3: *1925–1927:* Compur shutter.
Zeiss Tessar f/4.5: *1928–1934:* Compur shutter. *1935–1937:* Compur-S shutter.
Ross Homocentric f/6.3: *1921:* Velosto shutter. *1921–1931:* Compur shutter. *1924–1926:* Kodamatic shutter.
Cooke Aviar f/6.3: *1924–1926:* Kodamatic shutter. *1925–1931:* Compur shutter.
Cooke Anastigmat f/6.3: *1935:* Compur shutter.
Kodak Anastigmat f/6.3: *1921:* Velosto shutter. *1921–1934:* Compur shutter. *1924–1933:* Kodamatic shutter.
Bausch & Lomb Kodak Anastigmat f/6.3: *1921:* Velosto or Compur shutter. *1924:* Kodamatic shutter.

Boy Scout Kodak

Type Folding rollfilm
Introduced July 1929
Discontinued 1934
Film size 127
Picture size 1⅝ × 2½in.
Manufactured US, UK (January 1931–July 1935)
Lens Meniscus
Shutter V.P. Rotary
Numbers made ?

Description/Remarks

Special version of Vest Pocket Kodak Model B camera, covered in olive drab leatherette (UK version in dark green crackle enamel), with Boy Scout insignia in enamel on baseplate (American eagle, vertical stripes – US version; fleur-de-lys, horizontal wavy lines – UK version).

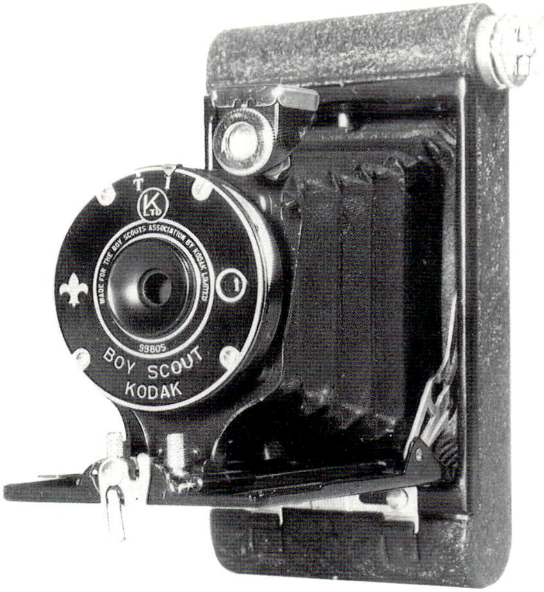

KM

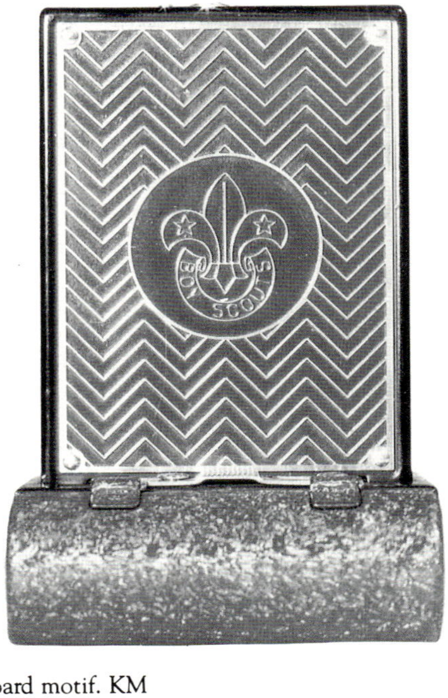

Baseboard motif. KM

Camp Fire Girls' Kodak

Type   Folding rollfilm
Introduced   April 1931
Discontinued   January 1934
Film size   127
Picture size   1⅝ × 2½in.
Manufactured   US
Lens   Meniscus
Shutter   V.P. Rotary
Numbers made   ?

Description/Remarks

Special version of Vest Pocket Kodak Model B camera, brown leatherette with Camp Fire Girls' insignia on baseplate.

No 3 Cartridge Kodak

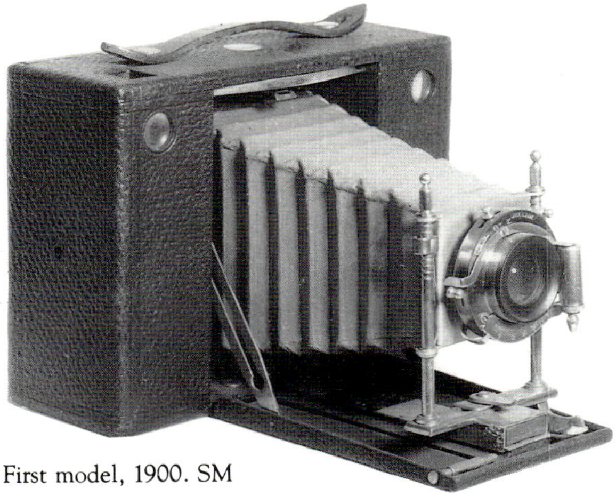

First model, 1900. SM

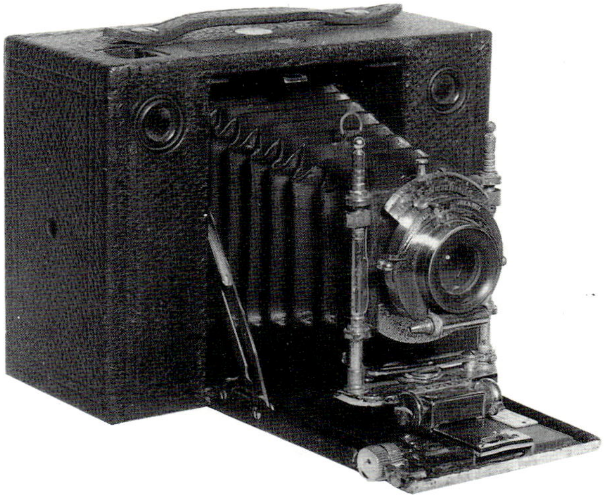

Second model, from 1900. RPS

Type Folding rollfilm
Introduced April 1900
Discontinued 1907
Film size 119
Picture size 4¼ × 3¼ in.
Manufactured US
Lens Rapid Rectilinear – but see below.
Shutter 1900: Eastman Triple Action Pneumatic (valve on right)
1901–1903: Eastman Triple Action Pneumatic (valve below lens)
1904–1907: Kodak Automatic
Numbers made ?, but more than 15,000

Description/Remarks

Rising and cross front; two brilliant finders; plate adaptor available. Serial numbers from 501; from December 1900 sliding focusing replaced by rack and pinion, with extra extension, from serial number 3,518. Spirit levels fitted from January 1904.

Variations

Goerz Anastigmat f/6.8: *Apr. 1901–July 1901:* Unicum shutter. *Oct. 1902–Mar. 1905:* Bausch & Lomb Automatic shutter. *Oct. 1902–1906:* Volute shutter. *Apr. 1904–1906:* Kodak Automatic shutter.
Bausch & Lomb Plastigmat f/6.8: *Apr.1901–1902:* Unicum shutter. *Jan. 1902–Mar. 1905:* Bausch & Lomb Automatic shutter. *1903–1907:* Volute shutter. *Apr. 1904–1907:* Kodak Automatic shutter.
Bausch & Lomb Zeiss Anastigmat f/8: *1900:* Unicum shutter.
Bausch & Lomb Zeiss Tessar f/6.3: *1906–1907:* Volute shutter.
Cooke Anastigmat f/6.5: *1907:* Volute shutter.

UK VARIATIONS
1901–1903: Beck-Steinheil Orthostigmat. *1907:* Ross Homocentric series C f/6.3 or series D, f/8. Aldis No 2 series II f/6. In Kodak Automatic, Unicum or Bausch & Lomb Automatic shutters.

No 4 Cartridge Kodak

Type Folding rollfilm
Introduced 1897
Discontinued 1907
Film Size 104
Pictures size 5 × 4 in.
Manufactured US
Lens Rapid Rectilinear – but see below
Shutter 1897–1900: Eastman Triple Action Pneumatic, (valve on right of lens).
Nov. 1900–1903: Eastman Triple Action, (valve below lens).
Jan. 1902–1903: Bausch & Lomb Automatic.
Apr. 1904–1907: Kodak Automatic.
Numbers made 90.000+

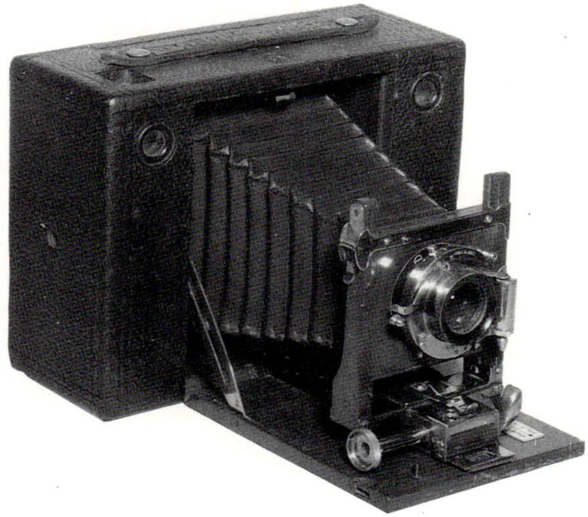

First model. RPS

Description Remarks

The first model of the Cartridge Kodak camera range. Plate adaptor available. Serial numbers from 501; camera underwent a series of changes – see below.

Variations

1897–Nov. 1900: wooden front, with screw clamped sliding focusing. Metalwork changed from brass to nickel plate from Feb.1899,from serial number 21,816. Brilliant finders fitted from Apr. 1900, from serial number 36,944.

From Nov. 1900 metal front fitted, with aluminium baseboard and extra extension, rack and pinion focusing, from serial number 50,000. From Sept. 1903 fitted with spirit levels, from serial number 80,138.

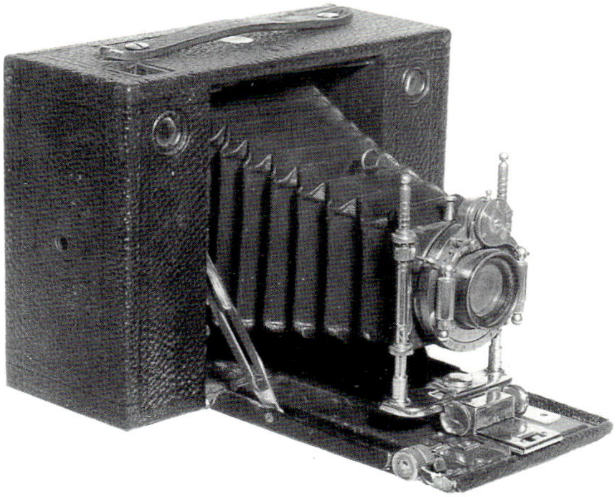

Model from 1900. RPS

Goerz Anastigmat f/6.8: *Apr. 1901–July 1901:* Bausch & Lomb Iris Diaphragm shutter. *Oct. 1902–Mar. 1905:* Bausch & Lomb Automatic shutter; Volute shutter. *Apr. 1904–1906:* Kodak Automatic shutter.
Bausch & Lomb Plastigmat f/6.8: *Apr. 1901–1902:* Bausch & Lomb Iris Diaphragm shutter. *Jan. 1902–Mar. 1905:* Bausch & Lomb Automat shutter. *1902–1907:* Volute shutter. *Apr.1904–1907:* Kodak Automatic shutter.
Bausch & Lomb Zeiss Anastigmat f/8: *1900:* Bausch & Lomb Iris Diaphragm or Unicum shutter.
Bausch & Lomb Zeiss Tessar f/6.3: *1905–1907:* Volute shutter.
Cooke Anastigmat f/6.5:*Mar. 1907–1907:* Volute shutter.

UK VARIATIONS
1901–1903: Beck-Steinheil Orthostigmat. *1907:* Ross Homocentric series C f/6.3 or series D f/8; Aldis No 2 series II f/6: in Kodak Automatic, Unicum or Bausch and Lomb Automatic shutters.

No 5 Cartridge Kodak

Type Folding rollfilm
Introduced 1898
Discontinued 1907
Film size 115
Picture size 7 × 5 in.
Manufactured US
Lens Rapid Rectilinear – but see below.
Shutter 1898–1900: Eastman Triple Action Pneumatic (valve on right of lens).
Nov. 1900–1903: Eastman Triple Action (valve below lens).
1902: Bausch & Lomb Iris Diaphragm.
April 1904–1907: Unicum or Bausch & Lomb Automatic.
Numbers made 17,500+

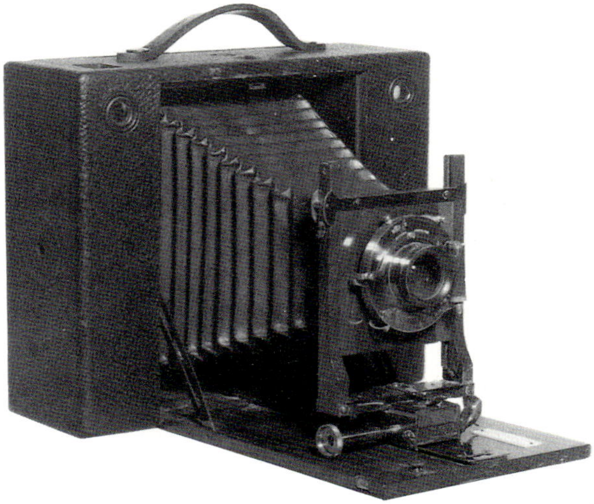

First model, 1898–1901. RPS

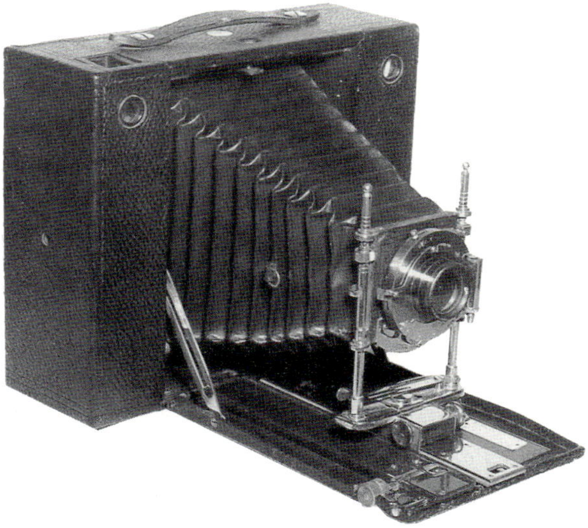

Model E, 1901–1907. RPS

Description/Remarks

The largest daylight-loading Kodak rollfilm camera. Plate adaptor back available. Serial numbers from 1. The camera underwent a number of changes – see below.

Variations

1898–Jan. 1901: Wooden front, with screw clamped sliding focusing. From March 1899 fittings changed from brass to nickel plate, from serial number 3,004. Brilliant finders fitted from April 1900.

Jan. 1901–1907: metal front, rack and pinion focusing, extra extension and aluminium baseboard, from serial number 7,500. Spirit levels fitted from August 1903, from serial number 14,100.

Bausch & Lomb Plastigmat f/6.8: *Apr. 1901–1902:* Bausch & Lomb Iris Diaphragm shutter. *Jan. 1902–1907:* Bausch & Lomb Automatic shutter. *1903–1907:* Volute shutter.
Goerz Anastigmat lens f/6.8: *Apr. 1901–July 1901:* Bausch & Lomb Iris Diaphragm shutter. *Oct. 1902–1906:* Bausch & Lomb Automatic or Volute shutter.
Bausch & Lomb Zeiss Anastigmat f/8: *1900:* Bausch & Lomb Iris Diaphragm or Unicum shutter.
Bausch & Lomb Zeiss Tessar f/6.3: *1905–1907:* Volute shutter.
Cooke Anastigmat f/6.3: *Mar. 1907–1907:* Volute shutter.

UK VARIATIONS

1901–1903: Beck-Steinheil Orthostigmat. *1907:* RossHomocentric series C f/6.3 or series D f/8. Aldis No 8, series III, f/7.7.Fitted with Kodak Automatic, Unicum or Bausch & Lomb Automatic shutters.

Flat Folding Kodak

Type Folding darkroom loaded rollfilm
Introduced 1895
Discontinued 1896
Film size 48 exposure darkroom loaded
Picture size 4 × 5 in.
Manufactured US, for UK market only
Lens Rapid Rectilinear
Shutter Kodet-type built-in
Numbers made 400

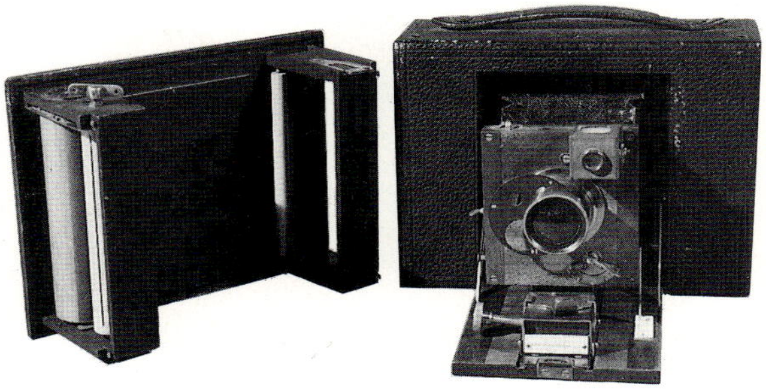

KM

Description/Remarks

Probably introduced as a rival to the Blair 400 camera, sold in the UK under the name Folding Kamaret. The Flat Folding Kodak camera was similar in appearance, but had a more basic specification, and sold for rather less. The lens and shutter, focusing arrangements and finder were the same as on the Kodet cameras. It was sold only on the English market for a short time in 1895–96. It was the most compact Kodak folding camera to date, and was advertised as "The Cyclist and Tourist's Comrade". Black morocco leather covering; brass fittings and mahogany baseboard; rackand pinion focusing.

No 3 Flush-Back Kodak

Type Folding rollfilm
Introduced February 1908
Discontinued 1915
Film size 118
Picture size 3¼ × 4¼ in.
Manufactured US
Lens Rapid Rectilinear
Lens Bausch & Lomb Automatic or 3FPK Automatic
Numbers made 12,000; 5,383 sold in UK, 6,398 in Europe, South Africa and India.

Description/Remarks

Essentially a No 3 Folding Pocket Kodak camera fitted with a special recessed combination plate back taking a single metal plate holder. This made the camera

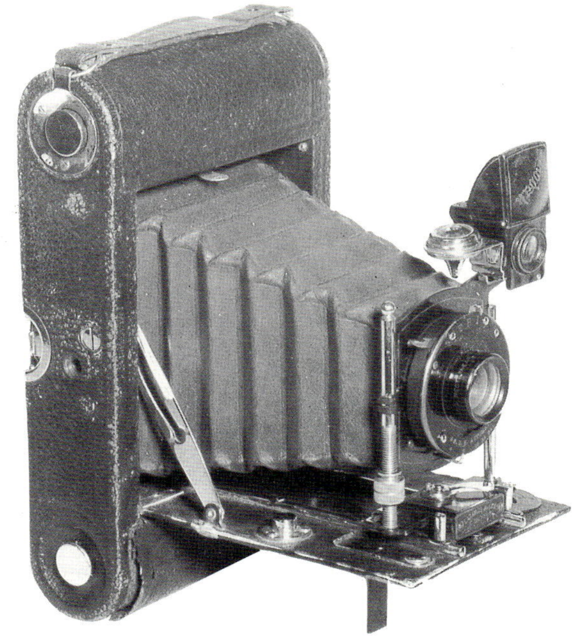

RPS

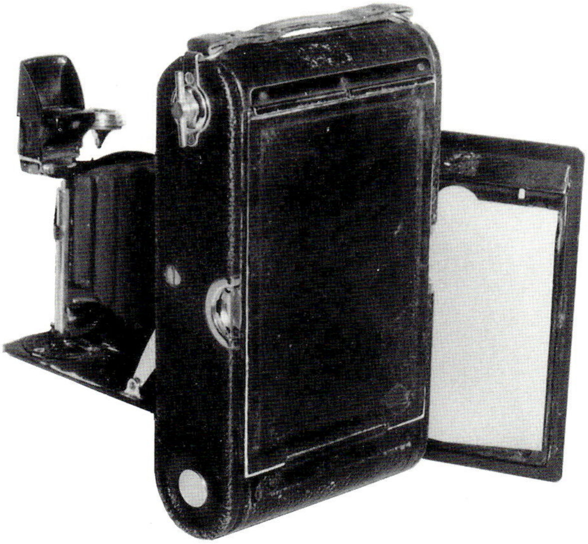

RPS

almost the same thickness as the normal model, unlike the standard Combination Back, which added about half an inch. It was supplied only to Kodak Limited for the European market, probably in response to the popularity of Butcher's Flush-back Carbine rollfilm camera, introduced in 1906. Curiously, it does not appear in Kodak Limited catalogues or trade circulars as such, although the July 1911 issue of the Kodak Trade Circular refers to a limited number of Flush Back Attachments being available for the 3 and 3A Folding Pocket Kodak cameras. Serial numbers from 1.

Variations

From Sept. 1910: improved focusing scale fitted, from serial number 6,001.

No 2 Folding Bulls-Eye

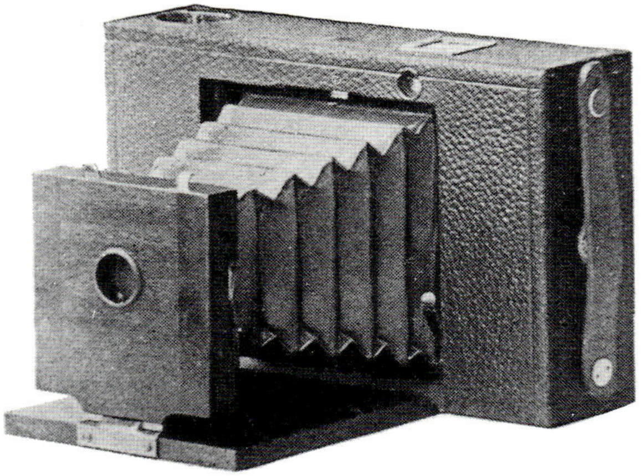

First model, to April 1899.

Type Folding rollfilm
Introduced 1899
Discontinued 1901
Film size 101
Picture size 3½ × ½ in.
Manufactured US
Lens Achromatic
Shutter Rotary
Numbers made 8,000

Description/Remarks

Simple specification; reflecting finder, fixed focus. Serial numbers from 1,001.

Variations

From Apr. 1899: improved film loading arrangement and baseboard runner with pull ring, from serial number 2001.

From Aug. 1899: metalwork changed from brass to nickel plate, from serial number 7,003.

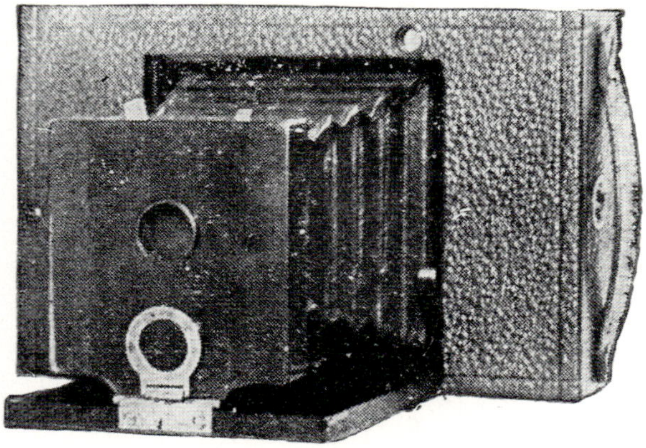

Second model, from April 1899.

No 4 Folding Kodak

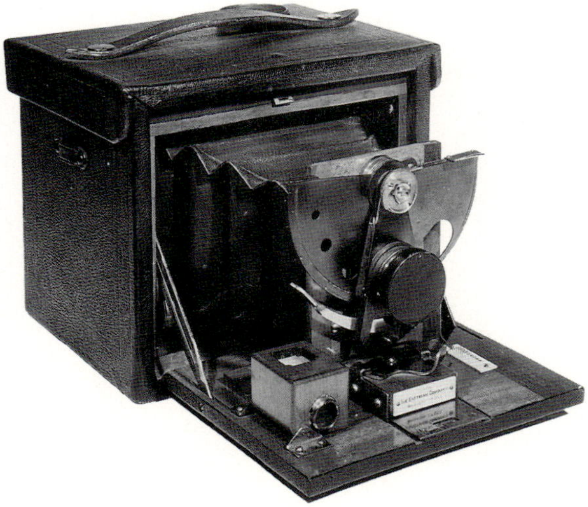

First model, 1890-1892. KM

Type Folding darkroom loaded rollfilm
Introduced July 1890
Discontinued 1897
Film size 48 exposure darkroom loaded
Picture size 4 × 5 in.
Manufactured US
Lens Bausch & Lomb Universal
Shutter 1890–1892: Special Kodak Winged Type
1892: Barker
1893–1897: Bausch & Lomb Iris Diaphragm
Numbers made 3,750

Description/Remarks

Box shaped leather covered case with hinged lid giving access to Eastman-Walker rollholder.

Variations

1890: Winding knob on case top engaged roll-holder key; small lens panel; sliding focusing; reflecting finder on baseboard.

1892: Asbury Barker shutter fitted; winding key

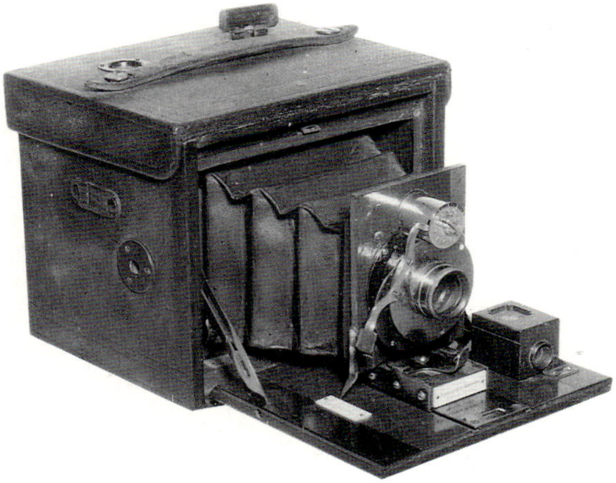

1892 model. RPS

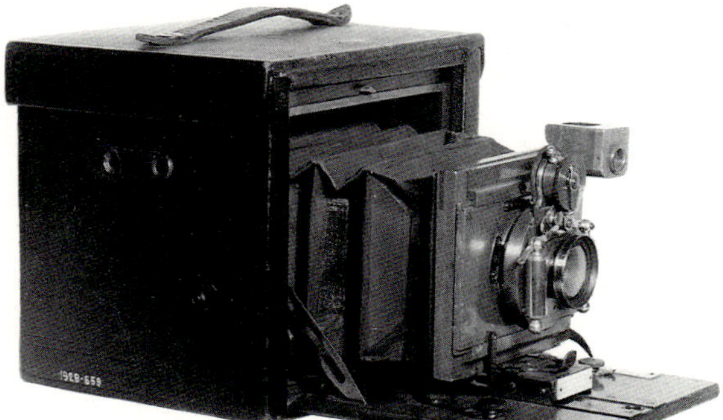

Improved model, 1893-1895. SM

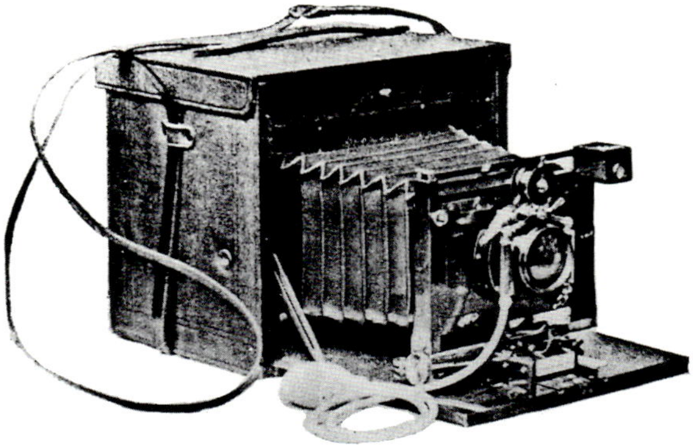

1895 model.

replaced knob; wider lens panel; peep hole for exposure counter.

1893: Improved model; Bausch & Lomb Iris Diaphragm shutter fitted; baseboard hinged to permit drop front movement when using wide angle lens; compartment within case for lens cells; double swing back and rising and cross front movements on lens panel; film wind within case; adapted to take ground glass screen and plate holders (older models could be adapted); finder on lens panel.

1895: Rack and pinion focusing replaced sliding focusing movement; improved lens panel and supports, with clamping screw for rising front, and cross movement of whole camera front, with locking lever.

No 4A Folding Kodak

Type Folding rollfilm
Introduced April 1906
Discontinued April 1915
Film size 126
Picture size 4¼ × 6½ in.
Manufactured US
Lens Rapid Rectilinear – but see below
Shutter Bausch & Lomb Automatic – but see below
Numbers made 15,000

Description/Remarks

Seal grain leather covering; largest size of convential rollfilm camera. Serial numbers from 1-L.

Variations

1904–1907: Wooden front, with rising and cross

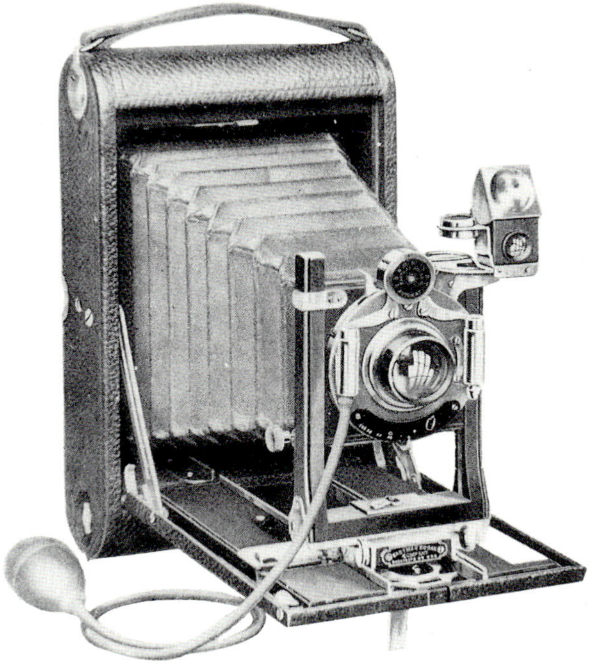

First model, 1904–1907.

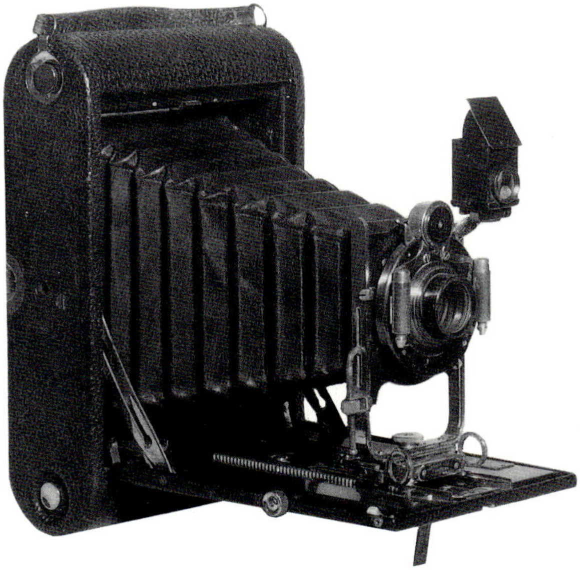

Model C, 1912–1915. RPS

movements; sliding focusing with automatic lock; cubical finder with level; key typespool centres.

Dec. 1907–Jan. 1912: Model B; metal front; screw adjusted rising front; rack and pinion focusing; prism shaped finder with no level; disc type spool centres; from serial number 7,200. From January 1911 longer screw gave increased rising front; lens bed plate screwed rather than riveted; from serial number 12,207.

Jan. 1912–1915: Model C; new finder with level; from serial number 13,207. From January 1912 all cameras fitted with black instead of red bellows, from serial number 13,907.

No 4A Autographic Kodak cameras were made from 1915 by adding Autographic backs; these were available also for converting earlier models.

Bausch & Lomb Zeiss Tessar f/6.3: *Apr. 1906–1912: Volute shutter. 1908:* Goerz X.L. Sector shutter. *Apr. 1909–1912:* Bausch & Lomb Automatic or Compound shutter.
Goerz Anastigmat f/6.8:
Apr. 1906–1906: Kodak Automatic or Volute shutter.
Cooke Anastigmat f/6.5: *Mar. 1907–1912:* Volute shutter.*1908:* Goerz X.L. Sector shutter. *Apr. 1909–1912:* Bausch & Lomb Compound or Automatic shutter.
Bausch & Lomb Plastigmat f/6.8: *1907:* Bausch & Lomb or Kodak Automatic or Volute shutter.
Goerz Dagor f/6.8: *1908:* Goerz X.L. Sector or Volute shutter.
Beck Isostigmar f/6.3: *1908:* Volute or Bausch & Lomb Automatic shutter.
Zeiss Kodak Anastigmat f/6.3:
Apr. 1909–1915: Bausch & Lomb Automatic or Compound shutter.*1909:* Volute shutter.

UK VARIATIONS
Goerz Series III f/6.8: *1907:* Kodak or Bausch & Lomb Automatic or Unicum shutter.
Goerz Dagor Series III f/6.8: *1908:* Unicum shutter. *1908–1910:* Bausch & Lomb Automatic, Koilos, or Compound shutter.
Goerz Syntor f/6.8: *1910:* Bausch & Lomb Automatic, Koilos, Compound or Goerz Sector shutter.
Goerz Celor f/4.8: *1910:* Bausch & Lomb Automatic, Koilos or Compound shutter.
Zeiss Tessar Series IIb f/6.3: *1908–1914:* Bausch & Lomb Automatic or Koilos shutter. *1908–1915:* Compound shutter. *1908–1910:* Goerz Sector shutter. *1912:* Kodak Automatic shutter.
Zeiss Tessar Series Ic f/5.3: *1912–1914:* Compound shutter.
Zeiss Double Amatar f/6.8: *1912:* Kodak Automatic, Koilos or Compound shutter.
Zeiss Protar f/9: *1908:* Unicum or Goerz Sector shutter. *1908–1910:* Bausch & Lomb Automatic, Koilos or Compound shutter.
Zeiss Double Protar Series IV f/6.3: *1910:* Bausch & Lomb Automatic, Koilos, Compound or Goerz Sector shutter.
Cooke Series III f/6.5: *1908–1914:* Bausch & Lomb Automatic or Koilos shutter. *1908–1915:* Compound shutter. *1908:* Unicum shutter. *1912:* Kodak Automatic shutter.
Goerz Dagor Series III f/6.8: *1908:* Unicum shutter.*1908–1910:* Bausch & Lomb Automatic, Koilos, or Compound shutter.
Goerz Syntor f/6.8: *1910:* Bausch & Lomb Automatic, Koilos, Compound or Goerz Sector shutter.
Goerz Celor f/4.8: *1910:* Bausch & Lomb Automatic, Koilosor Compound shutter.
Zeiss Tessar Series IIb f/6.3: *1908–1914:* Bausch & Lomb Automatic or Koilos shutter. *1908–1915:* Compound shutter.*1908–1910:* Goerz Sector shutter. *1912:* Kodak Automatic shutter.
Zeiss Tessar Series Ic f/5.3: *1912–1914:* Compound shutter.
Zeiss Double Amatar f/6.8: *1912:* Kodak Automatic, Koilos or Compound shutter.
Zeiss Protar f/9: *1908:* Unicum or Goerz Sector shutter.*1908–1910:* Bausch & Lomb Automatic, Koilos or Compound shutter.
Zeiss Double Protar Series IV f/6.3: *1910:* Bausch & Lomb Automatic, Koilos, Compound or Goerz Sector shutter.
Cooke Series III f/6.5: *1908–1914:* Bausch & Lomb Automatic or Koilos shutter. *1908–1915:* Compound shutter.*1908:* Unicum shutter. *1912:* Kodak Automatic shutter.
Cooke Series IV f/5.6: *1910–1914:* Bausch & Lomb Automatic, Koilos or Compound shutter. *1910:* Goerz Sector shutter.*1912:* Kodak Automatic shutter.
Cooke Series V f/8: *1910:* Bausch & Lomb Automatic, Koilos, Compound or Goerz Sector shutter.
Ross Homocentric Series C or III f/6.3: *1908–1910:*Koilos or Compound shutter. *1910:* Bausch & Lomb Automatic shutter.
Ross Homocentric Series D or V f/8: *1908–1910:* Bausch & Lomb Automatic, Koilos or Compound

shutter. *1908:* Unicum or Goerz Sector shutter.
Ross Homocentric Series II f/5.6: *1910:* Bausch & Lomb Automatic, Koilos or Compound shutter.
Ross Homocentric Series IV f/6.8: *1910:* Bausch & Lomb Automatic, Koilos or Compound shutter.
Aldis Series III f/7.7: *1908–1910:* Bausch & Lomb Automatic, Goerz Sector or Koilos shutter. *1908:* Unicum shutter.*1910:* Compound shutter.
Aldis Series II f/6: *1910:* Bausch & Lomb Automatic, Koilos, Compound or Goerz Sector shutter.
Aldis Oxys f/6: *1908–1910:* Bausch & Lomb Automatic, Koilos, Goerz Sector or Compound shutter. *1908:* Unicum shutter.
Dallmeyer Stigmatic Series II f/6: *1908–1910:* Bausch & Lomb Automatic, Koilos, or Compound shutter. *1908:* Unicum or Goerz Sector shutter.
Euryplan Series II f/5.6:
1908–1910: Bausch & Lomb Automatic, Koilos or Compound shutter.*1908:* Unicum or Goerz Sector shutter.
Euryplan Nulli Secundus f/6.8: *1908:* Bausch & Lomb Automatic, Unicum, Goerz Sector, Koilos or Compound shutter.
Euryplan Nulli Secundus f/6.5: *1910:* Bausch & Lomb Automatic, Koilos, Goerz Sector or Compound shutter.
Beck Isostigmar f/5.8: *1908:* Bausch & Lomb Automatic, Unicum, Koilos, Goerz Sector or Compound shutter.
Beck Isostigmar f/7.7: *1908:* Bausch & Lomb Automatic, Unicum, Koilos, Celverex, Goerz Sector or Compound shutter.
Beck Series I f/4.5: *1910:* Bausch & Lomb Automatic shutter.
Beck Series II f/5.8 or III f/7.7: *1910:* Bausch & Lomb Automatic, Koilos, Compound or Goerz Sector shutter.

No 5 Folding Kodak

Type Folding darkroom loaded rollfilm
Introduced 1890
Discontinued 1897
Film size 54 exposure darkroom loaded
Picture size 5 × 7 in.
Manufactured US
Lens Bausch & Lomb Universal
Shutter 1890–1892: Special Kodak Winged Type
1892: Barker
1893–1897: Bausch & Lomb Iris Diaphragm
Numbers made 4,900

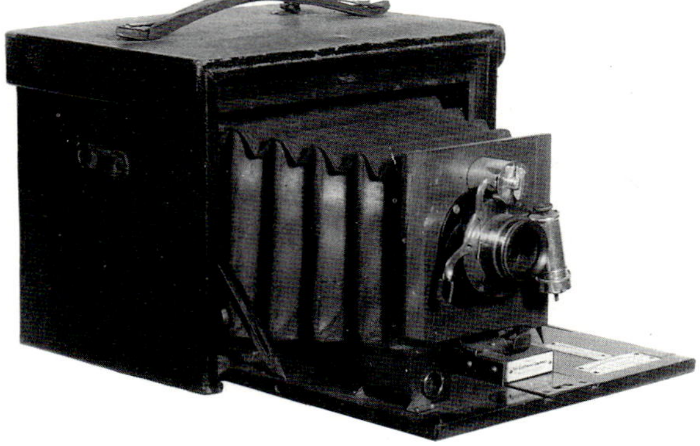

1892 model. SM

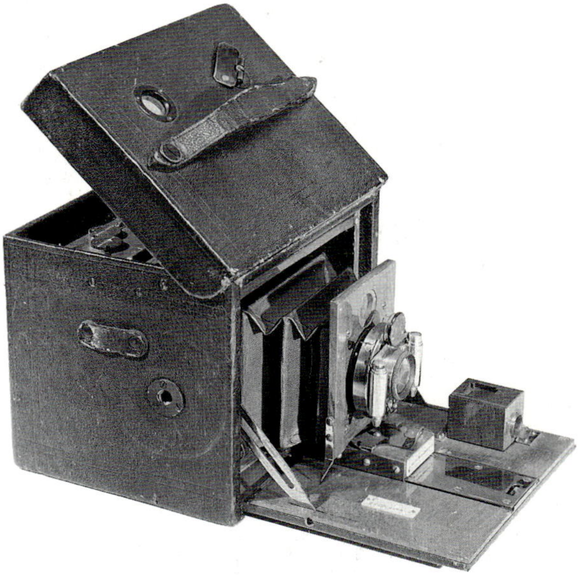

1892 model (not original lens and shutter). KM

Description/Remarks

Box shaped leather covered case with hinged lid giving access to Eastman-Walker rollholder.

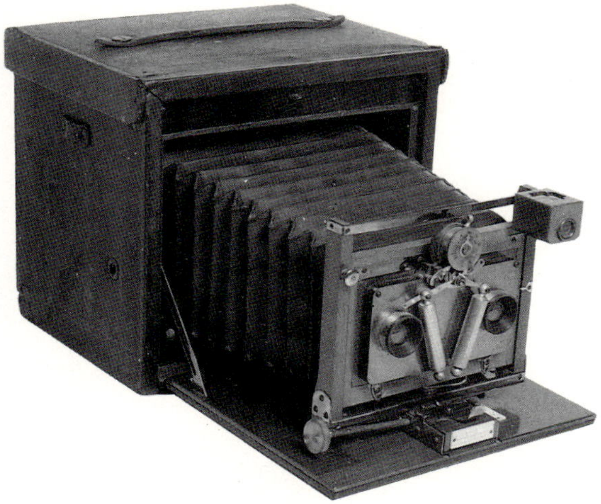

Improved model, 1893, fitted with stereo lens panel. TNC

Variations

1890: Winding knob on case top engaged roll-holder key; small lens panel; reflecting finder on baseboard; sliding focusing.

1892: Asbury Barker shutter fitted; winding key replaced by knob; wider lens panel; peep hole for exposure counter.

1893: Improved model; Bausch & Lomb Iris Diaphragm shutter fitted; baseboard hinged to permit drop front movement when using wide angle lens; compartment within case for lens cells; double swing back and rising and cross front movements on lens panel; rack and pinion focusing; film wind within case; adapted to take ground glass screen and plate holders (older models could be adapted); finder on lens panel; curved baseboard struts. An extra lens panel and partition were supplied to convert for stereoscopic use if desired.

1895: Improved lens panel and supports, with clamping screw for rising front, and cross movement of whole camera front, with locking lever; straight baseboard struts.

No 6 Folding Kodak

Type Folding darkroom loaded rollfilm
Introduced 1893
Discontinued 1895
Film size 48 exposure darkroom loaded
Picture size 6½ × 8½ in.
Manufactured US
Lens Bausch & Lomb Universal
Shutter Bausch & Lomb Iris Diaphragm
Numbers made 150 (?)

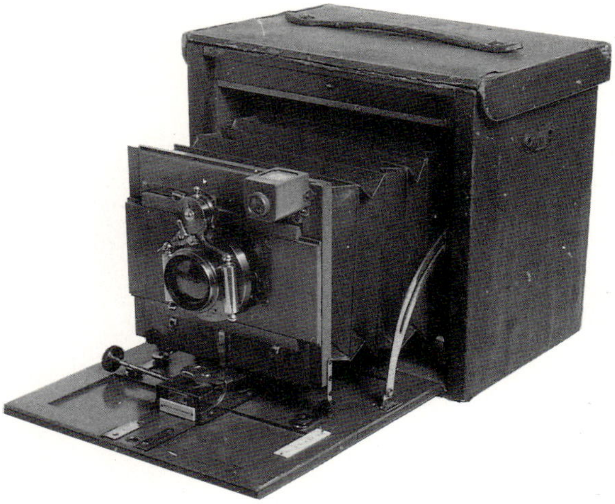

First model, 1893-1895. TNC

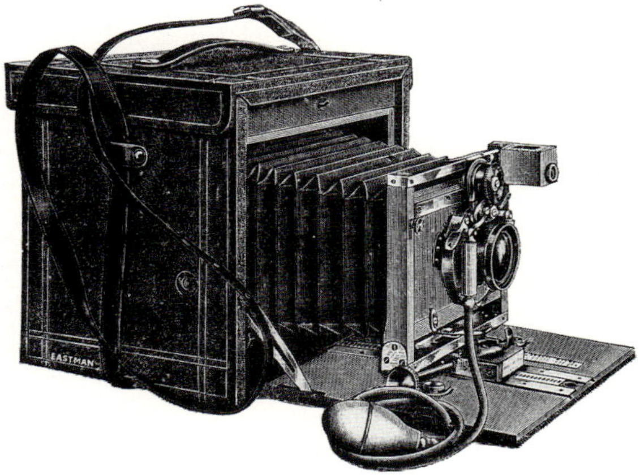

1895 model.

Description/Remarks

Box shaped leather covered case with hinged lid giving access to Eastman-Walker rollholder. The largest rollfilm camera ever, producing a whole-plate negative.

Baseboard hinged to permit drop front movement when using wide angle lens; compartment within case for lens cells; double swing back and rising and cross front movements on lens panel; rack and pinion focusing; film wind within case; adapted to take ground glass screen and plate holders; finder on lens panel; curved baseboard struts. An extra lens panel and partition were supplied to convert for stereoscopic use if desired.

1895: Improved lens panel and supports, with clamping screw for rising front, and cross movement of whole camera front, with locking lever; straight baseboard struts.

Folding Pocket Kodak

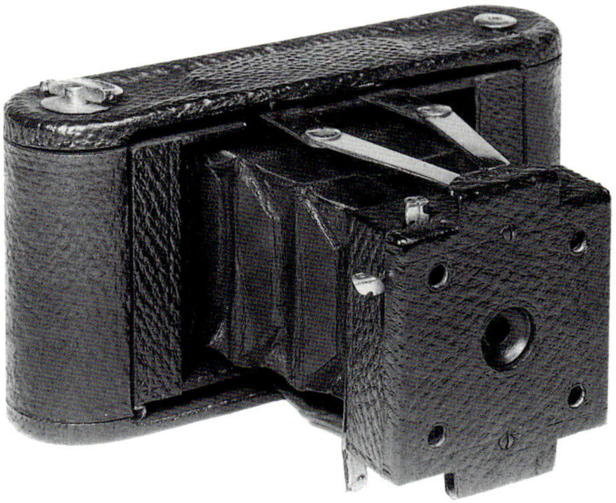

KM

Type Collapsing rollfilm
Introduced August 1897
Discontinued April 1899
Film size 105
Picture size 2¼ × 3¼ in.
Manufactured US
Lens Achromatic f/11
Shutter Eastman Automatic (built-in)
Numbers made 75,000 approximately

Description/Remarks

The first model of what became a best-selling range of folding rollfilm cameras, introducing the to-be-popular 2¼ × 3¼ inch negative format. Integral shutter; four 'windows' on lens panel, two only used for reflecting finder lenses; recessed conical lens window; sliding flat strip for supporting camera front. Serial numbers from 101.

Variations

From Dec. 1897: locking case catches fitted, from serial number 5,101.

From Mar. 1898: metalwork changed from brass to nickel plate, from serial number 12,200.

No 0 Folding Pocket Kodak

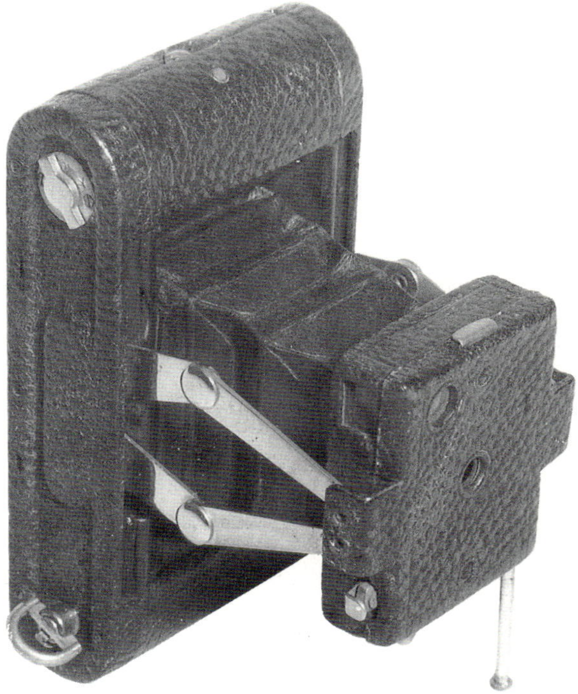

Model A-B. RPS

Type Collapsing rollfilm
Introduced March 1902
Discontinued November 1906
Film size 121
Picture size 1⅝ × 2½ in.
Manufactured US
Lens Meniscus
Shutter Eastman Automatic, built-in.
Numbers made 20,000

Description/Remarks

The smallest Folding Pocket Kodak camera, using the popular 'vest-pocket' format. Serial numbers from 101.

Variations

Model A – to June 1902. Model AB – from June 1902, fitted with centre pins for film spools, from serial number 5,100. Improved winding key from serial number 10,100, September 1902.

No 1 Folding Pocket Kodak

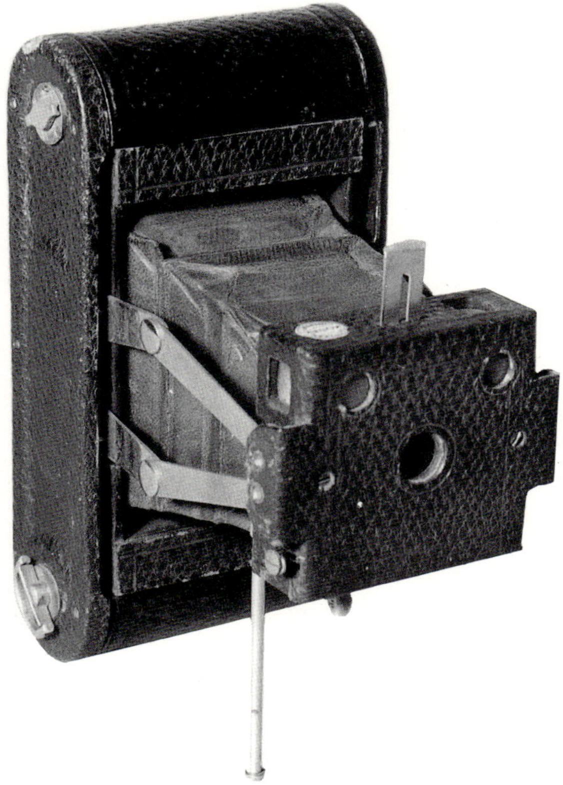

Model B. KM

Type Collapsing rollfilm
Introduced April 1899
Discontinued April 1915
Film size 105
Picture size 2¼ × 3¼ in.
Manufactured US
Lens Achromatic f/11 – but see below.
Shutter April 1899–June 1905: Eastman Automatic
June 1905–April 1915: Pocket Automatic
Numbers made 125,000

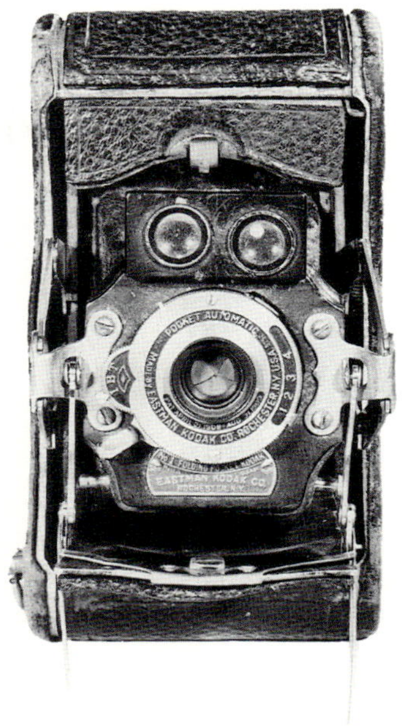

Model C. KM

Description/Remarks

The Folding Pocket Kodak camera was redesignated No 1, model B, with the introduction of the No 2 Folding Pocket Kodak camera. Only two, larger, finder windows on front panel; lens opening on front panel without conical recess; round rod front support.

This model underwent a number of changes of design – see below.

Variations

From Jan. 1901: brilliant finders and noiseless winding keys fitted, from serial number 95,146.

June 1905–Feb. 1907: Model C, with twin reflecting finders and Pocket Automatic shutter; self-erecting mechanism, with baseboard covering the lens when closed; from serial number 130,201.

Oct. 1906–Apr. 1910: Model D, with single reversible finder; camera numbers on exterior bottom of case instead of inside; new spool centre pins; from serial number 145,240. *From June 1907:* improved shutter with four apertures, from serial number 149,233. *From Jan.1908:* new shutter with 'star' opening, from serial number 153,234. *From Mar. 1909:* shutters fitted with iris diaphragms, from serial number 159,260.

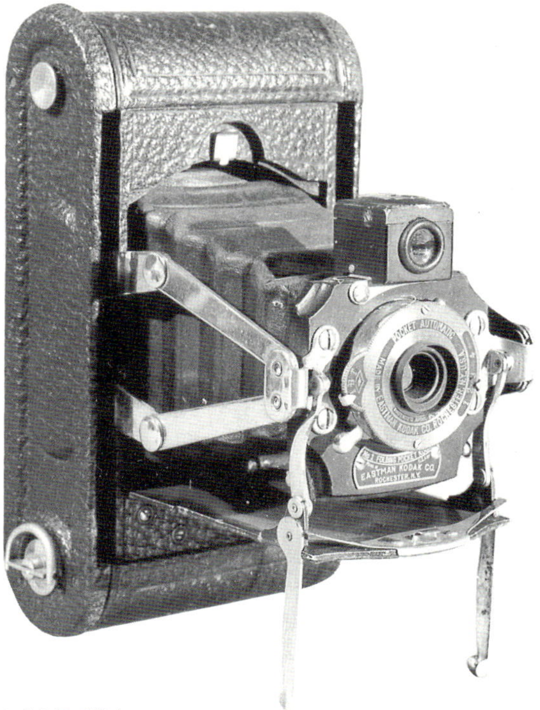

Model D. KM

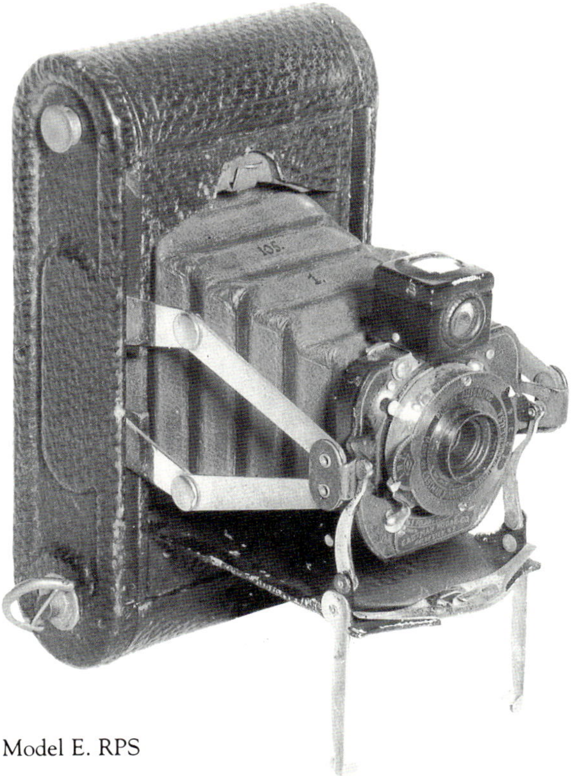

Model E. RPS

Aug. 1909–Apr. 1915: Model E, with metal replacing wood lens panel, from serial number 161,198.

Until 1911 all models had red bellows; from August 1911 those shipped to London had black bellows. From October 1912 all cameras fitted with black bellows, from serial number 178,201. (**Note:** red bellows on many early models will have been replaced by black during repairs.)

UK VARIATIONS

Goerz Doppel Anastigmat: *1901–1904:* Bausch & Lomb or Eastman Automatic shutter.
Goerz Series III Anastigmat f/6.8: *1906:* Compound shutter.
Goerz Dagor Series III f/6.8: *1908–1910:* Bausch & Lomb Simplex shutter.
Beck-Steinheil Orthostigmat: *1901:* Bausch & Lomb or Eastman Automatic shutter.
Cooke Series V f/8: *1906–1910:* Bausch & Lomb single valve shutter. *1910:* Koilos or Compound shutter.
Cooke Series III f/6.8: *1906:* Compound shutter.
Cooke Series III f/6.5: *1908–1910:* Bausch & Lomb Simplex shutter. *1910–1914:* Koilos shutter. *1910–1915:* Compound shutter. *1912–1914:* Ball Bearing.
Zeiss Tessar Series III f/6.5: *1914:* Compound shutter.
Zeiss Tessar Series IIb f/6.3: *1908–1910:* Bausch & Lomb Simplex shutter. *1910–1914:* Koilos shutter. *1910–1915:* Compound shutter,
Ross Homocentric f/6.3: *1908:* Minx shutter. *1910:*Bausch & Lomb single valve, Koilos or Compound shutter.
Beck Series II f/6.3 or III f/7.7: *1910:* Bausch & LombSimplex shutter.
Beck Isostigmar f/5.8 or f/7.7: *1908:* Simplex or Koilos shutter.
Plastigmat Series 00 f/6.8: *1908:* Bausch & Lomb Simplex shutter.
Dallmeyer Stigmatic f/6: *1910:* Koilos or Compur shutter.
Euryplan Series II f/5.6 or Nulli Secundus f/6.8: *1908:*Bausch & Lomb Simplex shutter.

No 1A Folding Pocket Kodak

Type   Collapsing rollfilm

Introduced December 1899
Discontinued April 1915
Film size 116
Picture size 2½ × 4¼ in.
Manufactured US
Lens Achromatic f/11 – but see below
Shutter 1899–June 1905: Eastman Automatic, built-in.
June 1905–1915: Pocket Automatic.
Numbers made 202,000

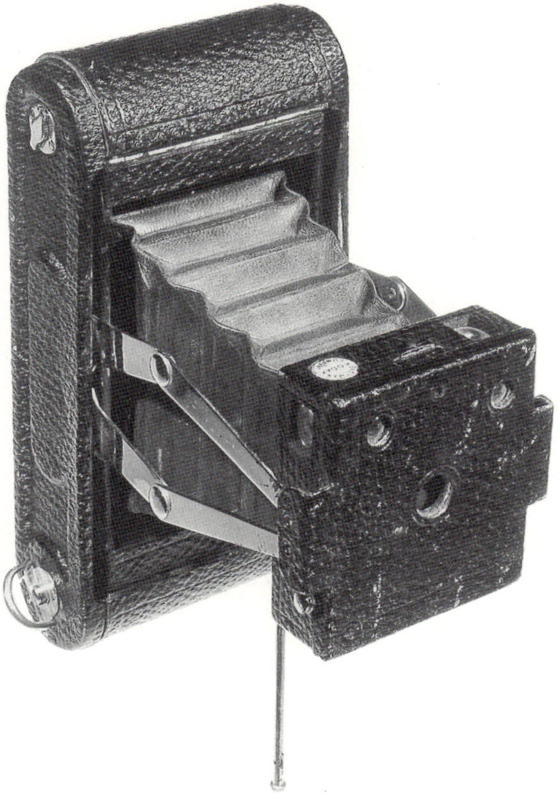

First model, 1899-1905. KP

Description/Remarks

This camera introduced the 116 rollfilm size. Serial numbers from 1,001.

Variations

1899–June 1905: first model; built-in shutter and reflecting finders; from January 1900 noiseless winding keys fitted, from serial number 4,982; brilliant finders fitted from April 1900, serial number 11,002.

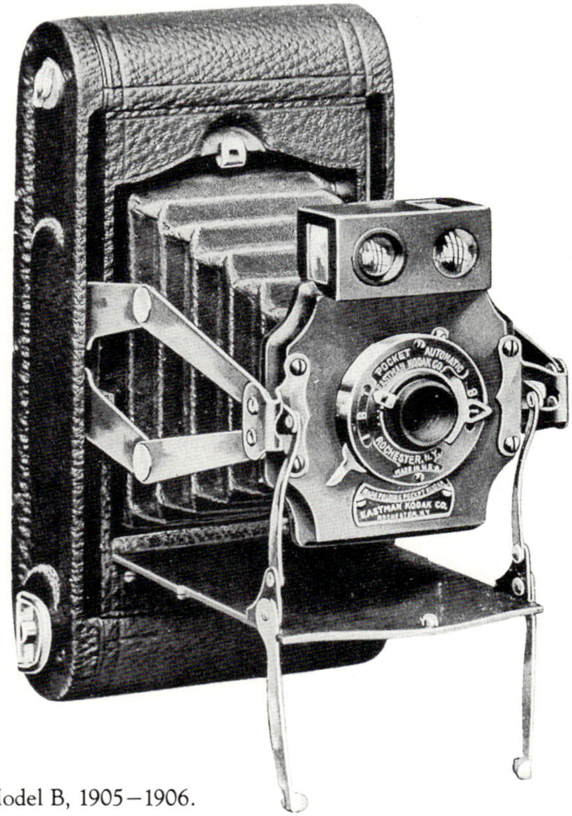

Model B, 1905–1906.

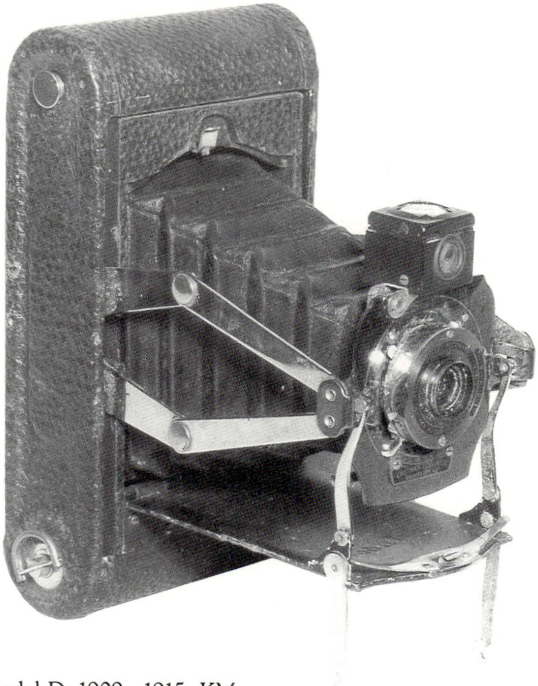

Model D, 1909–1915. KM

June 1905–Sept. 1906: Model B; fitted with Pocket Automatic shutter; self-erecting mechanism with metal baseboard protecting lens when closed; twin reflecting finders; from serial number 57,001.

Sep. 1906–July 1909: Model C; Single reversible finder; camera numbers on exterior bottom instead of inside back; from serial number 78,100. Improved shutter with four apertures from March 1907. Improved shutter with 'star' opening from Oct. 1907; from serial number 99,103.

From Mar. 1909: shutters fitted with iris diaphragm, from serial number 116,226.

July 1909–Apr. 1915: Model D; metal lens panel replaces wood of earlier models, from serial number 119,286.

UK VARIATIONS

Goerz Doppel Anastigmat: *1901:* Eastman Automatic shutter. *1901–1904:* Bausch & Lomb shutter.

Beck-Steinheil Orthostigmat: *1901:* Bausch & Lomb or Eastman Automatic shutter.

Cooke Series III, f/6.5: *1910–1914:* Koilos shutter.*1910–1915:* Compound shutter. *1914:* Ball Bearing.

Cooke Series V, f/8: *1907–1910:* Bausch & Lomb Simplex shutter. *1910:* Koilos or Compound shutter.

Plastigmat f/6.8: *1908:* Bausch & Lomb Simplex shutter.

Zeiss Tessar IIb, f/6.5: *1908:* Bausch & Lomb Simplex or Unicum shutter. *1908–1914:* Koilos shutter. *1908–1915:*Compound shutter.

Goerz Dagor f/6.8: *1908–1910:* Bausch & Lomb Simplex shutter.

Goerz Syntor f/6.3: *1910:* Bausch & Lomb shutter.

Ross Homocentric f/6.3 or f/8: *1908–1910:* Koilos or Compound shutter.

Ross Homocentric f/6.8: *1910:* Koilos or Compound shutter.

Beck Isostigmar f/5.8 or f/7.7: *1908:* Koilos or Bausch & Lomb Simplex shutter.

Beck Series II, f/5.8 or Series III, f/7.7: *1908:* Bausch & Lomb, Koilos or Compound shutter.

Dallmeyer Stigmatic f/6: *1910:* Koilos or Compound shutter.

Euryplan Series II, f/5.6: *1908:* Bausch & Lomb Simplex shutter.

Euryplan Nulli Secundus Series IV, f/6.8: *1908:* Bausch & Lomb Simplex.

No 1A Folding Pocket Kodak, RR Type

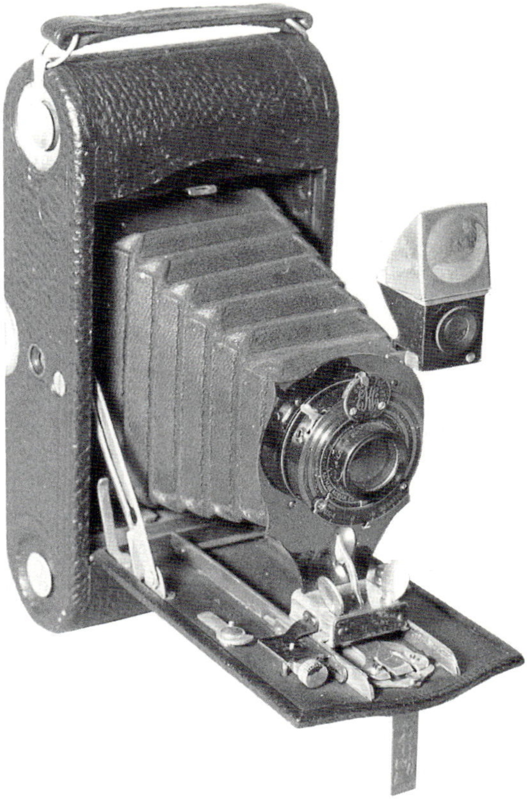

KM

Type Folding rollfilm
Introduced March 1912
Discontinued 1915
Film size 116
Picture size 2¼ × 4¼ in.
Manufactured US
Lens Rapid Rectilinear – but see below.
Shutter March 1912–September 1914: Kodak Ball Bearing
January 1913–September 1914: Kodak Automatic
Numbers made 46,000

Description/Remarks

This model was originally called No 1A Folding Pocket Kodak Special camera (q.v.), but was renamed from March 1912, from serial number 37,635. It became the 1A Autographic Kodak camera (q.v.) from September 1914, serial number 79,808.

Variations

Zeiss Kodak Anastigmat f/6.3: *1912–1914:* Kodak Automatic or Bausch & Lomb Compound shutter.
Bausch & Lomb Zeiss Tessar f/6.3: *1912–1914:* Bausch & Lomb Compound or Kodak Automatic shutter.
Cooke anastigmat f/6.5:
1912–1914: Bausch & Lomb Compound or Kodak Automatic shutter.

From Nov. 1914–1915: the Kodak Anastigmat f/8 lens was available as an exchange for owners of the Rapid Rectilinear/Ball Bearing shutter model.

UK VARIATIONS
Zeiss Tessar Series IIb f/6.3: *1912:* Kodak Automatic, Koilos, Compound or Ibso shutter.
Zeiss Tessar Series Ic f/4.9: *1912:* Koilos or Compound shutter.
Zeiss Double Amatar f/6.8: *1912:* Kodak Automatic, Koilos, Compound or Ibso shutter.
Zeiss-Kodak Anastigmat f/6.3: *1914–1915:* Koilos or Compound shutter. *1914:* Ibso shutter.
Cooke Series III f/6.5 or Series IV f/5.6: *1914:* Kodak Automatic, Koilos or Compound shutter.

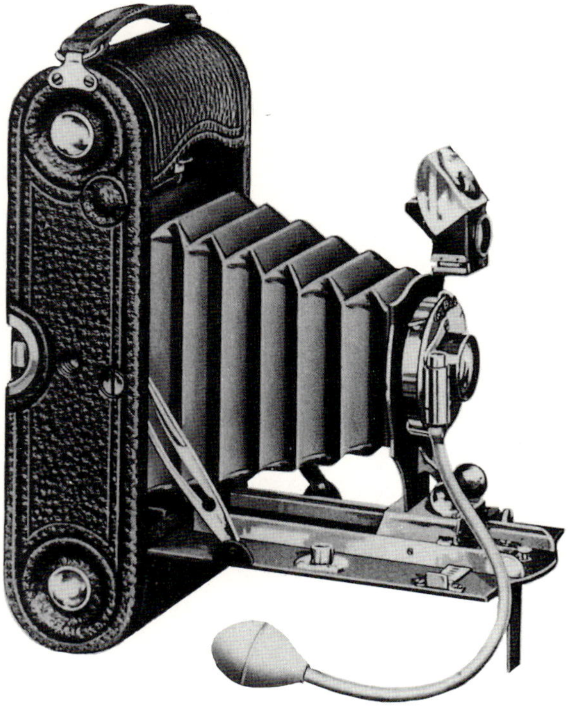

No 1A Folding Pocket Kodak Special

Type Folding rollfilm
Introduced April 1908
Discontinued March 1912
Film size 116
Picture size 2¼ × 4¼ in.
Manufactured US
Lens Rapid Rectilinear – but see below.
Shutter April 1908–1909: F.P.K. Automatic
April 1910–1912: Kodak Automatic
Numbers made 42,000

Description/Remarks

Different from the No 1A Folding Pocket Kodak camera, with folding as opposed to collapsing construction and superior lens and shutter equipment. Serial numbers from 1-S.

From March 1912 this model was renamed No 1A Folding Pocket Kodak – RR Type camera (q.v.), to avoid confusion with the newly introduced No 1A Kodak Special camera.

Variations

Sep. 1909–Nov. 1910: Model B; Ball Bearing shutter, No 3 FPKtype winding key; from serial number 12,082.

Nov. 1910–Apr. 1911: Model C; new style reflecting finder; from serial number 20,092.

Apr. 1911–Apr. 1912: Model D; new style baseboard; from serial number 24,135.

Bausch & Lomb Zeiss Tessar f/6.3: *Apr. 1908–1910:*Bausch & Lomb Automatic shutter. *Aug. 1908–1912:* Bausch & Lomb Compound shutter. *April 1909–1912:* Kodak Automatic shutter.
Zeiss Kodak Anastigmat f/6.3: *Apr. 1909–1910:* Bausch & Lomb Automatic shutter. *Apr. 1909–1912:* Kodak Automatic or Bausch & Lomb Compound shutter.
Goerz Dagor f/6.8: *1908:* Kodak or Bausch &

Lomb Automatic or Bausch & Lomb Compound shutter.
Cooke Anastigmat f/6.5: *Apr. 1909–1912:* Bausch & Lomb Compound or Automatic, or Kodak Automatic shutter.
Beck Isostigmar f/6.3: *1908:* Bausch & Lomb Automatic shutter.
Bausch & Lomb Plastigmat f/6.8: *1908:* Kodak Automatic shutter.

UK VARIATIONS
Zeiss Tessar Series IIb f/6.3: *1908–1910:* Bausch & Lomb Automatic shutter. *1908–1912:* Kodak Automatic shutter. *1908–1914:* Koilos shutter. *1910–1914:* Compound shutter. *1912:* Ibso shutter.
Zeiss Double Protar Series IV f/6.3: *1910:* Kodak or Bausch & Lomb Automatic, Koilos or Compound shutter.
Zeiss Tessar Series Ic f/4.9: *1912:* Koilos or Compound shutter.
Zeiss Double Amatar f/6.8: *1912:* Kodak Automatic, Koilos, Compound or Ibso shutter.
Cooke Series III anastigmat f/6.5: *1908–1910:* Bausch & Lomb Automatic shutter. *1908–1912:* Kodak Automatic shutter. *1908–1914:* Koilos shutter. *1910–1914:* Compound shutter.
Cooke Series IV f/5.6: *1910:* Bausch & Lomb Automatic shutter. *1910–1912:* Kodak Automatic, Koilos or Compound shutter.
Cooke Series V f/8: *1910:* Kodak or Bausch & Lomb Automatic, Koilos or Compound shutter.
Goerz Syntor f/6.8: *1910:* Kodak or Bausch & Lomb Automatic, Koilos or Compound shutter.
Goerz Dagor f/6.8: *1908–1910:* Koilos shutter.
Goerz Celor f/4.8: *1910:* Kodak or Bausch & Lomb Automatic, Koilos or Compound shutter.
Beck Series II f/5.8 or Series III f/7.7: *1910:* Kodak or Bausch & Lomb Automatic, Koilos or Compound shutter.
Beck Isostigmar f/7.7 or f/5.8: *1908:* Kodak or Bausch & Lomb Automatic or Koilos shutter.
Ross Homocentric Series III f/6.3, Series IV f/6.8 or Series V f/8: *1910:* Kodak or Bausch & Lomb Automatic, Koilos or Compound shutter.
Aldis Series II f/6: *1908–1910:* Kodak or Bausch & Lomb Automatic or Koilos shutter. *1910:* Compound shutter.
Aldis Series II Oxys f/5.6: *1910:* Kodak or Bausch & Lomb Automatic, Koilos or Compound shutter.
Dallmeyer Stigmatic f/6: *1910:* Kodak or Bausch & Lomb Automatic, Koilos or Compound shutter.
Euryplan f/5.6 or Nulli Secundus f/6.5: *1910:* Kodak or Bausch & Lomb Automatic, Koilos or Compound shutter.

No 2 Folding Pocket Kodak

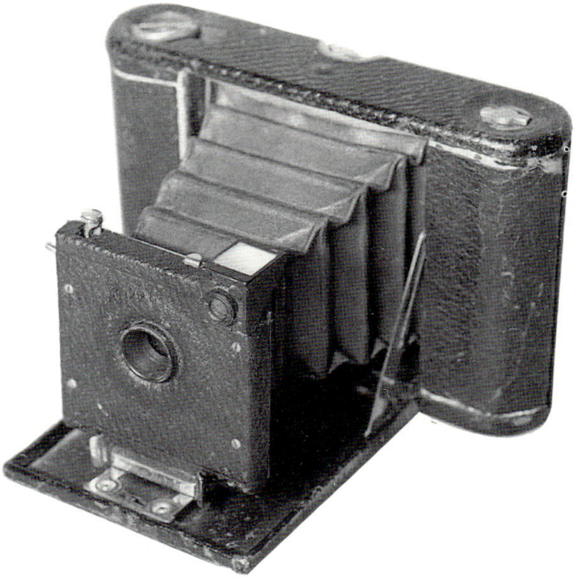

Model A, 1899–1902. KM

Type Folding rollfilm
Introduced April 1899
Discontinued April 1910
Film size 101
Picture size 3½ × 3½in.
Manufactured US
Lenses 1899–1903: Achromatic
1904–1910: Rapid Rectilinear
Shutters 1899–1903: Eastman Automatic, built-in
1904–1910: F.P.K Automatic
Numbers made 48,000+

Description/Remarks

Horizontally disposed body. Serial numbers from 101. Sliding focusing; reflecting finder.

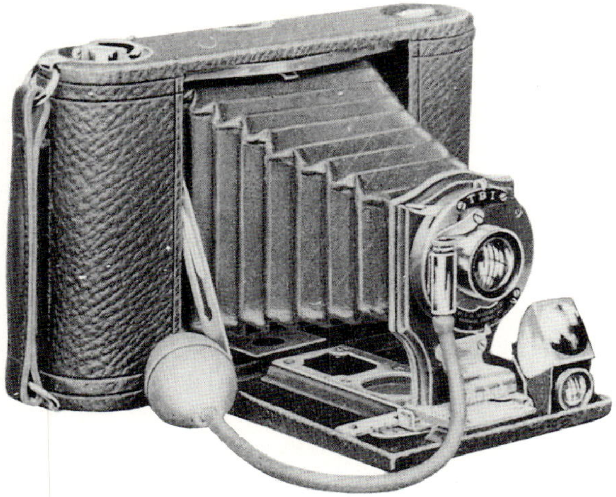

Model C, 1904-1907.

Variations

Apr. 1899–Nov. 1902: Model A. *From June 1900:* brilliant finders fitted, from serial number 20,134. *From Sept. 1900:* noiseless winding keys fitted, from serial number 32,139.

Nov. 1902–May 1904: Model B; hinged cover fitted to finder, from serial number 32,139.

May 1904–Apr. 1907: Model C; F.P.K. Automatic shutter fitted; automatic focusing lock at 8, 25 and 100 foot positions; finder moved to baseboard; from serial number 35,743.

Apr. 1907–Apr. 1910: Model D; improved film spool centring device; from serial number 45,992.

UK VARIATIONS

Goerz Doppel Anastigmat: *1901–1904:* Bausch & Lomb shutter.
Beck-Steinheil Orthostigmat: *1901:* Eastman Automatic or Bausch & Lomb shutter.
Goerz Series III, f/6.8: *1907:* Unicum shutter.
Goerz Syntor f/6.8: *1910:* Bausch & Lomb Simplex, Koilos or Compound shutter.
Goerz Dagor f/6.8: *1908:* F.P.K. Automatic shutter. *1910:* Bausch & Lomb Simplex, Koilos or Compound shutter.
Zeiss Protar Series IIIb f/9: *1908:* F.P.K. Automatic shutter. *1910:* Koilos or Compound shutter.
Zeiss Tessar f/6.3: *1910:* Koilos, Compound or Bausch & Lomb shutter.
Ross Homocentric Series III, f/6.3, Series IV, f/6.8 or Series V, f/8: *1910:* Koilos or Compound shutter.
Cooke Series III, f/6.5: *1908:* F.P.K. Automatic shutter.
Plastigmat f/6.8: *1908:* F.P.K. Automatic shutter.
Beck Isostigmar f/5.8 or f/7.7: *1908:* F.P.K. Automatic shutter.
Beck Series II, f/5.8 or Series III, f/7.7: *1910:* Koilos or Compound shutter.
Euryplan Series II, f/5.6: *1908:* F.P.K. Automatic shutter.
Euryplan Nulli Secundus f/6.8: *1908:* F.P.K. Automatic shutter.

No 3 Folding Pocket Kodak

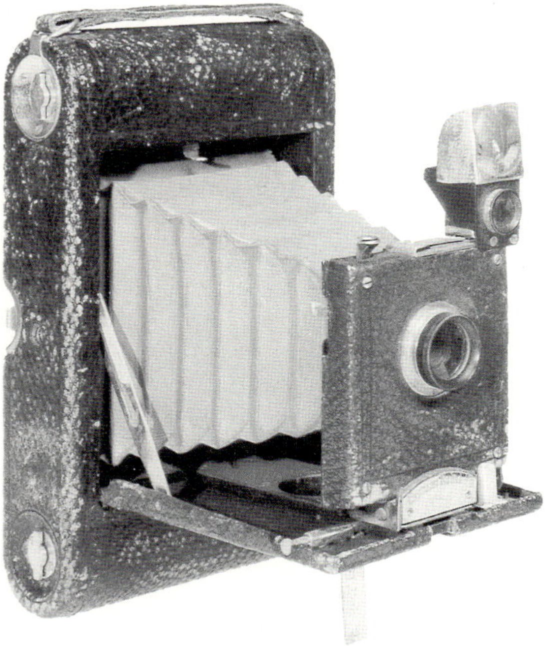

Model A. KM

Type Folding rollfilm
Introduced April 1900
Discontinued 1915
Film size 118
Picture size 3¼ × 4¼in.
Manufactured US
Lens Rapid Rectilinear – but see below.

Shutters 1900–1903: Eastman Automatic, built-in
April 1901–March 1902: Unicum
January 1902–March 1905: Bausch & Lomb Automatic
July 1903–1908: F.P.K. Automatic
March 1905–September 1914: Kodak Automatic
April 1909–1914: Kodak Ball Bearing
Numbers made 288,000+

Description/Remarks

The most popular of the FPK range, with a large number of design changes and lens and shutter combinations. Serial numbering was complicated by the existence of several number ranges and two basic models – one without rising front movement (*1900–Nov. 1909:* from serial number 301), and one with (*June 1903–1915:* from serial number 101). The latter, *between 1903 and Nov. 1909* have an -E suffix.

Variations

MODELS WITHOUT RISING FRONT

Apr.–Oct. 1900: Square, leather covered lens panel with "Eastman Kodak Co" engraved on plate at base. Flat strip lens slide on baseboard; pin baseboard support foot for horizontal pictures; from serial number 301.

Oct. 1900–Aug. 1901: Model A; "Eastman Kodak Co" on lens panel plate ; improved lens slide block, to protect bellows, from serial number 14,951. *From June 1901:* cloth lined bellows fitted, from serial number 40,000.

Aug. 1901–Feb. 1902: Model AB; rail type lens slide; leather lined baseboard; "Kodak" on plate at base of lens panel; strip baseboard support foot for horizontal pictures; from serial number 40,000.

Feb. 1902–Oct. 1902: Model C; locking cam fitted to lens slide block; from serial number 51,000. *From Apr. 1902:* tripod socket fitted in baseboard, from serial number 55,499.

Oct. 1902–May 1904: Model C-2; improved bellows frame; from serial number 68,005.

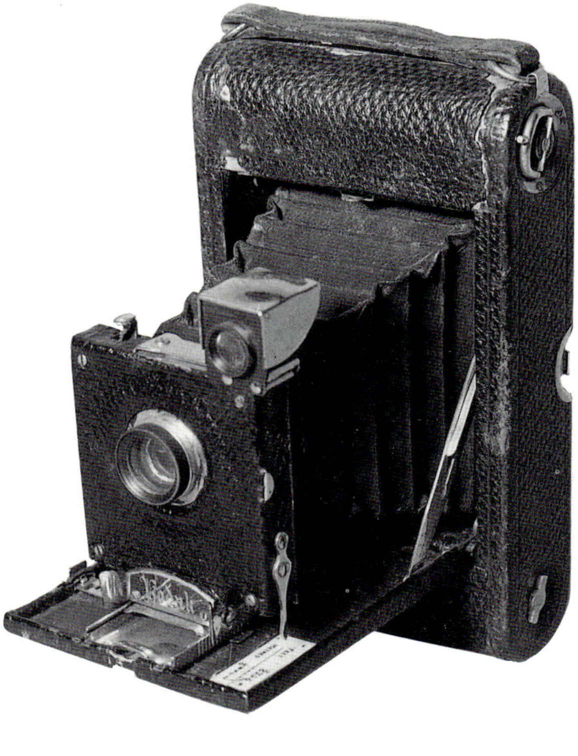

Model AB. KM

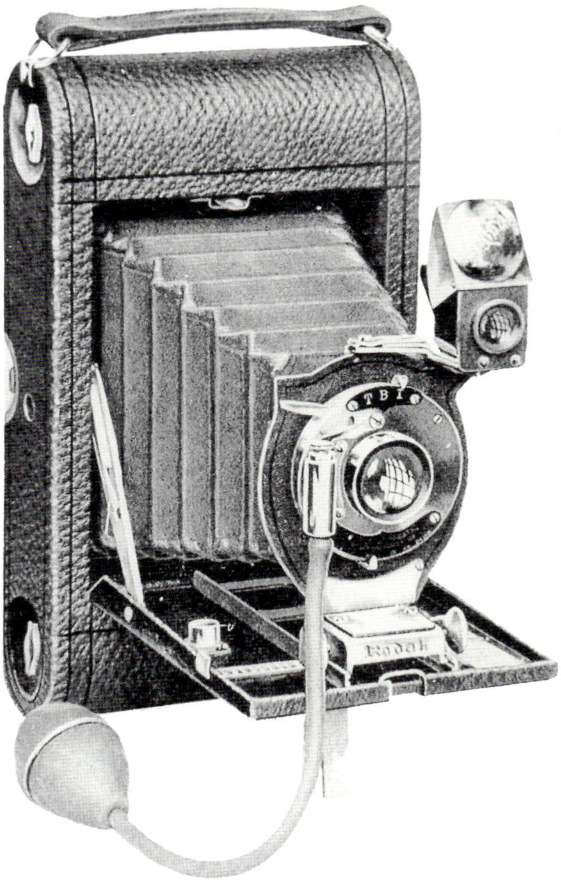

Model C-2.

Apr. 1904—Apr. 1907: Model C-3; automatic focusing lock; new non-reversible back with different-sized catches; from serial number 22,700-B. (A new serial number range with the -B suffix appears to have been introduced during the Model C-2 production, some time after serial number 78,000). *From Mar. 1906:* tension springs were fitted to the back, from serial number 34,003-B.

Apr. 1907—Aug. 1908: Model C-4; blackened nickel metal lens panel instead of leather covered wood, top with 'cat's-ears' shape; from serial number 40,522-B (some cameras in this range do not have the -B suffix, but appear to be in the same number sequence).

Aug. 1908—Nov. 1909: Model C-5; baseboard fitted with wooden strips; automatic focusing lock discontinued; combination film/plate focusing scales added; combination back fitted; from serial number 52,100. *After Nov. 1909:* all models fitted with rising front.

RISING FRONT MODELS

June 1903—Nov. 1903: Model D; sliding rising front locked by clip; metal lens panel, top with central dome; from serial number 101-E.

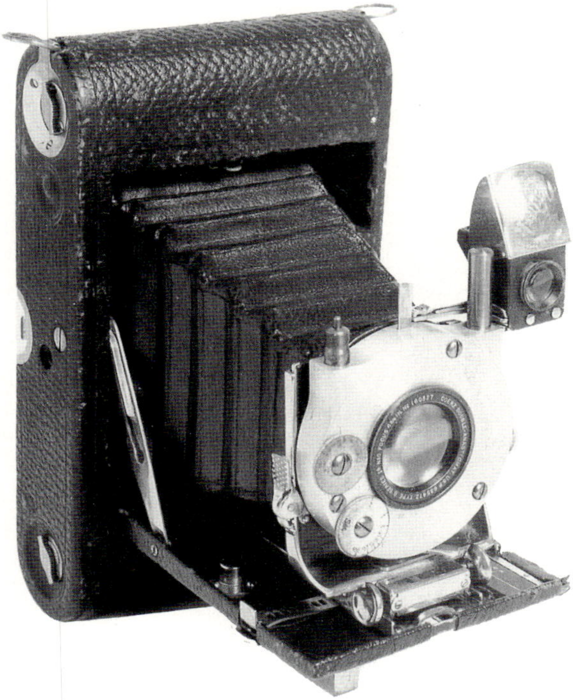

Model. D. TNC

Nov. 1903-May 1904: Model E; rack and pinion rising front; from serial number 4,910-E.

May 1904—Apr. 1907: Model E-2; new non-reversible back with catches of different sizes; automatic preset focusing lock; from serial number 9,000-E. *From Feb. 1906:* tension springs fitted to camera back, from serial number 28,080-E.

Apr. 1907—June 1908: Model E-3; new lens support frame —U-shaped square-section nickel plated frame with rounded knobs on ends; from serial number 36,599-E.

June 1908—Nov. 1909: Model E-4; wooden baseboard strips; automatic focus lock discontinued; combination plate/film focusing scales fitted; combination back fitted; from serial number 45,117-E.

Nov. 1909—May 1911: Model F; new baseboard (same as that on the No 1A Folding Pocket Kodak RR model camera), with edge not raised, front edge curved, upright rails; support foot for horizontal pictures

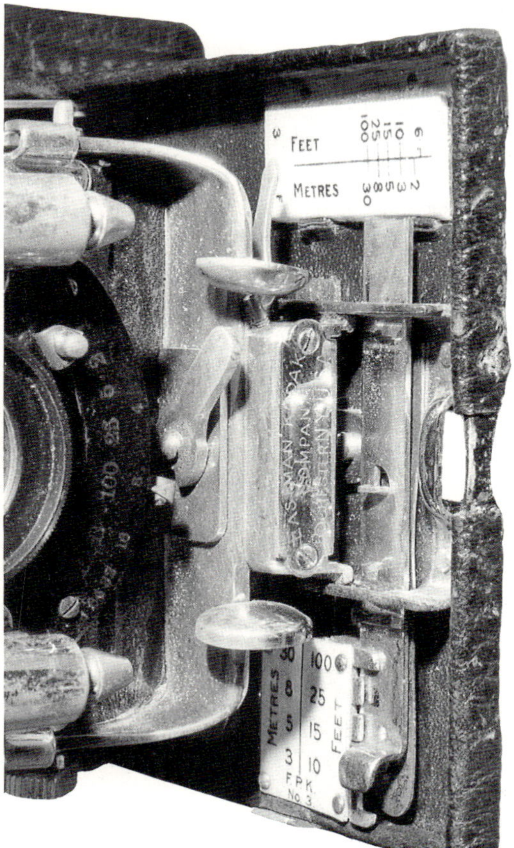

Model E-2, preset focusing lock on left. KM

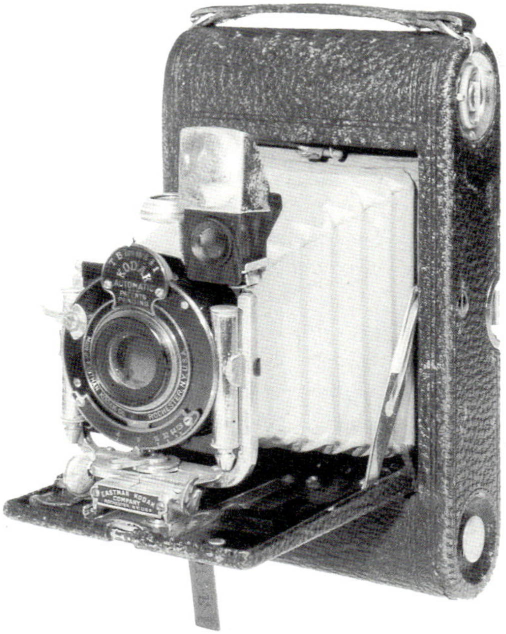

Model E-3. KM

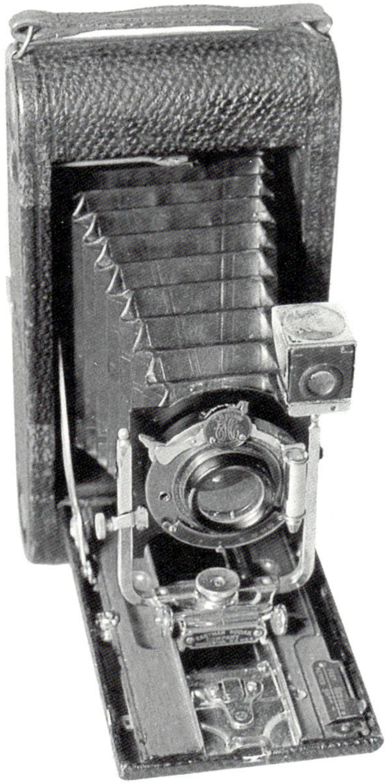

Model E-4. KM

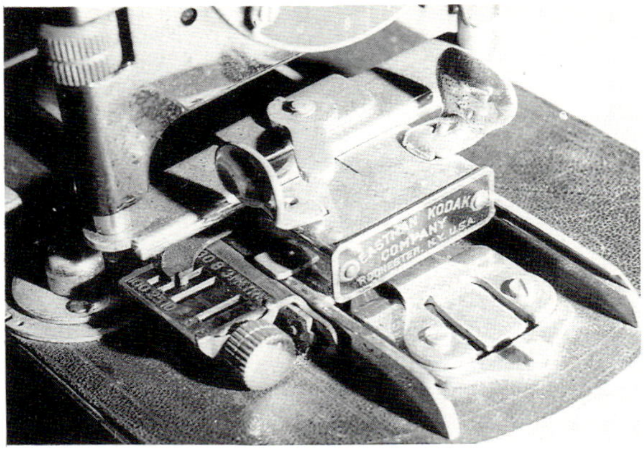

Model F and G, preset focusing lock. KM

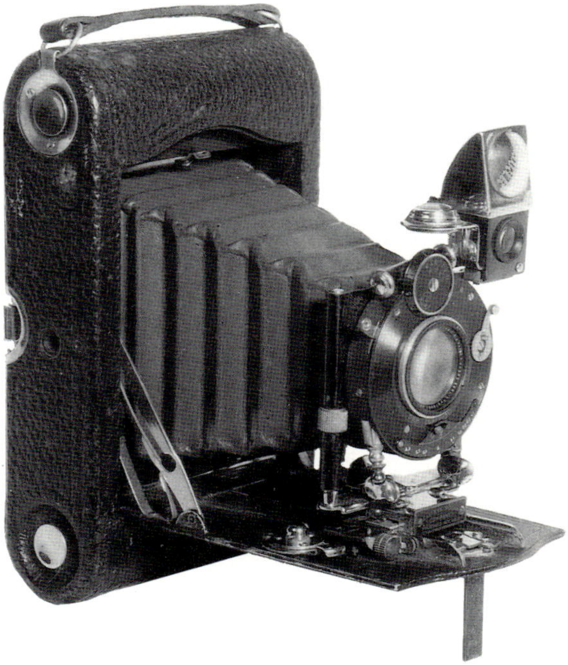

Model F. SM

attached to tripod bush in baseboard; preset focusing lock set by milled screw; reflecting finder opens for cleaning, with spirit level attached; lens panel wrapped around support standard, screw-operated rising front; from serial number 60,000-R. (The -R suffix appears to have been adopted with this model; the numbers seem to follow in sequence from the -E series).

May 1911–1914: Model G; new baseboard, with raised edge, but retaining curved front edge and upright rails; new lens panel with rack and pinion rising front, supported between square section uprights with rounded knobs at the top; support foot separate from tripod bush. These cameras have a new numbering sequence — examples range from serial numbers below 1,200 to over 87,000. *From June 1912:* centring clip added to the rising front pinion, from serial number 95,050.

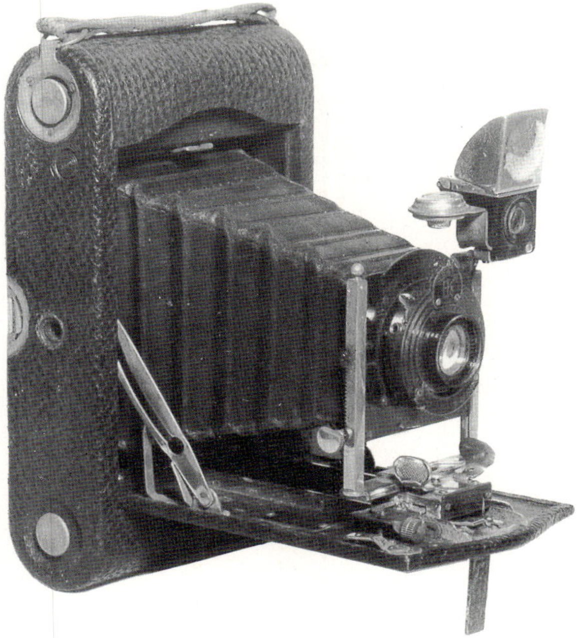

Model G. RPS

From Mar. 1910: cameras supplied to Kodak Limited had black instead of red bellows; *from Jan. 1913:* all cameras so fitted.(**Note** — earlier models may have had original red bellows replaced with black during repairs).

Model H cameras were mostly fitted with Autographic backs; lens front similar to Model F, otherwise like Model G, from serial number 85,050.

Goerz Anastigmat f/6.8: *Apr. 1901—July 1901:* Unicum shutter. *Oct. 1902—Mar. 1905:* Bausch & Lomb Automatic shutter.*Oct. 1902—1906:* Volute shutter. *Mar. 1905—1906:* Kodak Automatic shutter.
Goerz Dagor f/6.8: *1908:* Goerz Sector, Kodak Automatic, Bausch & Lomb Automatic or Volute shutter. *1909:* Bausch & Lomb Compound shutter.
Bausch & Lomb Plastigmat f/6.8: *Apr. 1901—Mar. 1902:*Unicum shutter. *Jan. 1902—Mar. 1905:* Bausch & Lomb Automatic shutter. *June 1902—1908:* Volute shutter. *Mar.1905—1908:* Kodak Automatic shutter. *1908:* Goerz Sector shutter.
Bausch & Lomb Zeiss Tessar f/6.3: *Apr. 1906—1912:* Volute shutter. *1908:* Goerz Sector shutter. *Aug. 1908—1912:* Bausch & Lomb Compound shutter. *Apr. 1909—1912:* Kodak or Bausch & Lomb Automatic shutter.
Cooke Anastigmat f/6.5: *Feb. 1907—1912:* Volute shutter. *1908:* Goerz Sector shutter. *Apr. 1909—1912:* Bausch & Lomb Compound shutter. *1909:* Kodak or Bausch & Lomb Automatic shutter.
Beck Isostigmar f/6.3: *1908:* Bausch & Lomb Automatic or Volute shutter.
Zeiss Kodak Anastigmat f/6.3: *April 1909—1912:* Kodak Automatic, Bausch & Lomb Automatic or Compound shutter. *1909:* Volute shutter.

In 1914-1915: Rapid Rectilinear lenses in Ball Bearing shutters could be exchanged for Kodak Anastigmat f/8 lenses.

UK VARIATIONS
Beck-Steinheil Orthostigmat: *1901:* Eastman Automatic or Unicum shutter.
Goerz Doppel Anastigmat: *1901:* Eastman Automatic or Unicum shutter.
Goerz Dagor Series III, f/6.8: *1908—1910:* Kodak or Bausch & Lomb Automatic, Unicum, Koilos, Compound or Goerz Sector shutter.
Goerz Celor f/4.8: *1910:* Kodak or Bausch & Lomb Automatic, Koilos or Compound shutter.
Goerz Syntor f/6.8: *1910:* Kodak or Bausch & Lomb Automatic, Koilos, Compound or Goerz Sector shutter.
Ross Homocentric f/8: *1907—1910:* Kodak or Bausch & Lomb Automatic shutter. *1907—1908:* Unicum shutter. *1910:*Koilos or Compound shutter.
Ross Homocentric f/6.3: *1908—1910:* Kodak or Bausch & Lomb Automatic, Koilos, Compound or Goerz Sector shutter. *1908:*Unicum shutter.
Ross Homocentric f/6.8 or f/5.6: *1910:* Kodak or Bausch & Lomb Automatic, Koilos or Compound shutter.
Aldis No 2 Series II f/6: *1907—1910:* Kodak or Bausch & Lomb Automatic shutter. *1907—1908:* Unicum shutter. *1908—1910:* Koilos or Compound shutter. *1908:* Goerz Sector shutter.
Aldis Series II Oxys f/5.6: *1908—1910:* Kodak or Bausch & Lomb Automatic, Koilos or Compound shutter. *1908:* Unicum or Goerz Sector shutter.

Zeiss Tessar IIb f/6.3: *1908–1912:* Kodak Automatic, Koilos or Compound shutter. *1908–1910:* Bausch & Lomb Automatic or Goerz Sector shutter. *1912:* Ibso shutter.
Zeiss Tessar Ic f/4.5: *1912:* Kodak Automatic, Koilos or Compound shutter.
Zeiss Protar f/9: *1908:* Kodak or Bausch & Lomb Automatic, Unicum, Koilos, Compound or Goerz Sector shutter.
Zeiss Double Protar Series II f/6.3: *1910:* Kodak or Bausch & Lomb Automatic, Köilos, Compound or Goerz Sector shutter.
Zeiss Double Amatar f/6.8: *1912:* Kodak Automatic, Koilos, Compound or Ibso shutter.
Zeiss-Kodak Anastigmat f/6.3: *1914–1915:* Compound shutter. *1914:* Koilos or Ibso shutter.
Cooke Series III f/6.5: *1908–1912:* Kodak Automatic, Koilos or Compound shutter. *1908–1910:* Bausch & Lomb Automatic or Goerz Sector shutter. *1908:* Unicum shutter.
Cooke Series IV f/5.6: *1910–1912:* Kodak Automatic, Koilos or Compound shutter. *1910:* Bausch & Lomb Automatic shutter. *1912:* Ibso shutter.
Cooke Series V f/8: *1910:* Kodak or Bausch & Lomb Automatic, Koilos, Compound or Goerz Sector shutter.
Beck Series I f/4.5, Series II f/5.6, Series III f/7.7:*1910:* Kodak or Bausch & Lomb Automatic, Koilos or Compound shutter.
Beck Isostigmar f/7.7 or f/5.8: *1908:* Kodak or Bausch & Lomb Automatic, Unicum, Koilos, Compound, Goerz Sector or Beck Celverex shutter.
Dallmeyer Stigmatic Series II f/6: *1908–1910:* Kodak or Bausch & Lomb Automatic, Koilos or Compound shutter. *1908:* Unicumor Goerz Sector shutter.
Euryplan f/5.6 or Euryplan Nulli Secundus f/6.5: *1908–1910:* Kodak or Bausch & Lomb Automatic, Koilos or Compound shutter. *1908:* Unicum or Goerz Sector shutter.
TT&H-Kodak Anastigmat f/6.8: *1914:* Kodak Automatic or Koilos shutter. *1914–1915:* Compound shutter.

No 3 Folding Pocket Kodak DeLuxe

Type Folding rollfilm
Introduced October 1901 (1906 in UK)
Discontinued 1903 (1908 in UK)
Film size 118
Picture size 3¼ × 4¼in.
Manufactured US
Lens Bausch & Lomb Plastigmat f/6.8
Shutter Bausch & Lomb Automatic
Numbers made ?

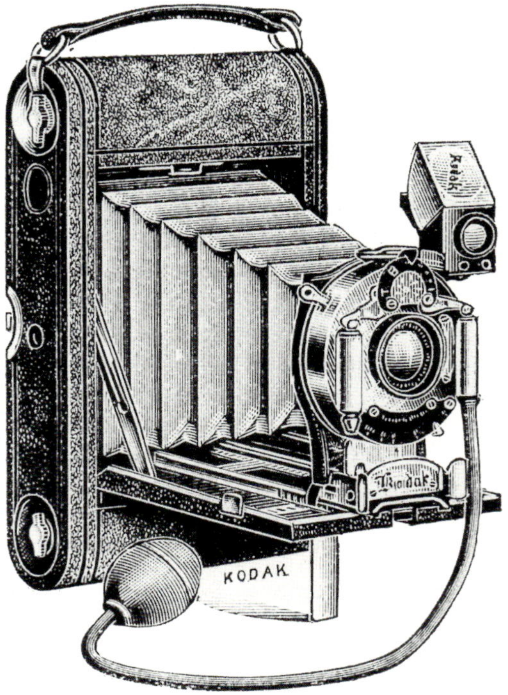

Description/Remarks

"One of the richest and daintiest Kodak" cameras, said the catalogue. A No 3 Folding Pocket Kodak camera covered in specially selected Persian Morocco leather, fine brown silk covered bellows and a silver nameplate. The matching case had silver fittings.

No 3A Folding Pocket Kodak

Type Folding rollfilm
Introduced May 1903
Discontinued 1915
Film size 122
Picture size 3¼ × 5½in.

Manufactured US
Lens Rapid Rectilinear – but see below
Shutters May 1903–1908: F.P.K. Automatic.
May 1903–1904: Bausch & Lomb Automatic.
March 1905–1914: Kodak Automatic.
April 1908–1910: Bausch & Lomb Automatic.
May 1908–1910: Volute.
April 1909–1914: Kodak Ball Bearing.
April 1909–1911: Bausch & Lomb Compound.
Numbers made 360,000+

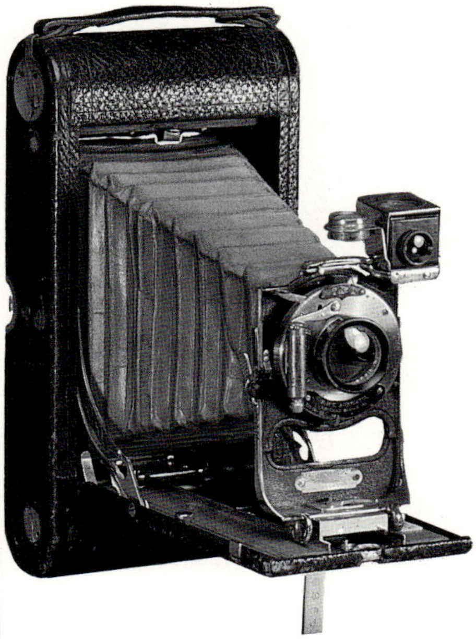

Model A. KM

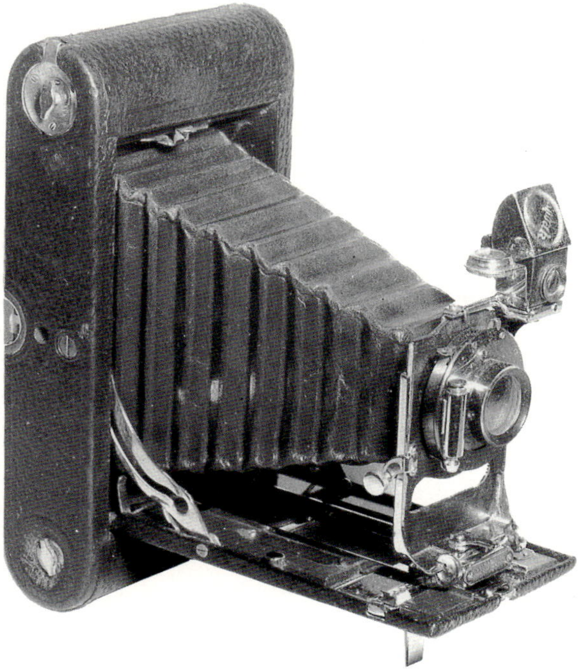

Model B–2. RPS

Description/Remarks

Very popular postcard format camera, with a wide range of variations. Serial numbers from 101.

Variations

June 1903–Sept. 1903: first model; sliding rising front with locking catches.

Sept. 1903–June 1904: Model B; rack and pinion rising front; improved baseboard locking catch; from serial number 5,101. *From Feb.1904:* "Kodak" engraved on support foot, from serial number 8,486.

June 1904–Nov. 1906: Model B-2; automatic preset focusing lock; non-reversible back with different size

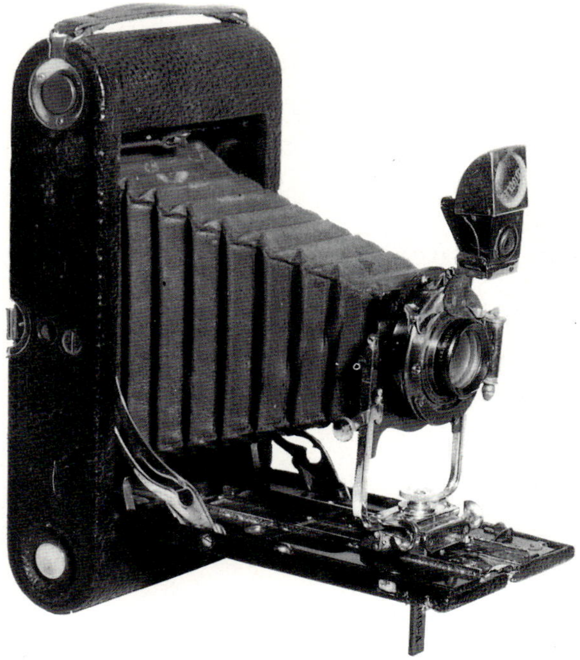

Model B–3, later version. KM

catches; from serial number 20,200. *From Jan. 1906:* tension springs fitted to back; from serial number 58,062.

Nov. 1906–June 1908: Model B-3; Improved bracket for finder; knob replacing lever locking of cross front; from serial number 80,350. *From Mar. 1907:* leather covered lens panels replaced by blackened nickel; new U-shaped square section lens standard with rounded ends; finder shape changed from cube to prism; levels discontinued; from serial number 85,353.

June 1908–Apr. 1909: Model B-4; focus locking device replaced by plate/film combination scale; from serial number 126,700.

Apr. 1909–Jan. 1912: Model B-5; back tension springs changed for film spool springs; from serial number 147,775.

Jan. 1912–1915: Model C; changed baseboard design; new finder with spirit level ; from serial number 266,801.

From Apr. 1910: cameras supplied to Kodak Limited had black rather than red bellows; *from Aug. 1912:* all cameras had black bellows, from around serial number 295,00 (**Note** red bellows on earlier models may have been replaced by black during servicing).

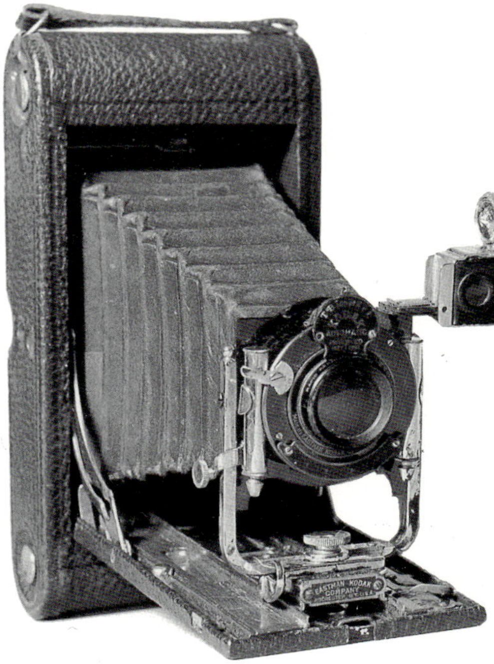

Model C. KM

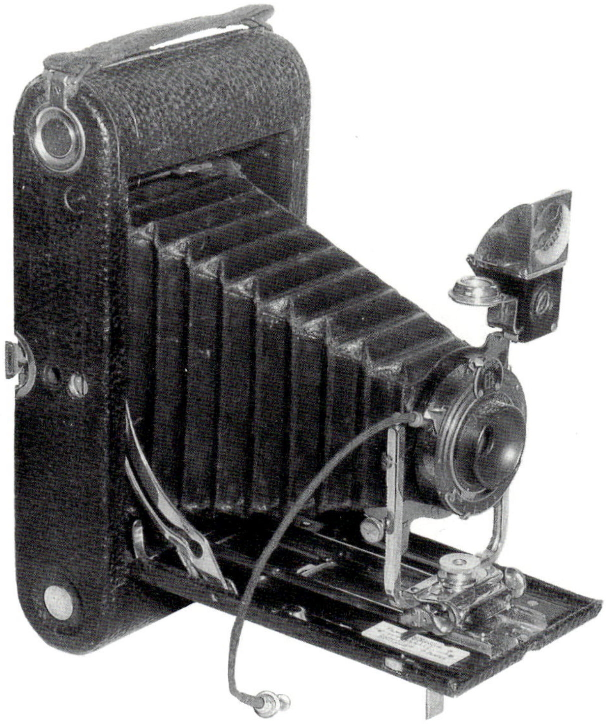

Model B-4. RPS

From Aug. 1914: models were fitted with Autographic backs, from serial number 368,668.

This camera became the 3A Autographic Kodak from September 1914.

Bausch & Lomb Plastigmat f/6.8: *May 1903–1904:* Bausch and Lomb Automatic shutter. *May 1903–1908:* Volute shutter. *Mar. 1905–1908:* Kodak Automatic shutter. *Apr.1908–1908:* Bausch & Lomb Automatic shutter. *May 1908–1908:*X.L. Sector or Volute shutter.
Goerz Anastigmat f/6.8: *May 1903–1905:* Volute shutter. *May 1903–1904:* Bausch & Lomb Automatic shutter. *Mar.1905–1905:*Kodak Automatic shutter.
Bausch & Lomb Zeiss Tessar f/6.3: *Apr. 1906–1909:* Volute shutter. *May 1908–1908:* X.L. Sector shutter. *Aug.1908–1912:* Bausch & Lomb Compound shutter.
Goerz Dagor f/6.8: *Apr. 1906–1908:* Kodak Automatic or Volute shutter. *May 1908–1908:* X.L. Sector or Bausch & Lomb Automatic shutter. *Aug.*

1908–1908: Bausch & Lomb Compound shutter.
Cooke Anastigmat f/6.5: *Mar. 1907–1908:* Volute shutter.*May 1908–1908:* X.L. Sector shutter. *May 1908–1910:* Volute shutter. *May 1908–1911:* Bausch & Lomb Automatic shutter. *May 1908–1912:* Kodak Automatic shutter. *Apr.1909–1912:* Bausch & Lomb Compound shutter.
Isostigmar f/6.3: *May 1908–1908:* Bausch & Lomb Automatic or Volute shutter.
Zeiss Kodak Anastigmat f/6.3: *Apr. 1909–1912:* Bausch & Lomb Compound shutter. *Apr. 1909–1909:* Volute shutter.
Kodak Anastigmat f/8: *Sept. 1914–1915:* Kodak Automatic or Ball Bearing shutter. This combination of lens and shutters was available as an exchange conversion for owners of Rapid Rectilinear models.

UK VARIATIONS
Ross Homocentric f/8: *1907–1910:* Kodak or Bausch & Lomb Automatic shutter. *1907–1908:* Unicum shutter.*1908–1910:* Goerz Sector, Koilos or Compound shutter.
Ross Homocentric f/6.8: *1910:* Kodak or Bausch & Lomb Automatic, Koilos, Compound or Goerz Sector shutter.
Ross Homocentric f/6.3: *1907–1910:* Kodak or Bausch & Lomb Automatic shutter. *1907–1908:* Unicum shutter.*1910:* Koilos, Compound or Goerz Sector shutter.
Ross Homocentric f/5.6: *1908–1910:* Goerz Sector, Koilosor Compound shutter. *1910:* Kodak or Bausch & Lomb Automatic shutter.
Aldis No 2A Series II f/6: *1907–1910:* Kodak or Bausch & Lomb Automatic shutter. *1907–1908:* Unicum shutter.*1908–1910:* Goerz Sector, Koilos or Compound shutter.
Aldis Oxys f/6.9: *1908–1912:* Kodak or Bausch & Lomb Automatic, Goerz Sector, Koilos or Compound shutter. *1908–1910:*Unicum shutter.
Zeiss Tessar series IIb f/6.3: *1908–1910:* Kodak or Bausch & Lomb Automatic or Goerz Sector shutter. *1908:* Unicum shutter. *1908–1912:* Koilos or Compound shutter. *1912:* Ibso shutter.
Zeiss Protar Series IIIa f/9: *1908:* Kodak or Bausch & Lomb Automatic, Goerz Sector, Koilos, Unicum or Compound shutter.
Zeiss Double Protar Series IV f/6.3: *1910:* Kodak or Bausch & Lomb Automatic, Goerz Sector, Koilos or Compound shutter.
Zeiss Double Amatar f/6.8: *1912:* Kodak or Bausch & Lomb Automatic, Ibso or Compound shutter.
Zeiss-Kodak Anastigmat f/6.3: *1914–1915:* Koilos shutter. *1914:* Ibso shutter.
Cooke Series III f/6.5: *1908–1912:* Kodak Automatic, Koilos or Compound shutter. *1908–1910:* Bausch & Lomb Automatic shutter. *1908:* Unicum shutter. *1912:* Ibso shutter.
Cooke Series IV f5.6: *1910–1912:* Koilos or Compound shutter. *1910:* Goerz Sector shutter. *1910:* Kodak Automatic or Ibso shutter.
Cooke Series V f/8: *1910:* Kodak Automatic, Koilos, Compound or Goerz Sector shutter.
Goerz Dagor Series III f/6.8: *1908–1910:* Bausch & Lomb Automatic, Koilos or Compound shutter. *1908:* Unicum shutter.
Goerz Syntor f/6.8: *1910:* Kodak or Bausch & Lomb Automatic, Goerz Sector, Koilos or Compound shutter.
Goerz Celor f/4.8: *1910:* Kodak or Bausch & Lomb Automatic, Goerz Sector, Koilos or Compound shutter.
TT&H-Kodak Anastigmat f/6.8: *1914–1915:* Compoundshutter. *1914:* Kodak Automatic or Koilos shutter.
Dallmeyer Stigmatic f/6: *1908–1912:* Kodak or Bausch & Lomb Automatic, Goerz Sector, Koilos or Compound shutter. *1908–1910:* Unicum shutter.
Beck Isostigmar Series II, f/6.3 or Series III, f/7.7:*1908–1910:* Kodak Automatic, Goerz Sector, Koilos or Compound shutter. *1908:* Unicum or Celverex shutter.
Euryplan Series II f/5.6 or Euryplan Nulli Secundus f/6.8: *1908–1910:* Kodak or Bausch & Lomb Automatic, Goerz Sector, Koilos or Compound shutter. *1908:* Unicum shutter.

No 4 Folding Pocket Kodak

Type Folding rollfilm
Introduced February 1907
Discontinued April 1915
Film size 123
Picture size 4 × 5in.
Manufactured US
Lens Rapid Rectilinear – but see below
Shutters February 1907–1908: F.P.K Automatic
February 1907–1914: Kodak Automatic

April 1909–April 1915: Ball Bearing
Numbers made 28,000

Description/Remarks

Large format vertically folding camera, which would just about fit into a coat pocket. Similar to the contemporary No 3A Folding Pocket Kodak camera. Serial numbers from 1-C.

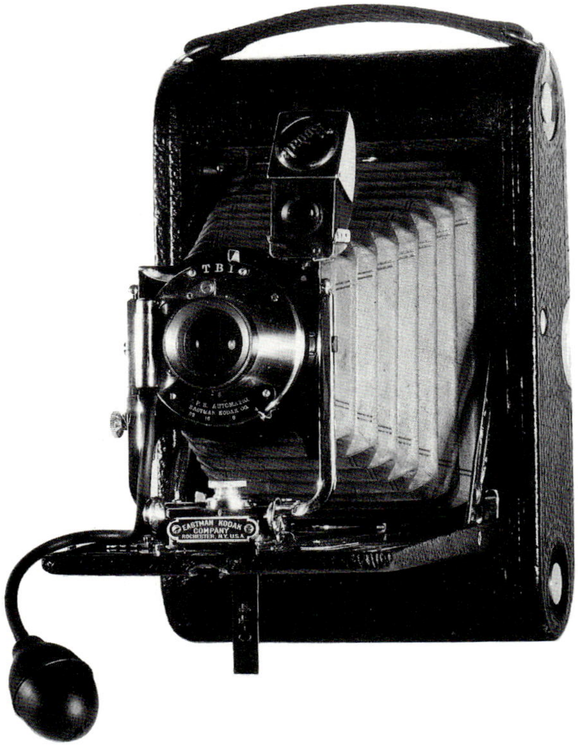

Model A. KP

Variations

From Jan. 1910: automatic focusing lock replaced by a plate/film combination scale, from serial number 16,280.

From Sept. 1911: cameras shipped to Kodak Limited had black instead of red bellows. *From June 1913:* all cameras fitted with black bellows, from serial number 13,907 (**Note:** some early examples may have had red bellows replaced by black during servicing).

A small number of the last production batch, from December 1914, serial number 26,046, were fitted with Autographic backs.

Bausch & Lomb Zeiss Tessar f/6.3: *Feb. 1907–1909:* Volute shutter. *May 1908–1908:* X.L. Sector shutter. *Aug.1908–1912:* Bausch & Lomb Compound shutter.
Bausch & Lomb Plastigmat f/6.8: *Feb.1907–1909:* Kodak Automatic shutter. *Mar. 1907–1908:* Volute shutter. *May 1908–1908:* X.L. Sector shutter.
Cooke Anastigmat f/6.5: *Mar. 1907–1909:* Volute shutter. *May 1908–1908:* X.L. Sector shutter. *Apr. 1909–1912:* Kodak or Bausch & Lomb Compound shutter.
Goerz Dagor f/6.8: *May 1908–1908:* Volute or X.L. Sector shutter. *Aug. 1908–1908:* Bausch & Lomb Compound shutter.
Beck Isostigmar f/6.3: *May 1908–1908:* Volute shutter.
Zeiss Kodak Anastigmat f/6.3: *Apr. 1909–Apr. 1915:*Bausch & Lomb Compound shutter. *Apr. 1909–1909:* Volute shutter.

UK VARIATIONS
Zeiss Tessar Series IIb f/6.3: *1908–1912:* Bausch & Lomb Automatic, Koilos, Compound shutter. *1908-1910:* Kodak Automatic or Goerz Sector shutter. *1908:* Unicum shutter.*1912:* Ibso shutter.
Zeiss Protar Series IIIa f/9: *1908:* Kodak or Bausch & Lomb Automatic, Unicum, Goerz Sector, Koilos or Compound shutter.
Zeiss Double Protar Series IV f/6.3: *1910:* Kodak or Bausch & Lomb Automatic, Goerz Sector, Koilos or Compound shutter.
Zeiss Double Amatar f/6.8: *1912:* Kodak or Bausch & Lomb Automatic, Koilos, Compound or Ibso shutters.
Zeiss-Kodak Anastigmat f/6.3: *1914–1915:* Compound shutter.
TT&H-Kodak Anastigmat f/6.8: *1914-1915:*Compound shutter.
Cooke Series III f/6.5: *1908–1912:* Kodak Automatic, Koilos or Compound. *1908–1910:* Bausch & Lomb Automatic or Goerz Sector shutter. *1908:* Unicum shutter.
Cooke Series IV f/5.6: *1912:* Kodak Automatic shutter. *1910–1912:* Koilos or Compound shutter. *1910:* Goerz Sector shutter.
Cooke Series V f/8: *1908:* Kodak or Bausch & Lomb Automatic, Goerz Sector, Koilos or Compound shutter.
Goerz Dagor Series III f/6.8: *1908–1910:* Kodak

or Bausch & Lomb Automatic, Goerz Sector, Koilos or Compound shutter. *1908:*Unicum shutter.
Goerz Syntor f/6.8: *1910:* Kodak or Bausch & Lomb Automatic or Goerz Sector shutter.
Goerz Celor f/4.8: *1910:* Kodak or Bausch & Lomb Automatic, Koilos or Compound shutter.
Ross Homocentric f/6.3 or f/8: *1908–1910:* Kodak or Bausch & Lomb Automatic, Goerz Sector, Koilos or Compound shutter.*1908:* Unicum shutter.
Ross Homocentric f/5.6: *1908–1910:* Goerz Sector, Koilosor Compound shutter. *1910:* Kodak or Bausch & Lomb Automatic shutter.
Ross Homocentric f/6.8: *1910:* Kodak or Bausch & Lomb Automatic, Goerz Sector, Koilos or Compound shutter.
Aldis Series II f/6.3 or Oxys f/6.9: *1908–1910:* Kodak or Bausch & Lomb Automatic, Goerz Sector, Koilos or Compound shutter.*1908:* Unicum shutter.
Dallmeyer Stigmatic Series II f/6: *1908–1910:* Kodak or Bausch & Lomb Automatic, Goerz Sector, Koilos or Compound shutter.
Euryplan Series II f/5.6 or Nulli Secundus f/6.5: *1908–1910:* Kodak or Bausch & Lomb Automatic, Goerz Sector, Koilos or Compound shutter. *1908:* Unicum shutter.
Beck Isostigmar f/6.3 or f/7.7: *1908:* Kodak or Bausch & Lomb Automatic, Goerz Sector, Unicum, Koilos or Compound shutter.
Beck Series I f/4.5: *1910:* Kodak or Bausch & Lomb Automatic shutter.
Beck Series II f/6.3: *1910:* Kodak or Bausch & Lomb Automatic, Goerz Sector, Koilos or Compound shutter.
Beck Series III f/7.7: *1910:* Kodak or Bausch & Lomb Automatic or Goerz Sector shutter.

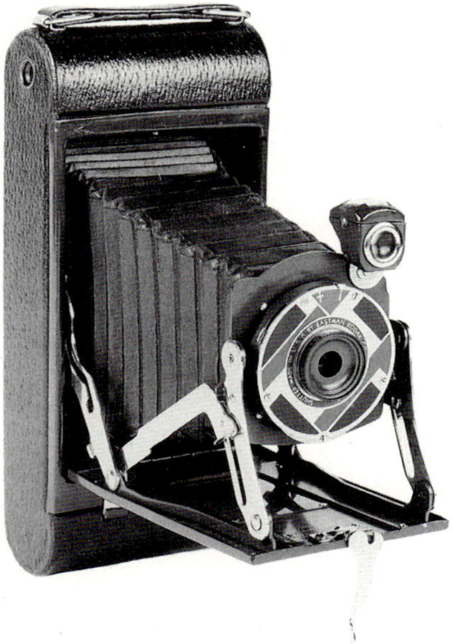

Photo: Michael Pritchard

No 1A Gift Kodak

Type Self-erecting folding rollfilm
Introduced October 1930
Discontinued November 1931
Film size 116
Picture size 2¼ × 4¼in.
Manufactured US
Lens Achromatic
Shutter Kodo
Numbers made 10,000

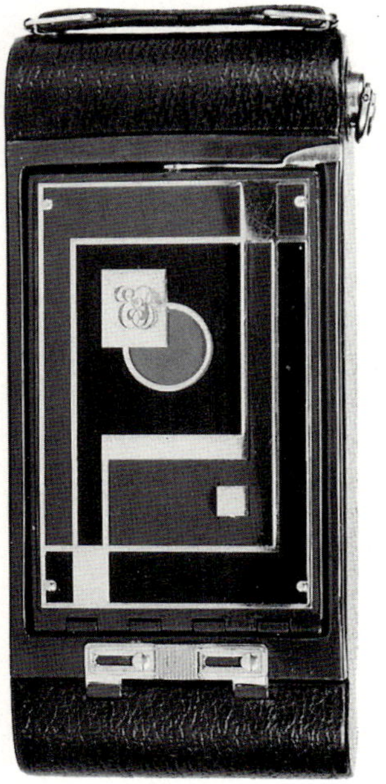

Photo: Michael Pritchard

Description/Remarks

A special version of the No 1A Pocket Kodak Junior

camera, covered in brown leather and with Art Deco motifs on baseplate and shutter plate. Supplied in a cedar-wood box with matching design.

Girl Guide Kodak

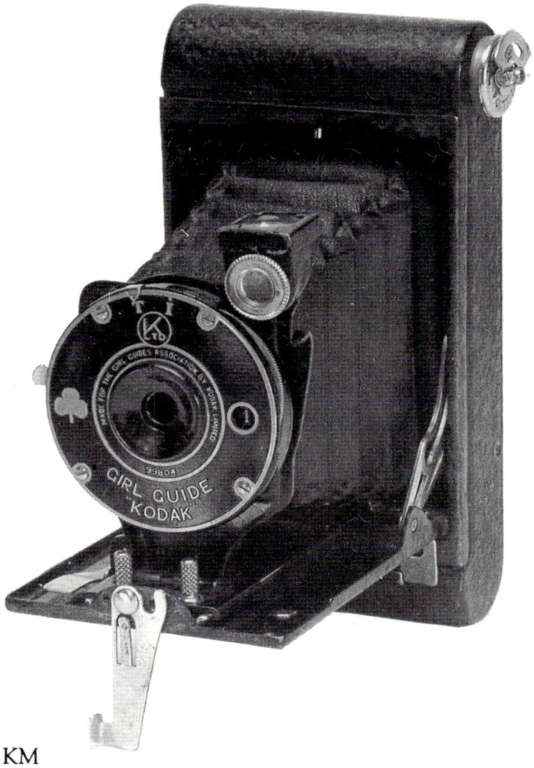

KM

Type Folding rollfilm
Introduced January 1931
Discontinued 1935
Film size 127
Picture size $1\frac{5}{8} \times 2\frac{1}{2}$in.
Manufactured UK
Lens Meniscus
Shutter Vest Pocket Rotary
Numbers made ?

Description/Remarks

A special version of the Vest Pocket Kodak Model B camera for the Scouting movement in Great Britain. Dark blue crackle enamelled body, with Girl Guide emblem on baseboard. Supplied with matching case.

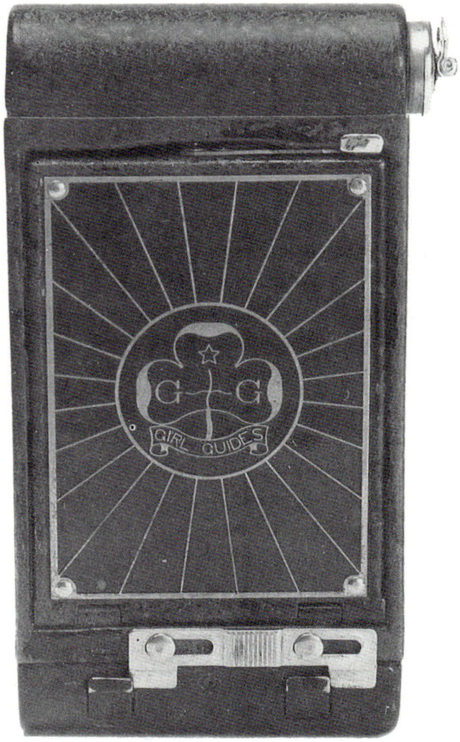

Baseboard motif. KM

Girl Scout Kodak

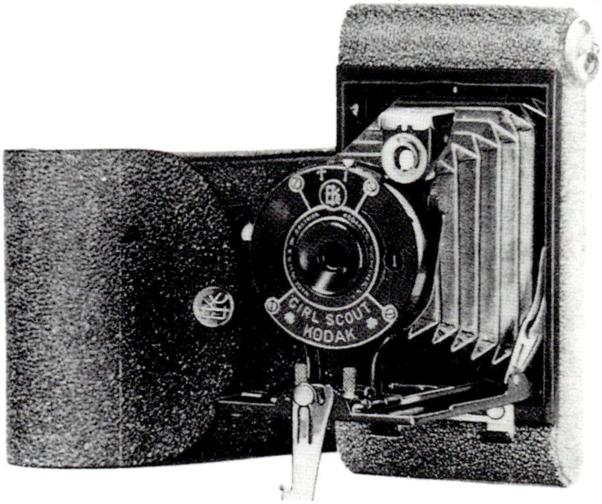

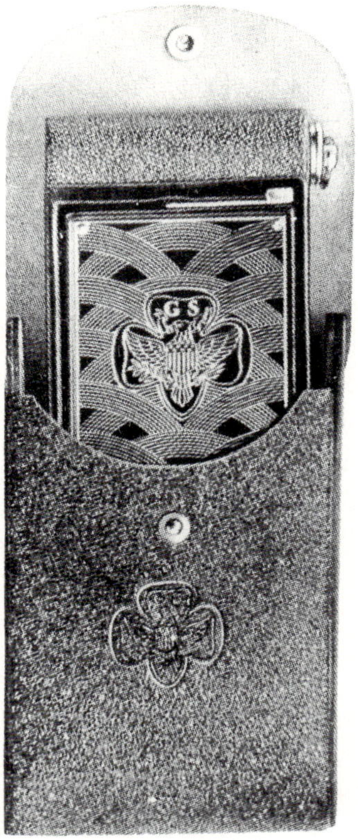

With matching case.

Type Folding rollfilm
Introduced December 1929
Discontinued January 1934
Film size 127
Picture size 1⅝ × 2½in.
Manufactured US
Lens Meniscus
Shutter Vest Pocket Rotary
Numbers made ?

Description/Remarks

A special version of the Vest Pocket Kodak Model B camera for the Scouting movement in America. Covered in green leatherette, with green enamelled Girl Scout emblem on baseboard. Supplied with matching case.

No.2 Hawkette

Type Collapsing rollfilm
Introduced 1930
Discontinued 1930
Film size 120
Picture size 2¼ × 3¼in.
Manufactured UK
Lens Meniscus
Shutter Rotary
Numbers made ?

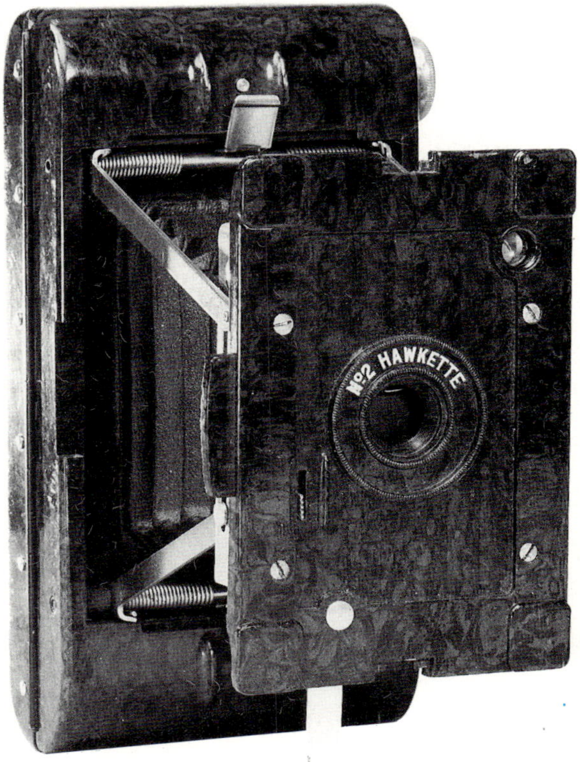

KM

Description/Remarks

The first Kodak plastic body camera. Constructed from brown Bakelite mouldings fabricated by E.K. Cole Ltd., and assembled, using some parts imported from Rochester, at Kodak Limited's Harrow factory. This model was made for premium sales only, and its production may have been inspired by the appearance of the rival APEM Rajar No.6 camera in 1928, also made from Bakelite, and with a similar construction.

Jiffy Kodak Six-16

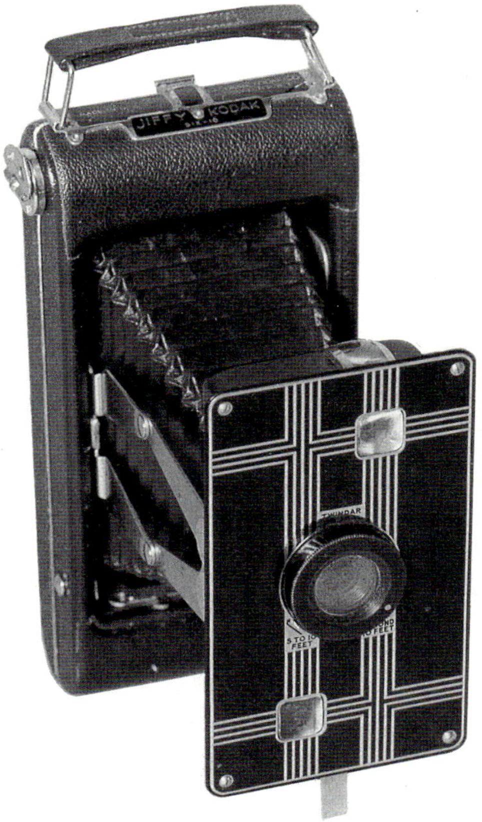

KM

Type Collapsing rollfilm
Introduced April 1933
Discontinued July 1937
Film size 616
Picture size 2½ × 4¼in.
Manufactured US
Lens Twindar periscopic
Shutter Built-in
Numbers made ?

Description/Remarks

Spring actuated extension. Two-position focusing lens. Two brilliant finders. Etched metal front with Art Deco design.

Jiffy Kodak Six-16, Series II

Type Collapsing folding rollfilm
Introduced July 1937
Discontinued October 1942
Film size 616
Picture size 2½ × 4¼in.
Manufactured US
Lens 'Twindar periscopic
Shutter Built-in
Numbers made ?

Description/Remarks

Similar to Jiffy Kodak Six-16 camera, but with morocco grain imitation leather covering to front panel.

Jiffy Kodak Six-20

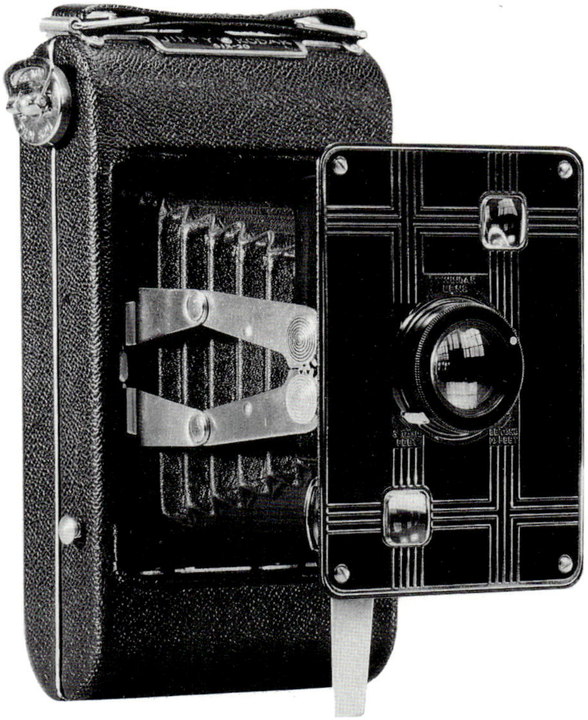

KP

Type Collapsing rollfilm
Introduced April 1933
Discontinued July 1937

Film size 620
Picture size 2¼ × 3¼in.
Manufactured US
Lens Twindar periscopic
Shutter Built-in
Numbers made ?

Description/Remarks

Spring actuated extension; 2-position focusing lens. Front panel in etched metal with Art Deco design.

Jiffy Kodak Six-20 Series II

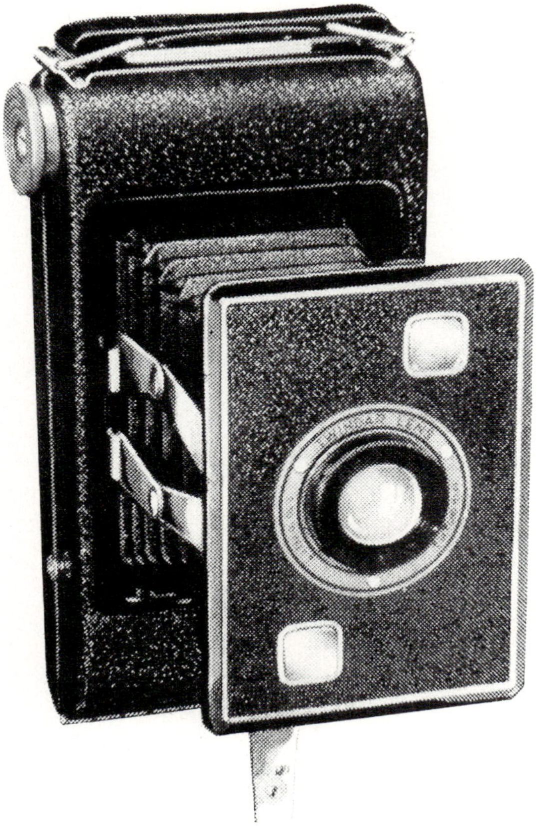

Type Collapsing rollfilm
Introduced July 1937
Discontinued June 1948
Film size 620
Picture size 2¼ × 3¼in.
Manufactured US
Lens Twindar periscopic
Shutter Built-in
Numbers made ?

Description/Remarks

Similar to Jiffy Six-20 Kodak camera, but with front covered in morocco grain imitation leather.

Jiffy Kodak V.P.

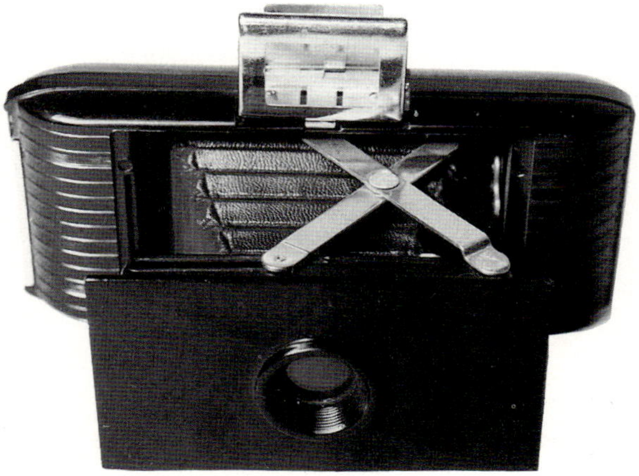

KM

Type Collapsing rollfilm
Introduced April 1935
Discontinued October 1942
Film size 127
Picture size 1⅝ × 2½in.
Manufactured US
Lens Doublet, fixed focus
Shutter Jiffy V.P.
Numbers made ?

Description/Remarks

Moulded Bakelite plastic body and lens panel; folding frame finder. Similar to the Kodak Bantam camera, f/6.3 model.

Kodak Bantam

Type Collapsing self-erecting rollfilm
Introduced June 1935
Discontinued June 1948

Film size 828
Picture size 28 × 40mm
Manufactured US
Lens Various – see below
Shutter Built-in
Numbers made ?

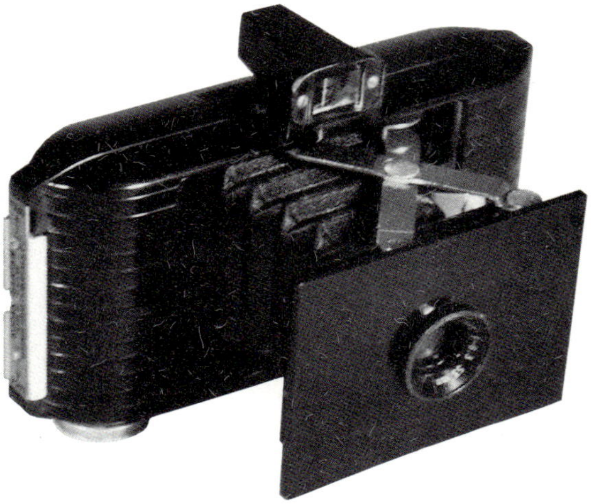

F/6.3 model, 1935–1937. PDM

Description/Remarks

A range of miniature rollfilm cameras which introduced the 828 rollfilm size. Most had moulded plastic bodies; some had plastic lens panels.

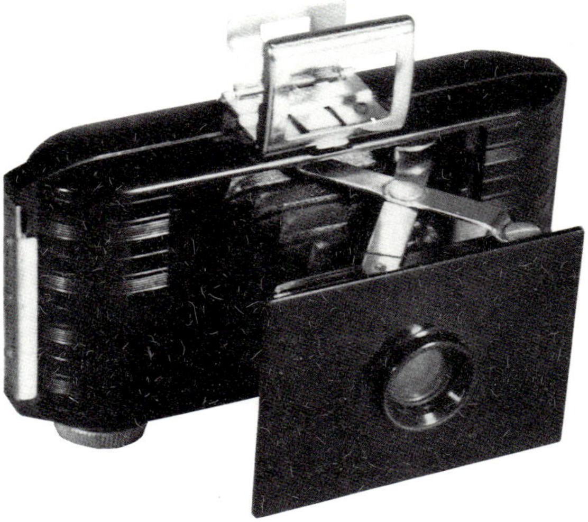

Doublet model, 1935–1938. PDM

Variations

June 1935–1937: Kodak Anastigmat f/6.3; rigid direct vision finder.

June 1935–July 1938: Doublet f/12.5; metal folding frame finder. (Replacement folding optical frame finders were available from February 1938.)

Feb. 1938–Jan. 1947: Kodak Anastigmat f/6.3; folding optical frame finder.

The above had plastic bodies and lens panels.

July 1938–May 1941: Kodak Anastigmat f/5.6; folding optical frame finder; plastic body, metal lens panel.

July 1938–June 1948: Kodak Anastigmat Special f/4.5; folding optical frame finder; metal lens panel and body with angled ends; lens coated from July 1946.

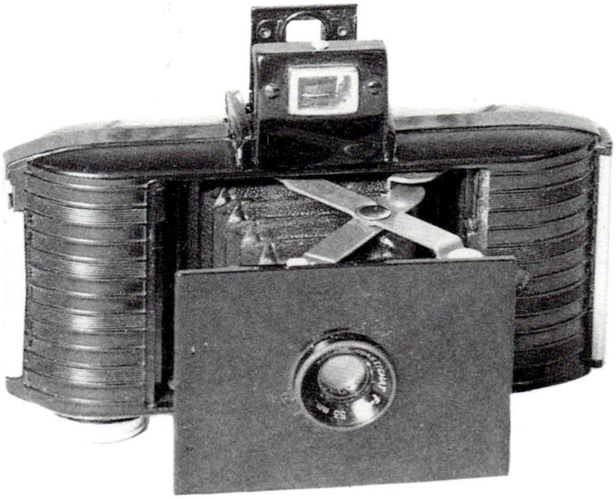

F/6.3 model, 1938–1947. KM

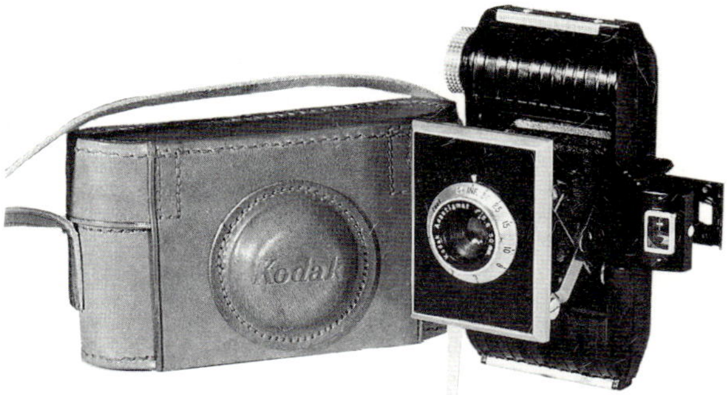

F/5.6 model, 1938–1941. KP

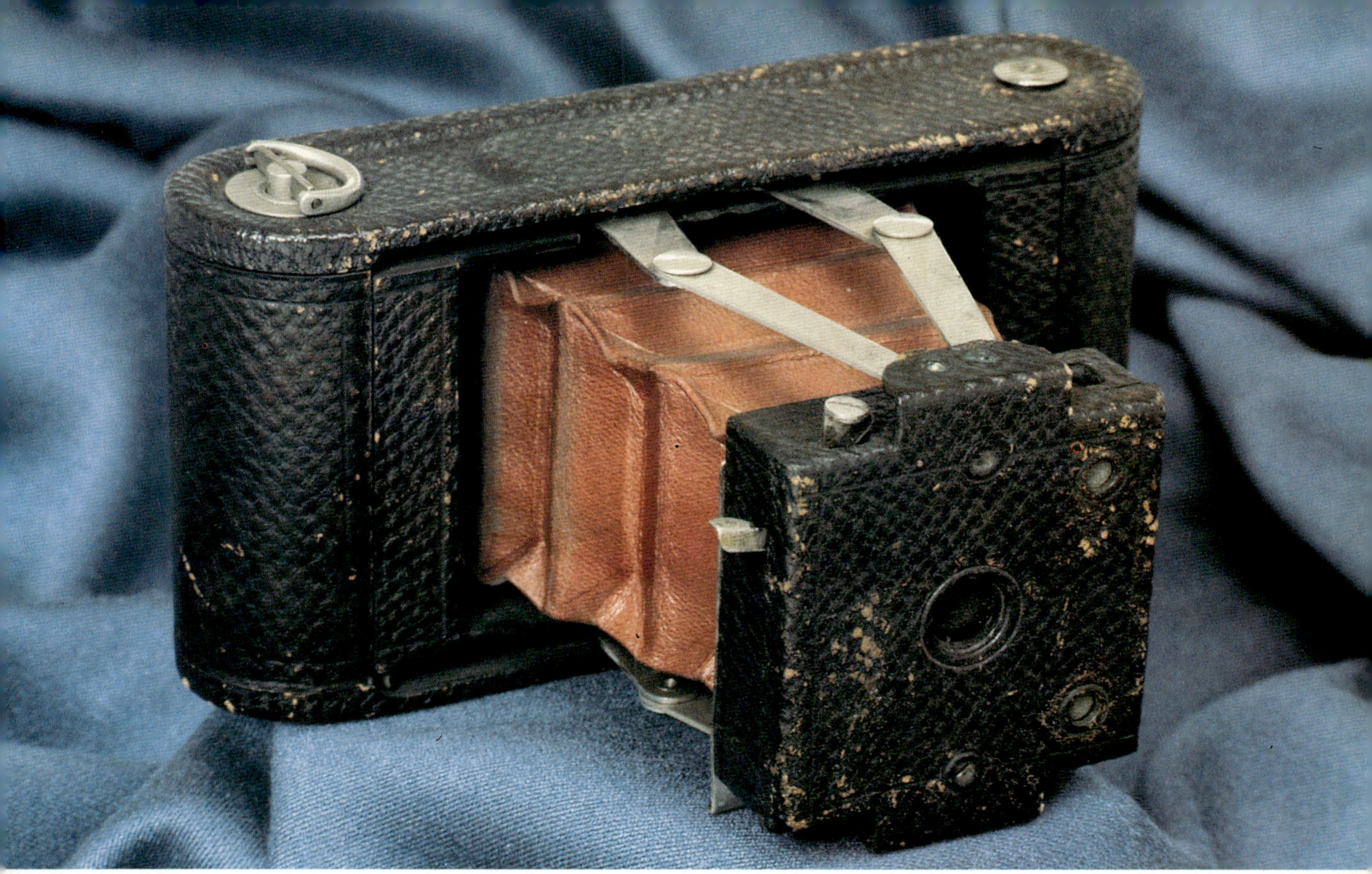

Above: No.1 Folding Pocket Kodak camera (see page 97). KM   Below: No.2 Brownie camera model F, coloured versions marketed in the UK 1929-1933 (see page 36). KM

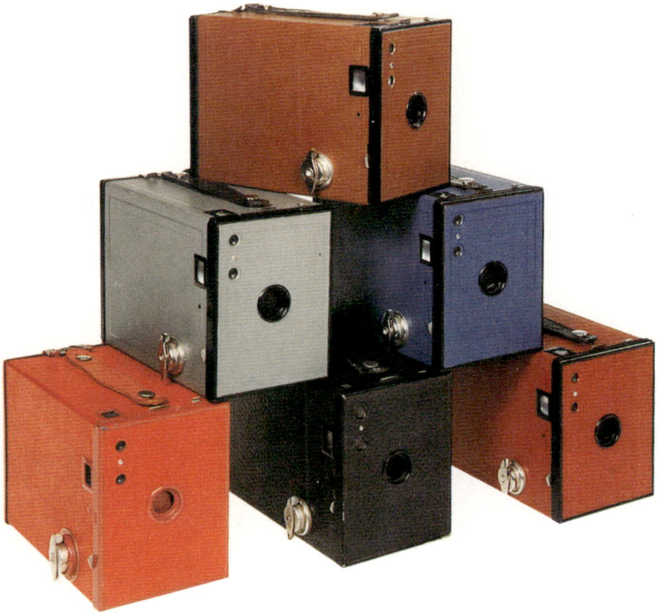

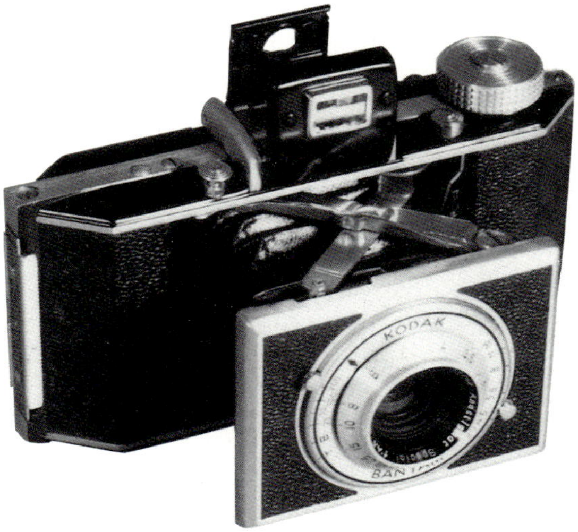

F/4.5 model, 1938-1948. PDM

Kodak Bantam Special

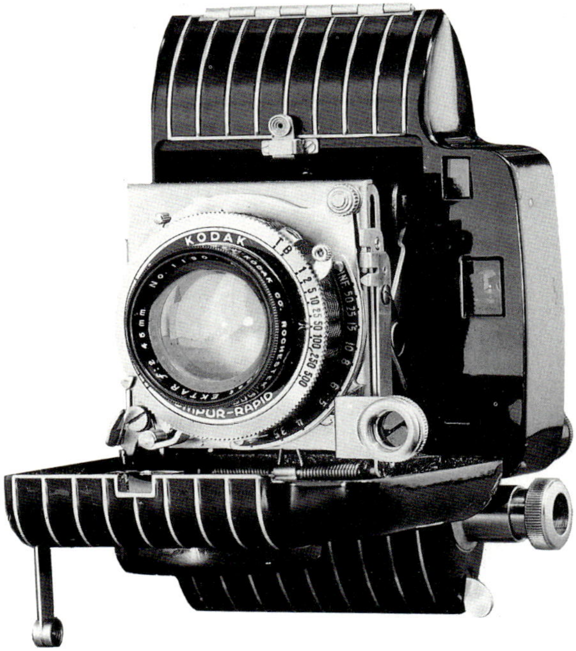

KP

Type Self-erecting folding rollfilm
Introduced July 1936
Discontinued June 1948
Film size 828
Picture size 28 × 40mm
Manufactured US
Lenses 1936–1940: Kodak Anastigmat Ektar f/2.0
1941–1948: Kodak Ektar f/2.0
Shutters Compur Rapid (Anastigmat Ektar)
Supermatic (Ektar)
Numbers made ?

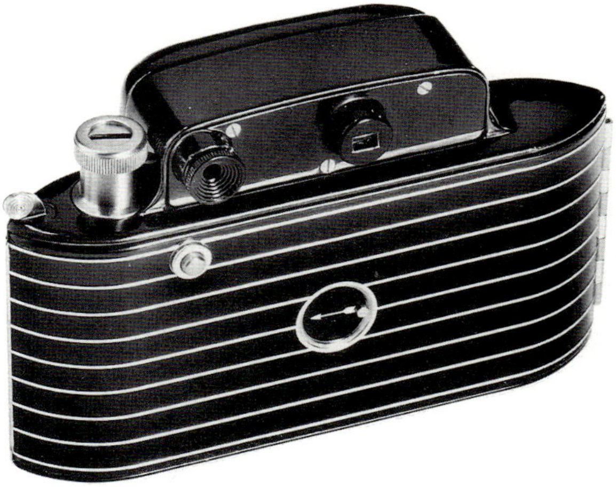

KP

Description/Remarks

Another striking design by Walter Dorwin Teague. Black enamelled body with bright metal lines. Coupled rangefinder with helical focusing; direct vision optical finder; sideways opening baseboard.

Kodak Coquette

Type Folding rollfilm
Introduced October 1930
Discontinued January 1932
Film size 127
Picture size 1⅝ × 2½in.
Manufactured US
Lens Meniscus
Shutter Vest Pocket Rotary
Numbers made ?

Description/Remarks

Blue Kodak Petite camera in case with matching

powder compact and lipstick holder with Art Deco designs. The cosmetics were supplied by Coty.

Kodak Duo Six-20

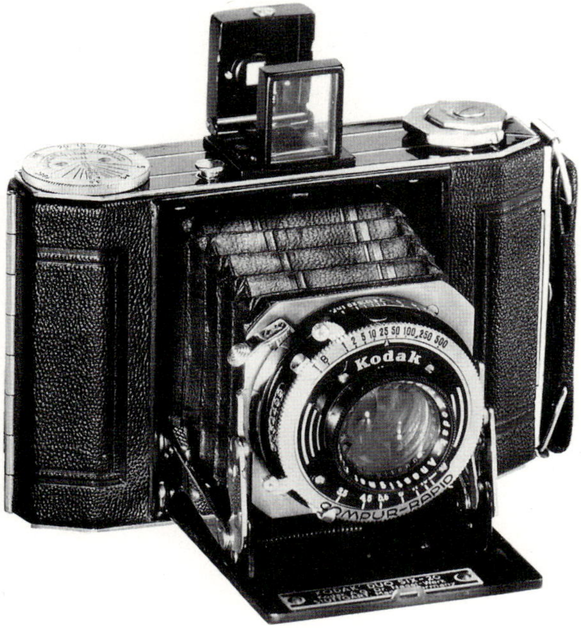

First model, 1933–1937. KP

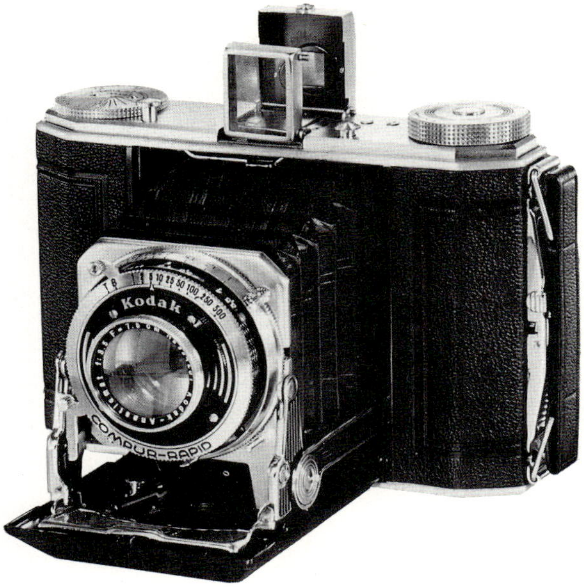

Second model, 1937–1939. KP

Type Self-erecting folding rollfilm
Introduced 1933
Discontinued 1939
Film size 620
Picture size 2¼ × 3¼in.
Manufactured Germany
Lens Kodak Anastigmat f/3.5 or f/4.5 – but see below
Shutter Pronto S, Compur or Compur Rapid – see below
Numbers made 81,000 approximately

Description/Remarks

Precision-made folding rollfilm camera; folding optical frame finder. Models with f/3.5 lenses had helical focusing mounts, those with f/4.5 lenses had front-cell focusing.

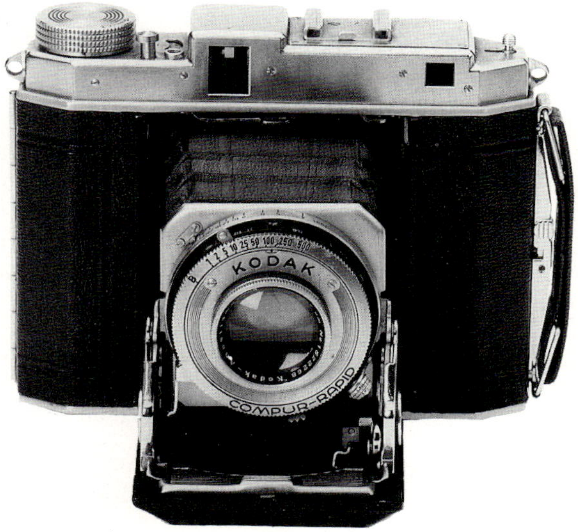

1939 model. KAG

Variations

First model with lined enamelled top plate, key wind-on.
From 1937: fitted with body release, chromed top plate; changed baseboard struts with lined pattern; wind-on knob; baseboard release bar at front; accessory shoe.
From Sept. 1939: fitted with combined viewfinder/rangefinder,and with shutter and wind-on interlocked.

Kodak Anastigmat f/4.5: *1933–1934:* Pronto S shutter. *1933–1939:* Compur shutter. *1935–1936:* Kodak S shutter. *1935–1939:* Compur Rapid shutter.
Kodak Anastigmat f/3.5: *1933–1939:* Compur shutter. *1935–1939:* Compur Rapid shutter.
Schneider Xenar f/3.5 or f/4.5: *1933–1939:* Compur shutter. *1935–1939:* Compur Rapid shutter.
Zeiss Tessar f/3.5: *1933–1939:* Compur shutter. *1935–1939:* Compur Rapid shutter.
Zeiss Tessar f/4.5: *1934:* Compur shutter.

Kodak Ensemble

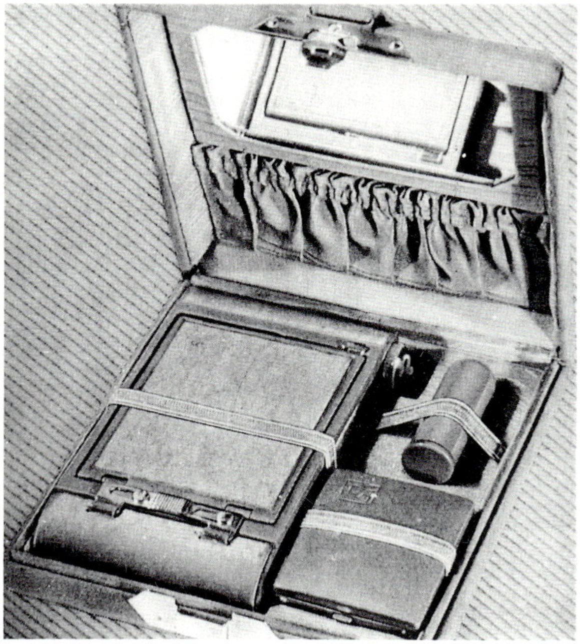

Type Folding rollfilm
Introduced October 1929
Discontinued 1933
Film size 127
Picture size 1⅝ × 2½in.
Manufactured US
Lens Meniscus
Shutter Vest Pocket Rotary
Numbers made ?

Description/Remarks

Kodak Petite camera in range of colours – beige, rose and green – in suede case with matching powder compact, lipstick and mirror. Cosmetics supplied by The House of Tre Jur.

Kodak Flash Bantam

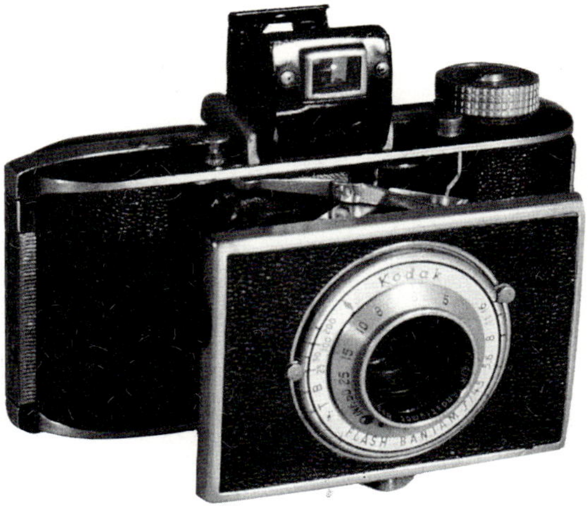

PDM

Type Self-erecting collapsing rollfilm
Introduced July 1947
Discontinued October 1953
Film size 828
Picture size 28 × 40mm
Manufactured US
Lenses 1947–1948: Kodak Anastigmat Special f/4.5
1948–1953: Kodak Anastar f/4.5
Shutter Built-in, flash synchronised
Numbers made ?

Description/Remarks

Developed from f/4.5 model Bantam camera, but with rounded rather than angled body; folding optical frame finder; body release.

No 1 Kodak Junior

Type Folding rollfilm
Introduced April 1914
Discontinued December 1914
Film size 120
Picture size 2¼ × 3¼in.

Manufactured US
Lens Meniscus achromatic or Rapid Rectilinear
Shutter Kodak Ball Bearing
Numbers made 33,000

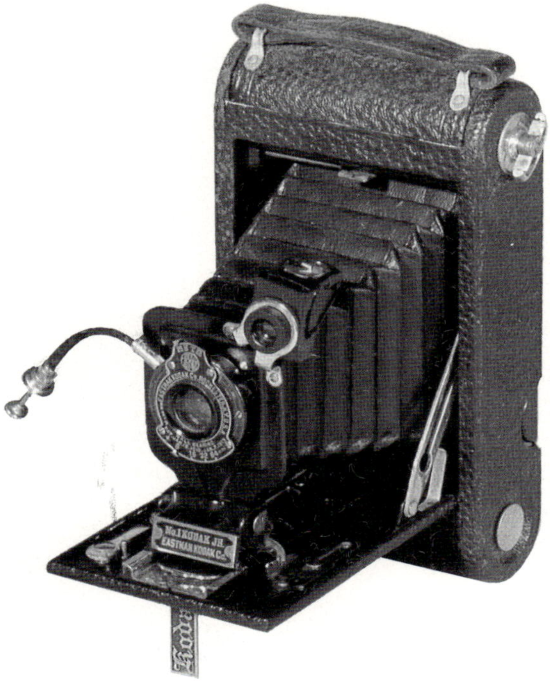

KM

Description/Remarks

J-shaped back with below-centre catches; serial numbers from 1,001. It became the No 1 Autographic Kodak Junior camera after December 1914, from serial number 33,901.

No 1A Kodak Junior

Type Folding rollfilm
Introduced April 1914
Discontinued December 1914
Film size 116
Picture size 2½ × 4¼in.
Manufactured US
Lens Meniscus achromatic or Rapid Rectilinear
Shutter Kodak Ball Bearing
Numbers made 48,000

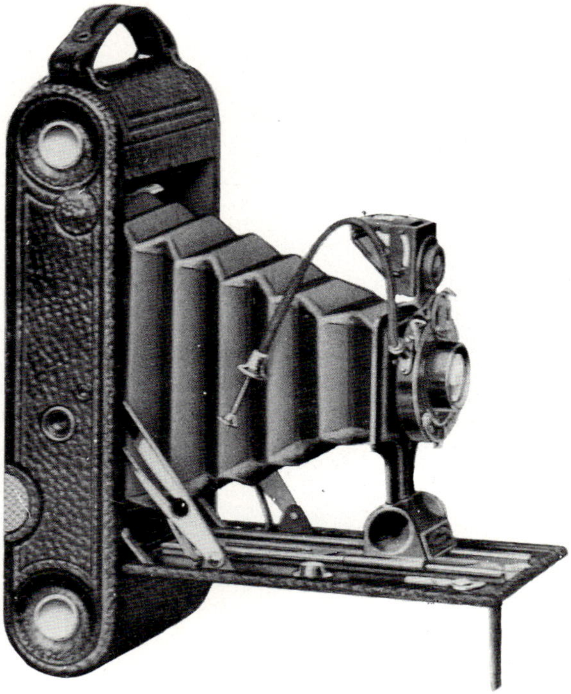

Description/Remarks

J-shaped back with below-centre catches. From serial number 1,001. It became the No 1A Autographic Kodak Junior from December 1914, from serial number 49,101.

Kodak Junior 0

Type Self-erecting folding rollfilm
Introduced 1939
Discontinued 1939
Film size 620
Picture size 2¼ × 3¼in.
Manufactured Germany
Lens Kodak Triskop f/11
Shutter Kodak Special
Numbers made 27,198

Description/Remarks

Front cell focusing; folding frame and brilliant finders.

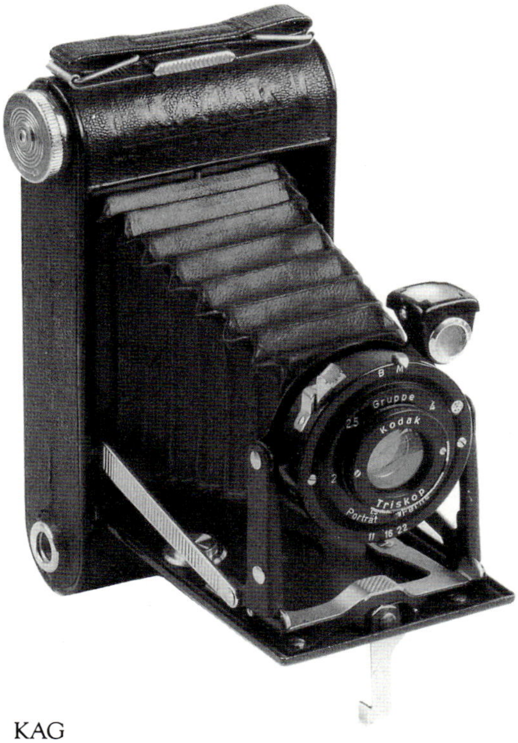

KAG

Type Self-erecting folding camera
Introduced June 1954
Discontinued 1959
Film size 620
Picture size 2¼ × 3¼in.
Manufactured UK
Lens Meniscus, fixed focus
Shutter Kodette III
Numbers made ?

Description/Remarks

Moulded plastic top incorporating direct vision optical finder.

Variations

From 1957: lens panel side supports chromed rather than black.

Kodak Junior I

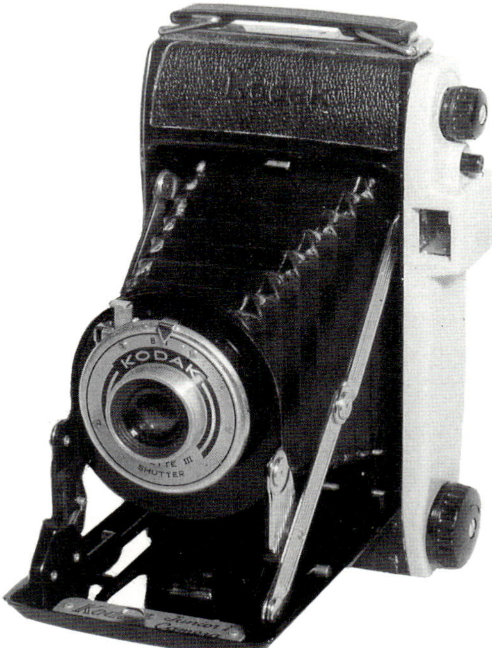

RPS

Kodak Junior II

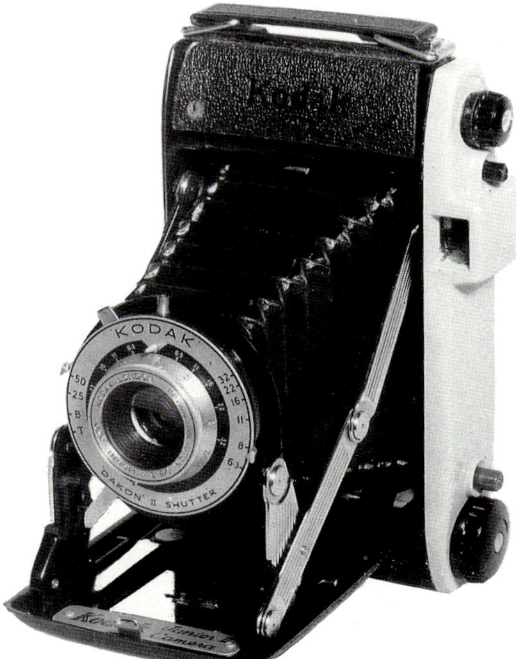

RPS

Type Self-erecting folding rollfilm
Introduced June 1954
Discontinued 1959
Film size 620
Picture size 2¼ × 3¼in.
Manufactured UK
Lens Kodak Anaston f/6.3
Shutter Dakon II
Numbers made ?

Description/Remarks

Similar to Kodak Junior I camera, but with better lens; flash synchronised shutter.

Variations

From 1957: lens panel side supports chromed rather than black.

Kodak Junior Six-16 (US model)

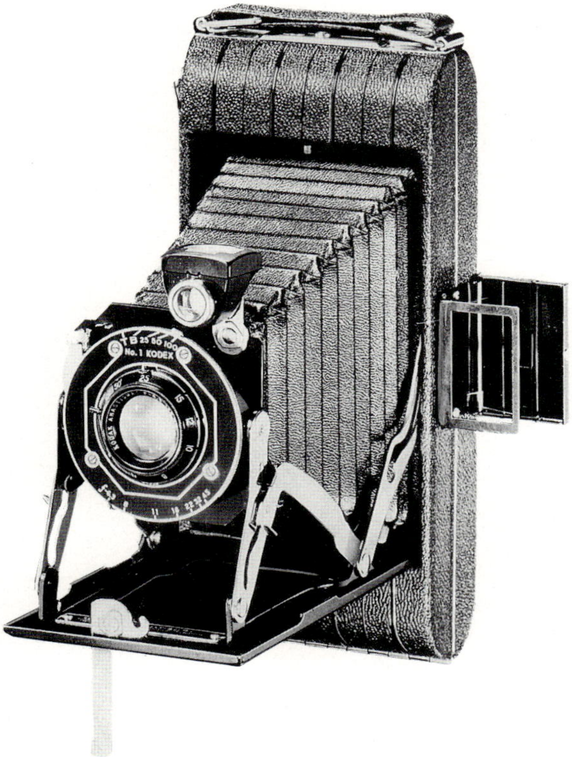

KP

Type Self-erecting folding rollfilm
Introduced February 1935
Discontinued April 1937
Film size 616
Picture size 2½ × 4¼in.
Manufactured US, UK, Germany
Lenses Doublet or Kodak Anastigmat f/6.3
Shutters Kodon (with Doublet) or Kodex (with Anastigmat).
Numbers made ?

Description/Remarks

Reflecting and folding frame finders; banded finish to leatherette covering.

For UK version (*1934–1940*) see Six-16 Kodak Junior camera.

For German version (*1934–1939*) see Kodak Junior 616 camera.

Kodak Junior Six-16 Series II

Type Self-erecting folding rollfilm
Introduced May 1937
Discontinued June 1940
Film size 616
Picture size 2½ × 4¼in.
Manufactured US
Lens Bimat, 3-position focusing – but see below
Shutter Kodon – but see below
Numbers made ?

Description/Remarks

Baseboard release bar at front, smooth finish leatherette covering.

Variations

May 1937–June 1940: Fixed focus single lens, Kodal shutter.

May 1937–July 1938: Kodak Anastigmat f/6.3 lens, Kodex shutter.

Kodak Junior Six-16 Series III

Type Self-erecting folding rollfilm

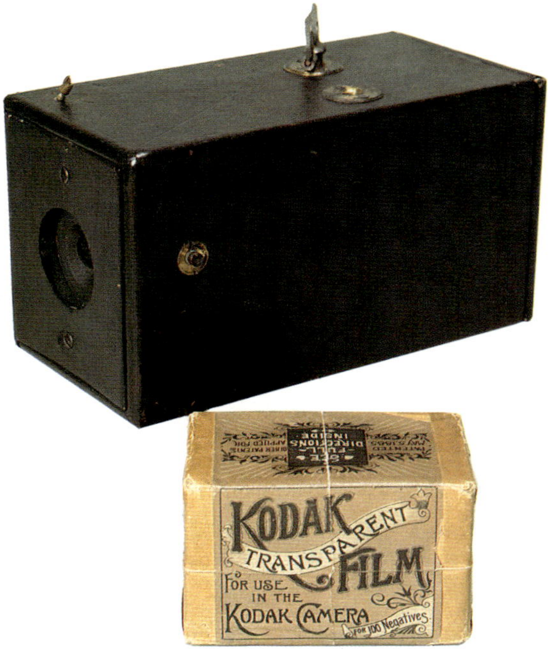

Above: The Kodak camera, 1888, with a carton of the celluloid film developed for it in 1889 (see page 11). KM Below: Girl Guide and Boy Scout Kodak cameras – UK models (see pages 85 & 114). KM

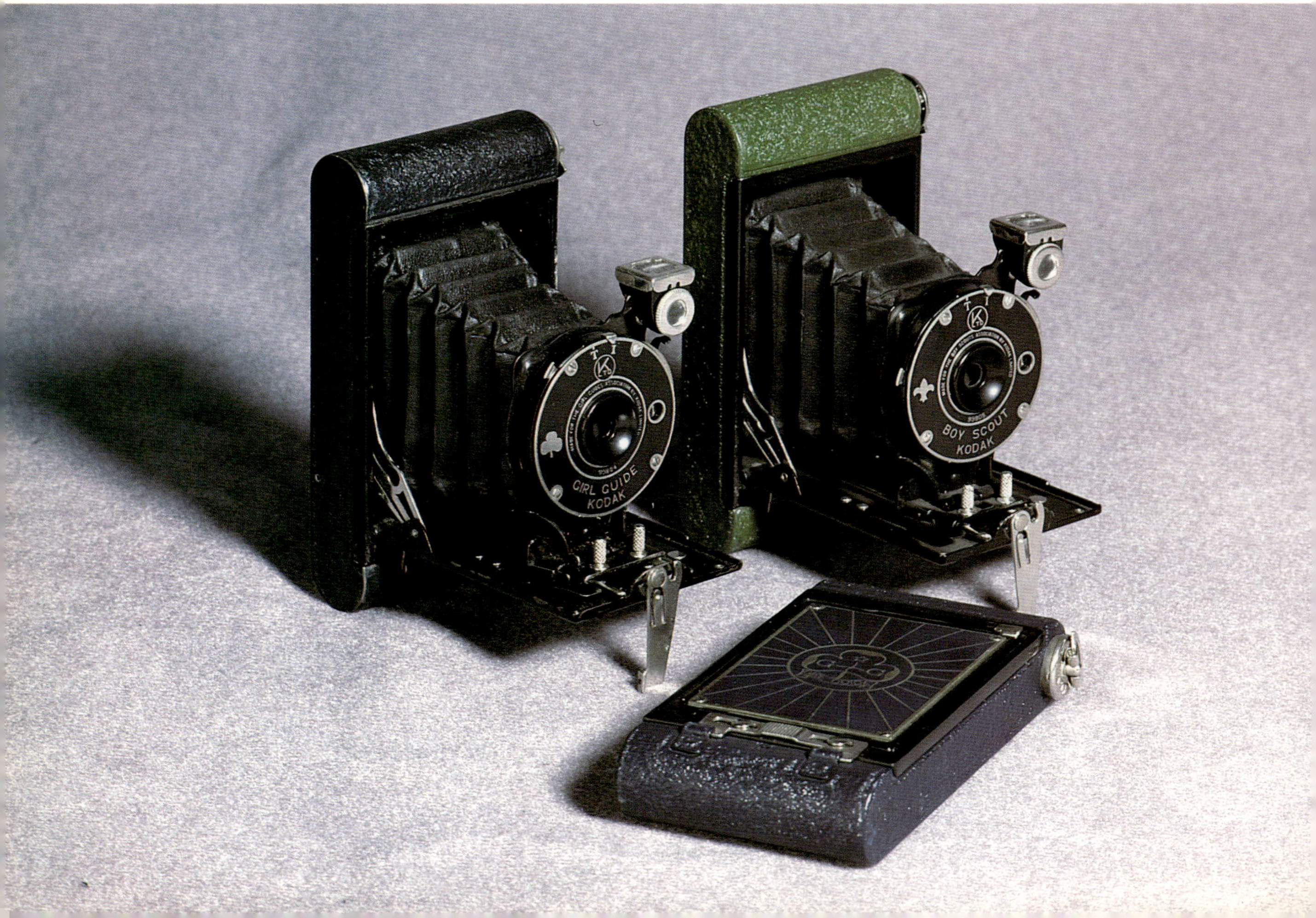

Introduced July 1938
Discontinued October 1939
Film size 616
Picture size 2½ × 4¼in.
Manufactured US
Lenses Kodak Anastigmat f/8.8 or f/6.3 – but see below
Shutter Kodex – but see below
Numbers made ?

Description/Remarks

Redesigned; dished baseboard; optical frame finder only; simplified support struts.

Variations

July 1938–Oct. 1939: Kodak Anastigmat f/4.5 lens and Diomatic shutter.

Kodak Junior 616

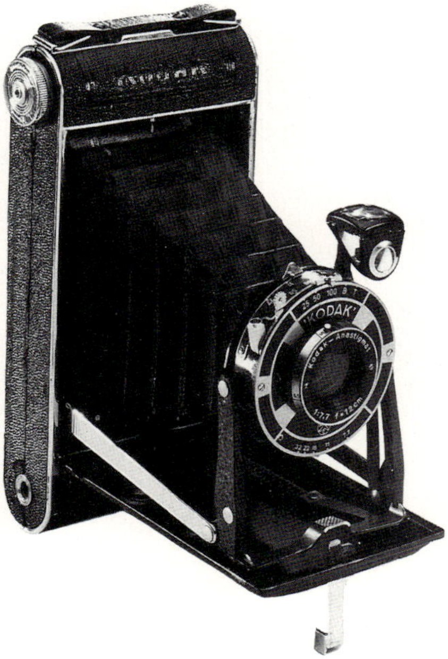

1934–1937 model. KAG

Type Self-erecting folding rollfilm
Introduced 1934
Discontinued 1939
Film size 616
Picture size 2½ × 4¼in.
Manufactured Germany
Lenses Kodak Anastigmat f7.7 or f/6.3
Shutters Kodak K 1 (f/7.7 lens) or K 8S (f/6.3 lens)
Numbers made 12,077 (7,403 with English markings)

Description/Remarks

Folding frame and brilliant finders; front cell focusing.

Variations

1937: design change, with simplified baseboard strut system, body release, folding winding key replacing knob, angled ends to body replacing rounded ends.

Kodak Junior Six-20 (US model)

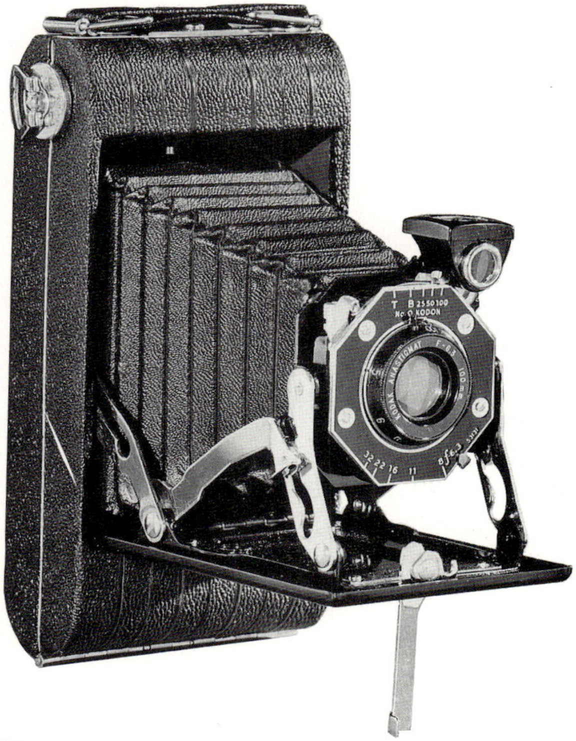

KP

Type Self-erecting folding rollfilm
Introduced February 1935
Discontinued April 1937
Film size 620

Picture size 2¼ × 3¼in.
Manufactured US (also UK and German models)
Lenses Doublet or Kodak Anastigmat f/6.3
Shutter Kodon
Numbers made ?

Description/Remarks

Octagonal shutter housing; folding frame and brilliant finders; banded finish on leatherette covering.

For UK version (*1933–1940*) see Six-20 Kodak Junior Camera.

For German version (*1933–1939*) see Kodak Junior 620 camera.

Kodak Junior Six-20 Series II

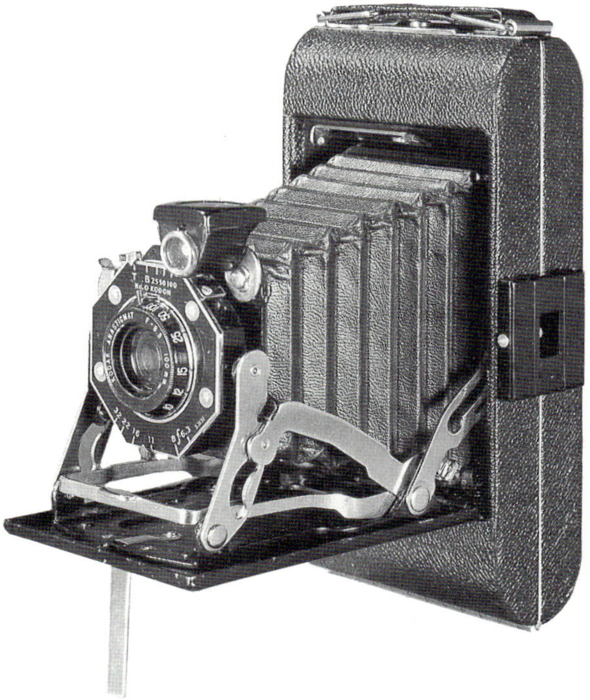

KP

Type Self-erecting folding rollfilm
Introduced May 1937
Discontinued June 1940
Film size 620
Picture size 2¼ × 3¼in.
Manufactured US
Lenses Single (fixed focus), Bimat (3-point focus) or Kodak Anastigmat f/6.3
Shutters Kodo, for single lens; Kodon for Bimat and Anastigmat
Numbers made ?

Description/Remarks

Baseboard release bar at front; smooth finish to leatherette covering. Folding frame and brilliant finders.

Kodak Junior Six-20 Series III

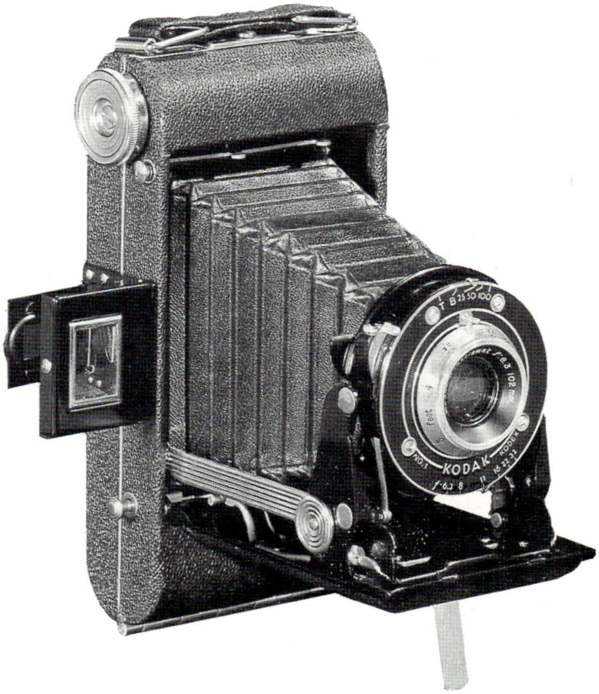

KP

Type Self-erecting folding rollfilm
Introduced July 1938
Discontinued October 1939
Film size 620
Picture size 2¼ × 3¼in.
Manufactured US
Lenses Kodak Anastigmat f/8.8, f/6.3, f/4.5
Shutters Kodex (f/8.8, f/6.3)

Diomatic (f/4.5)
Numbers made ?

Description/Remarks

Redesigned; dished baseboard, with simplified support struts; folding optical frame finder only; body release.

Kodak Junior 620

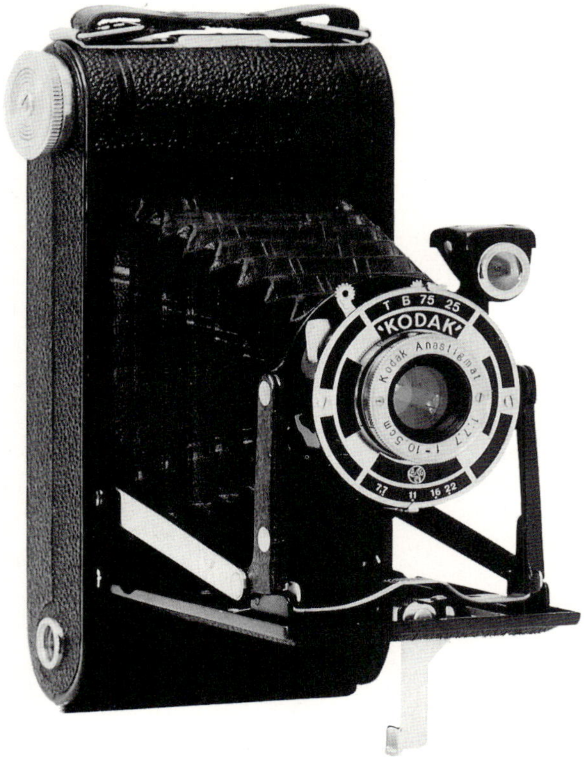

1933 model. KP

Type Self-erecting folding rollfilm
Introduced 1933
Discontinued 1939
Film size 620
Picture size 2¼ × 3¼in.
Manufactured Germany
Lenses Kodak Anastigmat f/8.8, f/7.7, f/6.3, f/4.5
Shutters Various: see below
Numbers made 581,000 (47,797 with English markings)

Description/Remarks

Folding frame and brilliant finders; folding optical frame finder on f/4.5 lens model.

Variations

1933: Knob wind, plated straight baseboard support struts. *1934:* Key wind, vertically ribbed baseboard struts. *1936:*Back catch changed from sliding button to hinged latch.

1937: Redesigned, with body release; simplified support struts with angled ends; folding frame finder moved to the left side (seen from front). *1937–1939:* Some models (with f/7.7, f/6.3 or f/4.5 lenses)had chromium plated side panels.

This camera was supplied with a variety of Kodak shutters, which were given a K number which indicated the number of shutter speeds; S indicated a self-timer.

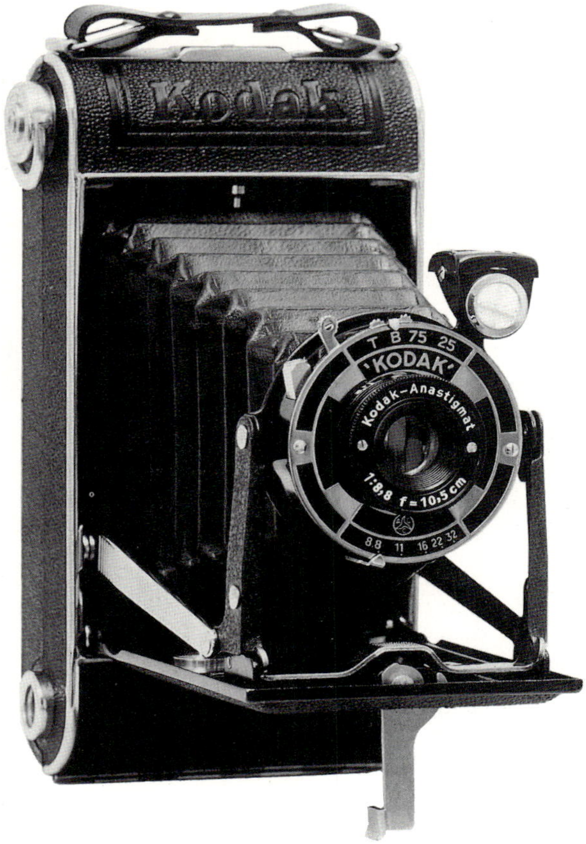

1935–1936 model. KP

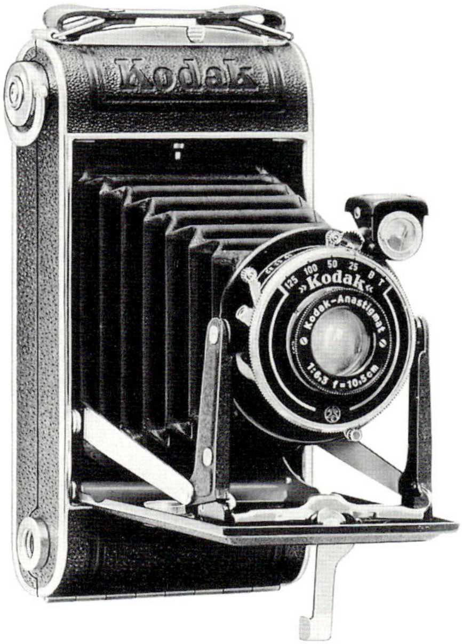

1936 model. KP

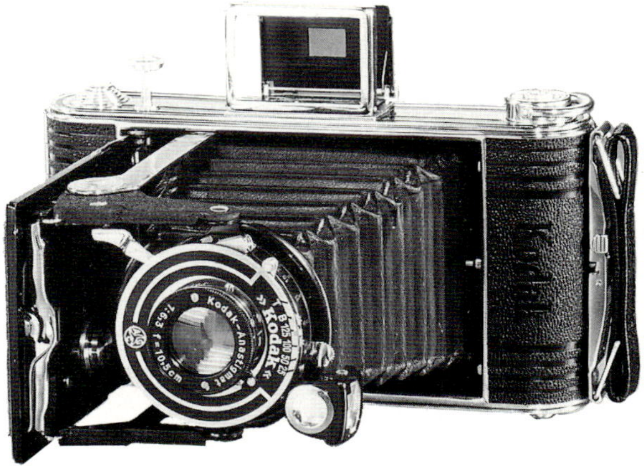

1937–1939 model, chrome panels. KP

Kodak Anastigmat f/8.8: *1935–1936:* Kodak shutter. *1937:* Kodak K2 shutter. *1937–1939:* Kodak K3 shutter.
Kodak Anastigmat f/7.7: *1933–1934:* Box-shutter *1935–1936:* Kodak or Kodak S shutter. *1937–1939:* Kodak K3 or K4S shutter.
Kodak Anastigmat f/6.3: *1935–1936:* Kodak S shutter.*1937–1939:* Kodak K4S shutter.
Kodak Anastigmat f/4.5: *1937–1939:* Kodak K4S or K8S shutter.

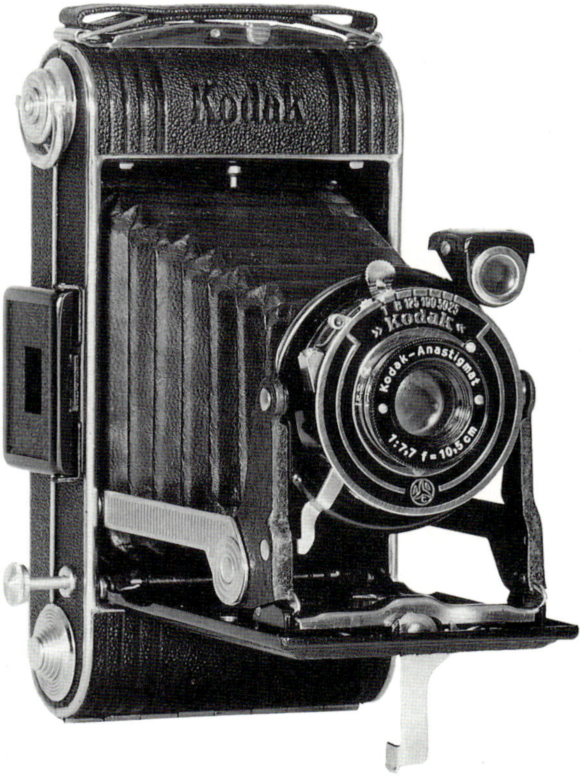

1937–1939 model. KP

Kodak Monitor Six-16

Type Self-erecting folding rollfilm
Introduced October 1939
Discontinued June 1948
Film size 616
Picture size 2½ × 4¼in.
Manufactured US
Lenses Kodak Anastigmat or Special Anastigmat f/4.5
Shutters Kodamatic (Anastigmat)
Supermatic (Special Anastigmat)
Numbers made ?

Description/Remarks

Folding optical frame and brilliant finders; body release; accessory shoe.

Kodak Monitor Six-20

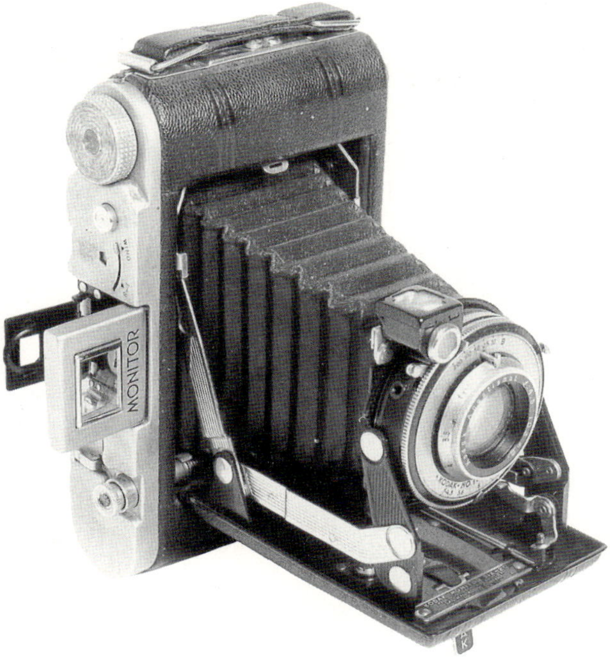

TNC

Type Self-erecting folding rollfilm
Introduced October 1939
Discontinued June 1948
Film size 620
Picture size 2¼ × 3¼in.
Manufactured US
Lenses Kodak Anastigmat or Special Anastigmat f/4.5
Shutters 1939–1948: Kodamatic (Anastigmat), Supermatic (Special Anastigmat)
October 1946–1948: Flash Supermatic
November 1946–1948: Flash Kodamatic
Numbers made ?

Description/Remarks

Folding optical frame and brilliant finders; body release; accessory shoe.

Kodak Petite

Type Folding rollfilm
Introduced June 1929
Discontinued 1934
Film size 127
Picture size 1⅝ × 2½in.
Manufactured US
Lens Meniscus
Shutter Vest Pocket Rotary
Numbers made ?

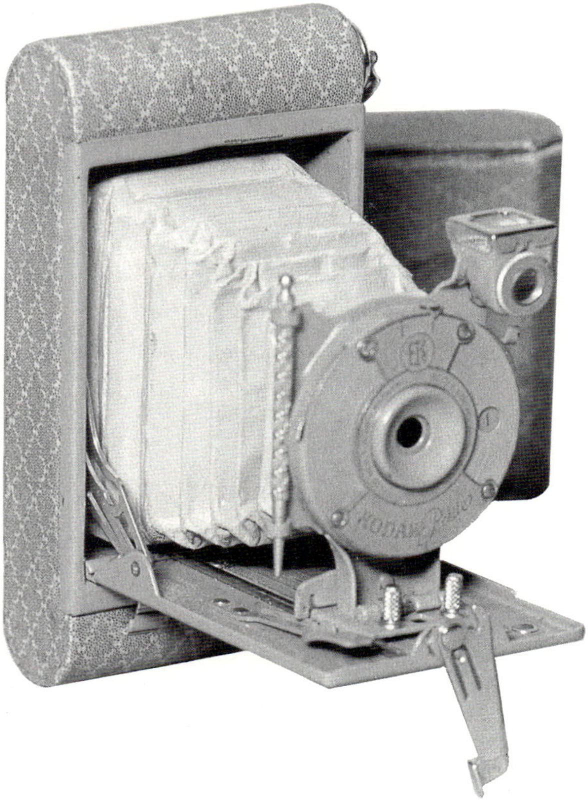

KM

Description/Remarks

The Vest Pocket Kodak Model B camera in a range of coloured finishes: blue, grey, green, lavender and old rose, with diamond patterning and coloured bellows. Sold with matching case.

Kodak Pliant

Type Self-erecting folding rollfiilm
Introduced c1950
Discontinued mid 1950s
Film size 620

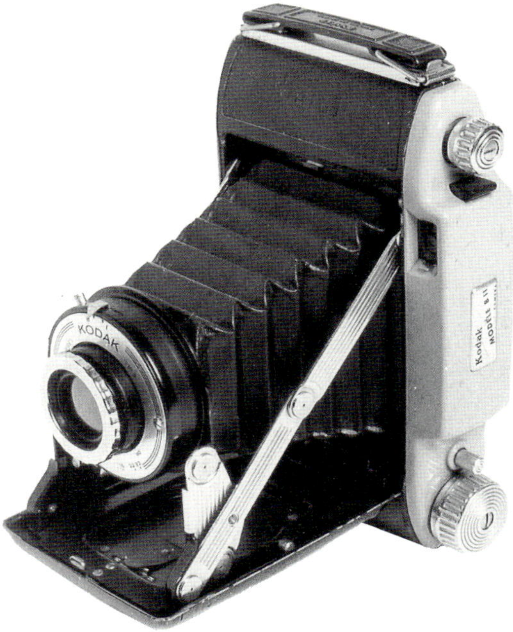

Model B 11. TNC

Picture size 6 × 9cm
Manufactured France
Lenses Angénieux or Berthiot – see below
Shutter Atos
Numbers made ?

Description/Remarks

For a few years after World War Two import of cameras into France was not possible. Kodak-Pathé began manufacture of a range of folding cameras to fill the gap.

Variations

First model: f/6.3 Angénieux or Som Berthiot lens, Atos I shutter, folding frame finder.
Second model: f/4.5 Angénieux lens, Atos or Royer shutter, satin chromed top, direct vision optical finder.
Third model: Model 40 – f/3.5 Angénieux or meniscus achromat lens, plastic top cover, 'periscopic' optical finder, with internal mirror system.
Model 42 – dual format, otherwise similar.
Fourth model: Series B – Plastic moulded body, Atos shutter; Series B11 – Meniscus achromat lens; Series B31 – Angénieux f/4.5 lens.

The early models had bodies with angled ends, similar to the pre-war German Vollenda Junior 620 cameras, and may have been made with press tools etc. from the Kodak Stuttgart factory. The plastic bodied version is very similar in construction to the Kodak Limited Junior and Sterling II cameras, except for the longer finder housing.

Kodak Regent

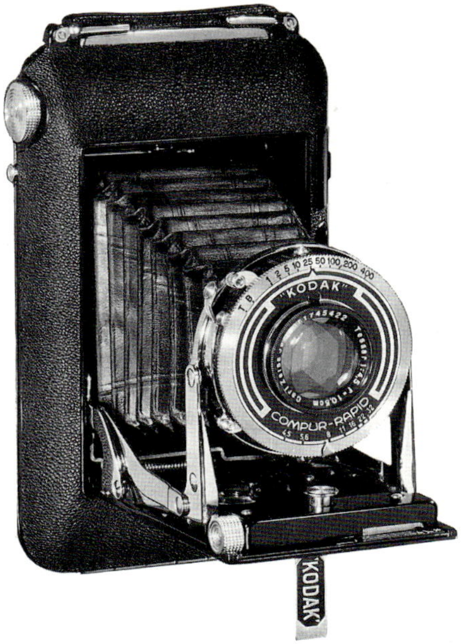

KP

Type Self-erecting folding rollfilm
Introduced 1935
Discontinued 1939
Film size 620
Picture size 2¼ × 3¼ or 2¼ × 1⅝in.
Manufactured Germany
Lenses Schneider Xenar f/4.5 or f/3.5
Zeiss Tessar f/4.5
Shutters Compur S or Compur Rapid
Numbers made 10,000 approximately

Description/Remarks

Dual format with inserted mask for smaller size; folding optical frame finder with adjustable mask for two formats; coupled rangefinder with focusing knob on baseboard front; morocco leather covering overall, streamlined shape when closed.

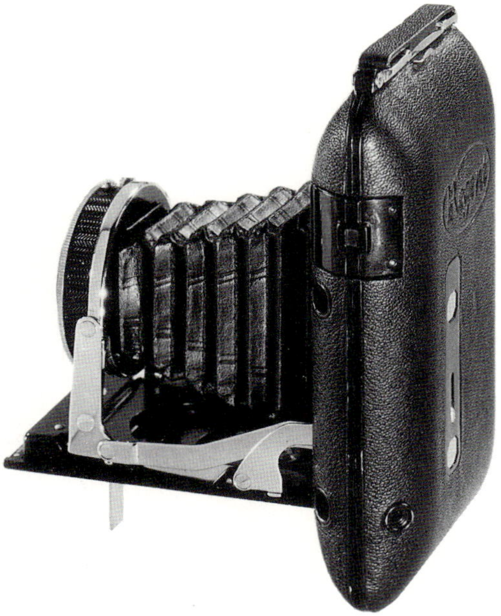

KP

Kodak Regent II

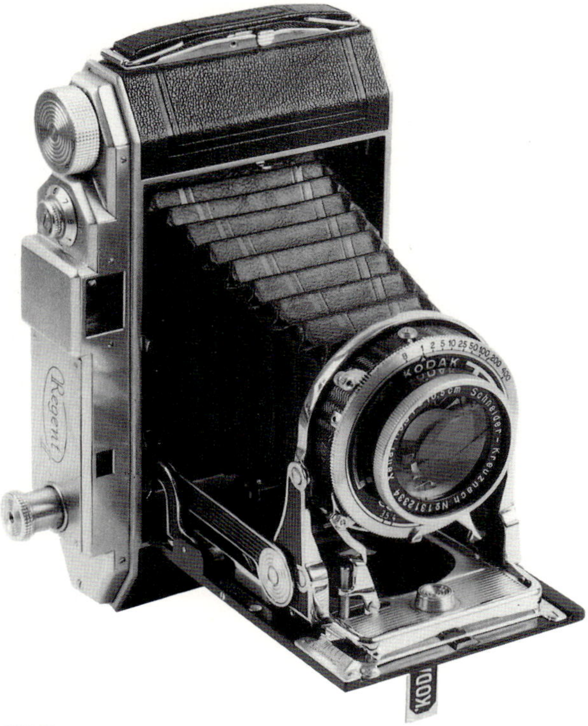

KAG

Type Self-erecting folding rollfilm
Introduced 1935
Discontinued 1939
Film size 620
Picture size 2¼ × 3¼ or 2¼ × 1⅝in.
Manufactured Germany
Lens Schneider Xenar f/3.5
Shutter Compur-Rapid
Numbers made 10,000

Description/Remarks

Redesigned model; chromed top mechanism cover; body release; combined direct vision optical finder and coupled rangefinder; focusing by milled wheel on back or by turning body release knob on top; automatic exposure counter.

Kodak Senior Six-16

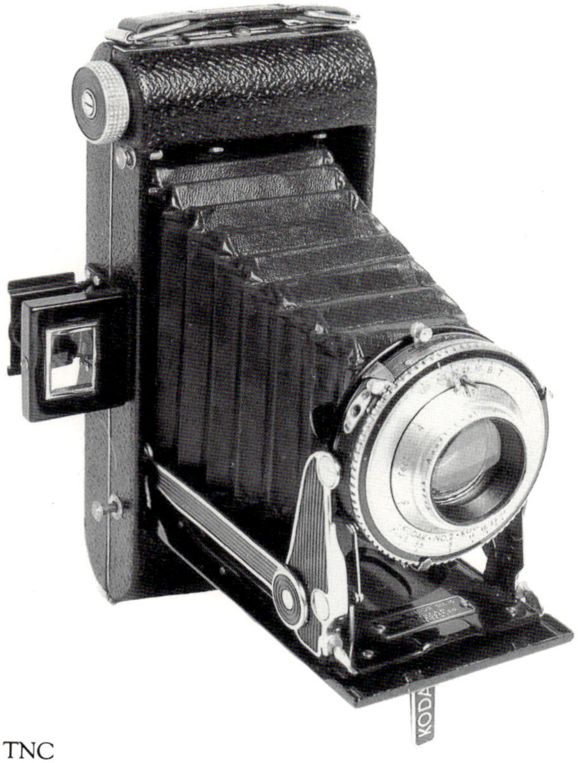

TNC

Type Self-erecting folding rollfilm
Introduced June 1937
Discontinued October 1939

Film size 616
Picture size 2½ × 4¼in.
Manufactured
Lenses 1937–1939: Bimat or Kodak Anastigmat f/6.3 or f/4.5
July 1938–1939: Kodak Anastigmat f/7.7
Shutters July 1937–1939: Kodex (Bimat, Anastigmat f/6.3 or f/7.7) Kodamatic (Anastigmat f/4.5).
July 1938–1939: Diomatic (Anastigmat f/6.3).
Numbers made ?

Description/Remarks

Folding optical frame finder; body release.

Kodak Senior Six-20

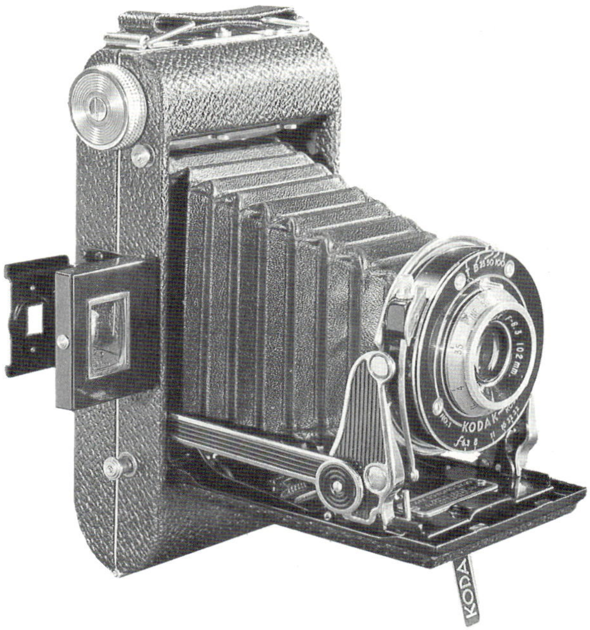

KP

Type Self-erecting folding rollfilm
Introduced June 1937
Discontinued 1939
Film size 620
Picture size 2¼ × 3¼in.
Manufactured US
Lenses 1937–1939: Bimat or Kodak Anastigmat f/6.3 or f/4.5.
1938–1939: Kodak Anastigmat f/7.7 or f/6.3.
Shutters 1937–1939: Kodex (Bimat, Anastigmat f/6.3) Kodamatic (Anastigmat f/4.5).
1938–1939: Kodex (Anastigmat f/7.7). Diomatic (Anastigmat f/6.3).
Numbers made ?

Description/Remarks

Optical frame finder; body release.

No 3A Kodak Series II

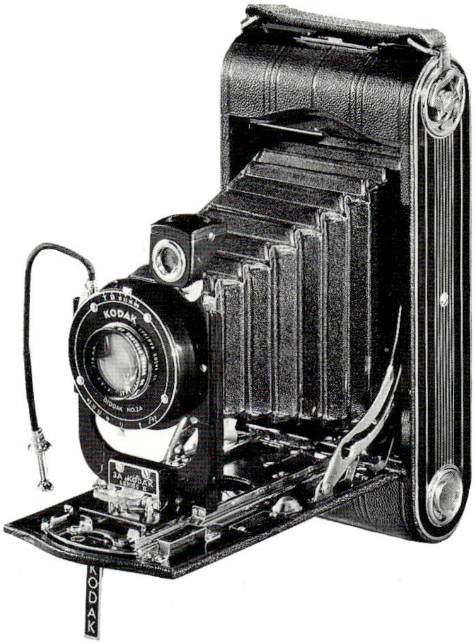

KP

Type Folding rollfilm
Introduced April 1936
Discontinued July 1941
Film size 122
Picture size 3¼ × 5½in.
Manufactured US
Lenses April 1936–July 1941: Kodak Anastigmat f/6.3
May 1937–July 1940: Kodak Anastigmat f/4.5
Shutter Diodak (f/6.3 lens) or Compur (f/4.5 lens)
Numbers made ?

Description/Remarks

Black grained leather covering, striped black enamel and chromium plate side panels.

No 1 Kodak Series III

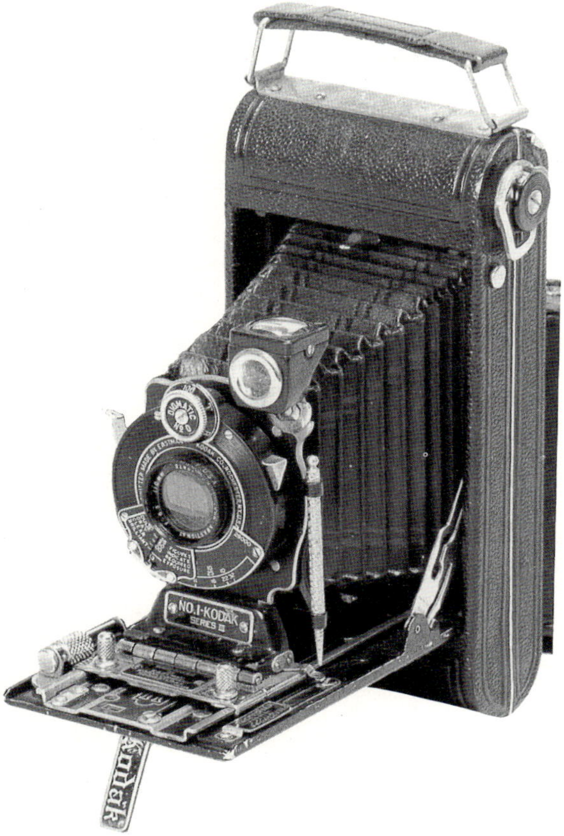

KM

Type Folding rollfilm
Introduced May 1926
Discontinued May 1932
Film size 120
Picture size 2¼ × 3¼in.
Manufactured US, and assembled in UK from 1929
Lens Kodak Anastigmat f/6.3
Shutter Diomatic
Numbers made ?

Description/Remarks

Differing from No 1 Pocket Kodak Series II camera by being without self-erecting front. Fine-grain leather covering; Autographic feature.

Variations

UK VARIATIONS
The following lenses were supplied in Compur shutters:
1927–1932: Kodak Anastigmat f/6.3, f/5.6 or f/4.5.
1927–1931: Cooke Aviar f/6.3.
1927–1930: Cooke Aviar f/4.5.
1927–1931: Ross Homocentric f/6.3.
1927–1932: Ross Xpres f/4.5.
1927–1931: Zeiss Tessar f/6.3.
1927–1932: Zeiss Tessar f/4.5.

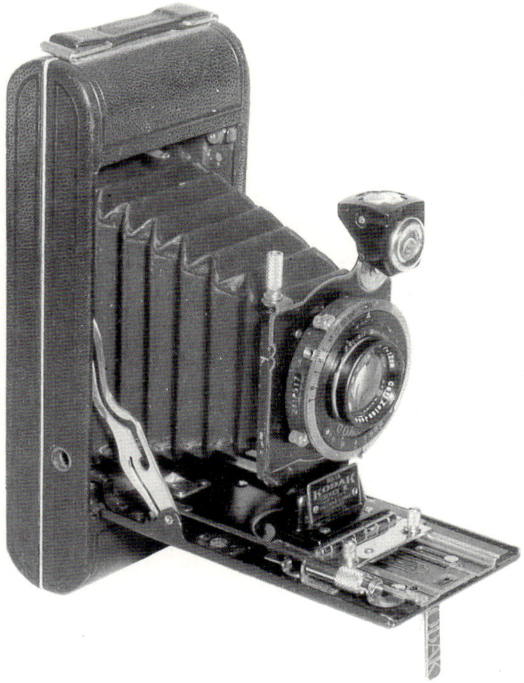

RPS

No 1A Kodak Series III

Type Folding rollfilm
Introduced July 1924
Discontinued 1931
Film size 116
Picture size 2½ × 4¼in.
Manufactured US, and assembled in UK from 1929.
Lenses July 1924–May 1926 Kodak Anastigmat f/7.7
May 1926–1928: Kodak Anastigmat f/6.3
1929–1931: Kodak Anastigmat f/5.6
Shutter Diomatic
Numbers made ?

Description/Remarks

Differing from 1A Pocket Kodak Series II camera by being without self-erecting front. Fine grain leather covering; Autographic feature.

Variations

UK VARIATIONS

The following lenses were supplied in Compur shutters:

1927–1932: Kodak Anastigmat f/6.3, f/5.6 or f/4.5.
1927–1930: Cooke Aviar f/6.3.
1927–1931: Cooke Aviar f/4.5.
1927–1930: Ross Homocentric f/6.3.
1926–1932: Zeiss Tessar f/6.3.
1927–1932: Zeiss Tessar f/4.5.

No 2C Kodak Series III

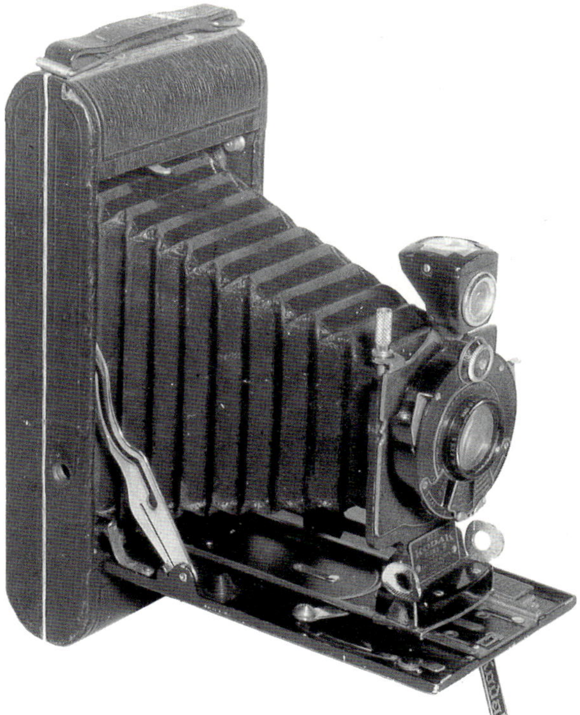

RPS

Type Folding rollfilm
Introduced 1924
Discontinued 1931
Film size 130
Picture size 2⅞ × 4⅞in.
Manufactured US
Lenses July 1924–June 1926: Kodak Anastigmat f/7.7
June 1926–1931: Kodak Anastigmat f/6.3
Shutter Diomatic
Numbers made ?

Description/Remarks

Fine grain leather covering; Autographic feature.

Variations

UK VARIATIONS

The following lenses were supplied in Compur shutters:

1926–1931: Zeiss Tessar f/6.3.
1927–1928: Kodak Anastigmat f/6.3; Cooke Aviar f/6.3; Ross Homocentric f/6.3.

No 3 Kodak Series III

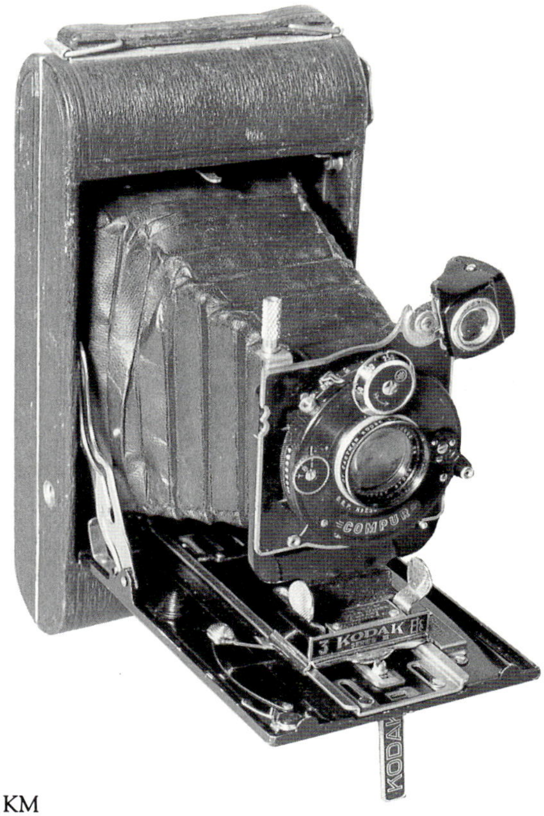

KM

Type Folding rollfilm
Introduced May 1926
Discontinued 1934
Film size 118
Picture size 3¼ × 4¼in.
Manufactured US
Lens Kodak Anastigmat – see below
Shutter Various – see below
Numbers made ?

Description/Remarks

Grained leather covering. Brilliant finder automatically compensated for rising front movement; Autographic feature.

Variations

Kodak Anastigmat f/6.3: *May 1926–1928:* Diomatic shutter. *Jan. 1931–1933:* Kodex shutter.
Kodak Anastigmat f/5.6: *1929–1933:* Diomatic shutter.
Kodar f/7.9: *May 1926–1934:* Kodex shutter.

UK VARIATIONS
The following lenses were supplied in Compur shutters:
1926–1932: Kodak Anastigmat f/6.3.
1927–1932: Kodak Anastigmat f/5.6 or f/4.5.
1926–1931: Zeiss Tessar f/6.3.
1927–1932: Zeiss Tessar f/4.5.
1926–1930: Ross Homocentric f/6.3.
1927–1930: Cooke Aviar f/6.3.
1927–1931: Cooke Aviar f/4.5.
1926–1927: TTH-Kodak Anastigmat f/6.8.
The following lenses were supplied in Kodamatic shutters:
1926: TTH-Kodak Anastigmat f/6.8; Kodak Anastigmat f/6.3; Zeiss Tessar f/6.3; Ross Homocentric f/6.3.

No 3A Kodak Series III

Type Folding rollfilm
Introduced July 1941
Discontinued August 1943
Film size 122
Picture size 3¼ × 4¼in.
Manufactured US
Lens Kodak Anastigmat f/6.3
Shutter Kodamatic
Numbers made ?

Description/Remarks

Similar to No 3A Kodak Series II camera, but with Kodamatic shutter.

Kodak 66 Model II

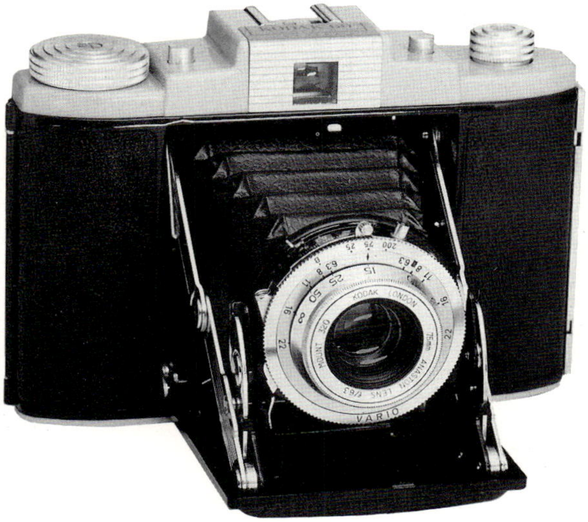

KP

Type Self-erecting folding rollfilm
Introduced July 1958
Discontinued 1960
Film size 120
Picture size 2¼ × 2¼in.
Manufactured UK
Lens Kodak Anaston f/6.3, 75mm
Shutter Vario 3-speed
Numbers made ?

Description/Remarks

This camera was to be called "Rapier" but was renamed before production; there was no Model I. Direct vision optical finder; flash synchronisation; moulded plastic top cover.

Kodak 66 Model III

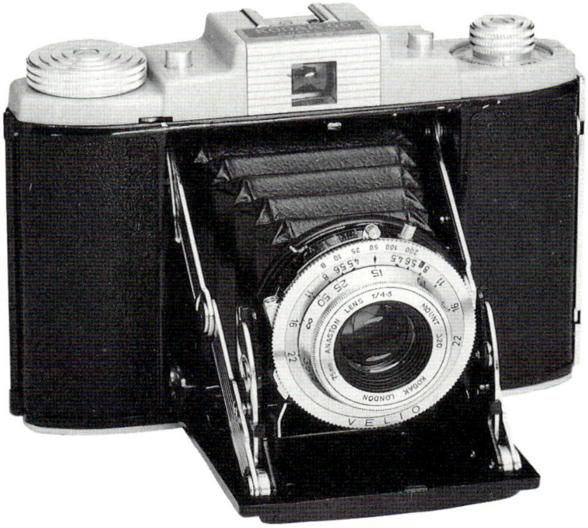

KP

Type Self-erecting folding rollfilm
Introduced July 1958
Discontinued 1960
Film size 120
Picture size 2¼ × 2¼in.
Manufactured UK
Lens Kodak Anaston f/4.5
Shutter Velio 5-speed
Numbers made ?

Description/Remarks

Improved lens and shutter, otherwise identical to Model II.

Kodak 616

Type Self-erecting folding rollfilm
Introduced 1934
Discontinued 1938
Film size 616
Picture size 6.5 × 11cm
Manufactured Germany
Lenses Kodak Anastigmat f/4.5, Schneider Xenar f/4.5 or Zeiss Tessar f/4.5
Shutter Compur S
Numbers made 12,702 (696 only with English markings)

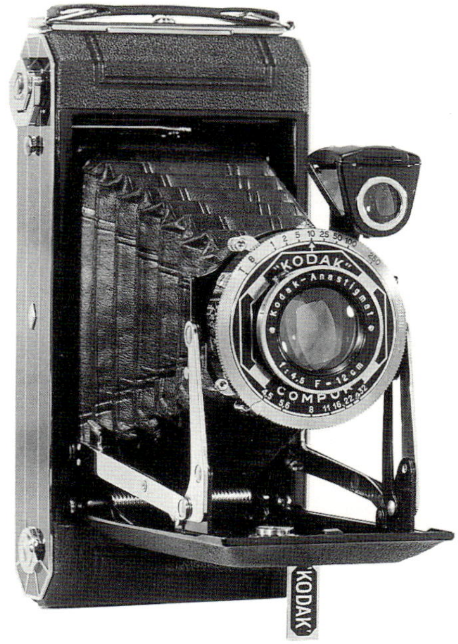

KP

Description/Remarks

Leather covered body with angled ends, enamelled side plates with nickel line design. Brilliant and folding frame finders.

Kodak 620

Type Self-erecting folding rollfilm
Introduced 1933
Discontinued 1937
Film size 620
Picture size 6 × 9cm
Manufactured Germany
Lenses Kodak Anastigmat f/6.3 or f/4.5, Schneider Xenar f/4.5 or Zeiss Tessar.
Shutters Pronto S (Kodak Anastigmat) Compur S (Xenar and Tessar)
Numbers made 34,000+ (490 only with English markings)

Description/Remarks

Leather covered body with angled ends, black enamelled side panels with nickel line design. Brilliant and folding frame finders.

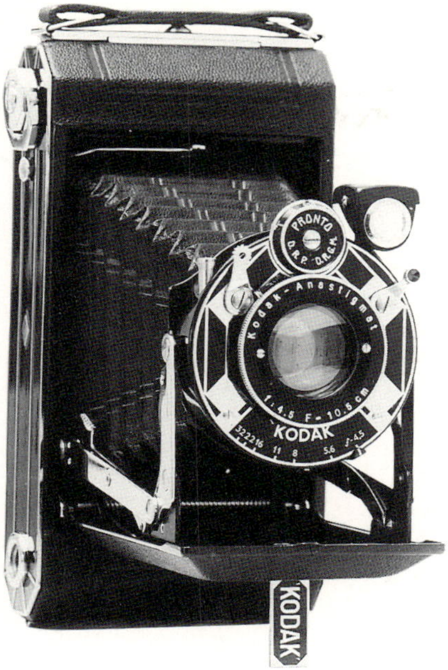

KP

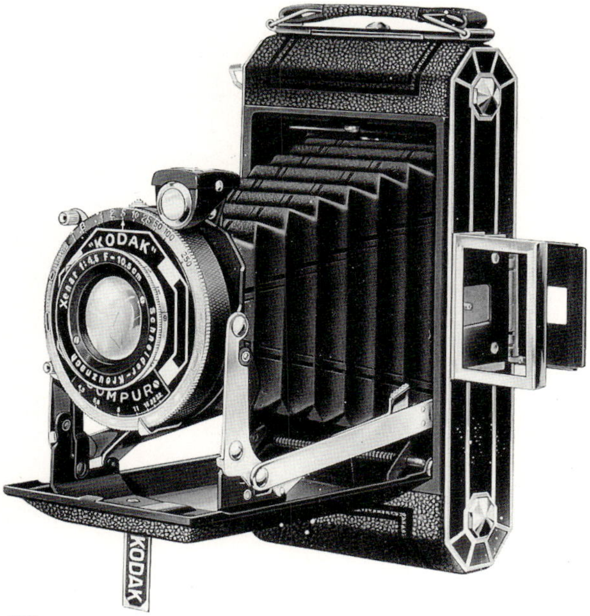

KP

Kodak Special Six-16

Type Self-erecting folding rollfilm
Introduced July 1937
Discontinued October 1939
Film size 616
Picture size 2¼ × 4¼in.
Manufactured US
Lenses July 1937–July 1938: Kodak Anastigmat f/4.5.
July 1937–October 1939: Kodak Anastigmat Special f/4.5.
Shutters July 1937–October 1939: Kodamatic
July 1937–October 1939: Compur Rapid
July 1939–October 1939: Supermatic
Numbers made ?

Description/Remarks

Body shutter release; folding optical frame finder, pin-seal grain leather covering.

Kodak Special Six-20

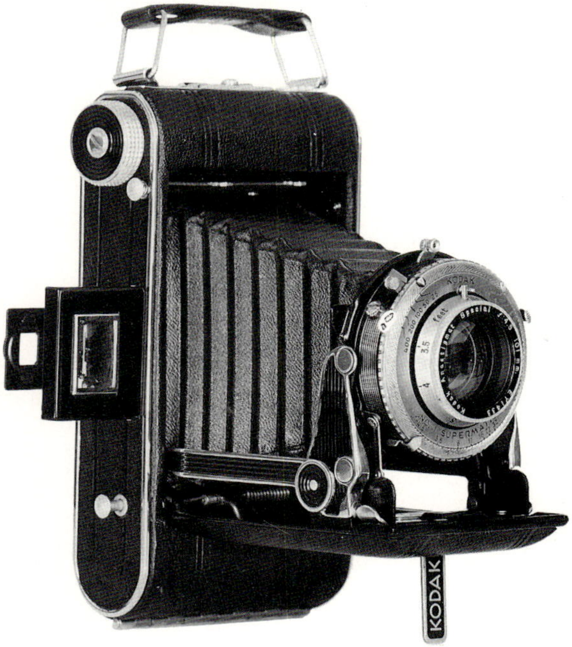

KP

Type Self-erecting folding rollfilm
Introduced July 1937
Discontinued October 1939
Film size 620
Picture size 2¼ × 3¼in.
Manufactured US
Lenses July 1937–July 1938: Kodak Anastigmat f/4.5
July 1937–October 1939: Kodak Anastigmat Special f/4.5

Shutters July 1937–October 1939: Compur Rapid
July 1937–October 1939: Kodamatic
May 1939–October 1939: Supermatic
Numbers made ?

Description/Remarks

Body shutter release; folding optical frame finder; pin-seal grain leather covering.

Kodak Sterling II

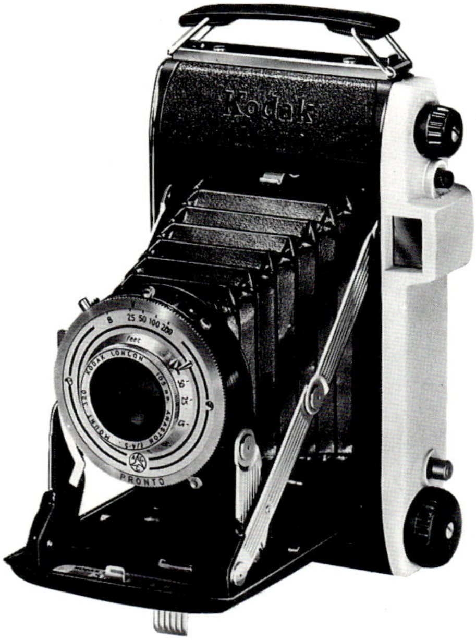

Early model. KP

Type Self-erecting folding rollfilm
Introduced May 1955
Discontinued 1959
Film size 620
Picture size 2¼ × 3¼in.
Manufactured UK
Lens Kodak Anaston f/4.5, 105mm
Shutter Pronto 4-speed
Numbers made ?

Description/Remarks

Grey plastic top cover incorporating direct vision optical finder; covered in morocco-grained leather cloth. There was no Model I.

Variations

Early models had plastic film knobs; *from mid-1956:* changed to metal.

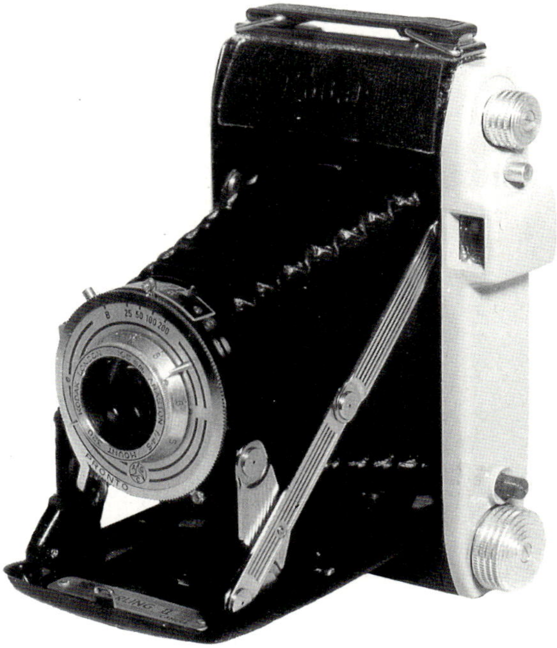

Late model. RPS

Kodak Suprema

Type Self-erecting folding rollfilm
Introduced 1938
Discontinued 1939
Film size 620
Picture size 2¼ × 2¼in. (6 × 6cm)
Manufactured Germany
Lens Schneider Xenar f/3.5, 80mm
Shutter Compur-Rapid
Numbers made 1,791 (only 183 with English scales)

Description/Remarks

Direct vision optical finder; body release; automatic exposure counter; matt chromed metal parts. Styling similar to the Kodak Retina camera.

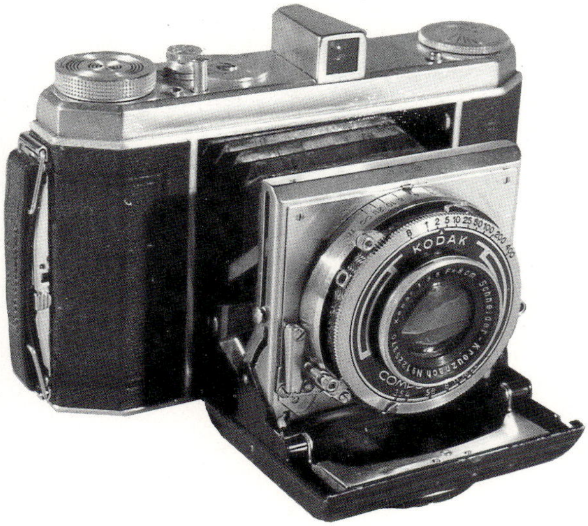

KM

Kodak Tourist

Type Self-erecting folding rollfilm
Introduced April 1948
Discontinued September 1951
Film size 620
Picture size 2¼ × 3¼in.
Manufactured US
Lenses Kodak Anaston, Anastar or Kodet – see below
Shutters Various – see below
Numbers made ?

Description/Remarks

Direct vision optical finder, plastic top cover.

Variations

Kodak Anaston f/4.5: *Apr. 1948–Sep. 1951:* Flash Kodamatic shutter.
Kodet f/12.5: *Aug. 1948–May 1951:* Flash Kodon shutter.
Kodak Anaston f/8.8: *Aug. 1948–Jan. 1951:* Flash Diomatic shutter.
Kodak Anaston f/6.3: *Aug. 1948–June 1951:* Flash Diomatic shutter
Kodak Anastar f/4.5: *Aug. 1949–Sept. 1951:* Synchro-Rapid 800 shutter.

The models with f/4.5 and f/6.3 lenses were fitted with an accessory shoe, and took the Tourist Adaptor kit which permitted four image sizes on 620 and 828 film.

Kodak Tourist II

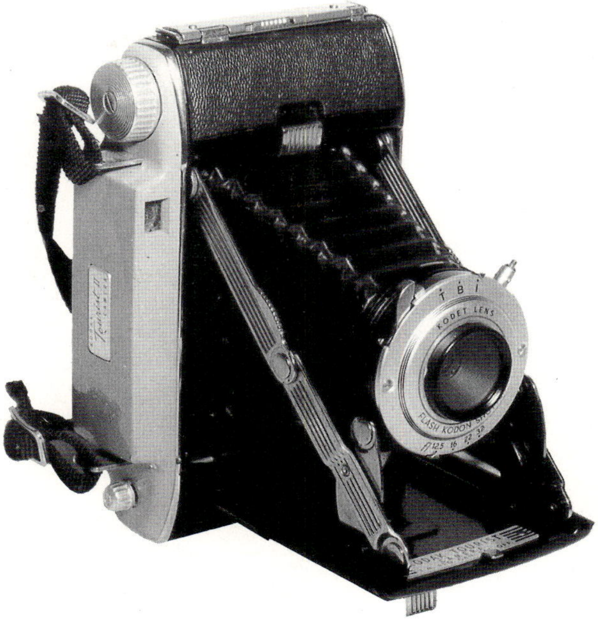

RPS

Type Self-erecting folding rollfilm
Introduced May 1951
Discontinued July 1958
Film size 620
Picture size 2¼ × 3¼in.
Manufactured US
Lenses Kodak Anaston, Anastar or Kodet – see below
Shutters Various – see below
Numbers made ?

Description/Remarks

Redesigned, with taller top housing incorporating direct vision optical finder.

Variations

Kodet f/12.5: *May 1951–May 1958:* Flash Kodon shutter.
Kodak Anaston f/6.3: *June 1951–May 1952:* Flash

Diomatic shutter. *Dec. 1951–July 1958:* Kodak Flash 200 shutter.
Kodak Anaston f/4.5: *Sept. 1951–Mar. 1953:* Flash Kodamatic shutter.
Kodak Anastar f/4.5: *Sept. 1951–June 1953:* Synchro-Rapid 800 shutter.

The f/4.5 lens models were fitted with an accessory shoe and larger finder window.

Kodak Vigilant Six-16

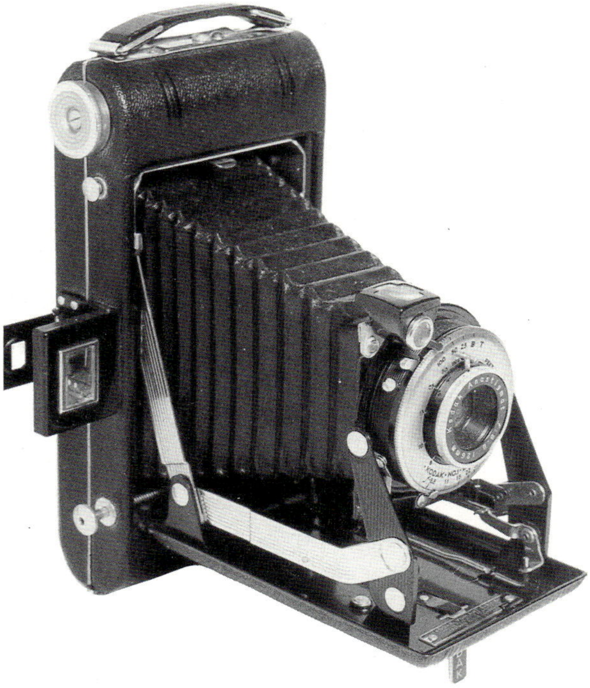

TNC

Type Self-erecting folding rollfilm
Introduced October 1939
Discontinued June 1948
Film size 616
Picture size 2½ × 4¼in.
Manufactured US
Lenses Kodak Anastigmat and Anastigmat Special – see below
Shutters Various – see below
Numbers made ?

Description/Remarks

Folding optical frame and brilliant finders; body release.

Variations

Kodak Anastigmat f/8.8: *Oct. 1939–Mar. 1940:* Kodex shutter. *Mar. 1940–Oct. 1942:* Diomatic shutter.
Kodak Anastigmat f/6.3: *Oct. 1939–July 1940:* Kodex shutter. *July 1940–June 1948:* Diomatic shutter.
Kodak Anastigmat f/4.5: *Oct. 1939–June 1948:* Kodamatic shutter.
Kodak Anastigmat Special f/4.5: *Oct. 1939–June 1948:*Supermatic shutter.

Kodak Vigilant Junior Six-16

Type Self-erecting folding rollfilm
Introduced April 1940
Discontinued June 1948
Film size 616
Picture size 2½ × 4¼in.
Manufactured US
Lenses Kodet or Bimat
Shutters Dak or Dakon
Numbers made ?

Description/Remarks

Cheaper version of Vigilant Six-16 camera, with folding frame and brilliant finders; no body release.

Kodak Vigilant Six-20

Type Self-erecting folding rollfilm
Introduced October 1939
Discontinued January 1949
Film size 620
Picture size 2¼ × 3¼in.
Manufactured US
Lenses Kodak Anastigmat or Anaston – see below.
Shutters Various – see below.
Numbers made ?

Description/Remarks

Body release; folding optical frame and brilliant finders.

Variations

Kodak Anastigmat f/8.8: *Oct. 1939–Mar. 1940:* Kodex shutter. *Mar. 1940–June 1948:* Diomatic shutter. *Nov.1946–June 1948:* Dakon shutter.
Kodak Anastigmat f/6.3: *Oct. 1939–June 1940:* Kodex shutter. *June 1940–June 1948:* Diomatic shutter. *Nov. 1946–June 1948:* Dakon shutter.
Kodak Anastigmat f/4.5: *Oct. 1939–June 1948:* Kodamatic shutter. *Aug. 1946–Apr. 1948:* Flash Kodamatic shutter.
Kodak Anastigmat Special f/4.5: *Oct. 1939–June 1948:* Supermatic shutter.
Kodak Anaston f/6.3: *Nov. 1947–Jan. 1949:* Flash Dakon shutter.

Kodak Vigilant Junior Six-20

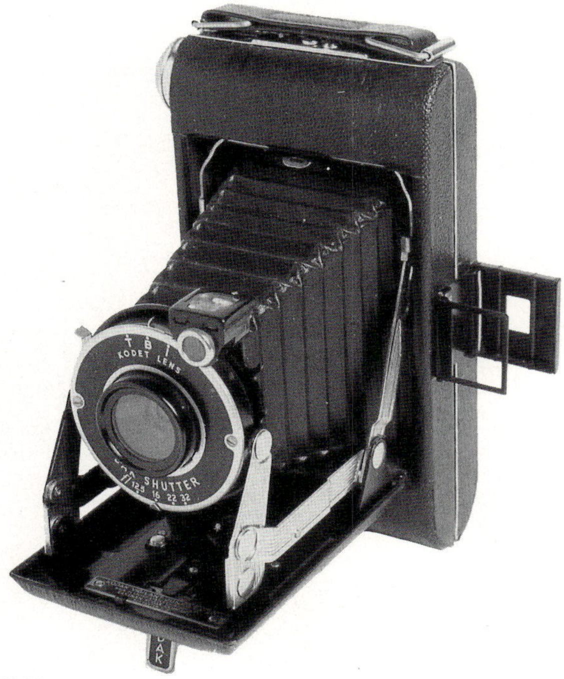

TNC

Type Self-erecting folding rollfilm
Introduced April 1940
Discontinued January 1949
Film size 620
Picture size 2¼ × 3¼in.
Manufactured US
Lenses 1940–1949: Kodet
1940–June 1948: Bimat
Shutters Dak (with Kodet lens)
Dakon (with Bimat lens)
Numbers made ?

Description/Remarks

Cheaper version of Vigilant Six-20 camera; folding frame and brilliant finders; no body release.

Kodak Vollenda No. 48

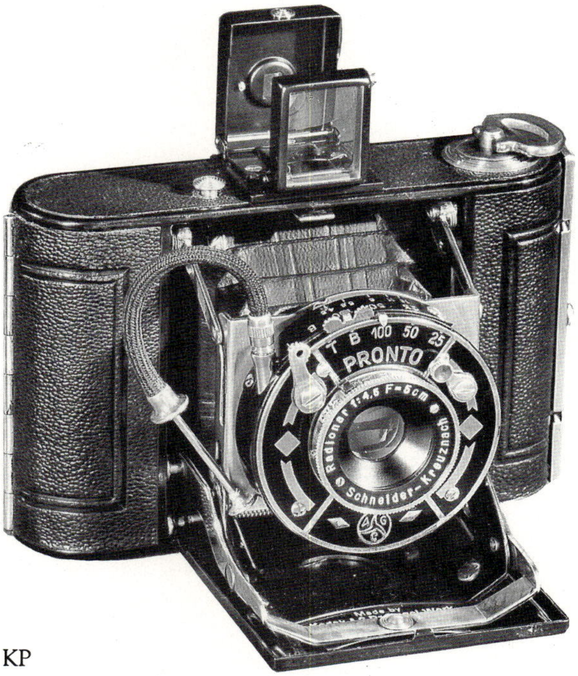

KP

Type Self-erecting folding rollfilm
Introduced 1932
Discontinued 1937
Film size 127
Picture size 3 × 4cm
Manufactured Germany
Lenses Schneider Radionar f/3.5 or f/4.5 – but see below.
Shutters Various – see below
Numbers made 43,000+

Description/Remarks

Introduced in 1931 by Nagel-Werke; a Kodak model from 1932. Folding frame or optical frame finders; front cell or helical focusing (on Tessar models).

Variations

Schneider Radionar f/4.5: *1932–1937:* Nagel shutter; Pronto S shutter.
Schneider Radionar f/3.5: *1933–1937:* Compur shutter.
Scheider Xenar f/3.5 or f/2.9: *1933–1937:* Compur shutter.
Zeiss Tessar f/3.5 or f/2.8: *1933–1937:* Compur shutter.
Leitz Elmar f/3.5: *1933–1937:* Compur shutter.

Kodak Vollenda No 52

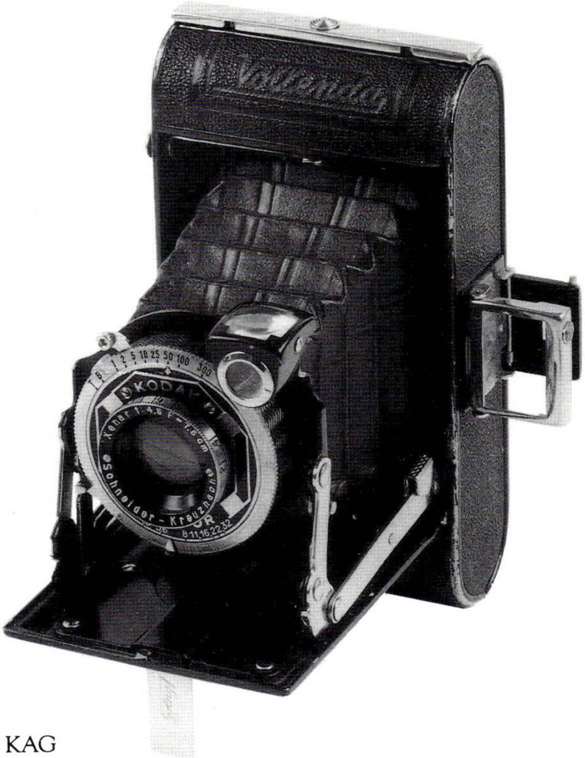

KAG

Type Self-erecting folding rollfilm
Introduced 1932
Discontinued 1937
Film size 127
Picture size 4 × 6.5cm
Manufactured Germany
Lens Schneider Radionar – but see below
Shutters Various – see below
Numbers made 6,000 approximately

Description/Remarks

Introduced by Nagel-Werke, then a Kodak model from 1932; folding frame and brilliant finders; models with front cell or helical focusing.

Variations

Schneider Radionar f/4.5, 75mm: *1932–1938:* Nagel shutter; Pronto-S shutter; Compur shutter.
Schneider Xenar f/4.5, 75mm or f/3.5, 70mm: *1932–1938:* Compur shutter.
Zeiss Tessar f/4.5, 75mm or f/3.5, 70mm: *1932–1938:* Compur shutter.

Kodak Vollenda 620

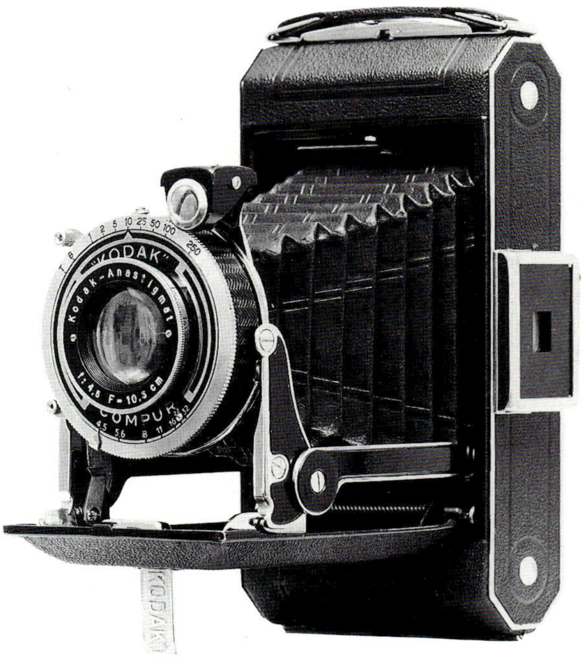

1934–1936 model. KP

Type Self-erecting folding rollfilm
Introduced 1934
Discontinued 1939
Film size 620
Picture size 2⅓ × 3¼in.
Manufactured Germany
Lens Kodak Anastigmat – but see below
Shutters Various – see below
Numbers made 100,890 (4,237 with English. scales)

Description/Remarks

Brilliant and folding frame finders; leather covering, nickel plated trim.
1936: Chromium plated trim; body release fitted; optical frame finder moved to left side (seen from front); stepped spool centres.

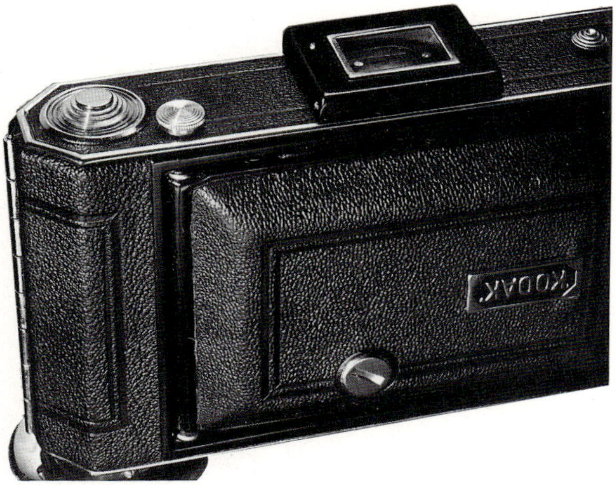

1936–1939 model, detail. KP

Variations

Kodak Anastigmat f/4.5, 50mm: *1934:* Compur S shutter. *1936–1939:* Compur S shutter.
Kodak Kodar Anastigmat f/4.5, 105mm: *1935–1936:* Kodak 4S or 8S shutter; Compur shutter.
Kodak Kodar Anastigmat f/6.3, 105mm: *1935–1936:* Kodak Sshutter.
Schneider Xenar f/4.5, 105mm: *1935–1936:* Compur shutter, *1936–1939:* Compur S Shutter.
Zeiss Tessar f/4.5, 105mm: *1936–1939:* Compur S shutter.

Kodak Vollenda Junior 616

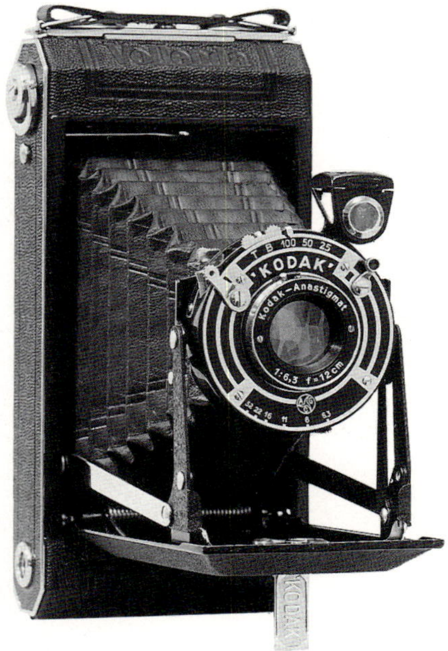

KP

Type Self-erecting folding rollfilm
Introduced 1934
Discontinued 1937
Film size 616
Picture size 6.5 × 11cm
Manufactured Germany
Lenses Kodak Anastigmat f/6.3 or f/4.5, 120mm
Shutter Pronto S
Numbers made 5,123 (1,893 with English markings)

Description/Remarks

Brilliant and folding frame finders; leatherette covering, nickel plated trim.

Kodak Vollenda Junior 620

Type Self-erecting folding rollfilm
Introduced 1933
Discontinued 1937
Film size 620
Picture size 2¼ × 3¼in.
Manufactured Germany

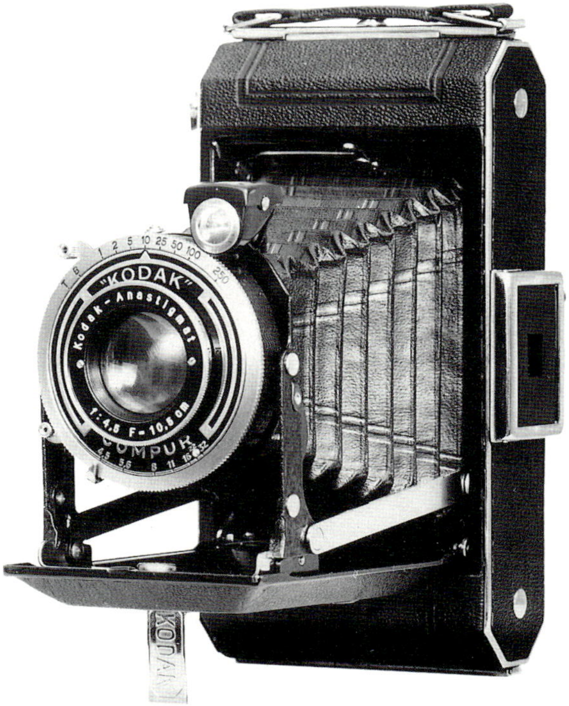

KP

Lenses Kodak Anastigmat f/6.3 or f/4.5
Shutters Kodak, Pronto or Compur – see below
Numbers made 25,000 (559 with English scales)

Description/Remarks

Cheaper version of Vollenda 620 camera. Brilliant and folding frame finders; leatherette covering, nickel plated trim.

Variations

Kodak Anastigmat f/6.3, 105mm: *1933–1935:* Pronto S shutter.
Kodak Anastigmat f/4.5, 105mm: *1933–1935:* Pronto S shutter; *1936–1937:* Kodak K4 S shutter; Kodak K8 S shutter; Compur S shutter; Compur-Rapid shutter.

Librette No.75

Type Folding rollfilm
Introduced 1933
Discontinued 1933
Film size 120
Picture size 6 × 9cm
Manufactured Germany
Lenses Schneider Radionar, Xenar or Zeiss Tessar f/4.5, 10cm.
Shutters Pronto, Pronto S or Compur S
Numbers made 4,000

Description/Remarks

Brilliant and frame finders.

No 1 Pocket Kodak

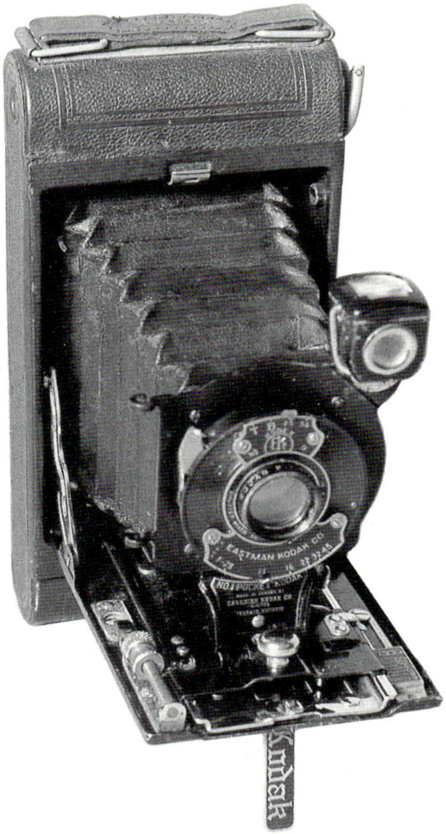

KM

Type Folding rollfilm
Introduced September 1926
Discontinued June 1932
Film size 120

Picture size 2¼ × 3¼in.
Manufactured US, UK 1929–1933
Shutter Achromatic or Kodar f/7.9 – but see below
Kodex
Numbers made ?

Description/Remarks

Brilliant finder; screw focusing; Autographic feature.

Variations

Apr. 1927–June 1932: Kodak Anastigmat f/6.3. *1927:* Kodak Anastigmat f/7.7.

June 1929–1931: In US only, Kodar f/7.9 model supplied in four colours – blue, brown, grey and green – as well as black.

No 1 Pocket Kodak Junior

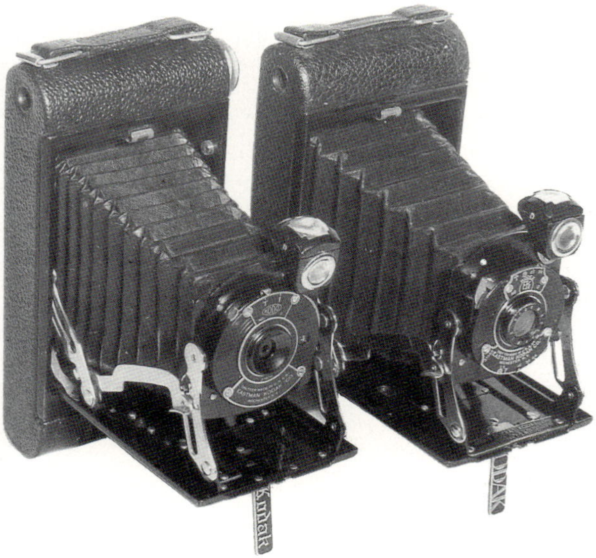

Left: meniscus lens. Right: doublet lens (US export model). RPS

Type Self-erecting folding rollfilm
Introduced October 1929
Discontinued June 1932
Film size 120
Picture size 2¼ × 3¼in.
Manufactured US, UK 1930–1933
Lens Meniscus achromat – but see below
Shutter Kodo – but see below
Numbers made ?

Description/Remarks

US models with coloured leatherette covering – black, blue, brown and green. UK models black only – 1930–1931 with 'iridescent' finish, 1931–1933 with leather grain finish.

UK VARIATIONS

Doublet lens: *1930–1931:* Kodex shutter.

Kodak Anastigmat f/7.7: *1930–1933:* Kodex shutter.

Kodak Anastigmat f/6.3 *1930–1933:* Ball Bearing shutter.

No 1 Pocket Kodak Series II

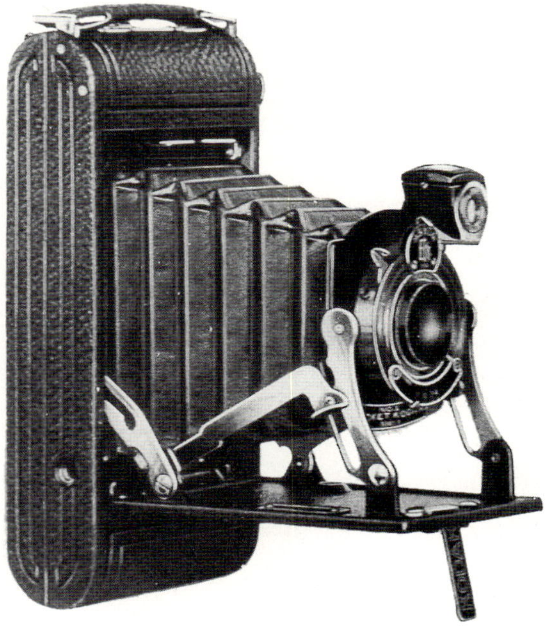

Type Self-erecting folding rollfilm
Introduced May 1922
Discontinued March 1932
Film size 120
Picture size 2¼ × 3¼in.
Manufactured US, assembled in UK 1929–1932

Lenses Kodak Anastigmat f/7.7 or f/6.3, Kodar f/7.9 or achromatic
Shutters Kodex, Ball Bearing, Diomatic or Compur
Numbers made ?

Description/Remarks

Leather covering; brilliant finder; Autographic feature.

Variations

Achromatic lens: *May 1922–1924:* Ball Bearing shutter; *Jan. 1925–Mar. 1932:* Kodex shutter.
Kodak Anastigmat f/7.7: *Oct. 1922–Jan. 1925:* Ball Bearing shutter; *Oct. 1924–Jan. 1932:* Diomatic shutter.
Kodar f/7.9: *May 1925–Mar. 1932:* Kodex shutter.

UK VARIATIONS

Kodak Anastigmat f/6.3: *1927–1928:* Diomatic shutter.
Zeiss Tessar f/6.3: *1927–1931:* Compur shutter.
Zeiss Tessar f/4.5: *1932:* Compur S shutter.

No 1 Pocket Kodak Special

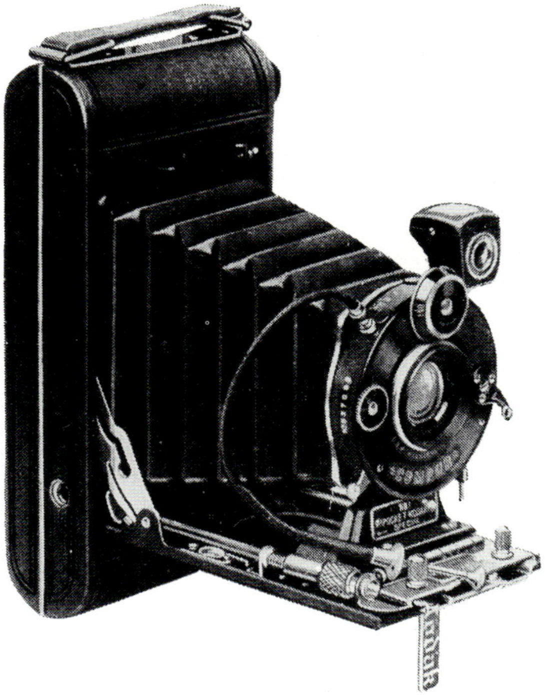

Type Folding rollfilm
Introduced May 1926
Discontinued 1934
Film size 120
Picture size 2¼ × 3¼in.
Manufactured US
Lenses Kodak Anastigmat f/6.3 (May 1926–Mar. 1927); f/5.6 (Nov. 1926–Feb. 1929); f/4.5 (May 1926–1934)
Shutter Kodamatic
Numbers made ?

Description/Remarks

Replaced the No 1 Autographic Kodak Special camera. Seal leather covering; screw focusing; Autographic feature.

UK VARIATIONS

The Kodak Trade Circular for October 1926 stated that Cooke, Ross and Zeiss Anastigmat lenses would be available. However, none were listed in the 1927 Catalogue, although it did illustrate a model with Kodak Anastigmat f/5.6 lens and Compur shutter, which was not listed.

1A Pocket Kodak

Type Folding rollfilm
Introduced September 1926
Discontinued June 1932
Film size 116
Picture size 2½ × 4¼in.
Manufactured US, UK from 1929–1935
Lens Achromatic meniscus – but see below
Shutter Kodex
Numbers made ?

Description/Remarks

Brilliant finder; Autographic feature (omitted from UK models after 1932).

Variations

Early models have shallow C-shaped support foot, later ones have "Kodak" on straight foot. *1929:* 'Iridescent' leatherette covering.

Early model. KM

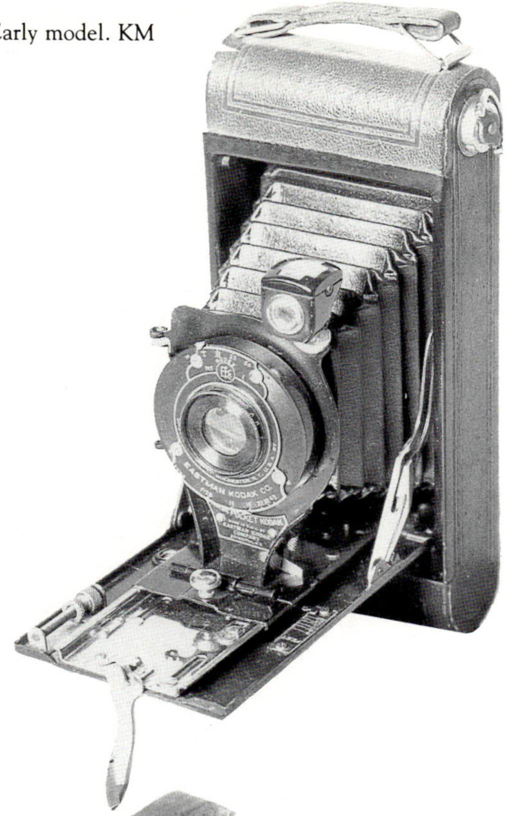

June 1929–June 1932: In US only, Kodar f/7.9 model supplied in four colours – blue, grey, green and brown – as well as black.

Sep. 1926–Dec. 1931: Kodar f/7.9 (1932-1935 in UK)
Apr. 1927–Dec. 1931: Kodak Anastigmat f/6.3 (1931-1935 in UK)
Jan. 1927–Sep. 1927: Kodak Anastigmat f/7.7

No 1A Pocket Kodak Junior

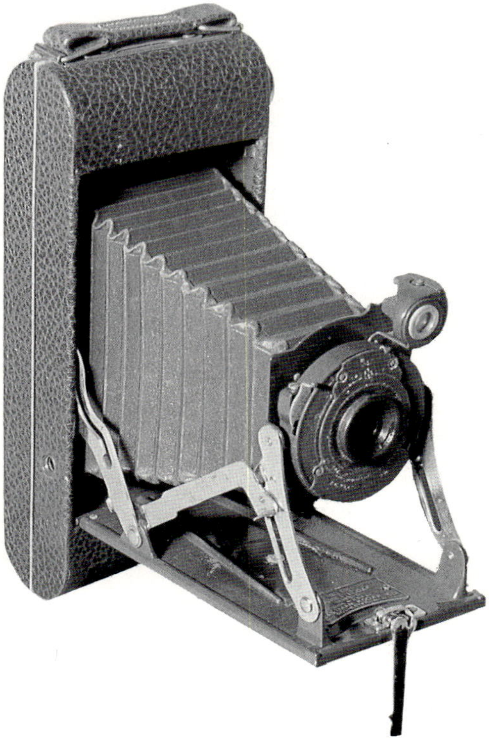

US model. KM

Type Self-erecting folding rollfilm
Introduced October 1929
Discontinued June 1932
Film size 116
Picture size 2½ × 4¼in.
Manufactured US, UK from 1930–1936
Lens Meniscus achromat – but see below
Shutter Kodo
Numbers made ?

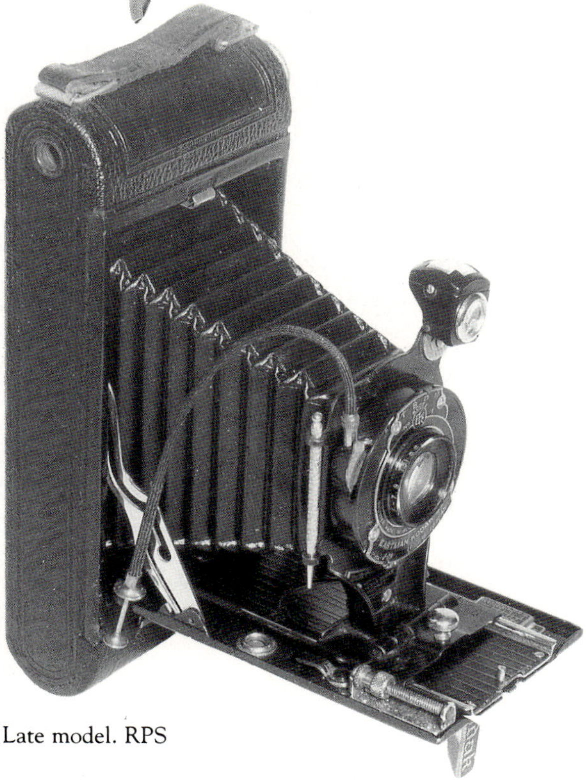

Late model. RPS

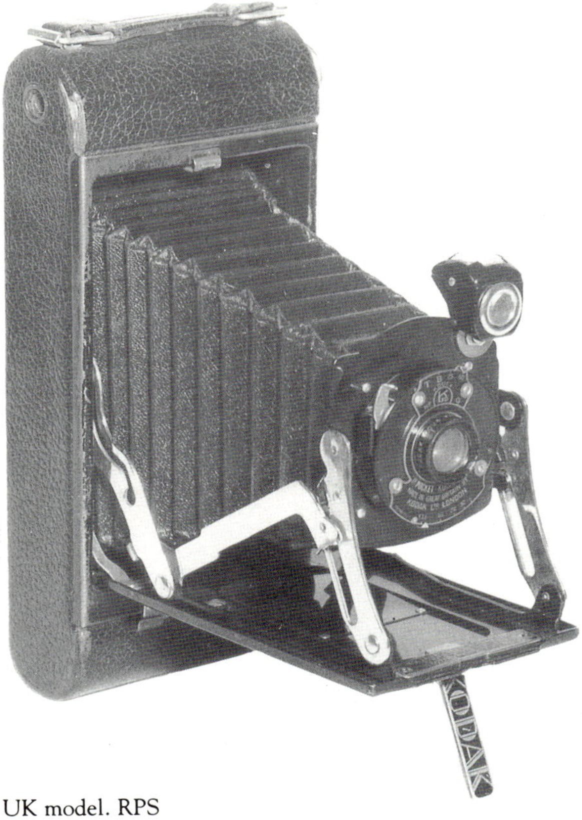

UK model. RPS

Description/Remarks

US models in coloured leatherette covering – black, blue, brown and green. UK models in black leatherette only – 1930–1931 with 'iridescent' finish, 1931–1936 with leather grain finish.

UK VARIATIONS

Kodak Anastigmat f/7.7 *1930–Autumn 1935:* Kodex shutter.
Doublet lens: *1931–July 1936:* Kodex shutter.
Kodak Anastigmat f/6.3 *1931–1935:* Kodex shutter.

No 1A Pocket Kodak Series II

Type Self-erecting folding rollfilm
Introduced April 1923
Discontinued 1931
Film size 116
Picture size 2½ × 4¼in.
Lens US, assembled in UK 1929–1936
Shutters Kodak Anastigmat f/7.7 or f/6.3, Kodar f/7.9 or achromatic
Shutters Ball Bearing, Kodex, Diomatic or Compur
Numbers made ?

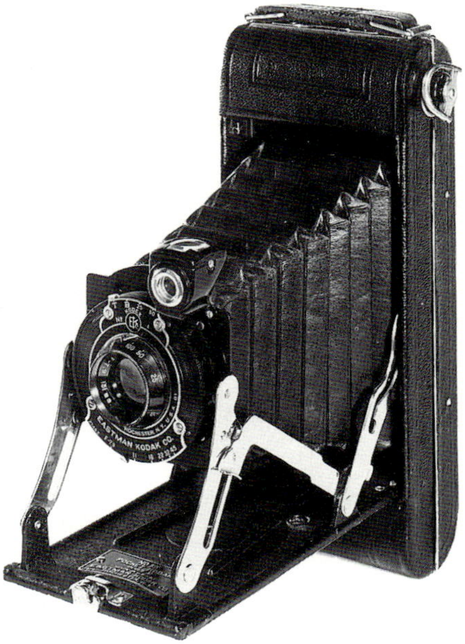

US model. KM

Description/Remarks

Leather covering; brilliant finder; Autographic feature.

Variations

1928–1931: Achromat lens/Kodex shutter models supplied in colour coverings – black, grey, blue, green (1929–1932), beige (1928–1929) and brown. Available in 1929 only in UK.

Achromatic lens: *Apr. 1923–1924:* Ball Bearing shutter. *Jan. 1925–1931:* Kodex shutter.
Kodak Anastigmat f/7.7: *Apr. 1923–Jan. 1925:* Ball Bearing shutter. *Oct. 1924–1931:* Diomatic shutter.
Kodar f/7.9: *May 1925–1931:* Kodex shutter.

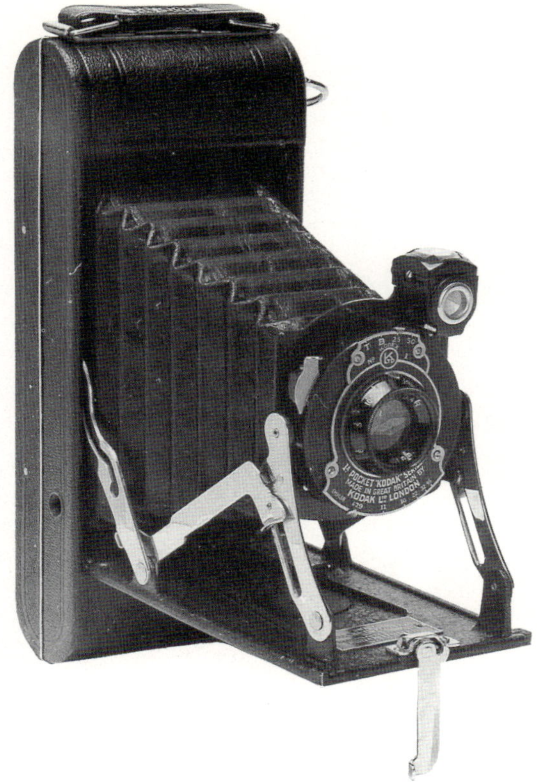

UK model. KM

UK VARIATIONS
Kodak Anastigmat f/6.3: *1927:* Diomatic shutter.
Zeiss Tessar f/6.3: *1927–1931:* Compur shutter.

No 1A Pocket Kodak Special

Type Folding rollfilm
Introduced May 1926
Discontinued 1934
Film size 116
Picture size 2½ × 4¼in.
Manufactured US
Lenses May 1926–March 1927: Kodak Anastigmat f/6.3
May 1926–1934: Kodak Anastigmat f/4.5
November 1926–February 1929: Kodak Anastigmat f/5.6
Shutter Kodamatic
Numbers made ?

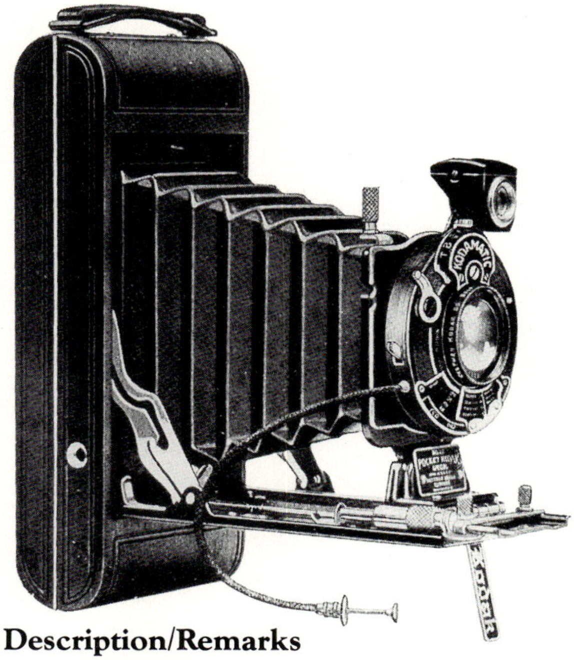

Description/Remarks

Replaced No 1A Autographic Kodak Special camera. Seal leather covering; screw focusing; Autographic feature.

UK VARIATIONS

The Kodak Trade Circular October 1926 stated that Cooke, Ross and Zeiss Anastigmat lenses would be fitted, but none were listed in the 1927 catalogue.

No 2C Pocket Kodak

Type Folding rollfilm
Introduced October 1926
Discontinued 1932
Film size 130
Picture size 2⅞ × 4⅞in.
Manufactured US
Lenses Achromatic or Kodar f/7.9 – but see below
Shutter Kodex – but see below
Numbers made ?

Description/Remarks

Brilliant finder; screw focusing; imitation leather covering; Autographic feature.

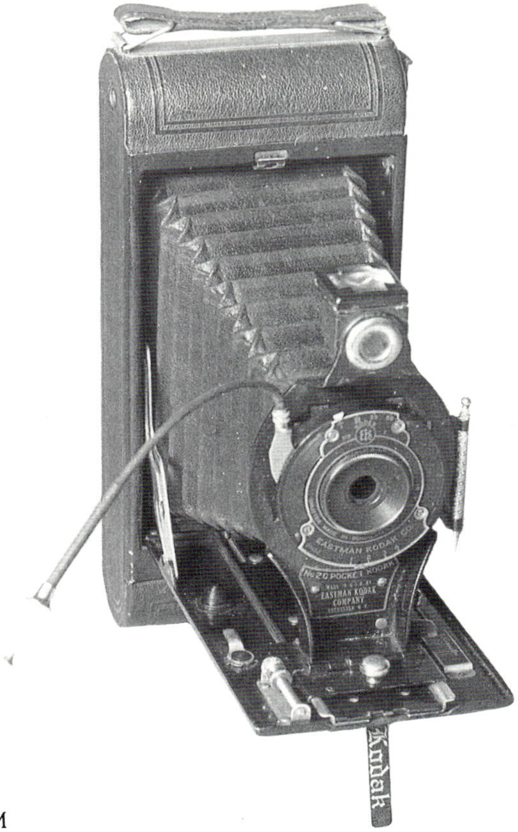

KM

Variations

Feb. 1927–1927: Kodak Anastigmat f/7.7
Apr. 1927–1932: Kodak Anastigmat f/6.3 with Ball Bearing shutter.

No 2C Pocket Kodak Special

Type Folding rollfilm
Introduced January 1928
Discontinued 1933
Film size
Picture size 2⅞ × 4⅞in.
Manufactured US
Lenses January 1928–February 1929: Kodak Anastigmat f/5.6
March 1929–March 1933: Kodak Anastigmat f/4.5
Shutter Kodamatic
Numbers made ?

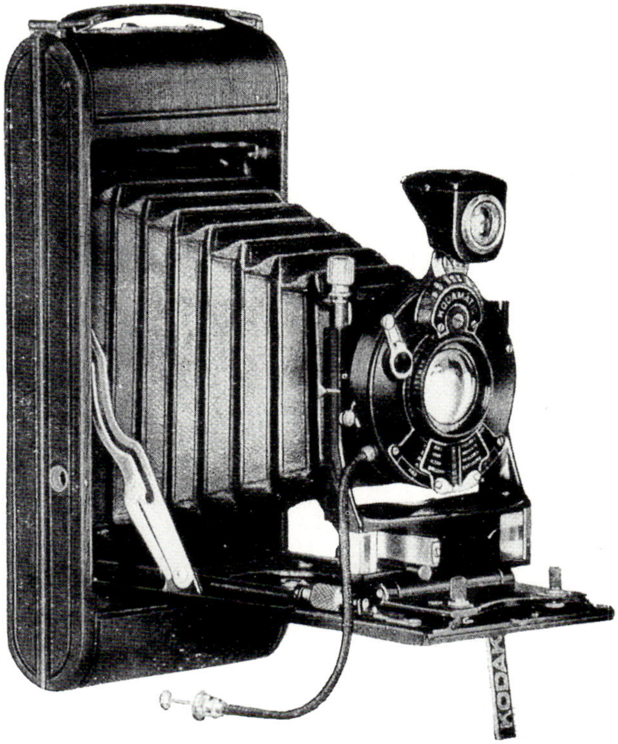

Description/Remarks

Replaced the No 2C Autographic Kodak Special camera. Seal leather covering; coupled rangefinder with screw focusing; Autographic feature.

UK VARIATIONS

Kodak Anastigmat f/6.3: *1930–1931:* Kodamatic or Compur shutter.
Zeiss Tessar f/6.3: *1930–1931:* Compur shutter.
Cooke Aviar f/6.3: *1930:* Compur shutter.
Ross Homocentric f/6.3: *1930:* Compur shutter.

In 1932 the camera was listed once again as the No 2C Autographic Kodak Special.

No 3 Pocket Kodak Special

Type Folding rollfilm
Introduced May 1926
Discontinued October 1933

Film size 118
Picture size 3¼ × 4¼in.
Manufactured US
Lenses May 1926–March 1927: Kodak Anastigmat f/6.3
May 1926–October 1933: Kodak Anastigmat f/4.5
November 1926–1928: Kodak Anastigmat f/5.6
Shutter Kodamatic
Numbers made ?

Description/Remarks

Replaced No 3 Autographic Kodak Special camera. Seal leather covering; lever focusing; Autographic feature.

UK VARIATIONS

The Kodak Trade Circular October 1926 stated that Ross, Cooke and Zeiss Anastigmats would be fitted, but none were listed in the 1927 catalogue.

No 3A Pocket Kodak

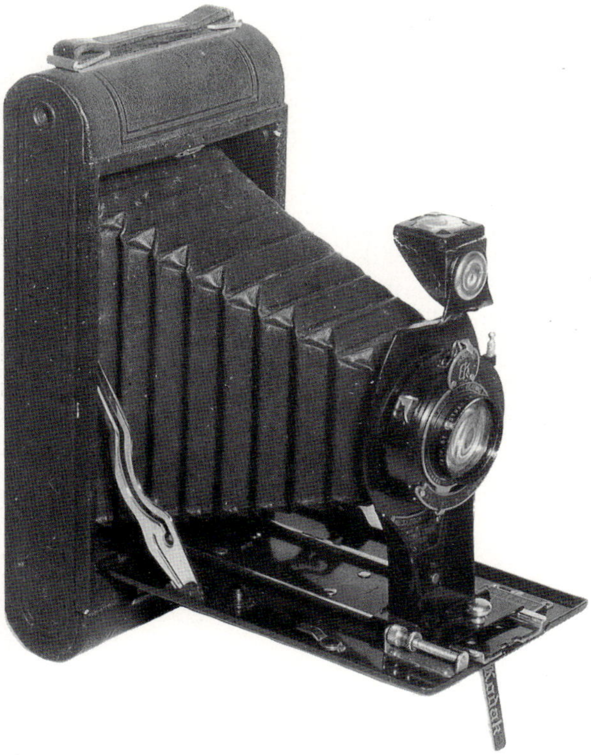

RPS

Type Folding rollfilm
Introduced February 1927
Discontinued 1933
Film size 122
Picture size 3¼ × 5½in.
Manufactured US
Lenses Achromatic or Kodar f/7.9 – but see below
Shutter Kodex – but see below
Numbers made ?

Description/Remarks

Screw focusing; imitation leather covering; brilliant finder; Autographic feature.

Variations

Feb. 1927–1927: Kodak Anastigmat f/7.7
Apr. 1927–1933: Kodak Anastigmat f/6.3 with Ball Bearing shutter.

No 4 Screen Focus Kodak

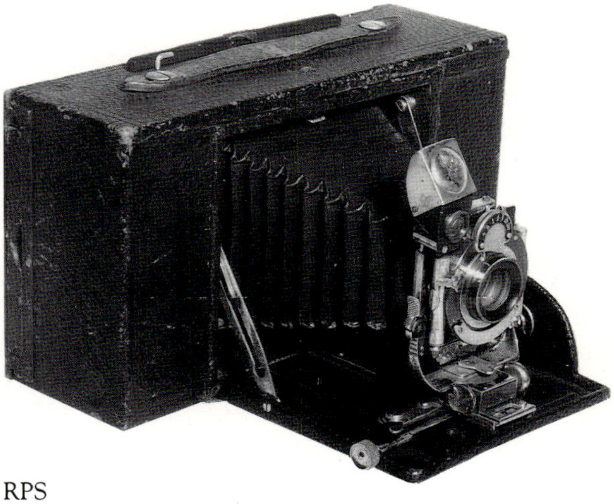

RPS

Type Folding rollfilm
Introduced April 1904
Discontinued April 1910
Film size 123
Picture size 4 × 5in.
Manufactured US
Lens Rapid Rectilinear – but see below
Shutter Kodak or Bausch & Lomb Automatic – but see below
Numbers made 4,000

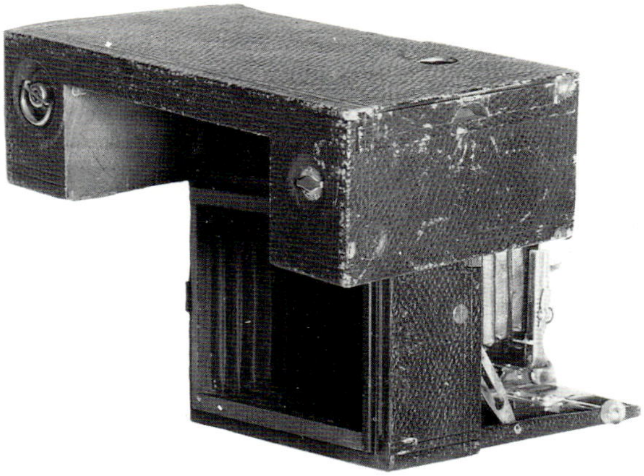

RPS

Description/Remarks

The rollfilm holder was pivoted at the top to the back of the camera body, allowing it to be swung up permitting a ground glass screen to be fitted for accurate focusing. A dark slide covered the film while the holder was out of position. It could be detached completely by withdrawing the pivot pins, and the camera used with plates. The first shipment of about 70 cameras in June 1904 were recalled to be remodelled. New model released January 1905, from serial number 101.

Variations

Bausch & Lomb Plastigmat f/6.8: *Apr. 1904–1908:* Kodak Automatic or Volute shutter. *Apr. 1904–March 1905:* Bausch & Lomb Automatic shutter.
Goerz Anastigmat f/6.8: *Apr. 1904–1906:* Kodak Automaticor Volute shutter. *Apr. 1904–March 1905:* Bausch & Lomb Automatic shutter.
Bausch & Lomb Zeiss Tessar f/6.3: *1906–1908:* Volute shutter. *Aug. 1908–Apr. 1910:* Bausch & Lomb Compound shutter.
Cooke Anastigmat f/6.5: *Mar. 1907-1909:* Volute shutter. *1909–Apr. 1910:* Kodak Automatic shutter.
Goerz Dagor f/6.8: *1908:* Volute shutter. *Aug.1908–Apr. 1910:* Bausch & Lomb Compound shutter.
Beck Isostigmar f/6.3: *1908:* Volute or Bausch & Lomb Automatic shutter.
Zeiss Kodak Anastigmat f/6.3: *1909–Apr. 1910:* Volute shutter.

Feb. 1906: Cover to dark slide opening fitted, from serial number2,094. *Sept. 1906:* Metal back frames fitted, from serial number 3,075.

UK VARIATIONS

Zeiss Tessar f/7: *1910:* Kodak Automatic, Koilos, Compound or Goerz Sector shutter.
Zeiss Tessar IIb f/6.3: *1908:* Kodak or Bausch & Lomb Automatic, Unicum, Goerz Sector, Koilos or Compound shutter.
Cooke Series III f/6.5: *1908:* Bausch & Lomb Automatic or Unicum shutter. *1908–1910:* Kodak Automatic, Koilos, Compound, or Goerz Sector shutter.
Cooke Series V f/8: *1910:* Kodak Automatic, Koilos, Compound or Goerz Sector shutter.
Beck Series II f/6.3 or Series III f/7.7: *1910:* Kodak Automatic, Koilos, Compound or Goerz Sector shutter.
Beck Isostigmar f/7.7: *1908:* Kodak or Bausch & Lomb Automatic, Koilos, Unicum, Celverex, Goerz Sector or Compound shutter.
Goerz Syntor f/6.8: *1910:* Kodak Automatic, Koilos, Compound or Goerz Sector shutter.
Goerz Dagor f/6.8: *1908:* Bausch & Lomb Automatic or Unicum shutter. *1908–1910:* Kodak Automatic, Koilos, Compound, or Goerz Sector shutter.
Ross Homocentric Series II f/5.6 or IV f/6.8: *1910:* Kodak Automatic, Koilos, Compound or Goerz Sector shutter.
Ross Homocentric Series III or C f/6.3: *1907–1908:*Bausch & Lomb Automatic or Unicum shutter. *1907–1910:* Kodak Automatic shutter. *1908–1910:* Koilos, Compound or Goerz Sector shutter.
Ross Homocentric Series V or D f/8: *1907–1908:* Bausch & Lomb or Unicum shutter. *1907–1910:* Kodak Automatic shutter. *1908–1910:* Koilos, Compound or Goerz Sector shutter.
Aldis Series II f/6.3: *1908:* Bausch & Lomb Automatic or Unicum shutter. *1908–1910:* Kodak Automatic, Koilos, Compound or Goerz Sector shutter.
Aldis Series III f7.7: *1907:* Kodak or Bausch & Lomb Automatic or Unicum shutter. *Aldis Oxys f/6.9: 1908:*Bausch & Lomb Automatic or Unicum shutter. *1908–1910:* Kodak Automatic, Koilos,

Compound or Goerz Sector shutter.
Dallmeyer Stigmatic Series II f/6: *1908:* Bausch & Lomb Automatic or Unicum shutter. *1908–1910:* Kodak Automatic, Koilos, Compound or Goerz Sector shutter.
Euryplan Series II f/6.8: *1908:* Bausch & Lomb Automatic or Unicum shutter. *1908–1910:* Kodak Automatic, Koilos, Compound or Goerz Sector shutter.
Euryplan Series II f/5.6: *1908:* Bausch & Lomb or Kodak Automatic, Koilos, Compound, Goerz Sector or Unicum shutter.
Euryplan Nulli Secundus f/6.8: *1908:* Bausch & Lomb or Kodak Automatic, Koilos, Compound, Goerz Sector or Unicum shutter.
Euryplan Nulli Secundus f/6.5: *1910:* Kodak Automatic, Koilos, Compound or Goerz Sector shutter.

Six-16 Kodak, UK model

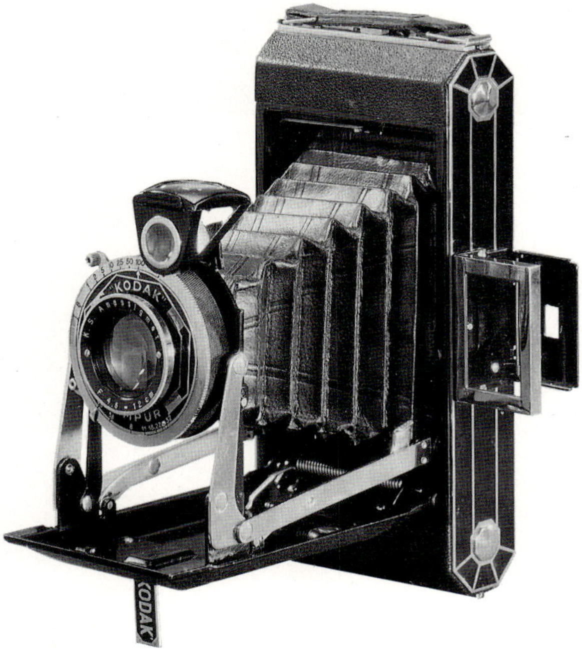

KP

Type Self-erecting folding rollfilm
Introduced 1934
Discontinued 1939
Film size 616
Picture size 2½ × 4¼in.
Manufactured UK
Lenses Kodak Anastigmat f/6.3 or f/4.5
Shutters Various Kodak or Compur – see below
Numbers made ?

Description/Remarks

Angled ends to body; black enamelled side plates with nickel lines; brilliant and folding frame finder; sliding red window cover.

Variations

Kodak Anastigmat f/6.3: *1934–1937:* O.V. 3-speed shutter; O.P.S. 3-speed shutter, delayed action.
Kodak Anastigmat f/4.5: *1934–1937:* O.P.S. 3-speed shutter, delayed action; Compur-S shutter. *1937:* Compur-Rapid shutter.
Zeiss Tessar f/4.5: *1935–1936:* Compur-S shutter.
From 1938 designated Model C:
Kodak Anastigmat f/6.3: *1938–1939:* O.V. 3-speed shutter, O.P.S. 3-speed shutter, delayed action.
Kodak Anastigmat f/4.5: *1938:* O.P.S. 3-speed, delayed action shutter, Compur-S shutter.

Six-16 Kodak, US model

Type Folding or self-erecting folding rollfilm
Introduced February 1932
Discontinued June 1936
Film size 616
Picture size 2½ × 4¼in.
Manufactured US
Lenses Various – see below
Shutters Various – see below
Numbers made ?

Description/Remarks

First model to use the slimmer 616 film spool. Pig-grain cowhide covering, in black or brown (1932–1934); angled ends to body; black enamelled side plates with nickel line motif; octagonal shutter casing or shutter plate (except on some Compur models); brilliant finder, folding frame finder fitted in addition from 1934.

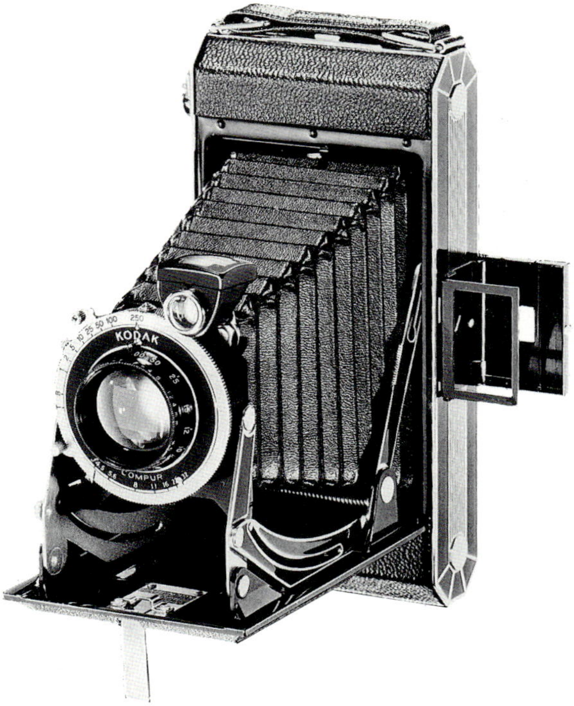

KP

Variations

FOLDING MODEL

Kodak Anastigmat f/4.5: *Aug. 1932–1933:* Diodak shutter.

SELF-ERECTING MODELS

Meniscus achromat: *1932:* Kodal shutter.
Doublet (fixed focus): *1932–1933:* Kodon shutter.
Doublet (focusing): *1934–June 1936:* Kodon shutter.
Kodak Anastigmat f/6.3: *Feb. 1932–Aug. 1935:* Diodak shutter.
Kodak Anastigmat f/4.5: *May 1934–June 1936:* Compur shutter.
Kodak Anastigmat f/6.3: *Aug. 1935–June 1936:* Dakar shutter.

The chromium plated baseboard locking struts were changed from May 1934 to an improved pattern finished in black enamel.

Six-16 Kodak Junior

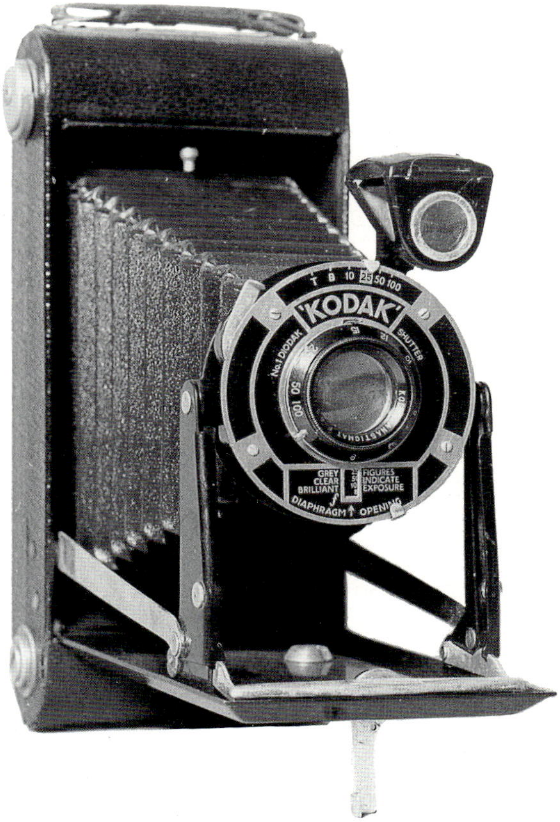

KM

Type Selferecting folding rollfilm
Introduced January 1934
Discontinued 1940
Film size 616
Picture size 2½ × 4¼in.
Manufactured UK
Lenses Twindar f/11 or Kodak Anastigmat f/6.3
Shutters Kodon (f/11)
Diodak (f/6.3)
Numbers made ?

Description/Remarks

Black leatherette covering; brilliant finder; from 1939 winding key replaced by knob.

Six-16 Kodak Senior

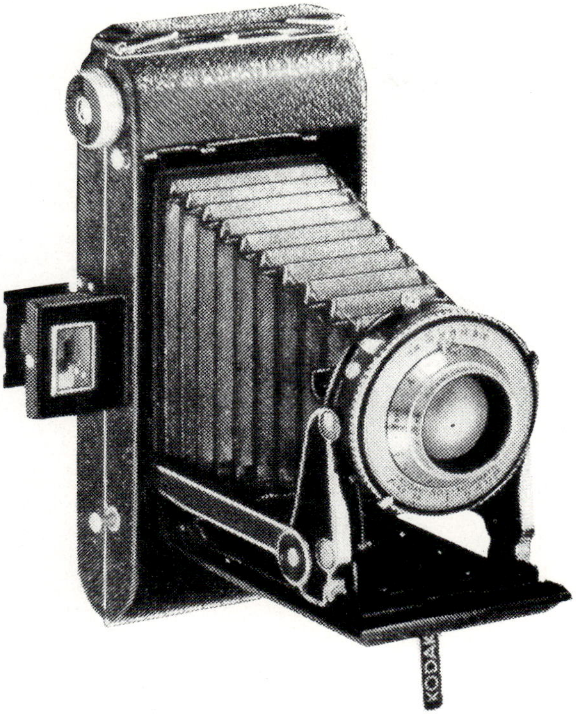

Type Self-erecting folding rollfilm
Introduced February 1938
Discontinued 1939
Film size 616
Picture size 2½ × 4¼in.
Manufactured UK
Lens Kodak Anastigmat f/4.5
Shutter Kodamatic
Numbers made ?

Description/Remarks

Body release; folding optical frame finder; knob wind.

Six-16 Kodak Special

Type Self-erecting folding rollfilm
Introduced February 1938
Discontinued 1939
Film size 616
Picture size 2½ × 4¼in.
Manufactured UK
Lens Kodak Anastigmat f/4.5
Shutter Compur-Rapid
Numbers made ?

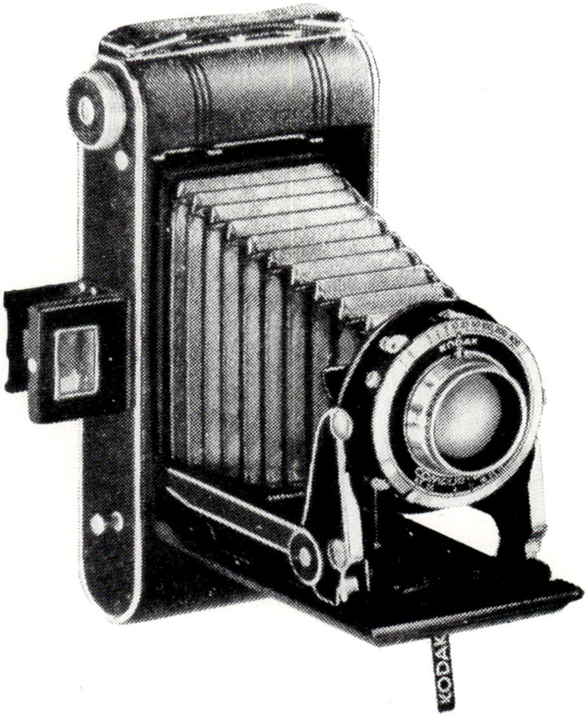

Description/Remarks

Pin-seal leather covering; body release; folding optical frame finder; wind knob.

Six-20 Kodak, UK model

Type Selferecting folding rollfilm
Introduced January 1932
Discontinued 1937
Film size 620
Picture size 2¼ × 3¼in.
Manufactured UK
Lenses Various – see below
Shutters Various – see below
Numbers made ?

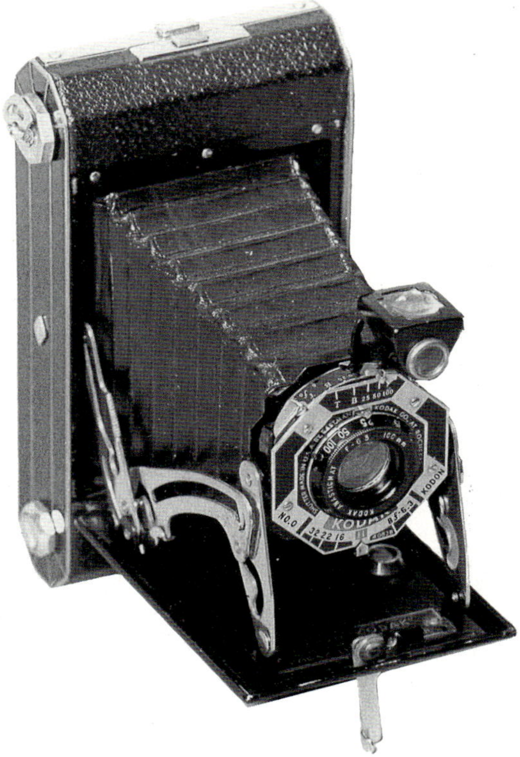

KM

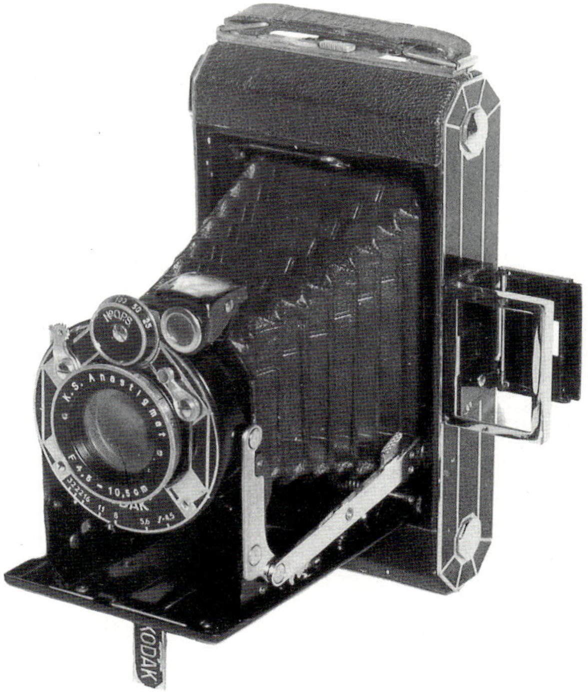

Model C. RPS

Description/Remarks

Angled ends to body, covered in pig-grained leatherette; enamelled side panels with nickel lines. Octagonal shutter housing or shutter plates.

Variations

Doublet: *1932–1933:* Kodon shutter.
Kodak Anastigmat f/6.3: *1932–1933:* Kodon shutter.

These early models had brilliant finders only. *From 1933:* redesigned model C with folding frame and brilliant finders (frame finders could be fitted to the earlier models by Kodak Limited); simplified baseboard struts; sliding red window cover. Not all models had "C"on the front plate.

Kodak Anastigmat f/6.3: *1933–1937:* O.P.S 3-speed shutter, delayed action. *1934–1937:* O.V. 3-speed shutter.
Kodak Anastigmat f/4.5: *1933–1937:* O.P.S. 3-speed shutter, delayed action Compur-S shutter. *1937:* Compur-Rapid shutter.
Cooke Anastigmat f/4.5: *1934–1936:* Compur-S shutter.

Six-20 Kodak, US model

Type Folding or self-erecting folding rollfilm
Introduced February 1932, but see below
Discontinued June 1937
Film size 620
Picture size 2¼1 × 3¼in.
Manufactured US
Lenses Various – see below
Shutters Various – see below
Numbers made ?

Description/Remarks

First cameras to use the slimmer 620 spool. Angled ends to body, covered in black or brown pig-grain cowhide; black enamelled side plates with nickel lines;

octagonal shutter housing or shutter plate; brilliant finder— folding reflecting finder added from 1934.

Although generally available from early 1932, some Six-20 Kodak cameras were in use the previous year; the UK Kodak Trade Circular for October—November 1931 advised dealers that stocks of the 620 film wereavailable if overseas visitors enquired.

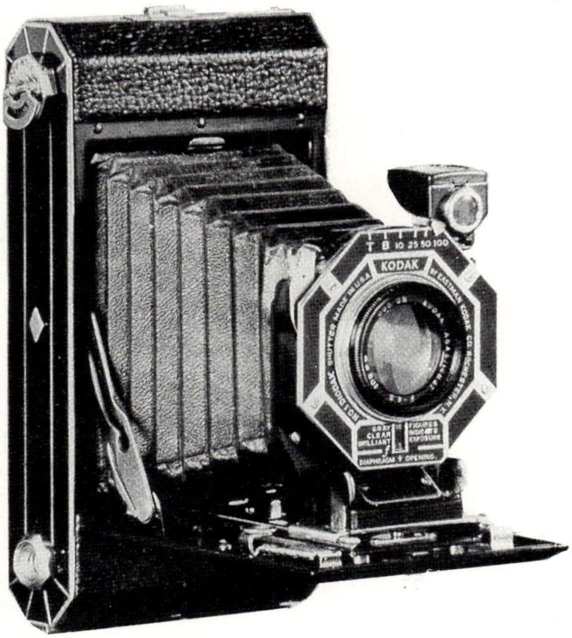

Variations

FOLDING MODEL

Kodak Anastigmat f/4.5: *Aug. 1932—1934:* Diodak shutter.

SELF-ERECTING MODELS

Meniscus achromat: *1932:* Kodal shutter.
Doublet (fixed focus): *Feb. 1932—1934:* Kodon shutter.
Doublet (2-position focusing): *1933—1934:* Kodon shutter.
Doublet (3-position focusing): *May 1934—June 1937:* Kodon shutter.
Kodak Anastigmat f/6.3: *Feb. 1932—1937:* Kodon shutter.
Kodak Anastigmat f/4.5: *Feb. 1934—June 1937:* Compurshutter.
From early 1934 the original chromed baseboard struts were replaced by an improved design, black enamelled.

Six-20 Kodak A

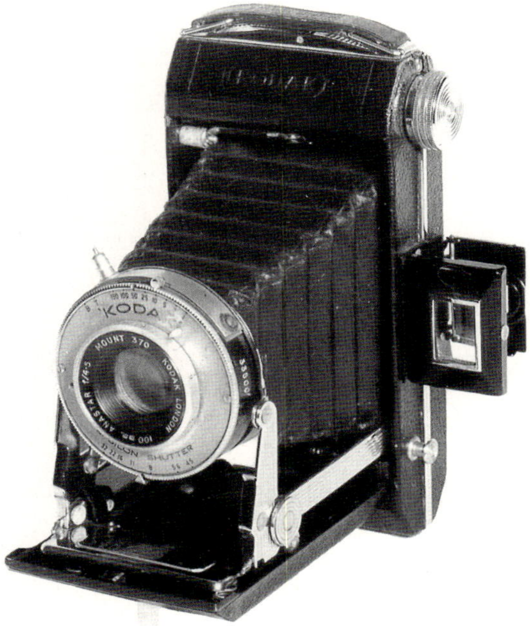

RPS

Type Self-erecting folding rollfilm
Introduced 1951
Discontinued January 1955
Film size 620
Picture size $2\frac{1}{4} \times 3\frac{1}{4}$in.
Manufactured UK
Lenses Kodak Anastar f/6.3 or f/4.5, 100mm
Shutters 1951—January 1955: Dakon (f/6.3)
1951—May 1954: Epsilon 4-speed (f/4.5)
1951—July 1953: Epsilon 8-speed (f/4.5)
Numbers made ?

Description/Remarks

Angled ends to body, fine-grained imitation leather covering; body release; bayonet flash contact; folding optical frame finder.

Six-20 Kodak B

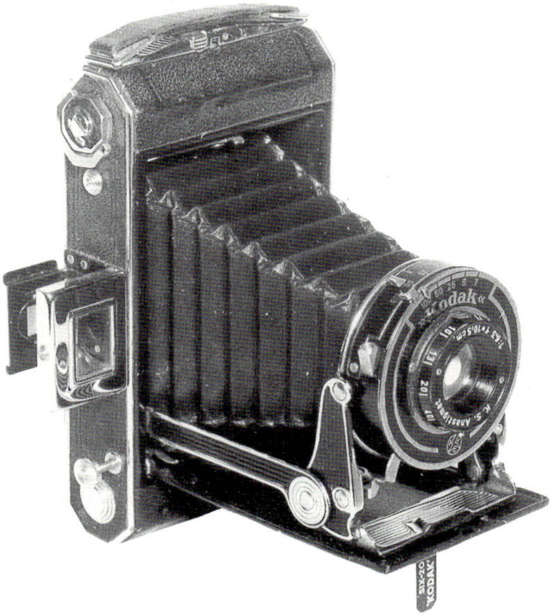

Type Self-erecting folding rollfilm
Introduced September 1937
Discontinued 1940
Film size 620
Picture size 2¼ × 3¼in.
Manufactured UK
Lenses Kodak Anastigmat f/6.3 or f/4.5
Shutters O.V. 3-speed, O.P.S. 3-speed (f/6.3, f/4.5); Compur-S (f/4.5).
Numbers made ?

Description/Remarks

Improved version of Six-20 Kodak camera, modelled on the Kodak AG Vollenda 620 camera; improved baseboard strut system; body release; winding knob instead of key; folding optical frame finder; red window safety cover; angled ends to body, grained leather covering.

Six-20 Kodak Junior

Type Self-erecting folding rollfilm
Introduced January 1933
Discontinued 1940
Film size 620
Picture size 2½ × 4¼in.
Manufactured UK
Lenses Various – see below
Shutter Kodon
Numbers made ?

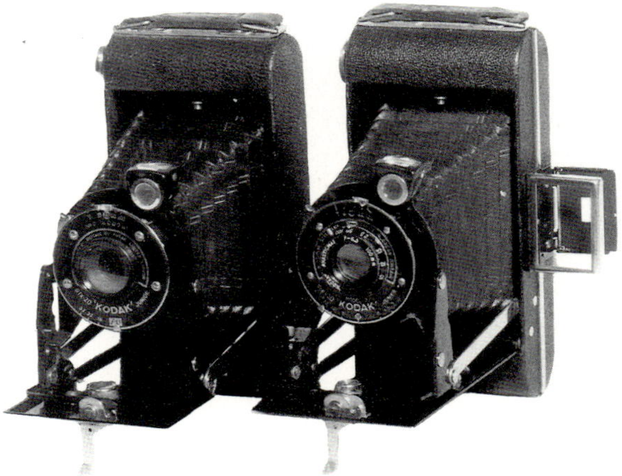

1933–1940 models. RPS

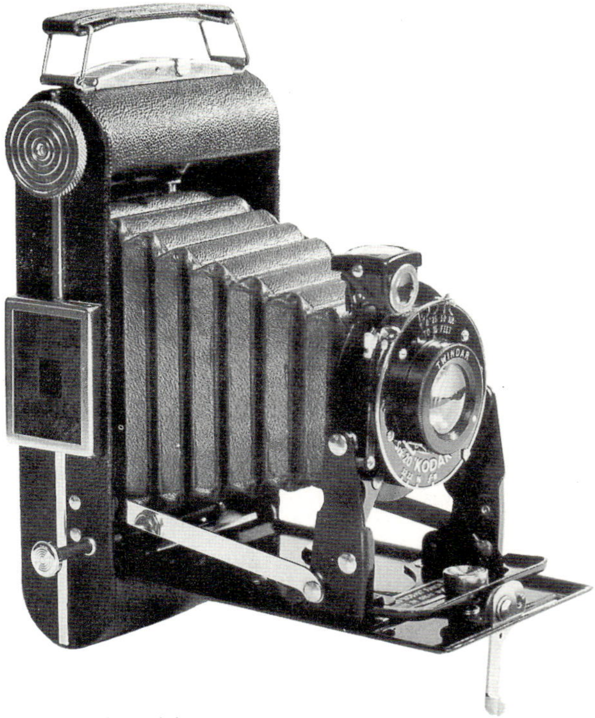

1939–1940 model. KP

Description/Remarks

Black leatherette covering; brilliant finder on right of lens panel (seen from front) until 1939, then on left.

Variations

Jan. 1933–1935: Doublet
Jan. 1934–1940: Twindar f/11 (*1934–5* – 2-point focusing; *1936–1940* – 3-point focusing)
Jan. 1933–1940: Kodak Anastigmat f/6.3
Feb. 1936–1940: Kodak Anastigmat f/7.7

1936–1940: Folding frame finder added to f/6.3 model. *1939–1940:* Optional body release; frame finder on left (seen from front) when fitted. Wind key changed to knob. *1934–1940* Red window cover fitted.

Six-20 Kodak Junior de Luxe

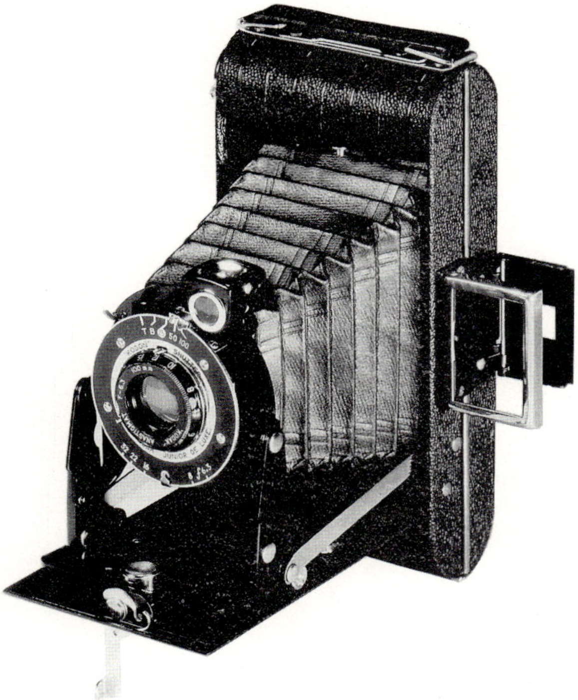

1935–1939 model. KP

Type Self-erecting folding rollfilm
Introduced November 1935
Discontinued 1940
Film size 620
Picture size 2¼ × 3¼in.
Manufactured UK
Lenses Kodak Anastigmat f/4.5 or f/6.3
Shutters Kodon (f/6.3)
Dakar (f/4.5)
Numbers made ?

Description/Remarks

Ribbed leatherette covering; bright chromium plated baseboard struts; brilliant and folding frame finders, on right (seen from front).

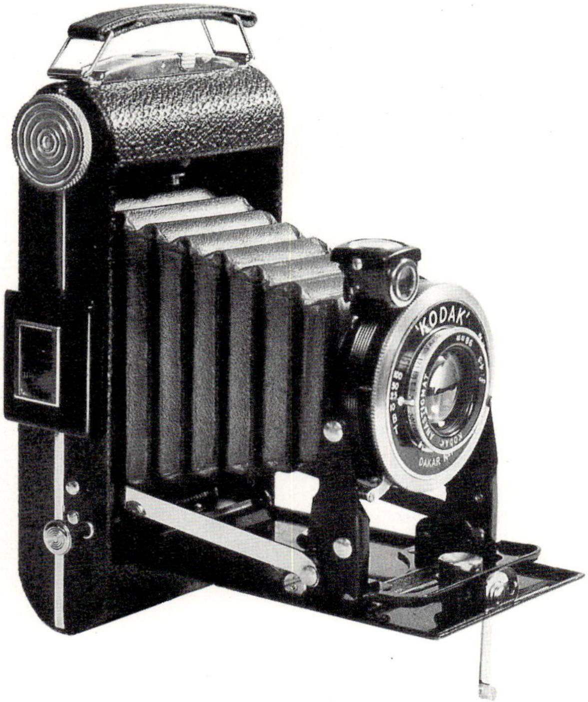

1939–1940 model. KP

Variations

1939–1940: Body release optional; optical frame finder, on left (seen from front) when body release fitted; some models have smooth pin-grain leatherette covering; knob wind instead of key.

Six-20 Kodak Special

Type Self-erecting folding rollfilm

Introduced February 1938
Discontinued 1940
Film size 620
Picture size 2¼ × 3¼in.
Manufactured UK
Lens Kodak Anastigmat f/4.5
Shutter Compur-Rapid
Numbers made ?

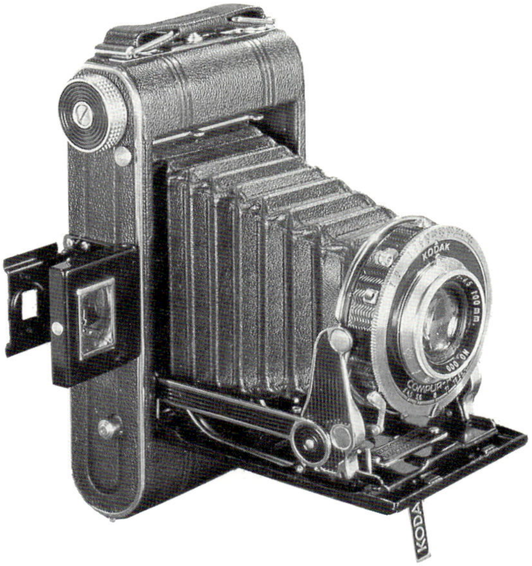

KP

Description/Remarks

De Luxe model, with pin-seal grain leather covering; body release; folding optical frame finder; wind knob.

Six-Three Kodak No 1A

Type Folding rollfilm
Introduced April 1913
Discontinued April 1915
Film size 116
Picture size 2½ × 4¼in.
Manufactured US
Lens Cooke Kodak Anastigmat f/6.3
Shutter Bausch & Lomb Compound
Numbers made ?

Description/Remarks

A variation of the No 1A Folding Pocket Kodak camera, which name is on the camera. It was described as 'Six-Three' only in catalogues and in the instruction book.

Six-Three Kodak No 3

Type Folding rollfilm
Introduced April 1913
Discontinued April 1915
Film size 118
Picture size 3¼ × 4¼in.
Manufactured US
Lens Cooke Kodak Anastigmat f/6.3
Shutter Bausch & Lomb Compound
Numbers made ?

Description/Remarks

A variation of the No 3 Folding Pocket Kodak camera, which name is on the camera. It was described as 'Six-Three' only in catalogues and in the instruction book.

Six-Three Kodak No 3A

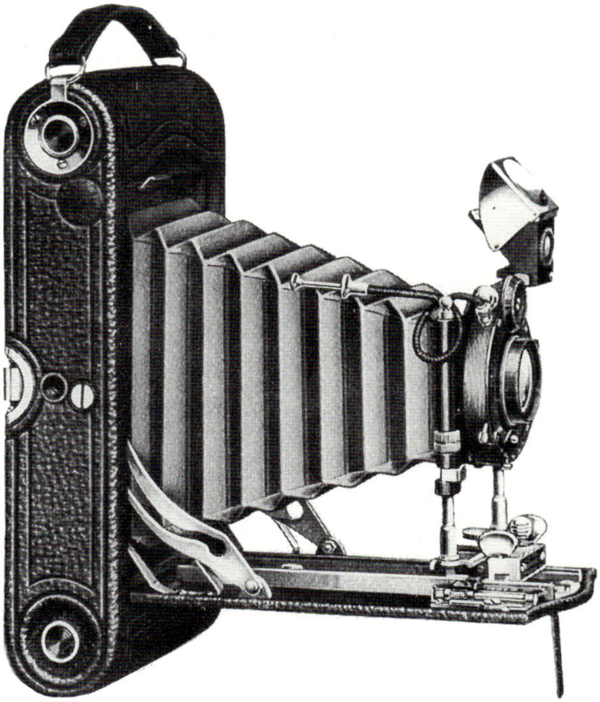

Type Folding rollfilm
Introduced April 1913
Discontinued April 1915
Film size 122
Picture size 3¼ × 5½in.
Manufactured US
Lens Cooke Kodak Anastigmat f/6.3
Shutter Bausch & Lomb Compound
Numbers made ?

Description/Remarks

A variation of the No 3A Folding Pocket Kodak camera, which name is on the camera. It was described as 'Six-Three' only in catalogues and in the instruction book.

No 1A Special Kodak

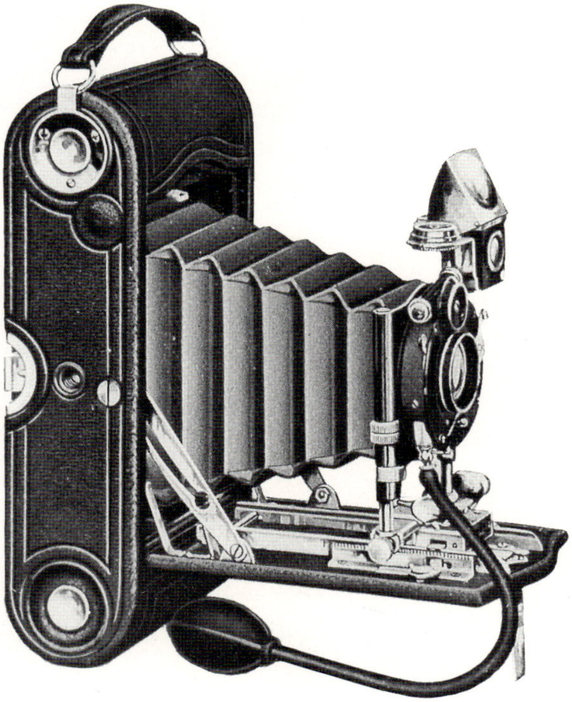

Type Folding rollfilm
Introduced April 1912
Discontinued 1914
Film size 116
Picture size 2½ × 4¼in.
Manufactured US
Lenses Zeiss Kodak f/6.3
Bausch & Lomb Zeiss Tessar f/6.3
Cooke Anastigmat f/6.5
Shutter Bausch & Lomb Compound
Numbers made 1,600 approximately

Description/Remarks

Persian morocco leather covering; rack and pinion focusing; brilliant finder with level; from serial number 1,001. Supplied with Autographic backs as No 1A Autographic Kodak Special camera from September 1914,serialnumber 2,686.

UK VARIATIONS

Cooke Series III f/6.5: *Nov. 1912–1915:* Compound shutter. *1914–1915:* Koilos shutter.
Zeiss Tessar f/6.3: *Nov. 1912–1915:* Compound shutter. *1914–1915:* Koilos shutter.
Ross Homocentric f/6.3: *1915:* Koilos or Compound.

No 3 Special Kodak

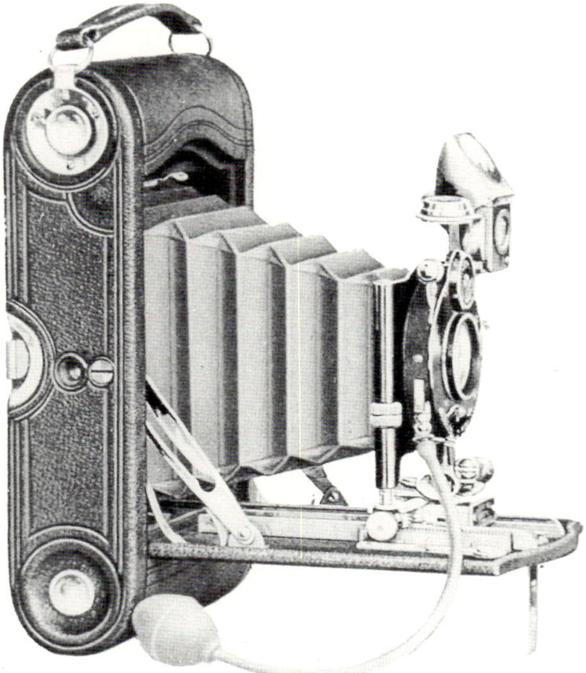

Type Folding rollfilm
Introduced April 1911
Discontinued 1914
Film size 118
Picture size 3¼ × 4¼in.
Manufactured US
Lenses Zeiss Kodak Anastigmat f/6.3
Bausch & Lomb Zeiss Tessar f/6.3
Cooke Anastigmat f/6.5
Shutter Bausch & Lomb Compound
Numbers made 5,000 approximately

Description/Remarks

Persian morocco leather covering; rack and pinion focusing; brilliant finder with level; from serial number 1.

Supplied fitted with Autographic backs as No 3 Autographic Kodak Special camera from September 1914, serial number 4,949.

UK VARIATIONS

Cooke Series III f/6.5: *June 1911–1915:* Compound shutter. *1912–1915:* Koilos shutter.
Cooke Series IV f/5.6: *1912–1914:* Koilos or Compound shutter.
Zeiss Tessar IIb f/6.3: *June 1911–1915:* Compound shutter. *1912–1915:* Koilos shutter.
Zeiss Tessar Ic f/4.9: *1912–1914:* Koilos or Compound shutter.
Zeiss Double Amatar f/6.8: *1912:* Koilos or Compound shutter.
Goerz Dagor f/6.8: *1911:* Compound shutter.
Ross Homocentric f/6.3: *1915:* Koilos or Compound shutter.

No 3A Special Kodak

Type Folding rollfilm
Introduced April 1910
Discontinued 1914
Film size 122
Picture size 3¼ × 5½in.
Manufactured US
Lenses Zeiss Kodak Anastigmat f/6.3
Bausch & Lomb Zeiss Tessar f/6.3
Cook Anastigmat f/6.5
Shutter Bausch & Lomb Compound
Numbers made 18,245

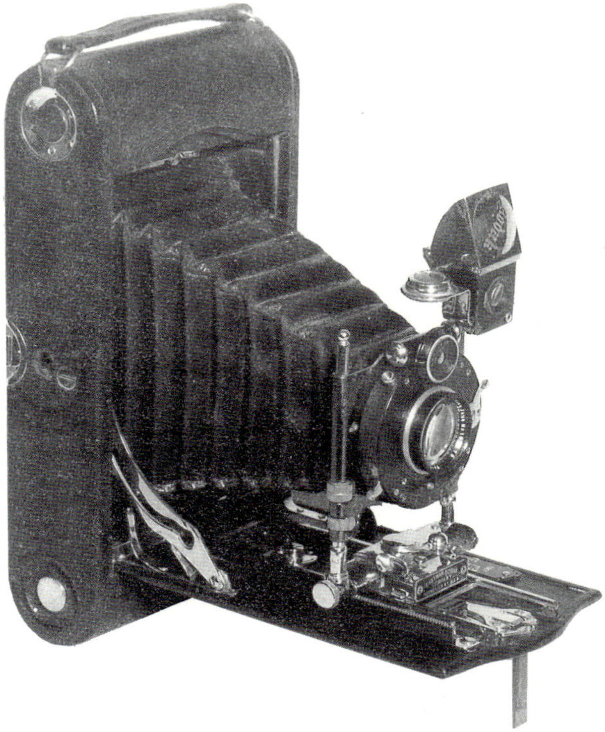

RPS

Description/Remarks

Persian morocco leather covering; rack and pinion focusing; brilliant finder with level; from serial number 1.

Supplied fitted with Autographic backs as No 3A Autographic Kodak Special camera from June 1914, serial number 18,246.

UK VARIATIONS

Goerz Dagor f/6.8: *1910–1911:* Compound shutter.
Cooke Series III f/6.5: *911–1915:* Compound shutter.*1912–1915:* Koilos shutter.
Zeiss Tessar Series IIb f/6.3: *1911–1915:* Compound shutter. *1912–1915:* Koilos shutter.
Zeiss Tessar Series Ic f/5.3: *1912–1914:* Compound shutter. *1914:* Koilos shutter.
Zeiss Double Amatar f/6.8: *1912:* Compound or Koilos.
Ross Homocentric f/6.3: *1915:* Compound or Koilos shutter.

No 1A Speed Kodak

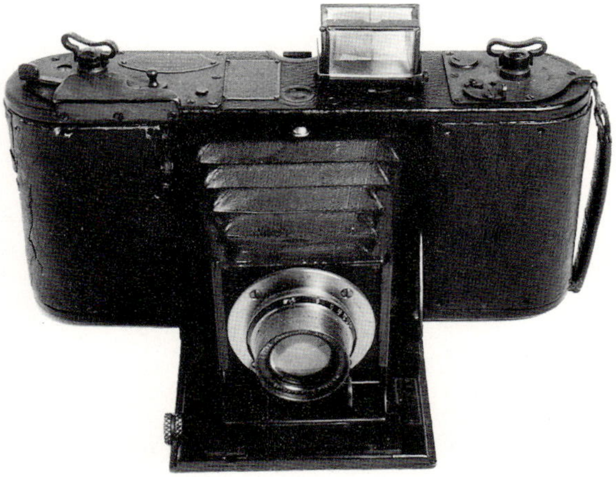

TNC

Type Folding rollfilm
Introduced April 1909
Discontinued 1913
Film size 116
Picture size 2½ × 4¼in.
Manufactured US
Lens Supplied without lens, or with choice of several – see below
Shutter Graflex Focal Plane
Numbers made 2,100 approximately

Description/Remarks

Multiple slot fabric focal plane shutter, 1/1000 sec. to 1/10 sec. Fine grain leather covering, gun metal finish on metal parts; optical folding frame finder with mirror; rack and pinion focusing. Serial numbers from 1,001.

UK VARIATIONS

Aug. 1910–1914: Zeiss Tessar IIb f/6.3; Zeiss Tessar Ic f/4.5
1912: Zeiss Double Amatar f/6.8.
Aug. 1910–1914 Cooke Series III f/6.5; Cooke Series IV f/5.6; Cooke Series II f/4.5.
1910: Beck Anastigmat f/5.8 or f/4.5; Beck No 4 Special Anastigmat f/5.6; Goerz Dagor f/6.8; Goerz Celor f/4.5.

No 4A Speed Kodak

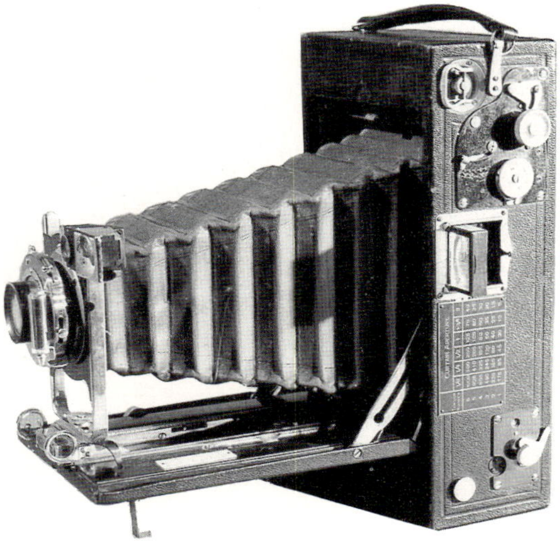

KM

Type Folding rollfilm
Introduced April 1908
Discontinued April 1913
Film size 126
Picture size 4¼ × 6½in.
Manufactured US
Lens Supplied without lens, or with choice from a range – see below
Shutter Kodak Focal Plane
Numbers made 1,000+

Description/Remarks

Variable aperture fabric focal plane shutter, speeds 1/1000 sec. to 1/5 sec. Brilliant and optical frame finders; rack and pinion focusing. From serial number 1-D

UK VARIATIONS

Feb. 1909–1915: Zeiss Tessar IIb f/6.3 or Ic f/4.5.
1912: Zeiss Double Amatar f/6.8.
Feb. 1909–1915: Cooke Series II f/4.5.
1910–1915: Cooke Series III f/6.5 or Series IV f/5.6.
1910: Beck Series I f/4.5 or Series II f/5.8.
1909: Beck Isostigmar f/5.8.
Feb. 1909–1910: Goerz Syntor f/6.8, Goerz Dagor f/6.8, Goerz Celor f4.8.

Stereo Kodak Model 1

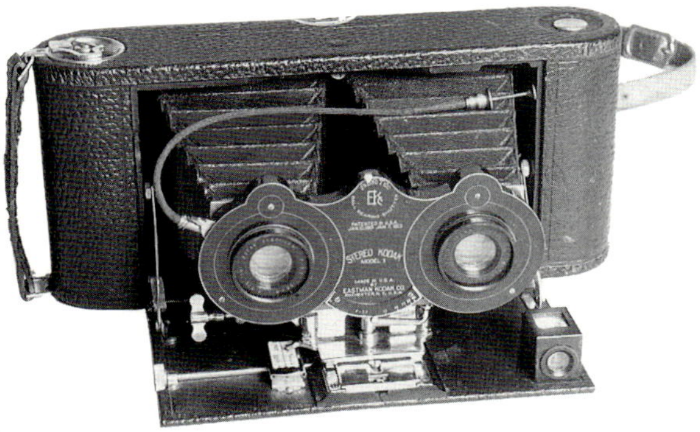

KM

Type Folding rollfilm
Introduced April 1917
Discontinued May 1925
Film size 101
Picture size Two 3⅛ × 3-3/16in.
Manufactured US
Lenses Two Kodak Anastigmat f/7.7
Shutters 1917–1918: Stereo Automatic
1919–May 1925: Stereo Ball Bearing
Numbers made ?

Description/Remarks

Seal grain leather covering; rack and pinion focusing; rising front.

UK VARIATIONS

Two Cooke Anastigmats f.6.5: *Oct. 1921–1922:* Stereo Automatic shutter.
Two Cooke Aviars f/6.3: *1924:* Stereo Ball Bearing shutter.
Two Ross Homocentrics f/6.3: *1922:* Stereo Automatic shutter. *1924:* Stereo Ball Bearing.

Super Kodak Six-20

Type Self-erecting folding rollfilm
Introduced August 1938
Discontinued August 1944
Film size 620
Picture size 2¼ × 3¼in.
Manufactured US
Lens Kodak Anastigmat Special f/3.5
Shutter Compur
Numbers made 719

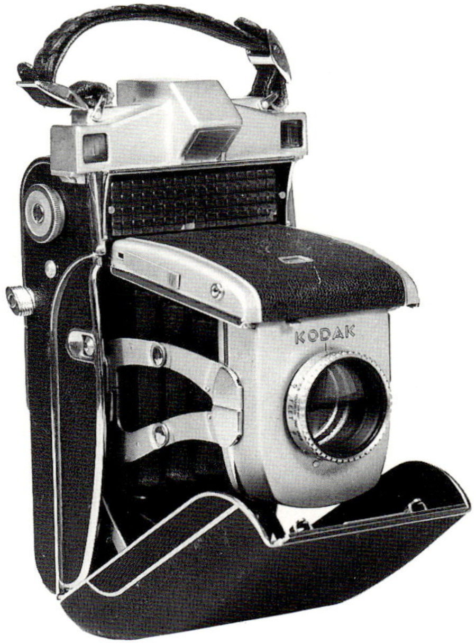

KP

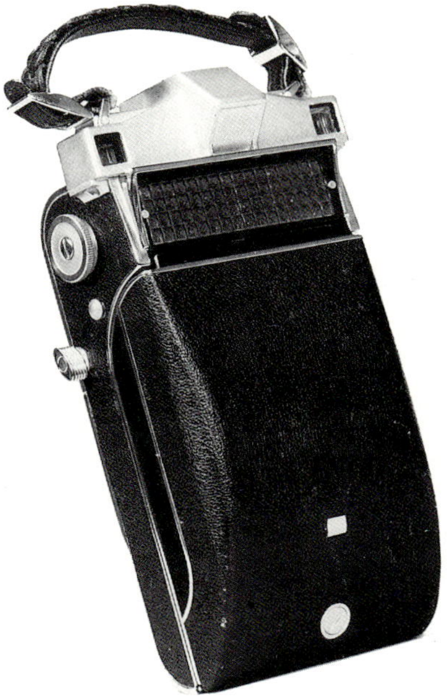

Closed. KP

Description/Remarks

Advanced design by Joseph Mihalyi and styling by Walter Dorwin Teague, 'clam-shell' construction. The first automatic exposure control camera. A large selenium photocell moved a meter needle, which was locked by the first pressure on the shutter release by a comb-like element. A spring-loaded sensor, connected to the aperture control, then moved until stopped by the locked needle; the exposure was then made. The camera was fully automatic for shutter speeds between $\frac{1}{25}$ and $\frac{1}{200}$ sec.; manual setting was possible.

Other innovative features were crank film wind and coupled wide-base rangefinder combined with direct vision optical viewfinder. It was very expensive – $225 (£75 at the rate of exchange then), much more than a Leica camera. This, together with a degree of unreliability – it was nicknamed 'the boomerang' by Kodak employees because of the regularity with which it returned to the Company for repair – led to it being the least widely sold Kodak camera aimed at the general market.

Vanity Kodak

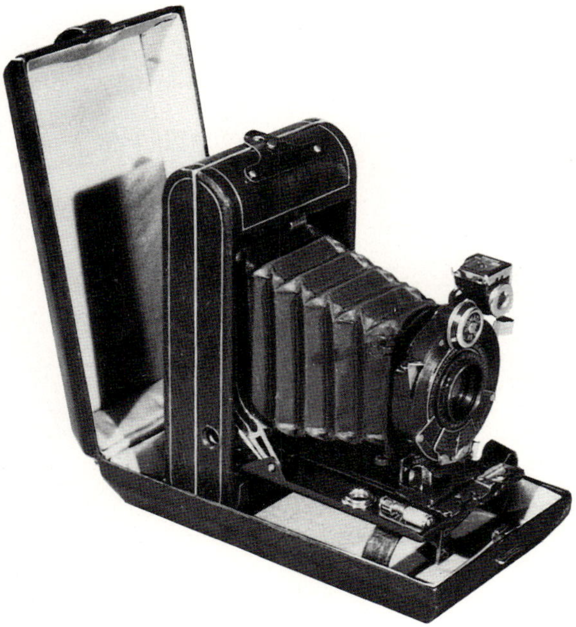

KM

Type Folding rollfilm
Introduced April 1928
Discontinued 1933
Film size 127
Picture size $1\frac{5}{8} \times 2\frac{1}{2}$in.
Manufactured US
Lens Kodak Anastigmat f/6.3
Shutter Diomatic
Numbers made ?

Description/Remarks

"The Modern Camera for the Modern Girl" – the Vest Pocket Kodak Series III camera in a range of grained coloured calf leathers – Sea Gull (grey), Redbreast (red), Jenny Wren (brown), Cockatoo (green) and Bluebird (blue)– with embossed gold lines and matching enamel on metal parts. The cameras were supplied in silk-lined matching cases.

Vanity Kodak Ensemble

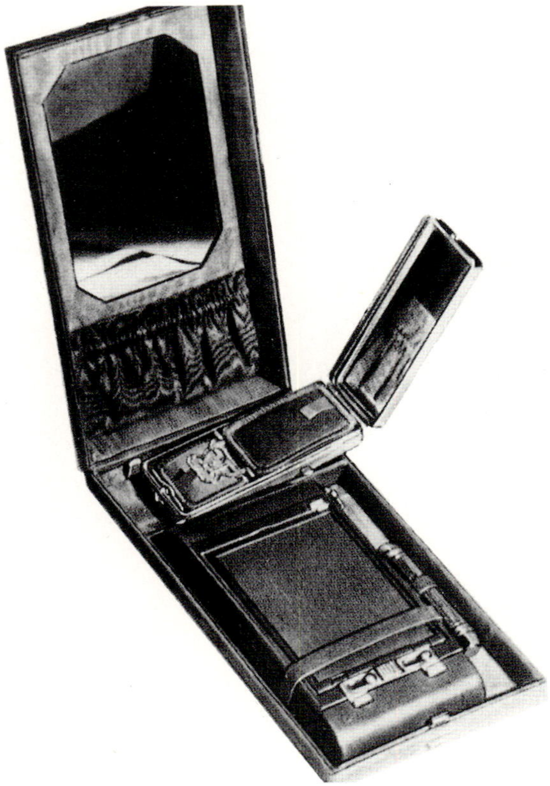

Type Folding rollfilm
Introduced October 1928
Discontinued 1929
Film size 127
Picture size 1$\frac{5}{8}$ × 2$\frac{1}{2}$in.
Manufactured US
Lens Meniscus
Shutter V.P. Rotary
Numbers made ?

Description/Remarks

A version of the Vest Pocket Kodak Model B camera in a coloured finish – green, grey or beige – packaged with matching lipstick, compact, mirror and change pocket. The cosmetics were supplied by Richard Hudnut.

Vest Pocket Autographic Kodak

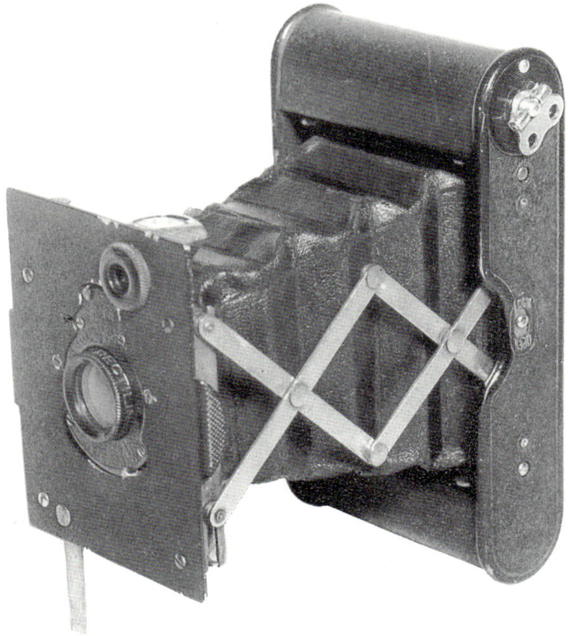

RPS

Type Collapsing rollfilm
Introduced January 1915
Discontinued September 1926
Film size 127
Picture size 1$\frac{5}{8}$ × 2$\frac{1}{2}$in.
Manufactured US
Lenses January 1915–January 1926: achromatic
1915: Kodak Anastigmat f/7.7 (fixed focus)
December 1917–September 1926
Shutter Ball Bearing
Numbers made 1,750,000 approximately

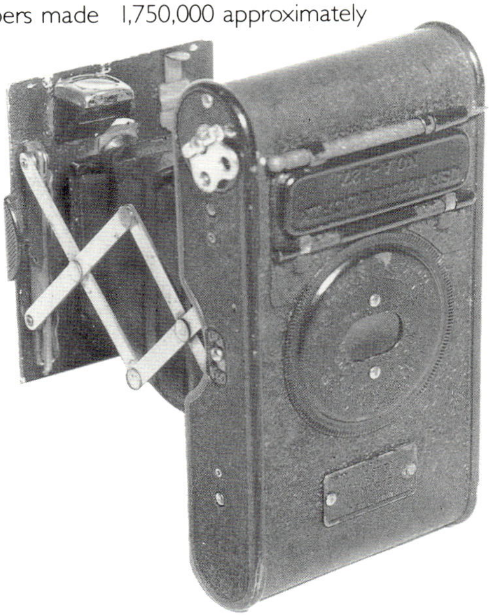

RPS

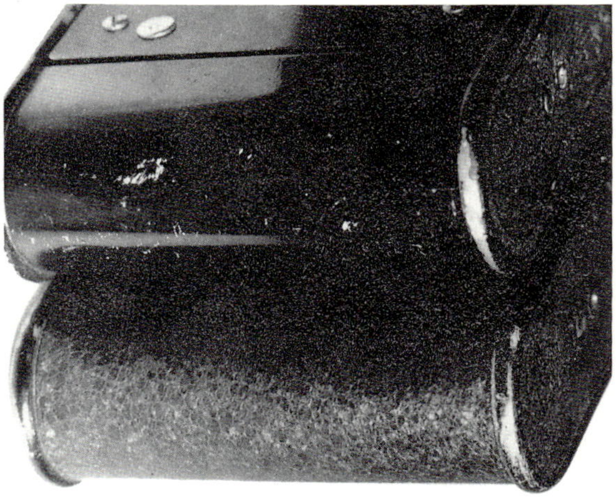

Above: Black enamel finish
Below: Japan crystal finish, from 1920. RPS

Description/Remarks

Autographic version of Vest Pocket Kodak camera. Serial numbers from around 200,000.

A best seller in World War I, when it was advertised as "The Soldier's camera".

Variations

Feb. 1915: Stop stud for vertical support eliminated, from serial number 231,401. *1920:* 'Japan Crystal' crackle enamel finish introduced.

Vest Pocket Autographic Kodak Special

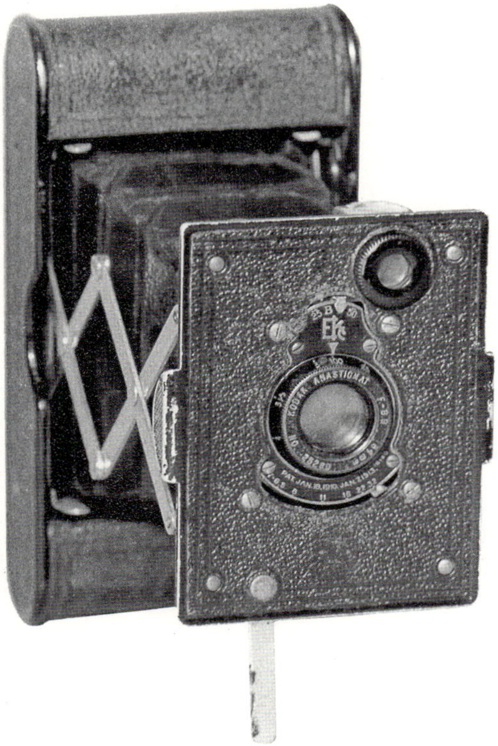

KM

Type Collapsing rollfilm
Introduced April 1915
Discontinued September 1926
Film size 127
Picture size 1⅝ × 2½in.
Manufactured US
Lenses Various – see below
Shutter Ball Bearing
Numbers made ?

Description/Remarks

Vest Pocket Autographic Kodak cameras with pin-grain leather covering and nickel-plated fittings.

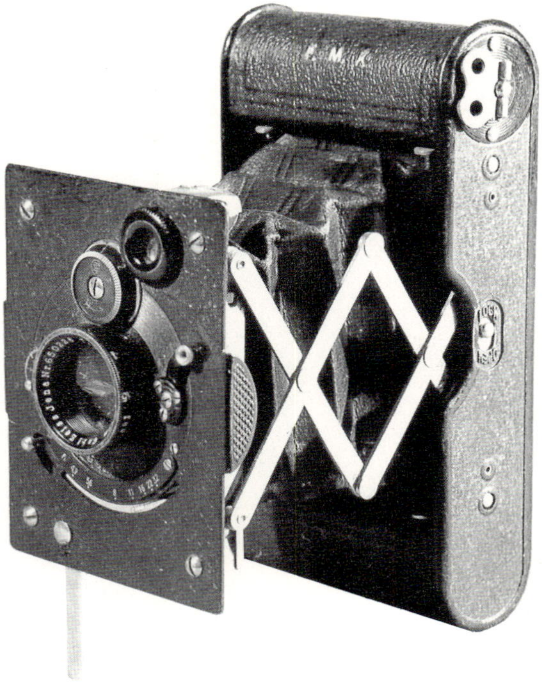

Tessar/Compur model. RPS

Variations

Apr. 1915–Apr. 1916: Zeiss Kodak Anastigmat f/6.9.
Apr. 1916–1926: Kodak Anastigmat f/7.7, fixed focus.
1916–1921: Kodak Anastigmat f/6.9, fixed focus.
Mar. 1921–Sept. 1926: Kodak Anastigmat f/6.9, focusing.
Apr. 1916–Sept. 1926: Bausch & Lomb Kodak Anastigmat f/6.9.
Mar. 1924–Sept. 1926: Kodak Anastigmat f/7.7, focusing.

UK VARIATIONS

1916–1927: TTH-Kodak Anastigmat f/6.5.
1916–1926: Ross Homocentric f/6.8.
1916–1926: Cooke Series III f/6.5, focusing.
1917: Lacour-Berthiot Olor.
1926: Zeiss Tessar F/6.8, focusing.
In Compur shutter:
1922: Cooke Anastigmat f/4.5, focusing.
1926–1927: Zeiss Tessar f/4.9, focusing.

Vest Pocket Kodak

Type Collapsing rollfilm
Introduced April 1912
Discontinued 1914
Film size 127
Picture size 1⅝ × 2½in.
Manufactured US
Lenses 1912–1914: Meniscus achromat
1914: Kodak Anastigmat f/8
Shutter Ball Bearing
Numbers made 200,000

Description/Remarks

Lazy-tongs strut construction; the first camera to take 127 size rollfilm. One of the most successful cameras of its day; a big seller during World War I in its Autographic version. Black smooth enamel finish; brilliant finder; film loaded from side.

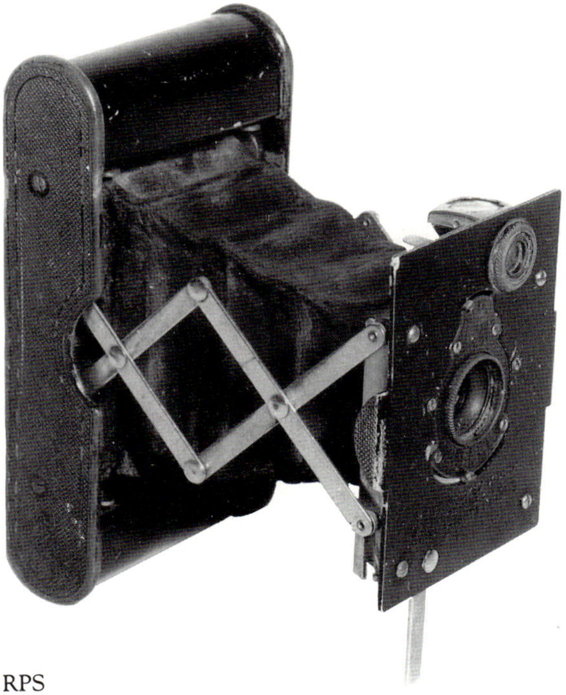

RPS

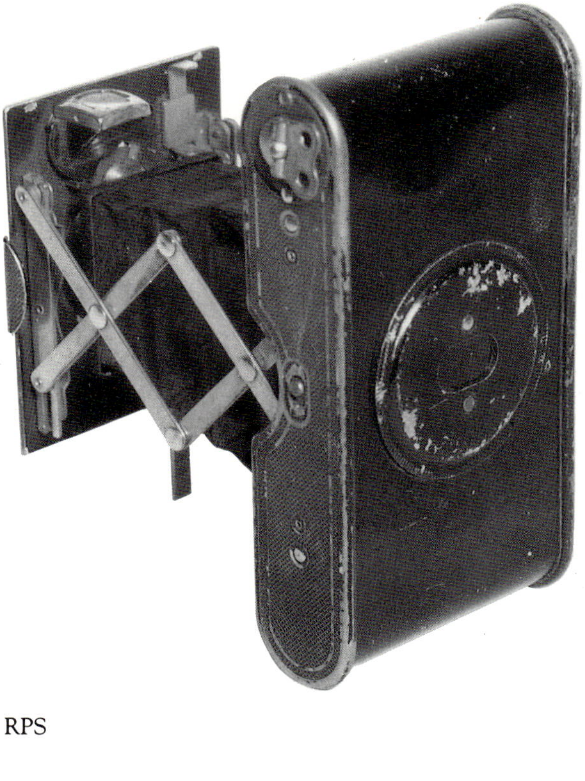

RPS

Vest Pocket Kodak Special

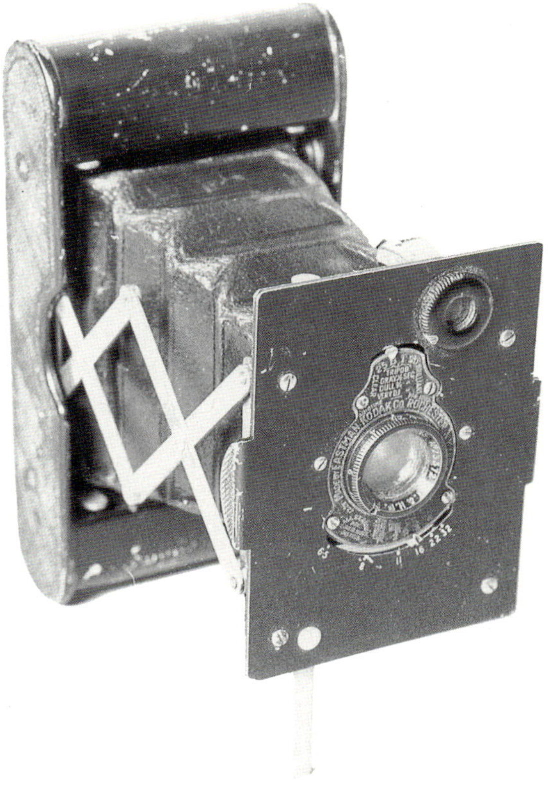

KM

Type Collapsing rollfilm
Introduced July 1912
Discontinued 1914
Film size 127
Picture size 1⅝ × 2½in.
Manufactured US
Lens Zeiss-Kodak Anastigmat f/6.9
Shutter Ball Bearing
Numbers made ?

Description/Remarks

Identical to Vest Pocket Kodak camera, but with improved lens.

UK VARIATIONS

1912–1915: Zeiss Tessar Series IIb f/6.3, Cooke Series III f/6.5.
1912–1914: Kodak Anastigmat f/6.3, TTH-Kodak Anastigmat f/6.8.
1914–1915: TTH-Kodak Anastigmat f/6.5.

Vest Pocket Kodak Special (later model)

Type Folding rollfilm
Introduced September 1926
Discontinued April 1935
Film size
Picture size 1⅝ × 2½in.
Manufactured US
Lenses Kodak Anastigmat f/5.6 or f/4.5
Shutter Diomatic
Numbers made ?

Description/Remarks

A de-luxe version of the Vest Pocket Kodak Series III camera with a superior lens and seal leather covering.

UK VARIATIONS
In Diomatic shutter:
1929–1936: Zeiss Tessar f/4.5, Ross Xpres f/4.5
In Compur shutter:
1927–1934: Ross Xpres f/4.5
1927–1936: Zeiss Tessar f/4.5.

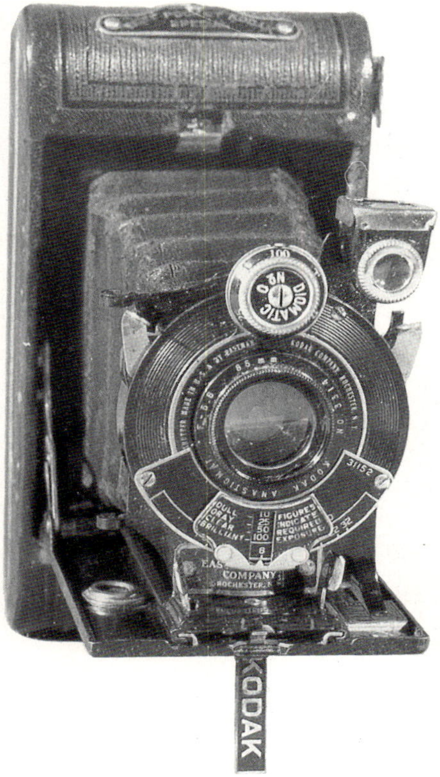

KM

Vest Pocket Kodak Model B

Type Folding rollfilm
Introduced October 1925
Discontinued 1934
Film size 127
Picture size 1⅝ × 2⅛in.
Manufactured US, UK from 1931 to 1933
Lenses October 1925–1934: Meniscus
September 1928–1931: Periscopic
1932–1934: Doublet
Shutter Vest Pocket Rotary
Numbers made ?

Description/Remarks

Imitation leather covering; with 'iridescent' finish from November 1926; Autographic feature until 1932; brilliant finder.

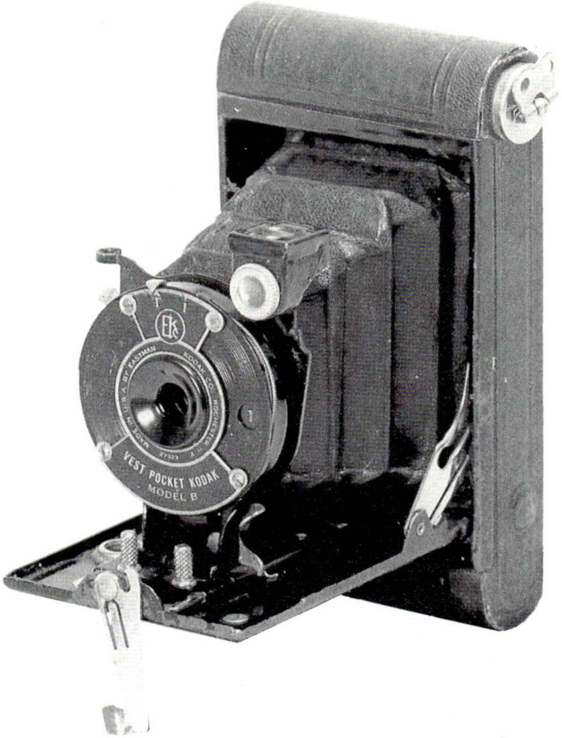

US model, imitation leather finish. KM

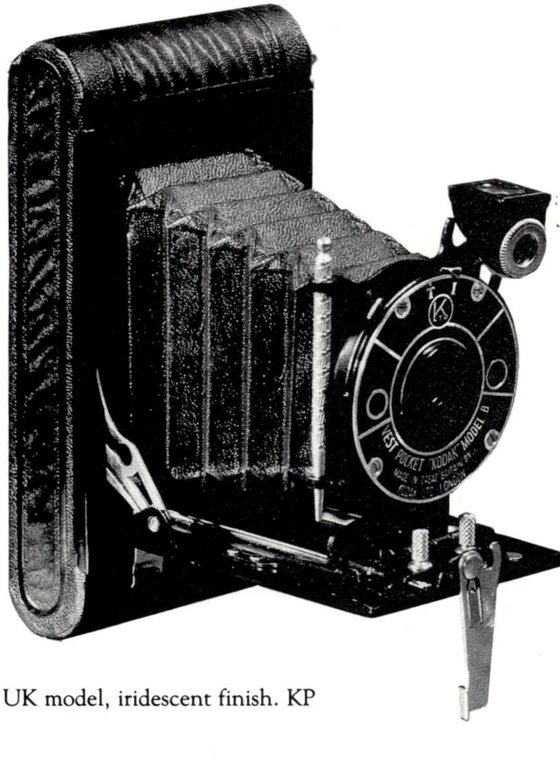

UK model, iridescent finish. KP

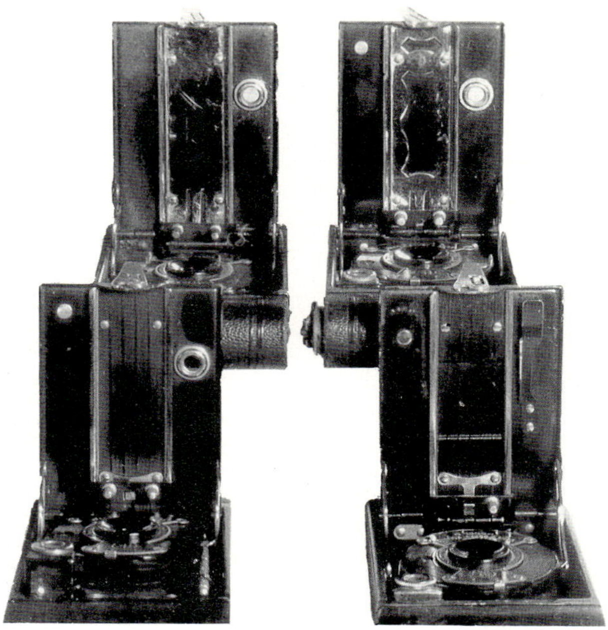

Changes in baseboard design, in chronological order left to right, top to bottom. RPS

Variations

1925–Sept. 1928: back released by concealed buttons. *Sept.1928–1934:* back released by sliding latch. Earliest models had plain metal lens slide; later models from 1926 had a scalloped aperture in the slide. *From 1928:* the slide had front to back ribbing. *From 1932:* no Autographic feature or tripod socket, focusing catch on the side of the baseboard.

Vest Pocket Kodak Series III

Type Folding rollfilm
Introduced September 1926
Discontinued 1934
Film size 127
Picture size 1⅝ × 2½in.
Manufactured US, UK from 1931 to 1937
Lenses September 1926–1934: Kodar f/7.9
September 1926–1930: Kodak Anastigmat f/6.3
1930–1934: Kodak Anastigmat f/5.6
Shutters Kodex (Kodar lens)
Diomatic (Kodak Anastigmat lens)
Numbers made ?

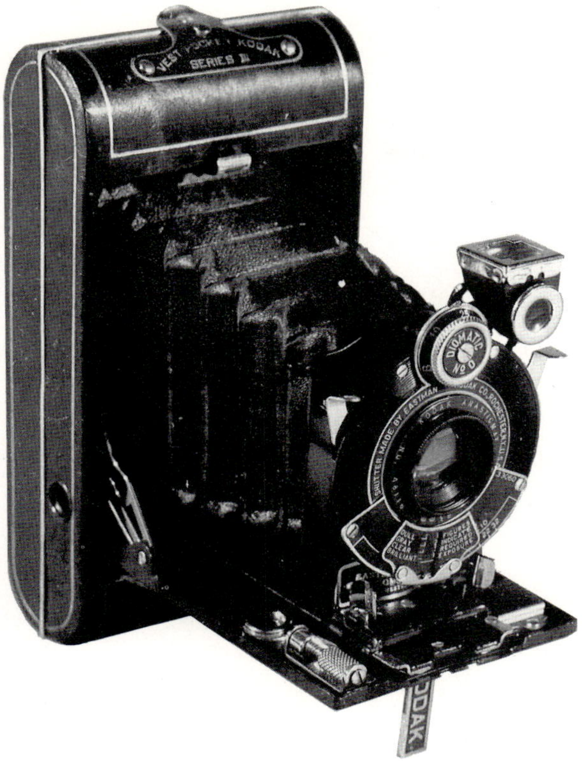

KM

Description/Remarks

Black leather covering; metal parts finished in nickel or enamel; versions with coloured finish called Vanity Kodak cameras (q.v.); Autographic feature; screw focusing.

UK VARIATIONS
Zeiss Tessar f/6.3: *1927–1936:* Diomatic shutter.
Ross Homocentric f/6.3: *1927–1931:* Diomatic shutter.

Vollenda No.68

Type Self-erecting folding rollfilm
Introduced 1930
Discontinued 1934
Film size 120
Picture size 6 × 9cm
Manufactured Germany
Lens Schneider Radionar f/6.3, 10.5cm
Shutters Nagel or Pronto S
Numbers made About 2,500 from 1933 with Kodak identification

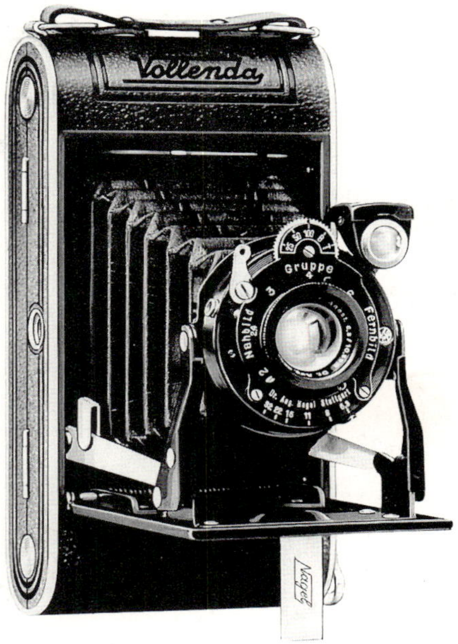

KP

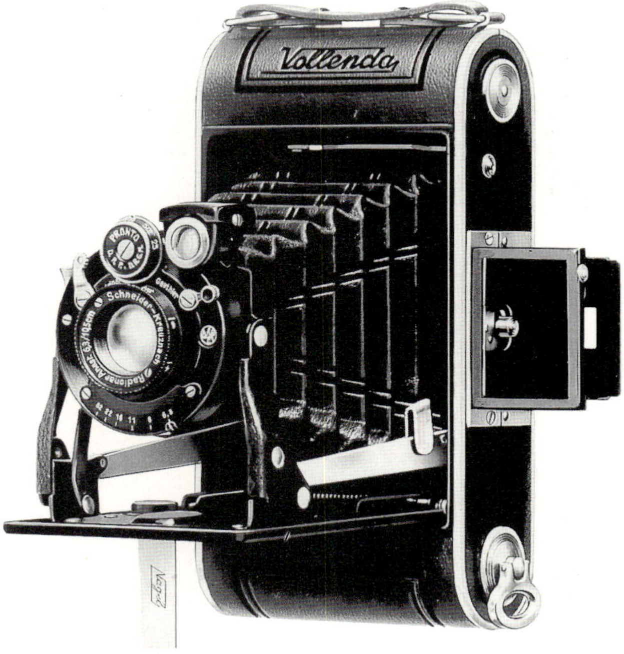

Model I. KP

Description/Remarks

Lens reset to infinity when camera closed; brilliant finder; leatherette covering.

Variations

Model I – as above, but leather covering and additional frame finder.
Model II – as model I, but with deluxe brown leather covering.

Vollenda No.70

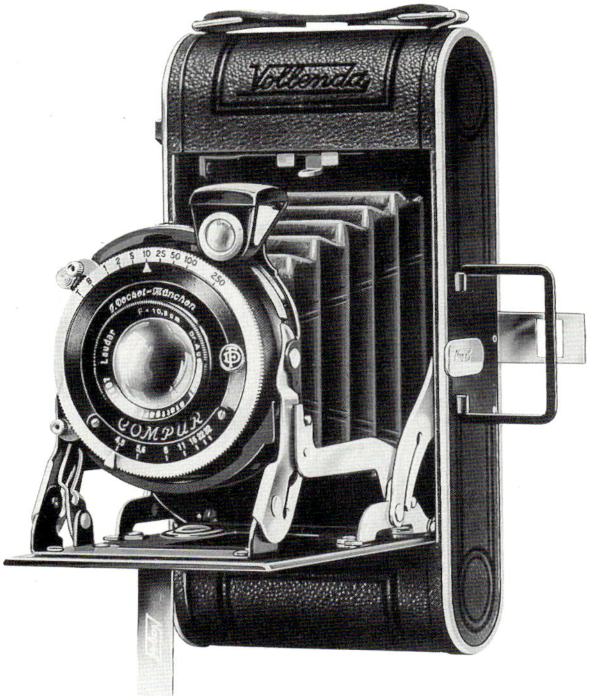

Model 70/1. KP

Type Self-erecting folding rollfilm
Introduced 1930
Discontinued 1934
Film size 120
Picture size 6 × 9cm
Manufactured Germany
Lenses Nagel Anastimat f/6.3 or f/4.5, 10.5cm
Shutters Nagel, Pronto or Pronto S
Numbers made ?

Description/Remarks

Lens reset to infinity on closing camera; brilliant finder.

Variations

No.70/1 – Nagel Laudar, Schneider Xenar or Leitz Elmar lenses. Ibsor, Compur, Compur S shutters.
No.70/2 – as 70/1, but deluxe finish.

Kodak Vollenda No.72

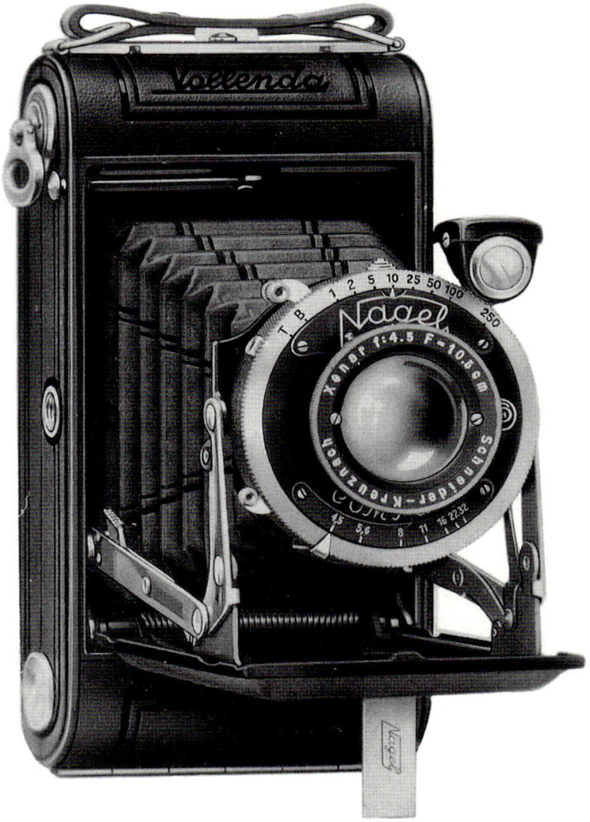

KP

Type Self-erecting folding rollfilm
Introduced 1933
Discontinued 1934
Film size 120
Picture size 6 × 9cm
Manufactured Germany

Lenses Schneider Radionar, Xenar or Zeiss Tessar f/4.5, 10.5cm.
Shutters Pronto S or Compur S
Numbers made ?

Description/Remarks

Focus reset to infinity when camera closed. Brilliant and frame finders.

CHAPTER 4 *Brownie Folding Cameras*

While the majority of Brownie cameras were low-cost box models, a limited number of folding cameras were made under this name. Most were made between 1904 and 1926, the later models having the Autographic feature. They had a more basic specification than their 'Kodak' counterparts, with little or no variation in lens and shutter options. While Eastman Kodak made no folding Brownie cameras after 1926, Kodak Limited in England made a Six-20 Folding Brownie model which was on sale in the late 1930s and for a few years after the War.

No 2 Folding Autographic Brownie

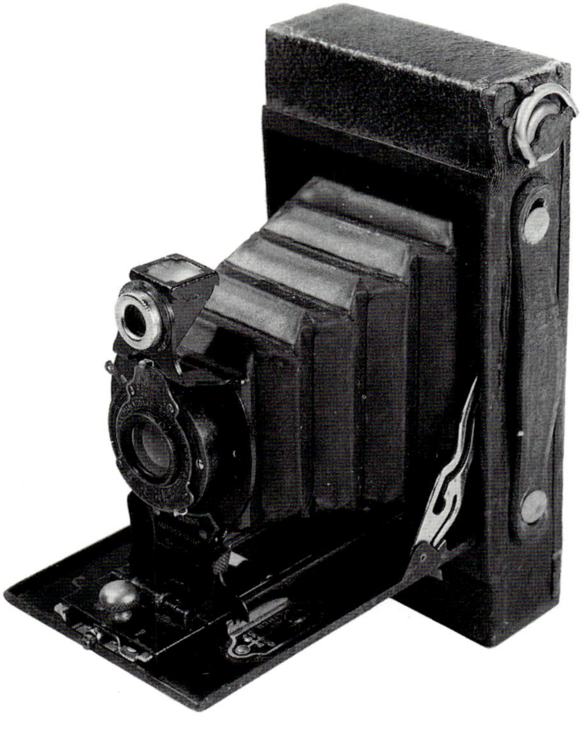

1915–1917 model. KM

Type Folding rollfilm
Introduced September 1915
Discontinued 1926
Film size 120
Picture size 2¼ × 3¼in.
Manufactured US
Lenses Achromatic or Rapid Rectilinear – but see below
Shutters Ball Bearing or Kodex – see below
Numbers made ?, but 540,000 before 1921

Description/Remarks

Imitation leather covering; reversible reflecting finder; sliding focusing with lock; from serial number 1,001.

Variations

Feb. 1916: new style Autographic attachment, from serial number 53,501. *Jan. 1917:* Square-ended cases changed to round, from serial number 133,301. *Oct. 1919:* support foot shape changed from shallow S curve to shallow C curve; from serial number 375,601.

Achromatic lens: *Sept. 1915–1923:* Ball Bearing shutter; *1924–1926:* Kodex shutter.
Rapid Rectilinear lens: *Nov. 1915–1923:* Ball Bearing shutter; *1924–Apr. 1926:* Kodex shutter.
Kodar f/7.9 lens: *May 1925–Sept. 1926:* Kodex shutter.

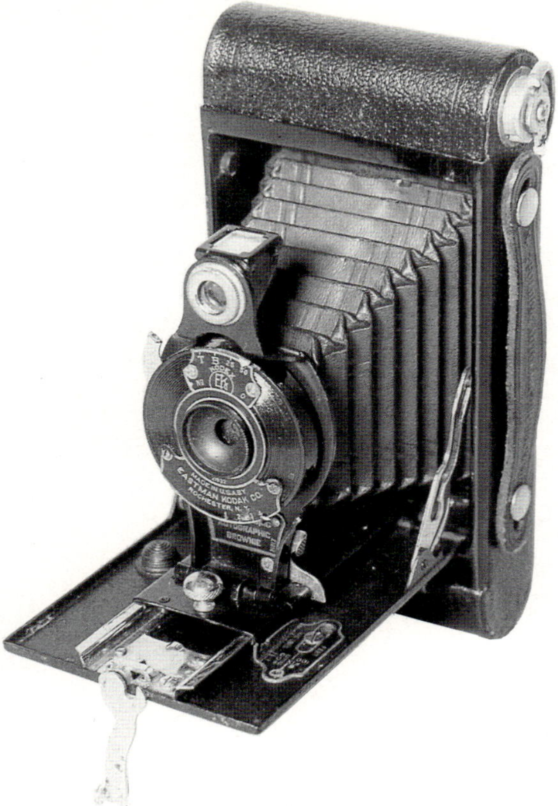

1917–1919 model. KM

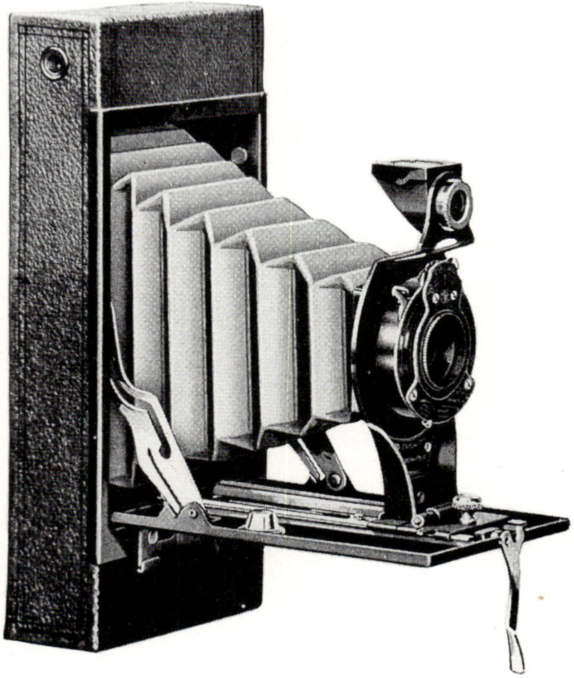

First model, 1915–1917.

UK VARIATION
Anastigmat f/6.3 lens: *1926:* Kodex shutter.

No 2A Folding Autographic Brownie

Type Folding rollfilm
Introduced November 1915
Discontinued 1926
Film size 116
Picture size 2½ × 4¼in.
Manufactured US
Lenses Achromatic or Rapid Rectilinear – see below
Shutters Ball Bearing or Kodex – see below
Numbers made ?, but 210,000 before 1921

Description/Remarks

Imitation leather covered; reversible reflecting finder; sliding focusing with lock; from serial number 951.

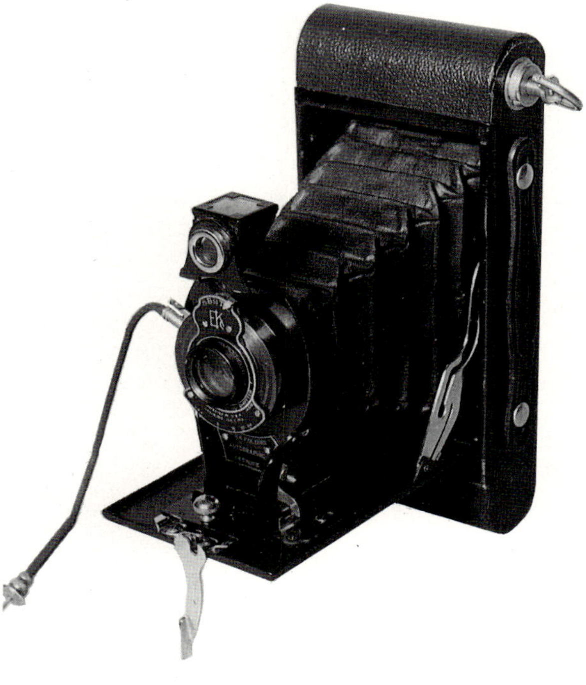

1919–1926 model. KM

Variations

Mar. 1916: New style Autographic attachment, from serial number 21,401. *Nov. 1917:* Square-ended case changed to rounded ends, from serial number 64,501. *Sept. 1919:* Support foot changed from shallow S shape to shallow C shape, from serial number 209,301.

Achromatic lens: *Nov. 1915–1923:* Ball Bearing shutter; *1924–Sept. 1926:* Kodex shutter.
Rapid Rectilinear lens: *Nov. 1915–May 1925:* Ball Bearing shutter; *1924–Jan. 1925:* Kodex shutter.
Kodar f/7.9 lens: *May 1925–1926:* Kodex shutter.

UK VARIATION
Anastigmat f/6.3 lens: *1926:* Kodex shutter.

No 2C Folding Autographic Brownie

Type Folding rollfilm
Introduced May 1916
Discontinued 1926
Film size 130
Picture size 2⅞ × 4⅞in.
Manufactured US
Lenses Achromatic or Rapid Rectilinear – but see below
Shutters Ball Bearing or Kodex – see below
Numbers made ?, but 130,000 before 1921

Description/Remarks

Imitation leather covered; reversible reflecting finder; sliding focusing with lock; from serial number 951.

Variations

Mar. 1917: Square-ended case changed to rounded ends, from serial number 38,501.

Achromatic lens: *July 1916–1925:* Ball Bearing shutter; *1925–Nov. 1926:* Kodex shutter.

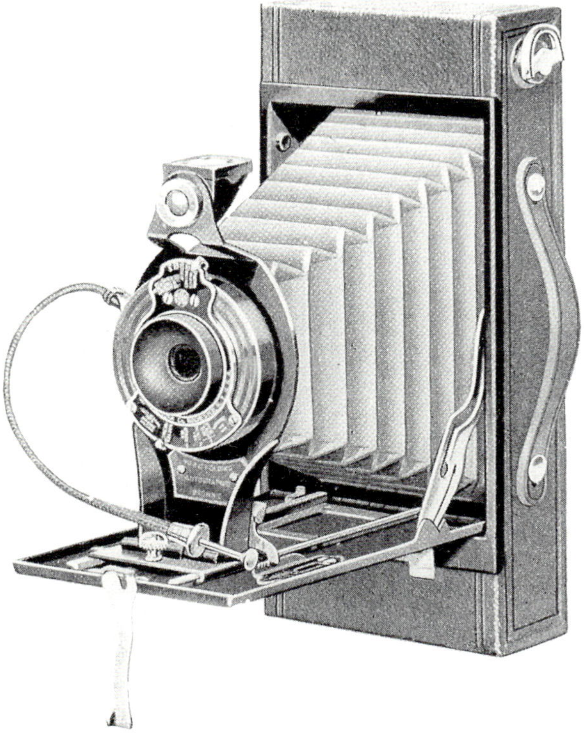

First model, 1916–1917.

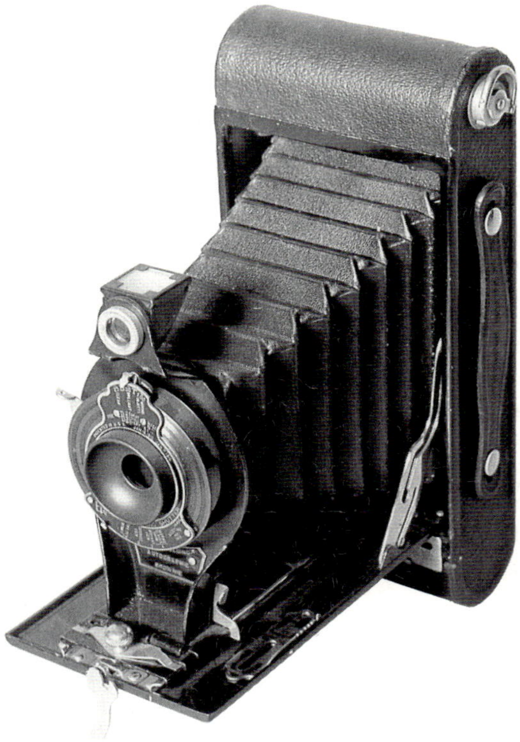

1917–1926 model. KM

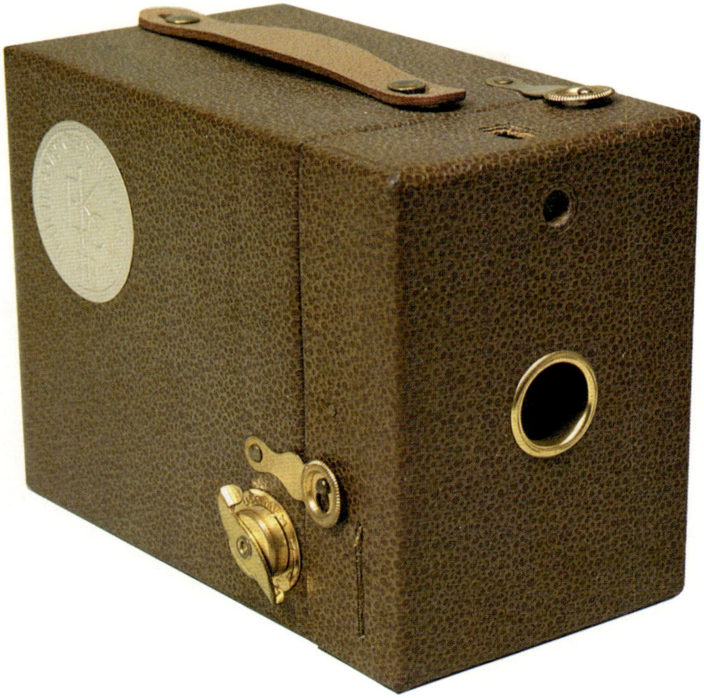

Above: The Eastman Anniversary camera (see page 8). KM Below: 1A Pocket Kodak Junior cameras in a range of colours (see page 149). KM

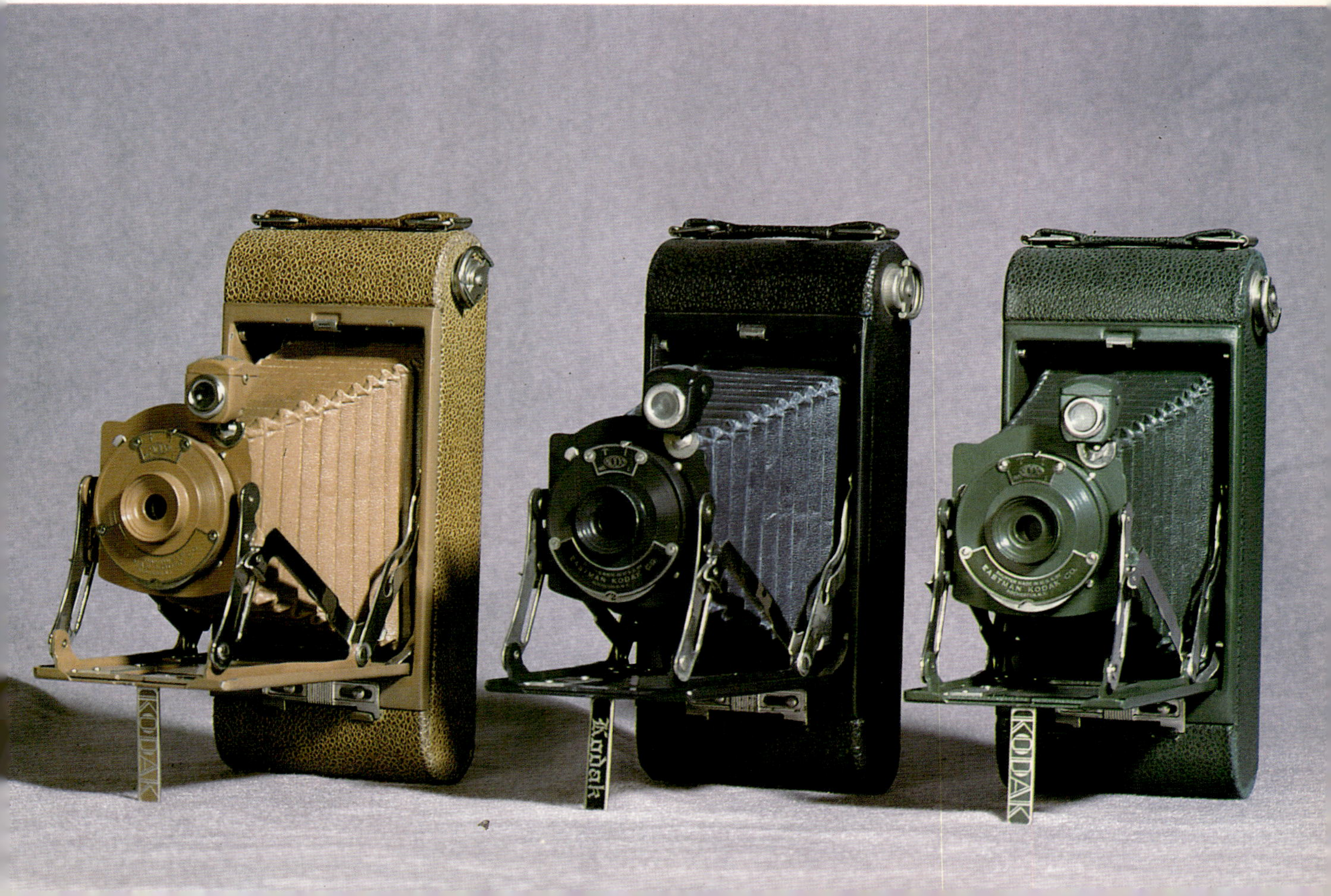

Rapid Rectilinear lens: *May 1916–1925:* Ball Bearing shutter. *Jan. 1925–Aug. 1925:* Kodex shutter.
Kodar f/7.9 lens: *May 1925–1926:* Kodex shutter.

No 3A Folding Autographic Brownie

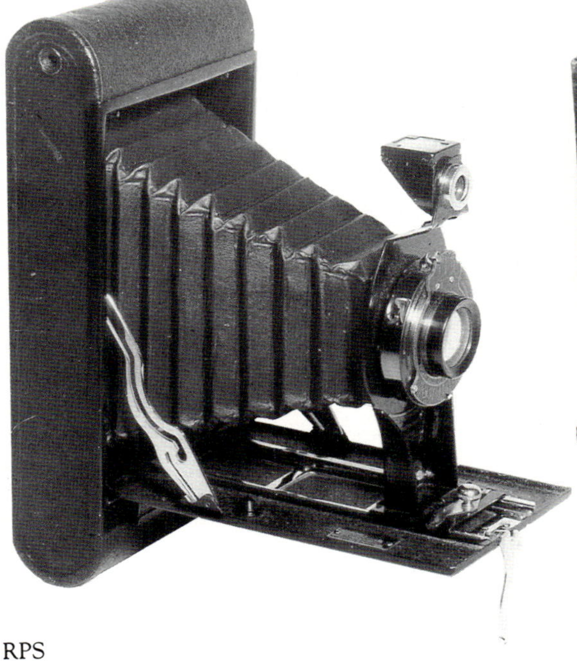

RPS

Type Folding rollfilm
Introduced July 1916
Discontinued November 1926
Film size 122
Picture size 3¼ × 5½in.
Manufactured US
Lenses Achromatic or Rapid Rectilinear – but see below
Shutters Ball Bearing or Kodex – see below
Numbers made ?, but 70,000 before 1921

Description/Remarks

Imitation leather covering; reversible reflecting finder; sliding focusing with lock; from serial number 1,001.

Variations

Achromatic lens: *July 1916–1925:* Ball Bearing shutter; *1925–Nov. 1926:* Kodex shutter.
Rapid Rectilinear lens: *July 1916–1925:* Ball Bearing shutter; *1925:* Kodex shutter.
Kodar f/7.9: *May 1925–1926:* Kodex shutter.

No 2 Folding Brownie

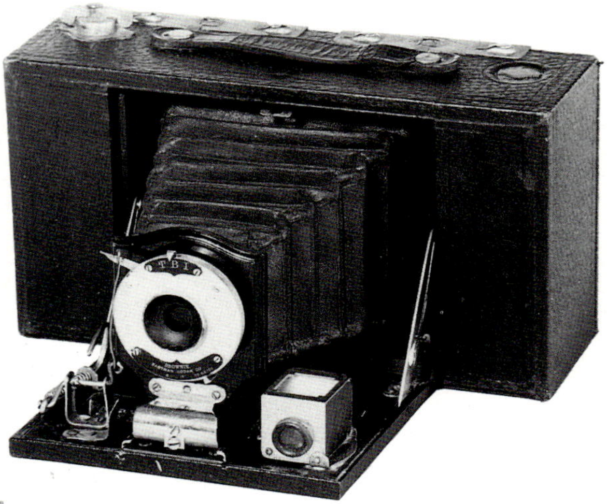

KM

Type Folding rollfilm
Introduced April 1904
Discontinued June 1907
Film size 120
Picture size 2¼ × 3¼in.
Manufactured US
Lens Meniscus achromat
Shutters 1904-5 Brownie Automatic
1905-1907: Pocket Automatic
Numbers made 76,000

Description/Remarks

Imitation leather covered wood body and baseboard; wood lens panel; reversible reflecting finder; sliding focusing with automatic catch; back released by sliding latch.

No 2 Folding Pocket Brownie, model B

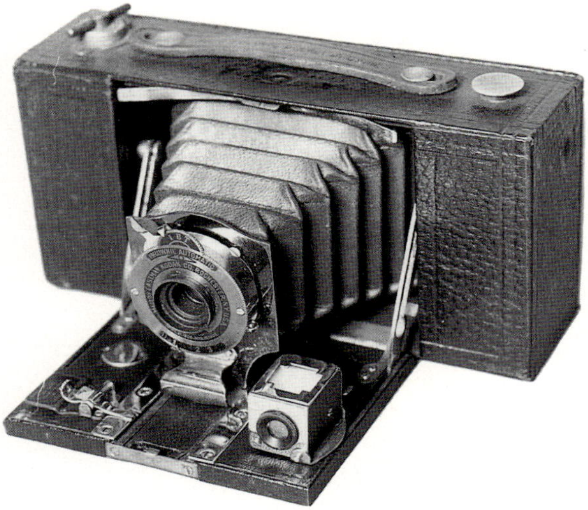

KM

Type Folding rollfilm
Introduced June 1907
Discontinued September 1915
Film size 120
Picture size 2¼ × 3¼in.
Manufactured US
Lens Meniscus achromat
Shutters Pocket or Brownie Automatic
Numbers made 174,000

Description/Remarks

Imitation leather covered wood, size reduced by 20% compared with the No 2 Folding Brownie camera. Reversible reflecting finder; metal lens panel; sliding focusing with automatic lock; hinged back released by concealed buttons.

Variations

Oct. 1907: Iris diaphragm fitted to shutter. *Feb. 1911:* metal finder lens mount. *From Aug. 1911:* black bellows fitted instead of red for cameras sent to UK. *Jan. 1913:* all cameras fitted with black bellows; new long baseboard hinge.

No 2A Folding Pocket Brownie

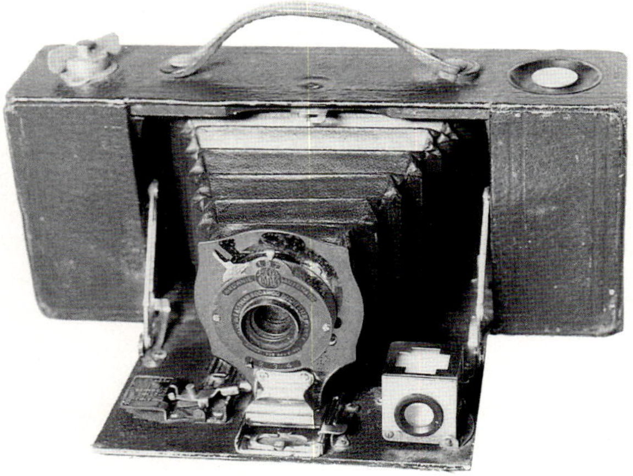

KM

Type Folding rollfilm
Introduced February 1910
Discontinued November 1915
Film size 116
Picture size 2½ × 4¼in.
Manufactured US
Lens Meniscus achromat
Shutters Pocket or Brownie Automatic
Numbers made 120,000

Description/Remarks

Imitation leather covered wood body; reversible reflecting finder; sliding focusing with automatic lock; sliding back released by concealed button; from serial number 1.

Description/Remarks

Dec. 1910: metal screw mount for finder lens; from serial number 25,918. *Aug. 1911:* black bellows instead of red fitted on cameras sent to UK. *Nov. 1912:* all cameras fitted with black bellows, from serial number 62,551.

No 3 Folding Brownie

Type Folding rollfilm
Introduced April 1905

Discontinued 1915
Film size 124
Picture size 3¼ × 4¼in.
Manufactured US
Lenses Meniscus achromat or Rapid Rectilinear – see below
Shutters F.P.K. Automatic or Ball Bearing – see below
Numbers made 108,000

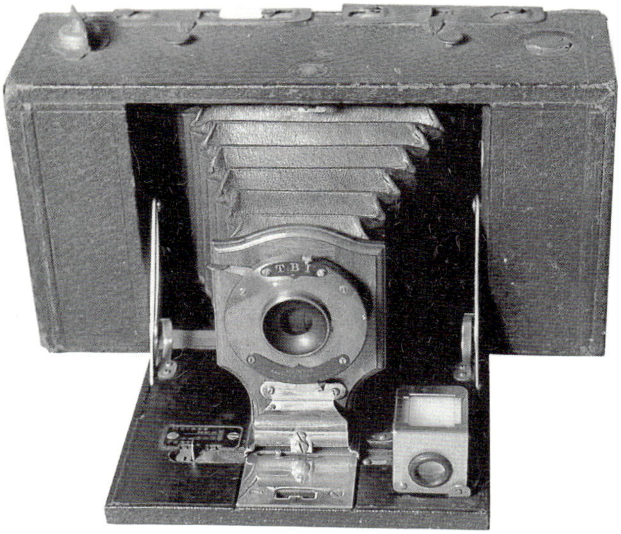

First model. KM

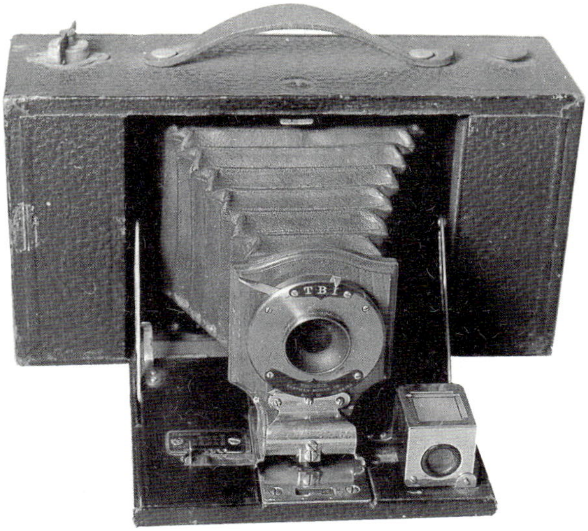

Model B. KM

Description/Remarks

Imitation leather covered wood; reversible reflecting finder; sliding focusing with automatic lock; from serial number 101-F.

Variations

May 1907: Model B; sliding back latch replaced by concealed buttons; spool centres changed from key shape to disc; from serial number 24,159.

June 1909: Model D; metal lens panel; new focusing scale; pneumatic release on F.P.K. shutter; from serial number 42,325.

Jan. 1912: Black bellows instead of red fitted on cameras sent to UK. *Feb. 1913:* Longer baseboard hinge fitted, from serial number 67,801.

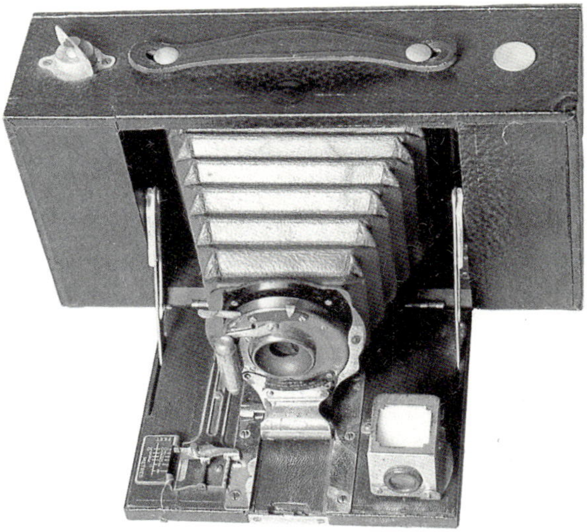

Model D. KM

Meniscus achromatic lens: *Apr. 1905–1913:* F.P.K. Automatic shutter. *1913–1915:* Brownie Ball Bearing shutter.
Rapid Rectilinear lens: *Apr. 1909–1912:* F.P.K. Automatic shutter. *1913–1915:* Brownie Ball Bearing shutter.

No 3A Folding Brownie

Type Folding rollfilm
Introduced April 1909

Discontinued 1915
Film size 122
Picture size 3¼ × 5½in.
Manufactured US
Lenses Meniscus achromat or Rapid Rectilinear
Shutters April 1909–1913: F.P.K. Automatic
April 1914–1915: Brownie Ball Bearing
Numbers made 114,000+

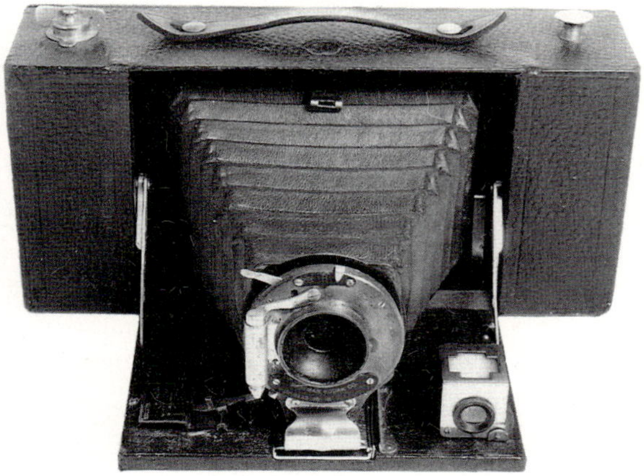

TNC

Description/Remarks

Imitation leather covered wood body; metal lens panel; reversible reflecting finder; sliding focusing with automatic lock; concealed release buttons for back; from serial number 1.

No 2 Stereo Brownie

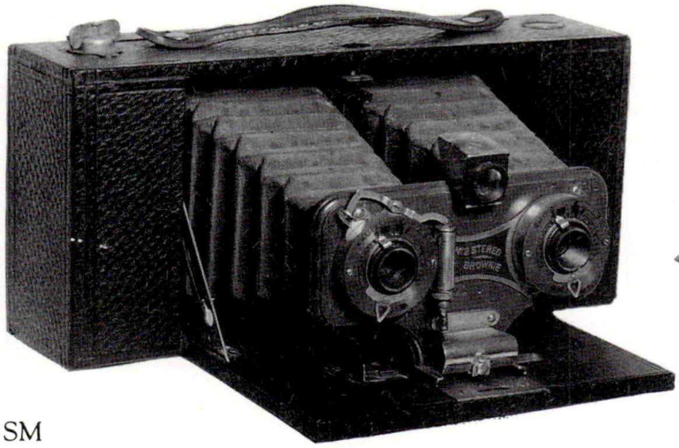

SM

Type. Stereoscopic folding rollfilm
Introduced April 1905
Discontinued 1910
Film size 125
Picture size 3¼ × 2½in.
Manufactured US
Lens Two meniscus achromats
Shutters 1905: Brownie Automatic
1906–1910 Pocket Automatic
Numbers made 4,000+

Description/Remarks

Imitation leather covered wood case; brilliant finder with hood; sliding focusing with automatic stop; twin bellows; pneumatic shutter release; from serial number 101-H.

Six-20 Folding Brownie

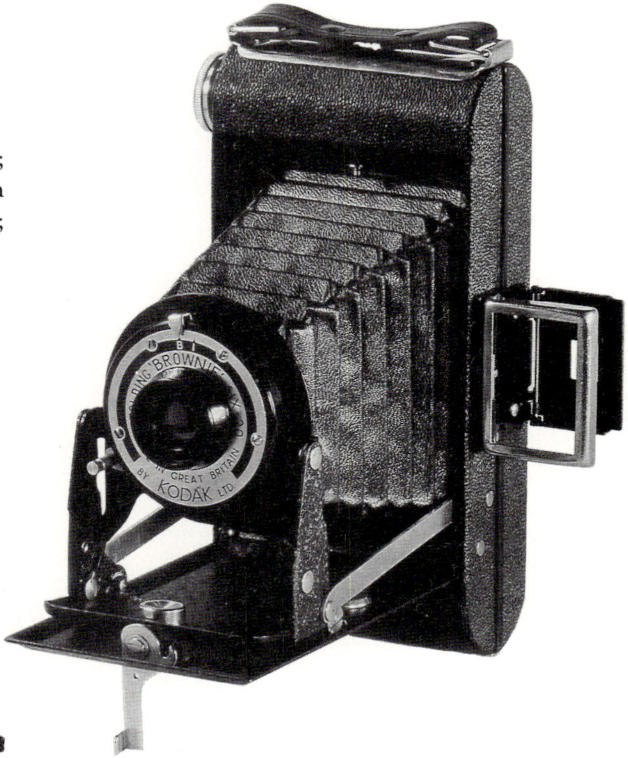

1937–1940 model. KP

Type Self-erecting folding rollfilm
Introduced January 1937
Discontinued 1940
Film size 620
Picture size 2¼ × 3¼in.
Manufactured UK
Lens Meniscus
Shutter Kodette II
Numbers made ?

Description/Remarks

Grained leatherette covering; folding frame finder, brilliant finder available as an optional extra from 1938.

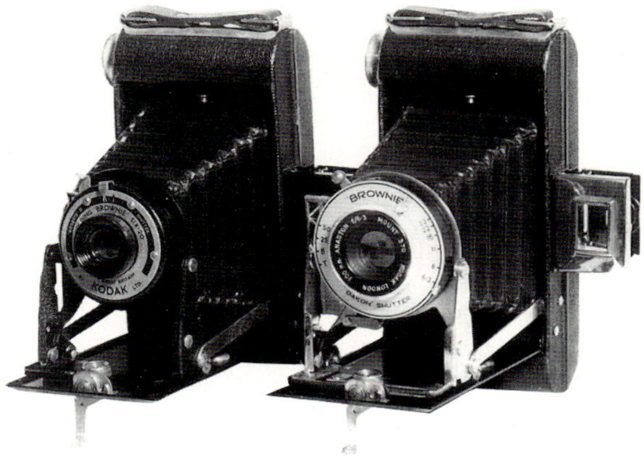

Left: meniscus lens. Right: Anaston lens, 1948–1954. RPS

Six-20 Folding Brownie, second model

Type Self-erecting folding rollfilm
Introduced 1948
Discontinued 1954
Film size 620
Picture size 2¼ × 3¼in.
Manufactured UK
Lenses Meniscus, fixed focus
Anaston f/6.3, 100mm focusing
Shutters Kodette II (meniscus lens)
Dakon (Anaston lens) with bayonet flash contacts
Numbers made Well over 300,000

Variations

Morocco grained imitation leather covering; folding optical frame finder; except for the optical frame finder, the menicus lens model is essentially the same as the pre-war version.

CHAPTER 5 *Kodak 35mm Cameras*

The first Kodak 35mm camera could be considered to be the small 00 Cartridge Premo box camera of 1916, which used an unperforated 35mm rollfilm. However, in this section we are concerned with the Kodak cameras which use perforated 35mm film in disposable cassettes. This format evolved from the cine film created by W.K.L. Dickson, Thomas Edison's assistant, in the early 1890s, for the Kinetograph movie camera and Kinetoscope viewer. These early experiments had been carried out on lengths of celluloid roll film obtained from George Eastman. The film for the original Kodak camera was 2¾ inches wide and about 23 feet long. Dickson wanted length rather than width, and cut the film down the middle to make two strips 1⅜ inches, or 35mm, wide. He perforated the film with rectangular holes along each edge to provide registration and traction in the mechanism, and set a frame size of about 24 × 18 mm. Since this film format was the first to bring moving pictures to the public, it was used by many other early film-makers, from the mid-1890s, and was adopted as a world-wide standard in 1909.

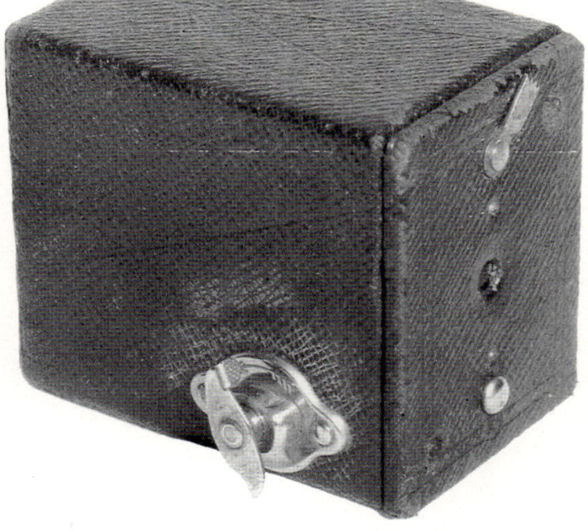

No.00 Cartridge Premo camera used 35mm wide rollfilm.

The ready availablity of 'short ends' of movie film led to the appearance of a number of cameras using perforated 35mm film. The first to be sold was the Tourist Multiple in 1913, which had a capacity for 750 exposures 18 × 24mm. The first commercially produced camera using the double

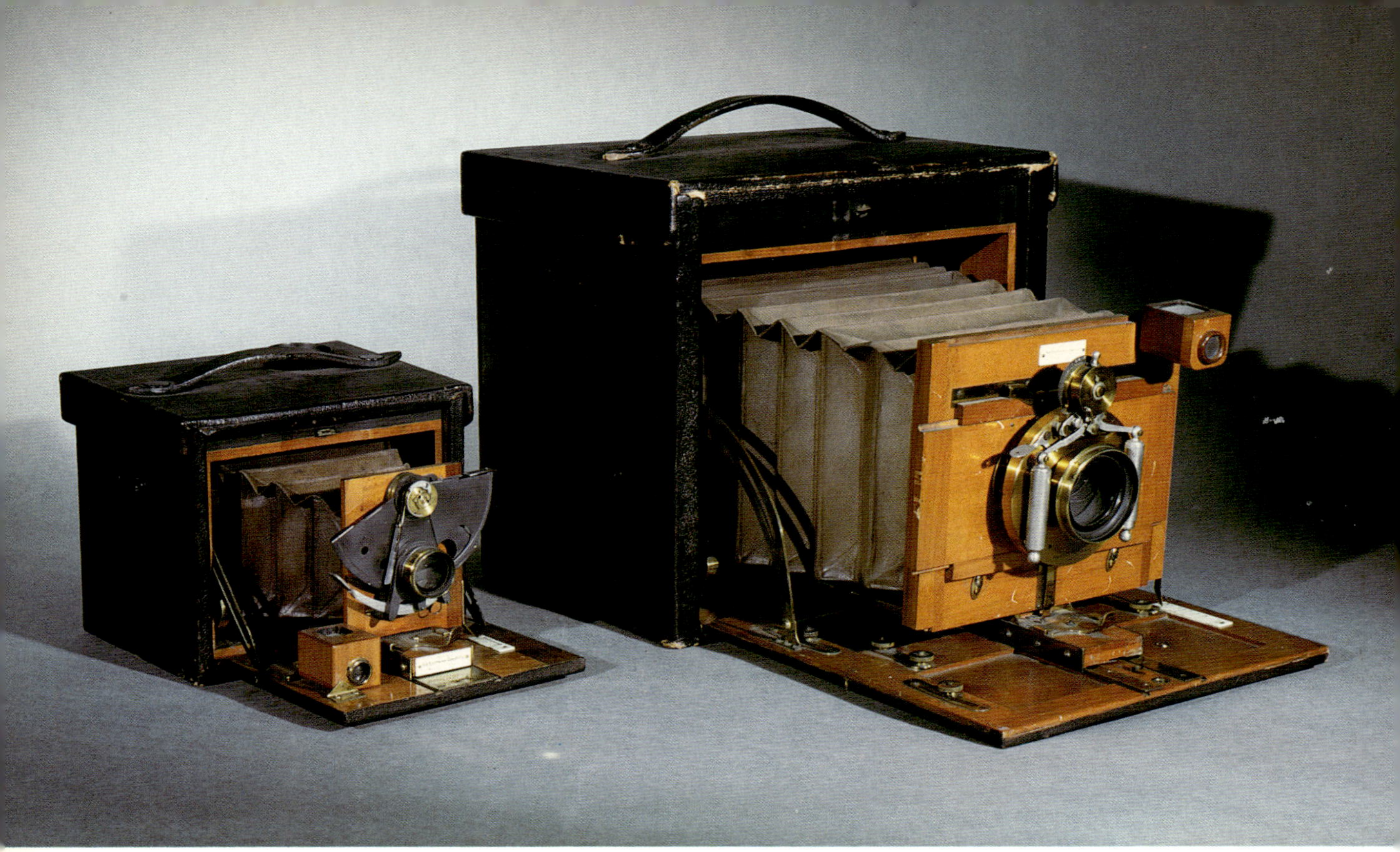

Above: No.4 and No.6 Folding Kodak cameras (see pages 91 & 95). KM Below: No.4 Kodak camera, covered with purple leather, which belonged to the Princess of Wales, later Queen Alexandra (see page 13). KM

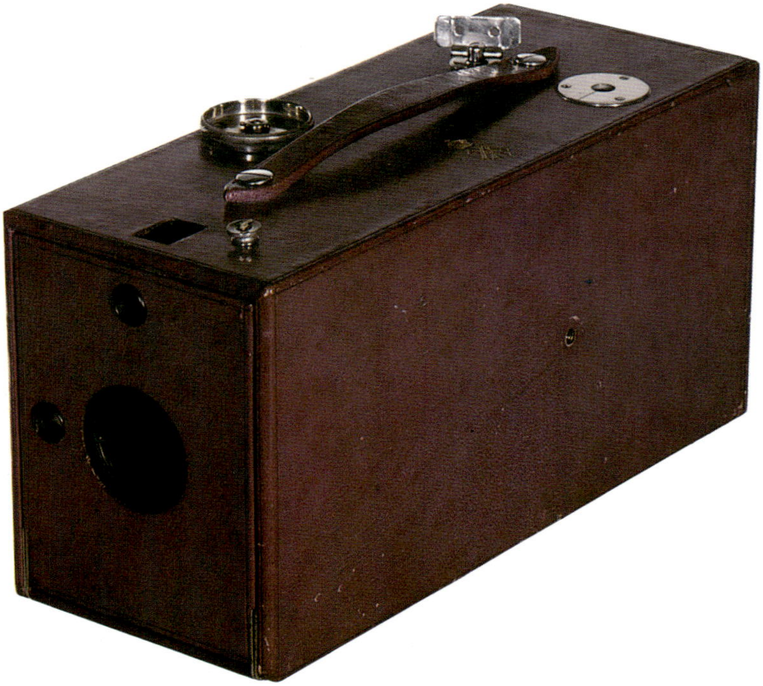

frame 24 × 36mm size was the 1914 Simplex, which also provided the option of 'single frame' 18 × 24mm. Jack Naylor has identified almost 30 camera models using 35mm film made before the appearance of the Leitz Leica camera in 1925. However, it was the success of this high precision miniature camera that encouraged photographers to take the small format seriously. The Leica, and Zeiss-Ikon's Contax camera which followed it, were quite expensive, and somewhat complicated to use, especially since the film had to be loaded into special cassettes before use. Following the acquisition of his company by Kodak at the end of 1931, Dr August Nagel designed a small, folding camera taking 35mm film, ready loaded in a disposable cassette. The Retina camera was launched in 1934, and its relatively low cost and convenience made it very popular. The ready availability of the 35mm cassette, too, encouraged the appearance of many other makes of 35mm camera in the 1930s, and by the beginning of World War Two 35mm photography had been firmly established.

The Kodak Retina camera evolved through many models, including a single lens reflex, before it was finally discontinued in the late 1960s. The range of Retinette cameras from 1939 provided a cheaper, but still precision made, alternative, and in post-war years sold in very large numbers. Eastman Kodak in Rochester manufactured a number of 35mm camera models, starting with the Kodak 35 camera in 1938, and Kodak Limited produced a 35mm version of their popular Colorsnap camera in 1959. After a break of almost twenty years, Kodak in 1986 re-entered the 35mm field with a range of 35mm compact cameras, many of which were manufactured in the Far East.

All Kodak 35mm cameras took 135 film, except for the ready loaded Kodak Fling 35, and all produced a picture size of 24 × 36mm, except for the Kodak Stereo.

Kodak AF1

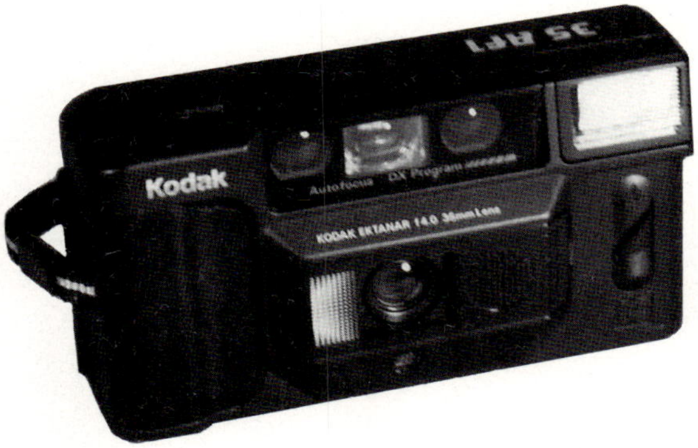

PDM

Type Solid body 35mm miniature
Introduced 1986
Discontinued –
Manufactured Japan
Lens Autofocus f/4.0, 35mm
Shutter Programmed, 1/90 – 1/333 sec.

Description/Remarks

Built-in electronic flash; fully automatic; DX film speed sensor. Made for European markets.

Kodak AF2

Type Solid body 35mm miniature
Introduced 1986
Discontinued –
Manufactured Japan
Lens Aspheric 4-element, autofocus f/2.8, 35mm
Shutter Programmed, 1/45 – 1/500 sec.

Description/Remarks

Sensalite electronic built-in flash. Self-timer; fully

automatic; DX film speed sensor; motorised film wind and rewind. Made for European markets.

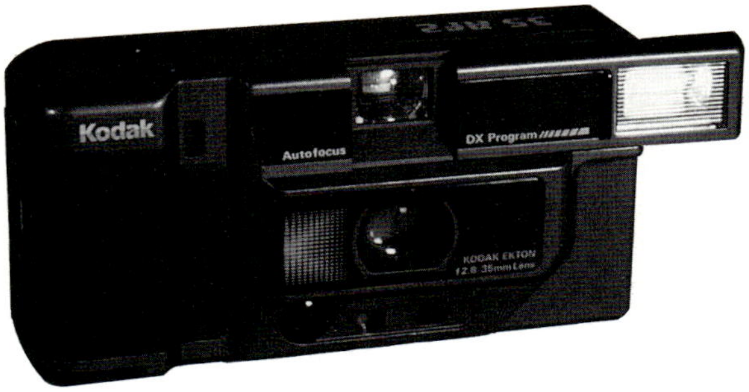

PDM

Kodak Automatic 35

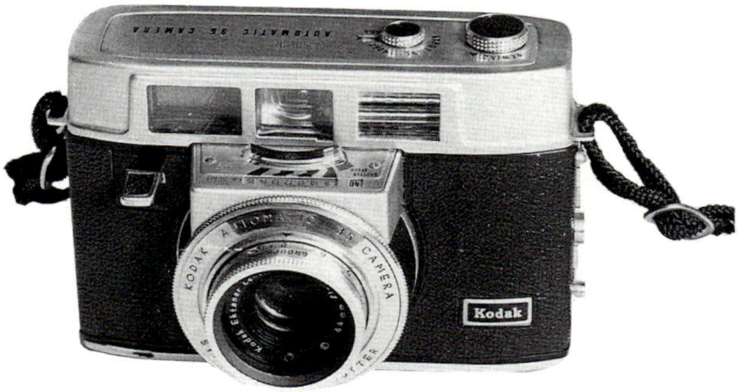

KM

Type Solid body 35mm miniature
Introduced April 1959
Discontinued September 1964
Manufactured US
Lens Kodak Ektanar f/2.8
Shutter Kodak Synchro 80
Numbers made ?

Description/Remarks

Aperture set by photocell as shutter release is operated; screw and pin flash contacts.

Kodak Automatic 35B

Type Solid body 35mm miniature
Introduced August 1961
Discontinued November 1962
Manufactured US
Lens Kodak Ektanar f/2.8
Shutter Kodak Automatic Flash
Numbers made ?

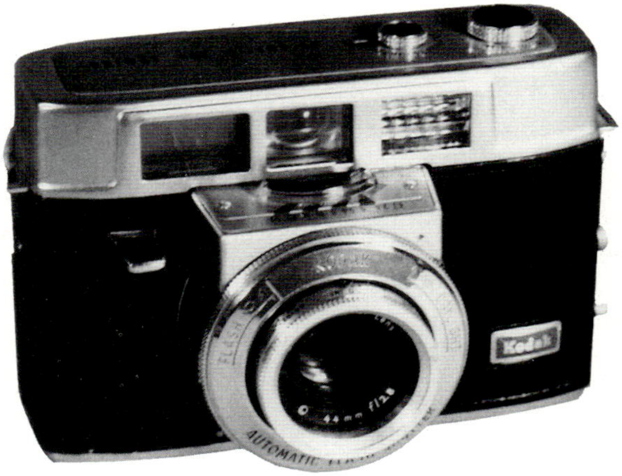

PDM

Description/Remarks

Similar to Automatic 35, but with automatic aperture setting for flash, with coupling between focus and aperture controls.

Kodak Automatic 35F

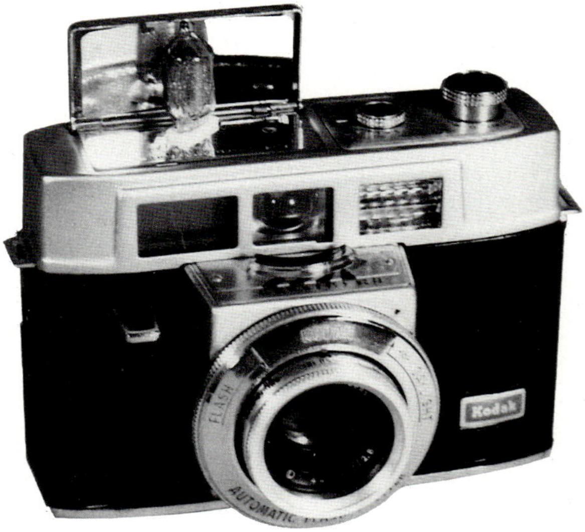

PDM

Type Solid body 35mm miniature
Introduced March 1962
Discontinued January 1966
Manufactured US
Lens Kodak Ektanar f/2.8
Shutter Kodak Automatic Flash
Numbers made ?

Description/Remarks

Similar to Automatic 35B, but with built in flashgun for AG-1 bulbs.

Kodak Automatic 35R4

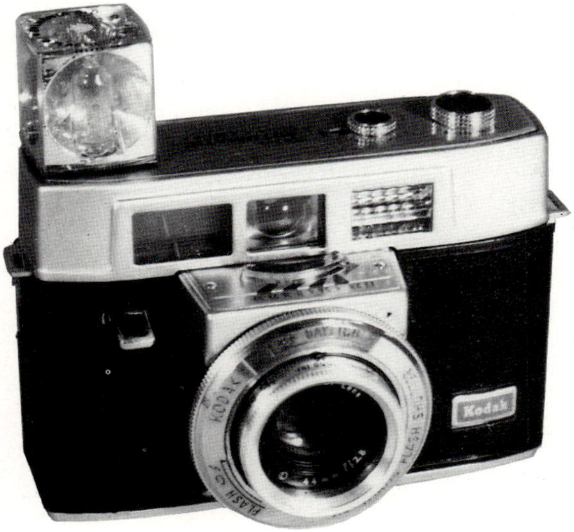

PDM

Type Solid body 35mm miniature
Introduced July 1965
Discontinued June 1969
Manufactured US
Lens Kodak Ektanar f/2.8
Shutter Kodak Automatic Flash
Numbers made ?

Description/Remarks

As Automatic 35F, but with socket for flash cubes.

Kodak Auto Colorsnap 35

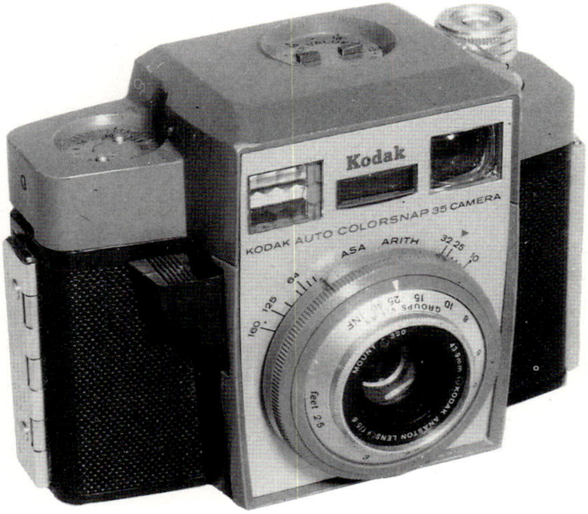

RPS

Type Solid body 35mm miniature
Introduced November 1962
Discontinued 1964
Manufactured UK
Lens Kodak Anaston f/5.6, 43.9mm
Shutter Self-setting
Numbers made ?

Description/Remarks

Automatic exposure version of Colorsnap 35.

Kodak Colorsnap 35

Type Solid body 35mm miniature
Introduced July 1959
Discontinued January 1964
Manufactured UK
Lens Kodak Anaston f/3.9, 43.9mm
Shutter Dakon self-setting
Numbers made ?

Description/Remarks

35mm version of the popular Bantam Colorsnap camera. Dial-the-weather calculator on camera front; shutter re-set lever for double exposure or reshooting

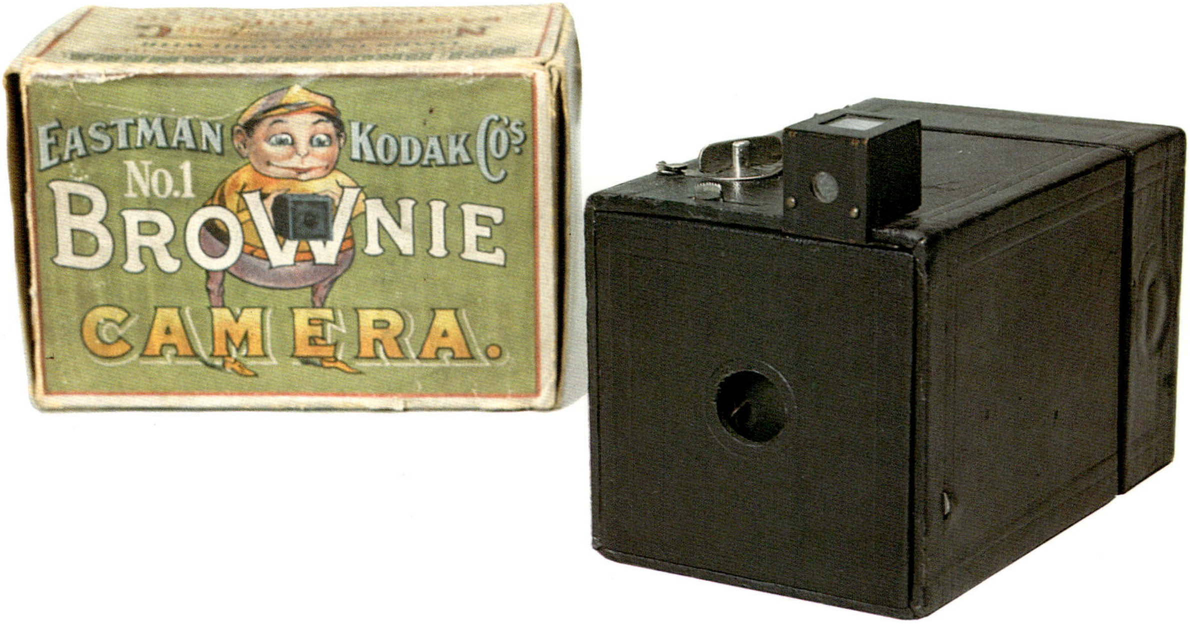

Above: No.1 Brownie camera, first model (see page 36). KM Below: The Brownie Flash B camera (see page 43). KM

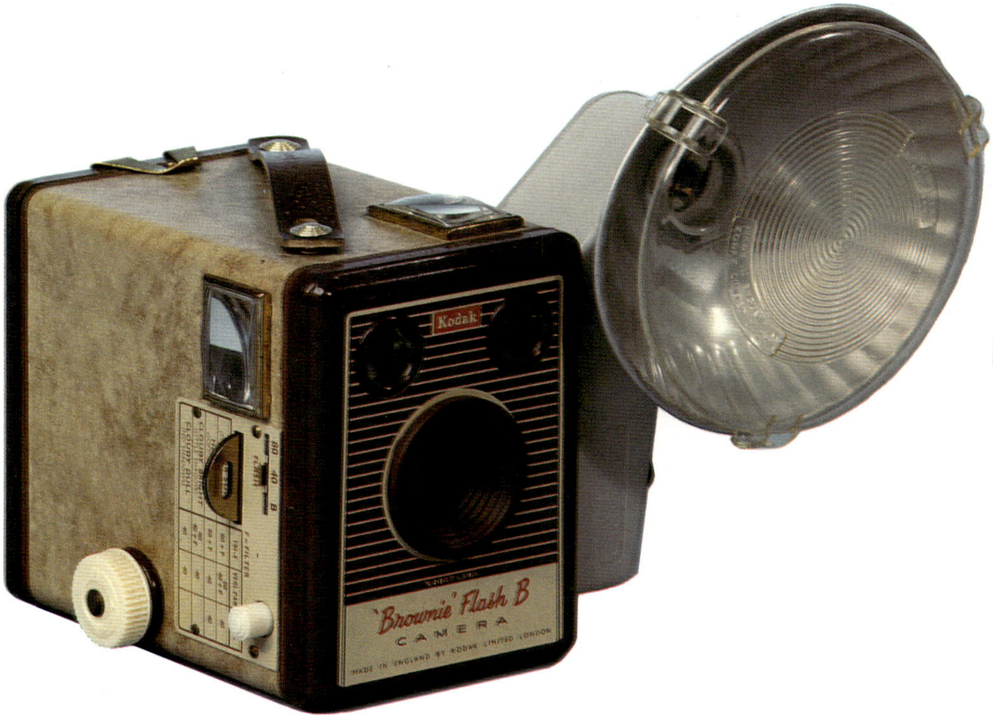

after failed flash; lever wind; pin and screw flash contacts.

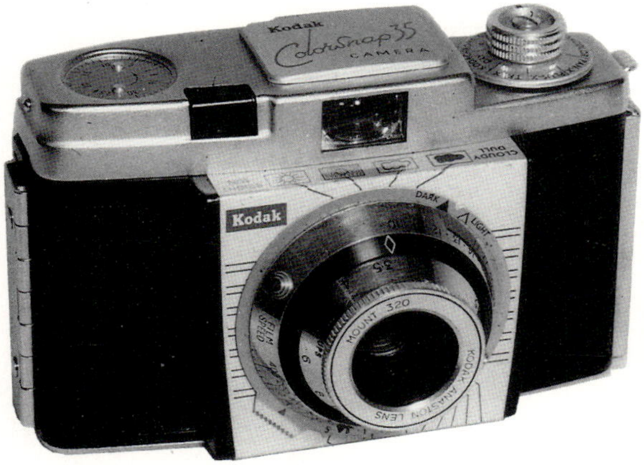

RPS

Kodak Colorsnap 35 model 2

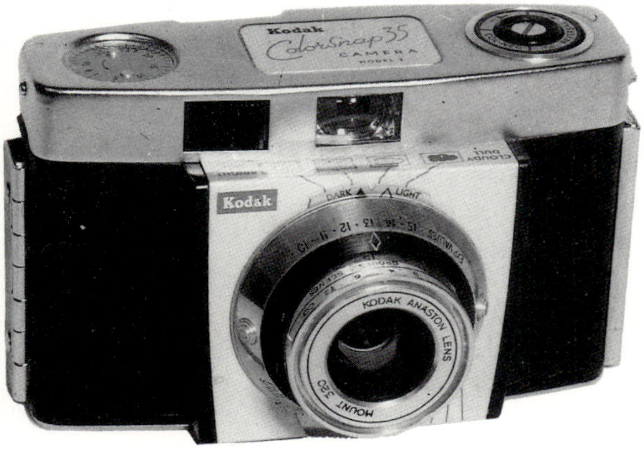

RPS

Type Solid body 35mm miniature
Introduced March 1964
Discontinued November 1967
Manufactured UK
Lens Kodak Anaston f/3.9, 43.9mm
Shutter Dakon
Numbers made ?

Description/Remarks

As Colorsnap 35, but with restyled body and mechanism cover, with recessed rewind knob; extended EV scale.

Kodak EF

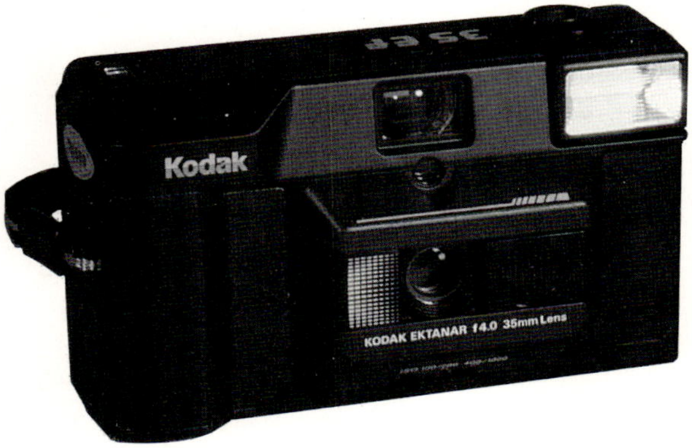

PDM

Type Solid body 35mm miniature
Introduced 1986
Discontinued –
Manufactured Japan
Lens Fixed focus f/4.0, 35mm
Shutter Single speed, $^{1}/_{125}$ sec

Description/Remarks

Built-in electronic flash.

Variations

Spring 1988: model available in red with black trim.

Kodak Ektra

Type Solid body 35mm miniature
Introduced January 1941
Discontinued June 1948
Manufactured US
Lenses Kodak Ektar f/1.9 or f/3.5, 50mm, interchangeable
Shutter Focal plane
Numbers made c2000

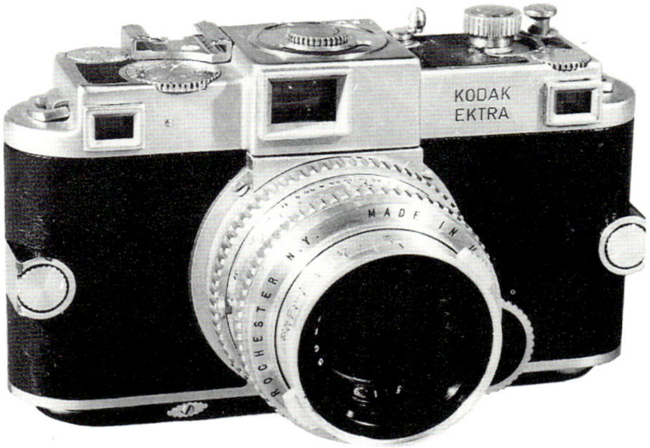

KM

Description/Remarks

A precision miniature camera developed to fill the gap left by the drying-up of supplies of German Leica and Contax cameras in World War Two. As well as a very accurate long-base coupled rangefinder, it included a number of innovative and original features, including interchangeable film backs, and automatic finder and parallax adjustment for the six Ektra lenses. Apart from the 50mm lenses, they were:

Kodak Ektar f/3.3, 35mm
Kodak Ektar f/3.5, 90mm
Kodak Ektar f/3.8, 135mm
Kodak Ektar f/4.5, 153mm

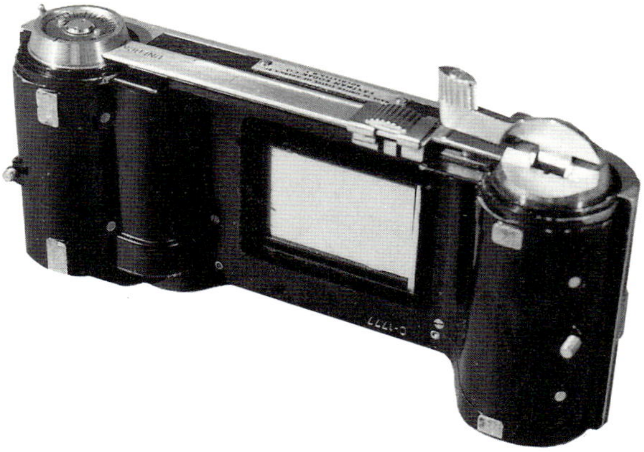

Interchangeable back. KM

Variations

Apparently, an Ektra II camera was intended, with clockwork motor film wind, but was not marketed. Although not officially listed, several examples exist, which may have been used for field trials. Apart from minor details the main difference is in the motor back, and the "II"designation.

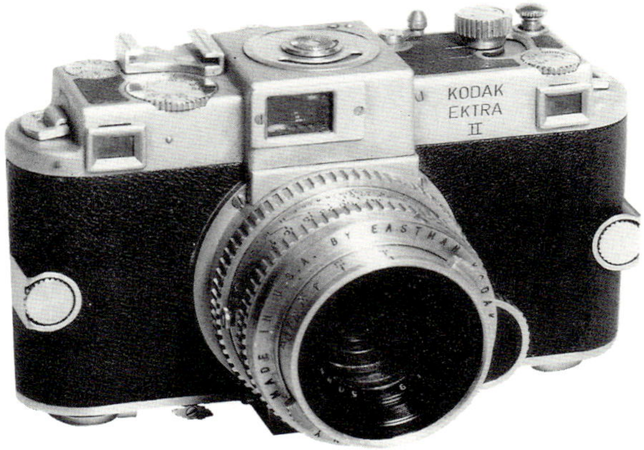

King Collection

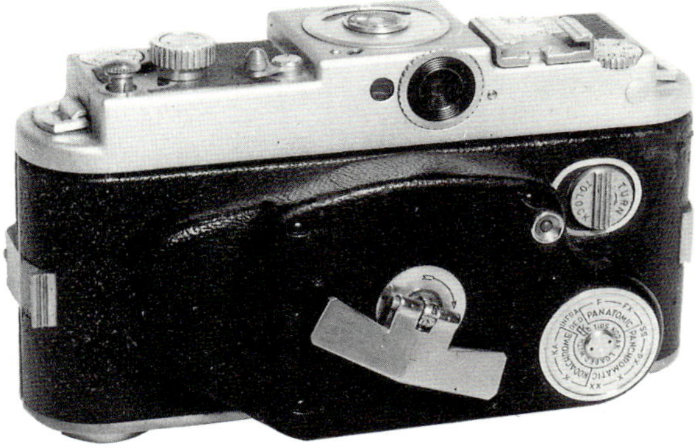

Motor back. King Collection

Kodak Fling 35

Type Solid body 35mm miniature
Introduced 1988
Discontinued –
Film size 24 exposure Kodacolor 400
Manufactured US
Lens Single f/11
Shutter Single speed 1/110 sec.

Description/Remarks

One-use disposable camera; returned to photo-laboratory.

Kodak Hobby

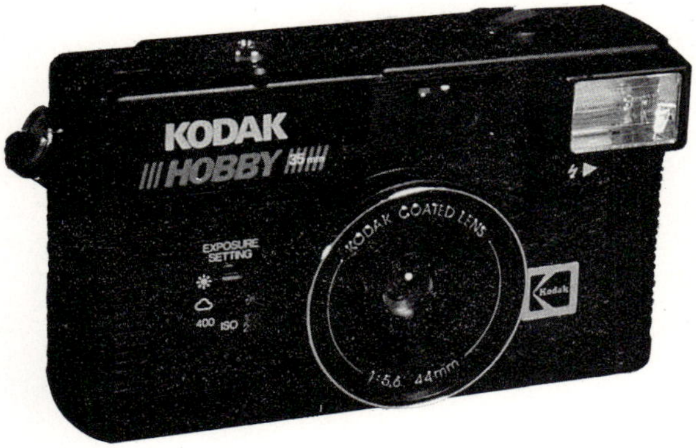

PDM

Type Solid body 35mm compact
Introduced 1988
Discontinued –
Manufactured Brazil
Lens f/5.6, 44mm
Shutter Single speed

Description/Remarks

Built-in electronic flash.

Kodak MD

Type Solid body 35mm miniature
Introduced 1987
Discontinued –
Manufactured Far East
Lens Kodak Ektanar f/4.0, 38mm
Shutter Electronic $^1/_{145}$ – $^1/_{400}$ sec

Description/Remarks

Integral electronic flash; automatic film speed setting for DX coded films; motorised film rewind and wind-on. Available in black and red (from Spring 1988) body colour. Identical to Kodak VR 35 model K40 camera.

Kodak Motormatic 35

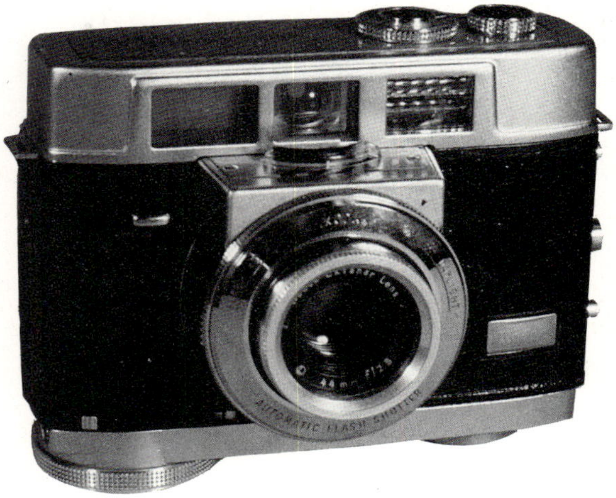

PDM

Type Solid body 35mm miniature
Introduced September 1960
Discontinued September 1962
Manufactured US
Lens Kodak Ektanar f/2.8
Shutter Kodak Automatic
Numbers made ?

Description/Remarks

Developed from Kodak Automatic 35 camera, with spring motor drive. Automatic exposure control; pin and screw flash contacts.

Kodak Motormatic 35F

Type Solid body 35mm miniature
Introduced March 1962
Discontinued April 1967
Manufactured US
Lens Kodak Ektanar f/2.8
Shutter Kodak Automatic Flash
Numbers made ?

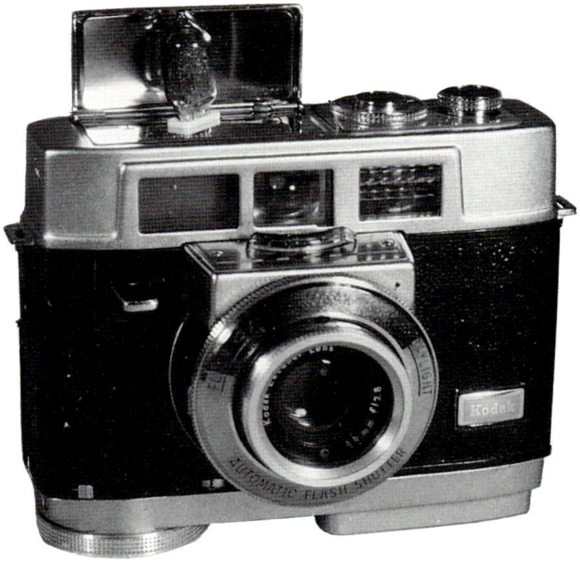

PDM

Description/Remarks

As Motormatic 35, with built-in flashgun for AG-1 bulbs.

Kodak Motormatic 35R4

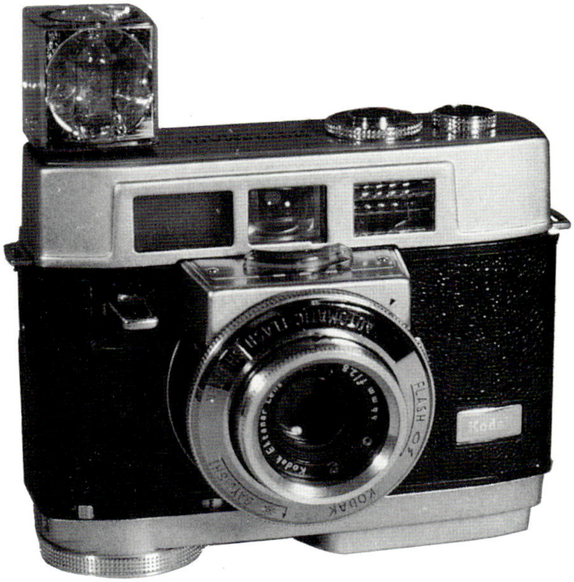

PDM

Type Solid body 35mm miniature
Introduced July 1965
Discontinued February 1969
Manufactured US
Lens Kodak Ektanar f/2.8
Shutter Kodak Flash Automatic
Numbers made ?

Description/Remarks

As Motormatic 35, but with flashcube socket.

Kodak Pony 135

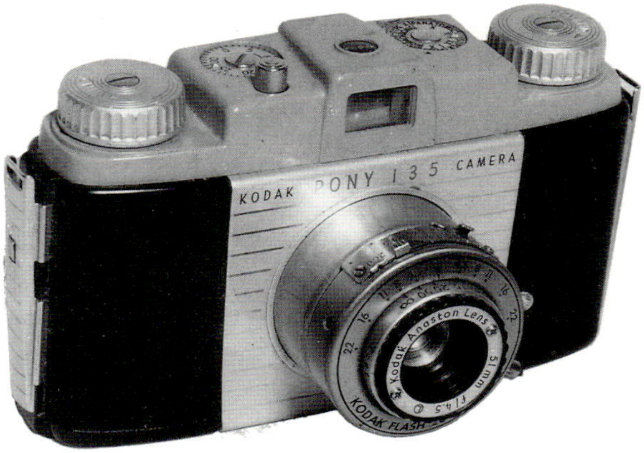

RPS

Type Solid body 35mm miniature
Introduced March 1950
Discontinued July 1958
Manufactured US
Lenses Kodak Anaston f/4.5, 51mm (1950–1954),
  44mm (1953–1955, Model B)
  Kodak Anaston f/3.5, 44mm (1955–1958, Model C)
Shutters Kodak Flash 200 (1950–1955)
  Kodak Flash 300 (1955–1958, Model C)
Numbers made ?

Description/Remarks

Black bakelite moulded body, telescoping lens mount; Model C brown body, fixed lens mount.

Variations

1956: Pony 135 (Le Pony) made in France, with Angénieux f/3.5, 45mm lens and everset 4-speed shutter.

Kodak Pony II

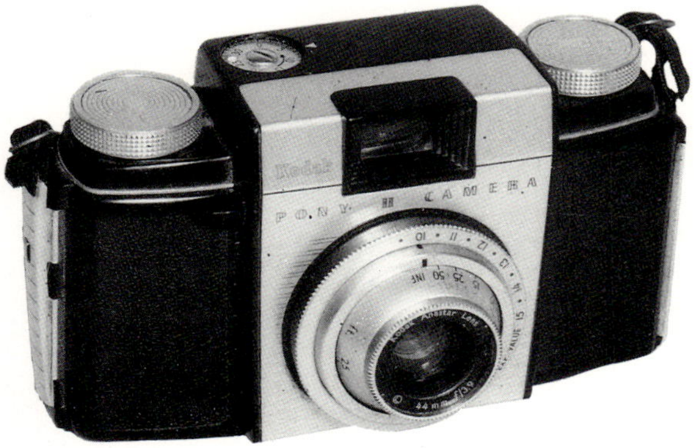

RPS

Type Solid body 35mm miniature
Introduced August 1957
Discontinued February 1962
Manufactured US
Lens Kodak Anastar f/3.9
Shutter Single speed
Numbers made ?

Description/Remarks

Redesigned body; simpler specification than other Pony cameras.

Kodak Pony IV

Type Solid body 35mm miniature
Introduced August 1957
Discontinued October 1961
Manufactured US
Lens Kodak Anastar f/3.5
Shutter Kodak Flash 250
Numbers made ?

Description/Remarks

Similar to earlier Pony 135 cameras, but calibrated in Exposure Value System settings.

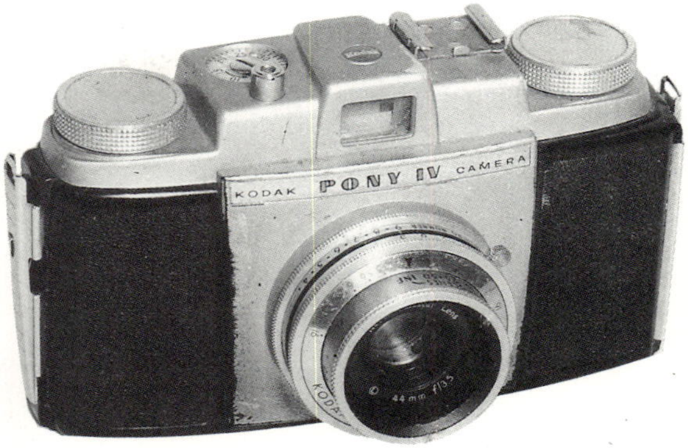

RPS

Kodak Signet 30

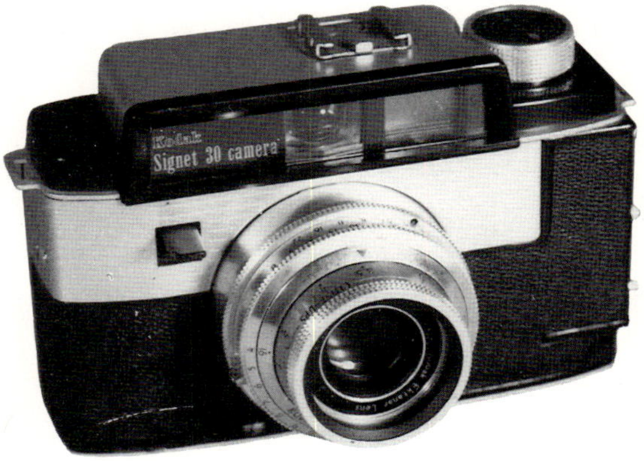

PDM

Type Solid body 35mm miniature
Introduced August 1957
Discontinued April 1959
Manufactured US
Lens Kodak Ektanar f/2.8
Shutter Kodak Synchro 250
Numbers made ?

Description/Remarks

Lever wind-on on base.

Kodak Signet 35

Type Solid body 35mm miniature

Introduced February 1951
Discontinued March 1958
Manufactured US
Lens Kodak Ektar f/3.5
Shutter Kodak Synchro 300
Numbers made ?

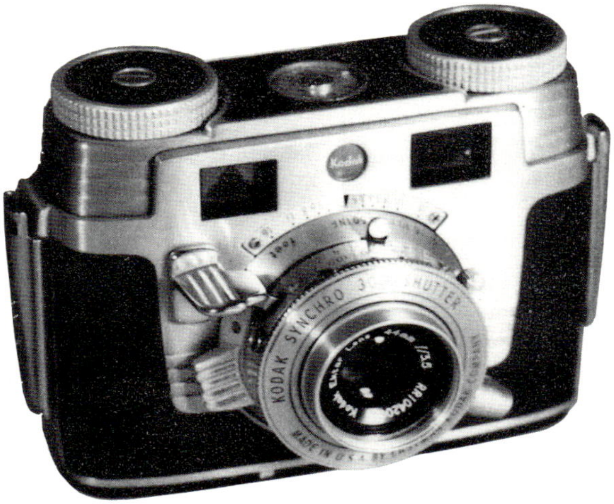

PDM

Description/Remarks

Coupled rangefinder.

Variations

American military version with black finish made for the Army Signal Corps.

Signet 40

Type Solid body 35mm miniature
Introduced October 1956
Discontinued April 1959
Manufactured US
Lens Kodak Ektanon f/3.5
Shutter Kodak Synchro 400
Numbers made ?

Description/Remarks

Thumb lever film advance on lens mount; pin and screw flash contacts.

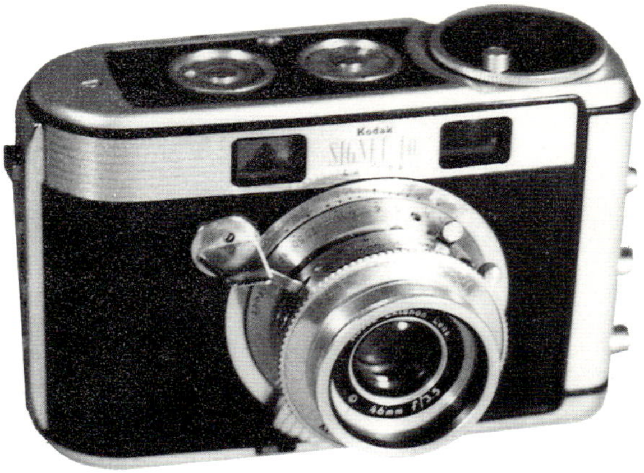

PDM

Kodak Signet 50

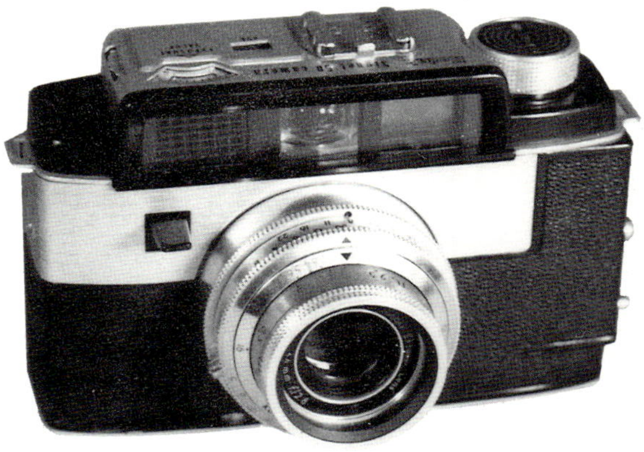

PDM

Type Solid body 35mm miniature
Introduced August 1957
Discontinued October 1960
Manufactured US
Lens Kodak Ektanar f/2.8
Shutter Kodak Synchro 250
Numbers made ?

Description/Remarks

Similar to Signet 30, but with built-in photoelectric meter.

Kodak Signet 80

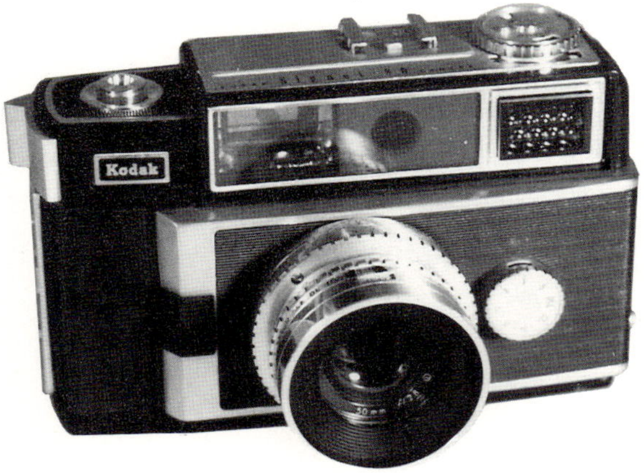

PDM

Type Solid body 35mm miniature
Introduced September 1958
Discontinued October 1962
Manufactured US
Lenses Kodak Ektanar f/2.8, with f/3.5, 35mm wide angle and f/4.0, 90mm telephoto accessory lenses
Shutter Behind-lens
Numbers made ?

Description/Remarks

Coupled rangefinder; interchangeable lenses, photoelectric exposure meter.

Kodak Stereo

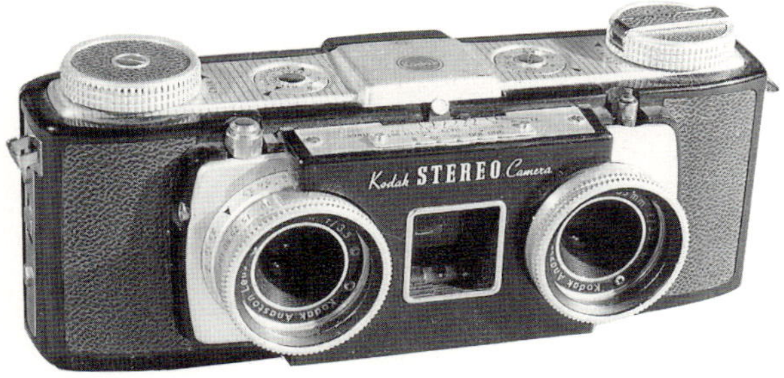

KM

Type Solid body 35mm stereoscopic miniature
Introduced May 1954
Discontinued February 1959
Picture size Two 23 × 24mm
Manufactured US
Lens Two Kodak Anaston f/3.5
Shutter Kodak Flash 200
Numbers made ?

Description/Remarks

Direct vision finder with spirit level.

Kodak S100 EF

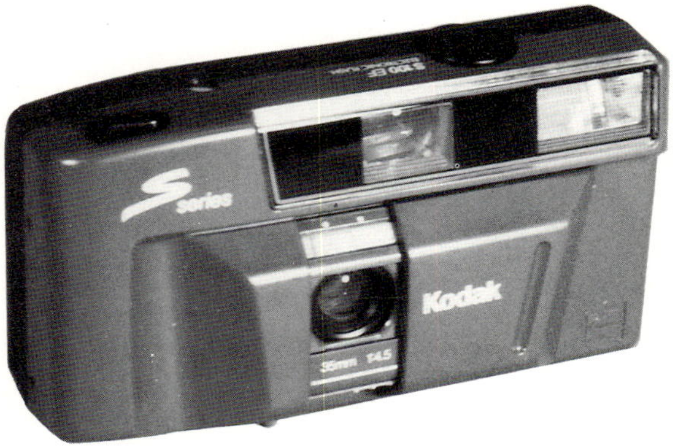

PDM

Type Solid body 35mm miniature
Introduced Autumn 1987
Discontinued –
Manufactured Far East
Lens 3-element f/4.5, 35mm
Shutter Single speed $^1/_{100}$

Description/Remarks

Built-in electronic flash. Available in black or red (from Spring 1988) body colour.

Kodak S900 Tele

Type Solid body 35mm miniature
Introduced February 1988
Discontinued –

Manufactured US
Lenses Fixed focus f/5, 34mm and autofocus f/7, 62mm
Shutter Single speed shutter 1/100 sec

Description/Remarks

Built-in Sensalite electronic flash; automatic exposure control; DX film sensor for automatic film speed setting.

Kodak 35

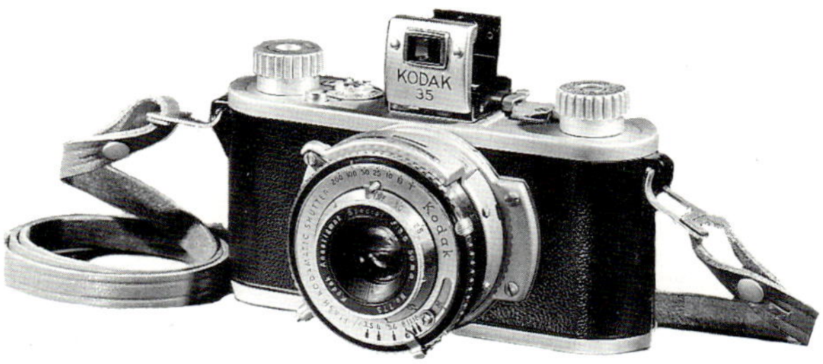

KP

Type Solid body 35mm miniature
Introduced 1938
Discontinued 1948
Manufactured US
Lens Kodak Anastigmat f/4.5 – but see below
Shutter Diomatic – but see below
Numbers made ?

Description/Remarks

The first 35mm Kodak camera to be manufactured outside Germany. It appeared in a number of lens and shutter combinations – see below. Models with f/5.6 lenses had black film knobs and finder; other models were satin chromed and had double exposure prevention.

Variations

Kodak Anastigmat f/5.6:*1938–1945:* Kodex shutter.
Kodak Anastigmat Special f/3.5: *1938–1949:* Kodamatic shutter.
Kodak Anastigmat f/4.5: *1946–1947:* Flash Diomatic shutter (lens coated after April 1947).
Kodak Anastigmat Special f/3.5: *1947–1948:* Flash Kodamatic shutter.
Kodak Anaston f/4.5: *1947–1948:* Flash Diomatic shutter.
A wartime military version was produced in olive drab finish.

Kodak 35 Rangefinder model

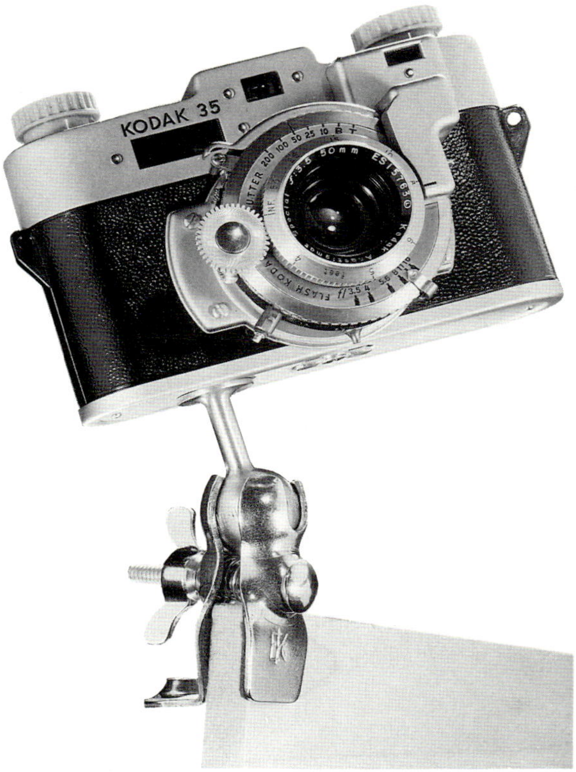

KP

Type Solid body 35mm miniature
Introduced 1940
Discontinued 1951
Manufactured US
Lenses Kodak Anastigmat Special f/3.5 1940–1948
Kodak Anastar f/3.5 1947–1951
Shutters Kodamatic 1940–1948
Flash Kodamatic 1947–1951
Numbers made ?

Description/Remarks

Coupled split-image rangefinder gear-coupled to front lens element in a manner which suggests that it was an after thought.

Kodak VR35 model K2a

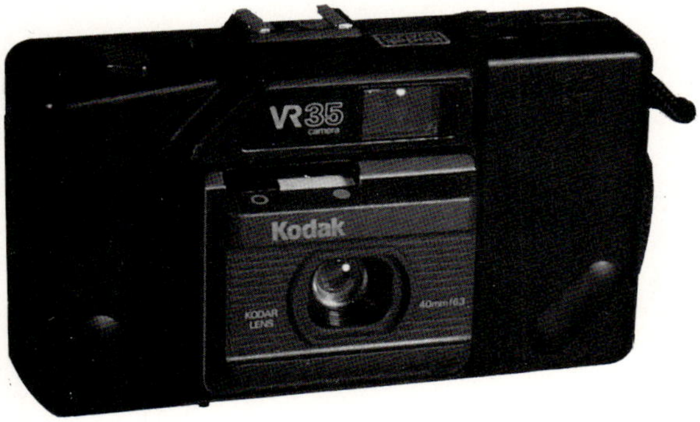

PDM

Type Solid body 35mm miniature
Introduced 1986
Discontinued –
Manufactured Hong Kong
Lens Fixed focus f/6.3, 40mm
Shutter Single speed, 1/125 sec.

Description/Remarks

Hot shoe. Made for Far Eastern markets.

Kodak VR35 model K4a

Type Solid body 35mm miniature
Introduced 1986
Discontinued –
Manufactured Hong Kong
Lens Fixed focus f/5.6, 38mm
Shutter Single speed, 1/125 sec.
Numbers made

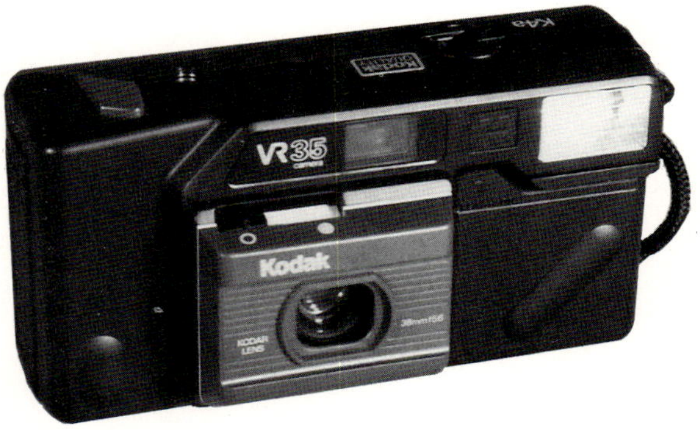

PDM

Description/Remarks

Built-in electronic flash. Made for Far Eastern markets. Same as Kodak VR 35 models K300, K400 and K500.

Kodak VR35 model K5

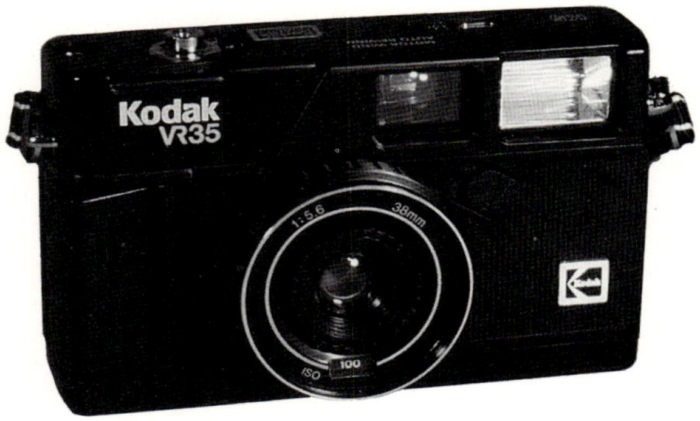

PDM

Type Solid body 35mm miniature
Introduced 1986
Discontinued –
Manufactured Hong Kong
Lens Fixed focus f/5.6, 38mm
Shutter Single speed, 1/125 sec.

Description/Remarks

Built-in electronic flash. Made for Far Eastern markets.

Kodak VR35 model K6

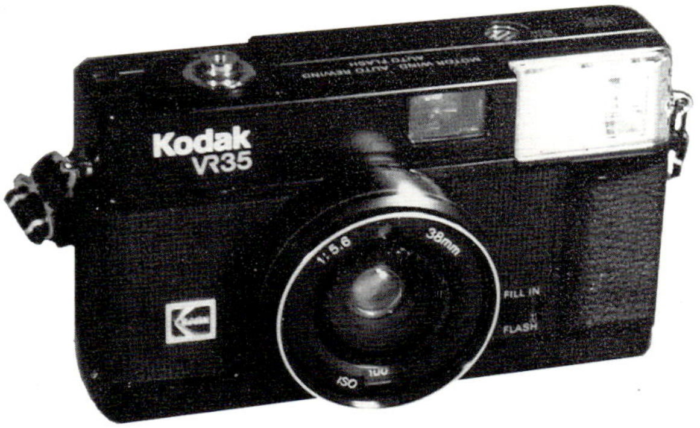

PDM

Type Solid body 35mm minature
Introduced 1986
Discontinued –
Manufactured Hong Kong
Lens Fixed focus f/5.6, 38mm
Shutter Single speed, 1/125 sec.

Description/Remarks

Built-in Sensalite electronic flash. Made for Far Eastern markets.

Kodak VR35 model K10

Type Solid body 35mm miniature
Introduced February 1986
Discontinued –
Manufactured US
Lens Autofocus f/3.5, 35mm
Shutter Programmed 1/8 – 1/500 sec.

Description/Remarks

Built-in Sensalite electronic flash.

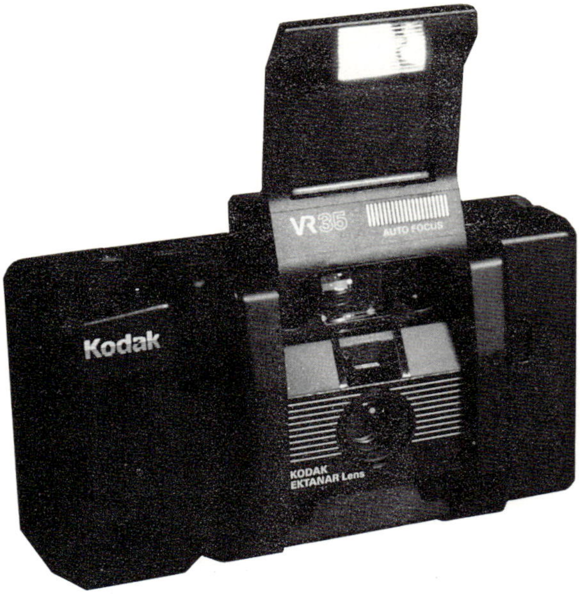

PDM

Kodak VR35 model K12

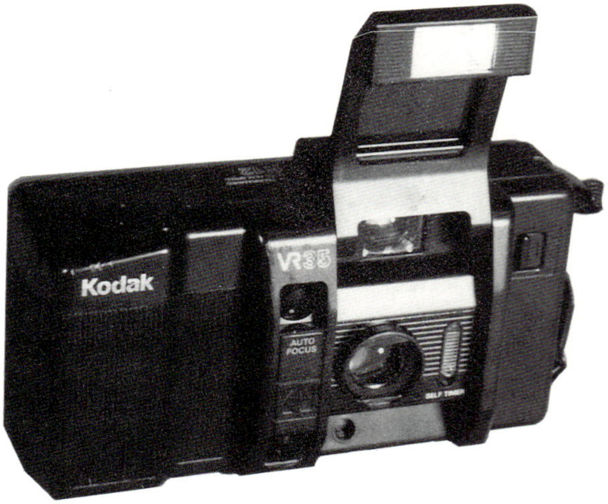

PDM

Type Solid body 35mm miniature
Introduced February 1986
Discontinued –

Manufactured US
Lens Autofocus f/2.8, 35mm
Shutter Programmed, 1/8 – 1/500 sec.

Description/Remarks

Built-in Sensalite electronic flash.

Kodak VR35 model K14 Medalist

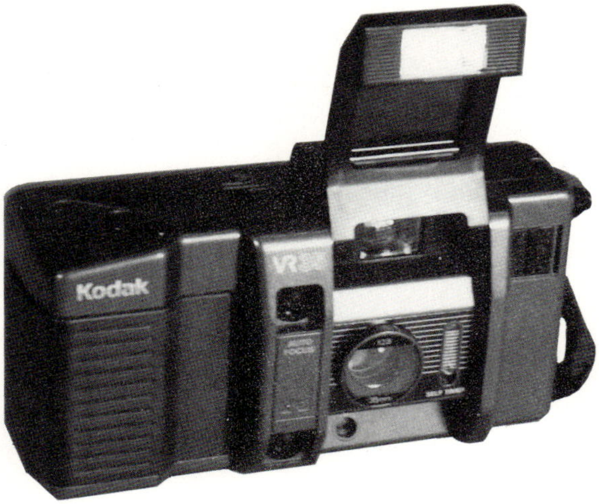

PDM

Type Solid body 35mm miniature
Introduced February 1986
Discontinued –
Manufactured US
Lens Autofocus f/2.8, 35mm
Shutter Programmed, 1/8 – 1/500 sec.

Description/Remarks

Special model with date back; built-in Sensalite electronic flash.

Kodak VR35 model K40

Type Solid body 35mm miniature
Introduced September 1986
Discontinued –
Manufactured US and Far East
Lens Fixed focus f/5.6, 35mm
Shutter Programmed electronic 1/145 – 1/400 sec.

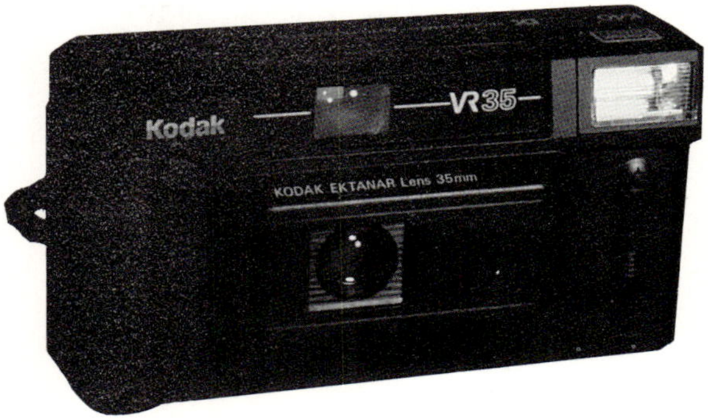

US-made model. PDM

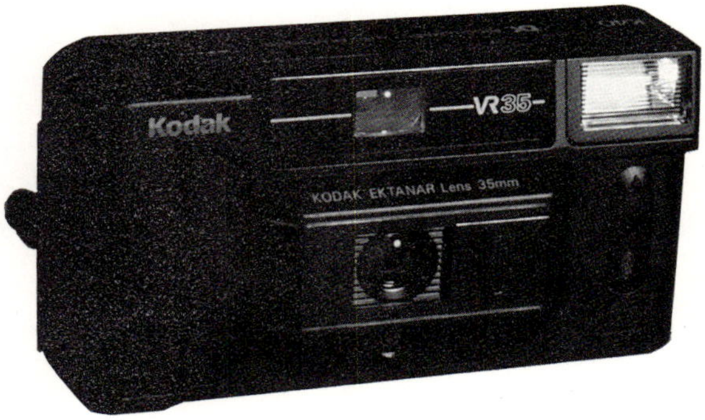

Chinon-made model. PDM

Description/Remarks

Motor drive and rewind; built-in electronic flash; DX film speed sensor. Sold as Kodak MD35 in non-US markets.

Kodak VR35 model K60

Type Solid body 35mm miniature
Introduced October 1986
Discontinued –
Manufactured US
Lens Fixed focus f/4.5, 35mm
Shutter Programmed

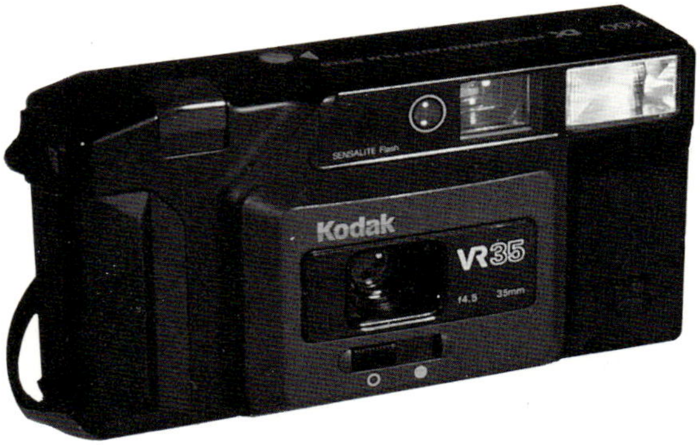

Kodak VR35 model K80

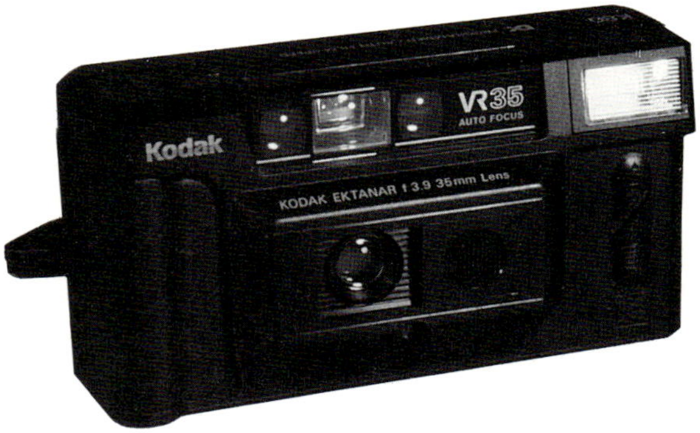

US-made model. PDM

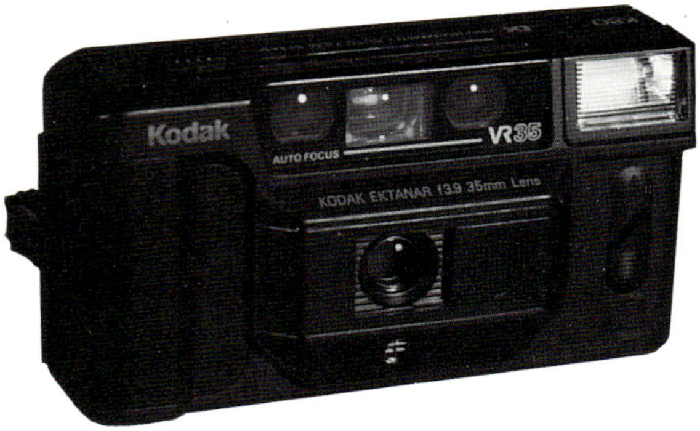

Chinon-made model. PDM

Type Solid body 35mm miniature
Introduced April 1987
Discontinued –
Manufactured US and Far East
Lens Autofocus f/3.9, 35mm
Shutter Programmed 1/100 – 1/500 sec.

Kodak VR35 model K300

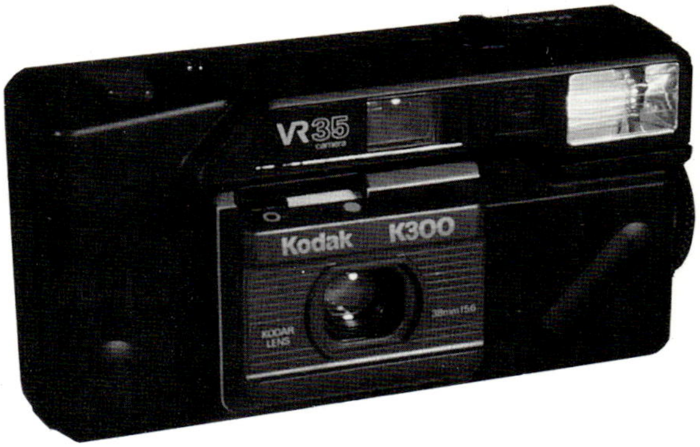

PDM

Type Solid body 35mm miniature
Introduced February 1987
Discontinued –
Manufactured Hong Kong
Lens Fixed focus f/5.6, 38mm
Shutter Single speed 1/125 sec.

Description/Remarks

Premium sales – identical to Kodak VR35, K400, K500 and K4a models.

Kodak VR35 model K400

Type Solid body 35mm miniature
Introduced February 1987
Discontinued –
Manufactured Hong Kong
Lens Fixed focus f/5.6, 38mm
Shutter Single speed 1/125 sec.

Description/Remarks

Made for premium sales – same as Kodak VR35 models K4a, K300 and K500.

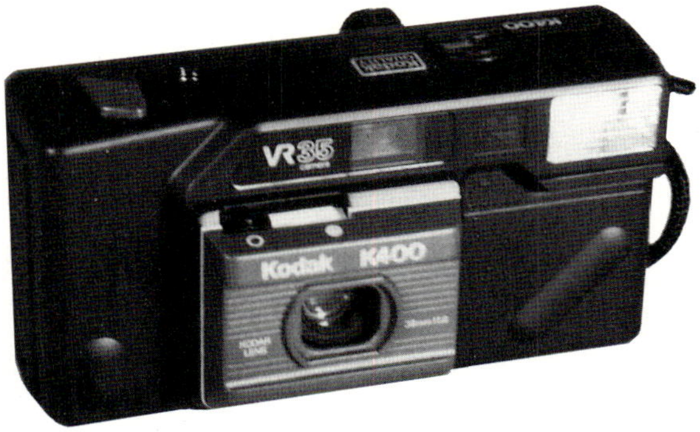

PDM

Kodak VR35 model K500

Type Solid Body 35mm miniature
Introduced February 1987
Discontinued –
Manufactured Hong Kong

Lens Fixed focus f/5.6, 38mm
Shutter Single speed $1/125$ sec.

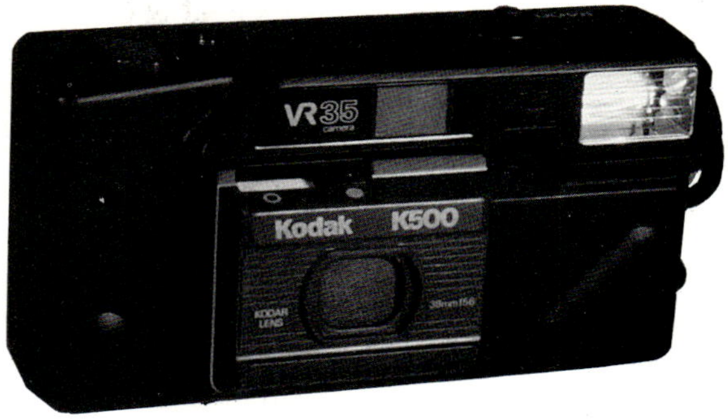

PDM

Description/Remarks

Made for premium sales – identical to Kodak VR35 models K4a, K300 and K400.

Kodak Retina Cameras

The Kodak Retina and Retinette cameras constitute the principal group of Kodak 35mm cameras. The Retinette cameras generally had a less advanced lens and shutter specification, although a number of the postwar models had the same body construction as the more expensive Retina cameras. The Kodak Retina and Retinette cameras are listed with their 'type' number – a production code allocated by Kodak AG. This provided a convenient means of distinguishing between various cameras with the same name and model number.

All the cameras were made in Germany.

Retina I (Type 117)

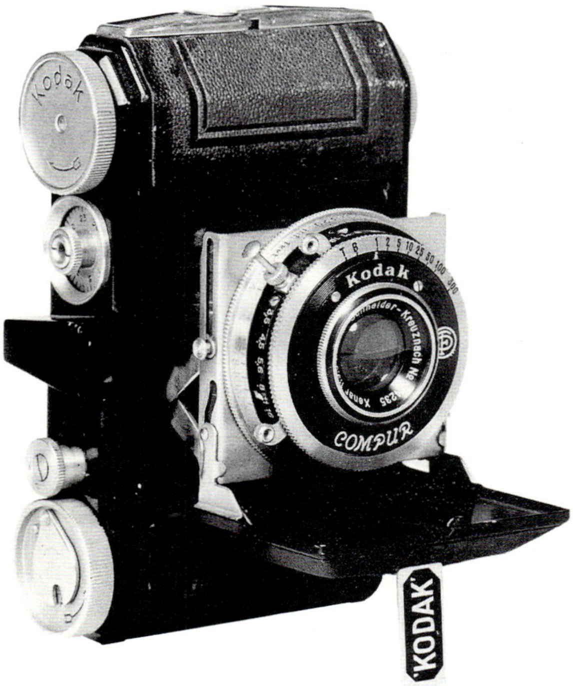

KP

Type Folding 35mm miniature
Introduced 1934
Discontinued 1935
Lens Schneider Xenar f/3.5, 50mm
Shutter Compur
Numbers made 60,000 approximately

Description/Remarks

The first Kodak 35mm miniature camera. Black enamelled bodywork, leather covering. Shutter release on shutter.

Retina I (Type 118)

Type Folding 35mm miniature
Introduced 1935
Discontinued 1936
Lens Schneider Xenar f/3.5, 50mm
Shutters Compur or Compur Rapid
Numbers made 9,144

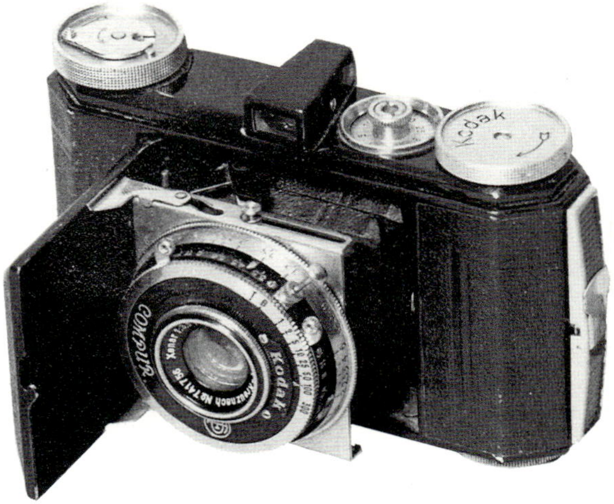

KM

Description/Remarks

Developed from Retina Type 117.

Retina I (Type 119)

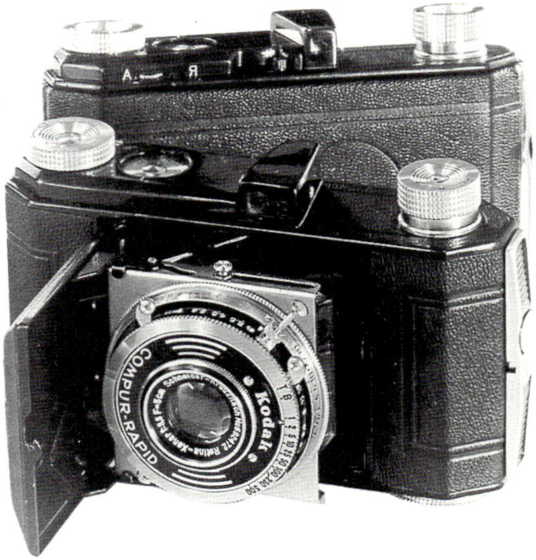

KP

Type Folding 35mm miniature
Introduced 1936
Discontinued 1938

Lenses Schneider Xenar or Kodak Ektar f/3.5, 50mm
Shutters Compur or Compur-Rapid
Numbers made 39,111

Description/Remarks

Black enamelled mechanism cover with inset finder and exposure counter. Taller rewind knob.

Retina I (Type 126)

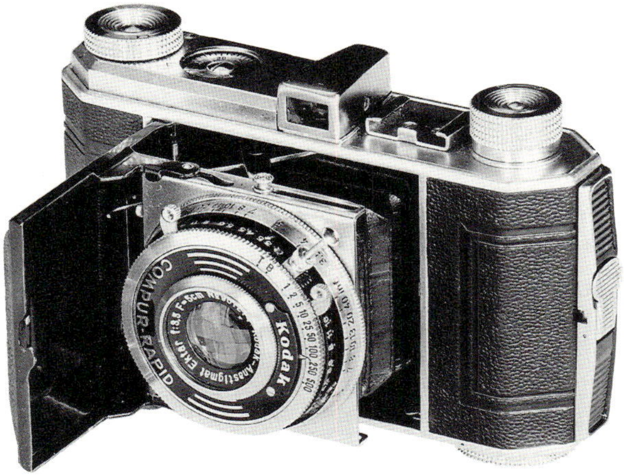

KP

Type Folding 35mm miniature
Introduced 1936
Discontinued 1938
Lenses Schneider Xenar, Kodak Ektar or Zeiss Tessar f/3.5, 50mm
Shutter Compur-Rapid
Numbers made 39,100

Description/Remarks

Similar to Retina I Type 119, but with chromed mechanism housing, top plate and body edges.

Retina I (Type 141)

Type Folding 35mm miniature
Introduced 1937
Discontinued 1939
Lenses Schneider Xenar or Kodak Ektar f/3.5, 50mm
Shutters Compur or Compur-Rapid
Numbers made 31,749

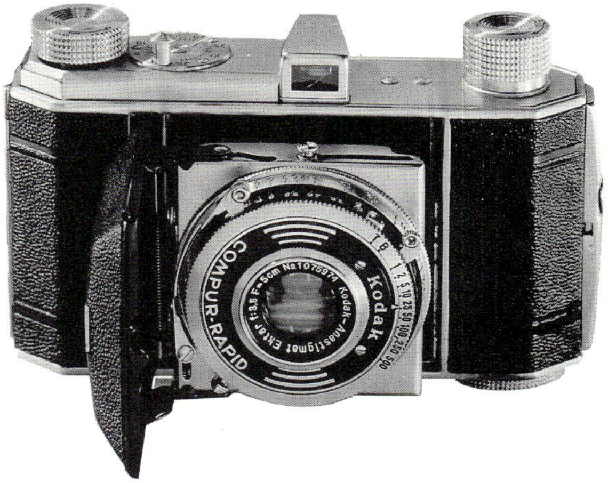

KP

Description/Remarks

Developed from Retina I Type 119; first model with body release; taller rewind knob, modified exposure counter.

Retina I (Type 143)

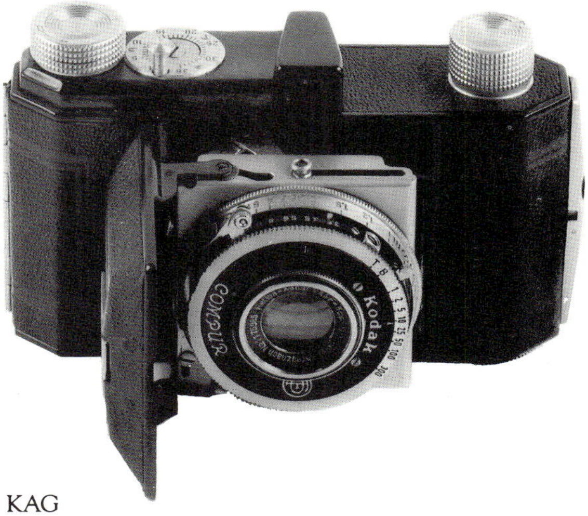

KAG

Type Folding 35mm miniature
Introduced 1938
Discontinued 1939

Lens Schneider Xenar f/3.5, 50mm
Shutter Compur
Numbers made 21,476

Description/Remarks

Black enamelled version of the Retina I Type 141.

Retina I (Type 148)

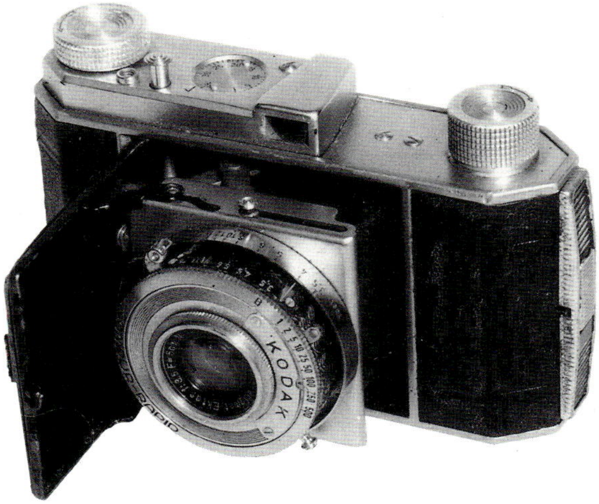

RPS

Type Folding 35mm miniature
Introduced 1939
Discontinued 1939
Lenses Schneider Xenar or Kodak Ektar f/3.5, 50mm
Shutters Compur or Compur-Rapid (Ektar only)
Numbers made 14,957

Description/Remarks

New raised mechanism cover with inset finder; repositioned frame counter.

Retina I (Type 149)

Type Folding 35mm miniature
Introduced 1939
Discontinued 1939
Lens Schneider Xenar f/3.5, 50mm
Shutter Compur
Numbers made 10,403

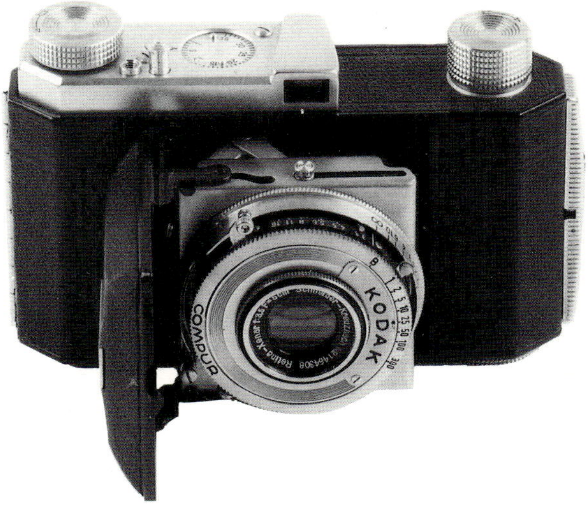

KAG

Description/Remarks

Developed from Retina I Type 148, but altered mechanism cover with finder built-in. Black enamelled edges to body, leather covering on top.

Retina I (Type 010)

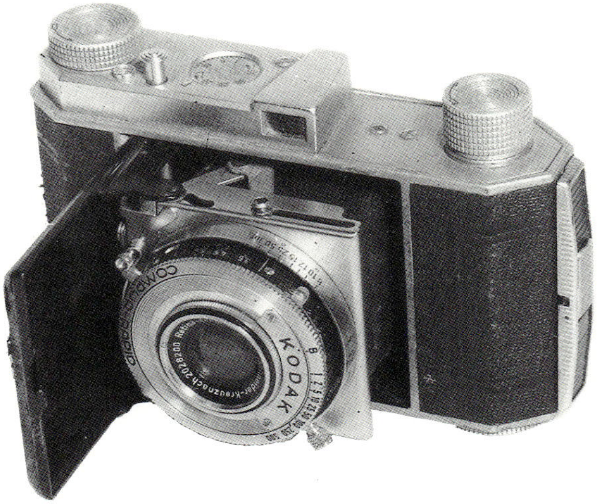

RPS

Type Folding 35mm miniature
Introduced 1946
Discontinued 1946

Lenses Schneider Xenar, Kodak Ektar or Ysar f/3.5,50mm
Shutters Compur or Compur-Rapid
Numbers made 413,708 (with Type 013)

Description/Remarks

The first post-War Retina, delivered only to occupying forces and for export. Based on Retina I Type 149, but with chromed top and body edges.

Variations

Several 'unofficial' variations exist, with non-standard combinations of bodies, lenses and shutters. They may well have been made up from parts obtained at the end of the War from Kodak AG's Stuttgart factory by occupying forces.

Retina I (Type 013)

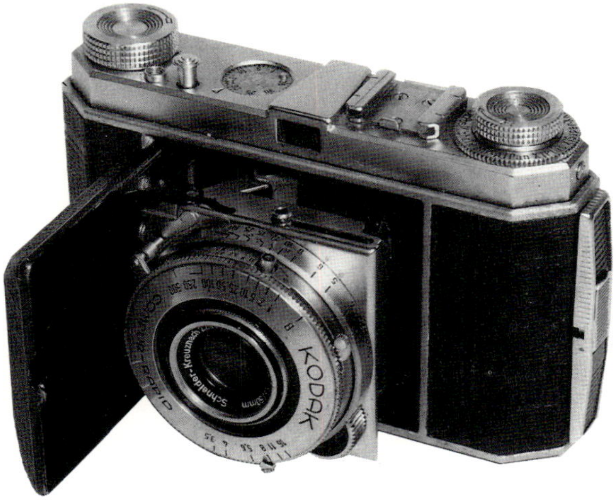

RPS

Type Folding 35mm miniature
Introduced 1949
Discontinued 1954
Lenses Schneider Xenar f/3.5, 50mm – 1949
Schneider Xenar f/2.8, 50mm – 1949–1954
Shutter Compur-Rapid
Numbers made 413,708 (with Type 010)

Description/Remarks

New design: chromed mechanism cover over whole body, with accessory shoe. Flash contact – coaxial socket. New rewind knob with depth of field scale; new focusing knob; no support foot. Coated lens.

Retina Ia (Type 015)

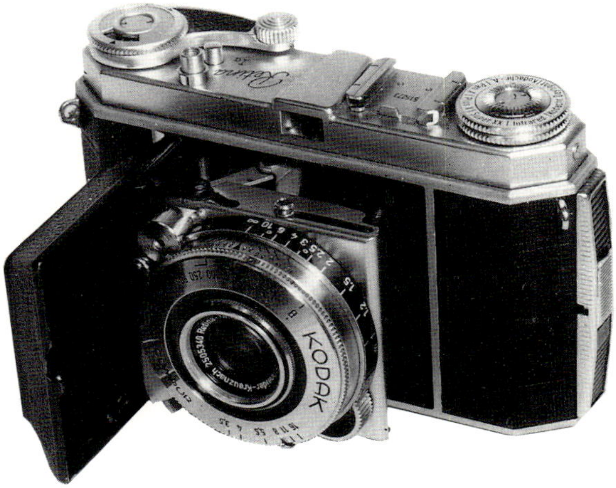

RPS

Type Folding 35mm miniature
Introduced 1951
Discontinued 1954
Lenses Kodak Ektar (1951), Schneider Xenar f/3.5 or f/2.8, 50mm
Shutters Compur-Rapid 1951
Synchro-Compur 1951–1954
Numbers made 137,000+

Description/Remarks

Lever wind-on with frame counter; deeper lens cover with no support foot; carrying strap fittings. From July 1951 lower rewind knob and Synchro-Compur fitted.

Retina Ib (Type 018)

Type Folding 35mm miniature
Introduced 1954
Discontinued 1958
Lens Schneider Xenar f/2.8 50mm
Shutter Synchro-Compur
Numbers made 160,893

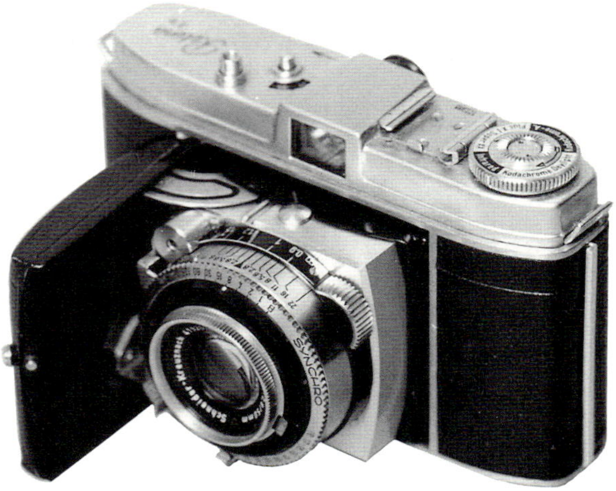

KM

Description/Remarks

Redesigned, with rounder shape. Taller, stepped mechanism cover with accessory shoe; wind-on lever on base; EV scale with coupled shutter and aperture setting. Reflected frame finder; new film transport mechanism. New strap fittings.

Retina IB (Type 019)

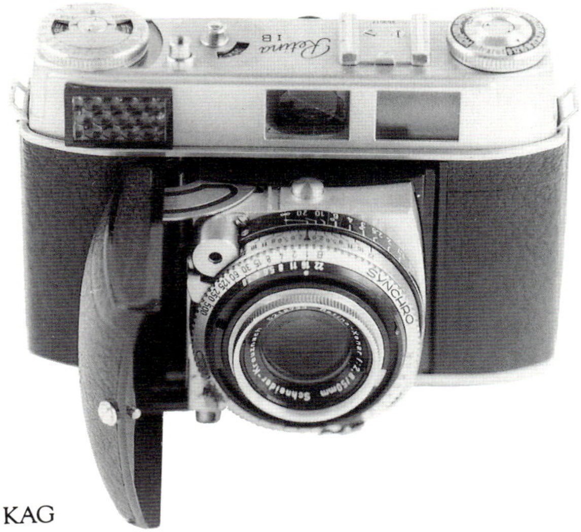

KAG

Type Folding 35mm miniature
Introduced 1957
Discontinued 1960
Lens Schneider Xenar f/2.8, 50mm
Shutter Synchro-Compur
Numbers made 76,000

Description/Remarks

Developed from Retina Ib Type 018; taller mechanism cover; built-in photoelectric exposure meter, with EV scale. From 1958 with brightline finder.

Retina I BS (Type 040)

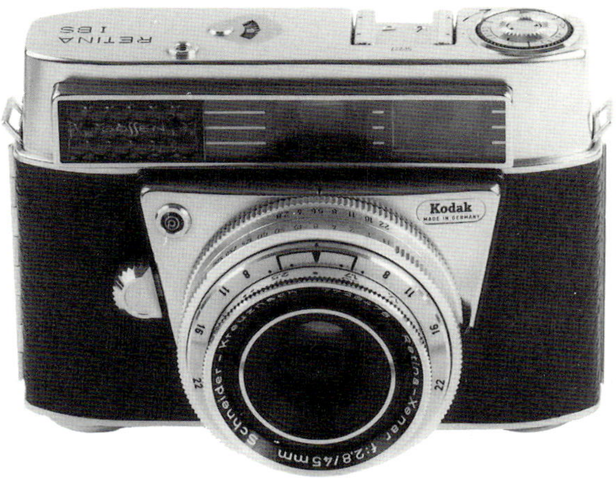

KAG

Type Solid body 35mm miniature
Introduced 1962
Discontinued 1963
Lens Schneider Xenar f/2.8, 50mm
Shutter Compur
Numbers made 13,000

Description/Remarks

New, non-folding design. Taller mechanism cover with recessed rewind knob and accessory shoe. Increased range exposure meter with alignment pointer in brightline finder; rectangular eyepiece.

Retina IF (Type 046)

Type Solid body 35mm miniature

Introduced 1963
Discontinued 1964
Lens Schneider Xenar f/2.8, 45mm
Shutter Prontor 500 LK
Numbers made 37,000+

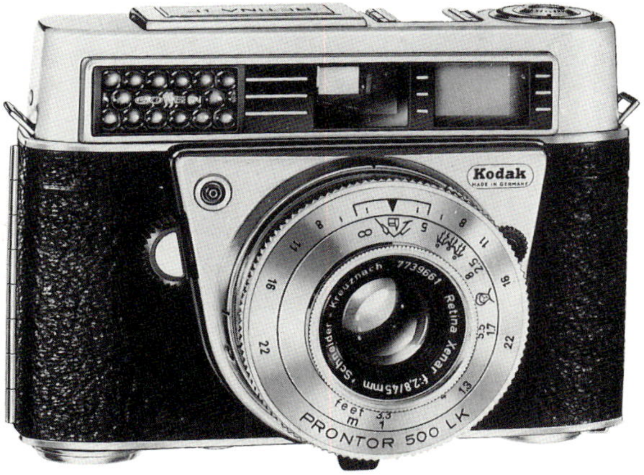

KP

Description/Remarks

Built-in photoelectric exposure meter with setting in brightline finder; recessed rewind knob; built-in flash gun for AG1 bulbs.

Retina II (Type 122)

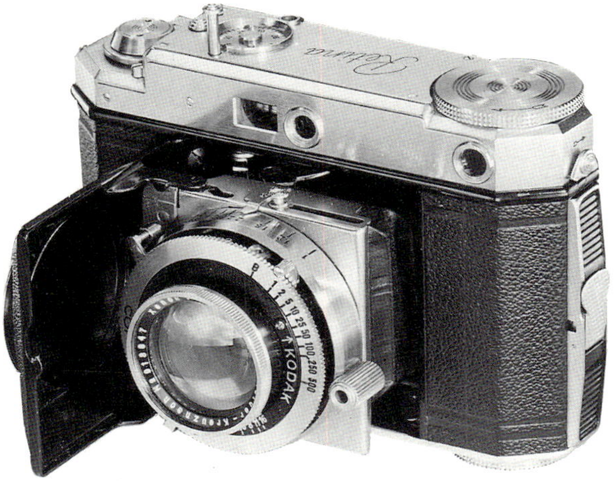

KP

Type Folding 35mm miniature
Introduced 1936
Discontinued 1937
Lenses Kodak Ektar f/3.5, 50mm or Schneider Xenon f/2.8 or f/2.0, 50mm
Shutter Compur-Rapid
Numbers made 4,611

Description/Remarks

Coupled rangefinder with separate finder eyepiece. Rangefinder window on the rewind axis. Lever wind-on on top.

Retina II (Type 142)

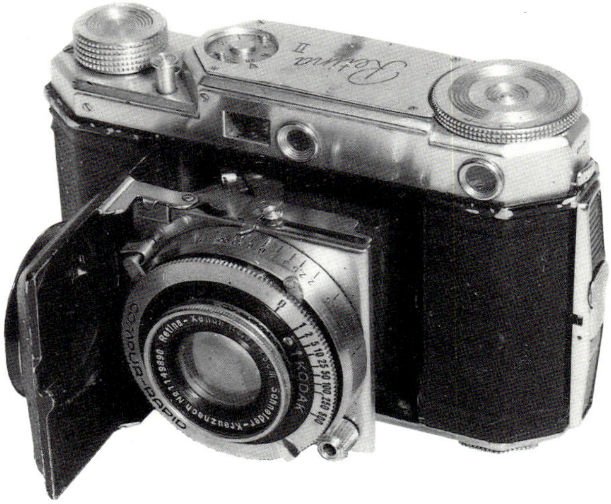

RPS

Type Folding 35mm miniature
Introduced 1937
Discontinued 1939
Lenses Kodak Ektar f/3.5, 50mm or Schneider Xenon f/2.8 or f/2.0, 50mm
Shutter Compur-Rapid
Numbers made 51,735

Description/Remarks

Developed from Retina II Type 122; altered mechanism cover with deeper step; wind-on knob; body release moved nearer wind-on.

Retina II (Type 011)

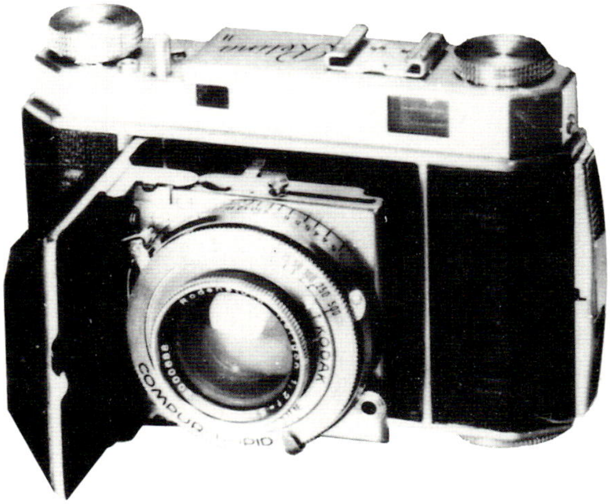

KP

Type Folding 35mm miniature
Introduced 1946
Discontinued 1949
Lenses Kodak Ektar f/2.0, 47mm, Schneider Xenon f/2.0, 50mm or Rodenstock Heligon f/2.0, 50mm
Shutter Compur-Rapid
Numbers made 268,924 (with Type 014 and 016)

Description/Remarks

Developed from Retina IIa Type 150; altered mechanism cover; body edges chromed; new model coupled rangefinder; no carrying strap fittings. Delivered only to occupying forces and for export.

Retina II (Type 014)

Type Folding 35mm miniature
Introduced 1949
Discontinued 1950
Lenses Schneider Xenon or Rodenstock Heligon f/2.0, 50mm
Shutter Compur-Rapid
Numbers made 268,924 (with Types 011 and 016)

Description/Remarks

Developed from Retina II Type 011; altered rewind knob, new polished shutter front plate, new focusing knob; coaxial flash synch socket; shutter release locked by closing camera; coated lenses.

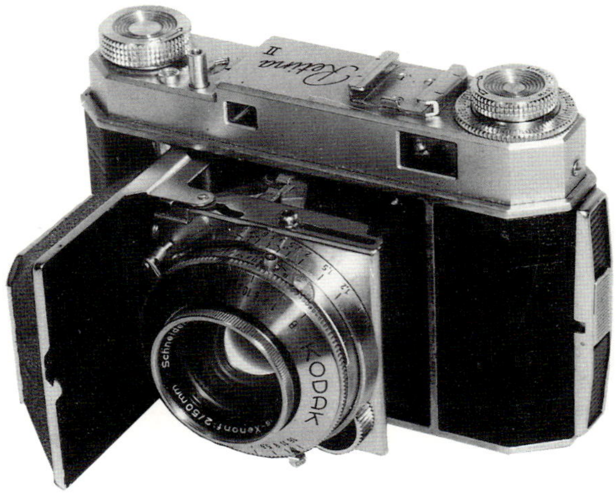

RPS

Retina IIa (Type 150)

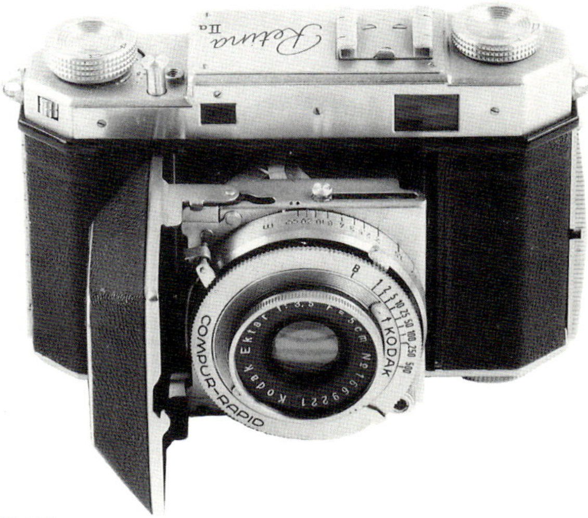

KAG

Type Folding 35mm miniature
Introduced 1939
Discontinued 1939
Lenses Kodak Ektar f/3.5, 50mm or Schneider Xenon f/2.8 or f/2.0, 50mm
Shutter Compur-Rapid
Numbers made 5,107

Description/Remarks

Developed from Retina II Type 142; redesigned mechanism cover with combined rangefinder; finder window off rewind axis. Accessory shoe; smaller rewind knob, on extending shaft. Redesigned lens cover; carrying strap fittings.

Retina IIa (Type 016)

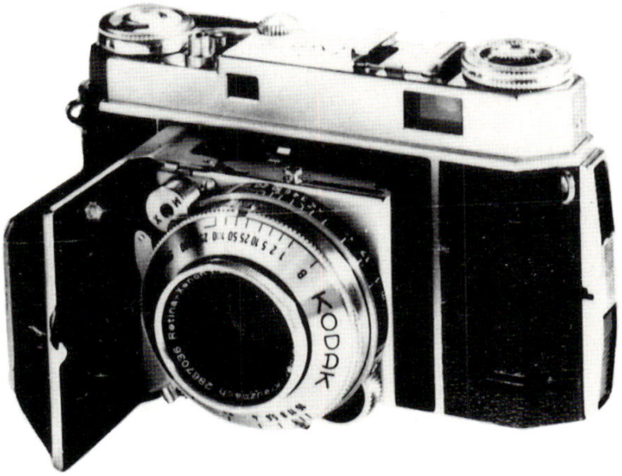

KP

Type Folding 35mm miniature
Introduced 1951
Discontinued 1954
Lenses Schneider Xenon or Rodenstock Heligon f/2.0, 50mm
Shutters Compur-Rapid to July 1951, then Synchro-Compur
Numbers made 268,924 (with Types 011, 014)

Description/Remarks

Lever wind-on with built-in exposure counter, locking on picture 36; new rewind knob with film type indicator; new focusing scale with white figures on black ground; new film transport mechanism; carrying strap fittings.

Retina IIc (Type 020)

Type Folding 35mm miniature
Introduced 1954
Discontinued 1957
Lenses Schneider Xenon C or Rodenstock Heligon C f/2.8, 50mm, interchangeable front elements – see below.
Shutter Synchro-Compur
Numbers made 136,000+

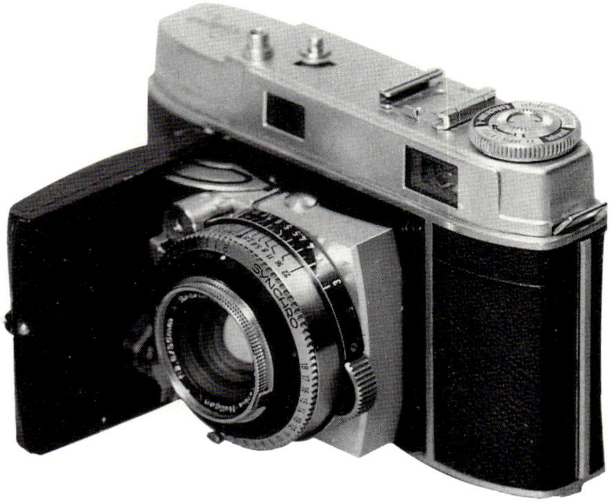

KM

Description/Remarks

New design, with rounded body; EV scale with coupled shutter and aperture settings; new carrying strap fittings; reflecting frame finder; front lens elements interchangeable:

Schneider Retina Curtar Xenon C or Rodenstock Curtar Heligon C f/5.6, 35mm (f/4 *from 1958*).

Schneider Retina Longar Xenon C or Rodenstock Longar Heligon C f/4.0, 80mm.

Retina IIC (Type 029)

Type Folding 35mm miniature
Introduced 1958
Discontinued 1958
Lenses Schneider Xenon C or Rodenstock Heligon C f/2.8, 50mm; interchangeable front elements – see below.
Shutter Synchro-Compur
Numbers made 18,700

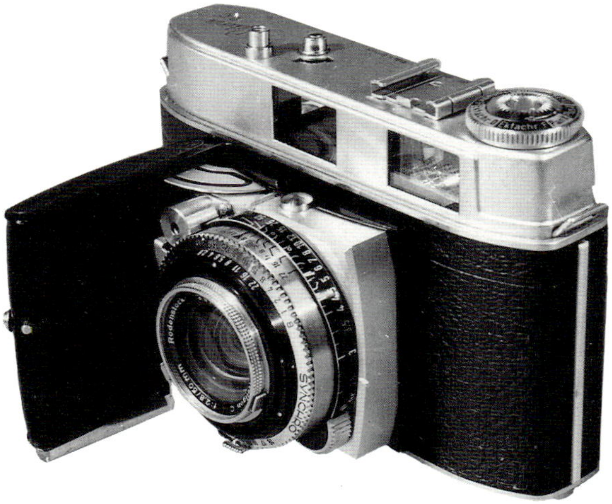

KM

Description/Remarks

Developed from Retina IIc Type 020. Brightline finder with frames for 35, 50 and 80mm lenses as available for Retina IIc.

Retina IIF (Type 047)

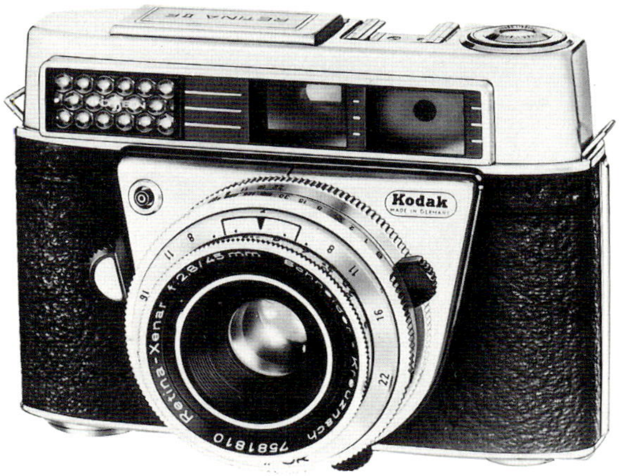

KP

Type Solid body 35mm miniature
Introduced 1963
Discontinued 1964
Lens Schneider Xenar f/2.8, 45mm
Shutter Compur
Numbers made 30,000

Description/Remarks

Built-in photoelectric exposure meter with setting in brightline finder, with coupled rangefinder. Recessed rewind knob; built-in flash unit for AG1 bulbs.

Retina IIS (Type 024)

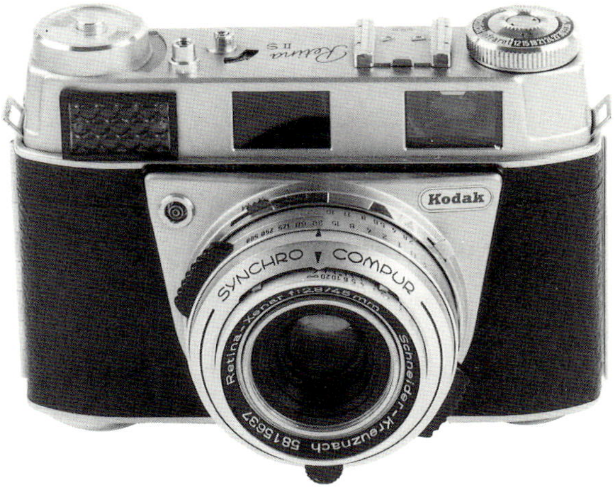

KAG

Type Solid body 35mm miniature
Introduced 1959
Discontinued 1960
Lenses Schneider Xenon or Rodenstock Heligon f/1.9, 50mm or Schneider Xenar f/2.8,50mm.
Fully interchangeable – see below.
Shutter Synchro-Compur
Numbers made 19,400

Description/Remarks

New design; built-in exposure meter, aperture set directly by aligning pointer after setting shutter speed; dynamic depth of field indicators; brightline finder combined with rangefinder. Range of interchangeable lenses:

Curtagon f/4, 28mm, f/2.8, 35mm
Eurygon f/2.8, 30mm, f/4.0,35mm
Tele Arton or Rotelar f/4.0, 85mm
Xenar or Rotelar f/4.0, 135mm

Retina IIIc (Type 021)

Type Folding 35mm miniature

Introduced 1954
Discontinued 1957
Lenses Schneider Xenon C or Rodenstock Heligon C f/2.0, 50mm; interchangeable front components
Shutter Synchro-Compur
Numbers made 209,765

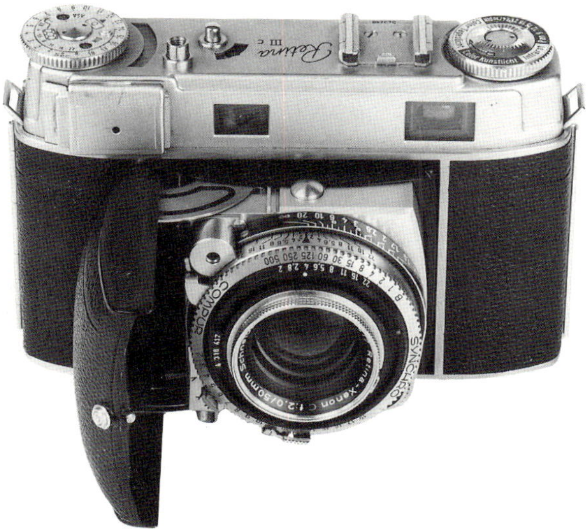

KAG

Description/Remarks

New body design, similar to Retina IIc, but with built-in meter with EV scale; same range of interchangeable front lens components – 35, 50 and 80mm.

Retina IIIC (Type 028)

Folding 35mm miniature
Introduced 1958
Discontinued 1960
Lenses Schneider Xenon C or Rodenstock Heligon C f/2.0, 50mm; interchangeable front components
Shutter Synchro-Compur
Numbers made 68,000 approximately

Description/Remarks

Similar to Retina IIC Type 029, but with exposure meter; large brightline finder with frames for 35, 50 and 80mm interchangeable front components.

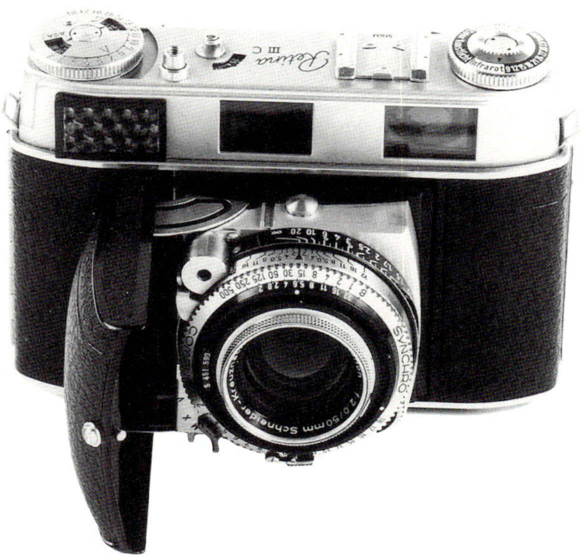

KAG

Variations

In 1977, to celebrate the 50th anniversary of the founding of Kodak AG, a limited number, about 120, were assembled from spare parts. Apart from the Gossen exposure meter, which had a longer film speed range (to 3200 ASA) than the earlier model, these were essentially the same as the earlier production models. The camera serial numbers always begin with '9.' on these re-makes; other differences were minor.

They were distributed to VIP customers, senior Kodak employees etc, and were not marketed.

Retina IIIS (Type 027)

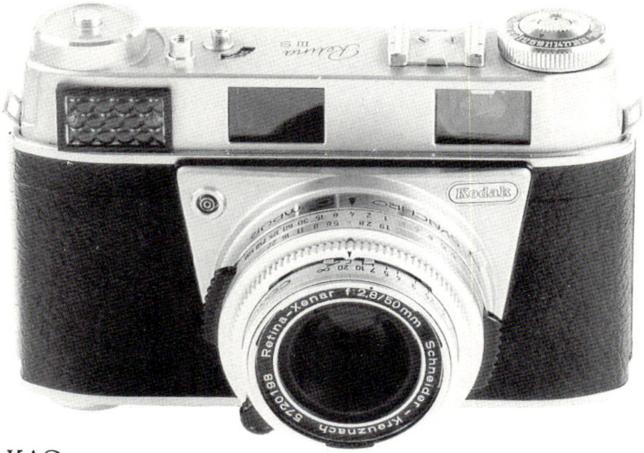

KAG

Type Solid body 35mm miniature
Introduced 1958
Discontinued 1960
Lenses Schneider Xenar or Rodenstock Ysarex f/2.8, 50mm or Schneider Xenon or Rodenstock Heligon f/1.9, 50mm, fully interchangeable
Shutter Synchro-Compur
Numbers made 45,050

Description/Remarks

Similar to Retina IIS Type 024 but with 8.5mm longer body; brightline finder with automatic selection of frames for 28 to 135mm lenses; behind-lens shutter.

Retina Automatic I (Type 038)

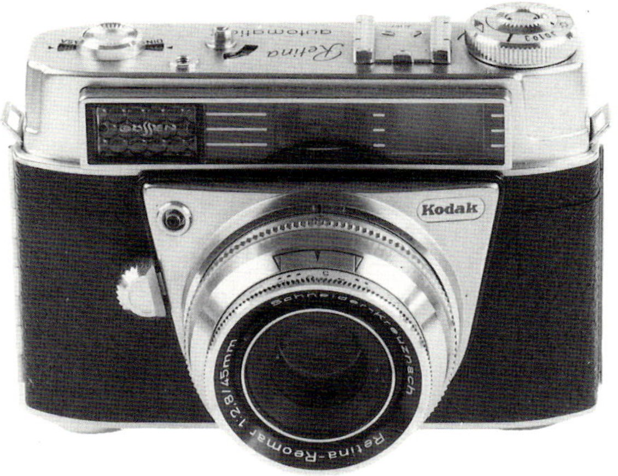

KAG

Type Solid body 35mm miniature
Introduced 1960
Discontinued 1962
Lens Retina Reomar f/2.8, 45mm
Shutter Prontormat-S
Numbers made 61,000+

Description/Remarks

Fully automatic exposure control, self-locking with low-light signal and 3-point focusing setting in brightline finder.

Retina Automatic II (Type 032)

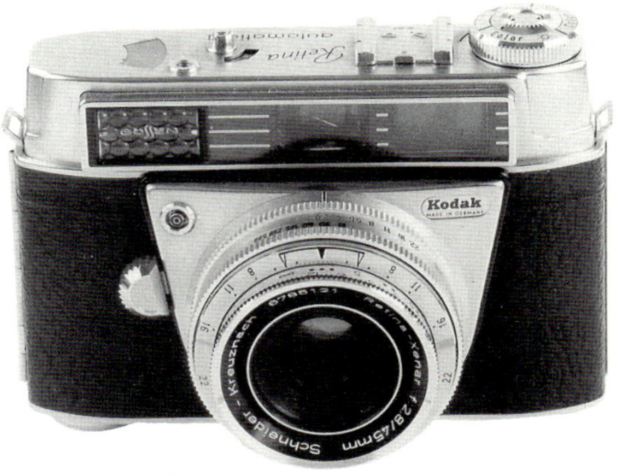

KAG

Type Solid body 35mm miniature
Introduced 1960
Discontinued 1962
Lens Schneider Xenar f/2.8, 45mm
Shutter Compur
Numbers made 48,000

Description/Remarks

Fully automatic exposure control, with shutter speed choice.

Retina Automatic III (Type 039)

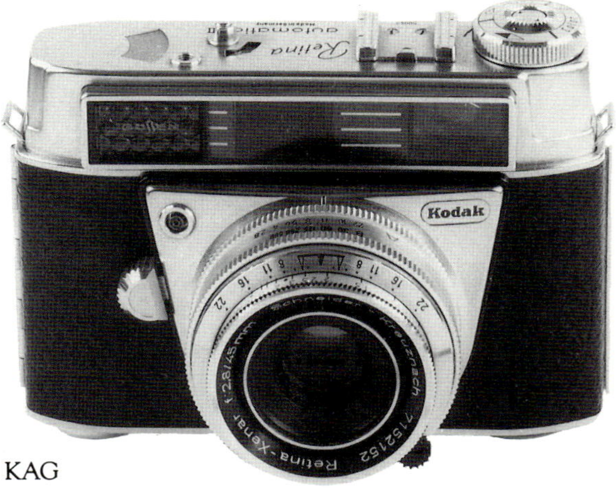

KAG

Type Solid body 35mm miniature
Introduced 1960
Discontinued 1963
Lens Schneider Xenar f/2.8, 45mm
Shutter Compur
Numbers made 77,000+

Description/Remarks

Similar to Retina Automatic II Type 039, but with coupled rangefinder.

Retina Reflex (Type 025)

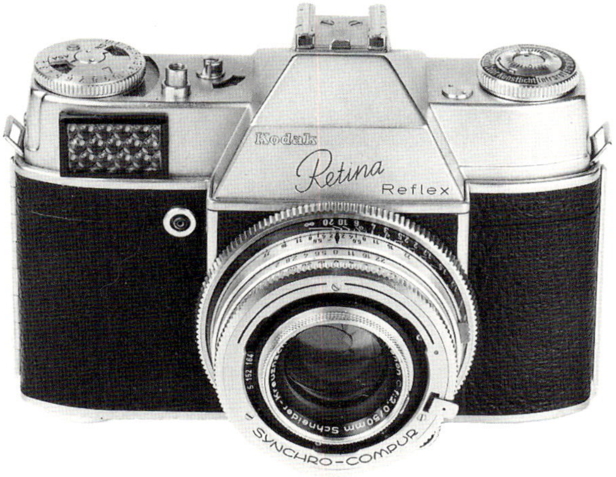

KAG

Type Solid body 35mm SLR miniature
Introduced 1956
Discontinued 1958
Lenses Schneider Xenon C or Rodenstock Heligon C f/2.0, 50mm, interchangeable front components
Shutter Synchro-Compur
Numbers made 65,000

Description/Remarks

Single lens reflex, focusing by ground glass and split-image rangefinder; photoelectric exposure meter; EV scale, shutter and aperture coupling; preset diaphragm; interchangeable front lens components:

Retina Curtar Xenon C or Heligon C f/4.0 or f/5.6, 35mm.

Retina Longar Xenon C or Heligon C f/4.0, 80mm

Retina Reflex S (Type 034)

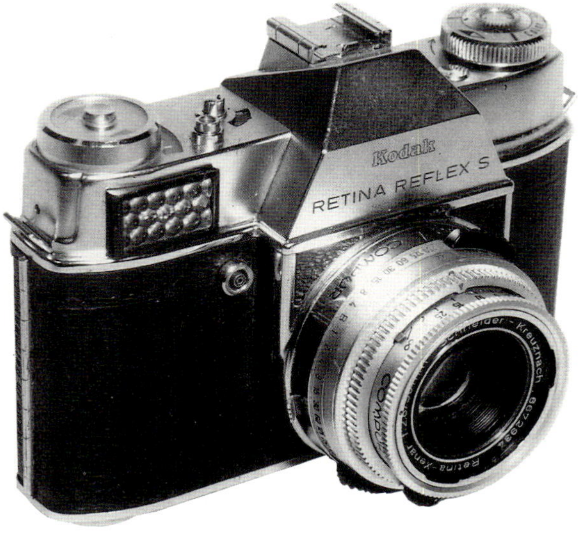

RPS

Type Solid body 35mm SLR miniature
Introduced 1959
Discontinued 1960
Lenses Schneider Xenar or Rodenstock Ysarex f/2.8, 50mm, or Schneider Xenon or Rodenstock Heligon f/1.9, 50mm, fully interchangeable
Shutter Synchro-Compur
Numbers made 78,000

Description/Remarks

Developed from Retina Reflex Type 025. Photoelectric meter, exposure set by aperture control after selecting shutter speed; coupled shutter/aperture rings. Interchangeable lenses with automatic depth of field indicators:

Curtagon f/4.0, 28mm or f/2.8, 35mm.
Eurygon f/2.8, 30mm or f4.0, 35mm.
Tele Arton or Rotelar f/4.0, 85mm.
Tele Xenar or Rotelar f/4.0, 135mm.

Retina Reflex III (Type 041)

Type Solid body 35mm SLR miniature
Introduced 1960
Discontinued 1964

Lenses Schneider Xenar or Rodenstock Ysarex f/2.8, 50mm or Schneider Xenon or Rodenstock Heligon f/1.9, 50mm, fully interchangeable
Shutter Synchro-Compur
Numbers made 116,000

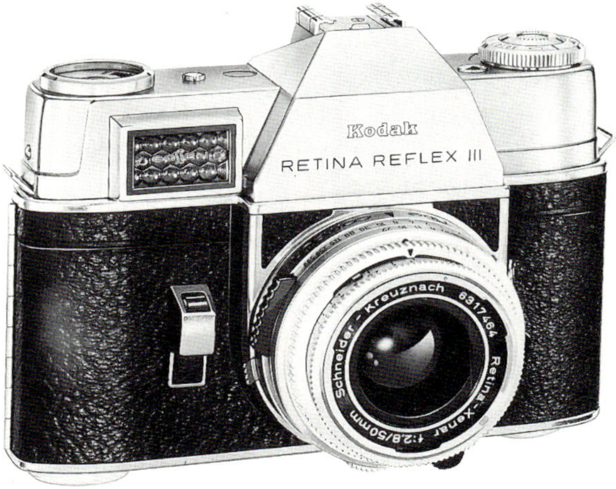

KP

Description/Remarks

Developed from Retina Reflex S Type 034; meter needle in reflex finder set by aperture control after presetting shutter. Exposure meter window built out; rectangular finder window; new release on body, next to lens. From Spring 1962 new meter with increased range; knob for film speedon side of mechanism cover. Interchangeable lens range as for Retina Reflex S Type 034; Tele Xenar f/4.8, 200mm available from October 1961.

Retina Reflex IV (Type 051)

Type Solid body 35mm SLR miniature
Introduced 1964
Discontinued 1967
Lens Schneider Xenar f/2.8, 50mm or Xenon f/1.9, 50mm, fully interchangeable
Shutter Synchro-Compur
Numbers made 524,000+

Description/Remarks

Developed from Retina Reflex III type 041; larger photocell; aperture and shutter scales in reflex finder; hot shoe; recessed rewind knob. Interchangeable lenses as for Retina Reflex III.

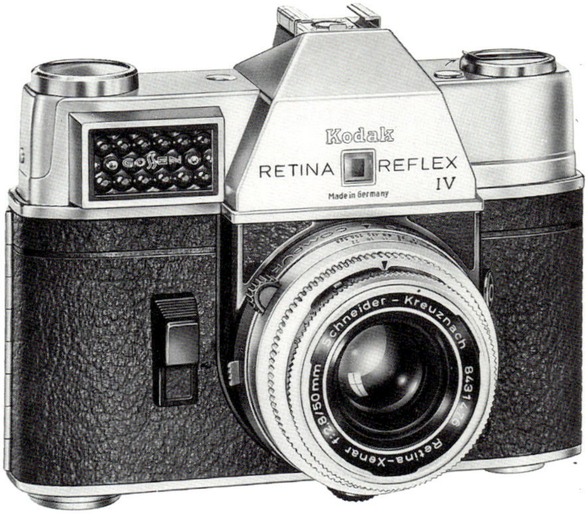

KP

Retina S1 (Type 060)

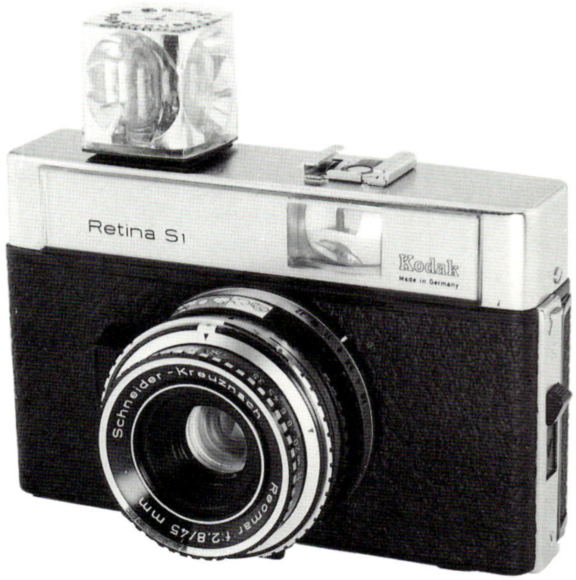

KP

Type Solid body 35mm miniature
Introduced 1966
Discontinued 1969

Lens Reomar f/2.8, 45mm
Shutter Kodak
Numbers made ?

Description/Remarks

Exposure setting by weather symbols; 3-symbol focusing scale; hot shoe and flashcube socket.

Retina S2 (Type 061)

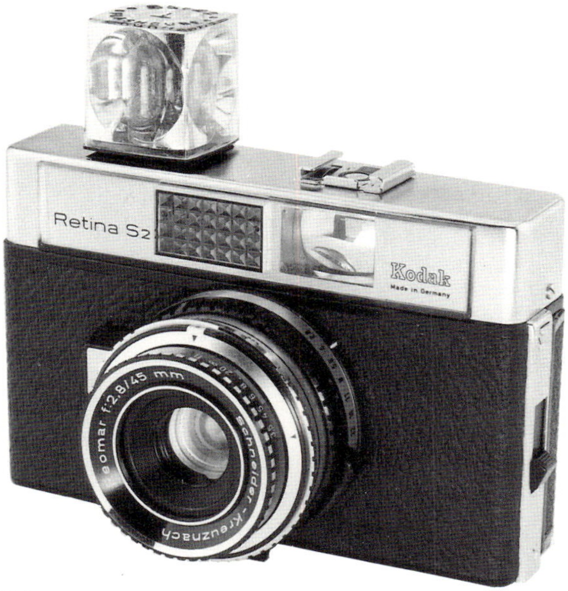

KP

Type Solid body 35mm miniature
Introduced 1966
Discontinued 1969
Lens Reomar f/2.8, 45mm
Shutter Kodak
Numbers made ?

Description/Remarks

As Retina S1 Type 060, but with photoelectric exposure meter reading in finder.

Retinette (Type 147)

Type Folding 35mm miniature
Introduced 1939
Discontinued 1939
Lens Kodak Anastigmat f/6.3, 50mm
Shutter Kodak K3
Numbers made 20,000

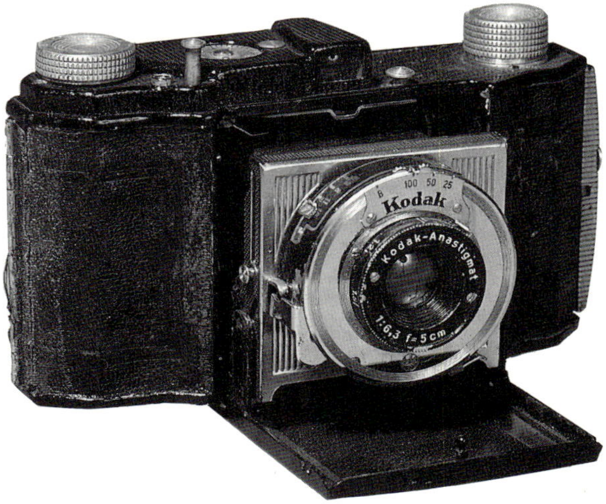

KM

Description/Remarks

The first model of what was to become a very popular range of budget-priced 35mm cameras.

It differed from later models in having a downward-opening baseboard/lens cover. The lens panel had vertical ribbing. It was on the market for only a short time, being introduced just before the outbreak of War.

Retinette (Type 012)

Type Folding 35mm miniature
Introduced 1949
Discontinued 1951
Lenses Ennatar or Kodak Anastigmat f/4.5, 50mm
Reomar f/4.5, 50mm from July 1949
Shutter Prontor-S
Numbers made 61,000+ (with Type 017)

Description/Remarks

Similar to the Retinette II, Type 160, with the Retina-type body, but with black enamelled top and satin chrome integral finder and counter housing. Plain lens panel. No support foot.

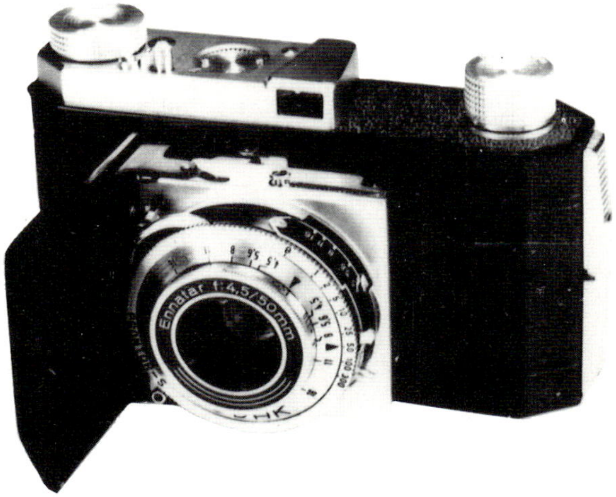

KP

Variations

Some of this production was supplied to Kodak-Pathé without lenses or shutters; French-made Angénieux f/2.8, 50mm lenses and Atom shutters were fitted. This version was designated Retinette 1A in France.

Retinette (Type 017)

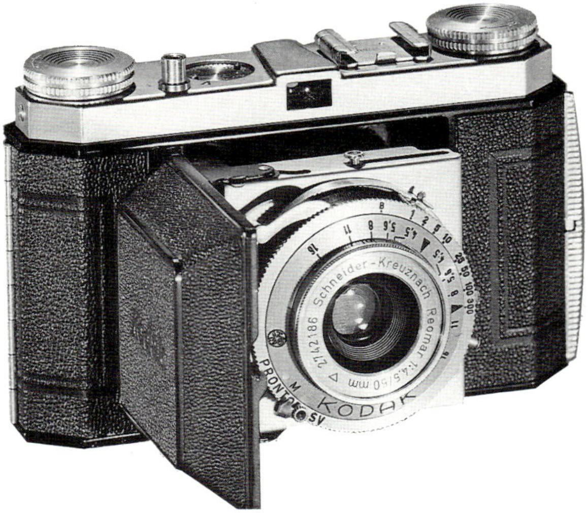

KP

Type Folding 35mm miniature
Introduced 1952
Discontinued 1954
Lenses Reomar f/4.5, 50mm
Xenar f/4.5, 50mm
Shutter Prontor-SV
Numbers made 61,000+ (with Type 012)

Description/Remarks

Redesigned longer satin chromed top mechanism cover with accessory shoe. Larger rewind knob. The last folding Retinette camera.

Variations

Some of this production was supplied to Kodak-Pathé without lenses and shutters; they were fitted with French-made Angénieux f/3.5 or f/4.5, 50mm lenses in Atom Atos-2 shutters.

Retinette (Type 022)

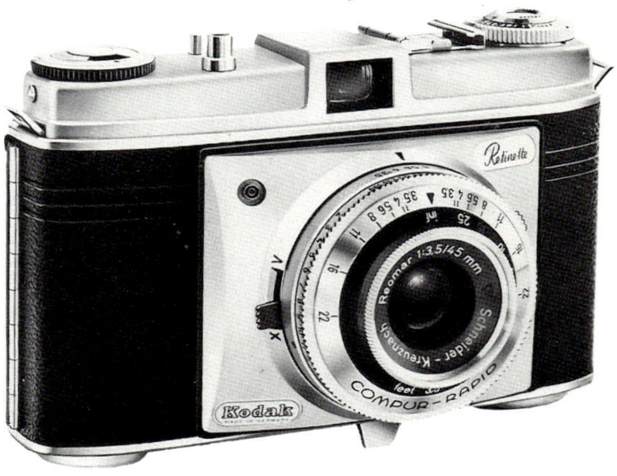

KP

Type Solid body 35mm miniature
Introduced 1954
Discontinued 1958
Lens Reomar f/3.5, 45mm
Shutter Compur-Rapid
Numbers made 238,000

Description/Remarks

Completely redesigned, with shorter focal length lens to permit a fixed body construction. Larger finder, accessory shoe, lever wind-on. EV scale, with coupled shutter and aperture.

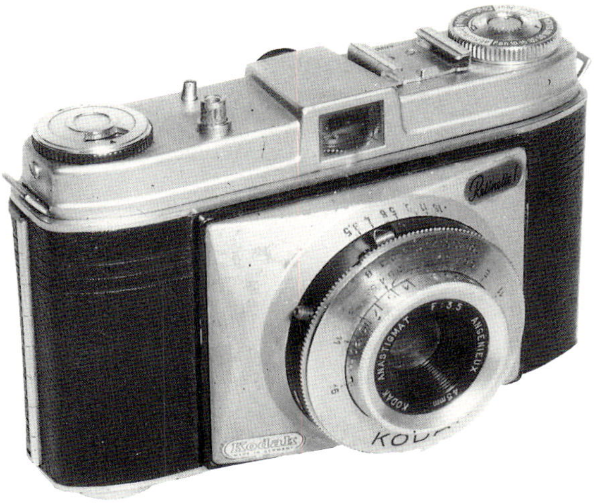

French version F. RPS

Variations

This model, designated Retinette F, was supplied to Kodak-Pathé without lens or shutter. French-made Angénieux f/3.5, 50mm lenses and Atom Atos-2 shutters were fitted.

Retinette I (Type 030)

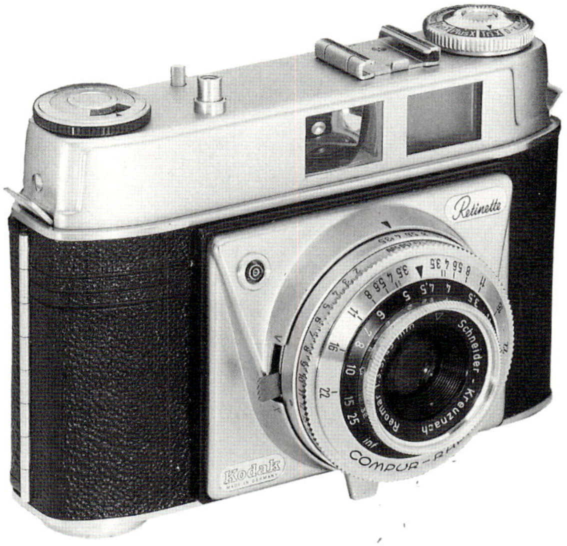

KP

Type Solid body 35mm miniature
Introduced 1958
Discontinued 1960
Lens Reomar f/3.5, 45mm
Shutter Compur-Rapid
Numbers made 118,000 approximately

Description/Remarks

Similar to Retinette II, but with smaller aperture lens.

Variations

Export models made for Kodak Limited, England (23,800+) and Kodak-Pathé, France (8,800+).

Retinette I A (Type 035)

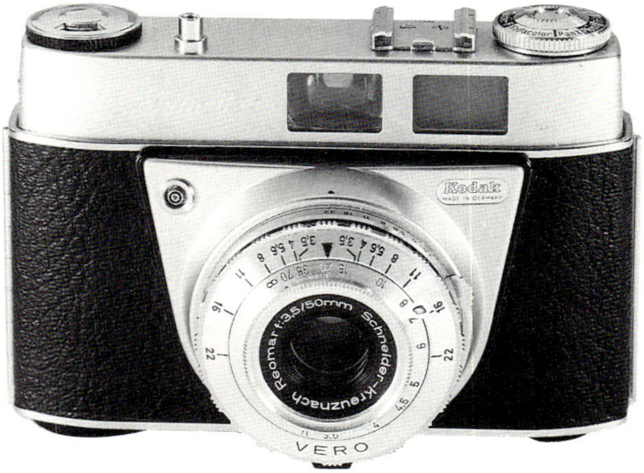

KP

Type Solid body 35mm miniature
Introduced 1959
Discontinued 1960
Lenses Reomar f/3.5, 45mm or 50mm
Shutters Pronto or Vero
Numbers made 40,000+

Description/Remarks

Cheaper version of the Retinette Type 030. Redesigned tapered front panel.

Variations

Export model produced for Kodak-Pathé, France.

The version with a Reomar f3.5 50mm lens and Vero shutter was sold in England from 1959 to 1961.

Retinette I A (Type 042)

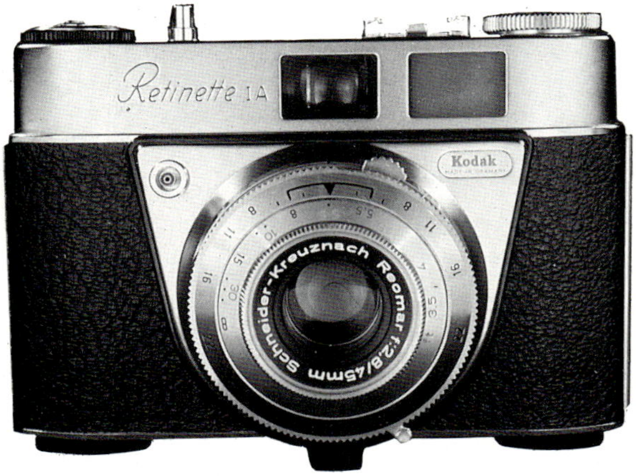

KP

Type Solid body 35mm miniature
Introduced 1960
Discontinued 1963
Lens Reomar f2.8 45mm
Shutter Pronto
Numbers made 217,000+

Description/Remarks

Brightline finder with 3-position focusing setting. Self timer.

Retinette I A (Type 044)

Type Solid body 35mm miniature
Introduced 1963
Discontinued 1967
Lens Reomar f/2.8, 45mm
Shutters Prontor 250 S
Prontor 300 S from 1965
Numbers made 343,000+

Description/Remarks

Focusing scale with distance symbols; hot shoe flash contact; brightline finder.

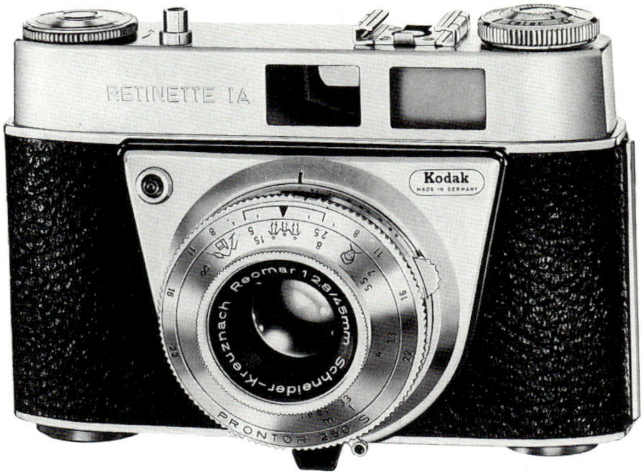

KP

Retinette I B (Type 037)

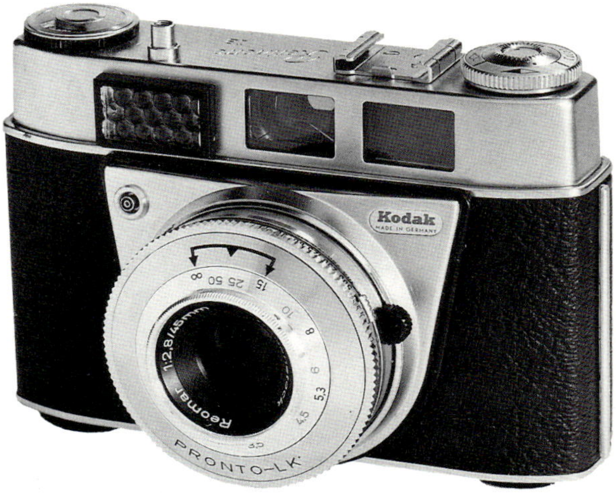

KP

Type Solid body 35mm miniature
Introduced 1959
Discontinued 1963
Lens Reomar f2.8 45mm
Shutter Pronto-LK
Numbers made 230,000+

Description/Remarks

Developed from Retinette IIA Type 036; 3-position focusing settings in brightline finder.

Variations

In 1978, Kodak AG decided to dispose of the spare parts for this model, but since there were enough to assemble about 100 cameras, this was done (as had been done for the Retina IIIC the previous year). These remakes were very similar to the original model, with minor differences in the engraving of the name etc., a larger meter window, and so on. The serial numbers began with "9."

These cameras were presented or sold to Kodak employees only.

Retinette I B (Type 045)

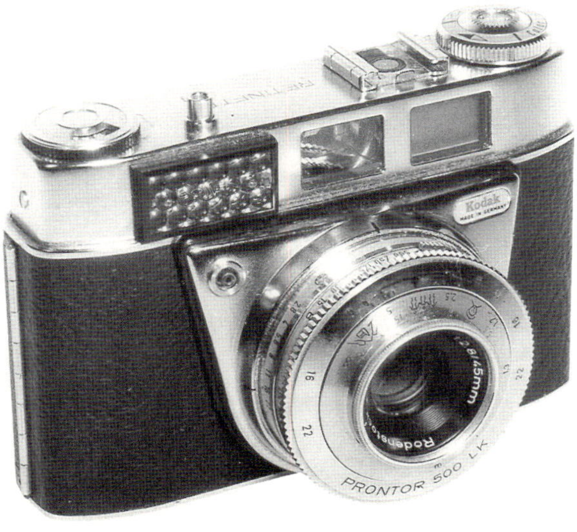

RPS

Type Solid body 35mm miniature
Introduced 1963
Discontinued 1966
Manufactured Reomar f/2.8, 45mm
Lens Prontor 500 LK
Numbers made 258,000 approximately

Description/Remarks

Built-in photoelectric meter, with needle in brightline finder. Distance symbols on focusing scale; hot shoe.

Retinette II (Type 160)

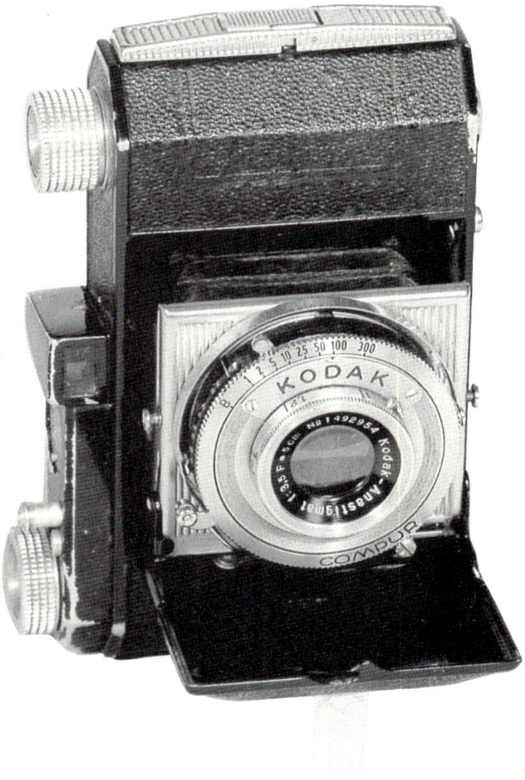

Private collection

Type Folding 35mm miniature
Introduced 1939
Discontinued 1939
Lenses Kodak Anastigmat f/3.5 or f/4.5, 50mm
Shutters Kodak K 4S with f/4.5 lens
Compur with f/3.5 lens
Numbers made 41,000

Description/Remarks

The second model, with essentially the same body as the current Retina camera. Sideways opening baseboard/lens cover, with horizontal ribbing on lens plate. Black enamelled finder/counter housing, leather covering on body top.

Retinette II (Type 026)

Type Solid body 35mm miniature

Introduced 1958
Discontinued 1958
Lens Reomar f2.8 45mm
Shutter Compur-Rapid
Numbers made 19,000

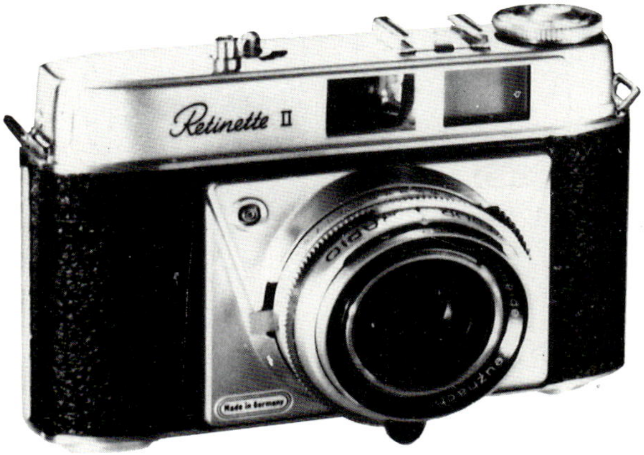

Description/Remarks

Redesigned, with taller top mechanism cover and new front panel. Brightline finder, EV scale and coupled aperture and shutter settings. Dynamic depth of field indicators.

Retinette II A (Type 036)

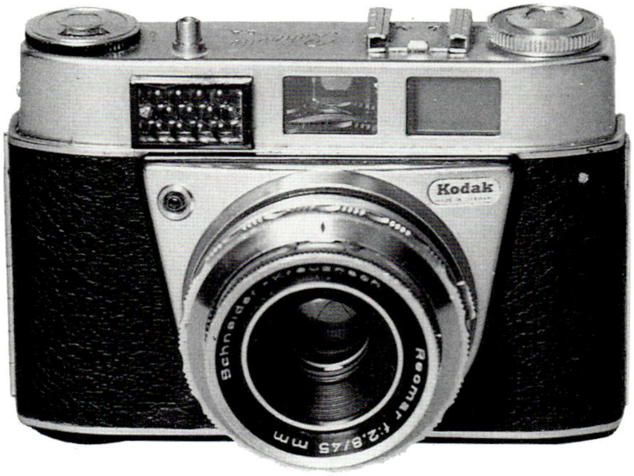

KM

Type Solid body 35mm miniature
Introduced 1959
Discontinued 1960
Lens Reomar f2.8 45mm
Shutter Prontormat
Numbers made 45,000+

Description/Remarks

Advanced version of the Retinette IA Type 035, with built-in photo-electric exposure meter, with the needle visible in the brightline finder.

Retinette II B (Type 031)

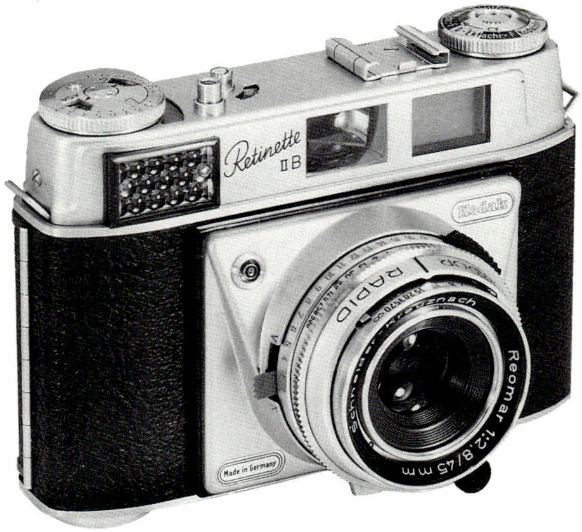

KP

Type Solid body 35mm miniature
Introduced 1958
Discontinued 1959
Lens Reomar f/2.8, 45mm
Shutter Compur-Rapid
Numbers made 40,000+

Description/Remarks

The most advanced of all the Retinette cameras. Dynamic depth of field indicators, built-in photo-electric light meter, EV scale coupled to shutter.

CHAPTER 6 *Kodak Cartridge Loading Cameras*

Film cameras which could be loaded by dropping in a cartridge of film, with no threading, have had a long history. Eastman's Daylight cameras of 1891 used light-tight cardboard containers for supplying and taking up the film, which was protected by black cloth or paper 'leaders', but they were not very successful. The Ticka, or Expo, watch-shaped camera of 1906 was loaded with a film carried in a one-piece drop-in cartridge, while many of the early 35mm cameras, in the 1920s, used a cassette-to-cassette system, which greatly simplified loading. Nonetheless, for very many years the mass market cameras used the paper-backed roll film popularised by Eastman from 1895.

Loading the roll film camera was an operation which many users were worried about. If not done correctly, the film might wind up incorrectly, damaging it, or letting light in to fog it. A very large proportion of snapshot camera users left the loading and unloading of the camera to the photo dealer. Kodak looked for ways in which this problem could be overcome. The advances in precision moulding of plastics that had taken place after World War Two made it possible to develop a new form of film cartridge which would load simply by dropping into the back of the camera, and which would fit only one, the correct, way. The new Kodapak cartridge, and the first generation of Instamatic cameras to use it, was launched in 1963. It was an immediate success. In only a few years approaching 70,000,000 Kodak Instamatic cameras had been sold worldwide, not to mention the large numbers made by other manufacturers.

Kodak Instamatic 126 Cameras

The Kodapak cartridge, given the number 126, used 35mm wide film with a single registration perforation for each frame. The film was equipped with a black backing paper, on which the exposure numbers were printed, and these, and the film type information on the back of the cartridge, could been seen through a rectangular transparent slot in the camera back. Moulded grooves on the cartridge engaged with ridges inside the camera to ensure exclusion of light from the film, but even if the camera back was opened and the cartridge displaced, only the uncovered and immediately adjacent exposures were affected. The image size was 28 × 28mm.

Kodak Instamatic 25

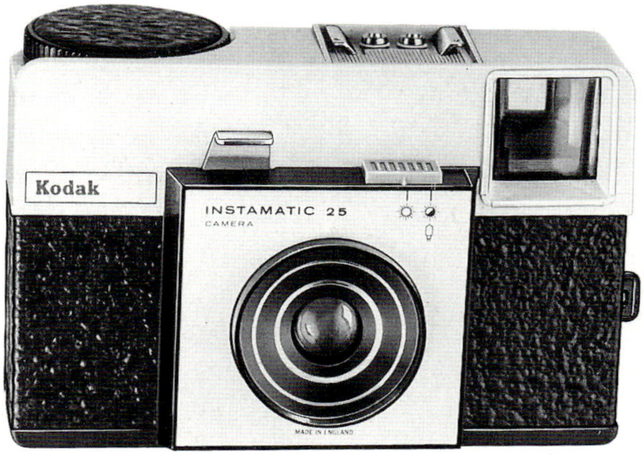

KP

Introduced January 1966
Discontinued 1971
Manufactured UK
Lens Fixed focus f/11, 43mm
Shutter 2-speed $\frac{1}{40}$ and $\frac{1}{90}$ sec.

Description/Remarks

Shutter settings with weather symbols; knob film wind; special hot shoe for Kodak Instamatic Flasholder.

Kodak Instamatic 26

Introduced 1968
Discontinued 1972
Manufactured UK
Lens Fixed focus f/11, 43mm
Shutter 2-speed $\frac{1}{40}$ and $\frac{1}{90}$ sec.

Description/Remarks

Made for premium sales only. Similar to Kodak Instamatic 25 camera.

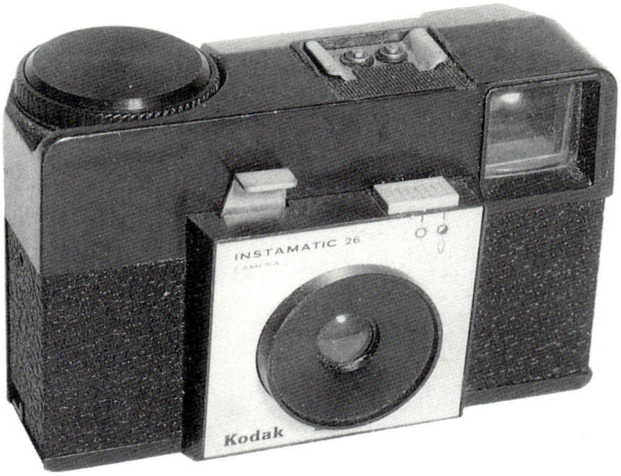

Kodak Instamatic 28

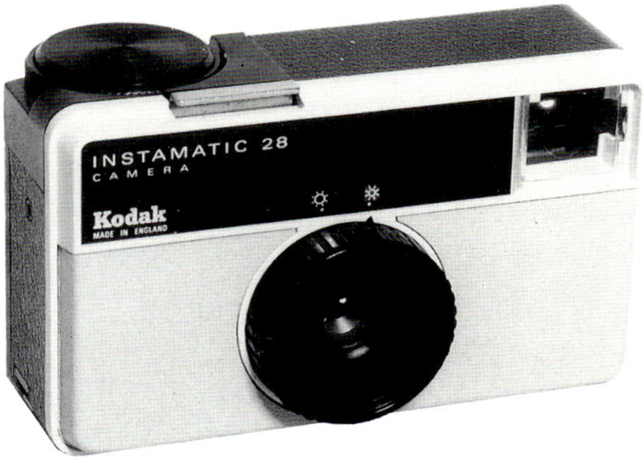

RPS

Introduced January 1972
Discontinued 1974
Manufactured UK
Lens Fixed focus f/11, 43mm
Shutter 2-speed $\frac{1}{40}$ and $\frac{1}{80}$ sec.

Description/Remarks

Weather symbols on shutter settings. No flash facility.

Kodak Instamatic 32

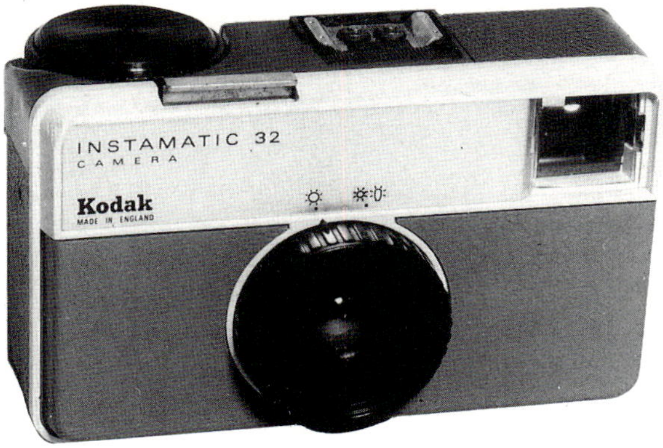

RPS

Introduced 1972
Discontinued 1973
Manufactured UK
Lens Fixed focus f/11
Shutter 2-speed 1/40 and 1/80 sec.

Description/Remarks

Identical to Kodak Instamatic 36 camera, but made for premium sales only.

Kodak Instamatic 33

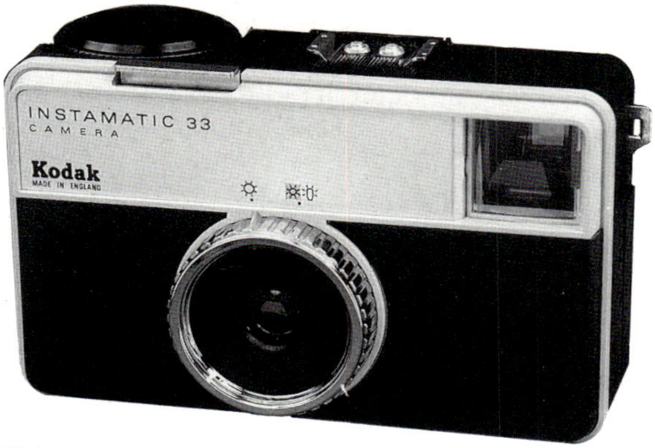

KM

Introduced September 1968
Discontinued 1973
Manufactured UK, Germany
Lens Fixed focus f/11, 43mm
Shutter 2-speed 1/40 and 1/80 sec.

Description/Remarks

Weather symbols on shutter speed setting; knob film wind; special hot shoe for Kodak Instamatic Flasholder.

Kodak Instamatic 36

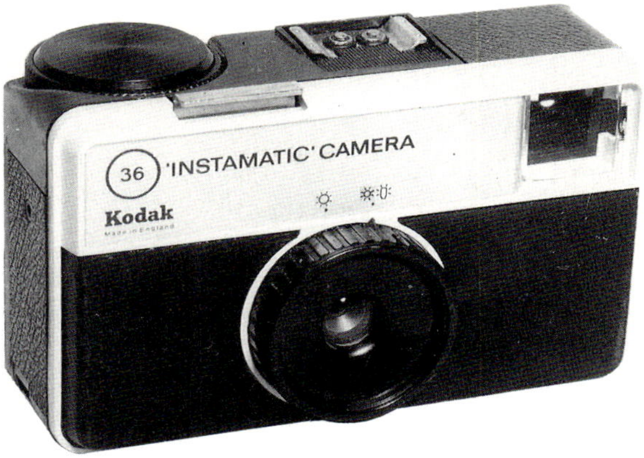

RPS

Introduced January 1973
Discontinued 1974
Manufactured UK
Lens Fixed focus f/11, 43mm
Shutter 2-speed 1/40 and 1/80 sec.

Description/Remarks

Special hot shoe for Kodak Instamatic Flasholder; weather symbols on shutter setting.

Kodak Instamatic 44

Introduced June 1969
Discontinued October 1973
Manufactured US
Lens Fixed focus f/11
Shutter Single speed, 1/50 sec.

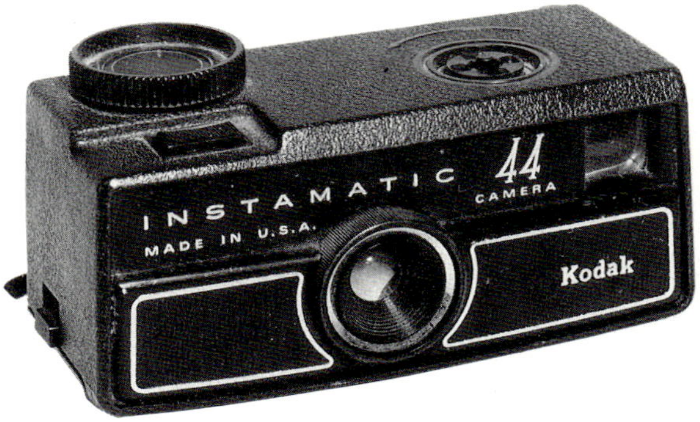

RPS

Description/Remarks

Moulded black plastic body; optical direct vision finder; flashcube socket.

Kodak Instamatic 50

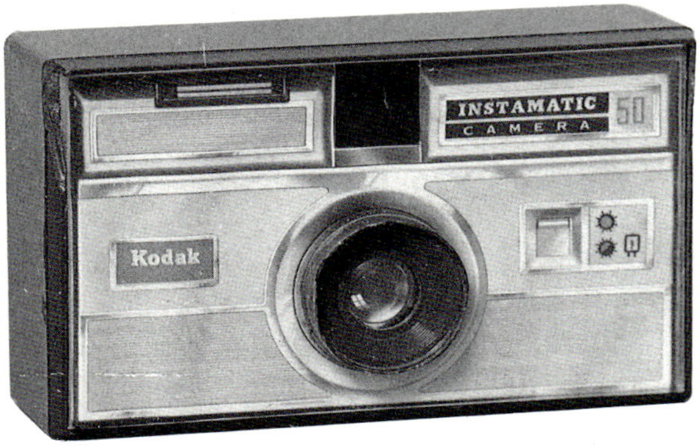

KM

Introduced February 1963
Discontinued January 1966
Manufactured UK
Lens Plastic meniscus f/11, 43mm
Shutter 2-speed 1/40 and 1/90 sec.

Description/Remarks

Special hot shoe for Kodak Instamatic Flasholder; lever wind.

Kodak Instamatic 55-X

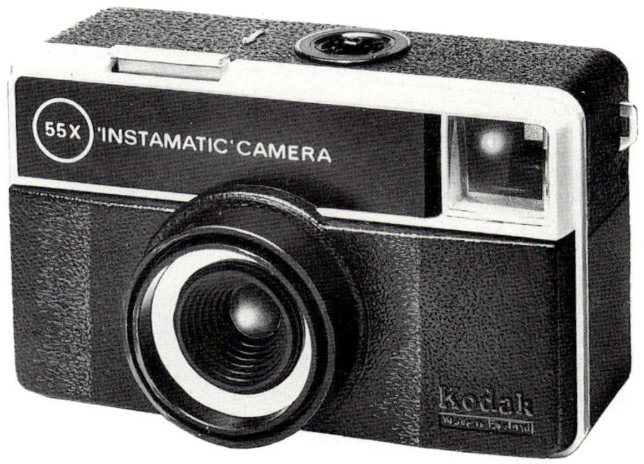

KP

Introduced September 1971
Discontinued 1972
Manufactured UK and Germany
Lens Fixed focus f/11, 43mm
Shutter Single speed 1/60 sec.

Description/Remarks

Magicube socket; lever film wind.

Kodak Instamatic 56-X

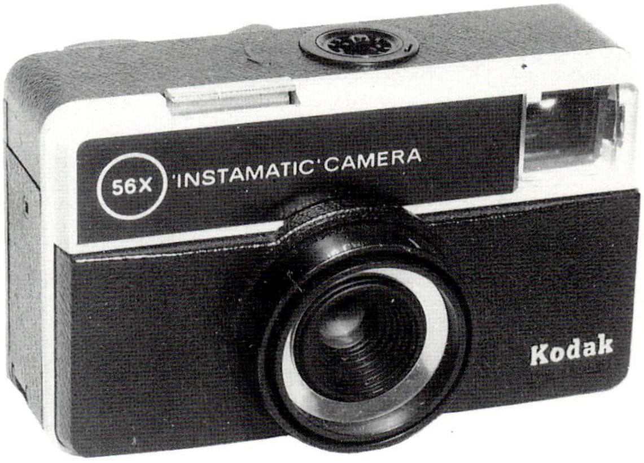

RPS

Introduced September 1972
Discontinued 1977
Manufactured UK
Lens Fixed focus f/11, 43mm
Shutter Single speed 1/50 sec.

Description/Remarks

Magicube socket, with used bulb signal in finder.

Kodak Instamatic 66-X

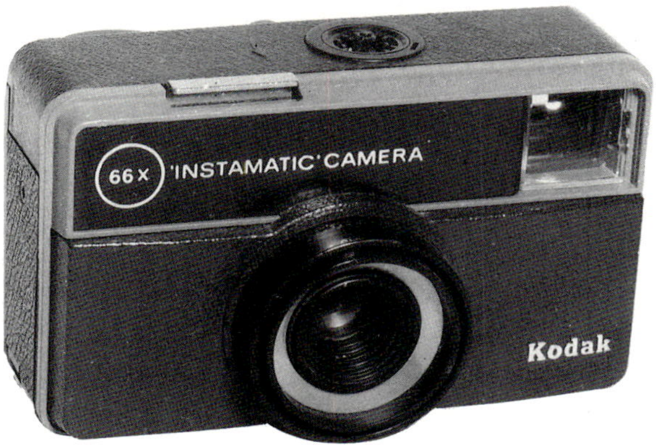

RPS

Introduced December 1973
Discontinued 1977
Manufactured UK
Lens Fixed focus f/11
Shutter Single speed 1/60 sec.

Description/Remarks

Premium sales only.

Kodak Instamatic 76-X

Introduced 1977
Discontinued –
Manufactured UK
Lens Fixed focus f/11, 43mm
Shutter Single speed 1/50 sec.

Description/Remarks

Version of Kodak Instamatic 77-X camera for premium sales only.

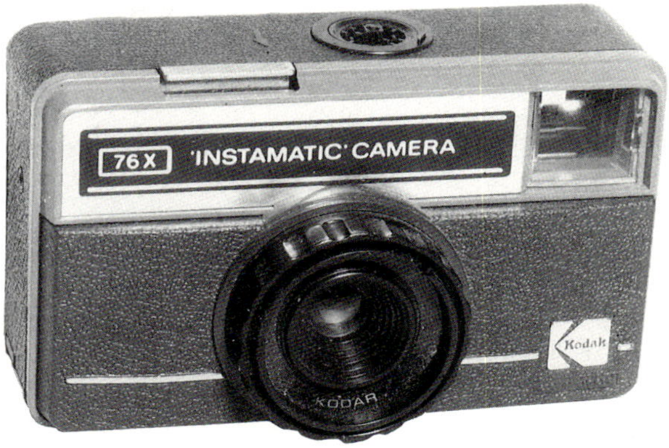

RPS

Kodak Instamatic 77-X

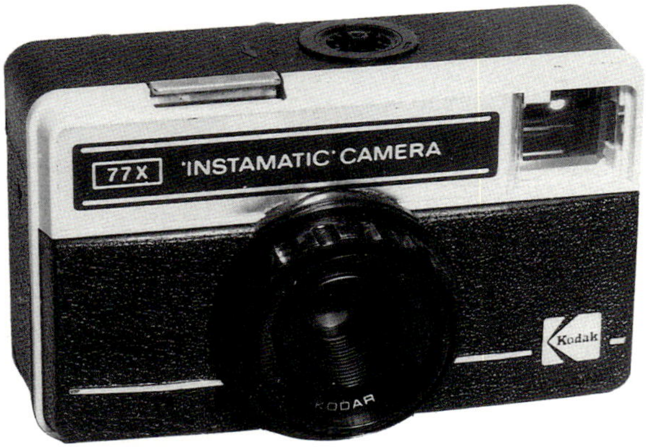

RPS

Introduced January 1977
Discontinued 1984
Manufactured UK and Germany
Lens Fixed focus f/11, 43mm
Shutter Single speed 1/50 sec.

Description/Remarks

Magicube socket, with used-bulb signal in finder; lever film wind.

Kodak Instamatic 100

Introduced March 1963

Discontinued June 1966
Manufactured US, UK
Lens Fixed focus f/11
Shutter 2-speed 1/40 and 1/90 sec.

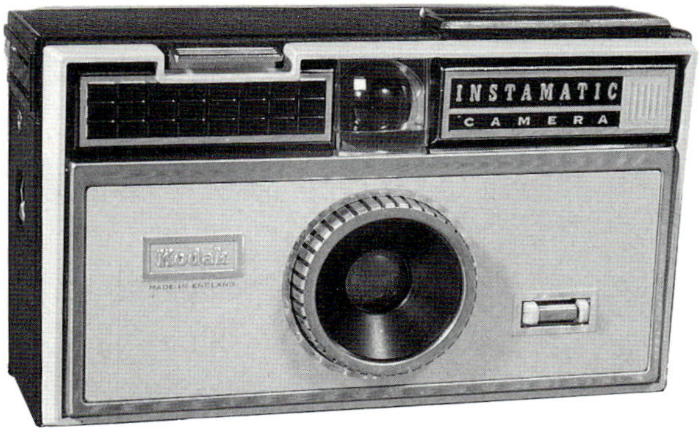

KP

Description/Remarks

Pop-up flash gun for AG1 bulbs; lever wind.

Kodak Instamatic 104

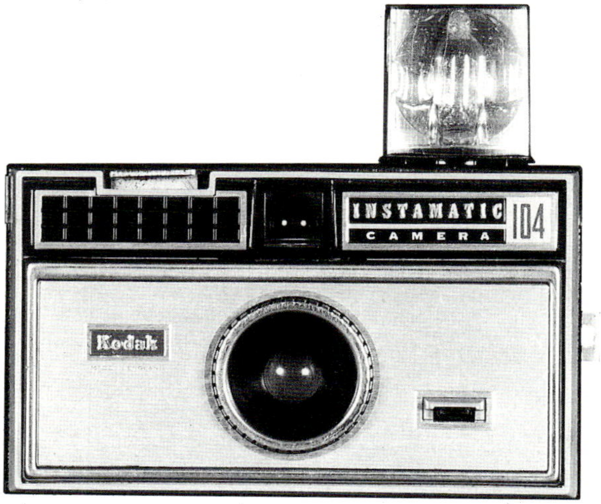

KM

Introduced July 1965
Discontinued September 1968
Manufactured US, UK
Lens Fixed focus f/11, 43mm
Shutter 2-speed 1/40 and 1/90 sec.

Description/Remarks

Flashcube socket; lever wind; optical direct vision finder.

Kodak Instamatic 124

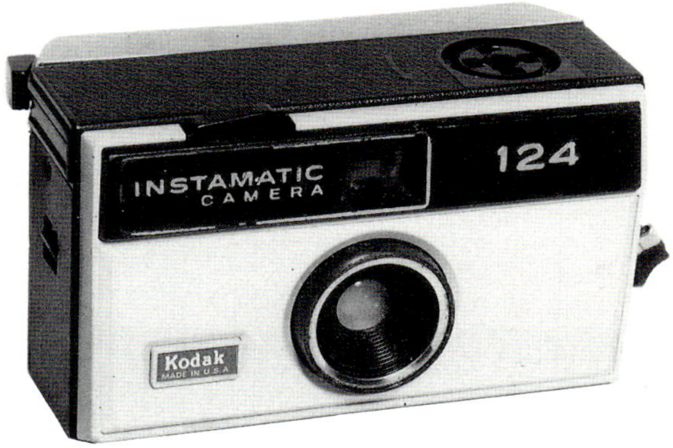

RPS

Introduced July 1968
Discontinued April 1971
Manufactured US
Lens Fixed focus f/11, 43mm
Shutter 2-speed 1/40 and 1/90 sec.

Description/Remarks

Flashcube socket; lever wind; optical direct vision finder.

Kodak Instamatic 133

Introduced September 1968
Discontinued 1970
Manufactured UK, Germany (Type 064) and Spain
Lens Fixed focus f/11, 43mm
Shutter 2-speed 1/40 and 1/80 sec.

Description/Remarks

Similar to Kodak Instamatic 33 camera but with flashcube socket and lever wind.

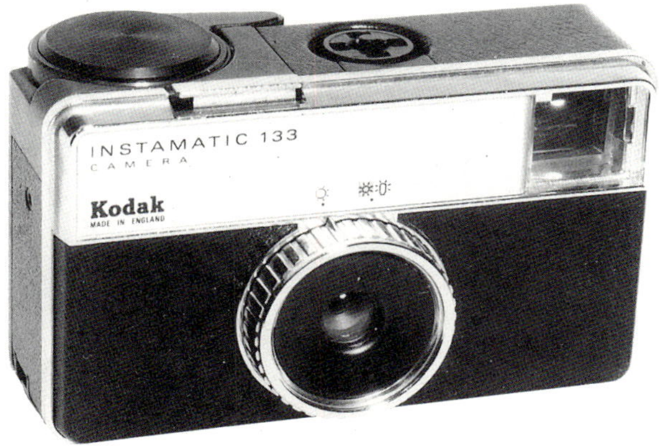

RPS

Kodak Instamatic 133-X

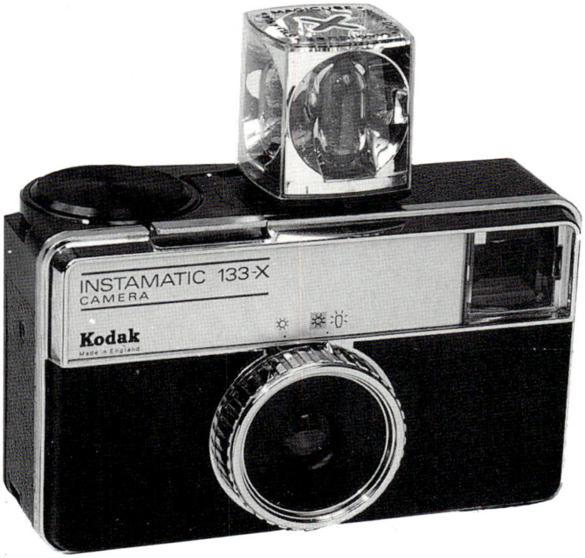

KP

Introduced September 1970
Discontinued 1971
Manufactured UK, Germany and Spain
Lens Fixed focus f/11, 43mm
Shutter 2-speed 1/40 and 1/80 sec.
Type

Description/Remarks

Similar to Kodak Instamatic 133 camera, but with Magicube socket; used-bulb warning in finder; weather symbols on shutter settings; lever wind.

Kodak Instamatic 134

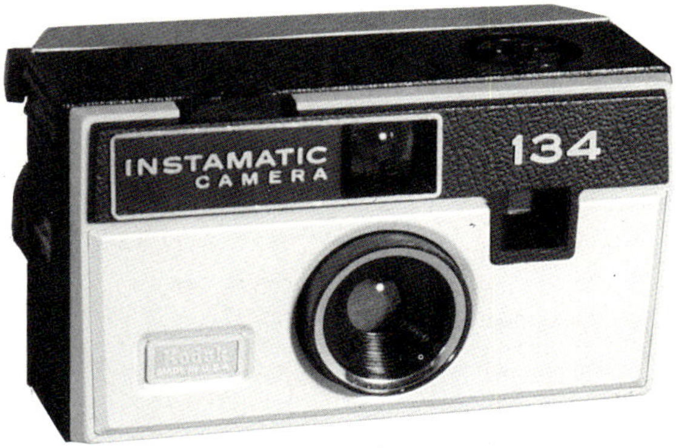

PDM

Introduced July 1968
Discontinued July 1971
Manufactured US
Lens Fixed focus f/11, 43mm
Shutter Single speed 1/50 sec.

Description/Remarks

Automatic exposure; flashcube socket; lever wind; direct vision optical finder.

Kodak Instamatic 150

Introduced August 1964
Discontinued July 1966
Manufactured US
Lens Fixed focus f/11, 43mm
Shutter 2-speed 1/40 and 1/90 sec.

Description/Remarks

Similar to Kodak Instamatic 100 camera, but with clockwork motor film advance.

Kodak Instamatic 154

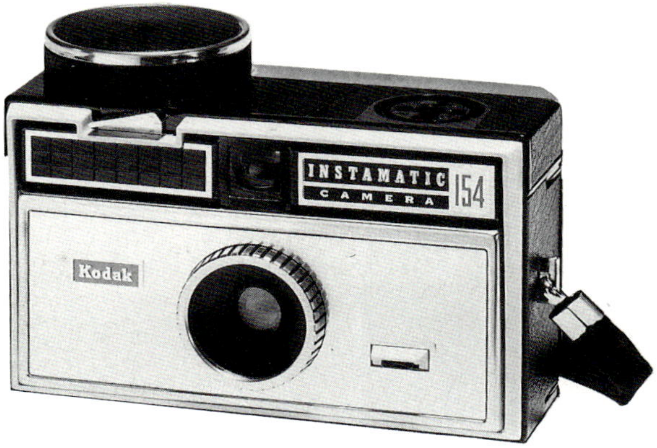

KP

Introduced July 1965
Discontinued January 1969
Manufactured US
Lens Fixed focus f/11, 43mm
Shutter 2-speed 1/40 and 1/90 sec.

Description/Remarks

Similar to Kodak Instamatic 150 but with flashcube socket. Clockwork motor film advance.

Kodak Instamatic 155-X

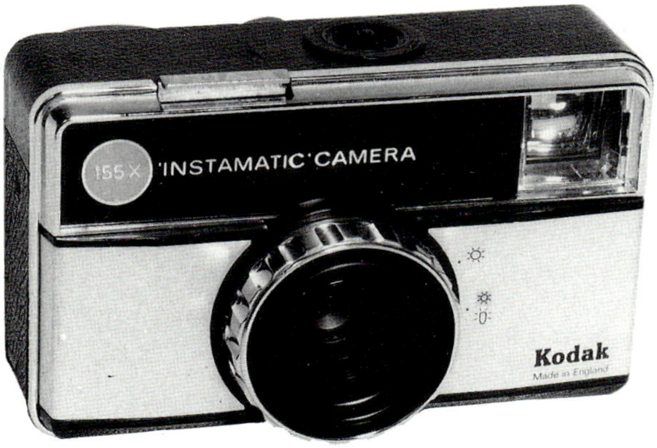

RPS

Introduced September 1971
Discontinued 1977
Manufactured UK and Germany
Lens Fixed focus f/11, 43mm
Shutter 2-speed 1/40 and 1/80 sec.

Description/Remarks

Magicube socket; brightline finder with used bulb signal; weather symbols on shutter setting.

Kodak Instamatic 174

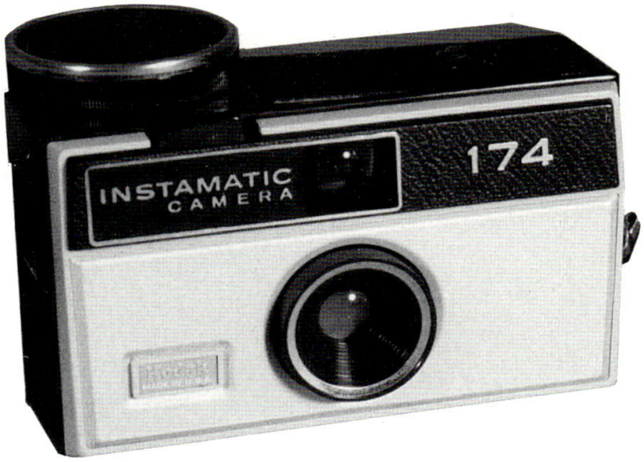

PDM

Introduced July 1968
Discontinued April 1971
Manufactured US
Lens Fixed focus f/11, 43mm
Shutter 2-speed 1/40 and 1/90 sec.

Description/Remarks

Clockwork motor film advance; flashcube socket; optical direct vision finder.

Kodak Instamatic 177-X

Introduced January 1977
Discontinued 1984
Manufactured UK and Germany

Lens Kodar f/11, 43mm fixed focus
Shutter 2-speed 1/40 and 1/80 sec.

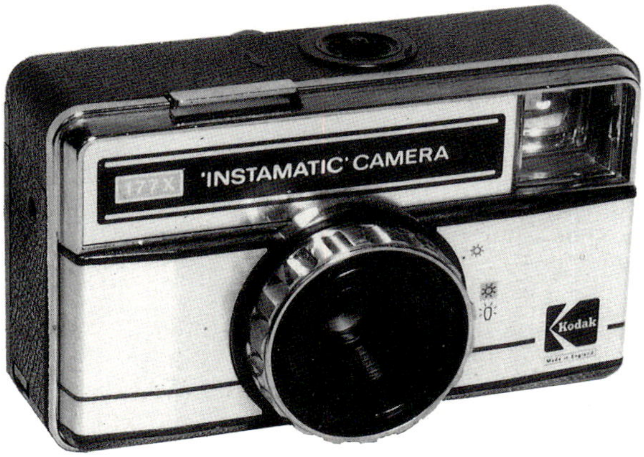

RPS

Description/Remarks

Magicube socket with used bulb signal in brightline finder; weather symbols on shutter setting; metallic finish on body.

Kodak Instamatic 200

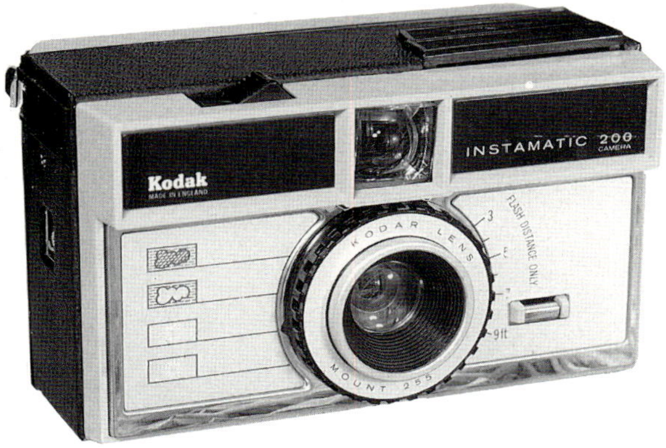

KP

Introduced January 1965
Discontinued 1966
Manufactured UK
Lens Kodar f/7.1, 41mm plastic
Shutter 2-speed 1/40 and 1/60 sec.

Description/Remarks

Dial the weather exposure guide on camera front; pop-up flash gun for AG1 bulbs; lever wind.

Kodak Instamatic 204

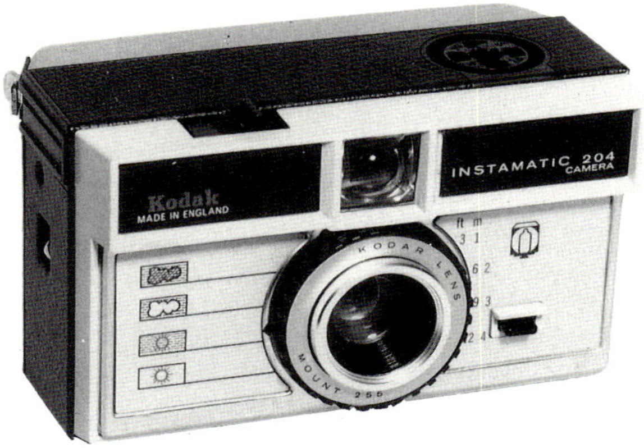

RPS

Introduced January 1966
Discontinued November 1968
Manufactured UK
Lens Kodar 3-element f/6.6, 41mm
Shutter 2-speed 1/40 and 1/60 sec.

Description/Remarks

Similar to Kodak Instamatic 200 camera, but with flashcube socket.

Kodak Instamatic 220 (Type 053)

Introduced 1965
Discontinued 1966
Manufactured Germany
Lens Reomar f/5.6, 38mm
Shutter 2-speed

Description/Remarks

Exposure setting by weather symbol scale; direct vision

optical finder; built-in flash gun for AG1 bulbs, with fold-up reflector.

Kodak Instamatic 224 (Type 059)

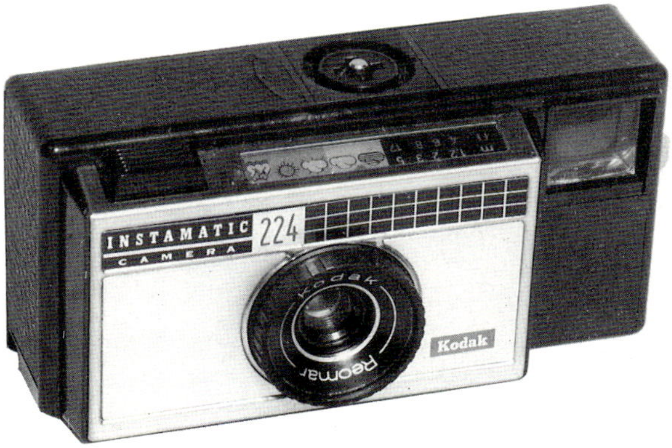

RPS

Introduced 1966
Discontinued 1968
Manufactured Germany
Lens Reomar f/5.6, 38mm
Shutter 2-speed

Description/Remarks

Very similar to Kodak Instamatic 220 camera, but with flash-cube socket.

Kodak Instamatic 233

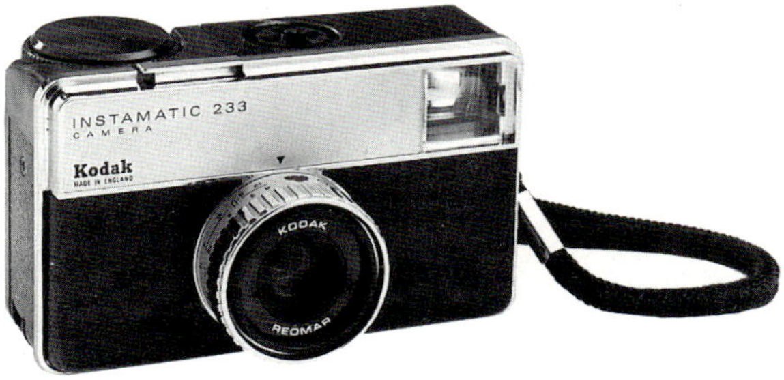

KP

Introduced September 1968
Discontinued 1970
Manufactured UK and Germany (Type 065)
Lens Reomar f/6.6, 41mm
Shutter 2-speed 1/40 and 1/80 sec.

Description/Remarks

Similar to Kodak Instamatic 133 camera, but with bright-line finder; weather symbol settings on lens barrel; knob film wind.

Kodak Instamatic 233-X

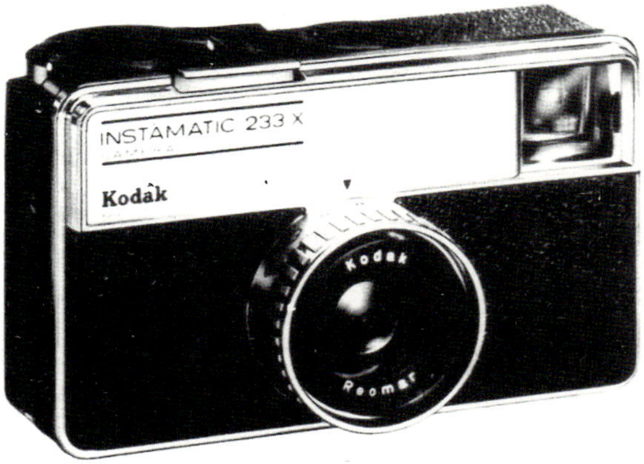

KP

Introduced September 1970
Discontinued 1971
Manufactured UK and Germany
Lens Reomar f/6.6, 41mm
Shutter 2-speed 1/40 and 1/80 sec.

Description/Remarks

Similar to Kodak Instamatic 233 camera but with Magicube socket, with used bulb warning in finder. Weather symbols on shutter setting.

Kodak Instamatic 250 (Type 052)

Introduced 1964
Discontinued 1965 (sold until 1967 in US)

Manufactured Germany
Lens Reomar f/2.8, 38mm
Shutter Compur 1/30 – 1/250 sec.

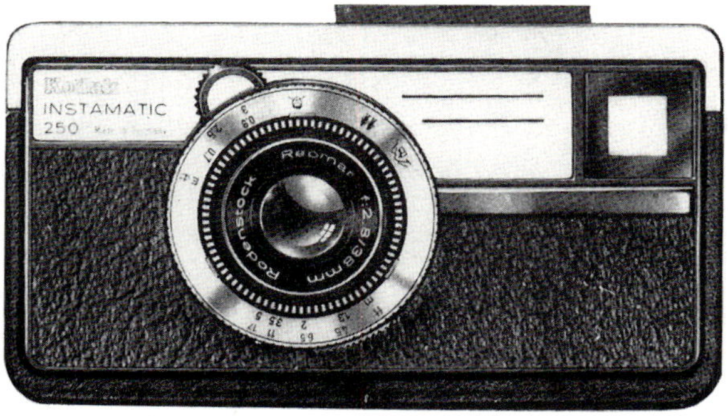

KP

Description/Remarks

Brightline finder; built-in flashgun for AG1 bulbs, hinged reflector.

Kodak Instamatic 255-X

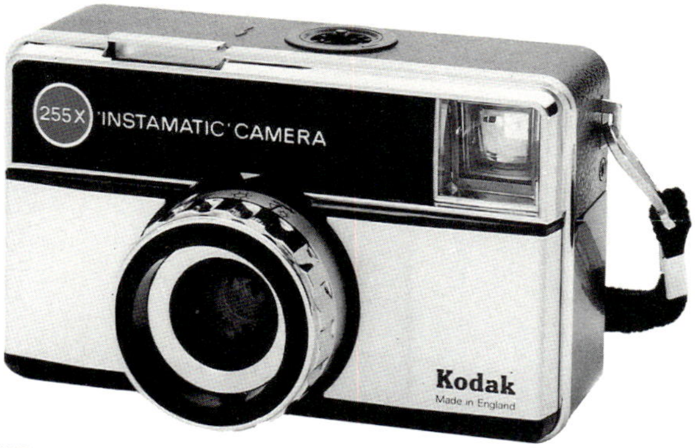

KP

Introduced September 1971
Discontinued 1977
Manufactured UK and Germany
Lens Reomar f/11, 41mm fixed focus
Shutter 2-speed 1/40 and 1/80 sec.

Description/Remarks

Magicube socket with used-bulb warning in brightline finder; lever film wind; weather symbols on lens barrel.

Kodak Instamatic 277-X

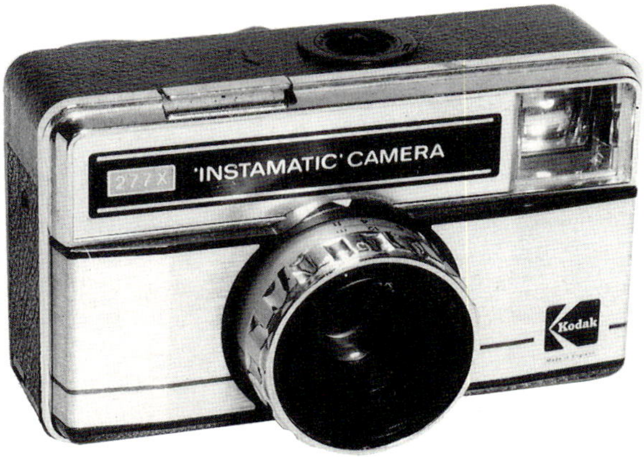

RPS

Introduced January 1977
Discontinued 1985
Manufactured UK and Germany
Lens Reomar f/6.6, 41mm
Shutter 2-speed 1/40 and 1/80 sec.

Description/Remarks

Magicube socket, with used-bulb signal in brightline finder; variable aperture with weather symbols.

Kodak Instamatic 300

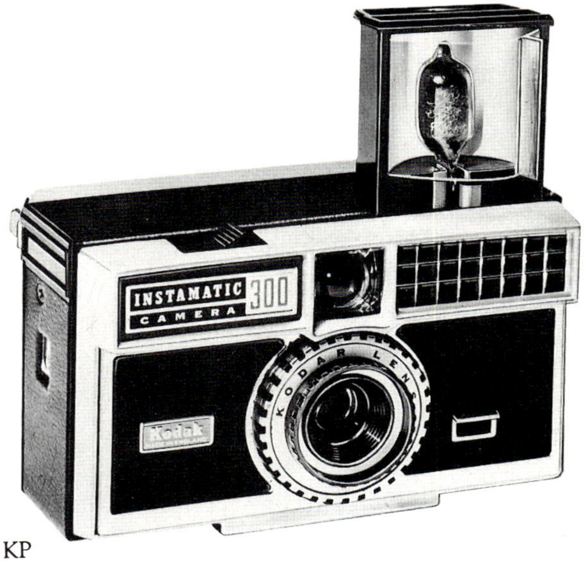

KP

Introduced March 1963
Discontinued June 1966
Manufactured US
Lens Kodar f/8, 41mm
Shutter 2-speed 1/40 and 1/90 sec.

Description/Remarks

Lever wind; automatic exposure, lowlight indicator in optical direct vision finder; pop-up flash gun for AG1 bulbs.

Kodak Instamatic 304

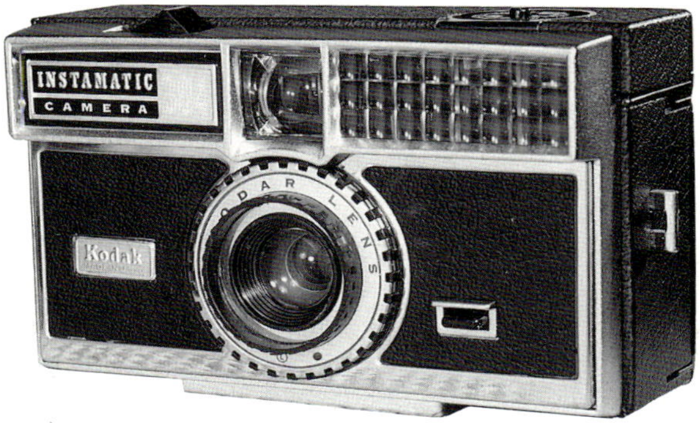

KP

Introduced July 1965
Discontinued April 1969
Manufactured US, UK
Lens Kodar f/8, 41mm
Shutter 2-speed 1/40 and 1/90 sec.

Description/Remarks

Similar to Kodak Instamatic 300, but with flashcube socket. Automatic exposure, lowlight indicator in optical direct vision finder; lever wind.

Kodak Instamatic 314

Introduced July 1968
Discontinued April 1971
Manufactured US
Lens Kodar f/8, 41mm
Shutter 2-speed 1/40 and 1/90 sec.

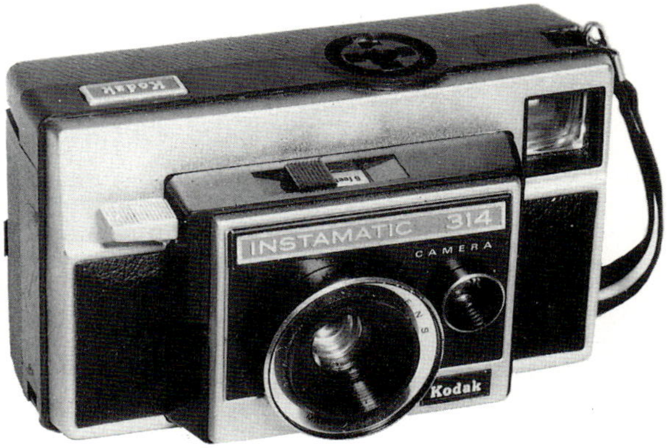

RPS

Description/Remarks

Automatic exposure setting by CdS cell; flashcube socket; lever wind; optical direct vision finder.

Kodak Instamatic 324 (Type 054)

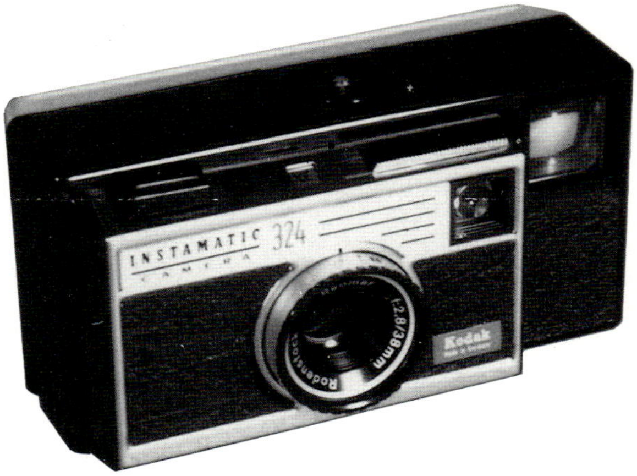

PDM

Introduced 1966
Discontinued 1967 (sold until June 1968 in US)
Manufactured Germany
Lens Reomar f/2.8, 38mm
Shutter Kodak 2-speed, 1/30 and 1/125 sec.

Description/Remarks

Automatic exposure control by CdS cell; brightline finder; flashcube socket.

Kodak Instamatic 333 (Type 066)

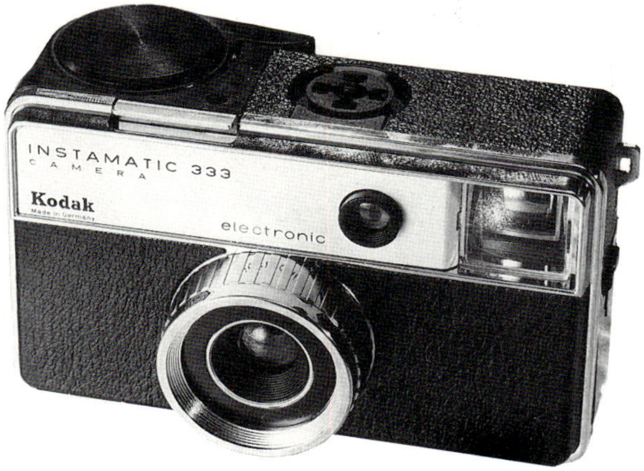

KP

Introduced September 1968
Discontinued 1974
Manufactured Germany
Lens Fixed focus f/11, 43mm
Shutter Electronic; 10 to 1/300 sec.

Description/Remarks

Automatic exposure setting by CdS cell; lowlight warning in finder; lever film wind.

Kodak Instamatic 333-X

Introduced September 1970
Discontinued 1971
Manufactured Germany
Lens Fixed focus f/11, 43mm
Shutter Electronic; 10 to 1/300 sec.

Description/Remarks

Similar to Kodak Instamatic 333 camera but with Magicube socket, with used bulb warning in finder; lever film wind.

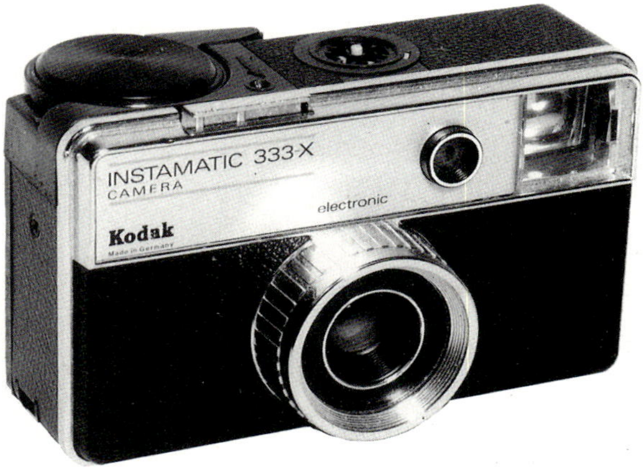

RPS

Kodak Instamatic 355-X

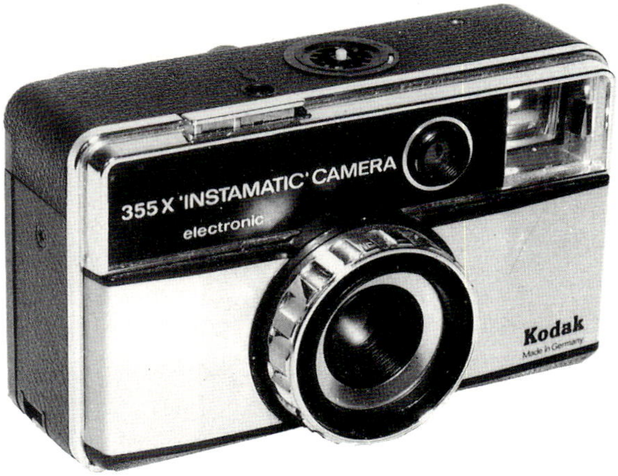

RPS

Introduced September 1971
Discontinued 1977
Manufactured Germany
Lens Fixed focus f/11, 43mm
Shutter Electronic; 30 to 1/300 sec.

Description/Remarks

Magicube socket, with used-bulb and low-light warning signals in brightline finder; lever film wind.

Kodak Instamatic 400

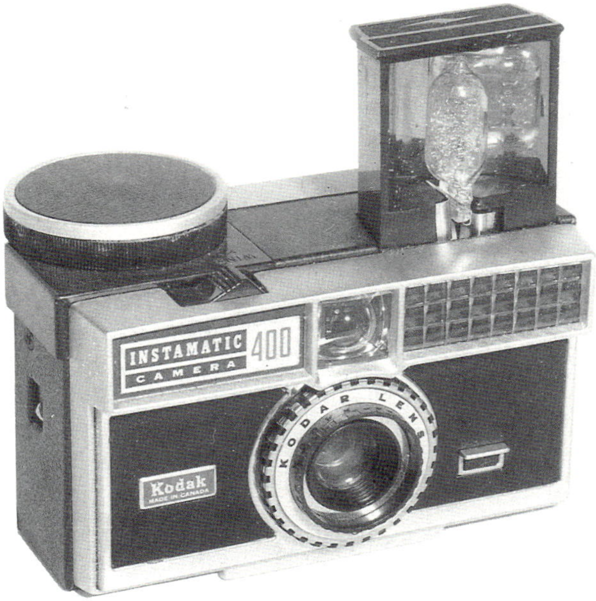

Introduced March 1963
Discontinued June 1966
Manufactured US
Lens Kodar f/8, 41mm
Shutter 2-speed 1/40 and 1/60 sec.

Description/Remarks

Automatic exposure setting by photocell, low-light indicator in optical direct vision finder; clockwork motor film advance.

Kodak Instamatic 404

Introduced July 1965
Discontinued April 1969
Manufactured US
Lens Kodar f/8, 41mm
Shutter 2-speed 1/40 and 1/60 sec.

Description/Remarks

Similar to Kodak Instamatic 304 camera, but with clockwork motor film advance. Automatic exposure by photocell; flashcube socket.

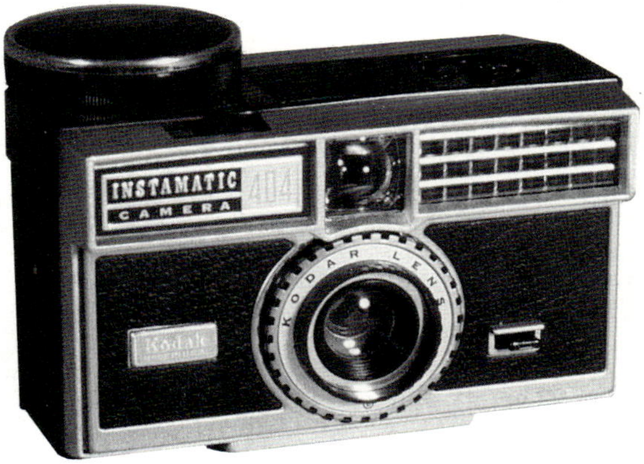

PDM

Kodak Instamatic 414

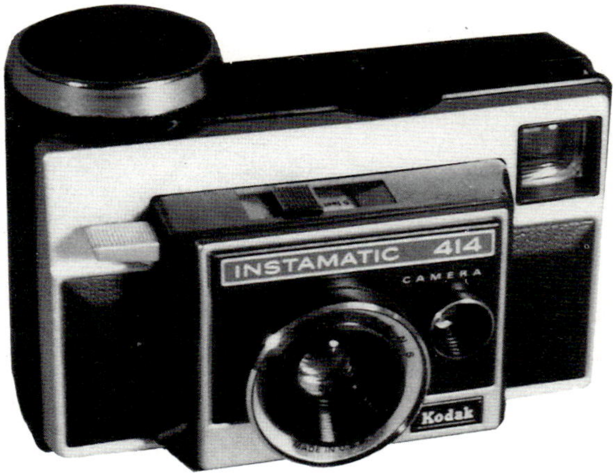

PDM

Introduced July 1968
Discontinued April 1971
Manufactured US
Lens Kodar f/8, 41mm
Shutter 2-speed 1/45 and 1/90 sec.

Description/Remarks

Similar to Kodak Instamatic 314, but with clockwork motor film advance. Automatic exposure setting by CdS photocell; optical direct vision finder.

Kodak Instamatic 500 (Type 048)

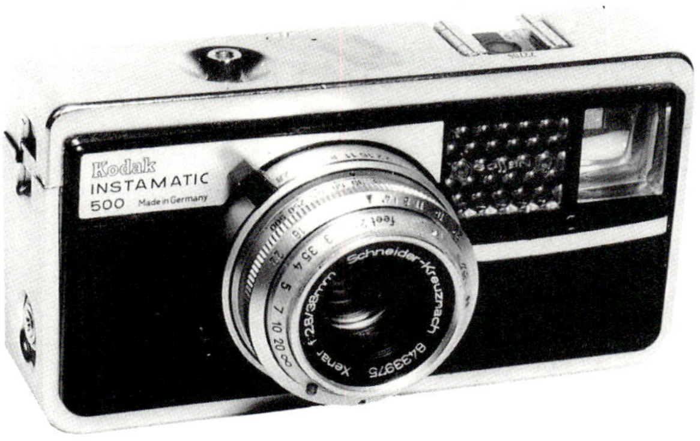

RPS

Introduced 1963
Discontinued 1965 (sold until August 1966 in US, 1968 in UK)
Manufactured Germany
Lens Schneider Xenar f/2.8, 38mm
Shutter Compur 1/30 to 1/500 sec.

Description/Remarks

Automatic exposure setting by photocell; brightline finder; retractable lens mount; lever wind; hot shoe and coaxial flash socket.

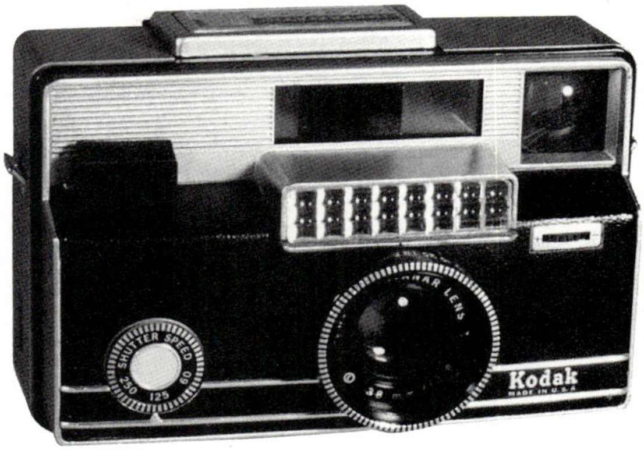

PDM

Kodak Instamatic 700

Introduced March 1963
Discontinued June 1966
Manufactured US
Lens Ektanar f/2.8, 38mm
Shutter 4-speed 1/30 to 1/250 sec.

Description/Remarks

Automatic exposure by photocell; built-in flash gun for AG1 bulbs, hinged reflector.

Kodak Instamatic 704

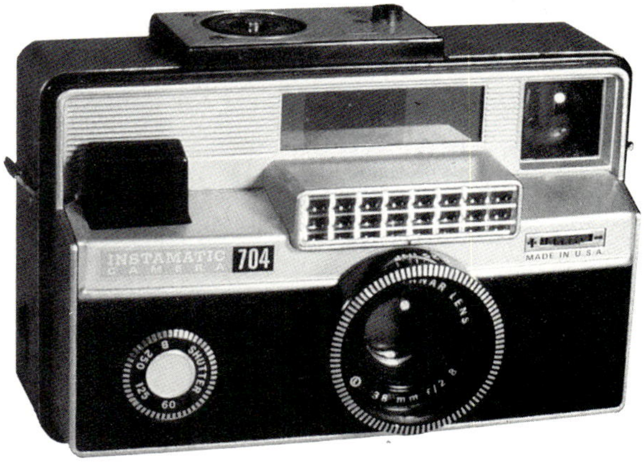

PDM

Introduced July 1965
Discontinued April 1969
Manufactured US
Lens Ektanar f/2.8, 38mm
Shutter 4-speed 1/30 – 1/250 sec.

Description/Remarks

Similar to Kodak Instamatic 700 camera, but with flashcube socket. Automatic exposure control by photocell.

Kodak Instamatic 714

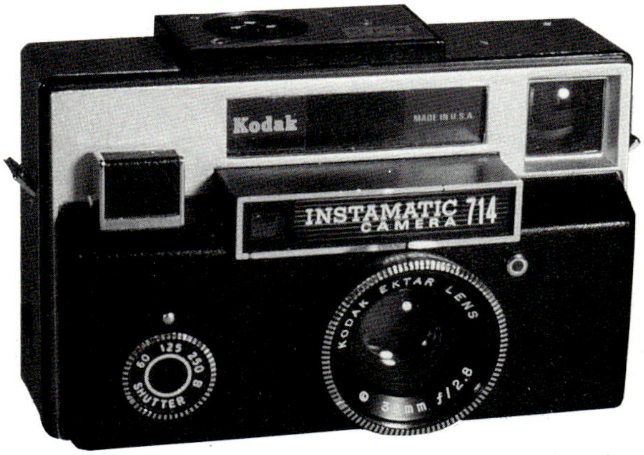

PDM

Introduced March 1968
Discontinued September 1970
Manufactured US
Lens Kodak Ektar f/2.8, 38mm
Shutter 4-speed

Description/Remarks

Similar to Kodak Instamatic 704 camera, but with automatic exposure control by CdS cell.

Kodak Instamatic 800

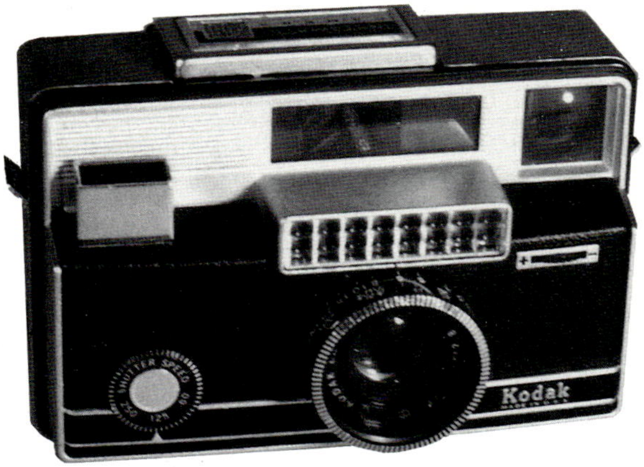

PDM

Introduced March 1964
Discontinued July 1966
Manufactured US
Lens Ektanar f/2.8
Shutter 4-speed 1/30 – 1/250 sec.

Description/Remarks

Similar to Kodak Instamatic 700 camera, but with coupled rangefinder and clockwork motor film advance, set by pulling tape in camera bottom.

Kodak Instamatic 804

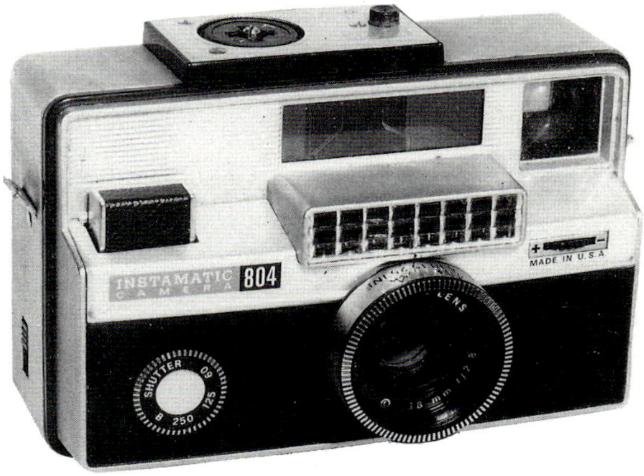

Introduced July 1965
Discontinued March 1970
Manufactured US
Lens Ektanar f/2.8, 38mm
Shutter 4-speed 1/30 – 1/250 sec.

Description/Remarks

Similar to Kodak Instamatic 800 camera, but with socket for flashcubes.

Kodak Instamatic 814

Introduced March 1968
Discontinued August 1970
Manufactured US

Lens Kodak Ektar f/2.8, 38mm
Shutter 4-speed 1/30 – 1/250 sec.

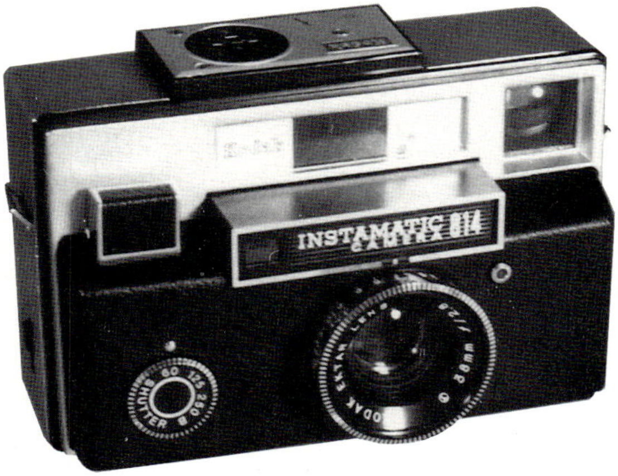

PDM

Description/Remarks

Similar to Kodak Instamatic 804 camera, but with automatic exposure set by CdS cell.

Kodak Instamatic Reflex (Type 062)

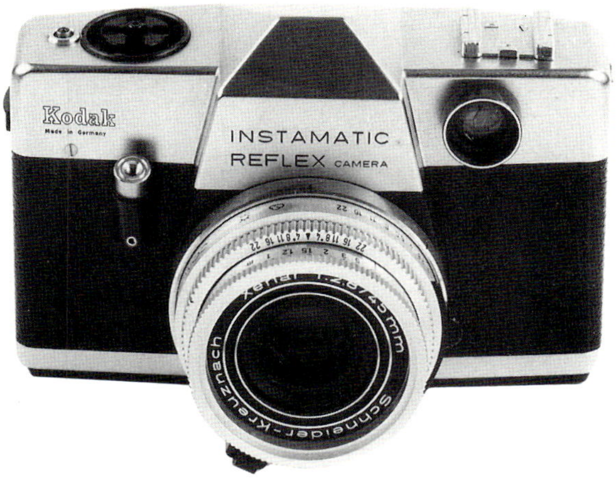

1968–1969 model. KAG

Introduced 1968
Discontinued 1970 (sold in US and UK until 1974)
Manufactured Germany
Lens Schneider Xenar f/2.8, 45mm or Xenon f/1.9, 50mm, interchangeable.
Shutter Compur-Electronic 20 to 1/500 sec.

Description/Remarks

Automatic exposure control by CdS meter; reflex focusing with split-image rangefinder; flashcube socket; coaxial flash socket; lever wind. The other lenses available were:

Curtagon f/4, 28mm wide-angle
Curtagon f/2.8, 35mm wide-angle
Tele-Arton f/4, 85mm telephoto
Tele-Arton f/4, 90mm telephoto
Tele-Xenar f/4, 135mm telephoto
Tele-Xenar f/4.8, 200mm telephoto

These lenses were introduced for the Kodak Retina Reflex cameras; the Kodak Instamatic Reflex camera was also supplied without lenses for the benefit of owners of these cameras. From March 1969 the chrome body top was changed for black.

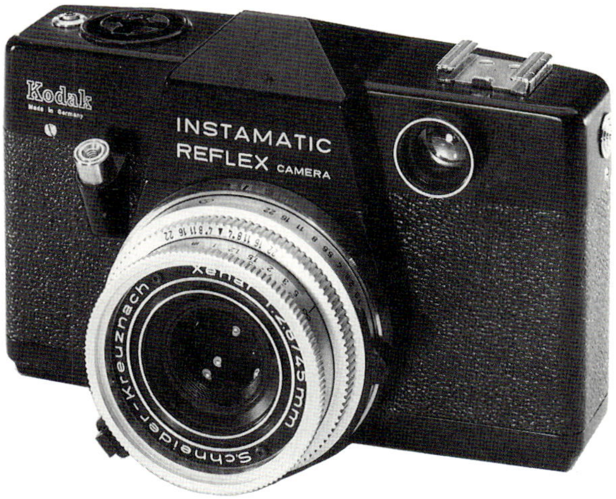

1969–1970 model. KAG

Kodak Instamatic S-10

Introduced March 1967
Discontinued March 1970
Manufactured US

Lens Kodar f/9.5, 35mm
Shutter 2-speed 1/40 and 1/125 sec.

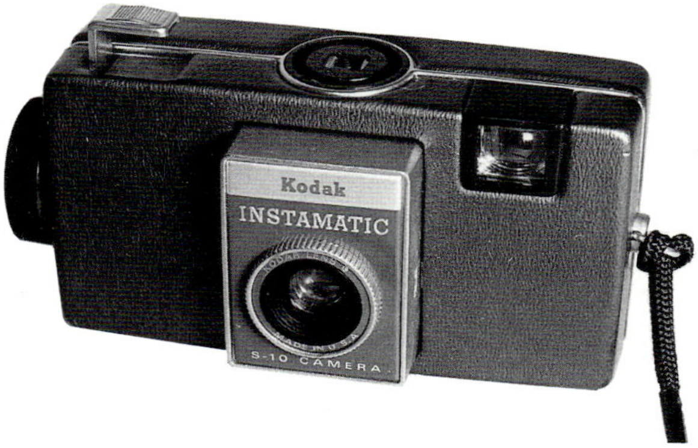

KM

Description/Remarks

Lens on retractable sprung rectangular tube; film wind knob on side; flashcube socket.

Kodak Instamatic S-20

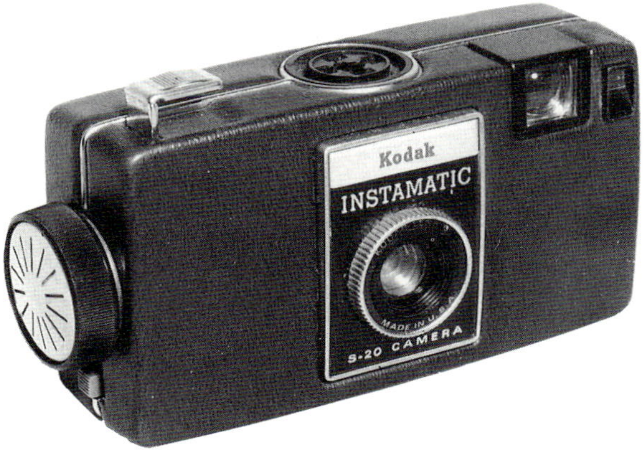

RPS

Introduced March 1967
Discontinued April 1971
Manufactured US
Lens Kodar f/9.5, 35mm
Shutter 2-speed 1/40 and 1/90 sec.

Description/Remarks

Similar to Kodak Instamatic S-10 camera, but with automatic exposure control by CdS cell.

Kodak Instamatic X-15

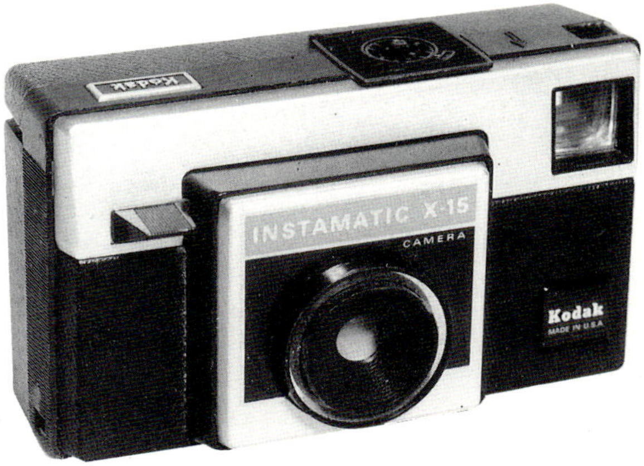

RPS

Introduced July 1970
Discontinued March 1976
Manufactured US
Lens Fixed focus f/11, 43mm
Shutter 2-speed 1/45 and 1/90 sec.

Description/Remarks

Magicube socket. From 1972 cameras carry the new Kodak logo.

Kodak Instamatic X-15F

Introduced March 1976
Discontinued ? 1981
Manufactured US
Lens Fixed focus f/11, 43mm
Shutter 2-speed 1/45 and 1/90 sec.

Description/Remarks

Brown plastic moulded case; flipflash socket.

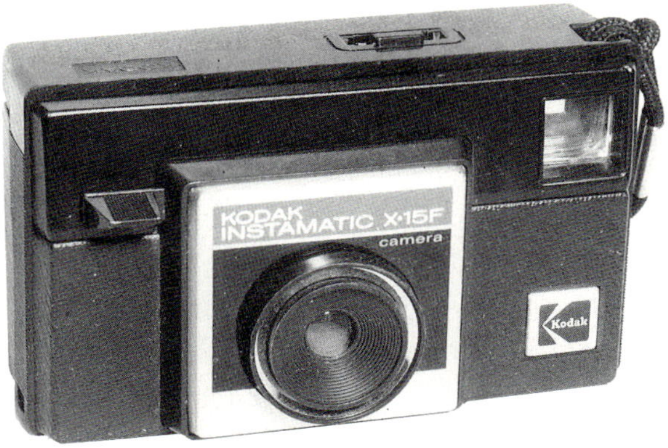

RPS

Kodak Instamatic X-25

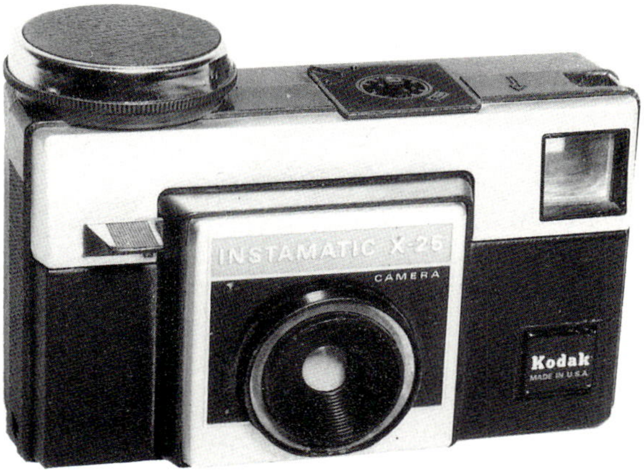

RPS

Introduced July 1970
Discontinued January 1974
Manufactured US
Lens Fixed focus f/11, 43mm
Shutter 2-speed 1/45 and 1/90 sec.

Description/Remarks

Like Kodak Instamatic X-15 camera, but with clockwork motor film advance; magicube socket.

Kodak Instamatic X-30

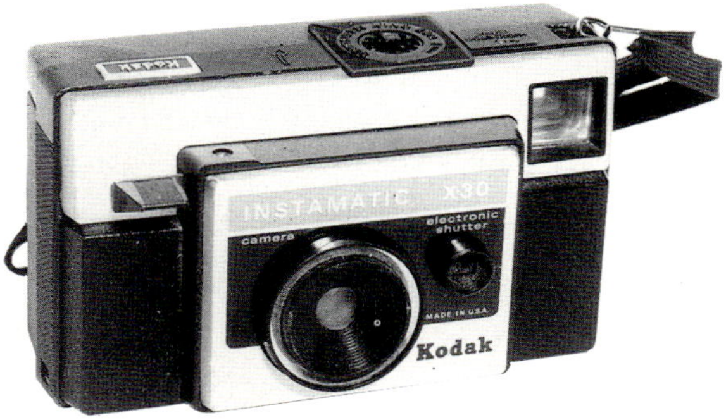

Introduced August 1971
Discontinued January 1974
Manufactured US
Lens Fixed focus f/11, 43mm
Shutter Electronic; 10 to 1/125 sec.

Description/Remarks

Automatic exposure control by CdS cell; magicube socket.

Kodak Instamatic X-35

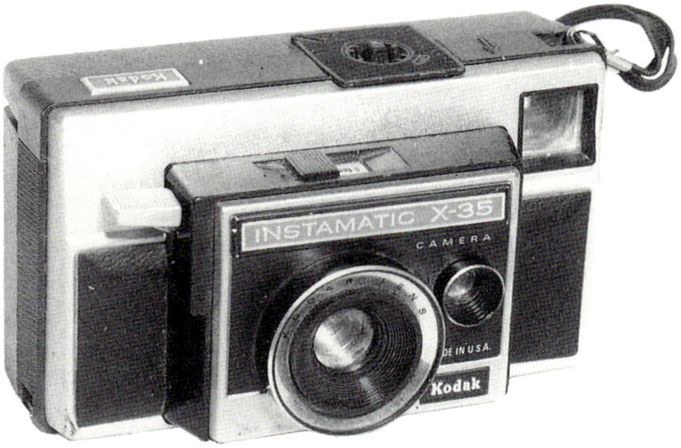

RPS

Introduced July 1970
Discontinued March 1976
Manufactured US

Lens 3-element f/8, 41mm
Shutter 2-speed 1/45 and 1/90 sec.

Description/Remarks

Similar to Kodak Instamatic 314 camera, but with magicube socket. Automatice xposure by CdS cell.

Kodak Instamatic X-35F

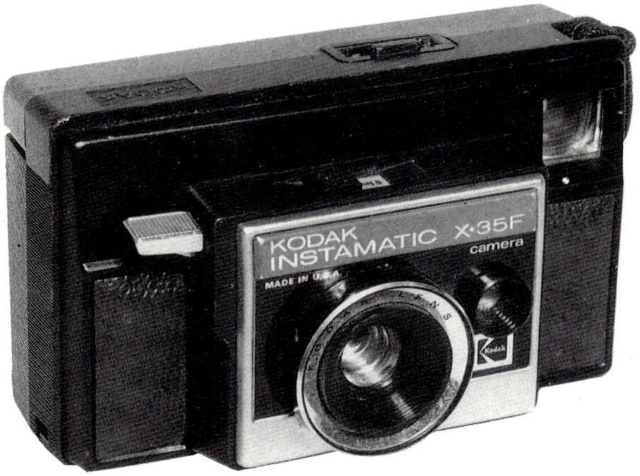

RPS

Introduced July 1970
Discontinued January 1974
Manufactured US
Lens 3-element f/8, 41mm
Shutter 2-speed 1/45 and 1/90 sec.

Description/Remarks

Similar to Kodak Instamatic X-15F, but with focusing adjustment and CdS cell automatic exposure control.

Kodak Instamatic X-45

Introduced July 1970
Discontinued January 1974
Manufactured US
Lens 3-element f/8, 41mm
Shutter 2-speed 1/45 and 1/90 sec.

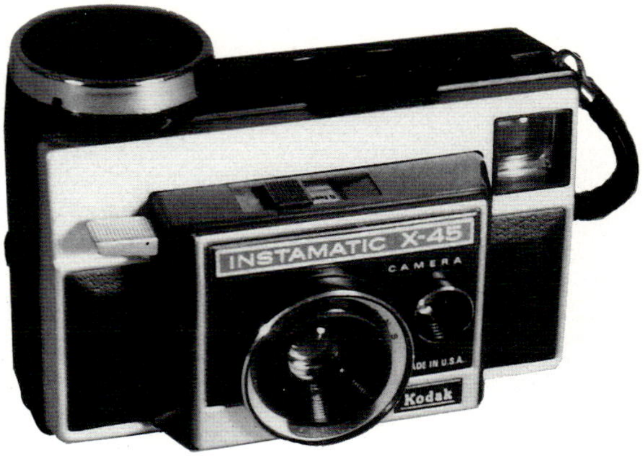

PDM

Description/Remarks

Automatic exposure control by CdS cell; focusing adjustment; clockwork motor film advance; magicube socket.

Kodak Instamatic X-90

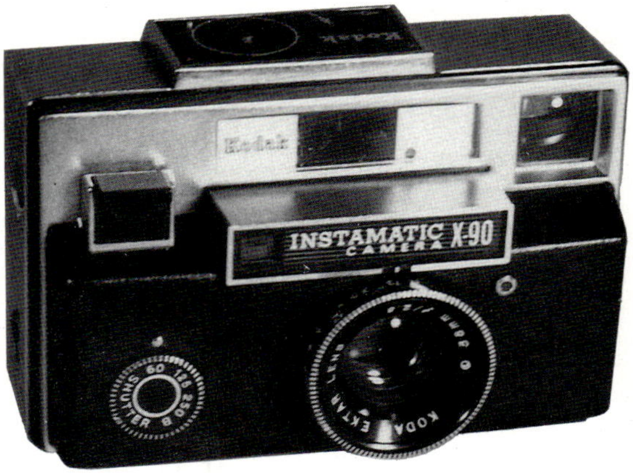

PDM

Introduced July 1970
Discontinued August 1973
Manufactured US
Lens Ektar f/2.8, 38mm
Shutter Automatic; 1/30 to 1/250 sec.

Description/Remarks

Coupled rangefinder; clockwork motor film advance; magicube socket.

Kodak Pocket 110 Cameras

The cartridge loading principle was extended to what had been hitherto known as the sub-miniature camera in 1972 with the introduction of the Kodak Pocket Instamatic cameras. New film manufacturing and processing technology made it possible to achieve good commercial quality from negatives made on a 16mm-wide film, with a single registration perforation. The construction of the new 110 cartridge was similar to that of the larger 126 type. The image size was 13x17mm. Further emulsion improvements made it possible to use 400 ASA as well as 100 ASA film, and from 1978 a new range of Ektra cameras incorporated a sensing device which 'read' notches on the cartridge, automatically adjusting the camera for the correct film speed. The faster shutter speeds this made possible helped to overcome the real problem of camera shake found with small cameras.

Fisher-Price

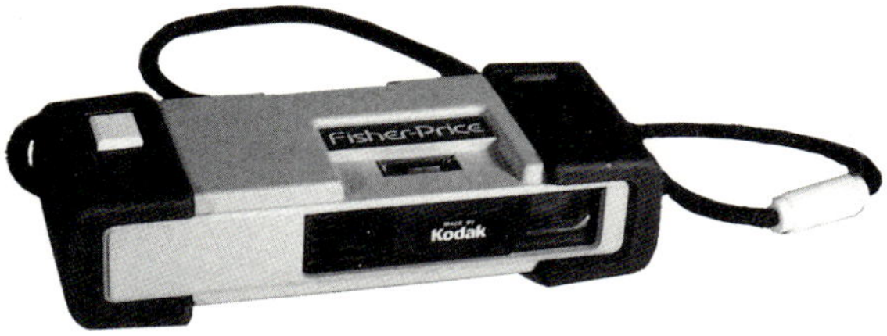

PDM

Introduced February 1984
Discontinued ?
Manufactured US
Lens Meniscus f/11, 25mm
Shutter 2-speed 1/60 and 1/150 sec.

Description/Remarks

Made by Kodak for Fisher-Price.

Kodak Brownie

Introduced 1980
Discontinued 1982
Manufactured UK
Lens Single element f/11, 25mm fixed focus
Shutter Single speed 1/50 sec.

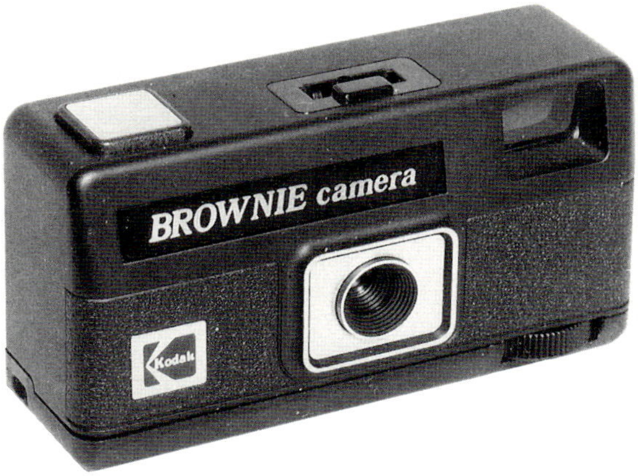

RPS

Description/Remarks

Identical to Kodak pocket A1 camera, but renamed in Kodak centenary year. The last camera to bear the Brownie name.

Kodak Ektra 1

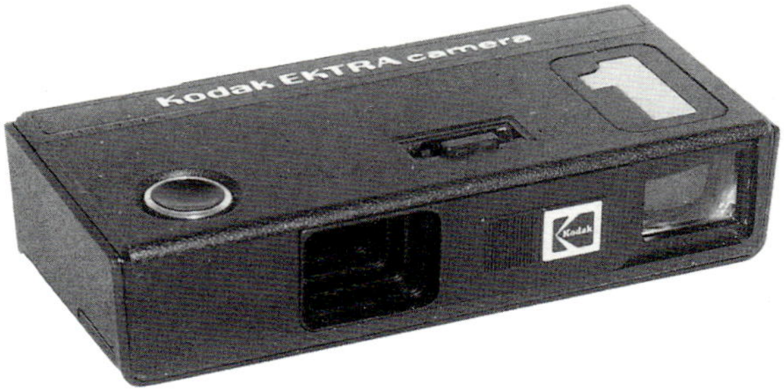

RPS

Introduced February 1978
Discontinued April 1984
Manufactured US
Lens Meniscus f/11, 25mm fixed focus
Shutter 3-speed 1/40, 1/100 and 1/170 sec.

Description/Remarks

Shutter set by film cartridge; flipflash socket.

Kodak Ektra 2

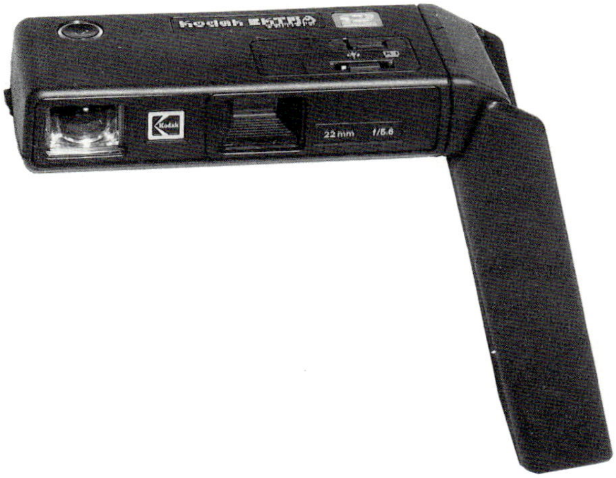

RPS

Introduced February 1978
Discontinued January 1980
Manufactured US
Lens 3-element f/5.6, 22mm fixed focus
Shutter 4-speed 1/60, 1/80, 1/250 and 1/500 sec.

Description/Remarks

Shutter speed set by film cartridge; flipflash socket.

Kodak Ektra 12

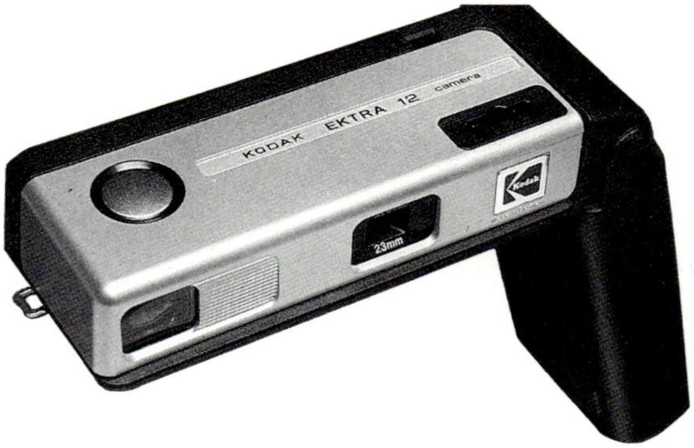

KP

Introduced January 1978
Discontinued 1981
Manufactured Germany
Lens Kodar single element f/11, 23mm fixed focus
Shutter 3-speed 1/40, 1/125 and 1/250 sec.

Description/Remarks

Folding cover/handle; shutter speed selected by film cartridge; flipflash socket.

Kodak Ektra 12-EF

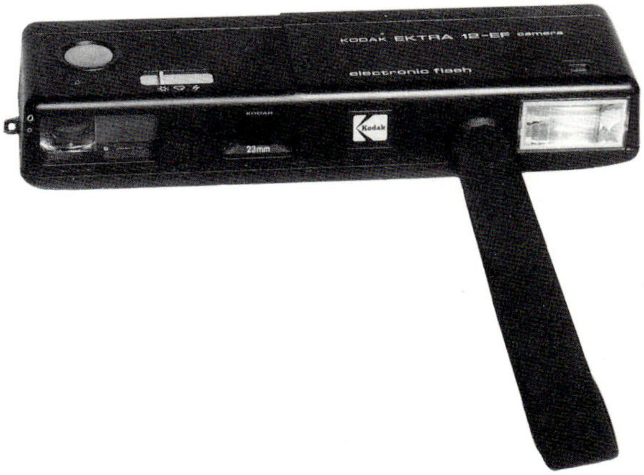

RPS

Introduced 1980
Discontinued 1981
Manufactured Germany
Lens Kodar f/11, 23mm
Shutter 3-speed 1/40 (flash only), 1/125 and 1/250 sec.

Description/Remarks

Similar to Kodak Ektra 12 camera, but with integral electronic flash.

Kodak Ektra 22

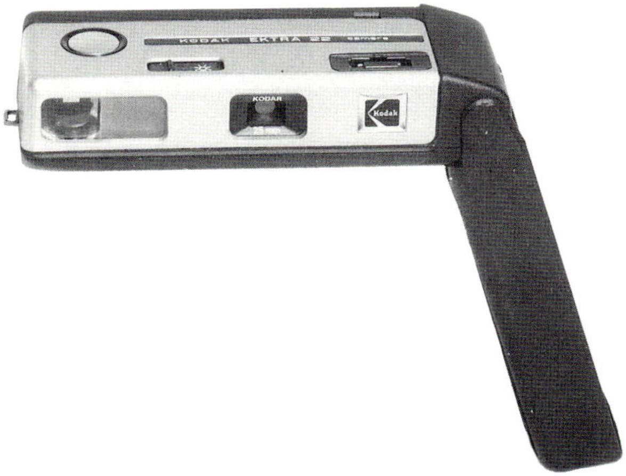

RPS

Introduced January 1978
Discontinued 1980
Manufactured Germany
Lens Kodar 2-element f/9.5, 25mm fixed focus
Shutter 3-speed 1/40, 1/125 and 1/250 sec.

Description/Remarks

Folding cover/handle; shutter speed selected by film cartridge; flipflash socket.

Kodak Ektra 22-EF

Introduced 1978
Discontinued 1980
Manufactured Germany
Lens Kodar f/9.5, 25mm fixed focus
Shutter 3-speed 1/40 (flash only), 1/125 and 1/250 sec.

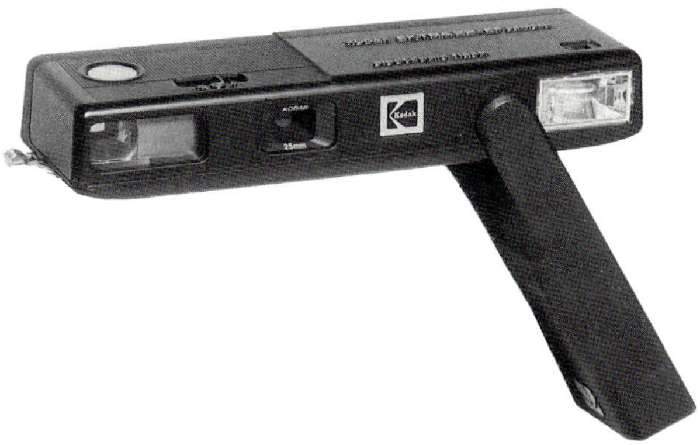

RPS

Description/Remarks

Similar to Kodak Ektra 22 camera, but with integral electronic flash.

Kodak Ektra 52

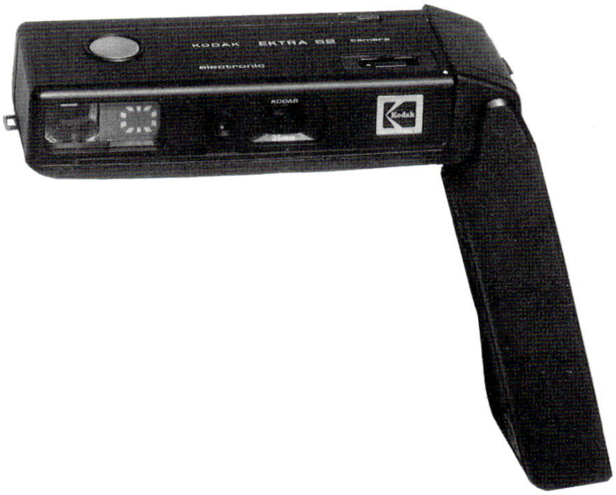

RPS

Introduced January 1978
Discontinued 1980
Manufactured Germany
Lens Kodar 2-element f/9.5, 25mm fixed focus
Shutter Electronic; 5 to 1/250 sec.

Description/Remarks

Folding cover/handle; flipflash socket; automatic exposure control.

Kodak Ektra 100

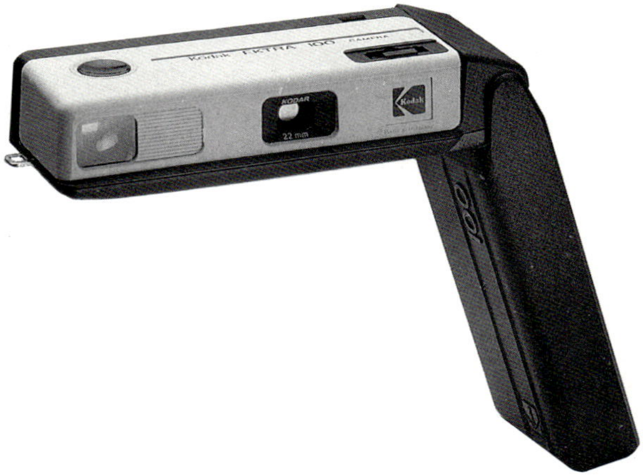

KAG

Introduced
Discontinued
Manufactured Germany
Lens Kodar 22mm
Shutter

Description/Remarks

Folding cover/handle; flipflash socket.

Kodak Ektra 200

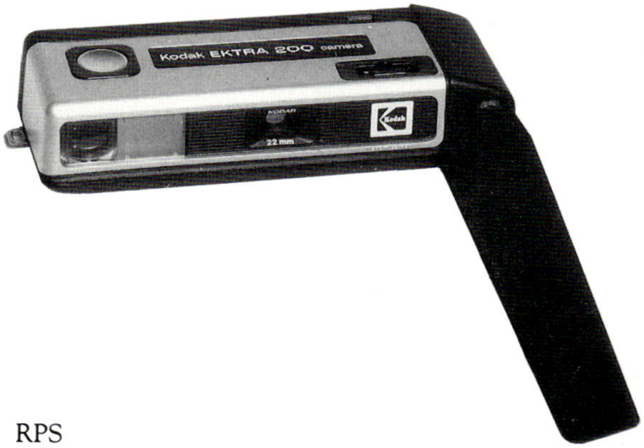

RPS

Introduced 1980
Discontinued 1987
Manufactured Germany
Lens Kodar f/11, 22mm fixed focus
Shutter 3-speed 1/40 (flash only), 1/125 and 1/250 sec.

Description/Remarks

Folding cover/handle; flipflash socket; shutter speed set by film cartridge.

Kodak Ektra 250

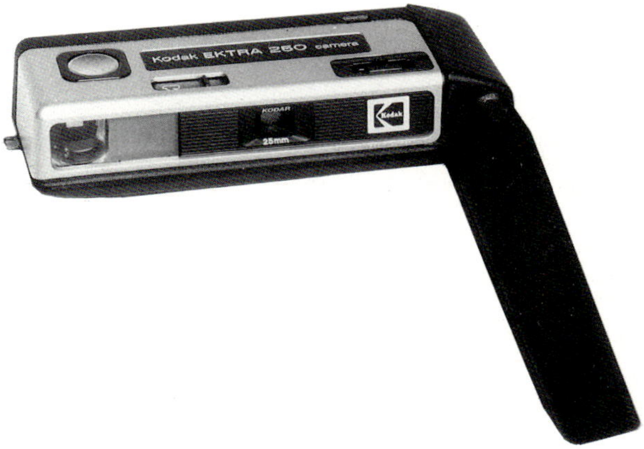

RPS

Introduced 1980
Discontinued 1983
Manufactured Germany
Lens Kodar doublet f/9.5, 25mm
Shutter 3-speed 1/50, 1/125 and 1/250 sec.

Description/Remarks

Folding cover/handle; shutter speed set by film cartridge; brightline finder with weather symbols; flipflash socket.

Kodak Ektralite 10

Introduced July 1978
Discontinued 1988
Manufactured US
Lens 3-element f/8, 25mm
Shutter 2-speed 1/125 and 1/210 sec.

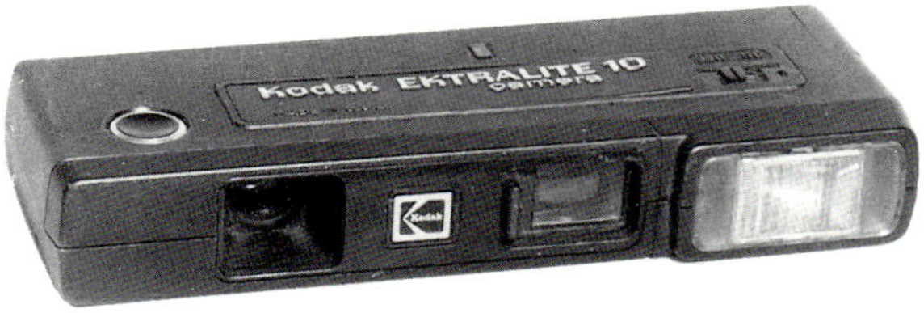

RPS

Description/Remarks

Integral electronic flash; fixed focus.

Kodak Ektralite 30

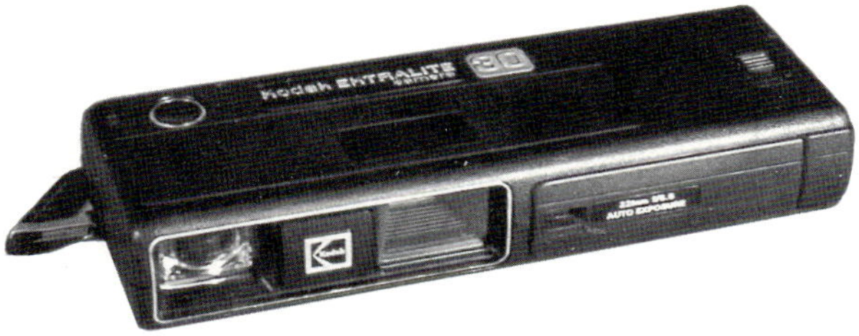

PDM

Introduced July 1979
Discontinued June 1981
Manufactured US
Lens 3-element f/5.6, 22mm
Shutter 2-speed 1/100 and 1/500 sec.

Description/Remarks

Integral swing-out electronic flash; automatic exposure control.

Kodak Ektralite 400

Introduced February 1981
Discontinued 1987
Manufactured Germany
Lens Reomar f/6.8, 24mm
Shutter 3-speed 1/60, 1/125 and 1/250 sec.

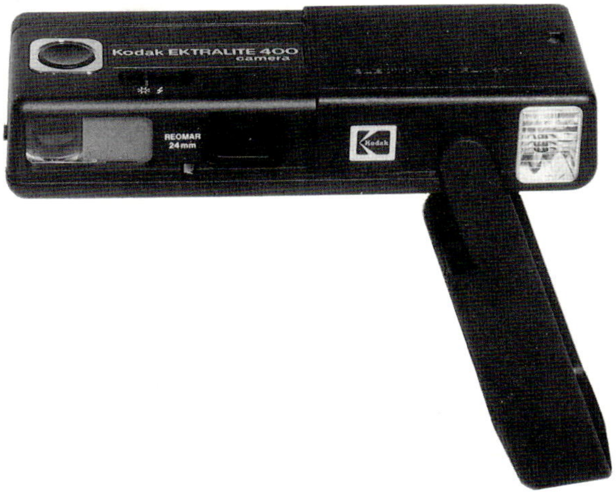

RPS

Description/Remarks

Folding cover/handle; fixed exposure for daylight or integral electronic flash; shutter speed set by film cartridge.

Kodak Ektralite 450

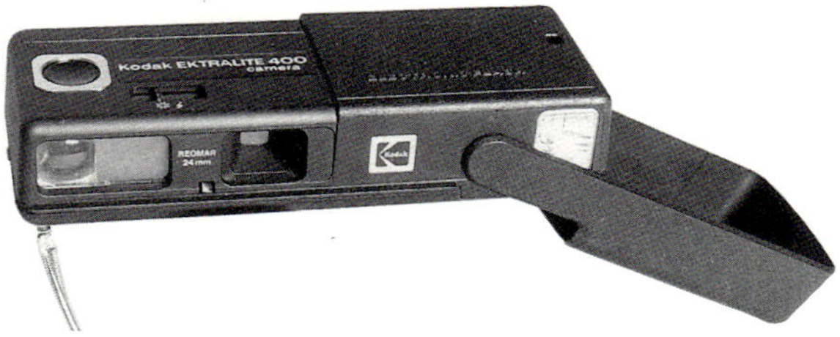

KM

Introduced 1980
Discontinued 1984
Manufactured Germany
Lens Reomar f/6.8, 24mm
Shutter 3-speed 1/60, 1/125 and 1/250 sec.

Description/Remarks

Folding cover/handle; brightline finder with weather and flash symbols; integral electronic flash; shutter speed set by film cartridge.

Variations

In 1980, a limited number of these cameras were overprinted in gold with the Kodak 100th anniversary motif and "100 Jahre Zukunst der Fotografie". About 1000 were distributed at Photokina 1980 to press and other visitors. A second edition, believed to be less than 1000, was made with white overprinting and was similarly distributed, apart from about 40 which were sold to Kodak staff.

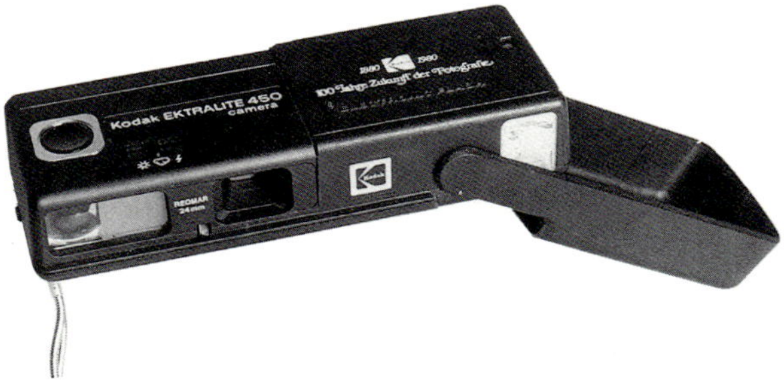

Over-printed model for Photokina 1980. KM

Kodak Ektralite 500

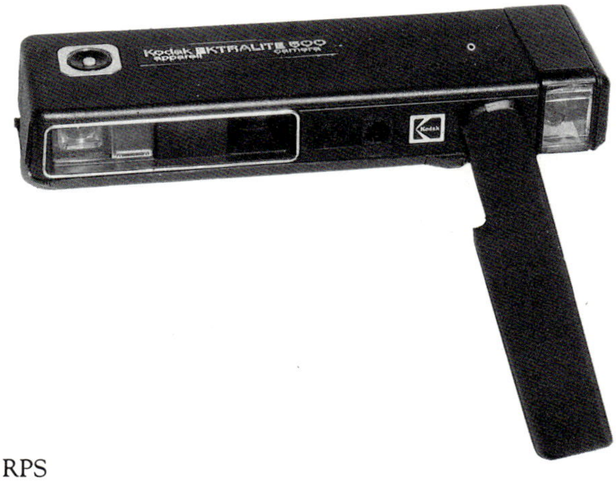

RPS

Introduced May 1980
Discontinued May 1982
Manufactured US, also French version made in Canada
Lens 3-element f/8, 22mm
Shutter 2-speed $^1/_{125}$ and $^1/_{250}$ sec.

Description/Remarks

Integral electronic flash, automatically activated in low light; shutter speed selected by film cartridge; hinged cover/handle.

Kodak Ektramax

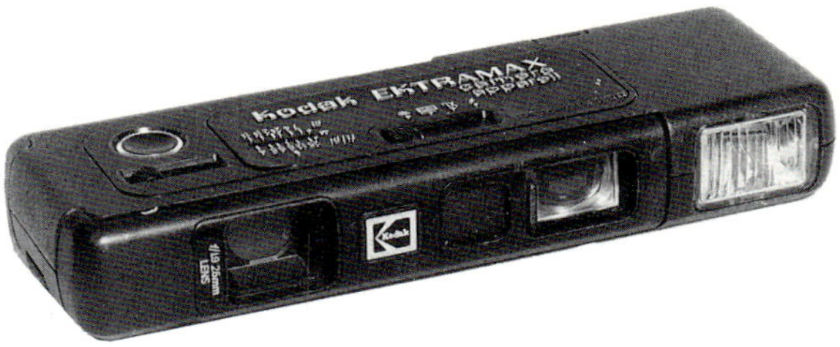

RPS

Introduced July 1978
Discontinued February 1981
Manufactured US (also French Canadian version)
Lens Aspheric 4-element f/1.9, 25mm focusing
Shutter 5-speed $^1/_{30}$ – $^1/_{350}$ sec.

Description/Remarks

Shutter speed set by film cartridge and weather symbols; combined aperture and shutter; integral electronic flash.

Kodak Fling

Introduced June 1987
Discontinued -
Manufactured US
Lens f/8
Shutter single speed $^1/_{120}$ sec

Description/Remarks

A simple one-use camera based on the 110 cartridge, reviving the concept behind Eastman's first Kodak camera. When the exposures were made, the whole camera was returned to the photo-finisher.

Kodak Gimini

Introduced Spring 1988
Discontinued -

Manufactured US
Lens meniscus
Shutter 2-speed, 1/125 or 1/250 sec.

Description/Remarks

Children's camera, in five body colours: red, blue, green, yellow and pink. Similar to Kodak Trimlite Instamatic 18 or Winner pocket cameras; flipflash socket.

Kodak Graffiti

Introduced July 1988
Manufactured US for UK market

Similar to Kodak Ektralite 10, but in red, blue, pink, green, purple or yellow, for teenage market.

Kodak Instamatic 91

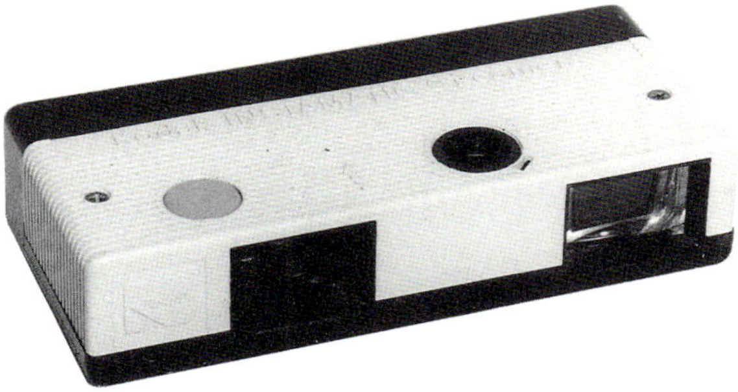

RPS

Introduced November 1974
Discontinued January 1976
Manufactured UK
Lens Kodak triplet f/11, 25mm fixed focus
Shutter Single speed 1/60 sec.

Description/Remarks

Premium sales version of Kodak Instamatic 92 camera.

Kodak Instamatic 92

Introduced September 1974
Discontinued January 1976

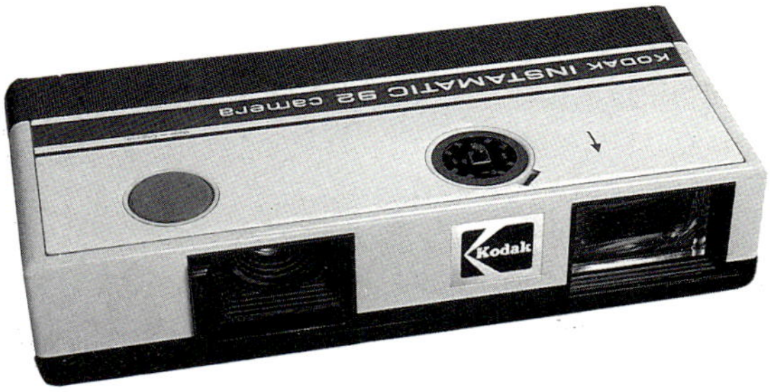

KP

Manufactured UK, Germany
Lens Kodak triplet f/11, 25mm fixed focus
Shutter Single speed 1/60 sec.

Description/Remarks

Magicube socket, used bulb warning in finder; sliding lens cover.

Kodak Instamatic 125

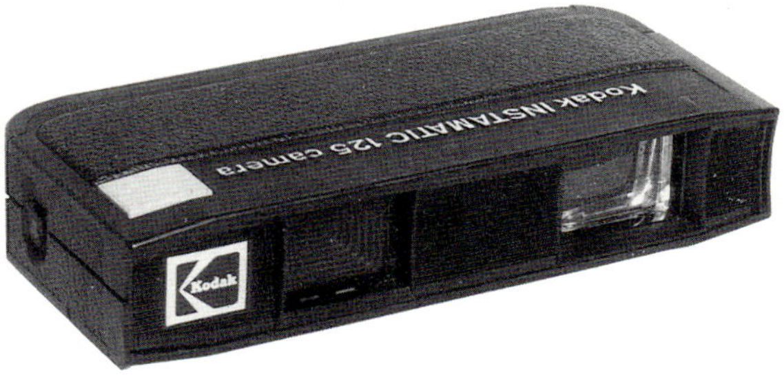

RPS

Introduced September 1976
Discontinued January 1978
Manufactured UK
Lens Meniscus f/11, 25mm
Shutter Single speed 1/60 sec.

Description/Remarks

Made for premium sales only.

Kodak Instamatic 130

Introduced January 1976

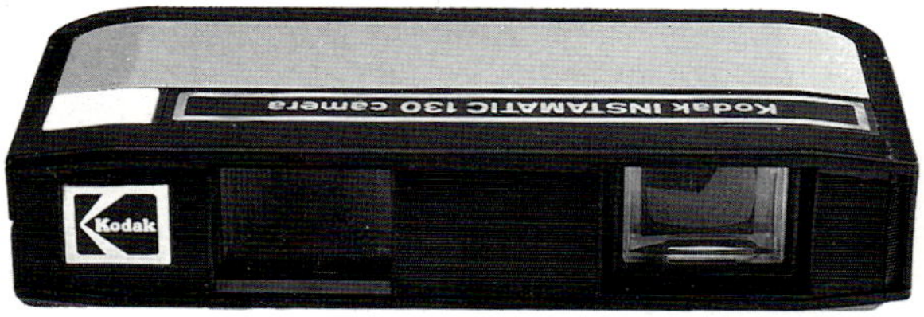

KP

Discontinued 1978
Manufactured UK, Germany
Lens Meniscus f/11, 25mm, fixed focus
Shutter Single speed 1/60 sec.

Description/Remarks

Body with tapering ends and back with curved corners; concealed magicube socket with used bulb signal in finder.

Kodak Instamatic 192

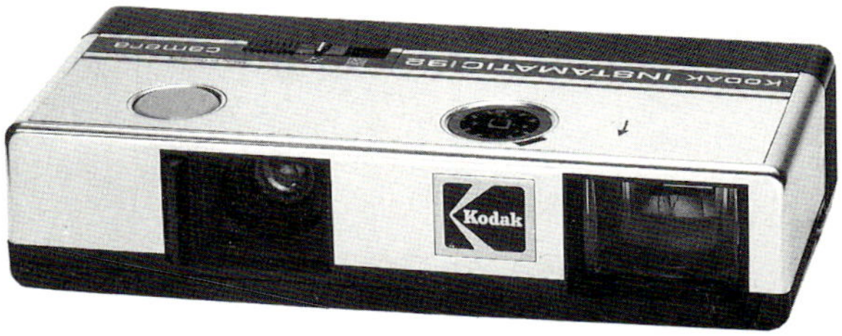

KP

Introduced January 1975
Discontinued January 1976
Manufactured UK, Germany
Lens Kodak triplet f/11, 25mm fixed focus
Shutter 2-speed 1/40 and 1/80 sec.

Description/Remarks

Shutter speed selected by weather symbol scale or insertion of magicube; used bulb signal in brightline finder.

Kodak Instamatic 230

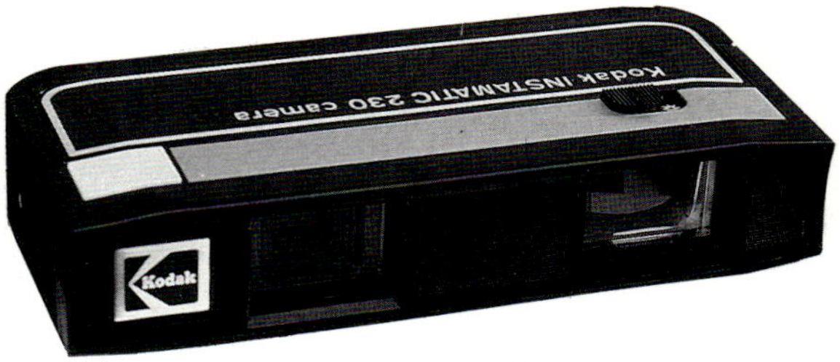

KP

Introduced January 1976
Discontinued January 1978
Manufactured UK, Germany
Lens Reomar f/11, 25mm
Shutter 2-speed 1/50 and /100 sec.

Description/Remarks

Shutter speed selected by weather symbol scale or magicube insertion, used bulb warning in brightline finder.

Kodak Mini-Instamatic S30

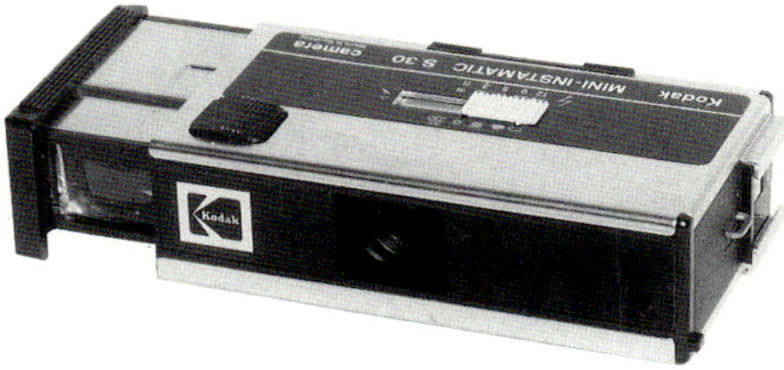

RPS

Introduced September 1976
Discontinued January 1978
Manufactured Germany
Lens Reomar f/5.6, 25mm fixed focus
Shutter 2-speed 1/40 anc 1/80 sec.

Description/Remarks

Telescoping body concealing lens and finder when closed; hot-shoe flash contact; brightline finder; exposure setting by weather symbol scale.

Kodak Mini-Instamatic S40

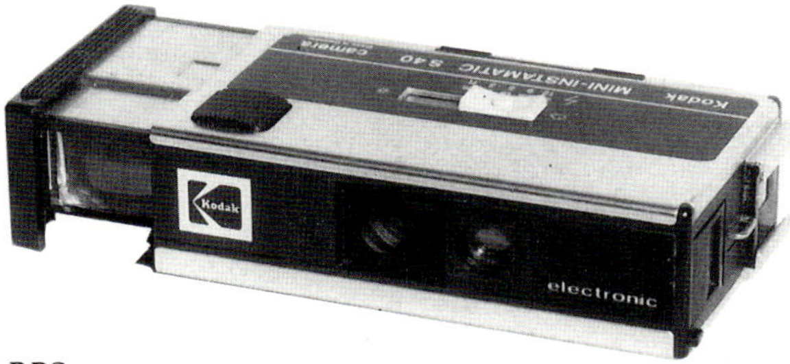

RPS

Introduced September 1976
Discontinued January 1978
Manufactured Germany
Lens Reomar f/5.6, 25mm fixed focus
Shutter 2-speed $\frac{1}{40}$ and $\frac{1}{80}$ sec.

Description/Remarks

Telescoping body concealing finder and lens when closed; exposure control by CdS cell with 'OK' light in brightline finder, aperture set by sliding control; hotshoe flash contact.

Kodak pocket A1

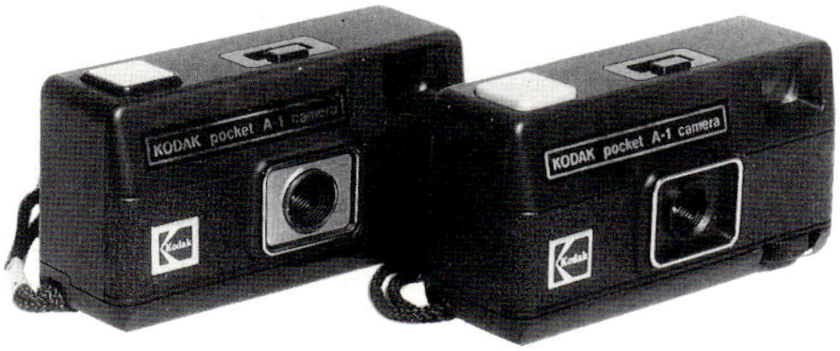

RPS

Introduced 1978
Discontinued 1980
Manufactured UK
Lens Single element f/11, 25mm fixed focus
Shutter Single $\frac{1}{50}$ sec.

Description/Remarks

Chunky design for easy holding; flipflash socket; thumbwheel film wind. Early models had yellow release buttons and matt black lens surround; later models had metalised release buttons and lens surrounds. This type was renamed Kodak Brownie camera in 1980.

Kodak pocket B1

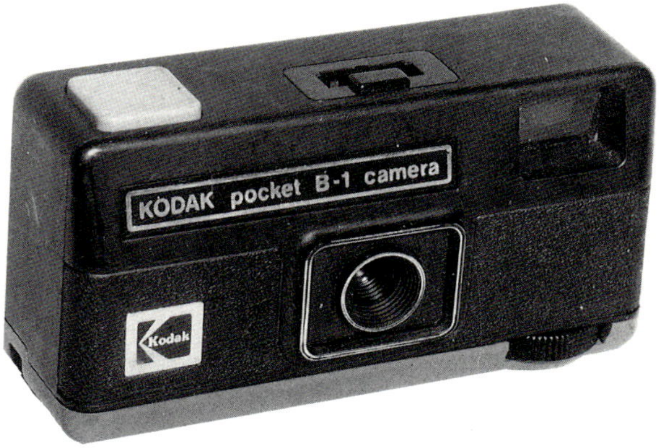

RPS

Introduced 1979
Discontinued 1980
Manufactured UK
Lens Single element f/11, 25mm
Shutter Single speed $\frac{1}{50}$ sec.

Description/Remarks

Premium sales version of Kodak pocket A1 camera.

Kodak pocket Instamatic 10

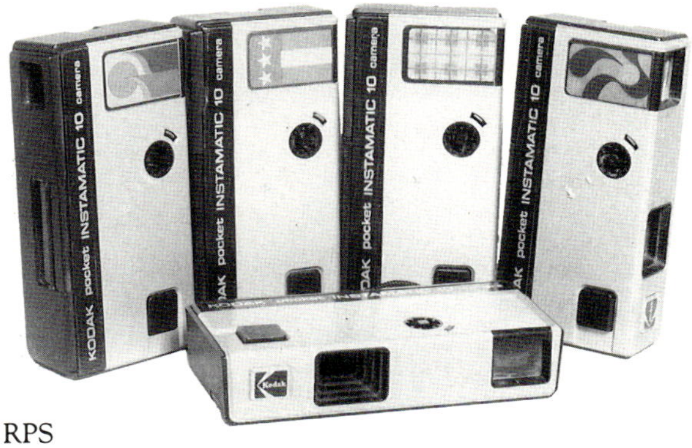

RPS

Introduced May 1973

Discontinued September 1976
Manufactured US
Lens Meniscus f/11, 25mm fixed focus
Shutter 2-speed 1/40 and 1/90 sec.

Description/Remarks

Basic model; version with choice of self-adhesive motifs above finder; Magicube socket.

Kodak pocket Instamatic 20

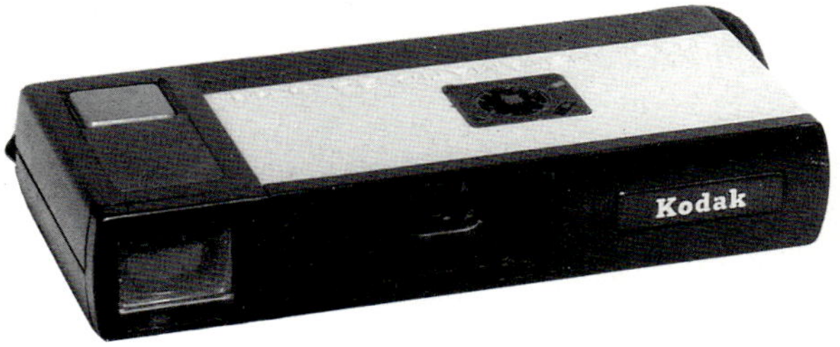

RPS

Introduced March 1972
Discontinued July 1976
Manufactured US
Lens 3-element f/9.5, 25mm fixed focus
Shutter 2-speed 1/40 and 1/100 sec.

Description/Remarks

Magicube socket.

Kodak pocket Instamatic 30

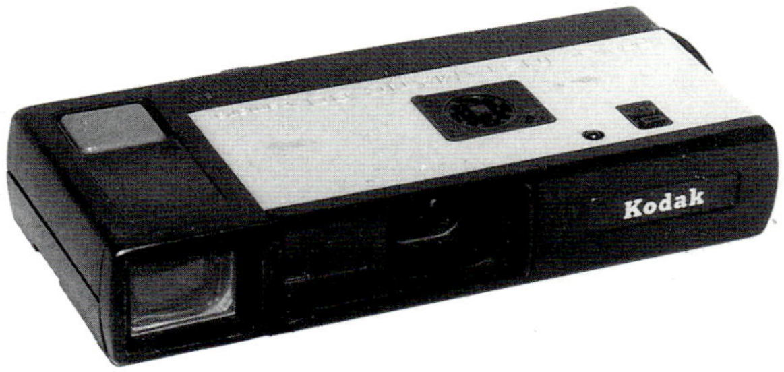

RPS

Introduced March 1972
Discontinued April 1976
Manufactured US
Lens 3-element f/9.5, 25mm fixed focus
Shutter Electronic; 10 to 1/160 sec.

Description/Remarks

Automatic exposure control by CdS cell; magicube socket.
May 1973: Parallax lines added to finder
July 1973: battery check button added.

Kodak pocket Instamatic 40

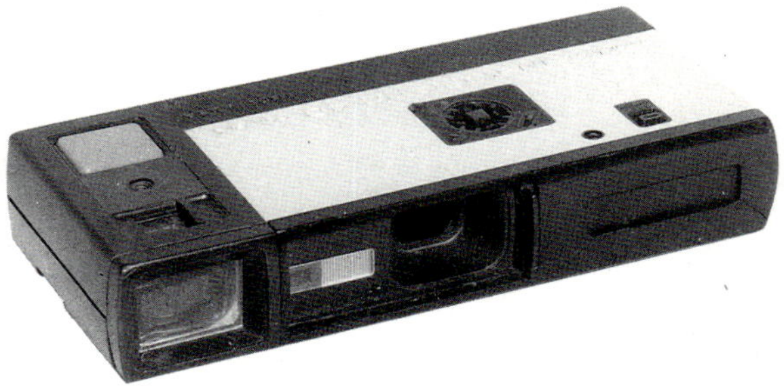

RPS

Introduced March 1972
Discontinued November 1975
Manufactured US
Lens 3-element f/8, 25mm, 2 position focusing.
Shutter Electronic; 10 to 1/225 sec.

Description/Remarks

Automatic exposure control by CdS cell; Magicube socket.
May 1973: Parallax lines added to finder.
July 1973: Battery check button added.

Kodak pocket Instamatic 50

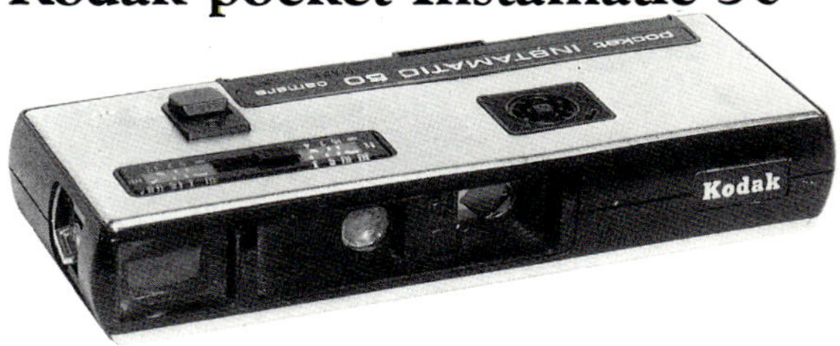

RPS

Introduced March 1972
Discontinued April 1976
Manufactured US
Lens Kodak Ektar f/2.7, 26mm, focusing
Shutter Electronic; 10 to $^1/_{250}$ sec.

Description/Remarks

Automatic exposure setting by CdS cell; aperture for flash exposure set by focusing scale; Magicube socket.
Apr. 1973: Battery check button added.
May 1973: Parallax lines added to finder.
Aug. 1973: Shutter release lock added.

Kodak pocket Instamatic 60

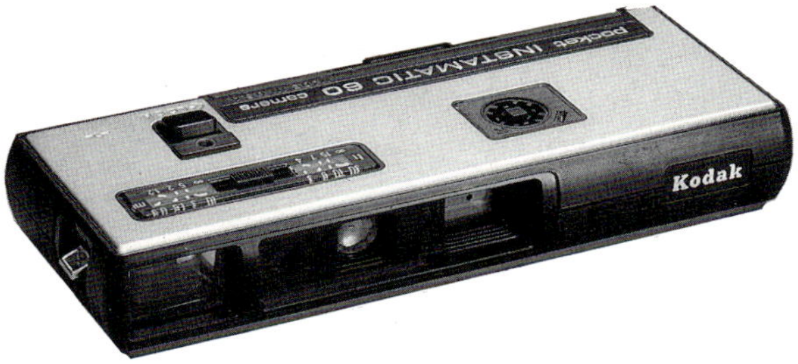

KP

Introduced March 1972
Discontinued September 1976
Manufactured US
Lens Kodak Ektar f/2.7, 26mm, focusing
Shutter Electronic; 10 to $^1/_{250}$ sec.

Description/Remarks

Coupled rangefinder; automatic exposure setting by CdS cell; Magicube socket.
Apr. 1973: Battery check button added.
May 1973: Parallax lines added to finder.
Aug. 1973: Shutter release lock added.
July 1973–Oct. 1975: De Luxe version in black and chrome with gold lettering, sold as outfit with matching case.

Kodak pocket Instamatic 100

Introduced September 1972
Discontinued December 1974
Manufactured UK, Germany
Lens Kodak triplet f/11, 25mm fixed focus
Shutter Single speed $^1/_{60}$ sec.

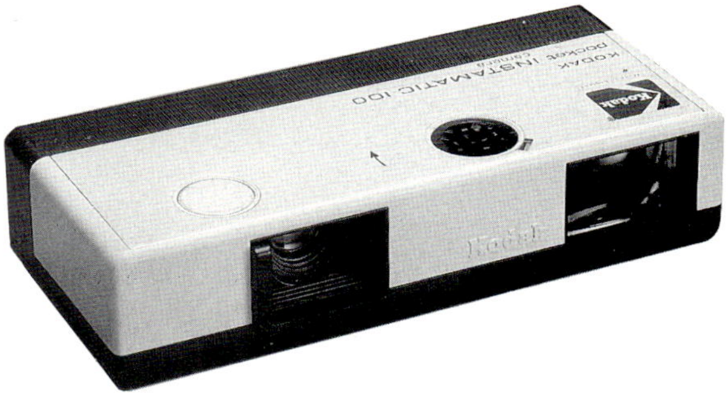

1973–1974 model. KP

Description/Remarks

Magicube socket; used bulb signal in finder. Sliding lens cover.

From 1973 a new light grey top and front cover replaced original black casing with light top panel.

Kodak pocket Instamatic 101

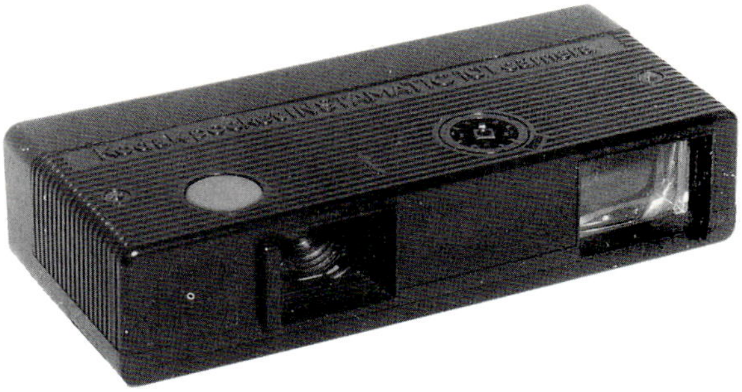

RPS

Introduced January 1974
Discontinued November 1974
Manufactured UK
Lens Kodak triplet f/11, 25mm
Shutter Single-speed $^1/_{60}$ sec.

Description/Remarks

Made for premium sales only.

Kodak pocket Instamatic 200

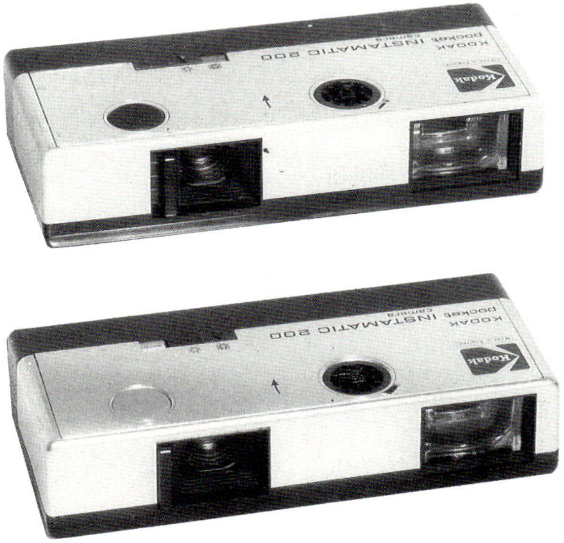

Above: Early model. Below: Late model. RPS

Introduced September 1972
Discontinued December 1974
Manufactured UK, Germany
Lens Kodak triplet f/11, 25mm fixed focus
Shutter 2-speed $1/40$ and $1/80$ sec.

Description/Remarks

Magicube socket; brightline finder with used bulb signal and parallax markings; shutter speed selected by weather symbols, or magicube insertion; sliding lens cover.

Early models had grey plastic cases with metal top plate and black release buttons. Later models had metalised cases with first red, then blue release buttons.

Kodak pocket Instamatic 300

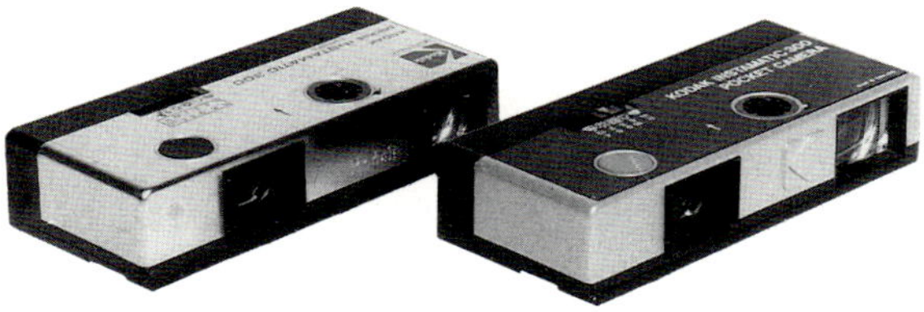

Left: Early model. Right: Late model. RPS

Introduced September 1972
Discontinued August 1976
Manufactured UK, Germany
Lens Kodak triplet f/5.6, 26mm fixed focus
Shutter 2-speed $1/40$ and $1/80$ sec.

Description/Remarks

Magicube socket, with used bulb signal in brightline finder, with parallax markings; aperture and shutter setting by single weather symbol scale or magicube insertion.

Early models had metal top plates and black release buttons, later red then blue. Late models were redesigned, with matt black tops.

Kodak pocket Instamatic 400

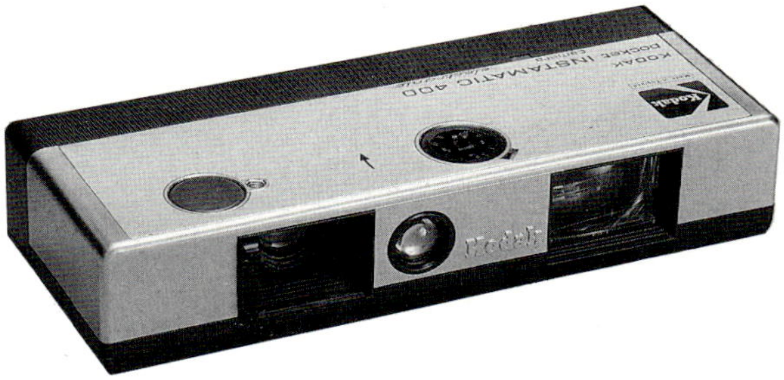

KP

Introduced September 1972
Discontinued 1976
Manufactured Germany
Lens Kodak triplet f/11, 25mm fixed focus
Shutter Electronic; 20 to $1/300$ sec.

Description/Remarks

Automatic exposure control by CdS cell, setting shutter speed; magicube socket, with used bulb signal in brightline finder, with low light signal and parallax markings.

Early models had black release buttons, later blue.

Kodak pocket Instamatic 500

Introduced September 1972

Discontinued 1976
Manufactured Germany
Lens Kodak triplet f/5.6, 25mm, fixed focus
Shutter Electronic; 20 to 1/300 sec.

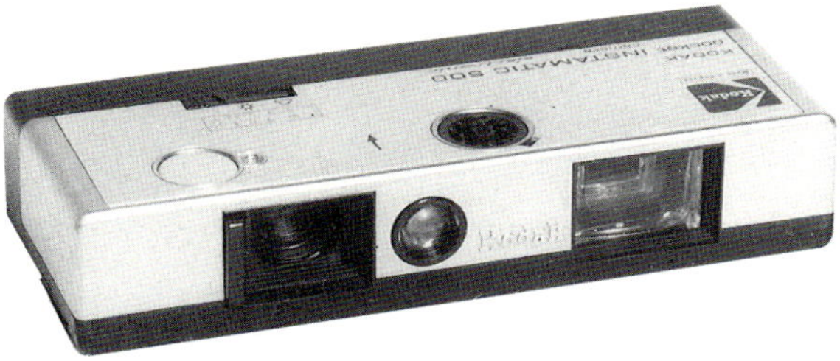

RPS

Description/Remarks

Automatic exposure control by CdS cell, setting shutter speed, aperture set manually by weather symbol scale; magicube socket with used bulb warning in brightline finder, with parallax markings and low light warning.

Early models had black release buttons, later blue.

Kodak Star

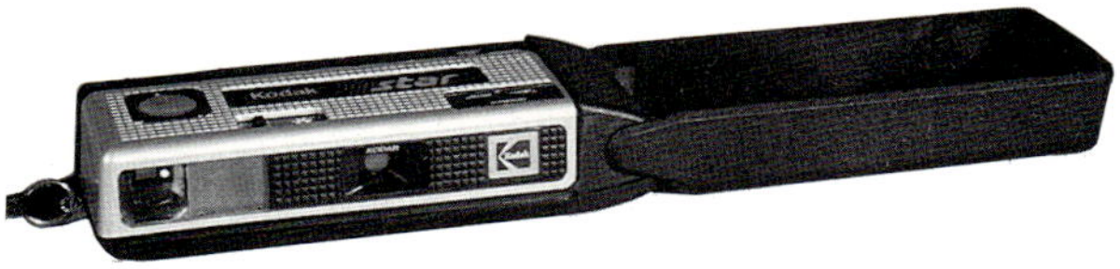

PDM

Introduced June 1985
Discontinued -
Manufactured US, Brazil
Lens Kodar meniscus f/11, 22mm
Shutter 3-speed 1/50, 1/125 and 1/250 sec.

Description/Remarks

Premium sales only in U.S.; shutter speed set by film cartridge; flipflash socket; folding cover/handle.

Kodak Stylite Pocket

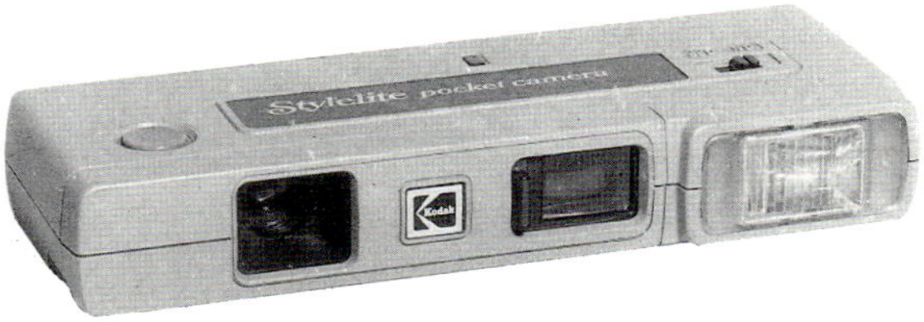

RPS

Introduced February 1979
Discontinued
Manufactured US
Lens 3-element f/8, 25mm fixed focus
Shutter 2-speed 1/125 and 1/210 sec.

Description/Remarks

Premium sales only; similar to Kodak Ektralite 10 camera, but with light buff colour scheme; integral electronic flash; shutter speed set by film cartridge.

Kodak Tele-Ektra 1

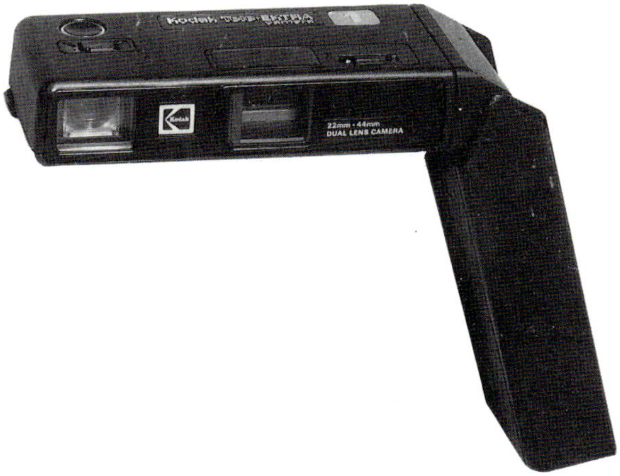

RPS

Introduced February 1978
Discontinued February 1981
Manufactured US, also French version made in Canada
Lens 2-element f/9.5, 22mm and f/11, 45mm
Shutter 3-speed 1/60, 1/125 and 1/210 sec.

Description/Remarks

Shutter speed set by film cartridge or flash; flipflash socket; hinged cover/handle; telephoto lens set by sliding button, finder changed automatically; fixed focus lens.

Kodak Tele-Ektra 2

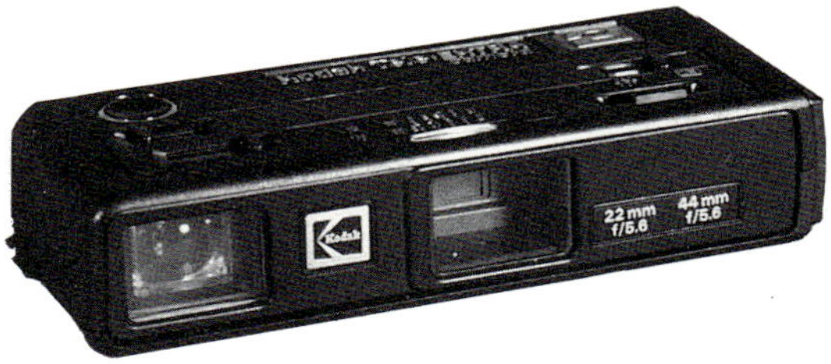

PDM

Introduced February 1978
Discontinued January 1980
Manufactured US, also French version made in Canada
Lenses 3-element f/5.6, 22mm and f/5.6, 44mm
Shutter 4-speed $^{1}/_{60}$, $^{1}/_{80}$, $^{1}/_{250}$ and $^{1}/_{500}$ sec.

Description/Remarks

Similar to Tele-Ektra 1 camera, but with focusing control and EX extended exposure setting.

Kodak Tele-Ektra 32

Introduced January 1978
Discontinued 1980
Manufactured UK
Lens Kodar single element f/11, 22mm and f/11, 37mm fixed focus
Shutter 3-speed $^{1}/_{40}$, $^{1}/_{125}$ and $^{1}/_{250}$ sec.

Description/Remarks

Folding cover/handle; shutter speed selected by film cartridge; flipflash socket.

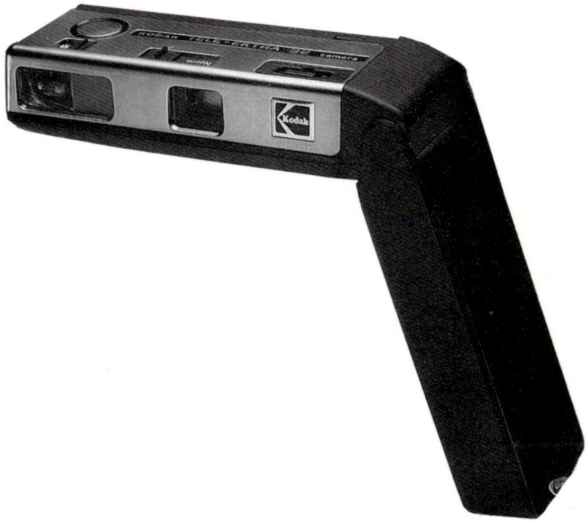

KP

Kodak Tele-Ektra 42

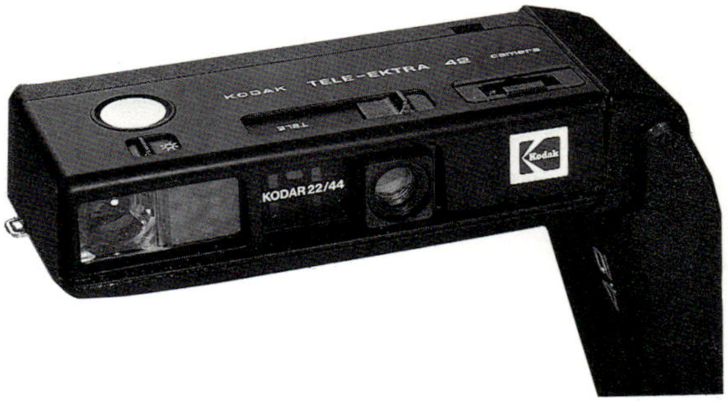

KP

Introduced 1978
Discontinued 1980
Manufactured Germany
Lens Kodar f/11, 22mm and f/11, 44mm fixed focus
Shutter 3-speed $^{1}/_{40}$ (flash only), $^{1}/_{125}$ and $^{1}/_{250}$ sec.

Description/Remarks

Folding cover/handle; flipflash socket; shutter speed set by film cartridge.

Kodak Tele-Ektra 300

Introduced May 1980

Discontinued May 1982
Manufactured US
Lens 3-element f/8, 22mm and f/8 44mm
Shutter 3-speed $^1/_{60}$, $^1/_{125}$ and $^1/_{250}$ sec.

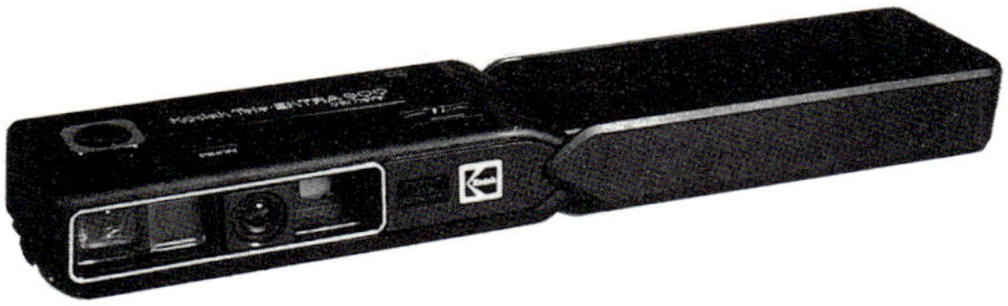

PDM

Description/Remarks

Integral cover/handle; shutter speed selected by film cartridge or flash; flipflash socket; focusing control for telephoto lens.

Kodak Tele-Ektra 350

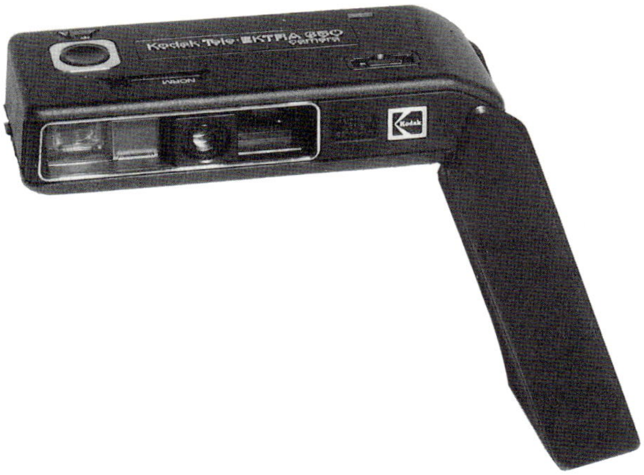

RPS

Introduced 1980
Discontinued 1983
Manufactured Germany
Lens Reomar f/8, 22mm (fixed focus) and Tele-Reomar f/8, 44mm (focusing)
Shutter 3-speed $^1/_{60}$, $^1/_{125}$ and $^1/_{250}$ sec.

Description/Remarks

Folding cover/handle; shutter speed set by film cartridge; flipflash socket; brightline finder with weather symbols and focusing symbols for telephoto lens.

Kodak Tele-Ektralite 20

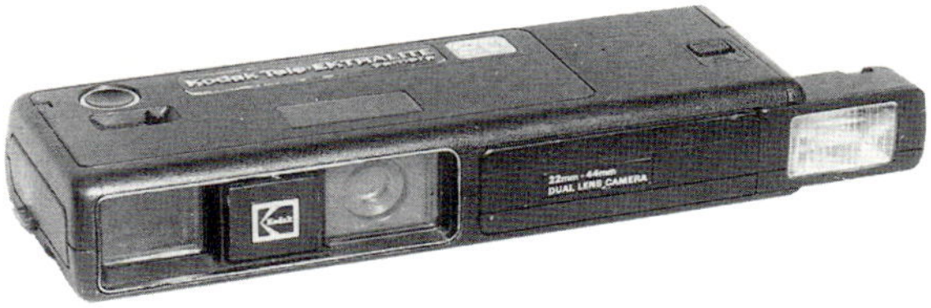

RPS

Introduced July 1979
Discontinued February 1981
Manufactured US
Lens 2-element f/9.5, 22mm and f/9.5, 44mm
Shutter 2-speed $^1/_{125}$ and $^1/_{210}$ sec.

Description/Remarks

Shutter speed selected by film cartridge; integral swing-out electronic flash; fixed focus.

Kodak Tele-Ektralite 40

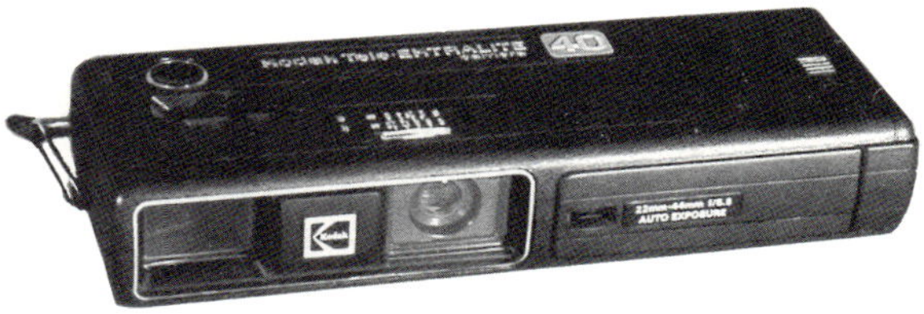

PDM

Introduced July 1979
Discontinued June 1981
Manufactured US
Lens 3-element f/5.6, 22mm and f/5.6, 44mm.
Shutter 2-speed $^1/_{100}$ and $^1/_{500}$ sec.

Description/Remarks

Automatic exposure control; integral swing-out electronic flash; focusing control for telephoto lens.

Kodak Tele-Ektralite 600

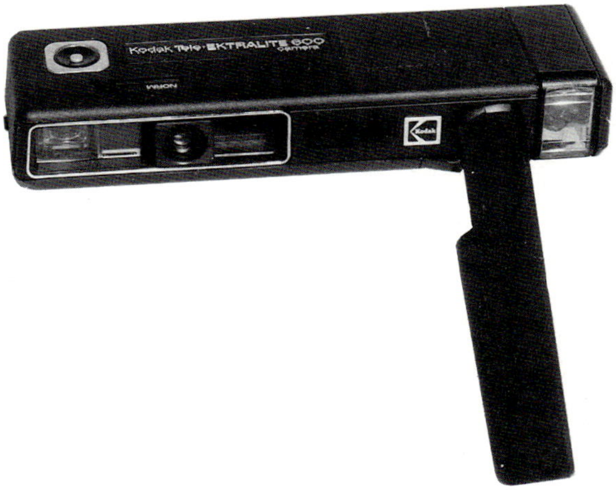

RPS

Introduced May 1980
Discontinued May 1982
Manufactured US
Lens Reomar 3-element f/8, 22mm and f/8, 44mm
Shutter 2-speed $^{1}/_{125}$ and $^{1}/_{250}$ sec.

Description/Remarks

Focusing control on telephoto lens; hinged cover/handle; integral electronic flash, automatically activated in low light; shutter speed selected by film cartridge; brightline finder.

Kodak Tele-Instamatic 330

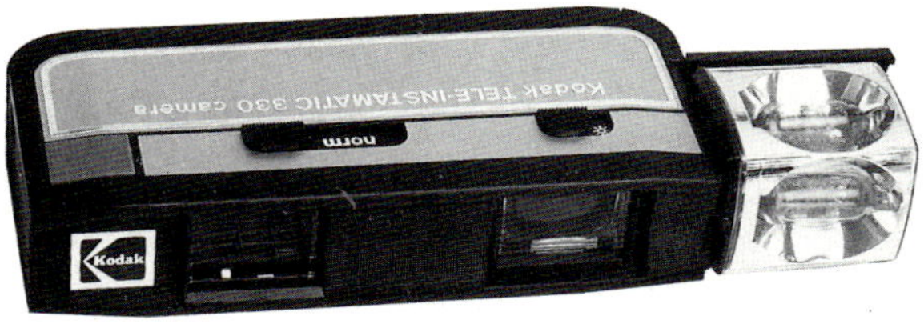

KP

Introduced September 1975
Discontinued 1978
Manufactured UK
Lens Kodak triplet f/11, 25mm and f/11 43mm
Shutter 2-speed $^{1}/_{50}$ and $^{1}/_{100}$ sec.

Description/Remarks

Body with slightly tapering ends and curved back corners; concealed magicube socket on one end.

Kodak Tele-Instamatic 430

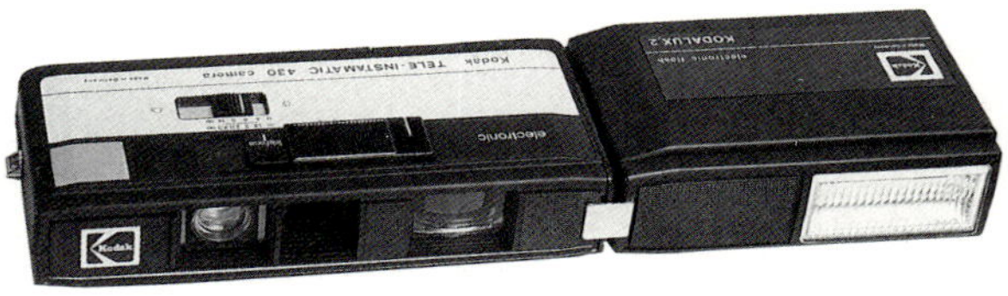

KAG

Introduced September 1975
Discontinued 1978
Manufactured Germany
Lens Reomar f/5.6, 25mm, fixed focus and
Tele-Reomar f/5.6, 42mm, focusing
Shutter 2-speed $^{1}/_{50}$ and $^{1}/_{100}$ sec.

Description/Remarks

Body with slightly tapering ends and back with curved corners; automatic exposure control by CdS cell, with lowlight warning in brightline finder; concealed magicube socket on one end.

Kodak Tele-Instamatic 608

Introduced April 1975
Discontinued June 1979
Manufactured US
Lens Meniscus f/11, 25mm and f/11, 43mm
Shutter 2-speed $^{1}/_{45}$ and $^{1}/_{125}$ sec.

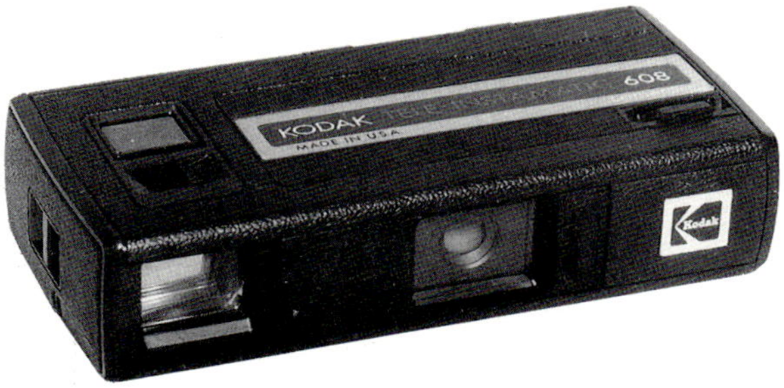

RPS

Description/Remarks

Telephoto lens selected by sliding button, finder changed automatically; flipflash socket; sliding lens and finder cover.

Kodak Tele-Instamatic 708

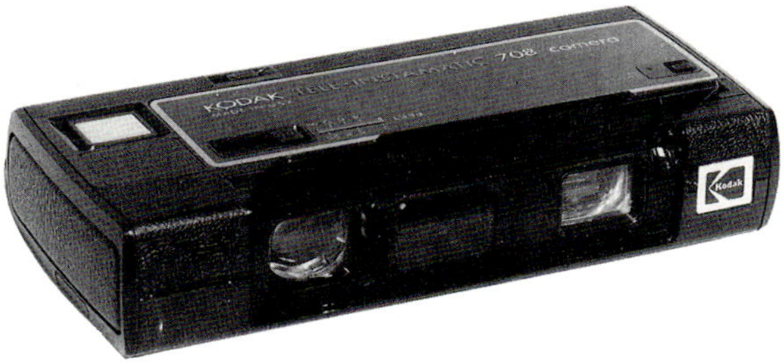

RPS

Introduced March 1976
Discontinued June 1979
Manufactured US
Lens 3-element f/5.6, 25mm and f/5.6, 43mm (with 4-element convertor)
Shutter Electronic; 1/30 to 1/300 sec.

Description/Remarks

Automatic exposure control by silicon cell; telephoto lens selected by sliding button, finder changed automatically; flipflash socket; hinged lens and finder cover.

Kodak Tele-Stylite

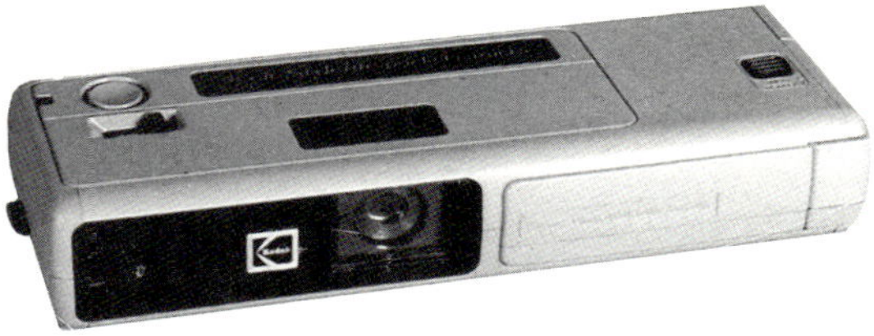

PDM

Introduced 1980
Discontinued 1982
Manufactured US
Lens
Shutter

Description/Remarks

Premium sales version of Kodak Tele-Ektralite 20 camera, (q.v.)

Kodak Trimlite Instamatic 18

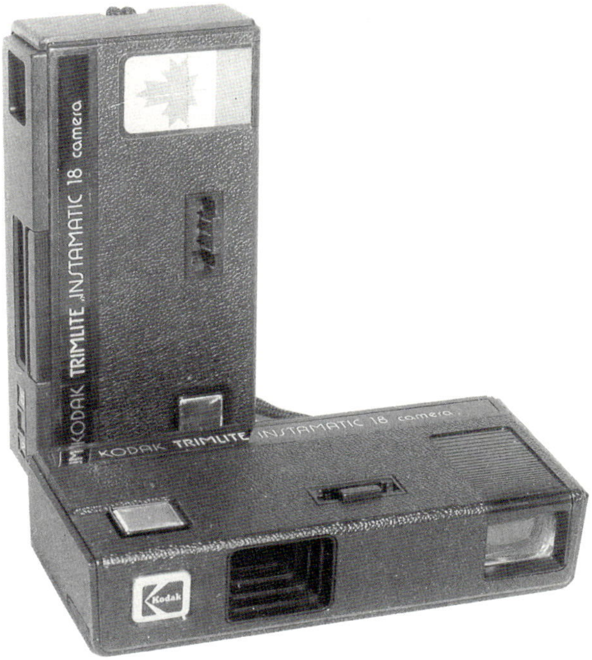

RPS

Introduced April 1975
Discontinued June 1979
Manufactured US
Lens Meniscus f/11, 25mm, fixed focus
Shutter 2-speed $\frac{1}{40}$ and $\frac{1}{90}$ sec.

Description/Remarks

Flipflash socket; variety of stick-on motifs available for recess above finder lens.

Kodak Trimlite Instamatic 28

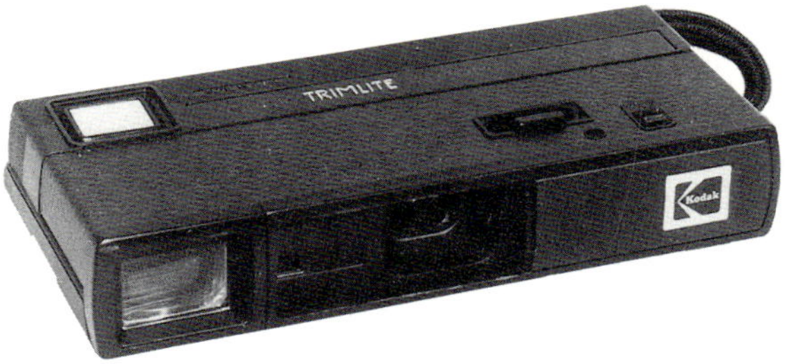

RPS

Introduced April 1975
Discontinued June 1979
Manufactured US
Lens 3-element f/8, 25mm
Shutter Electronic; $\frac{1}{30}$to $\frac{1}{60}$ sec.

Description/Remarks

Similar to Kodak Trimlite Instamatic 18 camera, but with automatic exposure controlled by CdS cell and two-position focusing.

Kodak Trimlite Instamatic 38

Introduced April 1975
Discontinued June 1979
Manufactured US
Lens 3-element f/8, 25mm
Shutter Electronic; 5 to $\frac{1}{225}$ sec.

Description/Remarks

Automatic exposure controlled by CdS cell, lowlight warning in finder; flipflash socket; battery tester; two-position focusing; brown and black vinyl covering.

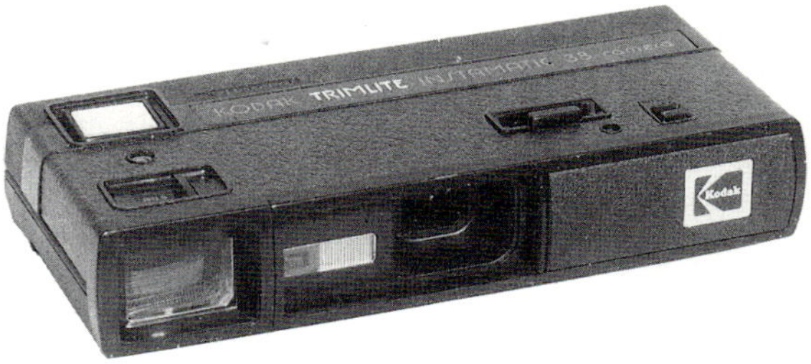

RPS

Kodak Trimlite Instamatic 48

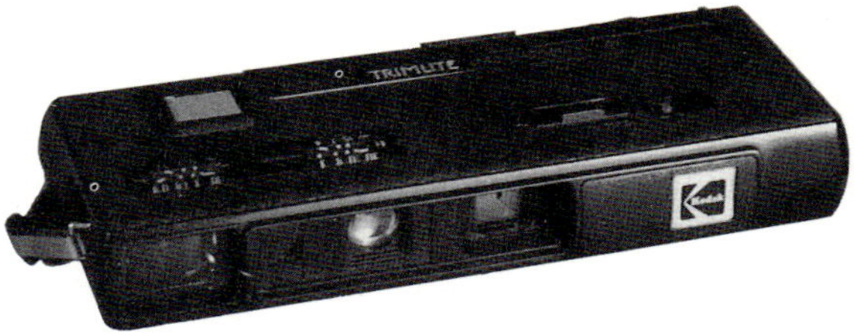

PDM

Introduced April 1975
Discontinued June 1979
Manufactured US
Lens Ektar f/2.7, 26mm
Shutter Electronic; $\frac{1}{30}$ to $\frac{1}{250}$ sec.

Description/Remarks

Coupled rangefinder focusing; brightline finder with parallax markings; automatic exposure controlled by CdS cell, lowlight warning in finder; flipflash, with automatic exposure setting through focusing control; pebbled brown and black vinyl covering.

Kodak Winner Pocket

Introduced January 1979
Discontinued –
Manufactured US

Lens Meniscus f/11, 25mm
Shutter Single speed 1/90 sec.

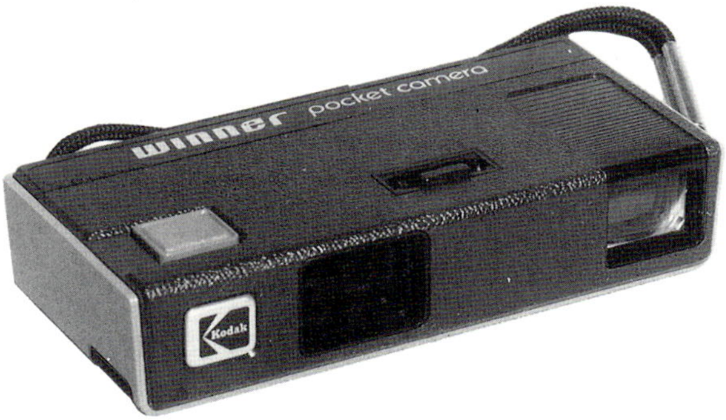

RPS

Description/Remarks

Premium sales only; similar to Kodak Trimlite Instamatic 18 camera, with brown and tan colour scheme, but with simpler finder.
Feb. 1988: made in blue and red, with 1988 Olympic Games logo; 2-speed shutter; direct sales.

Kodak Disc Cameras

Developing the philosophy behind the Instamatic and pocket cameras, Kodak moved further towards the completely foolproof, entirely automatic camera which would produce an acceptable results in almost any conditions. The Kodak disc cameras launched in 1982 replaced the traditional strip of film with a fairly rigid disc. Cameras exposing on film discs had been made before, including the Photoret of 1893, and the Japanese sub-miniature Petal camera made just after World War Two. They had been little more than novelties, since only very limited enlargement of small negatives was possible without great loss of quality. Emulsion technology now made possible a colour negative film for the disc cameras which would produce acceptable quality from a image only 8 × 10mm.

A number of features to simplify and improve the handling and printing of the disc films by photo-finishers were incorporated in the system, including the magnetic coding of information about printer settings during the printing operation, to facilitate matching reprints. The cameras were fitted with aspheric lenses, the mass production of which Kodak had developed, to give the best possible sharpness in the tiny negative. Entirely automatic exposure setting, including automatic flash control in most models, was provided. The very slim, flat case made it easy to slip into pockets or handbags. Despite all the apparent advantages, the disc cameras were not the runaway success that the cartridge and pocket cameras had been.

By 1988 the Kodak disc cameras had come almost to the end of their effective commercial life. The new generation of compact 35mm cameras, including Kodak's own, had replaced them in popular appeal. The superior quality given by negatives with over ten times the area of the disc images made all the difference.

Hawkeye disc 7000 camera

See Kodak disc 3100 camera

Kodak Challenger disc camera

See Kodak disc 3600 camera

Kodak disc 2000

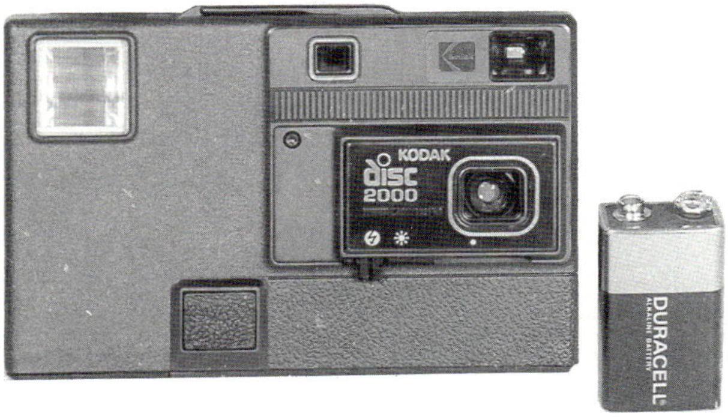

KM

Introduced October 1982
Discontinued 1984
Manufactured US, export only
Lens Aspheric f/2.8, 12.5mm fixed focus
Shutter 2-speed

Description/Remarks

Two exposures: daylight (1/200) sec., f/6 and flash (1/100) sec., f/2.8. Manual flash selection; replaceable 9 volt battery.

Kodak disc 3000

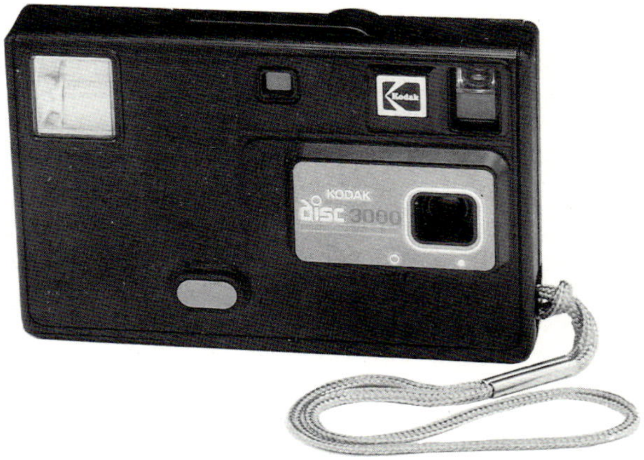

KP

Introduced March 1983
Discontinued July 1984
Manufactured US
Lens Aspheric f/2.8, 12.5mm fixed focus
Shutter 2-speed

Description/Remarks

Similar to Kodak disc 2000, but with automatic flash selection.

Kodak disc 3100

Introduced April 1984
Discontinued 1985
Manufactured US

Lens Aspheric f/2.8, 12.5mm fixed focus
Shutter 2-speed 1/100 and 1/200 sec.

Description/Remarks

Used replaceable 9 volt battery.

Variations

A version with a red front plate was made for the J.C. Penney Special Photo Outfit.

The Hawkeye disc 7000 camera (June 1985-December 1985) was a version made for premium sales.

Kodak disc 3500

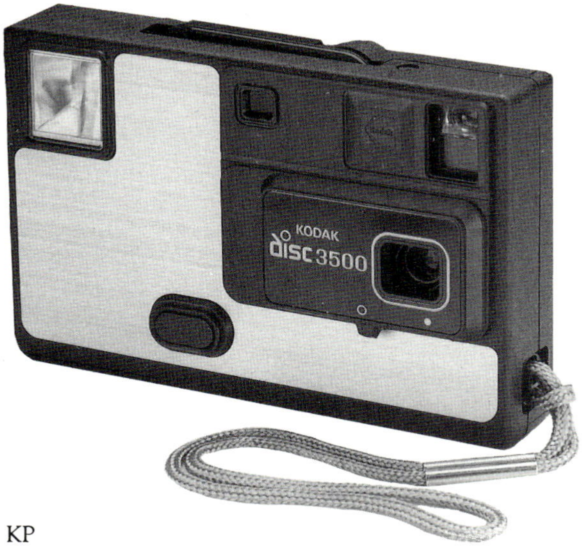

KP

Introduced September 1983
Discontinued 1984
Manufactured US, for export only
Lens Aspheric f/2.8, 12.5mm fixed focus
Shutter 2-speed

Description/Remarks

Similar to Kodak disc 3000 camera, for export markets.

Kodak disc 3600

Introduced February 1986
Discontinued 1988
Manufactured US
Lens f/4, 15mm
Shutter Single speed 1/300 sec.

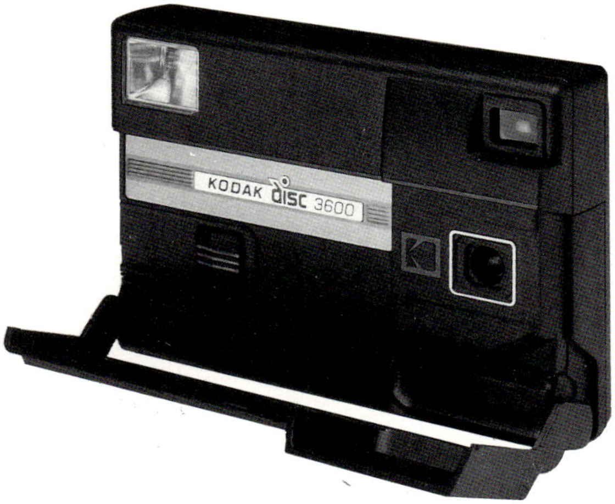

KP

Description/Remarks

Powered by two AA replaceable batteries.

The Kodak Challenger disc camera was a premium version of this model.

Kodak disc 4000

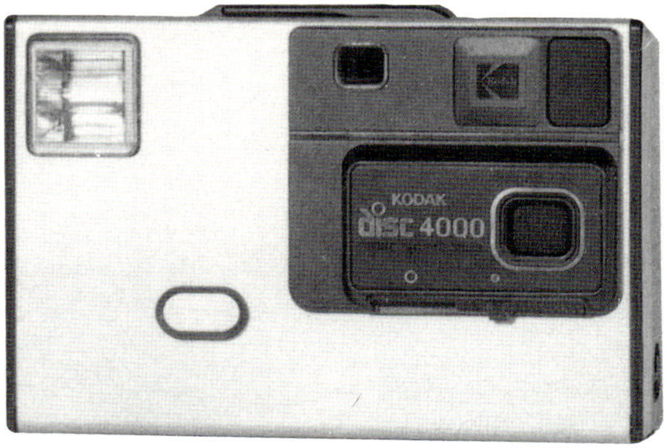

KM

Introduced May 1982
Discontinued April 1984

Manufactured US
Lens Aspheric f/2.8, 12.5mm fixed focus
Shutter 2-speed 1/100 and 1/200 sec.

Description/Remarks

Automatic flash selection; integral lithium battery.

Variations

About 1000 examples were over-printed with "photokina köln '82" for the European launch and distributed to the international press.

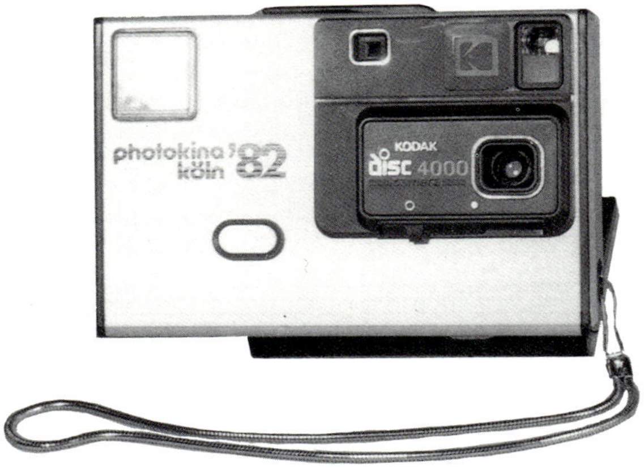

Over-printed for Photokina 1982. KM

Kodak disc 4100

Introduced April 1984
Discontinued 1987
Manufactured US
Lens Aspheric f/2.8, 12.5mm fixed focus
Shutter 2-speed 1/100 and 1/200 sec.

Description/Remarks

Similar to Kodak disc 3100 camera but with integral lithium battery.

The Kodak Medalist I disc camera (1986–) was a special edition of this camera.

Kodak disc 6000

Introduced May 1982
Discontinued April 1984 (sold until 1987 in UK)
Manufactured US
Lens Aspheric f/2.8, 12.5mm fixed focus, but with close-up lens
Shutter 2-speed 1/100 and 1/200 sec.

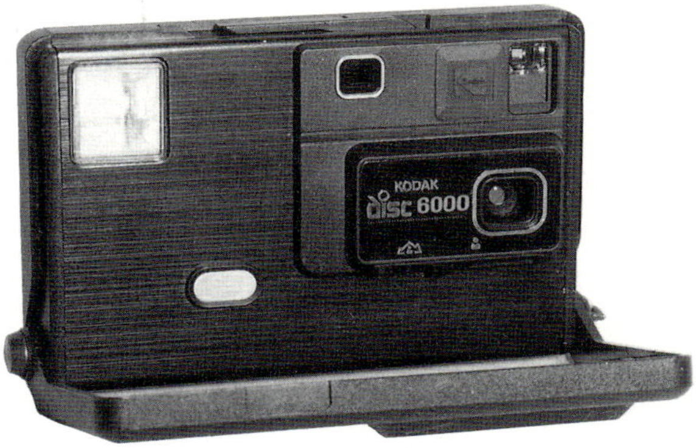

RPS

Description/Remarks

Similar to Kodak disc 4000 camera, but with close-up lens and folding cover.

Kodak disc 6100

Introduced April 1984
Discontinued 1987
Manufactured US
Lens Aspheric f/2.8, 12.5mm fixed focus, but with close-up lens.
Shutter 2-speed 1/100 and 1/200 sec.

Description/Remarks

Similar to Kodak disc 4100, but with close-up lens.

The Kodak Medalist II disc camera was a special edition version of this model.

Kodak disc 8000

Introduced May 1982
Discontinued April 1984 (sold until 1987 in UK)
Manufactured US

Lens Aspheric f/2.8, 12.5mm fixed focus, but with close-up lens.
Shutter 2-speed $1/100$ and $1/200$ sec.

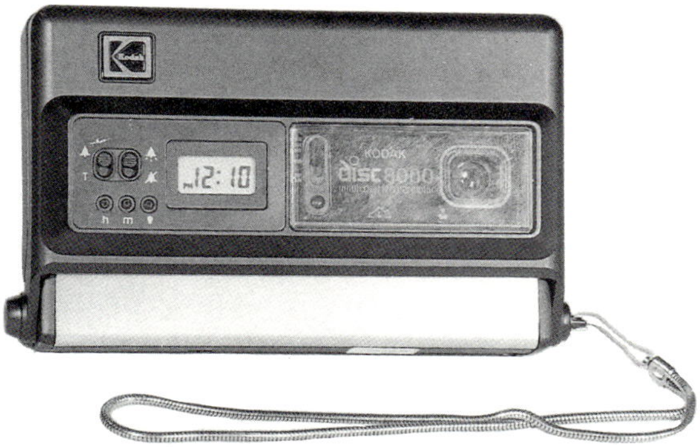

RPS

Description/Remarks

Simlar to Kodak disc 6000 camera, but with gold finish and electronic self-timer and digital clock built into hinged cover, which also acts as support stand.

Kodak Medalist I disc camera

See Kodak disc 3100 camera.

Kodak Medalist II disc camera

See Kodak disc 6100 camera.

Kodak Medalist Tele disc camera

See Kodak Tele disc camera.

Kodak Tele disc

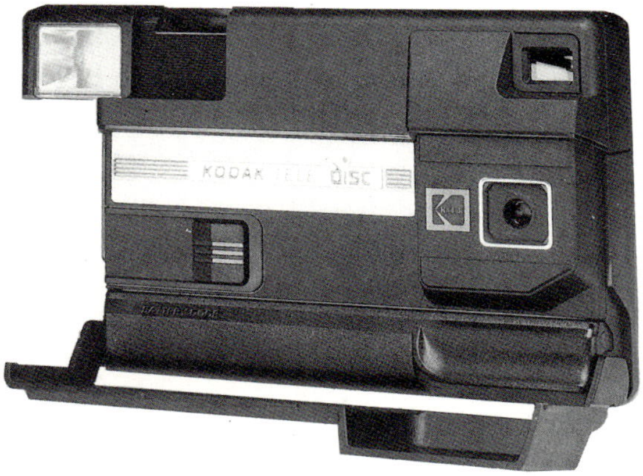

KP

Introduced September 1985
Discontinued 1988
Manufactured US
Lens f/4, 12.5mm and f/5.6, 22mm fixed focus
Shutter Single speed $1/300$ sec.

Description/Remarks

Similar to Kodak disc 3600 camera, but with telephoto lens.

The Kodak Medalist Tele disc camera was a special edition of this model.

The Kodak Tele Challenger disc camera (December 1985–1986) was a premium version of this model.

Kodak Tele Challenger disc camera

See Kodak Tele disc camera.

CHAPTER 7 *Kodak Instant Cameras*

Kodak entered the instant picture field in 1977 with a range of cameras and a new film, which, it claimed, differed from the Polaroid process which for so long had the market to itself. Polaroid disagreed, and a long drawn out litigation began over claimed patent infringement. This ended in 1985 with a judgement against Eastman Kodak. From 9th January 1986 all Kodak instant cameras and films were withdrawn from the market, users being offered various forms of compensation. As a result, only a very small proportion of the cameras sold remained in the hands of the public, and since the withdrawn cameras were destroyed, it is likely that in the future Kodak instant cameras will be among the rarest, and thus most sought after, of the Company's products.

The Kodak instant film differed from the Polaroid product in that the final image was formed on the back of the picture unit, so that a right-way-round picture was produced by direct exposure. No mirror was needed to reverse the image laterally, as in the rival Polaroid SX-70 and similar cameras. However, some early Kodak instant cameras had a double mirror system to fold the light path to make the camera more compact. The improved Trimprint film, introduced in 1984, enabled the relatively thick base with the processing chemical pods and negative image layers to be detached from the print shortly after the film had 'developed', leaving a thin, more convenient print. The picture size was 67 × 91mm, on a picture unit 98x102mm.

Champ Kodamatic Instant

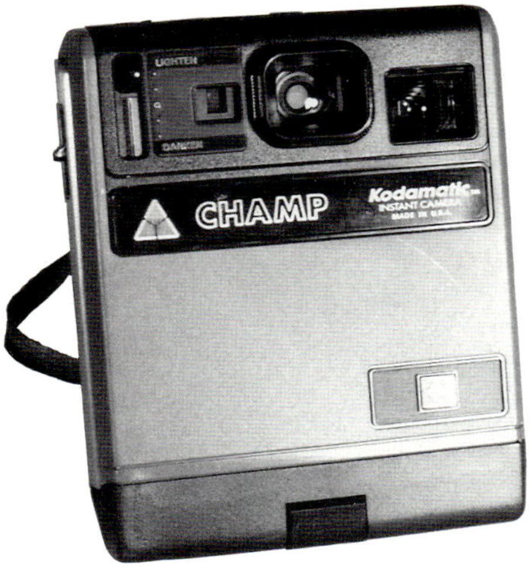

PDM

Introduced April 1982
Discontinued April 1984
Manufactured US
Lens f/12.8, 100mm fixed focus
Shutter Electronic $1/15$ – $1/400$ sec.
Numbers made

Description/Remarks

Designed for the faster HS144 Instant film packs. Renamed Kodak Trimprint 920 Instant camera from April 1984.

Produced as Partytime II Kodamatic camera for premium sales by Tupperware, 1982–1984.

Sold in Europe as Kodamatic 920 camera.

The Handle

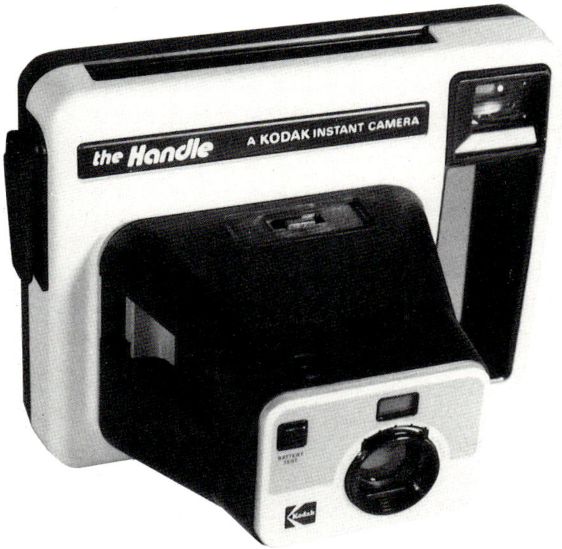

PDM

Introduced May 1977
Discontinued November 1979
Manufactured US
Lens 2-element f/12.7, 100mm fixed focus
Shutter Electronic 1/15 – 1/300 sec.

Description/Remarks

Solid body, direct light path; integral hand-hold; automatic exposure; flipflash socket; hand crank picture unit ejection.

Manufactured by Kodak Limited in UK as Kodak EK2 Instant camera.

Manufactured for Coca-Cola as the Happy Times camera, May 1978–1979.

Manufactured as the Pleaser Kodak Instant camera for premium sales only, November 1977–1982.

Handle 2 (EK22) Kodak Instant

Introduced May 1979
Discontinued January 1981
Manufactured US
Lens 2-element f/12.7, 100mm fixed focus
Shutter Electronic 2 to 1/300 sec.

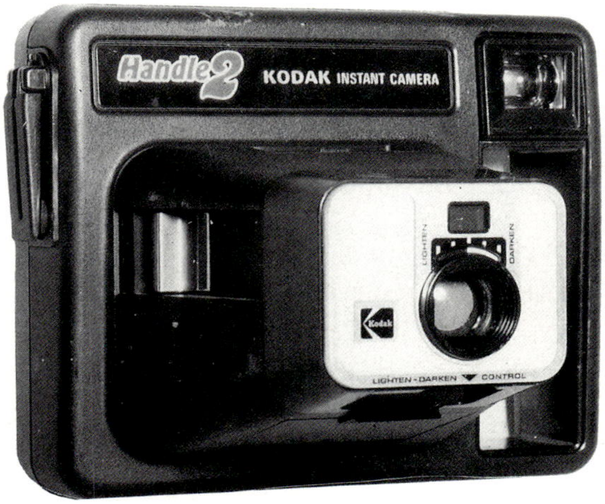

RPS

Description/Remarks

Similar to The Handle Kodak Instant camera, but with longer exposure range and all-black body.

Happy Times Kodak Instant camera

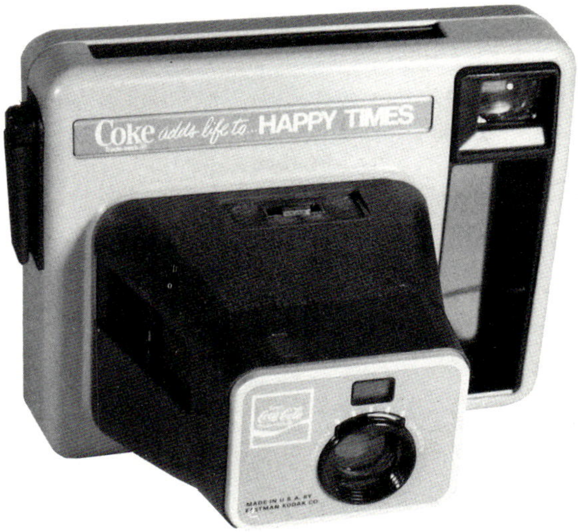

PDM

See The Handle Kodak Instant camera

Kodak Colorburst 50 Instant

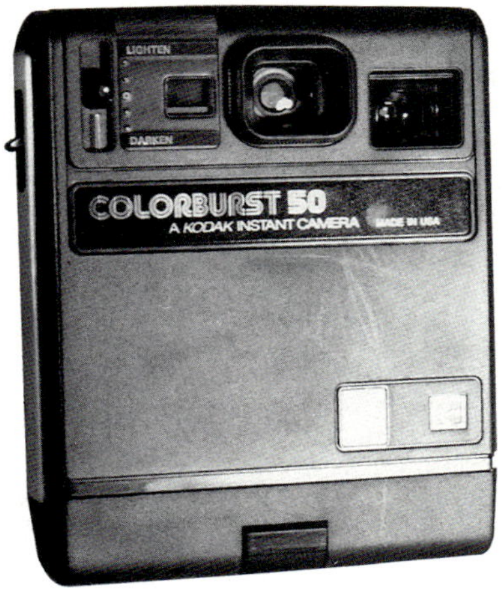

PDM

Introduced May 1979
Discontinued May 1982
Manufactured US
Lens 3-element f/12.8, 100mm fixed focus
Shutter Electronic 2 to 1/300 sec.

Description/Remarks

Double mirror folded light path; recessed rectangular lens mount; lighten-darken control; flipflash socket; motorised picture unit ejection.

Sold in Europe as Kodak EK160 Instant camera.

Produced as the Party time Instant camera for premium sales by Tupperware,1980–1982.

Kodak Colorburst 100 Instant

Introduced February 1978
Discontinued May 1880
Manufactured US
Lens 3-element f/11, 137mm focusing
Shutter Electronic 1/20 – 1/300 sec.

Description/Remarks

Similar to Kodak EK6 Instant camera, but with new 'arrow spectrum' motif.

Sold in Europe as Kodak EK100 Instant camera.

Kodak Colorburst 200 Instant

Introduced February 1978
Discontinued May 1980
Manufactured US
Lens 3-element f/11, 137mm focusing
Shutter Electronic 1/20 – 1/300 sec.

Description/Remarks

Similar to Kodak Colorburst 100 Instant camera, but with hinged cover protecting lens panel when not in use.

Sold in Europe as the Kodak EK 200 Instant camera.

Kodak Colorburst 250 Instant

Introduced July 1979
Discontinued May 1982
Manufactured US
Lens 3-element f/12.8, 100mm fixed focus
Shutter Electronic 2 to 1/300 sec.

Description/Remarks

Similar to Kodak Colorburst 50 Instant camera but with built-in self-quenching electronic flash, turned on by sliding to one side.

Sold in Europe as Kodak EK160-EF Instant camera.

Produced as Partyflash Instant camera for premium sales by Tupperware, 1981–1982, and as Partyflash II Instant camera 1982–1986.

Kodak Colorburst 300 Instant

Introduced February 1978
Discontinued May 1980
Manufactured US
Lens 3-element f/11, 137mm fixed focus
Shutter Electronic 1/20 – 1/300 sec.

Description/Remarks

Similar to Kodak Colorburst 100 Instant camera, but with built-in electronic flash unit, activated by sliding over top.

Sold in Europe as Kodak EK300 Instant camera.

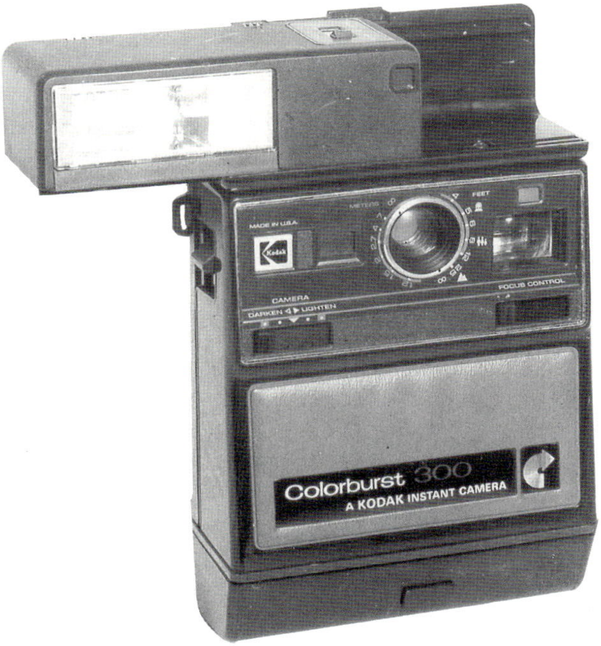

RPS

Kodak Colorburst 350 Instant

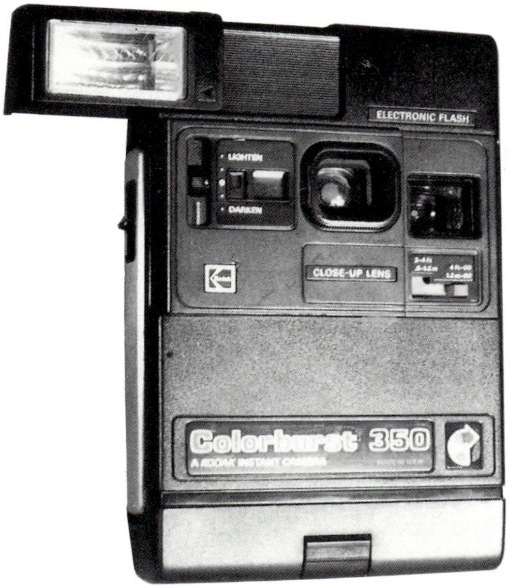

PDM

Introduced February 1981
Discontinued May 1982
Manufactured US
Lens 3-element f/12.8, 100mm fixed focus, but with close-up lens.
Shutter Electronic 2 to 1/300 sec.

Description/Remarks

Similar to Kodak Colorburst 250, but with close-up lens for pictures from 2 to 4ft.

Sold in Europe as Kodak EK260EF camera.

Kodak EK2 Instant

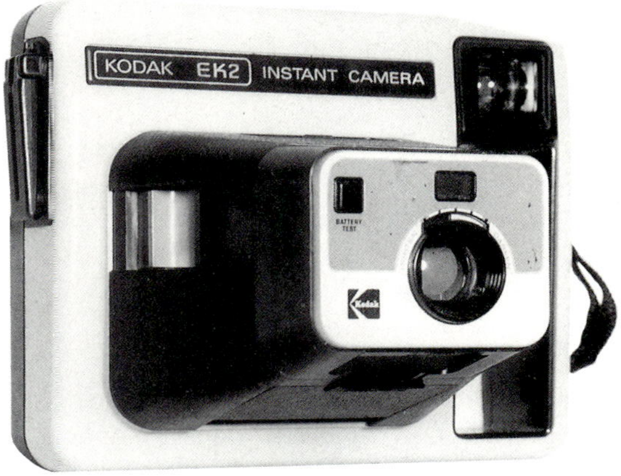

RPS

Introduced July 1977
Discontinued 1978
Manufactured UK
Lens 2-element f/12.7, 100mm fixed focus
Shutter Electronic 1/15 – 1/300 sec.

Description/Remarks

Solid body, with integral hand-hold; direct light path; automatic exposure; flipflash socket; hand crank picture unit ejection.

European version of The Handle Kodak Instant camera.

Kodak EK4 Instant

Introduced June 1976

Discontinued July 1978
Manufactured US
Lens 3-element f/11, 137mm focusing
Shutter Electronic 1/20 – 1/300 sec.

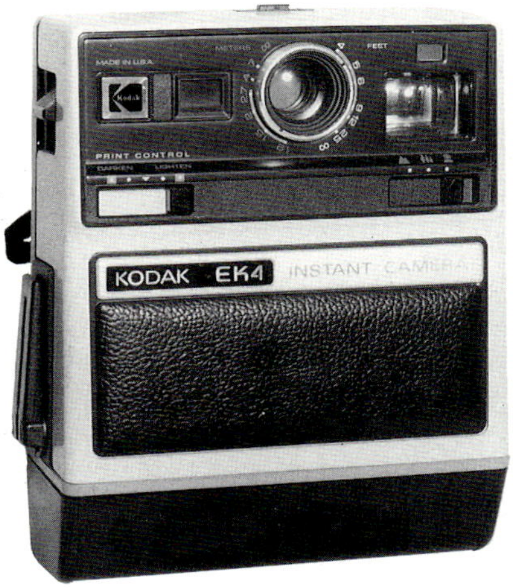

RPS

Description/Remarks

Double mirror folded light path; hand-crank picture unit ejection; automatic exposure with lighten-darken control; flipflash socket; 'zooming circle' focusing aid in finder.

Kodak EK6 Instant

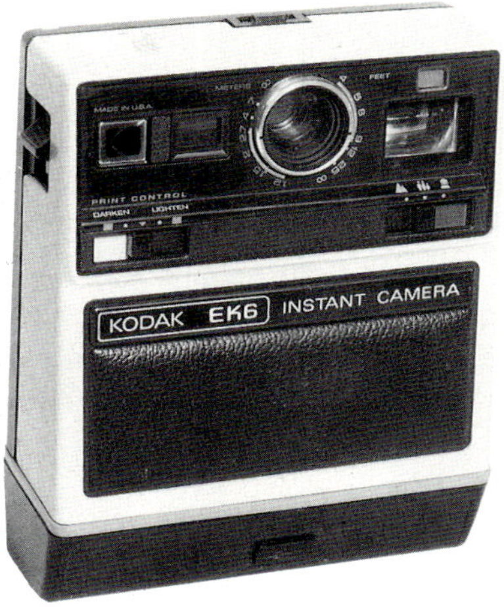

RPS

Introduced June 1976
Discontinued July 1978
Manufactured US
Lens 3-element f/11, 137mm focusing
Shutter Electronic 1/20 – 1/300 sec.

Description/Remarks

Similar to Kodak EK4 Instant camera but with motorised picture unit ejection.

Kodak EK8 Instant

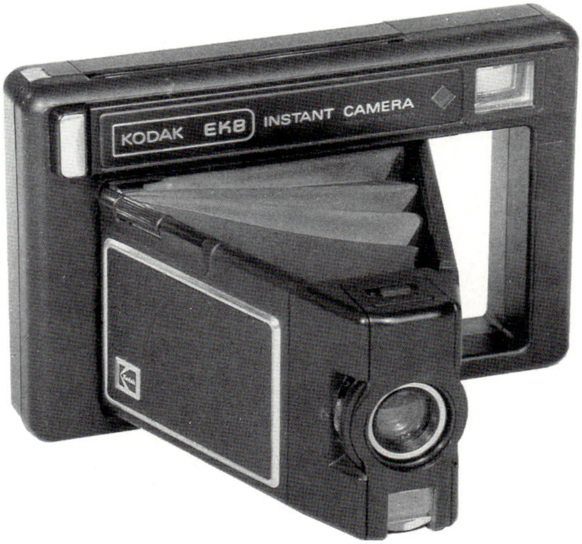

RPS

Introduced May 1977
Discontinued 1979
Manufactured Germany
Lens 3-element f/11, 137mm focusing
Shutter Electronic 1/20 – 1/300 sec.

Description/Remarks

Flat folding, opening to triangular shape with hand-hold; coupled rangefinder focusing; flipflash socket; automatic exposure with brighten-darken control; brightline finder.

Kodak EK100 Instant camera

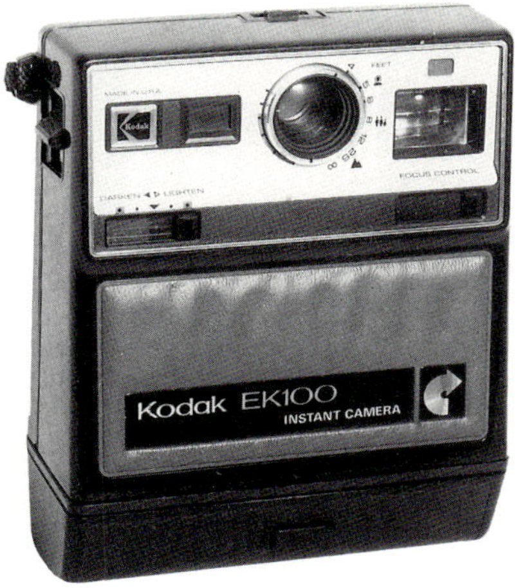

RPS

See Kodak Colorburst 100 camera.

Kodak EK160 Instant camera

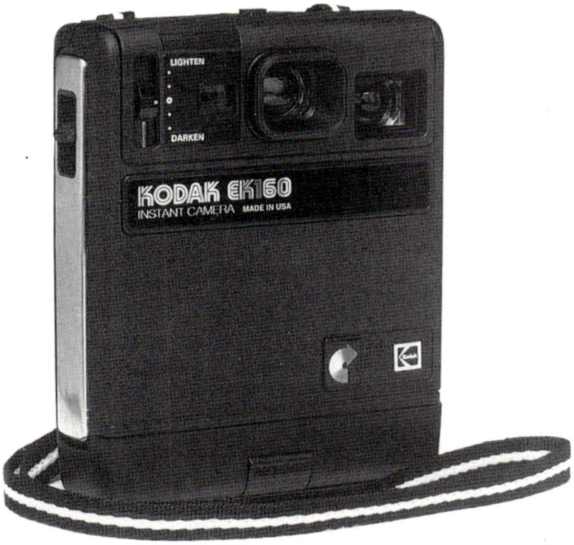

KP

See Kodak Colorburst 50 camera.

Kodak EK160-EF Instant camera

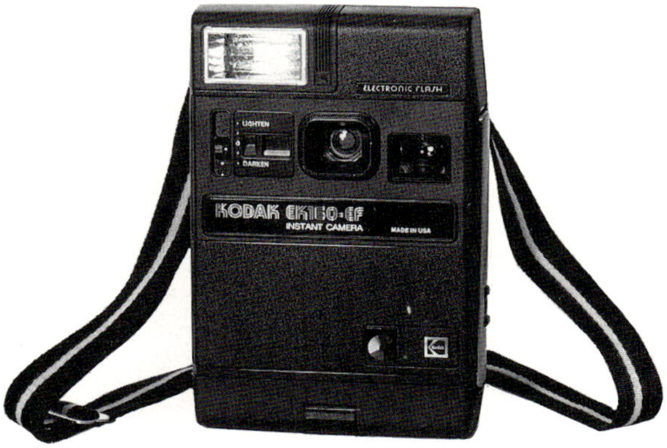

KP

See Kodak Colorburst 250 Instant camera.

Kodak EK200 Instant camera

See Kodak Colorburst 200 Instant camera.

Kodak EK260 EF Instant camera

See Kodak Colorburst 350 Instant camera.

Kodak EK300 Instant camera

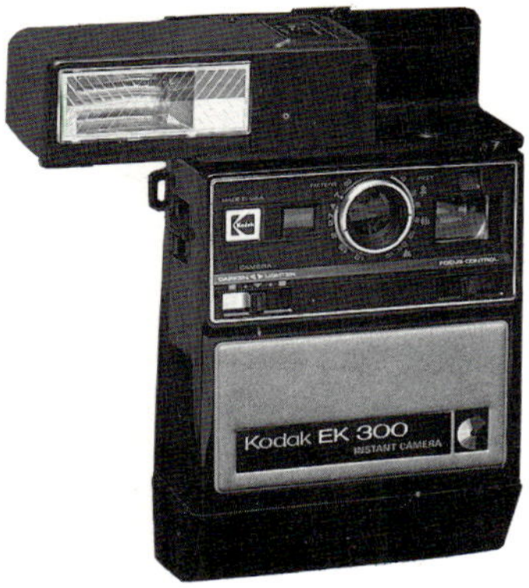

KP

See Kodak Colorburst 300 Instant camera.

Kodak Trimprint 920

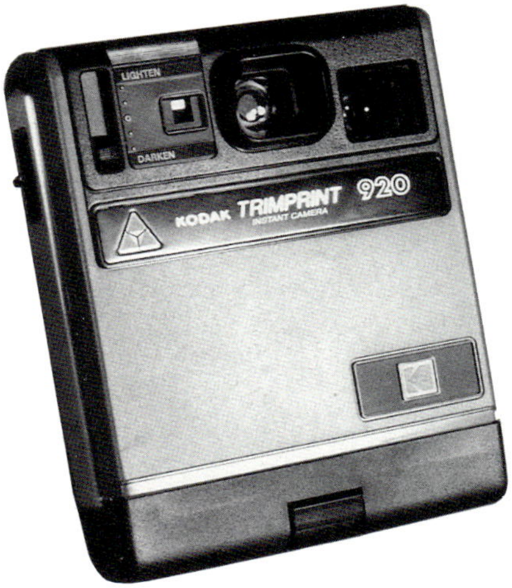

PDM

Introduced April 1984
Discontinued January 1986
Manufactured US
Lens f/12.8, 100mm fixed focus
Shutter Electronic 1/15 – 1/400 sec.

Description/Remarks

The Champ Kodamatic Instant camera renamed with the introduction of the improved Trimprint film packs.

Sold in Europe as the Kodamatic 920 camera.

Kodak Trimprint 940 Instant

Introduced April 1984
Discontinued January 1986
Manufactured US
Lens f/12.8, 100mm fixed focus
Shutter Electronic 1/15 – 1/250 sec.

Description/Remarks

Identical to Kodamatic 940 Instant camera; name changed with the introduction of the improved Trimprint film packs.

Kodamatic 920 Instant

See The Champ Instant camera.

Kodamatic 940 Instant

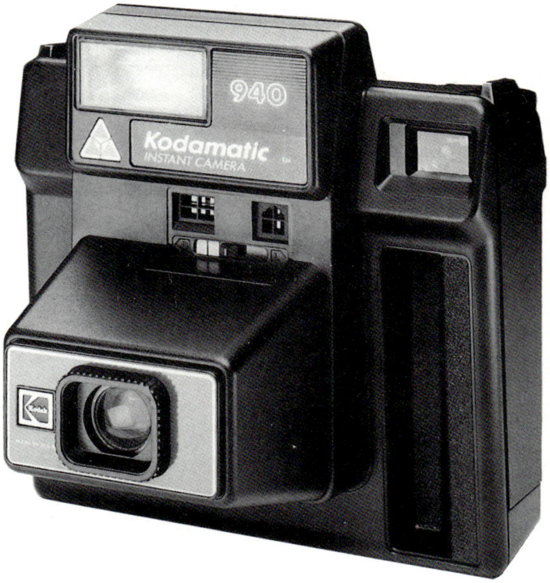

KP

Introduced April 1983
Discontinued April 1984
Manufactured US
Lens f/12.8, 100mm fixed focus
Shutter Electronic 1/15 – 1/250 sec.

Description/Remarks

Built-in electronic flash. Name changed to Kodak Trimprint 940 Instant camera from April 1984.

Kodamatic 950 Instant

Introduced 1983
Discontinued 1985
Manufactured Germany
Lens Single element f/12.8, 100mm.
Shutter Electronic 1/15 – 1/300 sec.

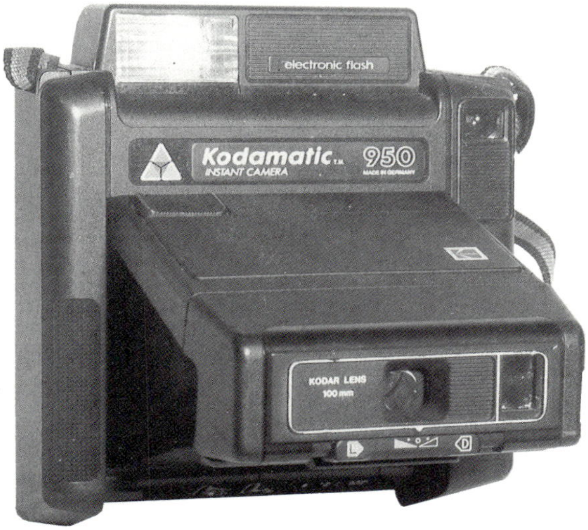

RPS

Description/Remarks

Folding model; automatic exposure; built-in electronic flash, firing automatically on each exposure.

Kodamatic 960 Instant

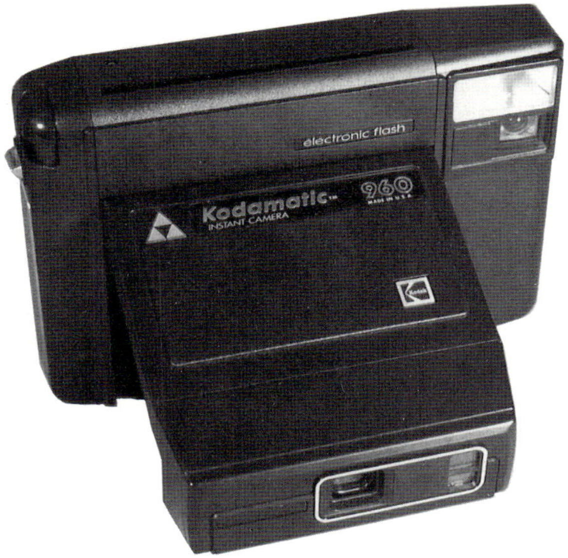

PDM

Introduced April 1982
Discontinued January 1986
Manufactured US
Lens f/12.8, 100mm fixed focus
Shutter Electronic 1/15 – 1/250 sec.

Description/Remarks

Folding model with built-in electronic flash, firing automatically on each exposure.

Produced as Party Star Kodamatic Instant camera for premium sales by Tupperware, 1983–1984, and as Party Star Trimprint Instant camera 1984–1986.

Kodamatic 970L Instant

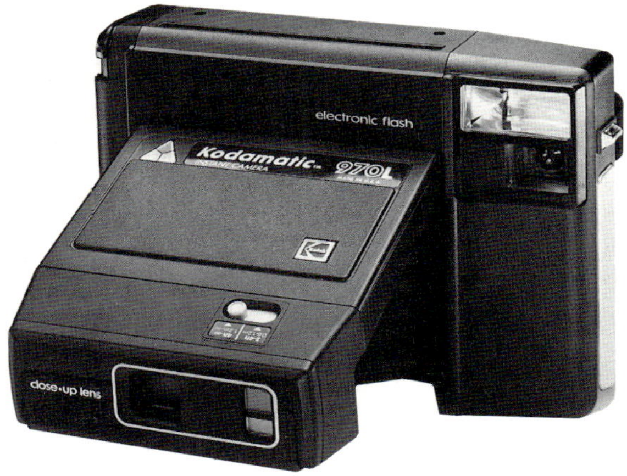

KP

Introduced April 1982
Discontinued January 1986
Manufactured US
Lens f/12.8, 100mm fixed focus, but with close-up lens.
Shutter Electronic 1/15 – 1/250 sec.

Description/Remarks

Folding model, similar to Kodamatic 960 Instant camera, but with close-up lens for pictures from 2 to 4ft.

Kodamatic 980L Instant

Introduced April 1982

Discontinued January 1986
Manufactured US
Lens f/11, 100mm autofocusing
Shutter Electronic $1/4$ – $1/150$ sec.

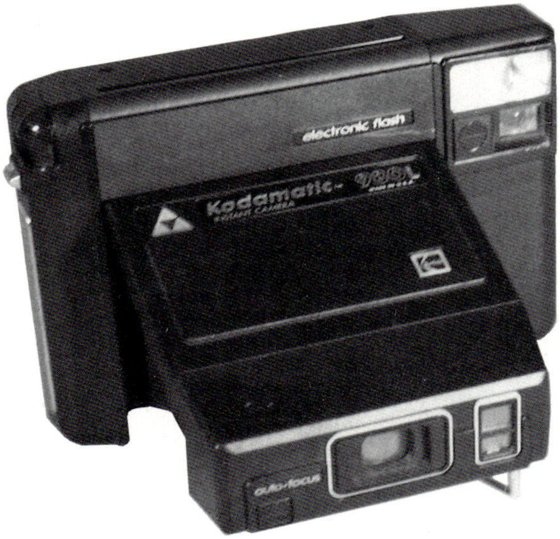

PDM

Description/Remarks

Folding model, similar to Kodamatic 960 Instant camera, but with autofocus feature.

Partyflash Instant camera

See Kodak Colorburst 250 Instant camera.

Partyflash II Kodamatic Instant camera

See Kodak Colorburst 250 Instant camera.

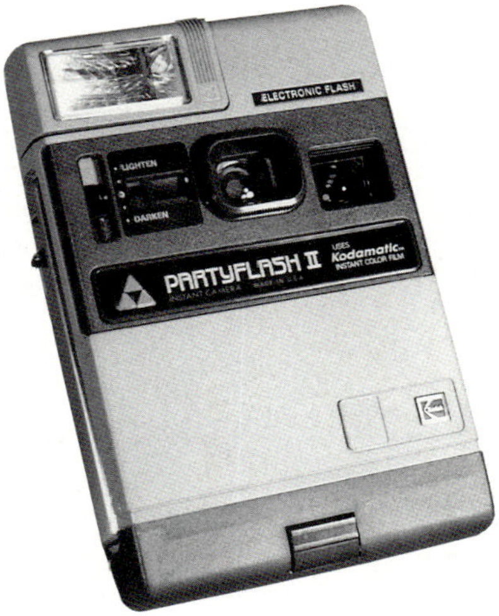

PDM

Party Star Kodamatic Instant camera

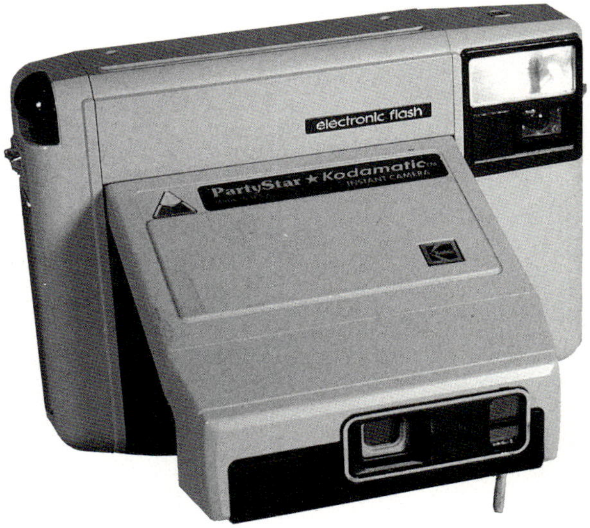

PDM

See Kodamatic 960 Instant camera.

Party Star Trimprint Instant camera

See Kodamatic 960 Instant camera.

Partytime Instant camera

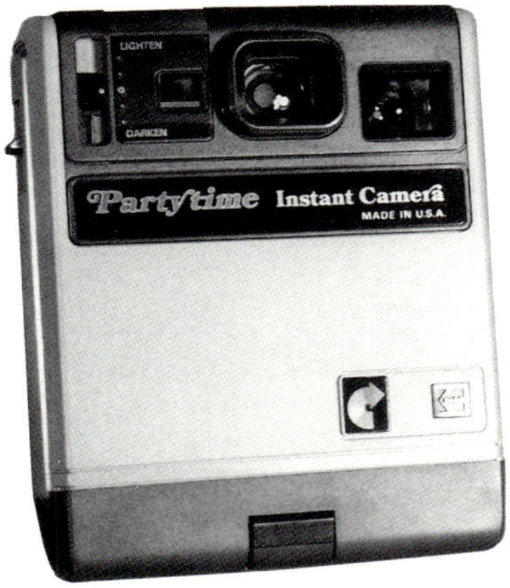

PDM

See Kodak Colorburst 50 Instant camera.

Partytime II Kodamatic Instant camera

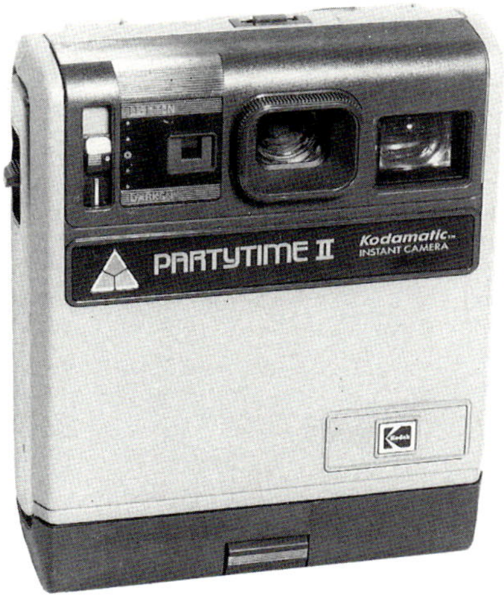

RPS

See Champ Kodamatic Instant camera.

Pleaser Kodak Instant camera

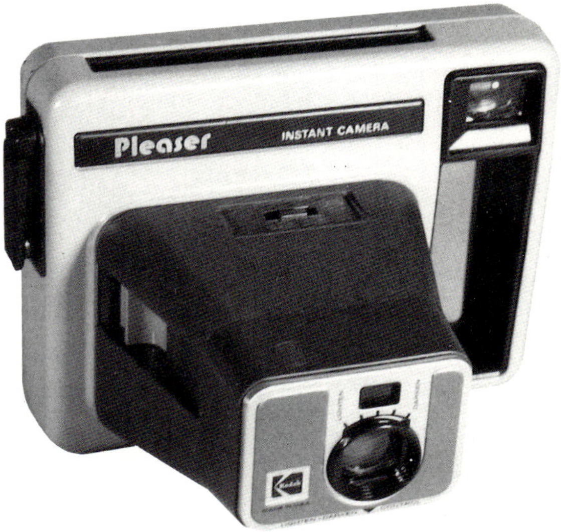

PDM

See The Handle Kodak Instant camera.

Pleaser II Kodamatic Instant

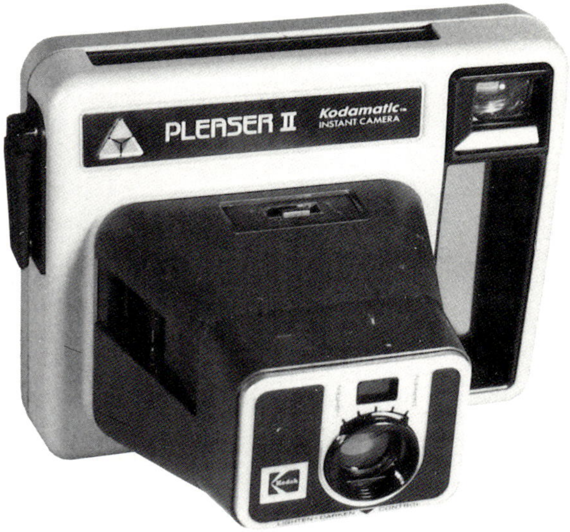

PDM

Introduced April 1982
Discontinued February 1985

Manufactured US
Lens f/12.8, 100mm fixed focus
Shutter Electronic 2 to 1/300 sec.

Description/Remarks

For premium sales only; similar to Champ Kodamatic Instant camera.

Pleaser Trimprint Instant

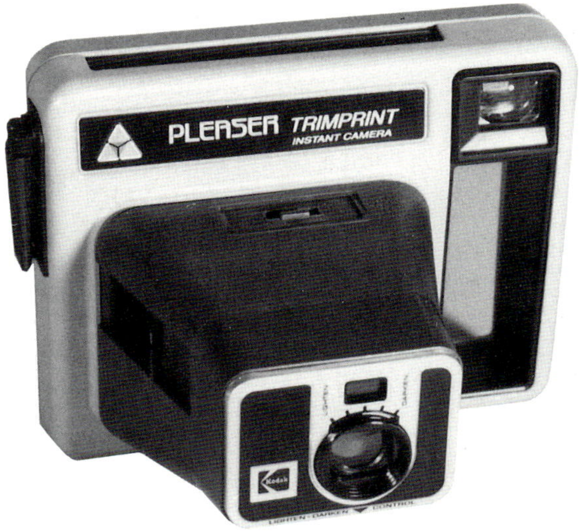

PDM

Introduced October 1984
Discontinued January 1986
Manufactured US
Lens f/12.8, 100mm fixed focus
Shutter Electronic 2 to 1/300 sec.

Description/Remarks

Similar to Pleaser II Instant camera, renamed with introduction of improved Trimprint film pack.

CHAPTER 8 *Kodak Plate Cameras*

Kodak from the beginning concentrated on film cameras. A very limited number of models, mostly early, were designed to take either plates or film, notably the Kodet cameras in the 1890s. Glass plate versions of several of the early string-set cameras were sold, without the roll holders, and the same was true of the first Folding Kodak cameras of the early 1890s. The Eastman Plate cameras of the early years of this century were the only models designed specifically for plate use. Several of the Nagel hand plate cameras continued in production after Dr Nagel-Werke was bought by Kodak in 1931. Otherwise, most of the plate cameras made by Kodak have been specialised professional models, beyond the scope of this book, or cameras made under the Premo or Folmer and Schwing marques, which are listed briefly in Appendix 1.

Anca No.10

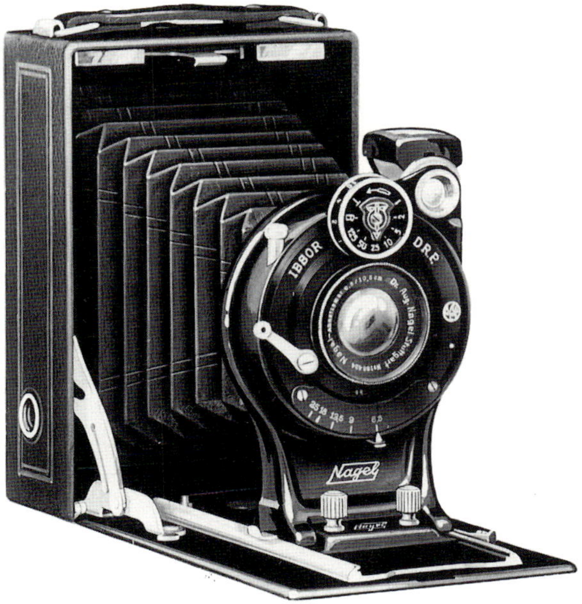

KP

Type Folding Plate
Introduced 1930
Discontinued 1934
Picture size 6 × 9cm
Manufactured Germany
Lens Nagel Anastigmat f/4.5, 10.5cm
Shutters Nagel, Pronto or Pronto S
Numbers made Probably less than 200 with Kodak identification.

Description/Remarks

A Nagel design which was produced from 1928 as Nagel No.10 camera, renamed Anca No.10 in 1930. Only a small number were made after the Kodak acquisition of Nagel Werke.

Single extension; sliding focusing; brilliant finder; leatherette covering.

Anca No.14

Type Folding plate
Introduced 1930
Discontinued 1934
Picture size 6.5 × 9cm
Manufactured Germany
Lenses Radionar f/6.3, 10.5cm, Nagel Anastigmat f/4.5, 10.5cm or Xenar f/4.5,10.5cm.

Shutter Pronto, Pronto S, Compur or Compur S
Numbers made Probably less than 400 with Kodak identification.

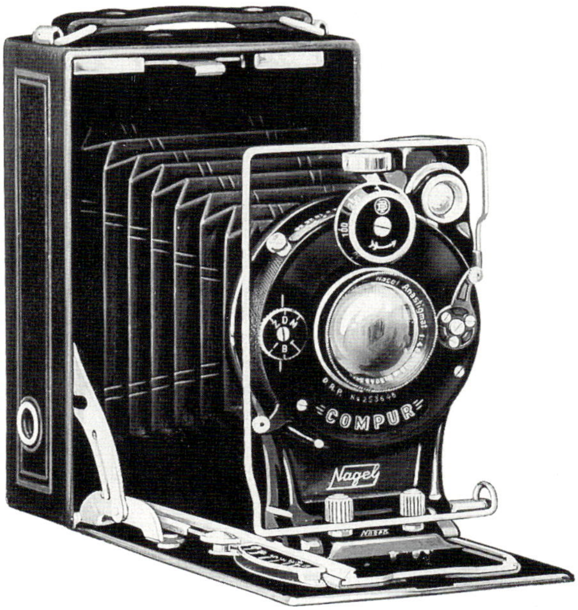

KP

Description/Remarks

A Nagel design produced from 1928 as Nagel No.14 camera, renamed Anca No.14 in 1930. Produced in small numbers only after acquisition of Nagel Werke by Kodak.

Single extension; lever focusing, brilliant and wire frame finders; leather covering.

Anca No.25

Type Folding plate
Introduced 1930
Discontinued 1934
Picture size 9 × 12cm
Manufactured Germany
Lenses Nagel Anastigmat f/6.3, 13.5cm or Nagel Laudar Anastigmat f/4.5, 13.5cm.
Shutters Pronto, Ibsor, Compur
Numbers made A small number only with Kodak identification

Description/Remarks

A Nagel design introduced in 1928 as Nagel No.25 camera, renamed Anca No.25 in 1930. Only limited production after acquisition of Nagel Werke by Kodak.

Slidng focusing, single extension; rising front; brilliant finder; leatherette covering.

Anca No.28

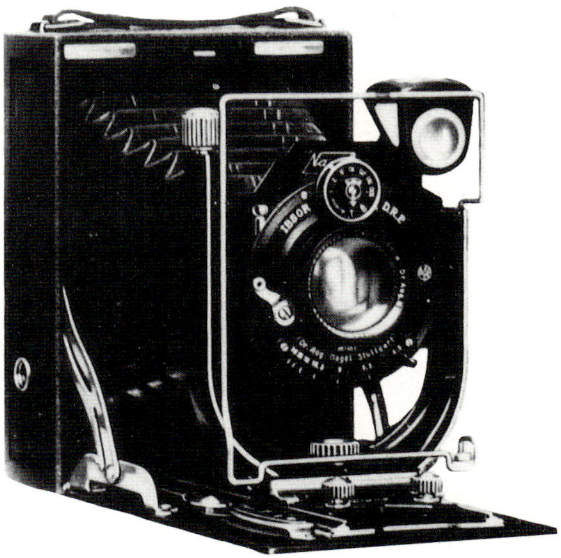

KP

Type Folding plate
Introduced 1930
Discontinued 1934
Picture size 9 × 12cm
Manufactured Germany
Lenses Radioar f/6.3, 13.5cm or Xenar f/4.5, 13.5cm
Shutters Pronto, Pronto S, Compur or Compur S
Numbers made Probably less than 300 with Kodak identification

Description/Remarks

A Nagel design introduced in 1928 as Nagel No.28 camera, renamed Anca No.28 in 1930. Small numbers only were made in 1933–1934 after acquisition by Kodak of Nagel Werke.

Lever focusing; rising front; brilliant and folding frame finders; leather covering.

No 3 Eastman Plate Series C and D

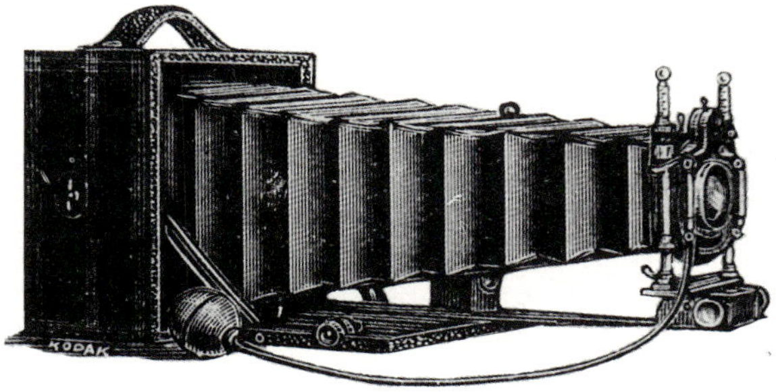

Series D

Type Folding plate
Introduced 1902
Discontinued 1904
Picture size 3¼ × 4¼in.
Manufactured US
Lens Rapid Rectilinear – but see below
Shutters Unicum, Volute or Bausch & Lomb Automatic
Numbers made 1,600 of each series

Description/Remarks

Fine grain leather covering; reversible reflecting finder; rising, falling and cross front; double swing back; ground glass screen with sprung shade; reversible spring back; rack and pinion focusing; Series D has extra long extension allowing use of either the front or back elements of the lens separately; both series numbered from 501. Could be fitted to take a Cartridge Roll Holder.

Sold in UK as Kodak Glass Plate Cameras.

Variations

May 1902: catch for reversible back changed from hook to eyelet and pin, from serial number 1,621.

Rapid Rectilinear: *Jan. 1902–1904:* Bausch & Lomb Automatic shutter; *Sept. 1901–1904:* Unicum shutter.
Plastigmat No 1 f/6.8: *Jan. 1902–1904:* Bausch & Lomb Automatic shutter; *Sept. 1901–1902:* Unicum shutter; *Apr. 1903–1904:* Volute shutter.
Goerz Series III No 0 or No 1 f/6.8: *Apr. 1903–1904:* Bausch & Lomb Automatic or Volute shutter.

No 4 Eastman Plate Series C and D

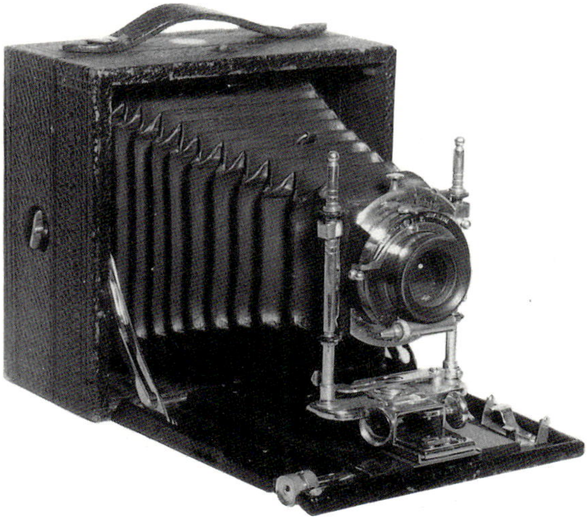

RPS

Type Folding plate
Introduced 1902
Discontinued 1903
Picture size 4 × 5in.
Manufactured US
Lens Rapid Rectilinear – but see below
Shutters Bausch & Lomb Automatic, Volute or Unicum
Numbers made 1,100 Series C
2,100 Series D

Description/Remarks

Fine grain leather covering; reversible reflecting finder; rising, falling and cross front; double swing back; ground glass screen with sprung shade; reversible spring back; rack and pinion focusing; Series D has extra long extension allowing use of either the front or back elements of the lens separately; Series C numbered from 510, Series D from 507. Could be fitted to take a Cartridge Roll Holder.

Sold in UK as Kodak Glass Plate cameras.

Variations

Mar. 1902: catch for reversible back changed from hook to eyelet and pin, from serial number 1,631.

Rapid Rectilinear: *Jan. 1902–1903:* Bausch &

Lomb Automatic shutter; *Sept. 1901–1902:* Unicum shutter.
Plastigmat No 2 f/6.8: *Jan. 1902–1903:* Bausch & Lomb Automatic shutter; *Sept. 1901–1902:* Unicum shutter; *Apr. 1903–1903:* Volute shutter.
Goerz Series III No 1 f/6.8: *Apr. 1903–1903:* Bausch & Lomb Automatic or Volute shutter.

No 5 Eastman Plate Series D

Type Folding plate
Introduced May 1902
Discontinued 1903
Picture size 5 × 7in.
Manufactured US
Lens Rapid Rectilinear – but see below
Shutters Bausch & Lomb Automatic, Volute or Unicum
Numbers made 500

Description/Remarks

Fine grain leather covering; reversible reflecting finder; rising, falling and cross front; double swing back; ground glass screen with sprung shade; reversible spring back; rack and pinion focusing; extra long extension allowing use of either the front or back elements of the lens separately; serial numbers from 501.

Sold in UK as No 5 Kodak Glass Plate camera, in 5x7 and 4¾ × 6½ inch sizes.

Variations

Rapid Rectilinear: *May 1902–1903:* Bausch & Lomb Automatic or Unicum shutter.
Plastigmat No 3 f/6.8: *May 1902–1903:* Bausch & Lomb Automatic shutter; *Apr. 1903–1903:* Volute shutter.
Goerz Series III No 2 f/6.8: *Apr. 1903–1903:* Bausch & Lomb Automatic or Volute shutter.

No 2 Eureka

Type Box plate
Introduced 1898
Discontinued 1899
Film size (106 with roll holder)
Picture size 3½ × 3½in.
Manufactured US
Lens Achromatic
Shutter Rotary shutter
Numbers made 14,000

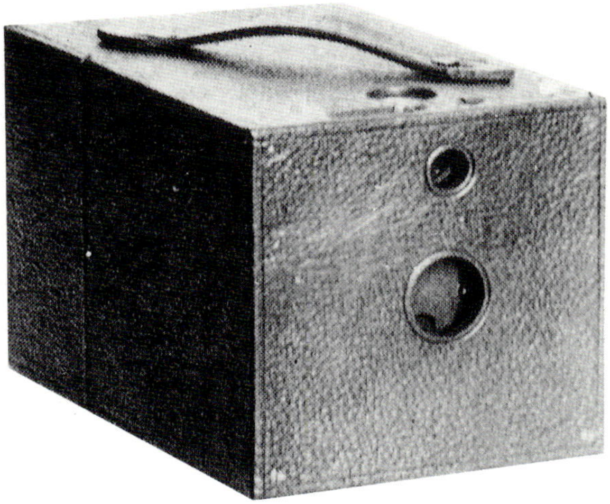

For glass plates

Description/Remarks

Fine grain leather covering; circular reflecting finder; pull-up strips for aperture and shutter setting. Takes double plate holder, but can be used with No 2 Cartridge Roll Holder for rollfilms. From serial number 1.

Variations

Mar. 1898: fitted with improved rotary shutter, from serial number 6,000.

No 4 Eureka

Type Box plate
Introduced 1899
Discontinued 1899
Film size (109 with roll holder)
Picture size 4 × 5in.
Manufactured US
Lens Achromatic
Shutter Rotary
Numbers made 4,500

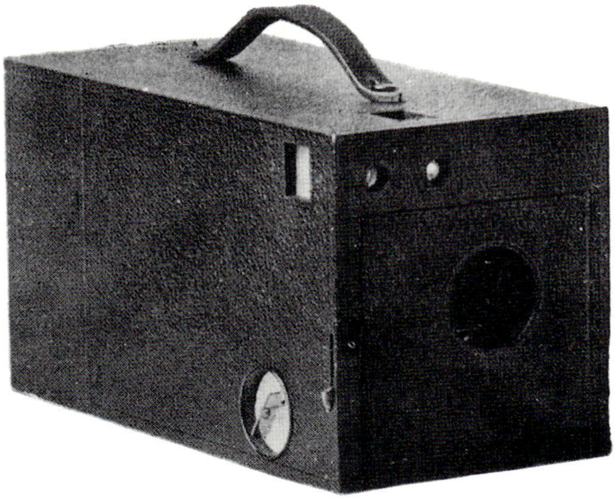

For glass plates

Description/Remarks

Fine grain leather covering; two reflecting finders; front opens for shutter and aperture setting; rack and pinion focusing; takes double plate holders, and can be used with No 4 (horizontal) Cartridge Roll Holder for rollfilms. Serial numbers from 200.

No 2 Eureka Junior

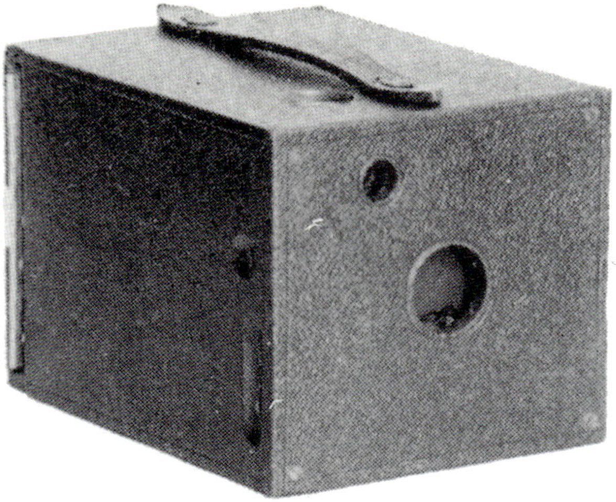

Type Box plate
Introduced 1898
Discontinued 1899
Picture size $3\frac{1}{2} \times 3\frac{1}{2}$in.
Manufactured US
Lens Achromatic
Shutter Rotary
Numbers made 10,000

Description/Remarks

Leatherette covered; circular reflecting finder; aperture adjustment only; takes single metal darkslide.

Nos 4, 5 and 6 Folding Glass Plate Kodak

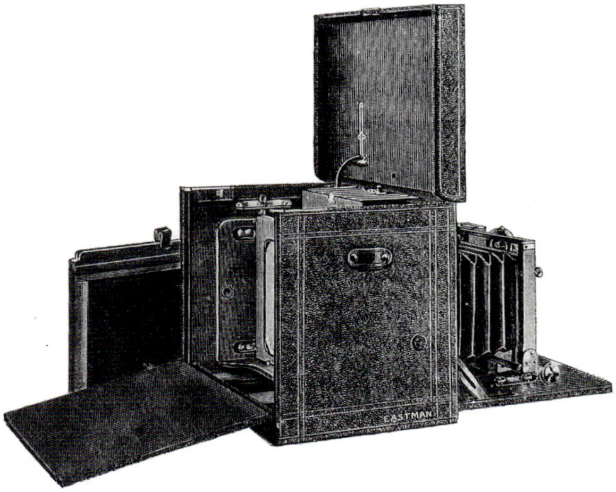

No.6 Glass Plate Kodak camera.

Type Folding plate

Nos 4, 5, and 6 Folding Kodak cameras (q.v.) supplied without roll holders.

Nos 3 and 4 Junior Glass Plate Kodak

Type Box plate

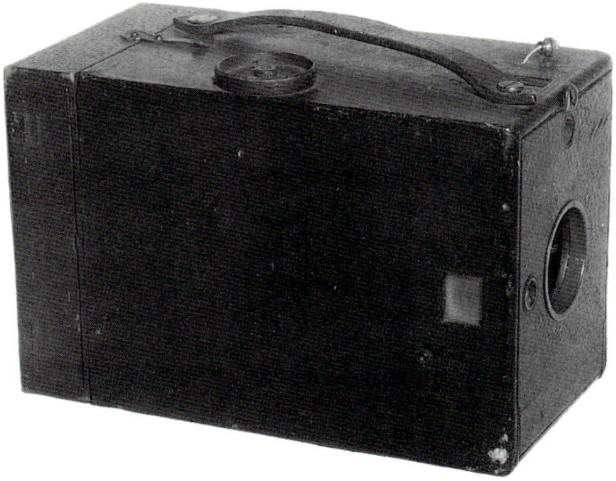

RPS

Nos 3 and 4 Kodak Junior cameras (q.v.) supplied without roll holders.

Kodak Recomar 18

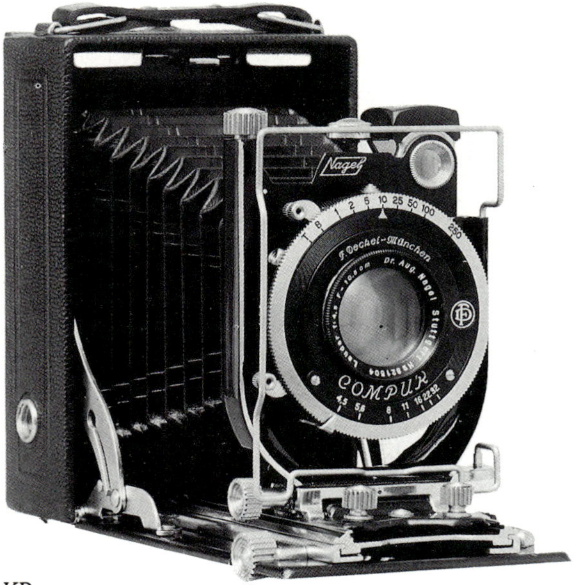

KP

Type Folding plate
Introduced 1930
Discontinued 1939
Picture size 6.5 × 9cm
Manufactured Germany
Lenses Various – see below
Shutters Various – see below
Numbers made 10,500 approximately from 1933.

Description/Remarks

Made first by Nagel-Werke from 1928 as Nagel No. 18, renamed Recomar in 1930. Sold by Kodak after acquisition of Nagel-Werke in 1932.

Leather covered metal body; rack and pinion focusing, double extension; rising and cross front; brilliant and folding wire frame finders.

Variations

Nagel Anastigmat f/6.3, 10.5cm: *1930–1931:* Ibsor shutter.
Nagel Doppel Anastigmat or Laudar Anastigmat f/4.5, 10.5cm: *1930–1931:* Ibsor or Compur shutter; *1931:* Compur S.
Schneider Xenar f/4.5, 10.5 or 12 cm, or f/3.8, 10.5cm: *1930–1931:* Compur shutter; *1931–1939:* Compur S shutter; *1935–1939:* Compur Rapid shutter.
Leitz Elmar f/4.5, 12cm: *1931:* Compur shutter.
Zeiss Tessar f/4.5, 10.5cm: *1933–1934:* Compur S shutter.

Kodak Recomar 33

Type Folding plate
Introduced 1930
Discontinued 1939
Picture size 9 × 12cm
Manufactured Germany
Lenses Various – see below
Shutters Various – see below
Numbers made 13,000+ from 1933

Description/Remarks

Made first by Nagel-Werke from 1928 as Nagel No. 33, renamed Recomar in 1930. Sold by Kodak after acquisition of Nagel-Werke in 1932.

Leather covered metal body; rack and pinion focusing, double extension; rising and cross front; brilliant and folding wire frame finders.

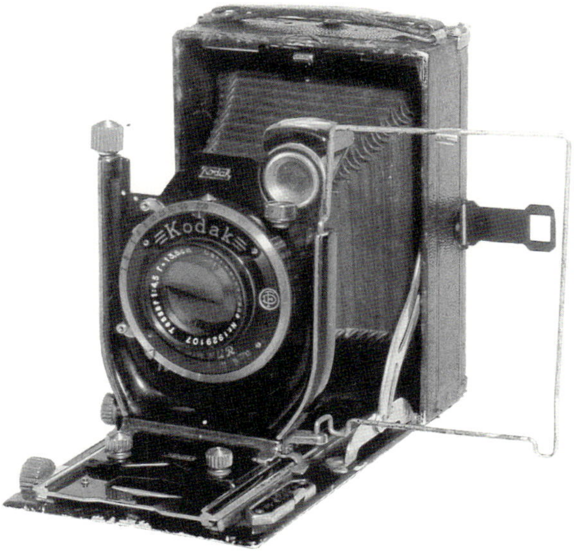

RPS

Variations

Nagel Doppel Anastigmat or Laudar Anastigmat f/4.5, 13.5cm: *1930–1931:* Compur shutter; *1931:* Compur S.
Schneider Xenar f/4.5, 15 or 13.5 cm, or f/3.8, 13.5cm: *1930–1931:* Compur shutter; *1931–1939:* Compur Sshutter; *1935–1939:* Compur Rapid shutter.
Leitz Elmar f/4.5, 12cm: *1931:* Compur shutter.
Zeiss Tessar f/4.5, 13.5cm: *1933–1934:* Compur S shutter.

No 3 Kodet

Type Box plate
Introduced 1894
Discontinued 1896
Picture size 3¼ × 4¼in.
Manufactured US, for UK market only
Lenses Achromatic or Rapid Rectilinear, wheel stops
Shutter Kodet, adjustable
Numbers made 405

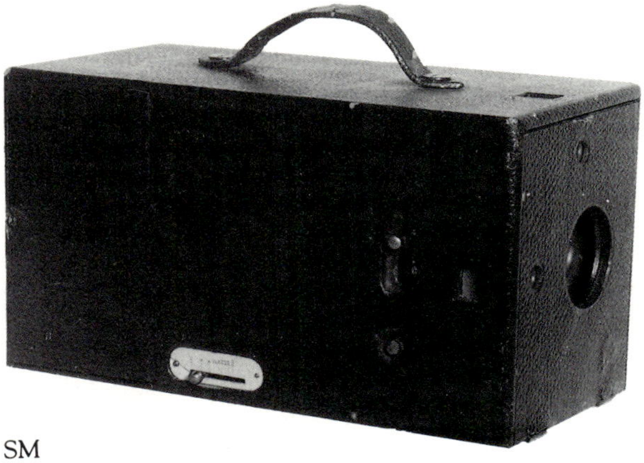

SM

Description/Remarks

Leather covered sycamore or mahogany wood box; focusing control, ground glass screen; two reflecting finders; took double plateholders.

Could be used for darkroom loaded 48-exposure rollfilms by adding Kodet roll holder.

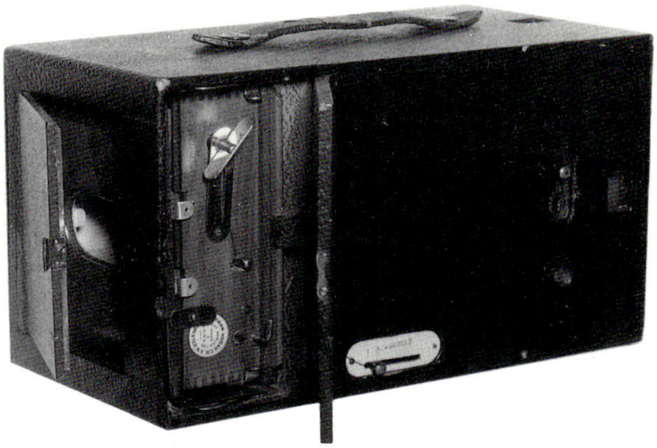

Fitted with roll holder. SM

No 3 Folding Kodet

Type Folding plate
Introduced 1894
Discontinued 1896
Picture size 3¼ × 4¼in.
Manufactured US, for UK market only
Lenses Achromatic or Rapid Rectilinear, wheel stops
Shutter Kodet, adjustable
Numbers made 625

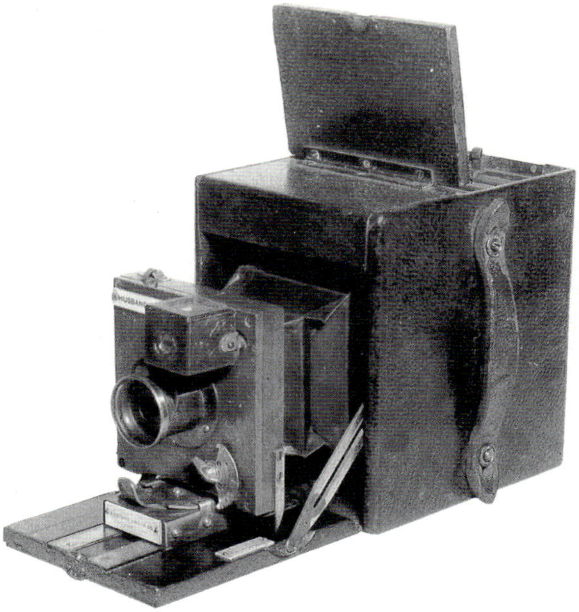

RPS

Description/Remarks

Leather covered mahogany wood box case; reflecting finder on lens panel; sliding focusing; took double plateholder.

Could be used for 48-exposure darkroom loaded rollfilms by adding Kodet roll holder.

No 4 Kodet

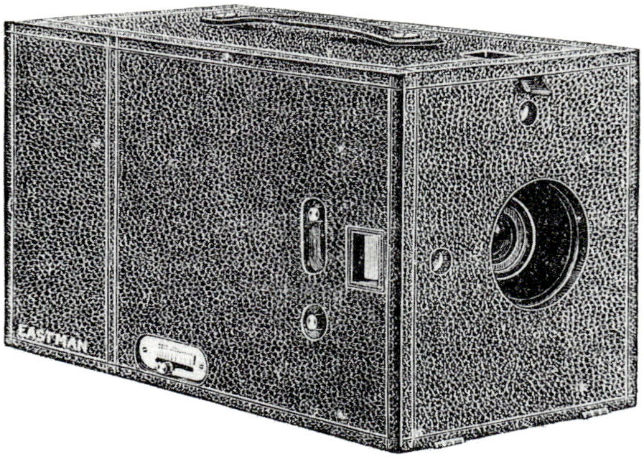

Type Box plate
Introduced 1894
Discontinued 1897
Picture size 4 × 5in.
Manufactured US
Lens Achromatic or Rapid Rectilinear, wheel stops
Shutter Kodet, adjustable
Numbers made 1,413

Description/Remarks

Leather covered sycamore or mahogany wood case; focusing control, ground glass screen; two reflecting finders; took double plateholders.

Could be used with darkroom loaded 48-exposure rollfilms by adding a Kodet roll holder.

No 4 Folding Kodet

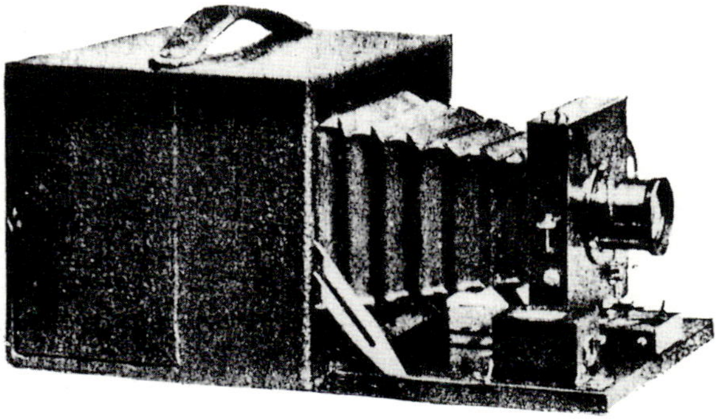

Type Folding plate
Introduced 1894
Discontinued 1897
Picture size 4 × 5in.
Manufactured US
Lenses Achromatic or Rapid Rectilinear
Shutters 1894–1897: Kodet, adjustable
1896–1897: Bausch & Lomb Kodak (with Rapid rectilinear)
1896: Gundlach (with Rapid Rectilinear)
Numbers made 2,246

Description/Remarks

Leather covered mahogany (or sycamore in 1895) wood box case; sliding focusing; reflecting finder on lens panel; took double plateholder.

Could be used for 48-exposure darkroom loaded rollfilms by adding Kodet roll holder.

No 4 Folding Kodet Junior

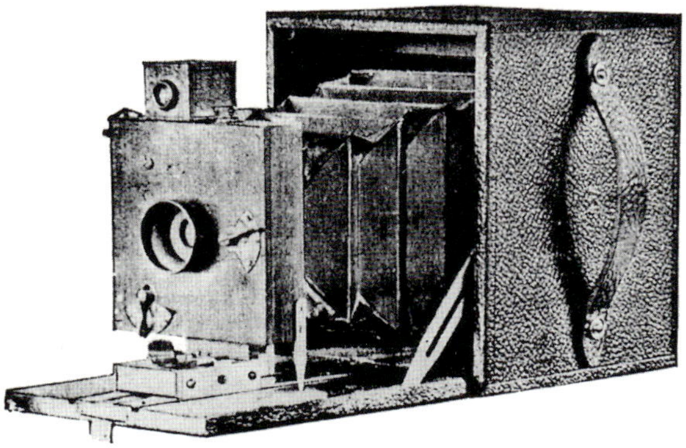

Type Folding plate
Introduced 1894
Discontinued 1897
Picture size 4 × 5in.
Manufactured US
Lens Achromatic
Shutter Kodet, adjustable
Numbers made 1,500

Description/Remarks

Similar to No 4 Folding Kodet, but with lever-set aperture; shutter-setting quadrant to left, below lens, instead of central; central reflecting finder on lens panel; took double plateholder. Could be used for 48-exposure darkroom loaded rollfilm by adding Kodet plateholder.

No 4 Folding Kodet Special

Type Folding plate
Introduced 1895
Discontinued 1897
Picture size 4 × 5in.
Manufactured US
Lenses Achromatic, wheel stops or Rapid Rectilinear, wheel stops or iris, depending on shutter
Shutters Kodet, adjustable
1896: Gundlach, wheel or iris stops
1896–1897: Bausch & Lomb Kodak or Iris Diaphragm
Numbers made 1,950

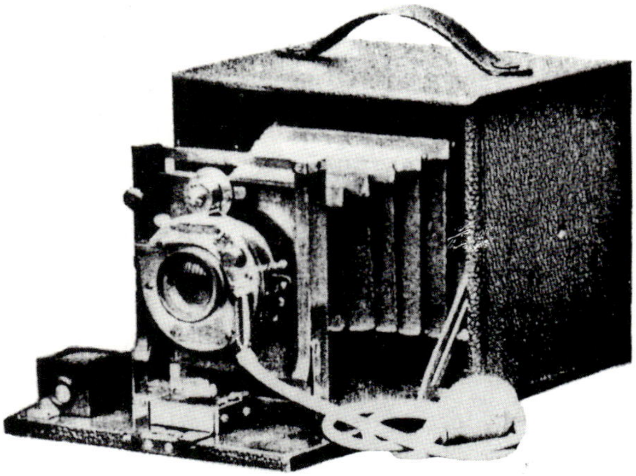

Description/Remarks

Leather covered mahogany wood box case; rising front movement; reflecting finder on baseboard; takes double plateholder.

Could be used for 48-exposure darkroom loaded rollfilm by adding Kodet roll holder.

No 5 Folding Kodet

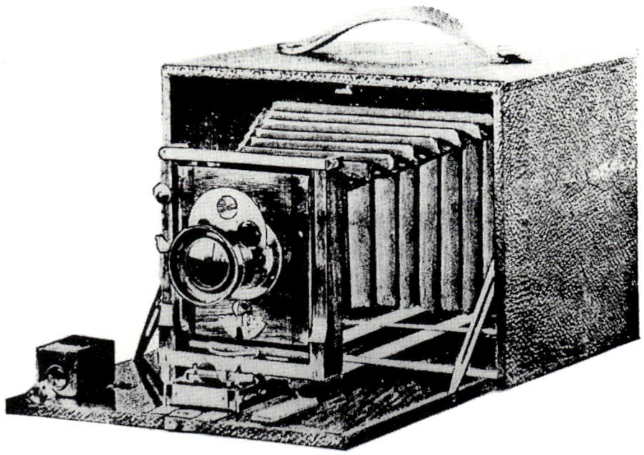

Type Folding plate
Introduced 1895
Discontinued 1897

Picture size 5 × 7in.
Manufactured US
Lenses Achromatic, wheel stops or Rapid Rectilinear, wheel stops or iris, depending on shutter.
Shutters Kodet, adjustable
1896: Gundlach (Rapid Rectilinear)
1896–1897: Bausch & Lomb Kodak (Rapid Rectilinear)
Numbers made 1,300

Description/Remarks

Leather covered mahogany box case; reflecting finder on baseboard; sliding focusing; took double plateholder.

Could be used for 48-exposure darkroom loaded rollfilm by adding Kodet roll holder.

No 5 Folding Kodet Special

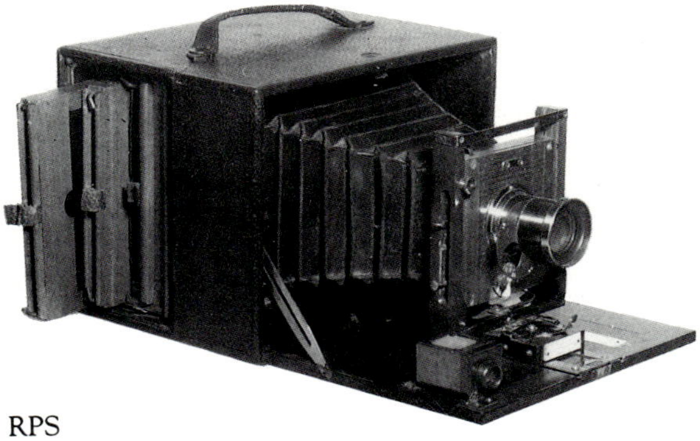

RPS

Type Folding plate
Introduced 1895
Discontinued 1897
Picture size 5 × 7in.
Manufactured US
Lens Rapid Rectilinear, wheel stops or iris, depending on shutter
Shutter Kodet, adjustable
1896: Gundlach
1895–1897: Bausch & Lomb Iris Diaphragm
1896–1897: Bausch & Lomb Kodak
Numbers made 400

Description/Remarks

Leather covered mahogany wood box case; reflecting finder on baseboard; sliding focusing; rising front on some models; took double plateholder.

Could be used for 48-exposure darkroom loaded rollfilm by adding Kodet roll holder.

C Ordinary Glass Plate

Type Box plate

Version of C Ordinary Kodak rollfilm camera (q.v.) supplied without roll holder.

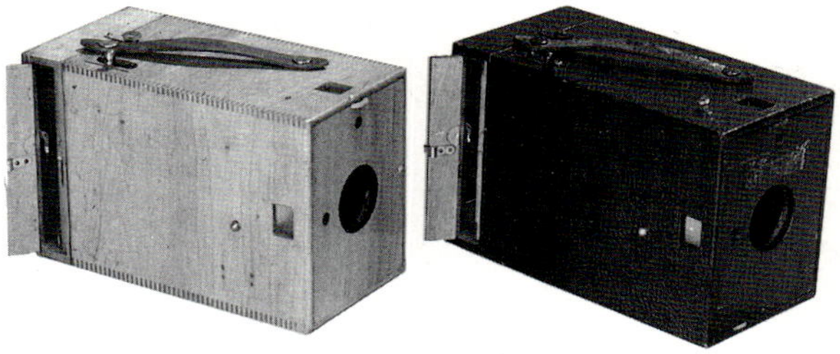

Left: C Ordinary Glass Plate. Right: C Special Glass Plate.

C Special Glass Plate

Type Box plate

Version of C Daylight Kodak rollfilm camera (q.v.) supplied without roll holder.

No 3 Zenith

Type Box plate
Introduced 1899
Discontinued 1900
Film size Cartridge Roll Holder
Picture size 3¼ × 4¼in.
Manufactured US, for UK market only
Lens Achromatic
Shutter Rotary
Numbers made 2,000 (+ 1,000 in 9 × 12cm size)

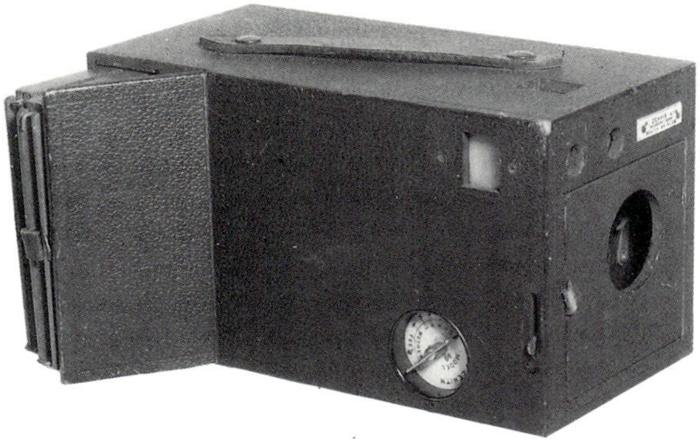

'99 Model. RPS

Description/Remarks

A quarter-plate version of the No 2 Eureka camera made for the English market only, where the Eureka name was already in use by another manufacturer, W.W. Rouch & Co. A quantity were made in the metric 'quarter-plate' size, 9 × 12cm, for the European market. Serial numbers from 200.

Model B, 1900, had an aperture in the front door for a release catch.

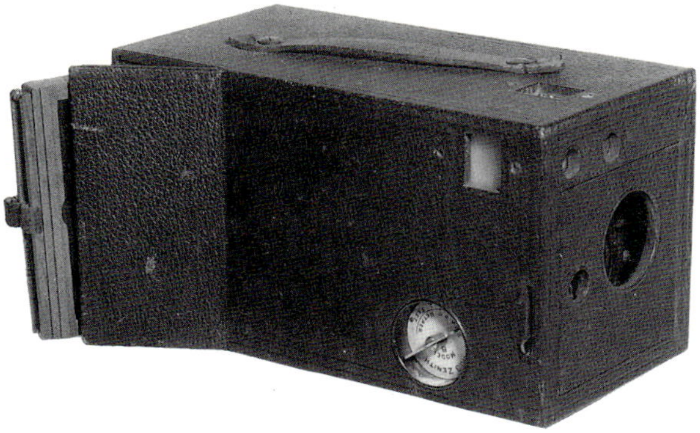

Model B. RPS

No 4 Zenith

Type Box plate
Introduced 1899
Discontinued 1900
Film size 109 with roll holder
Picture size 4 × 5 in.
Manufactured US, for UK market only
Lens Achromatic
Shutter Rotary
Numbers made 1,000+

Description/Remarks

Renamed version of No 4 Eureka camera for UK market, where that name was already in use by another manufacturer; from serial number 701.

CHAPTER 9 *Kodak Specials and Curiosities*

In this chapter are included a small number of Kodak or Kodak-connected items which do not fit easily into the other categories. One, the Queen Mary's Doll's House camera, is unique. Only one example each of a tiny scale model of a box and an Autographic Kodak camera were made. One or two were prototypes, which never reached distribution, but which are included for the reader's interest. The (external) replica of the original Kodak camera, created to celebrate the 100th anniversary of its appearance, may, in time, become a collector's item in its own right.

Anniversary Brownie

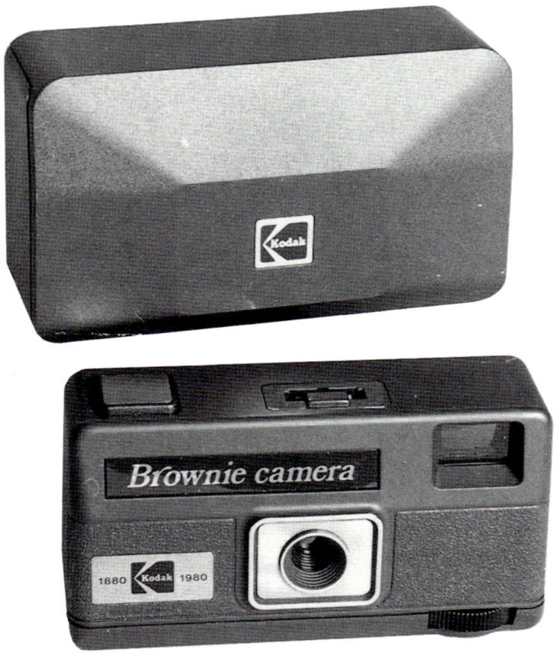

KM

Type Eyelevel 110 cartridge loading

Description/Remarks

A renamed version of the Kodak Limited pocket A1 camera was designed in 1979 for the 100th anniversary, in 1980, of the founding of George Eastman's company. The body was moulded in milk-chocolate-brown plastic, with gilt nameplate, lens panel and centenary motif. A matching hard ever-ready case was also designed. A small number were made for evaluation, but the decision was made not to market this attractive model. However, the standard A1 model in black plastic with silver trim, but no anniversary logo, was renamed the Kodak Brownie camera (q.v.) in Spring 1980.

Eastman Detective

Type Darkroom loaded rollfilm box
Introduced 1886
Discontinued 1888
Film size Darkroom loaded stripping film
Picture size 4 × 5in.
Manufactured US
Lens Not known
Shutter Special slit
Numbers made 40 approximately

Description/Remarks

Not strictly speaking a Kodak camera, since it was designed two years before the first Kodak camera. A modified Eastman-Walker roll holder (removable to

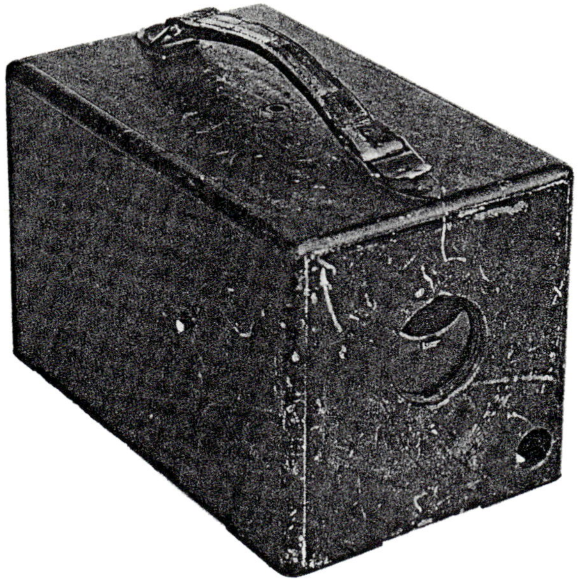

Photo courtesy of History of Photography Collection, Smithsonian Institution

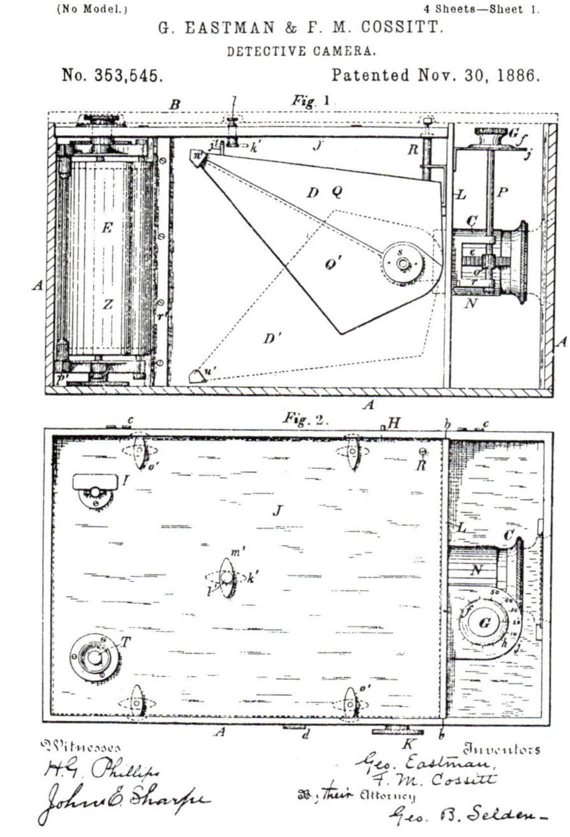

Extract from patent application

allow plates to be used) was fitted in a wooden box. The shutter was unusual – a prism-shaped pivoted metal box, the narrow apex of which swung close to the focal plane. Eastman found it too expensive to produce in quantity, and after making about forty, he sold them as a lot to W.H. Walmsey, a Philadelphia dealer for sale at $50 each.

Only one is known to have survived, and is in the Smithsonian Institution in Washington.

Eastman M.B., or Match Box

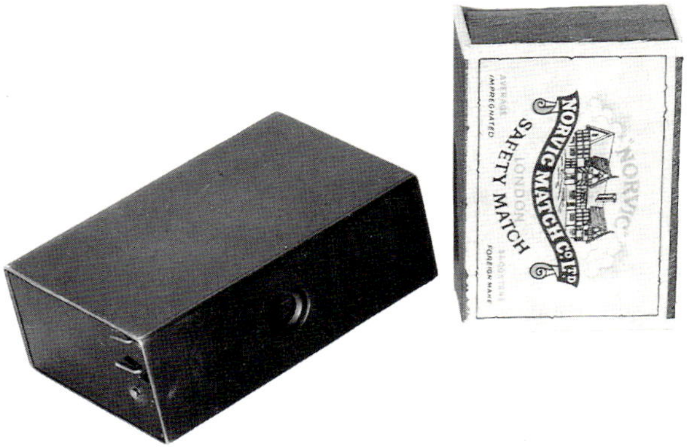

KM

Type Subminiature 16mm box camera
Introduced 1944
Discontinued 1945
Film size 16mm film in 30-exposure cassettes
Picture size 12.5 × 12.5mm
Manufactured US
Lens f/5, 1 inch fixed focus
Shutter Single speed 1/50 sec., and time
Numbers made About 1,000

Description/Remarks

Created for the OSS, and used by American and European agents and members of Resistance movements in occupied Europe. The featureless metal case was the size of a standard match box, and it could be disguised as such, with controls recessed at one end. The lens covered from 8 feet to infinity with a 45 degree angle of view. A processing kit and close-up stand for document copying were also available.

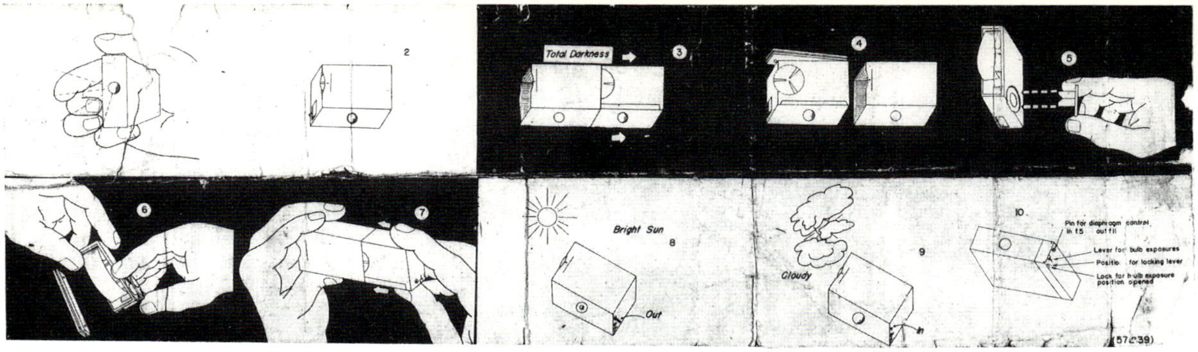

Instruction sheet for Eastman Match-box camera. KM

Eastman Pinhole

Type Box camera kit
Introduced June 1930
Discontinued 1950s
Film size Cut film
Picture size 3¼ × 4¼in.
Manufactured US
Lens Pinhole
Shutter Pivoted card cover

Description/Remarks

Kit for making a box camera; five scored card pieces, with gummed paper tape, to assemble into sliding box-form camera, together with a pin to make the pinhole. Full instructions supplied.

The G.E.C. Transistomatic

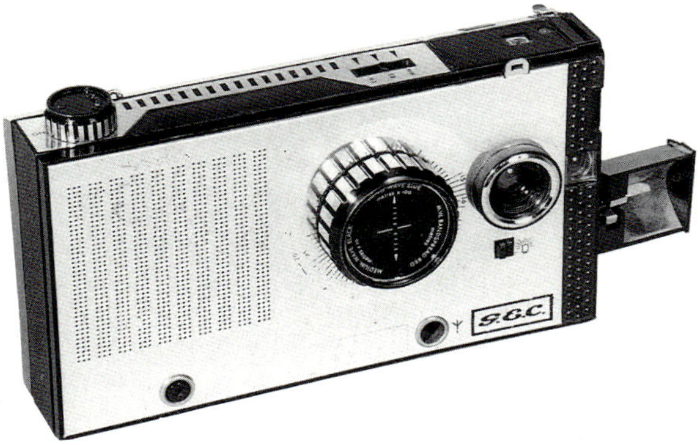

KM

Type Cartridge loading camera combined with radio
Introduced 1964

Description/Remarks

A Kodak Instamatic 100 camera, made in the UK, incorporated into a General Electric Company transistor radio. Not a particularly happy combination— awkward to use as a camera and adding to the bulk of the radio.

George Washington Kodak

Type Box roll film
Introduced 1932
Discontinued 1932
Film size 120
Picture size 2¼ × 3¼in.
Manufactured US
Lens meniscus
Shutter rotary

Description/Remarks

Very similar to the Eastman Anniversary camera, but with silver badge and motifs on front panel. Intended as a celebration of George Washington's bi-centenary, but not distributed.

The Kodak camera, 1988 facsimile

Type Copy of darkroom loaded rollfilm box

Description/Remarks

An external facsimile of the first Kodak camera (no working parts) made in England to celebrate its centenary. Manufacture (by a maker of musical instruments in Bradford, England) was coordinated by Kodak Limited, in association with the Kodak Museum at the National Museum of Photography, Film and Television in Bradford. Approaching 2,500 were manufactured and distributed world-wide through the Kodak organisation. The copy was sealed with a reproduction of the original quality seal, and supplied with reproductions of the instruction manual and exposure memorandum book.

Peer 100

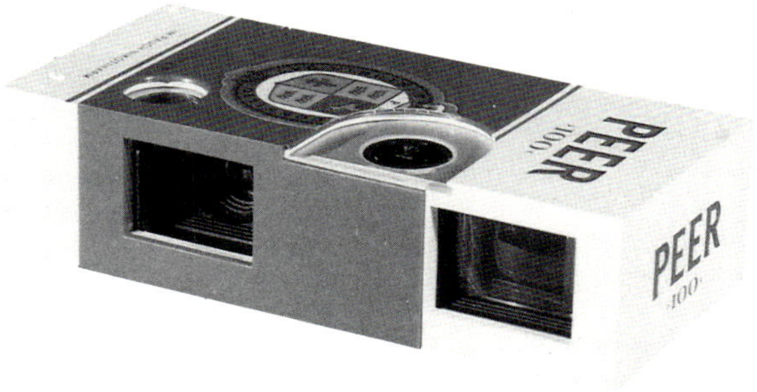

KM

Type Disguised pocket
Introduced 1976
Discontinued –
Film size 110 cartridge
Picture size 13 × 17mm
Manufactured Germany
Lens Kodak triplet f/11, 25mm fixed focus
Shutter Single speed 1/60 sec.
Numbers made ?

Description/Remarks

A Kodak pocket Instamatic 100 mechanism in a red and white plastic case closely resembling a pack of Peer cigarettes, with sliding covers for lens, finder etc. when not in use. A promotional model for the cigarette manufacturer.

Queen Mary's Doll's-house cameras

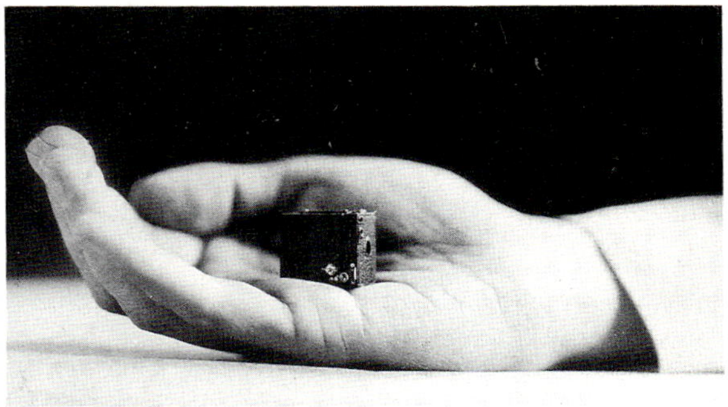

Scale model No 2C Brownie camera. KM

Type Miniature model rollfilm

Description/Remarks

In 1924 Queen Mary set up a project to create and furnish a large doll's-house with miniature versions of products by leading manufacturers, with the object that the completed work would be exhibited for charity. Kodak Limited craftsmen created first a 1/8th scale fully working model of a No 2C Brownie box camera, using a microscope objective lens, and watchmaker's jewels for the viewfinder lenses. Clear photographs were made with it, on small pieces of cut film placed in the back. Presumably on the assumption that such a grand house would have something rather more impressive than the humble box camera, a second camera was built, a scale model of a No 3A Autographic Kodak camera, which was presented to the project. The doll's-house is now at Windsor Castle. The box camera went to the Kodak

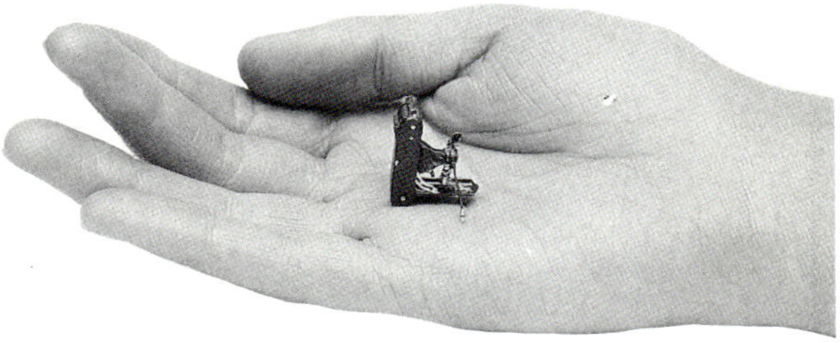

Scale model No 3A Autographic Kodak camerea. KP

Museum and is now with that collection at the National Museum of Photography, Film and Television at Bradford.

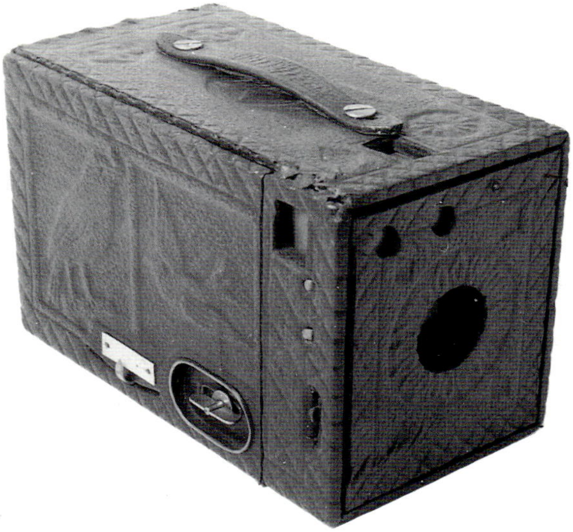

No.4 Bulls-eye Special camera, with original covering replaced by hand-tooled leather by an Alaskan hunter. TNC

Glossary

Accessory shoe – A flat socket, usually on the camera top, by which accessories may be attached.

AG1 bulb – A small capless bulb with two wire contacts on a flattened base.

Aspheric lens – A lens in which the radius of curvature of the lens surface varies across its diameter, enabling a high degree of correction of aberrations to be achieved.

Autofocus – A feature whereby the lens focusing is set by an automatic mechanism using a ranging method employing infra-red or other optical systems.

Autographic feature – An invention by Henry Gaisman, in which information could be 'written' on the film with a metal stylus at the time of exposure through a hinged flap on the camera back.

Automatic focusing lock – A pre-set stop on the camera baseboard by which the lens panel may be drawn out to a selected focusing position.

Baseboard – The hinged panel which covers the lens and bellows when closed, and which when pulled down provides a bed with rails along which the lens panel may be drawn into the operating position.

Bayonet flash socket – A flash connection in which an outer cylindrical contact carries two studs which are engaged by L-shaped slots on the flash lead plug, providing a secure connection.

Body release – A shutter release button on the camera body, usually convenient to the forefinger of the right hand, connected by mechanical linkage to the shutter mechanism.

Brightline finder – A direct vision optical finder with a bright frame suspended in the field of view, produced by optical means.

Brilliant finder – A reflecting finder with a field lens rather than a ground glass screen for receiving the image, giving a clearer, brighter image.

Capless bulb – A flash bulb without a metal base cap, with two contact wires on a tapering cylindrical glass base.

Cartridge film – 1. An early name for the paper-backed rollfilm, named for its similarity in shape to a shot-gun cartridge, and for its comparative ease of loading.
2. A drop-in loading film in a plastic casing, introduced first in 1963 for the Kodak Instamatic cameras.

CdS cell – A photo-conductive cell using Cadmium sulphide as the active agent. The electrical resistance of the cell falls progressively with increasing brightness, and the cell, in series with a small battery, can thus be used for exposure meters or automatic setting of a lens aperture or shutter. Silicon or other cells may be used for the same purpose. Such cells may be quite small, and require only a small window, unlike photo-electric cells (q.v.).

Click stops – Pre-set positions on a lens focusing setting, allowing it to be set rapidly to particular distances.

Coaxial flash socket – A flash connection consisting of a narrow central tubular contact with a concentric insulating layer and outer cylindrical contact.

Coincidence rangefinder – An optical device for accurate measurement of distance, using the principle of adjusting two superimposed images until they form one, when the correct focus is obtained.

Combination back – A removable back for folding cameras permitting the camera to be used with a plate holder instead of a rollfilm when required.

Coupled rangefinder – An optical device for accurate measurement of distance, the setting of which is directly coupled to the lens focusing mechanism.

Dual format – Cameras in which two picture sizes are possible, by means of a removable mask in the camera back.

Direct vision finder – An optical viewfinder usually taking the form of an inverted Galilean telescope, with negative front and positive rear lenses. Some later 'DV' finders have a 'brightline' feature (q.v.).

EV scale – Exposure value settings, in which the

shutter speed and aperture settings are expressed as a single scale of numbers.

Film carrier – The internal frame on which the film spools are carried.

Film guide rollers – Rollers on either side of the exposure aperture, over which the roll film passes through the camera back.

Film tension springs – Springs bearing on the ends or centre of the rollfilm, preventing it from unwinding too readily and thus maintaining flatness in the exposing aperture.

Flash cube – A combination of four AG1 size flash bulbs with associated reflectors in a small transparent cube. This structure requires only a suitable socket and a battery in the camera.

Flipflash – An vertical array of ten flash bulbs in a plastic mount. Thermal switches automatically connect the next bulb as each is fired. Connection is made via a flat rectangular socket on the camera.

Frame finder – A folding viewfinder with a front frame and rear peep-sight.

Front-cell focusing – A focusing method using a rotation of the front element only of the lens.

Helical focusing – A focusing method in which the whole lens is moved for focusing by means of a multi-start helical threaded mount.

Hot shoe – A flash connection in which electrical contacts are incorporated in an accessory shoe.

Lazy-tong struts – Scissor-shaped side struts by which the lens panel may be extended and held in position.

Lever focusing – A focusing method in which the lens panel is moved backwards and forwards by moving a pivoted lever.

Magicube – A four-bulb cube similar in appearance to the earlier flash-cube, but in which the bulbs are fired by the release of a spring striker hitting a percussion cap in the base of the bulb. The camera requires only a mechanical release, with no electrical power.

Noiseless winding key – A winding key mechanism in which back-winding is prevented by a quiet mechanism, instead of a noisy ratchet.

Optical frame finder – A folding viewfinder with, usually, negative front and positive rear lenses.

Photo-electric cell – A selenium cell which generates an electric current in proportion to the light falling on it. Used in exposure meters and early automatic exposure systems.

Reflecting finder – A finder with a front lens, a mirror at 45 degrees behind it and a ground glass screen above, on which an image is cast. Sometimes called a waist-level finder, since the image is seen by looking down into it.

Roll holder – An attachment for a camera designed to use plates, by which a rollfilm may be used instead.

Screw and pin flash contacts – A flash connection by which electrical contact is made with the flash gun through the attaching screw and a separate pin.

Self-erecting construction – A mechanical system whereby the lens panel of a camera is brought automatically into operating position as the baseboard is drawn down.

Self-quenching flash – An electronic flash unit in which a photo-cell measures the light reflected from the subject and turns off the flash as soon as sufficient exposure has been given.

Silicon cell – A photo-conductive cell; see CdS cell

Split-image rangefinder – A optical system for accurate measurement of distance which operates by aligning the top and bottom halves of a split view of the scene.

Spool centres – The pins on which the film spool is held and rotates in the camera back. Often, these could be retracted from outside the camera.

String-set shutter – Used on the early Kodak cameras; the shutter was cocked by pulling a gut string from outside the camera.

Stripping film – A paper negative 'film' used in the earliest Kodak cameras, in which after exposure, the processed image could be removed from the paper base and laid down on glass or other clear support for printing.

Support foot – A folding, pivoted or retractable support at the front of the baseboard, used to allow the camera to stand upright on a flat surface during time exposures.

Two-pin flash contact – a connection for a flash gun using two short pins on an insulating strip.

Zooming circle – A focus-setting optical system used in some Kodak Instant cameras, in which a bright circle in the finder could be enlarged or diminished until it just enclosed the head of the subject, when the focusing was approximately correct.

Appendix 1

Hawk-Eye cameras

The Hawk-Eye trademark was originally owned by the Boston Camera Company, and passed to the Blair Camera Company when they bought the Boston firm in 1890. In 1907 Eastman Kodak Company bought Blair outright and moved the plant to Rochester to form the Blair Camera Division. The production of Hawk-Eye cameras continued, but after World War One the majority of cameras bearing this name were made for premium sales only, and are not always listed in regular catalogues. Some Hawk-Eye cameras were manufactured in England by Kodak Limited from 1927 to 1939, including locally designed models, among them the first Kodak all-plastic camera, the No 2 Hawkette. In later models, including those of Kodak Limited, the hyphen was dropped from the name.

Only those Hawk-Eye cameras made after the takeover by Kodak are listed here.

Name	*Dates*	*Film type*
Baby Hawkeye (UK)	1949–1951	620
Brownie Hawkeye	1949–1951	620
Brownie Hawkeye Flash model	1950–1961	620
2 Cartridge Hawk-Eye	1924–1925	120
2 Cartridge Hawk-Eye mod B	1926–1933	120
2 Cartridge Hawk-Eye mod C	1926–1934	120
2 Cartridge Hawk-Eye mod CC (UK)	1927–1930	120
2A Cartridge Hawk-Eye	1924–1925	116
2 Film-Pack Hawk-Eye	1922–1925	520
2A Film-Pack Hawk-Eye	1923–1925	516
2 Folding Cartridge Hawk-Eye mod B	1926–1934	120
2A Folding Cartridge Hawk-Eye mod B	1926–1934	116
3A Folding Cartridge Hawk-Eye mod B	1926–1935	122
2 Folding Film-Pack Hawk-Eye	1923–1923	520
1A Folding Hawk-Eye mod 1	1908–1912	116
1A Folding Hawk-Eye mod 2	1913–1915	116
2 Folding Hawk-Eye Special	1929–1933	120
2A Folding Hawk-Eye Special	1929–1933	116
3 Folding Hawk-Eye mod 5	1908–1909	118
3 Folding Hawk-Eye mod 6	1908–1910	118
3 Folding Hawk-Eye mod 7	1910–1912	118
3 Folding Hawk-Eye mod 8	1911–1915	118
3 Folding Hawk-Eye mod 9	1913–1915	118
3A Folding Hawk-Eye mod 1	1908–1909	122
3A Folding Hawk-Eye mod 2	1908–1909	122
3A Folding Hawk-Eye mod 3	1910–1915	122
3A Folding Hawk-Eye mod 4	1910–1915	122
3A Folding Hawk-Eye Special	1929–1933	122
4 Folding Hawk-Eye mod 3	1905–1913	123
4 Folding Hawk-Eye mod 4	1905–1913	123
2 Folding Rainbow Hawk-Eye mod B	1931–1932	120
2 Folding Rainbow Hawk-Eye Special	1930–1933	120
2A Folding Rainbow Hawk-Eye mod B	1930–1933	116
2A Folding Rainbow Hawk-Eye Special	1930–1933	116
0 Hawkeye (UK)	1938–1938	127
2 Hawkette (UK) (see Chapter 3)	1930–1930	120
2 Hawk-Eye	1914–1915	120
2 Hawk-Eye Special	1928–1930	120
2A Hawk-Eye	1914–1915	116
2A Hawk-Eye Special	1928–1930	116
Hawkeye Ace (UK)	1938–1938	127
Hawkeye Ace de Luxe (UK)	1938–1938	127
Hawkeye Flashfun	1961–1967	127
Hawkeye Flashfun II	1965–1969	127
Hawkeye Instamatic	1964–1964	126
Hawkeye Instamatic II	1969–1972	126
Hawkeye Instamatic A1	1969–1972	126
Hawkeye Instamatic F	1964–1968	126

Name	Dates	Film type
Hawkeye Instamatic R4	1966–1971	126
Hawkeye Instamatic X	1971–1978	126
Hawkeye Pocket Instamatic	1973–1979	110
Hawkeye Pocket Instamatic III	1974–1979	110
Hawkeye Tele-Instamatic	1976–1979	110
2 Portrait Hawkeye (UK)	1930–1930	120
2 Rainbow Hawk-Eye mod B	1930–1933	120
2 Rainbow Hawk-Eye mod C	1930–1933	120
2A Rainbow Hawk-Eye mod B	1931–1932	116
Six-16 Folding Hawk-Eye	1933–1934	616
Six-16 Target Hawk-Eye	1933–1933	616
Six-20 Folding Hawk-Eye	1933–1934	620
Six-20 Hawkeye (UK)	1938–1938	620
Six-20 Hawkeye mod HB (UK)	1933–1933	620
Six-20 Hawkeye Major (UK)	1935–1935	620
Six-20 Target Hawk-Eye	1933–1933	620
Six-20 Portrait Hawkeye (UK)	1933–1933	620
Six-20 Portrait Hawkeye A Star A (UK)	1933–1933	620
Six-20 Portrait Hawkeye Star (UK)	1933–1933	620
Stereo Hawk-Eye mod 3	1907–1911	101
Stereo Hawk-Eye mod 4	1907–1911	101
Stereo Hawk-Eye mod 5	1912–1913	101
Stereo Hawk-Eye mod 6	1912–1913	101
2A Target Hawk-Eye	1932–1932	116
Vest Pocket Hawk-Eye	1927–1934	127
Vest Pocket Rainbow Hawk-Eye	1931–1933	127
2 Weno Hawk-Eye	1904–1915	101
4 Weno Hawk-Eye	1904–1915	103
5 Weno Hawk-Eye	1905–1915	118
7 Weno Hawk-Eye	1908–1915	122

Premo cameras

The Premo trademark was assigned to the Rochester Optical and Camera Company in 1899; it had been in use since 1893. Rochester Optical was bought by Eastman Kodak Company in 1907, to form the Rochester Optical Divison, Eastman Kodak Company. The name changed to Rochester Optical Department in 1918, and was finally dropped in 1922.

The Premo camera range had been mainly plate cameras; in 1903 a new form of camera was introduced. It was based on an invention by the English camera maker J.E. Thornton, co-founder of the famous Thornton-Pickard camera company. A set of celluloid cut films were held in a flat container. Each had a numbered paper tab attached; after each exposure the tab was pulled, drawing the exposed film from the front to the back of the pack, and torn off. Adaptors for the film pack were made to fit many cameras, and Rochester Optical designed new cameras with integral holders for the new medium, which was popular with photographers, being compact and light, compared with plates in their holders. Most of the cameras made by Kodak under the Premo trademark after 1907 were film pack models.

The cameras listed here are only those made after the take-over of Rochester Optical by Eastman Kodak.

Name		Type	Dates
00 Cartridge Premo		No 35	1916–1922
2 Cartridge Premo		120	1916–1922
2A Cartridge Premo		116	1916–1922
2C Cartridge Premo		130	1917–1922
Film Premo No 1	3 sizes	filmpack	1906–1916
Film Premo No 3	3 sizes	filmpack	1906–1910
Filmplate Premo	3 sizes	plate/ filmpack	1906–1916
Filmplate Premo Special	4 sizes	plate/ filmpack	1912–1916
2 Folding Cartridge Premo		120	1916–1922
2A Folding Cartridge Premo		116	1916–1922
2C Folding Cartridge Premo		130	1917–1922
3A Folding Cartridge Premo		122	1917–1922
Pocket Premo		filmpack	1918–1922
Pocket Premo C		plate/ filmpack	1904–1916
2 Pony Premo	3 sizes	filmpack	1904–1912
3 Pony Premo	3 sizes	plate	1904–1912
4 Pony Premo	2 sizes	plate	1906–1912
6 Pony Premo	3 sizes	plate	1906–1912
7 Pony Premo	3 sizes	plate	1907–1912
8 Premo	3 sizes	plate/ filmpack	1913–1922
9 Premo	3 sizes	plate/ filmpack	1913–1922
10 Premo		plate/ filmpack	1913–1922
12 Premo		plate/ filmpack	1916–1922
Premo Junior	5 sizes	filmpack	1908–1916
Premoette Junior		filmpack	1911–1911
Premoette Senior	3 sizes	filmpack	1915–1922
1 Premoette		filmpack	1909–1912
1 Premoette Junior		filmpack	1912–1922

Camera	*Type*	*Dates*
1 Premoette Junior Special	filmpack	1913–1918
1 Premoette Special	filmpack	1909–1911
1A Premoette	filmpack	1909–1912
1A Premoette Junior	filmpack	1912–1916
1A Premoette Junior Special	filmpack	1913–1918
1A Premoette Special	filmpack	1909–1911
Premograph	filmpack	1907–1908
2 Premograph	filmpack	1908–1909
4 Stereo Pony Premo	plate	1904–1912
6 Stereo Pony Premo	plate	1904–1912
7 Stereo Pony Premo	plate	1904–1912

Folmer and Schwing cameras

William F. Folmer and William E. Schwing formed a partnership in 1887 to manufacture bicycles in New York City. They became involved in camera making, using the trade name "Graphic". Folmer invented a focal plane shutter using a fabric curtain with a number of slits of different widths, incorporating it in a single lens reflex plate camera called the Graflex.

The company was acquired by Eastman in 1905, and formed the Folmer and Schwing Division of Eastman Kodak Company from 1907. The name changed to Folmer-Century Division in 1917. Eastman Kodak was obliged to divest itself of the Division in 1926, and the Folmer Graflex Corporation took over the assets and operated independently from then on.

The Graflex single lens reflex plate cameras were thought of as the best of their kind by amateurs and professionals alike. The Speed Graphic hand/stand camera evolved into the standard tool for press photographers in the 1930s, 1940s and 1950s. The Cirkut cameras could make panoramic pictures of up to 360 degrees, the film being moved behind an exposing slot while the camera was rotated by clockwork on the tripod head.

The cameras listed here are only those from the period of manufacture by Eastman Kodak.

Camera		*Type*	*Dates*
Auto Graflex (slr)	3 sizes	plate	1907–1923
Auto Graflex Junior (slr)	2 sizes	plate	1914–1924
5 Cirkut (panoramic)		5″ film	1915–1923
6 Cirkut (panoramic attachment)		6½″ film	1907–1925
8 Cirkut (panoramic attachment)		8″ film	1907–1926
10 Cirkut (panoramic)	3 sizes	6–10″ film	1907–1926
16 Cirkut (panoramic)	5 sizes	8–16″ film	1906–1924
Compact Graflex (slr)	3 sizes	plate	1915–1925
1A Graflex (slr)		116 film	1909–1916
1A Graflex Autographic (slr)		116 film	1917–1927
3A Graflex (slr)		122 film	1907–1916
3A Graflex Autographic (slr)		122 film	1917–1927
Graflex Series B (slr)	2 sizes	plate	1923–1926
RB Graflex Series B (slr)	2 sizes	plate	1923–1926
0 Graphic		121 film	1910–1923
Naturalists' Graflex (slr)		plate	1907–1921
Press Graflex (slr)		plate	1907–1923
RB Auto Graflex (slr)	2 sizes	plate	1909–1926
RB Auto Graflex Junior (slr)		plate	1915)-)1924
RB Cycle Graphic	2 sizes	plate	1921–1926
RB Home Portrait Graflex (slr)		plate	1912–1926
RB Tele Graflex (slr)	2 sizes	plate	1912–1923
Speed Graphic	4 sizes	plate	1912)-)1926
Stereo Auto Graflex (slr)		plate	1906–1922
Stereo Graphic		plate	1904–1921

Appendix 2

Roll film sizes

The table below gives the Kodak roll film sizes in the order they were introduced, with the first camera in which they were used; the film numbers were not allocated until 1913.

Number	*Date*	*Camera*	*Picture size (inches)*
101	1895	2 Bullet	3½ × 3½
102	1895	Pocket Kodak	1½ × 2
103	1897	4 Bullet	4 × 5
104	1897	4 Cartridge Kodak	5 × 4
105	1897	Folding Pocket Kodak	2¼ × 3¼
106	1898	2 Eureka	3½ × 3½
107	1898	Rollholder	3¼ × 4¼
108	1898	Rollholder	4¼ × 3¼
109	1898	Rollholder	4 × 5
110	1898	Rollholder	5 × 4
111	1898	Rollholder	6½ × 4¾
112	1898	Rollholder	7 × 5
113	1898	Rollholder	9 × 12cm
114	1898	Rollholder	12 × 9cm
115	1898	5 Cartridge Kodak	7 × 5
116	1899	1A Folding Pocket Kodak	2½ × 4¼
117	1900	The Brownie	2¼ × 2¼
118	1900	3 Folding Pocket Kodak	3¼ × 4¼
119	1900	3 Cartridge Kodak	3¼ × 4¼
120	1901	2 Brownie	2¼ × 3¼
121	1902	0 Folding Pocket Kodak	1⅝ × 2½
122	1903	3A Folding Pocket Kodak	3¼ × 5½
123	1904	4 Screen Focus Kodak	4 × 5
124	1905	3 Folding Brownie	3¼ × 4¼
125	1905	2 Stereo Brownie	3¼ × 5½
126	1906	4A Folding Kodak	4¼ × 6½
127	1912	Vest Pocket Kodak	1⅝ × 2½
128	1913	1 Ensignette	2¼ × 1½
129	1913	2 Ensignette	3 × 2
130	1916	2C Autographic Kodak	2⅞ × 4⅞
616	1931	Kodak Six-16	2½ × 4¼
620	1931	Kodak Six-20	2¼ × 3¼

Number	*Date*	*Camera*	*Picture size (inches)*
135	1934	Kodak Retina	24 × 36mm
828	1935	Kodak Bantam	28 × 40mm
No 35	1916	00 Cartridge Premo	32 × 44mm

(This special roll film for the smallest Premo camera used unperforated 35mm film)

Autographic films

The special films for Kodak Autographic cameras were made in the following sizes: A116, A118, A120, A122, A123, A126, A127, A130. They were identical to the standard films of those sizes except for the special construction. Standard films could be used in the Autographic cameras, although of course not giving the facility for writing on the film.

Film packs

The film packs used in the Premo cameras and in film pack adaptors were also given a number sequence in 1913; the name was changed from Premo Film Packs to Kodak Film Packs in June 1922, and the 300 series numbers were changed to a 500 series.

Premo no.	*Kodak no.*	*Date*	*Picture size (inches and cm.)*	
300	500	1911	1¾ × 2⅜	4.5 × 6
		1921	1⅝ × 2 7/16	4.5 × 6
315	515	1905	5 × 7	13 × 18
316	516	1909	2½ × 4¼	6.5 × 11
318	518	1903	3¼ × 4¼	8 × 10.5
320	520	1906	2¼ × 3¼	6 × 9
322	522	1904	3¼ × 5½	8 × 14
323	523	1904	4 × 5	10 × 12.5
326	526	1920	4¾ × 6½	12 × 16.5
	531	1926	2 9/32 × 5 11/32	6 × 13
340	540	1920	1¾ × 4¼	4.5 × 10.7
341	541	1920	3½ × 4¾	9 × 12
342	542	1911	3 × 5¼	7.5 × 13.5
343	543	1920	3¾ × 5½	10 × 15